Management Task Quick Look

This section is intended to give you a quick look at the management tasks that you'll have to perform regularly.

Task	Where to Make the Change	Task	Where to Make the Change
Create a hard drive or directory share	Properties | Sharing | New Share	Remove an NT service	Control Panel | Network | Service | (select a service) | Remove
Change permissions for a share (NTFS)	Properties | Security | Permissions	Add an NT network protocol	Control Panel | Network | Protocol | Add
Change permissions for a share (FAT)	Properties | Sharing | Permissions	Change TCP/IP information	Control Panel | Network | Protocol | (select TCP/IP) | Properties
Change maximum concurrent users on a share	Properties | Sharing | Allowed *number*	Change display properties	Right-click anywhere on the desktop, choose Properties
Start directory auditing	Properties | Security | Auditing | Add	Check server events	Start | Programs | Administrative Tools (common) | Event Viewer
Take ownership of a directory	Properties | Security | Ownership	Add a user account	Start | Programs | Administrative Tools (common) | User Manager for Domains | User | New User
Stop a server service	Control Panel | Services | (select a service) | Stop		
Start a server service	Control Panel | Services | (select a service) | Start	Add a local group	Start | Programs | Administrative Tools (common) | User Manager for Domains | User | New Local Group
Change a service startup condition	Control Panel | Services | (select a service) | Startup		
Discover active users	Control Panel | Server | Users	Add a global group	Start | Programs | Administrative Tools (common) | User Manager for Domains | User | New Global Group
Disconnect an active user	Control Panel | Server | Users | (select user) | Disconnect		
Discover active users per share	Control Panel | Server | Shares | (select share)	Change a user name	Start | Programs | Administrative Tools (common) | User Manager for Domains | (select the account) | User | Rename
Start directory replication	Control Panel | Server | Replication | (select)		
Modify alert notification list	Control Panel | Server | Alerts	Remove a user account	Start | Programs | Administrative Tools (common) | User Manager for Domains | (select the account) | User | Delete
Change domain name	Control Panel | Network | Identification | Change		
Change computer name	Control Panel | Network | Identification | Change	Observe hard drive configuration	Start | Programs | Administrative Tools (common) | Disk Manager
Add an NT service	Control Panel | Network | Service | Add		

Tasks Accessible from the Control Panel

Some control panels may or may not appear on your system, based on the options you have installed.

Control Panel	Purpose
Accessibility Options	Change NT usability for impaired users
Add/Remove Programs	Interface meant to help in the setup and removal of applications
Console	Properties of the DOS-style command prompt used in NT
Date/Time	Location for controlling the date and time of the system
Devices	Used to control the start, stop, and startup condition of devices
Dial-Up Monitor	View and control the condition of modems in the RAS system
Display	Monitor and video adapter properties
Find Fast	Aggressive file-finding utility (not really a control panel)

continues on back

Tasks Accessible from the Control Panel *continued*

Control Panel	Purpose
Fonts	Portal to the Fonts folder on the PC, and a tool for adding fonts
GSNW	Control for the Gateway Service for NetWare
Internet	Internet Explorer properties
Keyboard	Custom keyboard possibilities
Licensing	Client licensing options, licensing type, number of licenses
Mail and FAX	Basic Microsoft Exchange mailbox control
Microsoft Mail Postoffice	Workgroup post office creation and management interface
Modem	Modem installation and management
Mouse	Mouse control—including pointers, switching between left- and right-hand operation, speed
Multimedia	Multimedia driver control, including video, audio, MIDI, others
Network	Control and installation of network services, protocols, and drivers
PC Card (PCMCIA)	Install, remove, or configure a PCMCIA device driver
Ports	Specify the communications settings for a serial (COM) port
Printers	Combination control panel and print-management application
Regional Settings	Country and cultural changes that apply to the interface
SCSI Adapters	Control and installation of hard drive and CD-ROM drivers
Server	View and manage the server properties of this computer
Services	Start, stop, and set the startup condition of the server services
Sounds	System sound choices
System	Change environment variables, including startup, profiles, performance
Tape Devices	Add and control tape device drivers
Telephony	General telephone communications parameters

Performance Monitor Counters

There are literally hundreds of different counters that can be used to monitor your server in the Performance Monitor. This list gives you a launching point in the utility and a fast resource for things to watch.

Object	Counter	Description
Browser	Announcement Server/sec	Rate at which the servers in this domain have announced themselves to this server.
Browser	Election Packets/sec	Rate of browser election packets that have been received by this workstation.
Cache	Data Map Hits	Percentage of data maps in the cache that could be resolved without having to retrieve a page from the disk.
Gateway Service for NetWare	Server Sessions	Counts the total number of security objects the redirector has managed.
LogicalDisk	Avg. Disk Queue Length	Average number of both read and write requests that were queued for the selected disk during the sample interval.
LogicalDisk	Avg. Disk sec/Read	Average time in seconds of a read of data from the disk.
LogicalDisk	Avg. Disk sec/Write	Average time in seconds of a write of data to the disk.
Memory	Pages/sec	Primary counter to observe if you're concerned about excessive memory constraints, and the excessive paging that may result.
Memory	Page Faults/sec	A page fault will not cause the page to be fetched from disk.
Objects	Processes	Number of processes in the computer at the time of data collection. Each process represents the running of a program.
Objects	Threads	Number of threads in the computer at the time of data collection. A thread is the basic executable entity that can execute instructions in a processor.
Page File	% Usage	The amount of the Page File instance in use, as a percentage.
RAS Port	Total Errors	Total number of CRC, timeout, serial overrun, alignment, and buffer overrun errors.

SAMS Premier

Peter Norton's®
Maximizing
Windows® NT Server 4
Premier Edition

Peter Norton
and
Todd C. Brown

SAMS 201 West 103rd Street
PUBLISHING Indianapolis Indiana 46290

To my children, Benjamin and Brittney, who I hope can see that homework never ends, but does pay off.

And in memory of William O. Newton (my grandfather), who said, "I am not the smartest man in the world, but I know where the books are." Here is another one, Grandpa…

Copyright © 1997 by Peter Norton

PREMIER EDITION

All rights reserved. No part of this book shall be reproduced, stored in a retrieval system, or transmitted by any means, electronic, mechanical, photocopying, recording, or otherwise, without written permission from the publisher. No patent liability is assumed with respect to the use of the information contained herein. Although every precaution has been taken in the preparation of this book, the publisher and author assume no responsibility for errors or omissions. Neither is any liability assumed for damages resulting from the use of the information contained herein. For information, address Sams Publishing, 201 W. 103rd St., Indianapolis, IN 46290.

International Standard Book Number: 0-672-30987-4

Library of Congress Catalog Card Number: 96-69721

2000 99 98 97   4   3   2   1

Interpretation of the printing code: the rightmost double-digit number is the year of the book's printing; the rightmost single-digit number, the number of the book's printing. For example, a printing code of 97-1 shows that the first printing of the book occurred in 1997.

Composed in Goudy, Helvetica, and MCPdigital by Macmillan Computer Publishing

Printed in the United States of America

Trademarks

All terms mentioned in this book that are known to be trademarks or service marks have been appropriately capitalized. Sams Publishing cannot attest to the accuracy of this information. Use of a term in this book should not be regarded as affecting the validity of any trademark or service mark. Peter Norton® is a registered trademark of Peter Norton. Windows® is a registered trademark of Microsoft Corporation.

President, Sams Publishing	*Richard K. Swadley*
Publishing Manager	*Dean Miller*
Director of Editorial Services	*Cindy Morrow*
Director of Marketing	*Kelli S. Spencer*
Product Marketing Managers	*Wendy Gilbride*
	Kim Margolius
Associate Product Marketing Manager	*Jennifer Pock*
Marketing Coordinator	*Linda Beckwith*

Acquisitions Editor
Grace M. Buechlein

Development Editor
Sunthar Visuvalingam

Production Editor
Robin Drake

Indexers
Erika Millen
Cheryl Jackson

Technical Reviewers
Robert Bogue
Brett Bonenberger
Kelly Held

Editorial Coordinators
Mandie Rowell
Katie Wise

Technical Edit Coordinator
Lynette Quinn

Resource Coordinator
Deborah Frisby

Editorial Assistants
Carol Ackerman
Andi Richter
Rhonda Tinch-Mize

Cover Designer
Tim Amrhein

Book Designer
Gary Adair

Copy Writer
David Reichwein

Production Team Supervisors
Brad Chinn
Charlotte Clapp

Production
Rick Bond
Mona Brown
Elizabeth Deeter
Ian A. Smith

Overview

Contents

Acknowledgments

Computer software books need to be written within practically impossible deadlines, and yet remain painstakingly accurate in order for them to be of any value to the audience. So, with that dilemma in front of me, I had to lean heavily on some really great people to get this book to you in a timely and accurate fashion.

My wife, DaRhonda, is at the top of the list of people to thank. She helped me with typing and also directly with the book. But most of all she cooked, parented, and played social liaison when I couldn't be supportive of her. Somehow she remembered that the back she saw sitting at the computer for seven months was her husband. I saw and I noticed.

This book also had a number of people involved who don't appear on the cover, but who worked hard to help me. A great deal of help came from contributing authors Chad Purviance (Chapters 21 and 29), Terry W. Ogletree (Chapters 27 and 28), Les Harrison (Chapter 25), and Brett Bonenberger (Chapter 26). These gentlemen really helped to bring this book home to you.

I would like to thank the great people at Sams Publishing and at Waterside Productions for the opportunity to work on this project: Grace Buechlein at Sams, who kept her word and remembered me when this project became available; Sunthar Visuvalingam, also at Sams, who kept me between the margins, provided great tools, and was incredibly patient; Matt Wagner with Waterside, who was introduced to me as my agent (odd, right?), but who has earned his title by going to bat for me and keeping me informed; and Robin Drake, an independent editor, who was the last of my helpers—she picked me up with direction, a lot of kind words, and a great sense of humor when it stopped being fun from time to time.

Finally, I want to say thank you to Peter Norton. Without the groundwork laid by Peter Norton, this book would not have been born. Peter Norton and his staff have not only given me this book opportunity, but have helped me and others like me do their job for years. Thank you.

Tell Us What You Think!

As a reader, you are the most important critic and commentator of our books. We value your opinion and want to know what we're doing right, what we could do better, what areas you'd like to see us publish in, and any other words of wisdom you're willing to pass our way. You can help us make strong books that meet your needs and give you the computer guidance you require.

Do you have access to CompuServe or the World Wide Web? Then check out our CompuServe forum by typing **GO SAMS** at any prompt. If you prefer the World Wide Web, check out our site at http://www.mcp.com.

Note: If you have a technical question about this book, call the technical support line at 317-581-4669.

As the team leader of the group that created this book, I welcome your comments. You can fax, e-mail, or write me directly to let me know what you did or didn't like about this book—as well as what we can do to make our books stronger. Here's the information:

FAX: 317-581-4669

E-mail: opsys_mgr@sams.mcp.com

Mail: Dean Miller
         Comments Department
         Sams Publishing
         201 W. 103rd Street
         Indianapolis, IN 46290

About the Authors

Computer software entrepreneur and writer **Peter Norton** established his technical expertise and accessible style from the earliest days of the PC. His Norton Utilities was the first product of its kind, giving early computer owners control over their hardware and protection against myriad problems. His flagship titles, *Peter Norton's DOS Guide* and *Peter Norton's Inside the PC* (Sams Publishing) have provided the same insight and education to computer users worldwide for nearly two decades. Peter's books, like his many software products, are among the best selling and most respected in the history of personal computing.

Peter Norton's former column in *PC Week* was among the most highly regarded in that magazine's history. His expanding series of computer books continues to bring superior education to users, always in Peter's trademark style, which is never condescending or pedantic. From their earliest days, changing the "black box" into a "glass box," Peter's books, like his software, remain among the most powerful tools available to beginners and experienced users alike.

In 1990, Peter sold his software development business to Symantec Corporation, allowing him to devote more time to his family, civic affairs, philanthropy, and art collecting. He lives with his wife, Eileen, and two children in Santa Monica, California.

Todd C. Brown is a field systems engineer with LMB Microcomputers in Indianapolis, Indiana. He has been involved in operating system support and PC networking for eleven years. His primary activity is designing, implementing, and troubleshooting networks and operating systems for clients throughout Indiana. In that time, Todd has had extensive experience with Windows NT, NetWare, Macintosh OS, and OS/2. He has designed networks and networking strategies for thousands of companies. Todd has completed both his Microsoft Certified Systems Engineer (MCSE) and Novell Master Certified Network Engineer (MCNE).

As an author and technical editor, Todd has been a part of the Macmillan Computer Publishing family since 1992. He was a contributing author for the titles *Absolute Beginners Guide to Networking*, *NetWare 4.1 Survival Guide*, and *Special Edition Using NetWare 4.1*.

When not involved with work projects, Todd can be found with his family in central Indiana—though, sadly, he is still probably not too far from his PC. You can reach him at `tbrown@iquest.net`.

Introduction

Writing a book about an operating system that's constantly changing is a process that can be hard to pin down. Such a book can only be a snapshot of the operating system as it is today. The best that can be hoped for is to give the reader a view that's clear, fair, accurate, and above all useful regarding the present state of the system.

The Windows NT operating system comes in two flavors: Windows NT Workstation and Windows NT Server. This book focuses on the features of the NT Server product. The Workstation product is covered in the book *Peter Norton's Complete Guide to Windows NT 4 Workstation* (1996, Sams Publishing, ISBN 0-672-30901-7).

Who Should Read This Book

This book has been put together as a desk reference for administrators, field system engineers, power users, and managers who need to make informed decisions. It nevertheless yields useful information for a casual reader. It isn't exactly the book that you want to take with you to the beach for a casual read, but being a field system engineer myself (who has to read these books), I wanted to give it some life. So hopefully you'll find tidbits of information and morsels of humor that will help you to get through the projects that you start.

You'll find that this book was not written to hammer home the technical nitty-gritty of the operating system. It doesn't try to teach you how to look up how many threads it takes, under the hood, to complete a certain transaction. It isn't intended primarily for the developers (programmers and application writers) of the NT world, although they will still find much that's illuminating and useful between these covers. This book is called *Maximizing* because it's meant to be your personal guide to getting the most out of the NT Server operating system.

Everyone who reads this book will glean something different from it. LAN/WAN administrators and people who (like me) are involved in the field engineering area are most likely counting on this book to introduce some of the hidden jewels that we have to find in order to be considered "experts." I think the book delivers that. But the book must also cater to that manager or non-computer-related engineer who needs the background information, the basics, and the extras. By looking at how the book is organized I think you'll see that you should be able to find both types of information easily.

How This Book Is Organized

This book is organized into major parts that allow you to thumb through and find the things that you're looking for. The fact that it's put together in these categories means that you may find some things repeated on some level, but at each point you should find the level of coverage that fits that part of the book. For example, in Part II, "The Windows NT Operating System Environment," you'll find some discussion of protocols and communications. But for in-depth coverage of NT Server's use of network protocols, you'll need to proceed to Part IV, "Network Services."

Each part covers a specific level of the operating system and should be used to drill down into that particular area.

Part I: Introducing Windows NT Server 4

The introductory chapters are meant to give the novice user (or the experienced user who is new to Windows NT Server 4) a launching point. If you're already familiar with Windows NT 4 to some degree, you may want to skip Part I. But you may still find this enjoyable to read as a refresher.

Chapter 1, "Windows NT Introduction," introduces the Windows environment in general, and quickly develops into an exploration of NT as an operating system. Chapter 2, "What's New in Version 4.0?" goes on to highlight the differences between previous versions of NT and NT 4.0, an essential topic if you're new to the latest version of NT. It provides a road map to the details of these new features throughout the rest of the book.

Part II: The Windows NT Operating System Environment

Windows NT was created in a modular form that allows for the flexibility and strength that makes a great operating system. Part II explores those separate building blocks—how they work together, and yet are protected from each other. Each chapter covers a basic piece of the operating system in the order that you'll need to understand each piece.

The operating system itself is modular in its construction, and this topic is covered in Chapter 3, "Windows NT Subsystems." Though not necessary to manage the server, familiarity with the contents of this chapter will help you to understand why some things behave the way they do. I find that if I understand the inner workings of a complex system, it's easier to see what's going wrong on the surface.

Installation of the operating system is covered in Chapter 4, "Installation Considerations." There are many different ways to install NT and many different situations in which you'll find yourself during installation. This chapter advises you on how best to use the install process and how to avoid some pitfalls.

The remaining chapters in this section concern the basic operation of the operating environment. Topics such as the file system (Chapter 5, "File System and Storage Considerations"), networking concepts (Chapter 6, "Networking Brief") and printing configuration (Chapter 7, "Printing"), will help you understand the more advanced concepts covered throughout the book.

Part III: Account and Domain Management

This section begins by covering the basic concepts of networks (Chapter 8, "Microsoft Network Access Concepts Brief") and network account management (Chapter 10, "User Account Creation and Management," and Chapter 11, "The User Manager Tool") as seen through the eyes of Microsoft. This will help administrators new to the Microsoft world to ramp up into more advanced concepts.

NT Server uses a unique paradigm for account management called *domains and workgroups*. This section covers the management of those domains, as well as offering practical views of the domain model in general (Chapter 9, "Domain Design").

Part IV: Network Services

To provide utility to the clients on the network, NT Server is equipped with numerous basic services. Everything that the user requires—from basic connectivity to e-mail—is handled through some form of network service.

This part of the book covers the administration of getting user workstations attached to the server (Chapter 16, "Client Workstation Considerations"), making it possible for those workstations to see resources on the network (Chapter 12, "Network Browsing"), and basic e-mail services (Chapter 14, "The Workgroup Post Office"). Connectivity considerations extend to accessing the network from a remote location, as covered in Chapter 13, "Remote Access Services (RAS)," and ensuring seamless coexistence between different protocols, as described in Chapter 15, "Surviving in a Multi-Protocol World."

Part V: Connectivity in a Heterogeneous World

Network servers in an enterprise rarely exist in a homogeneous environment that will allow them to communicate only with those systems that match their own way of doing things. This part of the book covers the many features in NT Server that allow you to connect with and access resources from non-NT systems.

If you're involved with a heterogeneous network environment that includes NetWare servers (Chapter 17, "NetWare Connectivity"), Macintosh systems (Chapter 18, "Macintosh Services"), or even UNIX-based hosts (Chapter 19, "UNIX Host to NT Server Connectivity"), this section gives specific solutions to the connectivity problems involved. We even get into the issues of mainframe connectivity (Chapter 20, "SNA Connectivity with BackOffice").

Part VI: TCP/IP and the Internet

In previous versions of the Windows NT operating system, the TCP/IP protocol was simply a nifty add-on that made NT a functional part of enterprise networks and ensured connectivity to university networks. In NT Server 4, the TCP/IP protocol has become the default protocol (replacing NetBEUI), and it's fundamental to the operation of the system. Most of the excitement over TCP/IP has come from the Internet, which has also become an integral part of the NT operating system.

This section covers the management and installation of TCP/IP as a protocol, and gives advice on how to make this protocol behave properly in larger NetBIOS environments (Chapter 21, "TCP/IP Networking").

The Internet Information Server (IIS) has now been added to the basic operating system (Chapter 22, "Internet Information Server"). This part of the book covers what other services are included, as well how to install and manage each of them (Chapter 23, "Other Internet Services for NT 4.0"). The point-to-point tunneling protocol, which allows you to create private virtual networks at minimal cost over the Internet, also receives special attention in Chapter 24, "Point-to-Point Tunneling Protocol (PPTP)."

Part VII: Server Administration

The server requires a great deal of care and feeding after it has been born, and this section is dedicated to that process. It covers topics such as managing the server (Chapter 25, "Server Management"), optimizing the system (Chapter 26, "Optimizing and Tuning Performance"), backup (Chapter 27, "Server Backup"), and disaster recovery (Chapter 28, "Recovering from a Disaster"). The added facilities provided by the Systems Management Server are covered in Chapter 29, "Systems Management Server (SMS)."

Part VIII: Appendixes

Finally, you'll find some useful reference information in the appendixes, such as the Windows NT Server 4.0 Hardware Compatibility List (Appendix A), a troubleshooting and error list (Appendix B), a table of decimal-to-binary-to-hexadecimal translation for IP addresses (Appendix C), and synopsis of the software developer's kits available for Windows NT (Appendix D). There's also a complete glossary of terms to help you find quick answers to those "What is that?" questions.

Conventions Used in This Book

When a book is put together, the author must find some way of pointing out to the user where instructions or special directions are being given. I have therefore used the following special characters and conventions in this book:

File | Open	Menus and selections are separated by a vertical bar. "File | Open" means "Access the File menu and choose Open."
`monospace`	Monospace type in this book is used for the following:

- Filenames, directory names, paths, and extensions (`pagefile.sys`, `d:\BILBO_PO`, `.csv`)
- System messages (`No login server available`)
- Registry parameters and settings (`HKEY_LOCAL_MACHINE`, `IsDomainMaster`)
- Server and HTML commands and switches (`diskperf /v`, `#PRE`)
- Internet addresses (`http://www.symantec.com`)

`italic monospace`	Sometimes you need to supply a value for a command or option. For example, when you use the `CONVERT` command, you need to supply the name of the drive that you want to convert (`CONVERT drive: /fs:NTFS`). Because *drive* appears in italic monospace, you know that the word is a placeholder (variable) that you need to replace with a value. The placeholder simply tells you what kind of value you need to provide.
`bold monospace`	Items in bold monospace indicate characters that the reader needs to type as part of a command or step procedure.
`[<filename>]`	Square brackets around a value, switch, or command indicate an optional component of a command line.

Icons

Throughout the book, I often have thoughts and bits of information that are of interest but don't exactly flow with the immediate text. These details appear in Notes, Tips, and Warnings. You'll also find passages within the main body of the text that deal with a particular aspect of the operating system—passages that you'll want to spot easily and return to at leisure. Such thoughts and passages are highlighted by distinct icons. The following is a list of the icons used in this book and what they mean (on the next page):

Note: Notes are interesting tidbits or facts that don't necessarily affect your capacity to use the other surrounding information. But a Note is given to you at a time when it will help you understand or further your knowledge about the subject at hand.

Tip: Tips are meant to be a suggestion about a particular way of doing things that works well or is easier than the standard way. Tips sometimes may even be found to contradict commonly accepted notions, but are derived from hands-on experience, often learned the hard way.

Warning: If a problem may possibly arise as the result of your actions, or if you are at a crossroads leading to a possible complication, a warning will be given to point you in the right direction.

Peter's Principle: Peter's Principles Are Helpful Information

Peter's Principles are facts, considerations, strategies, and techniques that will provide you with a unique or nifty way of getting something done. It may even be a particularly insightful way of looking at a subject. They help you manage your NT environment more efficiently. These special tips often contain references on where to find more information.

Looking Ahead: I'm often in the position, especially in the earlier chapters, where I'm obliged to anticipate topics that are covered adequately later in the book. This icon is a sort of road sign that helps you flip forward if you're impatient, or if you feel that you need more information than I thought relevant in the present context.

Whenever you see the Architecture icon, I'm explaining the internal workings of Windows NT. Knowing how the operating system is built and functions internally can help you understand why things sometimes don't work the way you'd otherwise expect them to in a practical context.

In a heterogeneous networking world with multiple protocols, diverse hardware, so many vendors, and changing connectivity requirements, you're bound to run into problems of compatibility. I use this icon to point out such hurdles, along with information and tips on how to surmount them.

There are times when it's helpful to see the technical origin of a networking principle or where such a standard comes from. Although this entire book is about networking, this icon highlights such networking considerations in contexts where you might not think they apply.

The Performance icon highlights a wide variety of optimization techniques. Because many of them may require a tradeoff of some kind, you have to decide which are suitable for your particular needs. I've tried in each case to provide you all relevant information to make the right decision.

Problems of incompatibility arise from adherence to differing standards. The Standards icon marks passages that spell out the specific standards that a protocol, component, or product complies with.

Whenever I provide you with more info than you need to understand the matter at hand—whether technical details, background history, or other circumstantial information—I indicate this fact with the Technical Note icon. Though you can skip such information, it may help you better understand the topic, or just be fun to know.

With a complex network environment, you're bound to run into bottlenecks, failures, and problems of every sort. The Troubleshooting icon attempts to help you put your finger on the source of the problem, and generally direct you to the tools and other resources needed to properly diagnose and resolve the issue.

At times, you need to be aware of a particularly important or threatening part of the security scheme that may not be part of a security section or chapter. When this occurs, I'll note it with this icon.

When a unique opportunity presents itself to point out a trick or shortcut in the administration of your network, I'll use this icon. Not just running NT—because the whole book would qualify—but instead something specific from my involvement in the network operating system administration of many companies.

NT has now incorporated TCP/IP and the Internet into facets of the operating system that you may not expect or know to look for. When those times arise, I've added a special icon to help you recognize the value of the Internet in that situation.

I

Peter Norton™

Introducing
Windows NT
Server 4

1

Windows NT
Introduction

Peter Norton™

Windows has existed for 10 years now in some capacity, but in the last 4 years a product has materialized that takes Windows from a helpful file manager and menuing environment to a true operating system. From Windows v1 to Windows for Workgroups v3.11, Windows has always suffered from having to admit that it wasn't really an operating system at all, but an environment that depended on the operating system to deliver the ground-level controls that Windows needed to make the work happen. Windows NT is Microsoft's second crack at the answer to those failings.

Windows NT has been around for that last four years, but has gained notoriety only in the last two. The product was born from the broken family that was IBM and Microsoft. Both companies were involved in a long-ignored and less-than-popular 32-bit operating system called OS/2. When OS/2 was introduced, it was misunderstood, and the hardware and software to make it truly fly just didn't exist in enough numbers to make it a marketing success. OS/2 had also become associated with the PS/2 line of computer systems that IBM introduced in 1987 to introduce the PC world to 32-bit hardware standards.

The 32-bit hardware needed a 32-bit operating system. When IBM chose a partner for its new operating system, it chose the company that provided the operating system that helped launch its first PC revolution, Microsoft. Microsoft began as part of the OS/2 team, but dropped out of the OS/2 project within a few years of its inception.

> **Note:** One lasting piece of the Microsoft-IBM relationship still exists. IBM retained some right to Windows code and Microsoft retained the right to some OS/2 code. If you ever wondered how Windows NT runs certain OS/2 applications and OS/2 continues to run many Windows applications, well, now you know.

Shortly after dropping from the OS/2 operating system, Microsoft announced that it intended to introduce its own 32-bit operating system—a new technology (NT). Originally this new technology was to be part of OS/2, but OS/2 was limited in its scope and vision at that point.

Microsoft's new operating system would be an open platform that would run on more than the Intel-based systems. Microsoft operating systems had been limited to Intel processors in the past; the new system would be powerful enough to invade the workstation world held by UNIX, but would still maintain the ease of use that had accompanied the Windows environment. The system was to be scalable, capable of taking advantage of multiple processors. It would be capable of functioning as a network operating system and would be secure enough to obtain the government security clearance necessary to be trusted by the information systems (IS) departments of large businesses.

This new 32-bit operating system didn't appear until 1993. It was introduced along with a new version of the standard Windows environment (version 3.1), and so was called Windows NT 3.1. Not to imply that it was the third revision of the operating system, but rather that Microsoft was going to make every effort to maintain the same look and feel in both its Windows environment and its new operating system. Windows 3.0 had been introduced a year earlier and had made great leaps in the Windows interface, but it had been picked on for being very susceptible to crashes and lockups. The rollout of Windows 3.1 and Windows NT 3.1 was a great leap forward for Microsoft, even though Windows NT 3.1 was relatively ignored until the introduction of NT 3.5 in 1994.

In 1996, Microsoft again released a new version of Windows. Amid many predictions that the new version of Windows would be a convergence of all Windows versions into one 32-bit operating system—NT with a new suit—Microsoft threw us all a curve. What it introduced was not a new NT version, but a completely new operating system called Windows 95 (first available in 1996—imagine that). This operating system was to be the next logical progression of the Windows environment. It was a 32-bit operating system, with 16-bit subsystems capable of still handling most of those 16-bit Windows- and DOS-based applications. But the biggest thing it offered users of the Windows environment was a helping hand to carry them along into some of the technologies that had left many Windows users standing on the sidelines.

We won't discuss Plug and Play in this book, and that isn't really the point behind bringing up Windows 95. The reason for mentioning it is to help the reader understand some of the pieces that went into the creation of the new version of Windows NT (NT 4.0).

As mentioned earlier, when Windows 95 was introduced, many people expected that the upcoming product would be a new version of NT that would finally converge the products into one. Not only was the new product not NT, but the two interfaces were now different. For many of the power users who used NT because of its 32-bit capabilities, Windows 95 was more friendly and accessible. Many people who would be better served by using the more robust fully-32-bit Windows NT really envied the new interface of Windows 95. They also found that many of the networking access options were easier to understand and control than those found in NT.

Shortly after the release of Windows 95, Microsoft delivered a service pack (something we'll discuss in more detail later) that put the new Windows 95 interface on Windows NT v3.51. Late in 1996, Windows NT 4.0 was finally released; it contained the Windows 95 interface as a basic piece.

This chapter gives you an introduction to the basics of Windows NT Server 4. The concepts introduced in this chapter won't be covered in depth, but instead are meant to get you started thinking about the NT operating system and the facilities that make it a solid option for your network.

A Network Operating System

Windows NT was released in two separate versions: Windows NT Workstation and Windows NT Advanced Server (now known simply as Windows NT Server). Both products offered the user the ability to log on as a network user, but NT Server had the pieces necessary to function in an enterprise server environment, not just to serve small groups (workgroups).

Peter's Principle: NT Server as a Workstation OS

The NT Server operating system carries a great deal of baggage in order to be a server operating system; for that reason, it doesn't make a good choice for a workstation operating system. NT Server has the following drawbacks as a workstation operating system:

- Price
- Processes necessary to provide domain control
- DHCP and WINS responsibilities

This book addresses the Server platform, but it's important to note that this operating system is a great server operating system because it's based on a solid operating system in general. If you are looking for help with the NT Workstation package in particular, look for the other book in the Peter Norton NT series, *Peter Norton's Complete Guide to Windows NT 4 Workstation* (1996, Sams Publishing, ISBN 0-672-30901-7).

Microsoft approached the network operating system from a different angle than was used with the most successful systems of the day. Instead of building just another file-sharing and peripheral-sharing device, Microsoft began with a strong multitasking and multiprocessing operating system. This isn't a completely new approach; UNIX has been just such an operating system and has been available for more than 20 years.

The difference that Windows NT offers is a familiar user interface and easily accessible client/server file and print services. For years, the information systems community has proclaimed that it was going to be the year of UNIX, but the interface and the complexity of management tools has scared away even some of the bravest launches. Microsoft has taken the concept of a scalable and portable operating system and has put the familiar Windows interface and tools there. In other words, it has given an operating system both power and ease of use. This is important because it opens the door to more powerful processes to the general public and allows the world of application servers to intersect with that of file and print servers.

In the past, the only choices that offered meat to the server issue were Novell's NetWare for serious file and print services, or UNIX or mainframe installations for application services. Windows NT offers the combination of a symmetrical multiprocessing and portable operating system to give strength to the application services, with the client/server-based file and print services necessary to avoid being bogged down by numerous connections.

The primary difference between Windows NT Server and many of the popular file and print network operating systems of today is the microkernel architecture that sits at the base of the NT operating system and UNIX. The microkernel allows NT to separate the processing of user-level operations and that of hardware interaction. Because the application interface and the hardware layers are separate, NT Server is capable of running on many different processors (Intel x86, DEC Alpha, MIPS, and PowerPC) without a complete rewrite. This also allows NT to maintain a robust and clean operating environment even in the event that certain programs become unstable.

Windows NT has two basic modes of operation: user mode and kernel mode operation. But these modes separate into several different layers to give NT the ability to remove and replace any one of these pieces without having to rewrite the entire system. The modular nature of the system allows Windows NT not only to address many different hardware schemes, but also to be addressed by many different applications based on other operating systems (OS/2, Posix, Windows 3.x, and Windows NT).

Note: Posix is a form of UNIX used in many government installations. Microsoft has made a great effort to make NT accessible to large companies and government contracts.

Note: Windows NT can run some OS/2-based applications, but not all of them. Only text-based OS/2 applications from v2.1 and earlier run under NT, not those that require the OS/2 Presentation Manager.

The Nuts and Bolts

The different components of the Windows NT operating system are subsystems that can be changed within that set without affecting the others. The subsystems in Windows NT Server are the user environment, the Executive services, the kernel, and Hardware services (called *HAL* or *hardware abstraction layer*). Each of these modules has a separate function and contributes to the ability of NT to separate the hardware from the user's ability to function in an NT environment (see Figure 1.1).

Note: Win32 (shown in Figure 1.1) is still part of the basic structure, but has been given a major face lift. This is discussed in Chapter 3, "Windows NT Subsystems."

This modularity is a very important point because it's unique to mainstream systems today. Most operating systems in the mainstream are hardware-dependent; for this reason, information systems professionals are making decisions on hardware based on the limitations of the operating system and not the capabilities of the equipment.

Figure 1.1.
The basic architecture of Windows NT.

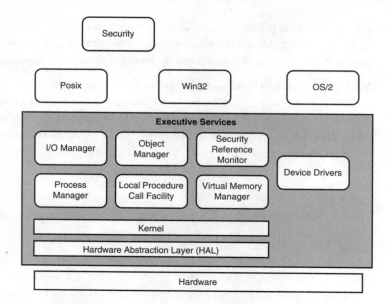

The Hardware Abstraction Layer (HAL)

The layer at the base of the NT operating system is the HAL (hardware abstraction layer). This layer is unique for each of the different processor families. As mentioned earlier, NT Server runs on the Intel x86, MIPS, PowerPC, and DEC Alpha processor families. To this point, other attempts to create an operating system that would make this leap have been commercially successful only in the UNIX family of products. Microsoft has managed to do it in the NT family and has delivered it in a more palatable package.

You communicate with the hardware subsystem only through the NT Executive. This relationship is not seen by the user or the applications, but instead occurs in the background. Each new class of processor requires that the HAL be rewritten to accommodate the special requirements of that family. Because of the relationship between the different modules, it's only necessary to rewrite the HAL and not the remainder of the operating system.

This relationship doesn't prevent all application writers from having to be aware of the processor, but if they write specifically to the Win32 API they only need to worry about being compatible with Windows NT. If the application is written to the Win16 or DOS environment, it may not require direct calls to the hardware; if direct calls are required, the application won't run properly. This problem includes previously written legacy applications that many companies may have become dependent on.

Looking Ahead: Keep in mind when you get to Chapter 4, "Installation Considerations," that this is one point when you need to be aware of the particular installation directory. Each processor has a different directory (MIPS, Alpha, I386).

The Kernel

The NT kernel is the base level of any software operation; it's necessary to use the kernel to speak to a processor. If it helps, think of the kernel as a colonel. Its job is to marshal the processes as they pass to the different processors.

Each processor in the system contains some portion of the kernel, and that portion controls the flow of threads coming to and from the processor. By controlling the priority and time consumption of items using the processor, the kernel stops ill-behaved processes from holding a processor too long and/or locking it up.

The Executive Services

The kernel is actually the primary part of a greater set of subsystems known as the Executive services. The pieces of the Executive subsystems are responsible for the fundamental functions of the operating system. The Executive services are responsible for functions such as memory management, hard disk access, printing, and so on.

You could think of the NT Executive like the dock for a trucking company. The Executive doesn't directly deliver anything. Instead, it receives requests and commands from applications and user interaction, and then ports these items to the proper subsystem. If any communication is needed back to the application, that communication also must go through the Executive.

The Executive is a combination of seven major subsystems. First is the kernel (discussed in the preceding section). The others are the I/O Manager, the Object Manager, the Virtual Memory Manager, the Process Manager, the Local Procedure Call Facility, and the Security Reference Monitor. The Executive is covered in more detail at the beginning of the next chapter; simply put, the combination of these facilities makes the connection between the user level and the hardware level.

The Application and User Interface

In user mode, applications interface with the appropriate application subsystem. Applications don't directly interface with the kernel of the operating system at all. This setup makes NT different from previous versions of Windows because even previous versions that had been updated to include the Win32 API capabilities still relied on DOS as the operating system.

The DOS operating system really has no way of protecting one application from another. All DOS applications have the ability to write to any desired block of memory. Even though most applications are well-behaved, an ill-behaved application can still cross memory boundaries and bring the entire system to its knees. The problem is like allowing a group of children to eat at a buffet. There can be many conflicts, confusion, and lockups in the system. (This subject is covered in more detail in Chapter 3.)

Multiple Platforms

It can be assumed that Windows NT Server will allow other Windows-based products to attach as clients, but one of the strengths of this system is its ability to allow workstations of many different types to log on and make use of the peripherals that it has available to share. NT allows for native logon of Windows 95, DOS-based clients, Macintosh-based clients—even users on a Novell NetWare network client.

Microsoft has approached network communications with the same open arms it used for hardware issues. Microsoft's Windows products, including NT Server, have a very open approach when it comes to allowing native controllable logon. Unlike NetWare, which until very recently required that all clients use IPX/SPX protocol to log onto a NetWare server, Microsoft's products support many different logon protocols. NT Server supports the following logon protocols:

- TCP/IP
- IPX/SPX
- NetBEUI
- AppleTalk

Looking Ahead: Protocols and communications methods are covered in much greater detail in later chapters, but we'll cover the effects of multiple-platform communications to some extent here.

TCP/IP: An Opening to the World

Through a very concentrated effort to bring the Internet and TCP/IP standards along with this product, Microsoft has managed to allow almost any machine to at least have access. The TCP/IP protocol isn't a new effort—as a matter of fact, it's very old. TCP/IP is a publicly owned protocol and the base protocol for communication across the Internet. The fact that the protocol is owned by the public, is incredibly routable, and that no one gets credit for its existence, has launched it into the forefront.

NT Server 4.0 uses TCP/IP as the default protocol for communicating with clients on LAN or WAN. Prior versions of NT used a protocol called NetBEUI by default, but the protocol couldn't be routed across different network segments and was never accepted by the rest of the networking world. By choosing TCP/IP, Microsoft has solved those problems.

The TCP/IP suite of protocols offers NT many ways of getting clients to the data and peripherals they want. Almost any operating system worth its salt has had some TCP/IP tools written for it, even if the system doesn't support it natively. Windows NT provides access to its systems natively through TCP/IP.

TCP/IP also brings along with it the granddaddy of all wide area networks, the Internet. By including the Internet Information Server suite, Microsoft opens NT Server to access through products available on almost any workstation. The Internet Information Server brings file transfer through the FTP protocol, information and usable applications through the World Wide Web or HTTP protocol, and the Gopher protocol for document storage and presentation.

Novell NetWare

Windows NT has two primary tools for speaking to the Novell world: the IPX/SPX protocol, and Gateway Service for NetWare. While both of these things will help with NetWare communications, IPX/SPX isn't just for NetWare and Novell-based systems.

IPX/SPX

IPX/SPX as a protocol has existed for 10 to 12 years and is the product of Novell. Novell NetWare has, until very recently, been unable to authenticate a user that came to it in any other protocol. Novell made this protocol public shortly after its release in hopes of gathering forces behind its NetWare operating system. The advantages offered by the IPX/SPX protocol suite are its routability and ease of installation.

When you install the IPX/SPX protocol, you don't need to specify an address manually on a per-workstation basis. This is not to say that you don't have to set addresses at all, but the addresses you set are at the network segment level. Each workstation's individual address is a combination of the segment address and the machine's MAC address. The point is that for small to medium-sized networks that involve little or no WAN communications, the IPX/SPX scheme makes life much easier on the administrator.

Note: A media access control address (MAC *address*) is a unique number assigned to individual network interface cards by the IEEE. Each manufacturer is given a range of numbers to assign to their cards, and those numbers must remain unique. This system allows all stations to be identified on a hardware level.

Windows NT supports the use of the IPX/SPX protocol suite through the NWLink IPX/SPX protocol. It not only supports the use of the protocol, but also allows users communicating with IPX/SPX to use all NT services. In fact, an NT server or workstation can use the IPX protocol as its only form of communication (although I wouldn't recommend this because of the tools that are made available through TCP/IP). I think you'll see in Chapter 15, "Surviving in a Multi-Protocol World," and Chapter 21, "TCP/IP Networking," that TCP/IP on NT offers even the smallest network such tools as Ping, FTP, HTTP, and WINS, which greatly expand the manageability of the network.

Gateway Service for NetWare

In an extremely controversial product introduced with Windows NT v3.5, Microsoft introduced a way to allow Windows NT clients to access a Novell server by using an NT authentication. The service, called Gateway Service for NetWare (see Figure 1.2), allows the administrator(s) of the NT and NetWare servers to coordinate to allow the NT server to share the resources of the NetWare server through the authentication of the NT server. The NetWare server's volumes, for example, would appear to be a share on the NT server.

Figure 1.2.
The Gateway Service setup dialog box.

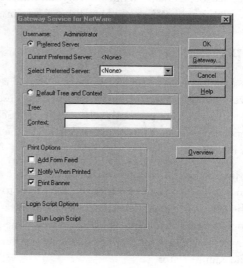

The complication here comes when this scheme is used by companies to bypass the licensing of NetWare. Microsoft goes to great lengths in its training and documentation to make sure that no one believes that they are doing this with Microsoft's permission. But, as you can imagine, Novell has been less than impressed.

Apple Macintosh

Communicating with the Macintosh system requires more magic than most systems in the office, if you want it to attach to the local network. The Macintosh system has its own way of doing things and until recently wasn't capable of networking using any form of communication other than AppleTalk.

The Windows NT Server approach to this issue is to give the Macintosh client what it wants. Through the use of the Macintosh service, Windows NT appears to the Macintosh user to be just another Macintosh sharing its hard drive or printer (see Figure 1.3). The Macintosh user needs only to open the Chooser and look in the right zone.

Figure 1.3.
The Macintosh Chooser.

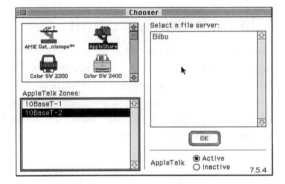

The Macintosh service supports the use of zones and allows for variable naming conventions for Macintosh versus NT users.

C2 Certified Security

From the inception of Windows NT as an operating system, the goal has been to secure the system from the basic level—which is to say that Windows NT Server is built on secure ground. Windows NT in both forms has been C2 certified by the United States government only on the workstation level, but workstation-level certification has value throughout the product line. If you can subvert the base product, the rest of the product is doomed.

NT Security Basics

Windows NT gives you control over user accounts, policies, and rights even at the workstation level. This isn't just for users who log onto the server from the outside, but also for users sitting at the server unit.

User accounts are controlled by the Administrator account created when the system is installed or when the first system is added to a new domain. The control of these accounts includes such items as

- Access to directories and files
- Access to printers
- User environment variables for Windows NT or Windows 95 users
- The ability to manage other users or groups
- Creating and managing shared resources

By default, NT creates three accounts: Administrator, Guest, and the initial user.

The Administrator Account

The Administrator account is created as an initial management account. The account is used to create users, install software, install printers, and generally manage the other accounts on the system. But most often this account will not be directly used after the initial setup of the NT system. It's best to set up accounts that are members of the Administrator group to perform the daily functions of managing the system. This strategy allows the manager to make changes to his or her own account and environment without affecting the Administrator account.

The Guest Account

The Guest account is a very dangerous account to leave on the system. It's initially set up as a convenience account that allows the occasional user to sit down and make use of certain files and printers. The issue that needs to be addressed is the fact that guest users are initially able to access anything to which they haven't specifically been denied access—in other words, every new object that is created—until you remove the rights.

Because no problem is created by deleting this account, I recommend deleting it. Create specific accounts to allow guest users to gain access to public objects. But be aware that NT by nature is an open system.

> **Warning:** If you are used to the NetWare form of administering users, you may be caught with the server open by assuming that new objects in the system are closed until you open them. For the most part, objects are open to the general public until you specifically exclude them.

The Initial Account

The third account is created to allow for another Administrator account on the system immediately. If you've ever forgotten the Administrator account on a system, this setup makes perfect sense to you. It's strongly suggested that you don't delete this initial account. Rename the account if you must, but if you delete this account without making another Administrator account, you may find yourself locked out of the castle with the key in the moat.

Groups

Groups are the preferred method of distributing rights and permissions to users. By definition, a group is really an account that contains accounts. The purpose of the grouping of these accounts is to allow the administrator to make changes to several accounts in one stroke. Changes include anything that you could allow a single user. By making the user a member of a group and then changing the group's permissions, you can make the same changes to any other user by simply adding the user to the group. The idea is to allow the administrator to cut down on the workload by performing fewer steps. Even if the group is created initially with one or two users, administration will be easier in the future if you make changes within the group framework.

The initial groups that are created with the installation process are as follows:

- **Users.** Users allowed to use the computer system.
- **Administrators.** Users with complete control of the system. Includes the Administrator and initial user.
- **Backup Operators.** Users allowed to back up and restore files from the server or domain.
- **Guests.** Users allowed limited access to the system. Includes the Guest account.
- **Power Users.** Users allowed to perform certain local administrative tasks, such as the creation and management of local shares.
- **Replicators.** Special users involved in the replication of the server directory structure.

NT Server Security

The primary difference between NT Workstation security and NT Server security is the existence of domain security for large enterprise-level installations. Both contain usernames, passwords, and policies that govern the behavior and appearance of NT to a given user. But NT Workstation maintains the workgroup model that existed in Windows for Workgroups. NT Server is capable of functioning in a workgroup model, but by offering a domain model it allows for security that better fits the needs of large network installations.

A *domain* is a logical collection of servers that share security accounts. This scheme allows users and shares to be created just once. It also allows for the management of security from centralized management tools. In a domain model, the users, printers, and storage shares are created and managed as part of the domain—not as part of a single server. When a user logs onto a domain-based server, he logs into the domain, not the server itself.

Domains are ruled by servers that are designated to be *domain controllers*. A domain controller responds to user requests for authentication. Each domain should contain one *primary domain controller* (*PDC*) and it's recommended that two *backup domain controllers* (*BDCs*) be available for quicker validation and fault tolerance.

The primary domain controller is the system on the network that is updated when changes are made in the user permissions, account names, passwords, and so on. It then updates the backup domain controllers over time. This setup allows users to be validated by several machines on the network and allows for smooth operation in the event of a server failure.

To understand the strength of this approach, you should understand that in a workgroup model the user attaches directly to the server and is authenticated by the server. If the server is down, the user isn't authenticated and doesn't have access to network resources. Also, you must consider that in a workgroup model every change that is made to a user account is unique to the server where the change has been made. Workgroup servers don't share information or permissions.

What Is C2 Certification?

Windows NT Server has been found by the United States government to meet the requirements of C2 Orange Book certification. A great deal of noise has been made about the security certification of network operating systems, but I would guess that very few people know what is meant by the term *C2 certified*. It's like saying that something has been hermetically sealed—we're all very impressed, but what does it really mean?

C2 Orange Book certification means that, according to the U. S. government, this operating system meets the criteria set forth by the National Computer Security Center (NCSC). The color of the book (Orange Book) is simply a division of the separate levels of the certification. A detailed explanation of the process might be just what you are looking for; that can be found on the Internet.

Instead of a long, boring description, I think it serves our purpose to look at it from the practical view of what is necessary to get this certification.

To begin, what does Orange Book mean? Each certification level, A through D, contains groups that evaluate the product for certification. The first level of certification is Workstation or Stand Alone. The group involved in this particular evaluation process records those meeting the requirements in a book called the Orange Book. So, Orange Book certification means that the operating system is secure as a workstation. This is important because it implies that the C2 certification that is so often heralded for NT Server is valid only if you don't attach it into a network. Red Book or Server certification is still being evaluated for NT as an operating system.

As mentioned earlier, several levels of compliance are associated with NCSC C2 certification. To begin with, to be certified an operating system must require a logon name and password for the user to make use of the system. Once a user is in the system, the operating system must be able to keep track of all interaction that the user has with the system and system objects. Users must be given the power to control the objects they create. Each user must be granted ownership of her own objects and must be able to be given control of who has access to those objects. Once files have been removed by the user, those files must be able to be completely eliminated from possible recovery.

If you have used Windows NT or any other C2 certified operating system, you know that you don't have to implement all of these rules, but only need to have them available for the administrator to put them in place. There are many other requirements and procedures, but I hope that this section has given you a flavor for what Microsoft is driving toward.

Backup

In Windows NT Server, much like other client/server network operating systems, backup is available through an integrated set of tools.

Archiving server-based data is critical to the success of your network not only for disaster recovery, but for the recovery of aged data and recovery from possible corruption. Many companies think of the tape backup system as simply a tool for the recovery of data from a failed hard drive or any other form of permanent storage. But it has been my experience that the majority of the time when data recovery is needed, it isn't due to a failure. It's usually to recover legacy or corrupted data.

The NT Backup utility included in NT Server is capable of backing up and restoring files and directories from any drive that the system is capable of accessing by the operating system. Again, the interface of Windows NT becomes a strength. The utility is simple enough to use that most administrators could back up the server without assistance.

The NT Backup utility is a graphical tool that allows you to back up files from sources that are formatted in FAT, HPFS, and NTFS file formats. That would include the server itself, OS/2 servers, Novell NetWare servers, and even Windows 95 or Windows 3.x PCs that share storage. This makes the NT Backup utility unique when compared to the NetWare backup utility, which requires each workstation to run a special program to send the files across to the server.

NT Backup is not the answer to all your backup needs. It's meant to be an available tool for emergency situations or spartan installations when you need to get a backup. If you have been in the PC server world for any time, you begin to see that it's important for operating system companies to allow the industry to provide some portion of the services. These concessions appear to be aimed at maintaining support from those vendors. Vendors that create backup utilities seem to be in one of those protected groups.

Looking Ahead: NT Backup is covered in great detail in Chapter 27, "Server Backup."

Performance Monitoring

When a network system is installed in your company, a great mystery comes along with that system. How is the system performing? Did that new piece of hardware we added to the server really help? What's causing the system to slow down to a snail's pace at 3:00 p.m. everyday? These questions go unanswered for the most part because the users don't know about or understand how to use the applications present to monitor these variables. Windows NT has been equipped with a surprisingly simple set of monitors that will help you to conquer the mystery.

NT Performance Monitor is a graphical tool that allows you to see in easy-to-understand graphs and logs what is currently happening and to track what happens over a given span of time (see Figure 1.4). Performance Monitor tracks each piece of the server as a single object. Software and hardware events are tracked within the operating system; Performance Monitor presents that information in two different forms—charts and logs.

Figure 1.4.
*The NT Performance
Monitor.*

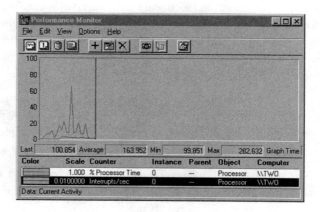

Charts enable you to view the effect systems changes are having on system performance. This gives you the opportunity to pinpoint bottlenecks and cure them.

Following is a brief list of the events that you can track with Performance Monitor:

- **Processor activity.** Monitors the activity of each of the processors in the system.
- **Pagefile activity.** Tracks the usage of virtual memory in the system.
- **Server processes.** Monitors the processes that communicate between the local machine and the network.
- **Threads.** Counts the threads that are being processed in the local system.
- **Memory.** Tracks memory usage.

Looking Ahead: For more specific information on Performance Monitor and the use of the tool, see Chapter 26, "Optimizing and Tuning Performance."

Summary

Windows NT is a mature and well-thought-out product capable of running a well-managed workstation; this makes it capable of supporting a strong server. It hasn't come about without great care being given to its future. We can see this in the planning and delivery of a scalable, portable, secure, and usable operating system.

NT's modular design has created an operating system capable of adjusting to change and to an ever-changing network environment. Through the use of a microkernel design, Microsoft has presented an operating system that is prepared to grow into the future of hardware without completely re-designing the software pieces that work. With a multi-protocol and multi-platform network interface, it's possible to serve many different types of clients with one server operating system scheme.

Servicing the system is made easier through the use of integrated tools—Performance Monitor to help pinpoint discrepancies and bottlenecks, and NT Backup to help recover from storage failures or corruption.

This opening chapter gave you some history of what has been and what is important about this operating system. In the chapters that follow, more detailed information is offered on almost everything mentioned here.

2

What's New in Version 4.0?

Peter Norton™

In 1996, when Microsoft introduced Windows 95, the information systems world was buzzing with reports that what was coming was a new version of Windows NT. In fact, many rumors quoted Bill Gates (CEO of Microsoft) as saying that the new version of Windows would be the convergence of all Windows versions into one robust 32-bit version based on Windows NT. Well, as we all know, that is not what happened. Windows 95 was introduced and with it a new easier-to-use interface.

It wasn't until late in 1996 that a new version of Windows NT was introduced. Windows NT 4.0 set out to change NT in three general categories: performance, ease of use, and communications. Many of the changes that came along with the new version of NT were available for NT 3.51 before the release of NT 4.0, but the release of the new operating system integrates these changes and delivers the performance that comes with the complete package.

Interface

The Windows 95 interface was a huge success with users of the Windows product line in both the Windows 3.1 world and the Windows NT world. The problem was that the NT interface didn't change at the same time. Microsoft released a Service Pack for Windows NT that included a version of the Windows 95 interface for NT 3.51, but the Service Pack was really only a "surface mounted" version of the interface and didn't include all the functionality of the true Windows 95 interface. It also slowed performance of the operating system because all the user was using was an environment, not really an integral part of the operating system.

Note: When Microsoft finds a way to improve a release of NT or any other software package, they release a Service Pack to allow users to access these improvements immediately. These Service Packs can generally be found in two locations:

- The Microsoft TechNet CD, a product to which you can subscribe in order to get updated information from Microsoft.

- On the Internet at http://www.microsoft.com or ftp://ftp.microsoft.com.

The importance of the Windows 95 interface is the ease of use factor toward which Microsoft has pushed since the creation of Windows. The Windows 95 interface allows the user to access the objects within an object-oriented operating system—easily and with more control. It isn't the intention of this book to make you an expert in the use of the NT 4.0 interface. But it is necessary to cover the interface differences to some degree in order to understand the approach differences. NT 4.0 is deeply rooted in object usage.

The Desktop

The most basic piece of this interface is the desktop. The desktop is the interface between the user and the operating system (see Figure 2.1).

Figure 2.1.
The Windows NT 4.0 desktop.

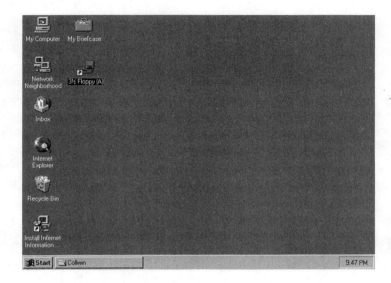

Although it's called the *desktop*, it's really a frame that allows the user to interact with tools that Windows provides. From the desktop, the user gains access to the Taskbar, the My Computer icon, the Network Neighborhood icon, and system's Recycling Bin. All these pieces are discussed separately in this text; suffice it to say that they're all extensions of what is called the *Explorer* (discussed in the following section).

The desktop allows the user to change the environment in which he or she will work. The changes that the user can make at the desktop level are visual and atmospheric. The placement of icons can be changed for better manageability, for example, or the desktop wallpaper can be changed for a little personal flair.

When a user initially approaches the NT 4.0 interface, he is asked to log in just as he would be from the NT 3.51 interface. Once the user provides his username and password, he is then in the desktop established specifically for him. The NT operating system keeps the interface changes made by the user in a profile for that user, so that each time the user logs in to the system it has the same look.

Looking Ahead: Chapter 16, "Client Workstation Considerations," explores how to control the changes that a user can make to the desktop and other areas of the interface by controlling these profiles.

The Explorer

Most of the items that you control on the desktop are really pieces of the Explorer. The Explorer is the backbone of the Windows NT interface. When you accessed previous versions of Windows (prior to Windows 95 or Windows NT 4.0), you interfaced with either File Manager or Program Manager. Explorer is more like the Macintosh Finder. If you have experience with that interface, you know that the Finder controls not only the file system, but also the user's access to programs and controls. The difference with Explorer is that instead of thinking of the file system (File Manager) and the program-launching interface (Program Manager) as separate entities, you now have a single interface that appears in many different ways.

Note: Macintosh users laugh at the rest of the world as we marvel at the advent of an operating system that allows us to put icons right on our desktop and access all of our programs from one starting point. As a matter of fact, they call this interface "Macintosh 89." The reason for all this laughter is the fact that the Macintosh world has had many of these interface features for years. But Microsoft delivers the interface with the ability to use many different processor platforms, and have multiple applications processing simultaneously.

The Explorer appears in different places and in different views. As you look at the desktop, you'll see icons that appear to be separate objects and appear to be run by different applications, but in fact they are really different views of the Explorer.

You could think of many Explorer objects the same way that you think of icons in the old Program Manager. If each drive, printer, network share, or computer was represented by an icon that would open the proper application to control or interface with that item, printer icons would open the printer's control panel or spool; drive icons would open File Manager, ready to present that drive's content; and a computer icon would open a File Manager session, showing all the drives controlled by that user.

The greatest difference between the Explorer and the old File Manager interface is that each object controlled by the Explorer can now be seen in a completely separate window. Within the File Manager interface, users had to open each separate drive in a window within the File Manager application—or open another instance of File Manager (see Figure 2.2). In the Explorer interface, each drive, folder, printer, or network share can become a separate icon that is accessed as a window. Folders (directories), control panels, and computer objects (computers, network shares, and printers) can all appear as separate objects (see Figure 2.3).

Figure 2.2.
A File Manager view of separate drives.

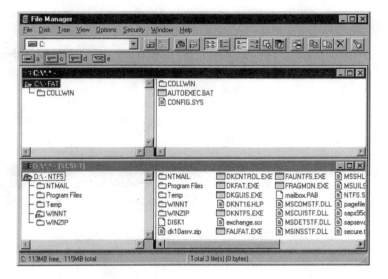

Figure 2.3.
An Explorer view of separate windows for each drive object.

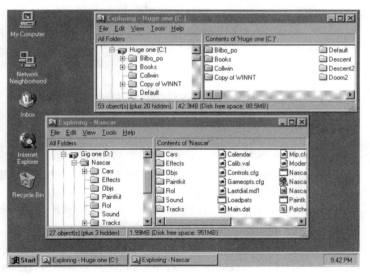

The Explorer has the ability to change the look of the separate windows in which it presents the objects. The windows that you see depend on the type of object that you are looking at; if the object contains other objects, you can select a particular view.

Computer-Based Objects

Computer-based objects appear closest to the old File Manager interface. When you look at the NT desktop, you initially see two computer-based icons: the My Computer icon and the Network Neighborhood icon. These icons are special desktop icons; you can't remove them from the desktop because of the special navigational abilities that they provide.

Within the My Computer icon are all the hardware peripherals that the local computer allows you to access, based on your logon. In other words, if someone's username is allowed access to drives C: and D: on the local computer, as well as to the local printer, she will see a presentation of both drive objects as well as the Printers control panel and the Control Panel object in the My Computer window, as shown in Figure 2.4. If the user also is attached to network drives, she will see those drives and the Network Neighborhood object.

Figure 2.4.
The My Computer window.

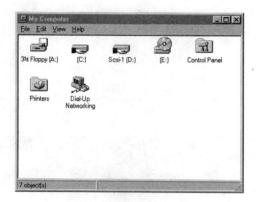

The drive objects are each separate objects that you can open and view; once you open a drive object, you can choose from some new views. Changing views is fairly simple. The reason for changing views is the utility of the different views:

- Large Icon view is best used when what you are looking at is a presentation of few objects or objects that are not files. The advantage of this view is that it presents objects in a very easy-to-read and usable fashion.
- Small Icon view is more of the same, but you get more on the screen at one time.
- List view is simply Small Icon view in a list format.
- The problem with the Large Icon, Small Icon, and List views is that when dealing with files you don't get the detailed file information—file size, creation date and time—that you get from a DOS DIR command. If you need this type of detail, choose the Detail view.

Beyond the general view of the file and folder objects, the user can also decide what he or she wants to view based on file attributes, file type, and whether to view extensions.

Printer Objects

Printer objects appear in several different forms and in many places. But they all break down to two different interfaces with printers and collections of printers.

Printer object icons are all viewed from inside the Printers control panel. The Printers control panel is a single point of access to all printer objects. Opening the Printers control panel displays a list of all of the printer objects to which the local computer has access. This includes local and network printers—just as it does in all other versions of Windows that are network-aware.

A printer object is essentially a combination of a printer driver and the port assignment to which Windows will send information in order to print to that printer. When the user creates a new printer object, he or she double-clicks the New Printer object and is led by a wizard (wizards are covered later in this chapter) through the process of creating a printer object. If you're familiar with the old Printers control panel, you will recognize this process as clicking the Add button, selecting a driver, and then connecting to a port.

Once you have created a printer, double-clicking the printer object shows you the jobs that are waiting to be printed on that printer. A single right-click on the printer object produces a menu that allows you to select the printer's properties.

When you display the properties of a printer object (see Figure 2.5), you are basically opening what Windows 3.1 users would have called the *control panel* for that printer. You can change printer options such as the port, paper selection, resolution, and so on. The ability to reach these control panel screens from a separate object-level menu is one of the changes that make the Windows NT 4.0 interface so much easier to work with than previous versions.

Figure 2.5.
The Properties dialog box for a printer.

Object Menus

As you make more use of the new interface, you'll find that it has hidden jewels. The second mouse button finally has been given a job in the mainstream. The button now presents case-sensitive menus when you right-click almost any object you encounter.

A good example of this is discussed in the preceding section; the properties menu for a printer is accessed through an object menu. Another example of a case-sensitive menu is accessed by placing the mouse pointer anywhere in the wallpaper portion of the computer screen and clicking the right mouse button (see Figure 2.6). Where did that menu come from? It's another example of a case-sensitive object menu.

Figure 2.6.
The screen/desktop properties menu.

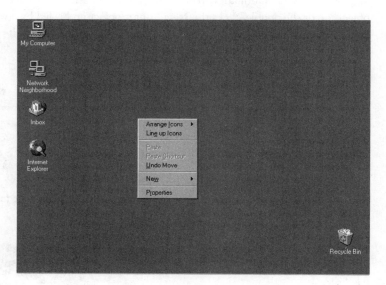

These menus can be found throughout the operating system; with them NT Explorer allows the user to have control over objects while interfacing with those objects, rather than by using some separate control panel or application.

By looking at the printer and screen/desktop object menus, you can see that Properties isn't the only option. The screen/desktop menu, for example, allows the user to do a little housekeeping, add new shortcuts, or create a folder. The concept is simple—if you have a task to perform that is specific to an object in Window NT, chances are that the object has a menu attached to it that will either perform that task or send it to a place that will.

Icons and Shortcuts

If you wanted to gain access to an application, control panel, or printer in previous versions of NT, you needed to open a Program Manager window to access the associated icon. Icons were directly associated with a program or a program information file (.PIF), and those icons had to live in Program Manager. A logical progression of the strong object orientation in NT 4.0 is that it now allows icons to be placed on the desktop. Because the desktop is actually a presentation of the Explorer, you can place icons that you use regularly on the desktop. Icons are still starting points for applications, control panels, and so on, but now they have gained power and mobility.

A new member of the icon family makes an appearance in the Windows interface: shortcut icons. Shortcuts are actually a variation on the .PIF files of old. Shortcuts are used to access .PIF files and Windows-based applications from locations other than the actual application file. The important distinction is that, in the NT 4.0 interface, application icons are accessible through the Explorer in many different places without having to exist in all of those places.

In order to understand the need for shortcuts, it may help to remember that computer objects contain drive, folder, and file icons. All the objects you see are actual files that exist within the Explorer—except for shortcuts. Shortcuts are small files that contain only enough information to take you to the actual application and launch that application. Because the separation between the file system and the Program Manager no longer exists, if you want an icon to launch an application it would be inefficient to make complete copies of the application files everywhere that you want access.

Shortcuts allow small, efficient files to lead you to what you actually want, without taking up extra space in your file system.

Control Panels

Control panels are applications that allow the user to change the behavior of system objects. Items such as printers, network access, and system services are controlled from these applications by making changes in the way the operating system interacts with the object.

Access to the control panel for each object can often be found in the object menu under Properties; if it isn't there, you'll find it in the Start menu under Settings. Real control panel objects are found in the Control Panel window. Most other ways of getting to the Control Panel are shortcuts.

NT 3.51 also has control panels. They are not a new idea in NT 4.0, but the look and utility of these objects is different from the earlier version.

The Network Control Panel

The Network control panel is a great example of a control panel that has changed a great deal in NT 4.0 (see Figure 2.7). The Network control panel in Windows 3.51 was considered difficult to understand by many users. It was difficult to tell what pieces could be manipulated and what couldn't.

NT users who used Windows 95 were envious of the ease of the Network control panel that Windows 95 offered.

The NT 4.0 Network control panel can be accessed by two different methods. The first is the obvious and standard method of opening the Control Panel and double-clicking the Networking control panel object. But another method is a lot easier to get to: Right-click the Network Neighborhood icon on the desktop and choose the Properties object menu choice. This method saves a few keystrokes and gets you where you want to be.

Figure 2.7.
The NT 4.0 Network control panel.

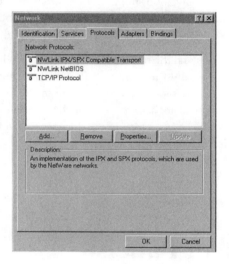

NT 4.0 delivers a look and feel that is very close to the Windows 95 Control Panel, but it's different. The pieces of the Control Panel that are the same are the clear separation of the services and settings. Adding tabbed pages and separating the operating system makes it easier to get to the objects you want to change and easier to see the relationships between services, protocols, and so on.

The differences are clear only if you have used the Windows 95 Control Panel. The Windows NT 4.0 version of the Control Panel has even deeper separation of the items that need to be controlled. Unlike in Windows 95, adapters, protocols, and services have been separated into different pages. This allows the administrator to have greater control over the behavior of those items. In the Windows 95 interface, the choice of an adapter or service may make further choices for you regarding services and protocols.

In previous versions of NT, the protocols and services were listed together as *Network Software*. The choices were less clear. The protocol and service items that could be manipulated were listed with the items that could only be kept or deleted.

Administrative Tools

The tool set that comes with Windows NT 4.0 is still fairly close to the set that came with NT 3.51. You still use the same tool set for the creation of users and to control domain relationships and accessibility. The differences lie primarily in the new tools that are available and the new ways in which they can be accessed.

Administrative Wizards

The ability to create users, groups, printers, and other multitasking operations has been made easier through the use of *wizards* (see Figure 2.8), found in the Administrative Tools. The idea is to be guided step by step through the process of creating NT objects.

Figure 2.8.
The Administrative Wizards toolbox.

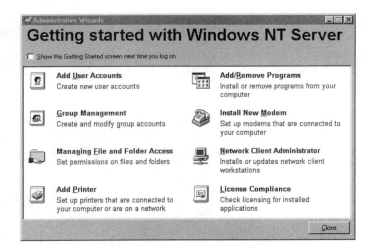

Windows 95 Client-Side Administration

In many office environments, it's impossible or at least inconvenient for administrators to sit at an NT workstation or server, but this doesn't prevent the administrator from having daily tasks to perform on the company network. Contained within the client install possibilities for Windows 95 clients is the ability to add tools that allow administrators using Windows 95 to control and monitor the servers and domains that have until now been the sole dominion of the NT servers themselves. Once you have installed these tools, you'll find a new choice in the Programs submenu off the Start menu called *Windows NT Server Tools*.

The tools that are available are

- User Manager for Domains
- Server Manager
- Event Viewer

The following sections describe these tools.

User Manager for Domains

The User Manager for Domains installed for Windows 95 (see Figure 2.9) is used to create, modify, and delete users and groups. Just like the User Manager for Domains tool in Windows NT Server, this tool allows the full range of features. The administrator can change passwords, set up user permissions, and even create home directories from the remote machine.

Figure 2.9.
The User Manager for Domains.

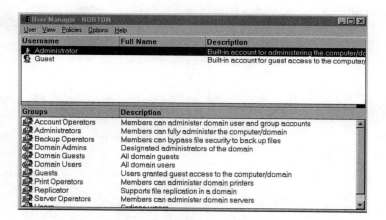

This tool is also helpful in allowing you to put department heads and group managers in charge of managing their own users and groups. In most cases, group managers are using Windows 95 and the same set of productivity tools that their employees use. The ability to use User Manager for Domains from the 95 environment allows you the freedom of putting file security and user management in the hands of the people in charge of users' other tasks.

The fact that the administrator isn't sitting at the server really affects the changes only if the primary domain controller is down for some reason, and then the changes take effect across the network once the primary domain controller is back online.

Server Manager

When you're looking at the Server Manager tool, you're looking at specific server computers on the network and in the domain. The purpose of this utility is to manage those computers and the relationship that they have with the domain.

Once you choose a particular computer to view in the Server Manager, you see a window that's the same as the Properties window for that computer—as if you were sitting at the computer itself (see Figure 2.10). Once inside, you can view the computer shares, users who are logged in, and alerts that have been generated by the computer.

Figure 2.10.
A Server Manager view of a server in a domain.

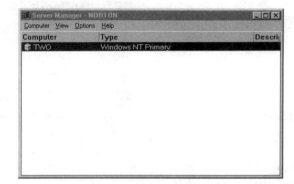

The relationships that these computers have in the domain can also be changed in the Server Manager window. Domains depend on domain controllers to maintain users and groups and the relationships that they have to the objects on the network. Through the Server Manager utility, an administrator can assign the roles of primary domain controller (PDC), backup domain controller (BDC), or server to the servers that participate in the domain.

The significance of this relationship is to maintain the ability to log into the domain even if a failure occurs in the server that controls the domain. It also allows users to attach to the network with more speed and convenience, because everyone is not depending on one machine to authenticate all network activity.

Looking Ahead: Domain controllers are covered at length in Chapter 6, "Networking Brief," and Chapter 8, "Microsoft Network Access Concepts Brief."

Event Viewer

The Event Viewer is like a detailed version of the Server Manager. Like the Server Manager, it makes it possible for remote administrators to find out from a remote location what's happening at the computer level on a server (see Figure 2.11). The Remote Event Viewer is a tool that reads the log files from specific servers. By looking at the log files, the administrator gets a more detailed view of the events and is then able to form a plan of action.

Figure 2.11.
The Windows NT Event Viewer.

Date	Time	Source	Category	Event
i 1/5/97	9:58:03 PM	Print	None	10
1/5/97	9:57:07 PM	Print	None	2
1/5/97	9:56:36 PM	Print	None	20
1/5/97	2:23:38 PM	BROWSER	None	8015
1/5/97	2:23:35 PM	BROWSER	None	8015
1/5/97	2:21:44 PM	EventLog	None	6005
1/5/97	2:23:34 PM	BROWSER	None	8015
12/31/96	1:04:02 AM	BROWSER	None	8033
12/31/96	1:04:02 AM	BROWSER	None	8033
12/31/96	1:04:00 AM	BROWSER	None	8033
12/30/96	10:30:07 AM	BROWSER	None	8015
12/30/96	10:30:05 AM	BROWSER	None	8015
12/30/96	10:28:12 AM	EventLog	None	6005
12/30/96	10:30:02 AM	BROWSER	None	8015
12/28/96	10:30:18 PM	BROWSER	None	8033
12/28/96	10:30:18 PM	BROWSER	None	8033

Event Viewer - System Log on \\TWO
Log View Options Help

The Event Viewer allows you to see the events that have occurred within applications, system hardware, and networking on that server. A few of the items that you can track are

- Failure to load drivers and services
- Time logged on the system by certain users
- New hardware and software components that have been added to the system
- Shutdown of the system and the startup time (viewable only when the machine is up, of course)

Imagine that you receive a call from the Seattle office, explaining that they can't log into the mainframe in St. Louis. You know that the personnel in Seattle access the mainframe through a leased phone line that connects to a Window NT server at their site. This server is running SNA Server for Windows NT. If you are able to look at the Event Viewer and see the events that are occurring on their server, you could see that the SNA Server application is registering an error on the DSU/CSU that it depends on for that SDLC connection.

Looking Ahead: If you're not familiar with the terms CSU/DSU and SDLC, you may want to explore the concepts in Chapter 20, "SNA Connectivity with BackOffice." A *CSU/DSU* is simply a device used to convert leased (dedicated) phone line signals to digital signals needed for your network. And *SDLC* is a communications protocol used by many host machines for these long-distance communications.

Now imagine not having that ability and trying to explain to a user in the Seattle office how to view the Event Viewer at the server while talking to you on the phone. It can be a nightmare trying to walk people through such situations; even if you get that accomplished, the information you get can often be inaccurate.

> **Looking Ahead:** The Event Viewer is one of the advantages that Windows NT 4.0 has over other network operating systems (NOSes). Knowing that something is wrong and knowing what caused it are two very different things. The ability to do both is what makes NT very strong. The Event Viewer is discussed at length in Chapter 25, "Server Management."

Microsoft Services for NetWare (FPNW and DSMN)

File and Print Services for NetWare (FPNW) and *Directory Services Manager for NetWare (DSMN)* together make up a product from Microsoft called *Microsoft Services for NetWare*. These two products are part of an effort by Microsoft to infiltrate the places in the networking world that have until now been dominated by Novell's NetWare product line. It's not that Microsoft feels that they don't have a superior product, but that Microsoft realizes just how powerful a tool market share can be. Novell has (depending on your source) upwards of 50 percent of the market share in the NOS world.

These are not new products for Microsoft, but they were released only in August 1996. These products did run under the NT v3.51 environment, but they function significantly better under the NT Server 4.0 platform. The NT Server 4.0 platform provides better multiprocessor support to this application than v3.51 does.

File and Print Services for NetWare (FPNW)

The FPNW product is what makes the Windows NT server emulate a Novell NetWare 3.12 server so that it can participate in file and print services in the NetWare environment. Access is done through bindery emulation, using any of the NetWare client software that will log into a NetWare 3.12 server. By creating a server that behaves as both a NetWare and Microsoft NT server, the client gets the benefit of Microsoft's powerful application server abilities without having the expense of converting all the NetWare clients.

Directory Services Manager for NetWare (DSMN)

DSMN is a tool that simplifies the life of network administrators who work in integrated NT and NetWare bindery environments. By installing the Directory Services Manager for NetWare package, the administrator can create and manage users from the NT directory structure and have the users automatically propagated to the NetWare servers in the network.

The NetWare servers are updated automatically; nothing needs to be done from the NetWare side to make this magic happen. But be aware that this is only a bindery emulation product. If your environment is a NetWare 4.1 NDS (NetWare Directory Services) environment, this product probably has limited value for you. NetWare 4.0 and higher versions use NDS as the primary means for administering the user account base. By creating users with bindery emulation, you're really creating users outside the normal management paradigm. This can create some real nightmares for your Novell administration.

Other NetWare Integration Tools

Windows NT has also included three other products that help to integrate an NT Server 4.0 plan into a NetWare world:

- **The NetWare Migration Tool.** This tool is used to pull the user, security, and file structure of a NetWare 2.x or 3.x server into an NT server. This tool can be used either to replace a NetWare server or to use it as a reference point for building a new user base in your NT server.

- **Gateway Services for NetWare.** This NT service is used by the NT server to allow any user of the Microsoft Client for NT to pass through the NT server and use NetWare server services. This is comparable to the reverse scenario provided by the File and Print Services for NetWare product, which allows NetWare clients to access the NT server.

- **NWLink IPX/SPX protocol.** By running an IPX/SPX protocol, the Windows NT server allows its services to be seen by Novell clients. It also allows the NT communications to be routed by NetWare servers that run only the IPX/SPX protocol.

These products are discussed in detail in Chapter 17, "NetWare Connectivity."

Until recently, the Windows NT platform had a great gap in interoperability when it came to IPX/SPX. The NT platform wasn't capable of routing IPX/SPX. Since the release of Service Packs for NT 3.51 and the release of NT 4.0, this problem has been solved. This is important because it prevented NT servers from replacing NetWare servers that were responsible for routing network traffic in IPX/SPX environments.

Workgroup Post Office

In the early years of PC networking, a network operating system came with some form of e-mail system. Early versions of NetWare had a very simplistic e-mail system; many peer-to-peer systems today still have these e-mail systems. Most of these e-mail systems were rudimentary but provided some form of basic communications that could be used by everyone on the network. That's what is found in the new NT 4.0 Workgroup Post Office.

Workgroup Post Office allows clients with the ability to access a Microsoft Mail post office to attach to the workgroup post office. This includes clients such as the Windows NT 4.0 and Windows 95 Exchange clients. Schedule+ and the new Outlook e-mail/scheduling client are also capable of using a workgroup post office to share schedules.

This isn't meant to be a robust full-featured post office. It won't exchange messages with other post offices and it doesn't handle large groups of users passing complex mail, but it's a convenient tool if you have a small group that wants to share messages and schedules.

Looking Ahead: You can get more detailed information on the installation and management of the workgroup post office in Chapter 14, "The Workgroup Post Office." You'll also want to look at Chapter 23, "Other Internet Services for NT 4.0," and see the section regarding Exchange Server. Exchange is a full-featured client/server e-mail system that will do all of the outside message handling that the workgroup post office won't.

The Internet/Intranet Is Now a Basic Right

The Internet has been around for 27 years (since 1969) and the protocols and standards that are used on that largest of large networks have been around for nearly as long. But until the invention of the World Wide Web in 1991, the Internet never really interested the business world the way it does today. Microsoft has seen this interest and probably better than any other NOS company has put the Internet and TCP/IP connectivity at the forefront of its product line.

In NT Server 4.0, Microsoft has made the TCP/IP protocol and the World Wide Web an integral part of the package.

TCP/IP

The TCP/IP protocol is the primary communications protocol used across the Internet. The fact that the protocol is owned by the public makes the protocol an open standard that allows any company to include it in their products. Microsoft has chosen to make the TCP/IP protocol an integral part of the NT operating system by making it the new default protocol for NT services.

NT has always allowed TCP/IP to be used as a protocol for authentication, but the default protocol was NetBEUI, a simplistic unroutable protocol that was based on the NetBIOS protocol from PC network days. To make many NT services run correctly, you had to install NetBEUI. This protocol is no longer the default NT protocol.

TCP/IP offers NT a robust, routable, and time-tested protocol that also fits well into the rest of the world.

Internet Information Server (IIS)

In 1996, Microsoft introduced a product called *Internet Information Server* (*IIS*). The product was a free add-on service for Windows NT Server, containing the services necessary to have an Internet presence on NT Server 3.5 and above. Yes, a free product from Microsoft—a very much for-profit company! But if you look closely at what Microsoft is doing with their whole product line, you'll see that the addition of IIS to the NT Server services is one more step to delivering a network operating system that's ultimately accessible and fits very well in a plan to make Microsoft the Internet leader.

Note: Within six months, Novell released a version of their NetWare product that includes the services necessary to make NetWare an Internet server. TCP/IP is also now an accepted protocol for authentication in NetWare.

Internet Information Server now comes as part of the Windows NT Server 4.0 package. IIS contains three products: FTP service, Gopher service, and an HTTP (World Wide Web) server. IIS integrates all three services into one shared management interface (see Figure 2.12) that allows the administrator to control the services. Through the interface you can control security, directory locations, and the logging of site usage.

IIS can be installed as part of the NT 4.0 server install or installed after the operating system install. If you wonder how interested Microsoft is in having you install this product, notice that after you install NT Server an icon is left on your desktop to start the install later (just in case you change your mind).

Figure 2.12.
The IIS management screen.

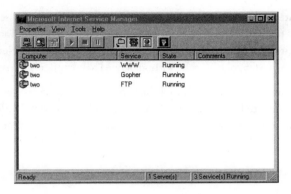

Because IIS uses NT's built-in security, it makes a good choice for an intranet site as well. Intranet sites offer the common Internet tools to deliver information to internal customers (employees, co-workers, and general human resources information). IIS uses NT security to require a username and password to log onto the server. It also makes it possible to allow the public to gain access to certain information and still leave other services private. Thus you can reserve certain information for select clients or for internal needs, while maintaining a public presence.

IIS security also allows you to log what users are looking at and which pages are most popular. You can selectively exclude certain users even from public sites, based on IP address and even subnet. You can be as secure as you care to maintain.

Installing IIS is very simple. The average time to install should be around 30 minutes if you read the screen carefully and TCP/IP isn't set up on your server yet. My record time for installation is 1 minute 50 seconds (no reading—just hitting Enter), and the server worked well. But if you are interested in a more involved installation with considerations for security, logging schemes, and recommendations for server performance, look to Chapter 22, "Internet Information Server."

Summary

This chapter looked at the new features and some of the philosophies that have gone into the creation of Windows NT Server 4.0. The basic structure of NT has progressed but Microsoft hasn't changed the underlying operating system that works well.

The interface has changed in many ways to meet the demands of a user base that was pleased with the utilities that came along with Windows 95. But the interface changes didn't sacrifice the operating system's separation of elements that gave the administrator control. All the pieces of the interface have come together in one product—the Explorer—which has replaced the Program Manager and File Manager of old.

The integration of NT into a multi-platform world has progressed with the introduction of products such as the Microsoft Services for NetWare. These products don't look to replace a NetWare world on their own, but to integrate NT servers into previously NetWare-only companies and let the operating system play its role, without a need to completely reinstall the client base in one fell swoop.

Microsoft has tightly integrated the protocols and services that make the Internet so popular into their entire product line, and NT Server is leading the way. TCP/IP and Internet Information Server (IIS) are now part of the NT Server package and not just interesting pieces that can be added.

II

Peter Norton™

The Windows NT Operating System Environment

3

Windows NT Subsystems

Peter Norton™

The opening section of this book takes a look at the basic structure and history of Windows NT and the changes that have come with the 4.0 version of the operating system. But the look we have taken to this point has been a surface sketch. In this chapter, we peel back the surface of the NT Executive and the user-level subsystems. You'll see that the NT subsystems have made some changes and some services have moved from the user mode to the kernel mode. We'll see how that helps and why those changes have occurred.

To get the maximum power and usability from an operating system, it's necessary to understand what's under the hood. Chapter 1, "Windows NT Introduction," covers the fact that the NT operating system was built on a microkernel model and that that basic structure allows the system to be robust and portable.

You'll remember that the microkernel allows NT to separate the processing of user-level operations and hardware interaction. Because the application interface and the hardware layers are separate, NT Server is capable of running on many different processors (Intel x86, DEC Alpha, MIPS, and PowerPC) without a complete rewrite. NT divides the tasks that must be done into separate sub-systems, each with different and distinct roles to perform. This also allows NT to maintain a robust and clean operating environment even in the event that certain programs become unstable.

Windows NT has two basic modes of operation: a user mode and a privileged processor mode (ker-nel mode). But these modes separate into several different layers to give NT the ability to remove and replace any one of these pieces without having to rewrite the entire system. The modular na-ture of the system allows Windows NT not only to address many different hardware schemes, but also to be addressed by many different applications based on other operating systems (OS/2, Posix, and Windows 3.x).

> **Note:** Be careful with the term *kernel* in this chapter; it's used in two contexts and it's important to keep them separated. The *kernel* is the executive process responsible for communicating with the processor. It does so in privileged processor mode, also called *kernel mode*.

The portion of Windows NT that runs in kernel mode is called the *Executive Services*. The following section describes the Executive Services.

Executive Services

The Executive Services portion of the Windows NT operating system is responsible for communi-cating between the user interface and the actual hardware. The Executive Services are not a single thing, but more of a collection of services responsible for managing hardware-related tasks and get-ting those tasks accomplished (see Figure 3.1).

Figure 3.1.
*The new look to the NT
Executive.*

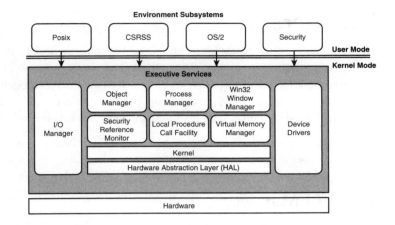

The major differences are found in the Win32 subsystem and the Window Manager placement. This chapter covers the changes in the Window Manager and the Win32 subsystem section, along with the other elements of the diagram.

If the application requires print activity, it can't access the printer directly. It must send that activity to the Executive and the managers it contains. Those managers, such as printer drivers, hardware interfaces, and memory to store the job, all work together within the Executive to get the job done (see Figure 3.2).

Figure 3.2.
*Follow the print job from
application to paper.*

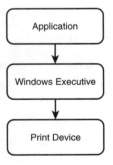

The Executive Services are composed of four major categories of services that each have specific services responsible for getting the real behind-the-scenes work done while the user types on the keyboard and moves the mouse:

- Managers
- Device drivers
- The hardware abstraction layer (HAL)
- The kernel

The following sections describe these services.

Managers

The Executive contains managers responsible for managing the specific items being handled by the Executive—such items as the basic I/O, security, and virtual memory. These systems are the software responsible for managing the events that the Executive makes happen. In other words, managers are not the document to be printed or the printer port on which it will print, but instead they constitute the code responsible for managing the functions between such items.

The following sections describe each of the managers and their areas of responsibility, but keep in mind that all of these items are part of the Executive Services.

The I/O Manager

It should be apparent by its name that the *I/O Manager* is involved in the management of the input and output devices—but it isn't quite that simple. The I/O system is packet-driven, which means that every I/O request is represented by an *I/O request packet* (IRP) as it travels from one I/O system component to another. An IRP is a data structure that controls how the I/O operation is processed at each stage along the way.

The I/O Manager defines an orderly framework within which I/O requests are delivered to file systems and device drivers. The I/O Manager doesn't actually manage I/O processing. Its job is to create an IRP that represents each I/O operation, pass the IRP to the correct driver, and dispose of the packet when the I/O operation is complete.

The Object Manager

In an object-based operating system, it's necessary to have a subsystem responsible for communicating between those objects and creating the objects necessary to make those communications possible. The *Object Manager* is responsible for that management.

The Object Manager is responsible for making sure that the objects needed to complete a task are available to the processes that need them. It tracks the objects that are needed for each process and also manages the objects throughout their life span.

Objects obviously are not physical objects that can be touched. Objects are operating system software tools used to manipulate the behavior of hardware and other software. The concept is for the Object Manager to make the requested objects available to the requesting process. But the manager doesn't stop there; it's also responsible for tracking objects as they pass through the system. The Object Manager is responsible for making sure that the objects that are no longer being used are removed. It's also responsible for making sure that these objects aren't monopolizing the system memory, much like the kernel is responsible for making sure that threads don't consume too much processor time.

The Virtual Memory Manager

Virtual memory isn't actually physical memory at all. Virtual memory is a virtual representation of memory that's really a portion of the hard drive used to fool the other portions of the operating system into believing that more memory exists. Later in the chapter we discuss the memory model on a deeper level, but it helps to understand that the NT memory model depends greatly on the existence of virtual memory to make some of its magic happen.

The *Virtual Memory Manager* is responsible for mapping the virtual memory addresses needed by applications into actual memory. This is needed because the applications need to have the appearance of physical memory. Like the other managers, the Virtual Memory Manager is responsible for making sure that the memory is located in areas with no conflict and is well-behaved.

The Process Manager

For an object to be processed, threads must be created and sent on the processor. Processors use threads to get things done; an activity that contains these threads is also called a *process*.

Threads are the granular form of each process as it passes through the processor. A process, in the simplest terms, is an executing program. One or more threads run in the context of the process. A thread is the basic unit to which the operating system allocates processor time. A thread can execute any part of the process code, including parts currently being executed by another thread.

The Process Manager is responsible for the creation of these processes and threads, and for moving them on the microkernel.

The Local Procedure Call Facility (LPC)

Processes running in the different application subsystems must communicate with one another in order to accomplish anything. For processes in the local machine to communicate with one another, they must use the *Local Procedure Call* (*LPC*) facility.

When an application makes an application program interface (API) call to an environment subsystem, the application process packages the parameters for the call and sends them to a server process that implements the call. It's the LPC facility that allows the procedure to pass the data to the server process and wait for a response.

The Security Reference Monitor

While communication among subsystems in the Executive is necessary, security must still be considered. The piece of the operating system that's responsible for this security at the base level is the *Security Reference Monitor*.

When users make requests and objects in the operating system are required, the Object Manager checks with the Security Reference Monitor to see that a user's security clearance allows him or her to use that object. After successful authentication, whenever the user tries to access a protected object, the Security Reference Monitor runs an access-validation routine against the user's security information to ensure that the user has permission to access the object.

The Window Manager and the Win32 Subsystem

NT 4.0 has made a severe change in the way that Win32 operations are handled and what part of the operating system contains those operations. Environmental subsystems are covered later in this chapter, but in order to understand the new Window Manager you must understand what the Win32 subsystem did prior to these changes.

Win32—Before

In previous versions of NT, the Win32 subsystem was part of the user mode operations. The Win32 environment was an independent environmental subsystem, no different from Posix or OS/2 subsystems. Each of the subsystems is intended to be a stand-alone environment, but the Win32 subsystem had become an integral part of the operating system.

The Win32 subsystem contained five different modules:

- **Window Manager.** Handled input and managed the screen I/O.
- **Graphics Device Interface (GDI).** A drawing library for graphics output devices.
- **Graphics Device Drivers (GDD).** Hardware-dependent graphics drivers (portions of the graphics device drivers were also implemented in the Executive).
- **Console.** Provides text-window support for such items as the DOS-style command-line prompt.
- **Operating System Communications Functions.** Error handling, shutdown, and the pieces of the client/server subsystem (CSRSS).

This close relationship between the operating system and the Win32 subsystem consumes a great deal of memory and CPU. To maintain the relationship with the Executive Services and the Win32 subsystem, the operating system (OS) must communicate with separate modes of operation over and over again. With increasingly graphically-intense applications, this relationship can severely hurt OS performance.

Win32—Today

In the 4.0 release of Windows NT, the majority of the Win32 subsystem has been moved into the kernel mode operations; more specifically, into the following components:

- Window Manager
- Graphics Device Interface (GDI)
- Graphics Device Drivers (GDD)

By moving these systems into kernel mode, the operating system becomes more realistic about what must be done to be efficient. The advantage to those of us who don't write applications and device drivers is that the processes that are written to this operating system can now use the Executive without first writing to the environment. In other words, the processes are now being managed in the place that's most efficient at management. Because the GDI is already in the Executive now, it can make kernel mode calls. Simply put, it's more efficient.

Device Drivers

A *device driver* by definition is a software program that allows specific pieces of hardware to speak to the operating system. You may be able to speak to the processor and memory of the system, but without device drivers you won't speak to much more. Windows NT can't communicate with any device until the proper driver has been installed for that device. With each new piece of hardware you install, you should receive a driver to install with it.

The Hardware Abstraction Layer (HAL)

The layer at the base of the NT operating system is the *hardware abstraction layer* (HAL). This layer is unique for each of the different processor families that NT Server runs on: the Intel x86, MIPS, PowerPC, and DEC Alpha processor families.

You communicate with the hardware subsystem only through the NT Executive. This relationship isn't seen by the user or the applications but instead occurs in the background. Each new class of processor requires that the HAL be rewritten to accommodate the special requirements of that family. Because of the relationship between the different modules, it's necessary only to rewrite the HAL and not the remainder of the operating system.

This relationship doesn't prevent all application writers from having to be aware of the processor, but if they are writing specifically to the Win32 API they need worry only about being compatible with Windows NT. If the application is written to the Windows 16 or DOS environments, direct calls to the hardware may not be required. If they do require direct calls, they won't run properly.

The Kernel

The NT kernel is the base level of any software operation; it's necessary to use the kernel to speak to a processor. If it helps, think of the kernel as a colonel. Its job is to marshal the processes as they pass to the different processors. Each processor in the system contains some portion of the kernel; that portion controls the flow of threads coming to and from the processor. By controlling the priority and time consumption of items using the processor, the kernel stops ill-behaved processes from holding a processor too long and/or locking it up.

User Mode Operations and Environmental Subsystems

So far you have been told over and over again that the NT operating system has managed to separate the protected processor (kernel) mode operations and the user mode. This separation not only allows the operating system to protect itself, but also allows the user a greater choice of applications.

It's the environmental subsystems that allow NT to run applications written for Windows 3.x, Windows NT, OS/2, and Posix. The separate environments in the user mode are comparable to the hardware abstraction layer (HAL) in the kernel mode.

Figure 3.3.
User mode environments.

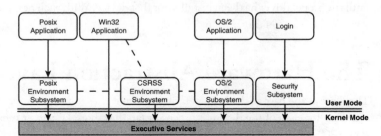

The Client/Server Runtime Subsystem (CSRSS)

In the 4.0 release of Windows NT Server, there are a few differences in the behavior of the user mode operations. The biggest differences have been discussed earlier in this chapter—namely, the transfer of the Win32 server and GDI from a user environment subsystem to an Executive subsystem.

But it's important to understand that the client/server services for the applications and environmental subsystems are still being provided inside the user mode. The services previously being provided by the Win32 subsystem are still being provided by the CSRSS subsystem. The Win32 applications, the Posix subsystem, and the OS/2 subsystem depend on the CSRSS subsystem for services.

The services provided by the CSRSS subsystem include the basic tools needed by the other environments to communicate with the OS and the user. The CSRSS subsystem owns the keyboard, mouse, and monitor. It also communicates with the other environments to convert the application programming interface (API) calls to the Win32 code.

NT Applications

Applications that have been written to utilize the Win32 APIs will run even cleaner in this new relationship between the Window Manager and the user-mode operations. In the new scheme, Win32 applications have a direct relationship with the other pieces of the Executive. By having Win32 inside the Executive, the Win32 application effectively has a friend in the OS business. I have already covered the advantages.

Win32 applications depend on the user mode only for the CSRSS subsystem that allows them access to the basic operating functions.

Win16 and DOS Applications

The way that Windows NT handles DOS and Windows 3.x applications is one of the great differences between NT and Windows 95. The Windows NT operating system is more particular about what it allows to happen and what it doesn't. The result is a far more robust operating system that doesn't allow a single out-of-control application to bring it to its knees.

When the original concept of protected-mode operating systems was introduced, it came along with a new concept called *virtual machines*. The idea was that a processor running in protected mode could create virtual machines that could run separate environments and thus allow for multitasking. This was all well and good, but most of the applications were written in DOS.

NT offers DOS the ability to multitask through the use of these virtual machines. In NT, the Virtual DOS Machine is a process that is created every time a DOS or Windows application is started. *Virtual DOS Machines* (VDMs) are capable of running just as any other Windows NT process, and so they offer DOS applications the ability to truly multitask.

Windows 3.x applications use the VDM for the basic operating system functions in the same way that the Windows environment has always depended on DOS to lay the groundwork. But, in the NT world, the Win16 subsystem relies on the ability of Windows NT to create Windows and deliver basic Windows services. This relationship is called *Windows on Windows NT* (WOW).

WOW is responsible for converting the Win16 application calls into Win32 calls. The biggest problem created by this relationship is the fact that Win16-based applications sometimes require sharing a virtual machine, due to memory requirements. This has caused Windows NT to have to handle these applications differently than any other DOS application. Win16 applications are all handled in the same VDM.

Because of this quandary, it's possible for NT to protect itself from poorly behaved Windows 3.x applications, but not from other Windows 3.x applications. Another odd consequence of this Win16 limitation is that DOS applications are effectively more reliable and able to be multitasked.

The Posix Subsystem

What the heck is Posix and why is your operating system concerned with being able to run applications written to its standard? Is Posix a bizarre unknown operating system that no one has heard of, but Microsoft doesn't want to ignore?

Posix isn't an operating system. Posix is an IEEE and government standard for the creation of applications to run on diverse operating systems. It's used primarily by companies that want to create applications for government-based needs. It's also used by operating system vendors to be sure that their operating system is capable of running applications on which government facilities are based. Until Windows NT, it was a standard used primarily by UNIX OS and application vendors.

Note: The IEEE (International Electronics and Electrical Engineers) is a standards organization that creates and/or monitors standards used by the electronics industry. This helps to assure that the public has a measuring stick for the performance and components of a given piece of software or hardware.

Like many other IEEE standards, there are different levels of Posix compliance. Windows NT is in compliance with Posix Library 1. Library 1 compliance means that NT is capable of doing the following for Posix applications:

- Case-sensitive file naming
- Hard links to provide the ability for files to have more than one name

The basic concept behind the Posix subsystem is to convert Posix API calls to Win32 APIs and send them on to the rest of the operating system. Some limitations do exist for the Posix subsystem. One of those limits is the inability to run more than one Posix session at a time. It's also unable to support networking of these applications.

Note: In the three years that I have been around Windows NT, I have yet to have one client ask a Posix question. I truly believe that the Posix subsystem is more of a milestone for this operating system than a strong market need. It may be a window to the future, though, and shouldn't just be passed off as a stupid OS trick. It does make NT unique in the larger operating system market.

The OS/2 Subsystem

Hopefully, by now you're starting to get the idea that the purpose of these environmental subsystems is to convert the native APIs into the Win32 API so that NT can run applications for the user. The difference with the OS/2 environment is that the OS/2 applications it will run don't include the full range of OS/2 applications written. Also, an OS/2 subsystem isn't part of the MIPS- or Alpha-based versions of NT.

The OS/2 subsystem hasn't progressed since the original NT version. This subsystem is only capable of running OS/2 character-based applications, not those written to Presentation Manager. But the OS/2 subsystem is capable of running different sessions for each OS/2 application, and it's also network-compatible.

The Logon and the Security Subsystem

The logon process and the Security subsystem together are responsible for gaining access for the user to the NT operating system and establishing just what that user is capable of doing. Just as with the other environmental subsystems, the Security subsystem is responsible for taking care of the security needs of the operating system in the user mode of the operating system.

When a user logs onto the operating system, she initially must supply a logon name and password to the logon process. From there, the user is assigned a *Security Access Token* (*SAT*) that will follow her requests throughout the operating system. When requests are made by the user, that SAT contains a complete description of what she is allowed to do.

Memory Model and Management

From the beginning of the Intel-based PC world, one of the most annoying problems for users was the concept of different memory pools—high memory, low memory, upper memory, extended, expanded, and so on. Memory considerations in the DOS/Windows 3.x world was consumed by a problem that had existed because no one in the original PC planning stage could imagine PC needing more than 1 megabyte of memory. You must understand that at the time even certain mainframe systems still ran programs in 64KB memory pools.

In order to solve this problem, Intel-based systems started adding memory above 1MB by doing magic tricks. Some of those tricks included pointing applications to places in the first 640KB that, in turn, would point to memory that existed elsewhere on expansion cards (expanded memory). And even when the processors could access more memory, the operating systems had to support legacy applications that didn't understand.

Memory should be memory. Windows NT maintains a memory system based on a flat linear address space. NT applications can consume up to 2GB of RAM directly.

The memory architecture is a demand-paged virtual memory model. Virtual memory means that the operating system can make it appear to applications that more memory is available than physically exists (see Figure 3.4).

Figure 3.4.
The NT memory model.

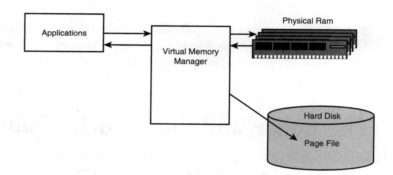

The operating system creates a paging system that involves presenting a portion of the system's hard drive storage as available memory. Obviously, hard drive storage doesn't respond as quickly as RAM, but versus not being able to make an application run or make a service available, speed becomes less of an issue.

Summary

Windows NT subsystems allow NT to be a robust and open system. By dividing the user and protected processor (kernel) modes of operation, Microsoft has succeeded in creating an operating system that is very accessible to the user's needs without exposing it to badly behaved applications.

The kernel mode operation of the NT operating system is primarily made up of a set of subsystems called the NT Executive. The Executive Services portion of the Windows NT operating system is responsible for communicating between the user interface and the actual hardware. The Executive Services aren't a single thing, but more of collective services that are responsible for managing hardware-related tasks and getting those tasks accomplished.

The user mode portion of NT is composed of different environmental subsystems that are created for each of the different faces NT can put on. It's the environmental subsystems that allow NT to run applications written for Windows 3.x, Windows NT, OS/2, and Posix. The separate environments in the user mode are comparable to the hardware abstraction layer (HAL) in the kernel mode.

Finally, we see that NT is a more open memory model than users of Intel-based systems have been used to. It finally allows the applications to have a flat memory model not encumbered by the old rules of DOS.

4

Installation Considerations

Peter Norton™

When maximizing an operating system, particularly a network operating system, there's no better time than during the initial install. There are some changes that just can't be made easily after that point. Every operating system experiences what could be called "OS decay," but if the system is set up properly the first time, you can avoid the majority of the server problems.

 OS decay is a term I first saw used by John Dvorak in a *PC Magazine* article. It describes very well a problem that PC users notice the longer they use a particular PC. As a user installs and removes applications, drivers, and utilities on an operating system, not everything gets removed or reset. Slowly but surely the system begins to slow down and even lock up for no obvious reason. The only solution is to reinstall the OS from scratch.

Here is a list of some of the major items that will be covered in this chapter:

- Minimum hardware requirements
- Preparing the hard disk for installation
- Checklist of hardware settings
- Hardware compatibility list (HCL)
- Installing Windows NT Server
- NT licensing options
- Migration and upgrade
- Windows NT 3.5x server upgrade
- The NetWare Migration Tool
- Power considerations
- UPS solutions
- Advanced hardware notes

System Requirements

When you're installing an operating system that's as hardware-intensive as Windows NT, it becomes very important to pay attention to the minimum requirements. It's also important to be aware of the realities involved. Often you find that the minimums are on the verge of ridiculous. You should imagine that you're putting together a work vehicle and not your first car as a teenager. This operating system won't tolerate a hardware scheme that doesn't meet or exceed the minimums.

Minimum Hardware Requirements

When putting together a hardware scheme for a file server, I like to imagine that I'm putting together a ship that will have to get my company and me across the ocean. In the planning of vital systems, you need to be aware of the quality of the parts. You must be confident that the pieces will carry you through your journey, because you can't make frequent stops to service your craft. Minimum requirements to get you across the ocean aren't what you want to find when things go a little off-course and the crew is getting restless.

You need to be careful where you save money or cut corners. A good rule of thumb when purchasing server computers is that there are three items for which you should always buy the best you can afford—and for one of them, you must always get as much as you can afford:

- **Memory.** Like the old adage about the most important thing in starting a new business being *location, location, location,* RAM, RAM, RAM is the one item that you can't ever have too much of in your file server. Windows NT is an extremely memory-intensive operating system; if you call for technical support, one of the first things they'll hang a problem on is lack of RAM. In the later section "Calculating Memory Requirements," I cover how to calculate the exact amount you need.

- **Hard drive.** The pieces of any machine most likely to fail first are the moving parts. In a PC file server, the only continuously-moving parts are the hard drives. Ironically, if the entire server melted into a pile of molten lava and you could save one piece, you would want the data on the hard drive. The piece of your server you most value is the most likely to fail. With that quandary, you can see that this is not a place to save money. Later in this book, we cover many different schemes for protecting yourself in the event of that meltdown.

- **Processor.** There are many things that you can change about your server later in its life— even the processor. But the processor can only be changed within its family. In other words, if you buy an Intel 80486, 66MHz machine today because it meets your minimum requirements, you need to be aware that you've trapped that machine in the 80486 line for the remainder of its life (see the note that follows). Pentium machines can be upgraded in the Pentium family line, Pentium Pro in the Pentium Pro line, and so on. If you can afford to purchase a machine with the top processor by that manufacturer, it will help your upgradeability later in the machine's life.

Note: The Intel company does make a Pentium Overdrive processor upgrade for machines equipped with the 80486 (486) processor. The problem is that the rest of the system containing the new Pentium processor is unable to utilize a Pentium processor. *PC Week*'s review stated that machines with the Pentium Overdrive processor actually performed slower than the machines with the 486/100MHz processors.

It's a good idea to be aware of the warranty that your server carries. Most top manufacturers offer a three-year on-site warranty for server-class machines. This type of warranty is important for two reasons. First, you don't really want to have to unplug your file server from the wall and carry it to the vendor. Second, the life cycle of any PC is three to five years. If you can get the vendor to cover a machine throughout the better part of its life cycle, you reduce your headaches considerably.

Intel x86 Systems

Following are the system minimums for NT Server running on an Intel x86 family machine:

- 16MB of RAM
- 125MB minimum of available disk space (*Note:* Additional space may be required, depending on your installation method.)
- VGA-level video support
- Keyboard
- IDE, EIDE, SCSI, or ESDI hard disk drive
- 486/33 processor or better
- CD-ROM drive, 1.44MB or 1.2MB floppy disk drive, or active network connection

Reality break: Throughout this section, I'll be breaking in to make sure that you realize what the reality of the installation process is.

When installing Windows NT Server, I wouldn't start the install without a minimum of the following hardware items:

- **Pentium processor or better.** This operating system is truly going to take advantage of the ability of a Pentium processor. You're going to really feel the difference in this version of NT with a 486 processor.
- **32 to 64 megabytes of RAM.** If you want to use NT Server for anything more than a nightlight, you need to have plenty of RAM.
- **Windows NT-compatible CD-ROM drive.** The reality of any software installation today is that you need a CD-ROM to get a smooth installation.

RISC Systems

This system has the same requirements as the x86 systems in the preceding section, except for these items:

- RISC processor compatible with Windows NT
- 160MB minimum available disk space (*Note:* Additional space may be required, depending on your installation method.)

Calculating Memory Requirements

Calculating the exact amount of RAM needed in a Windows NT server is possibly more of an art than a science. Microsoft provides a formula to calculate the memory needed, but I'll tell you right up front that it's a bit tough to follow. And it may be impossible to get it right on the first try.

The reason that I consider this calculation to be so difficult to get right is the fact that it involves predicting human behavior. In order to understand how much RAM is required, Microsoft would like you to know four things:

A. The base memory requirement of 16MB (see the note that follows for a more realistic number)

B. The average size of the data file opened by each user at peak network use

C. The number of active users at peak use

D. The memory required by all the executable files at peak load

> **Note:** The minimum requirement of 16MB of RAM is not nearly enough for most systems as a starting number. As you read through this book, you'll find place after place that mentions basic NT services not included in the minimum requirement for RAM. I strongly recommend that you use a base number of at least 32MB—and more is better.

Once you've compiled the information you need, follow the calculation below to determine the optimal amount of starting RAM:

$$A + (B \times C) + D = \text{Total Required RAM}$$

Example:

32MB	Base
+52MB	Data (1MB of data per 52 users at peak use)
+20MB	Server applications
104MB	RAM needed

The ability to run this calculation is a bit like the chicken-and-the-egg problem. If I don't have the server yet, how can I tell you what my average number of users will be at peak? If I don't have users, how can I tell what they'll use?

A possible solution to this problem is to coordinate user groups and/or users in the different departments that you trust to discuss what's being used by these users. Build a relationship with these people to help you better understand what their groups are doing at peak times of the day and what services they'll be counting on from you.

The NT operating system doesn't lend itself well to rules of thumb or quick fixes in this area. You have to know what will be done on this server before you install it. It has always been known that it's better to study your software needs before your hardware needs.

Hard Drive Space Requirements

The list that follows contains the requirements for hard drive space on NT Server:

- Standard installation: 124MB free drive space
- Using `WINNT.EXE` /b option: 124MB free drive space
- Standard installation from the local hard drive: 223MB free drive space

Reality break: If you can afford the disk space, set aside a 500MB FAT system partition. By creating a system partition with a FAT file format, you allow yourself the flexibility to later boot the server with another operating system or with utility disks.

Preparing the Hard Disk for Install

Before you can install NT 4.0 on an existing hard drive, it's necessary to make sure that the drive is compatible with or prepared to accept NT. Some of the items that need to be considered are the drive format, compression, and drive type.

NT is not compatible with any form of drive compression other than the compression that comes with NT. It's not compatible with Microsoft DoubleSpace or DriveSpace, Stacker, or any other compression software or hardware. If you're going to upgrade an NT server that is running a compressed boot drive, you can remove the compression. To remove NTFS compression from an NT drive, type the following command:

```
compact c:\ /u
```

If the system that you're upgrading is using HPFS, you must remove it before you install NT 4.0. In 4.0, Microsoft decided to stop all support for HPFS. The best idea if you need to access data on an HPFS drive is to back it up and format the hard drive. Then restore the data after installing NT 4.0. If the drive is on an NT machine before installing 4.0, you can simply convert the drive to NTFS, but don't assume that you can go without backing up the data first.

Windows NT supports only the following EIDE addressing schemes:

- Logical block addressing (LBA)
- OnTrak Disk Manager
- EZDrive
- Extended cylinder head sector (ECHS)

If you use one of these schemes, some implementations require special partitioning utilities and disk-preparation utilities. Don't format these drives under Windows NT.

Hardware Settings Checklist

Before you install NT, there are plenty of things to keep track of that can trip you up. There are also pieces of information that you won't be able to get during the installation. Having a checklist can help you to be prepared before you get to that point. The following sections provide the details.

Adapter Cards

For each item in the following list, I've left an open line to indicate that you'll want to fill in this information before you start. (You most likely won't want to do this in the book, but it will give you something that you can copy to create your own list.)

- Video adapter or chipset type_____
- Network card IRQ_____
  - I/O address_____
  - DMA (if used)_____
- Connector type (for example, BNC, twisted pair)_____
- SCSI controller adapter model or chipset_____
  - IRQ_____
  - bus type_____
- Mouse type and port (COM1, COM2, bus, or PS/2)_____
- I/O port IRQ_____
  - I/O address_____
  - DMA (if used) for each I/O port_____
- Sound card IRQ_____
  - I/O address_____
  - DMA_____
- External modem port connections (for example, COM1, COM2)_____
- Internal modem port connections or IRQ and I/O address (for nonstandard configurations)_____

Note: Before you trust your eye to catch all this information, you should be aware that NT 4.0 comes with two utilities that will help you find the information that you need:

- SCSITOOL—Found in the \support\scsitool directory on the NT CD-ROM. This tool is used to recover information about the SCSI devices attached to your machine before you begin installing. By running the MAKEDISK.EXE program, you create a boot disk that will collect the SCSI device and controller information from the machine. This presumes that the controller is a device supported by NT.

- NTHQ—Found in the \support\hqtool directory on the NT CD-ROM. This tool is used to recover hardware information from your machine before you begin the installation. By running the MAKEDISK.EXE program in this directory, you create a boot disk that will collect the PCI, EISA, and ISA system information on hardware components. A list will be put on the disk, called NTHQ.TXT.

To use these utilities, you need to use the MAKEDISK utility to create boot disks. These disks are created by opening the directory and typing **MAKEDISK** with a 1.44MB 3½-inch floppy disk in the floppy drive. The MAKEDISK utility will then make a boot disk that will launch the utility. After creating the disk, shut down and restart the PC with the disk in the floppy drive.

Unsupported BIOS Enhancements

Microsoft lists the following items as unsupported BIOS features. In this case, though, I suggest that you check with the specific hardware vendor to see whether they have further information. Some vendors have features that may sound like the same item as the listed items, but in fact may work fine.

- 32-bit I/O BIOS switch
- Enhanced drive access
- Multiple-block addressing or rapid IDE
- Write-back cache on disk controllers
- Power management features

Miscellaneous

There are a couple of items left that don't fall within the previously mentioned headings, but that are important to your installation:

- On some computers, shadow RAM and L2 write-back cache cause detection and hardware problems, including stopping responding and STOP error messages (blue screens). If you experience any problems, these features must be disabled at the BIOS level. Check your computer user manual for information on disabling these features.

- Verify that there are no power-on-self-test (POST) errors prior to starting Setup. Make certain that each adapter and peripheral device is set to an independent IRQ, memory address, and DMA channel.

Hardware Compatibility List (HCL)

When most network operating systems talk about a list of compatible hardware, the list is more a list of suggestions. When Microsoft says that they won't support any hardware not found on the HCL, I've found that they're not making a lame suggestion. The Windows NT HCL is a compilation of computers and system hardware that have been extensively tested with Windows NT for stability and compatibility. It's the guide used by Microsoft Product Support to determine whether a computer is supported for use with the Windows NT operating system.

If at all possible, I suggest that you use only hardware on the HCL, or that the vendor of the hardware be willing to stand firmly behind the hardware. Obviously, all of the hardware on the market that supports Windows NT 4.0 is not listed in the HCL. Perfectly good hardware is created everyday, and, for that matter, by the time someone gets through testing hardware for the HCL it may be obsolete. Use the list as a guide. Whenever possible, use an item found on the list, but don't abandon an item solely based on its not being listed.

My suggestion is that you stay with a vendor that has typically been approved on the HCL. These vendors will usually be willing and able to support you in your time of need, even if their product isn't on the list. If these vendors report that the product will work, it will—or they'll know how to help.

Because of the constantly changing nature of such a list, the easiest way to keep track of the HCL is through the World Wide Web. The Web site that Microsoft has established for finding HCL information is at the following site:

```
http://www.microsoft.com/isapi/hwtest/hsearchn4.idc
```

Domain Role

In general, Microsoft networks incorporate two different security schemes for sharing of information and peripherals: workgroups and domains. The domain model, as mentioned earlier in this book and again later in detail, involves a group of servers and workstations that agree to share a common list of user and group permissions.

As mentioned in Chapter 2, "What's New in Version 4.0?," domains depend on domain controllers to maintain users and groups and the relationships that they have to the objects on the network.

Administrators can assign the role of primary domain controller (PDC), backup domain controller (BDC), or server to the servers that participate in the domain.

The significance of this relationship is to maintain the ability to log in to the domain even if a failure occurs in the server that controls the domain. It also allows users to attach to the network with more speed and convenience, because everyone isn't dependent on one machine to authenticate all network activity.

Looking Ahead: The subject of domains and the relationships that are established in domains is covered in Part III of this book, "Account and Domain Management."

If you don't plan your domain before you begin installing your server(s), you'll find that you have quite a mountain to climb when you get done. The severity of not getting the domain name correct could include having to reinstall NT.

To add a server to an existing domain, you also have to do one of the following:

- Create a computer account in the Server Manager utility prior to installation.
- Grant the installing user account permission to create the computer account prior to installation.

If you're installing a new domain, the machine you're installing will be the PDC and you'll need to create the domain at that time.

Tip: Be careful about naming your domain the same as a workgroup that exists on the network already. It's fairly common to find that the company or division name is already taken. But this can really cause confusion in software (and humans). When someone's new installation asks what the name of their workgroup is, the natural response is *Company Name*. This may creep up and hurt you later if you've decided to give your domain the company name.

A possible variation is to name the domain *name* plus 1, 2, 3, and so on (for example, NORTON1). This scheme implies growth and keeps your domain out of the way of any renegade workgroups that might pop up.

Installing Windows NT Server

The actual installation of Windows NT server has changed very little from previous versions. The most obvious change is the extremely annoying auto-start that has been added to the CD-ROM when placed in a Windows 95 or NT 4.0 machine. The installation is started from a command-prompt level. But from there you have a lot of decisions to make.

Media Choice

Windows NT can be installed from the following media:

- Floppy boot disk and CD-ROM installation
- CD-ROM only
- Network installation from another server

Choosing an installation method has as much to do with efficiency as with equipment. When you're making the choice as to which method to use, consider the possible things that can go wrong and the method that will offer the smoothest transition to the new server. The following sections provide a few details to think about.

CD-ROM

When installing the NT operating system from CD-ROM, you have many choices to make. The possible options all have some specific reason that you might want to use them. Here's a quick checklist of items to consider in a CD-ROM based installation:

- **Does your CD-ROM exist on the HCL?** If you'll boot from the NT floppy disks to start the installation, your CD-ROM must be supported by NT.
- **How will you access the CD-ROM for the installation?** If you're installing directly from the CD-ROM, you must be able to access the CD-ROM from the operating system that you use to start the installation.
- **What processor does your server use?** If you're installing on a RISC-based machine, you must install from the CD-ROM.

Network Installation Considerations

Installing NT from a network drive is a choice that really makes sense only if you'll be doing installations on a number of NT machines. The idea is to provide a commonly-accessible place from which to start the installation. If you're installing NT on numerous computers with common drivers and a common network, it makes sense to place all the files that you'll need in a common place and access them over and over again—particularly when the alternative is to carry around a handful of driver disks.

The installation can be started from any drive that's accessible over the network and that the installing user has the right to use. The following network operating systems and others can be used to support this type of installation:

- Windows NT, any version (Server or Workstation)
- Windows 95
- Windows for Workgroups
- Novell NetWare 2.x, 3.x, 4.x
- Banyan Vines

Installation Method

Once you start installing Windows NT, you'll be given a choice of two basic forms of NT installation: Express and Custom. The choice amounts to the same choice that you've always had with Microsoft products: Do you want Microsoft to make the standard choices for you, or do you prefer to select the features you want?

If you choose to install NT with the Express method, you'll be given the standard network protocols and the monitor drivers that NT detects that you need. The drives will be partitioned that NT wants, and so on. This method allows you to get the operating system installed with the fewest number of questions possible.

The custom installation allows you to make changes. It will allow you to add network protocols and extra network cards—but it will also allow you to decide that you don't want certain items installed. Items like the game FreeCell, for example, may not fit into your server needs.

Note: Keep in mind that if you remove games such as FreeCell, you may have some very boring evenings on the phone waiting on Technical Support. Those games weren't added without some forethought.

Installing Windows NT Server from Floppy Disks

The installation of Windows NT on Intel x86-based PCs can be started by inserting Disk 1 of the three NT installation disks into floppy drive A: and placing the CD-ROM in the NT-supported CD-ROM drive. Then you must reboot the PC to start the installation.

Depending on the packaging of the NT version that you've purchased, you may not have boot floppies. If you don't have the floppies, you can create them by following these steps:

1. Place the Windows NT CD-ROM into the CD-ROM drive of a PC that can address the drive.

2. Type **D:** (replace **D** with the drive letter of the CD-ROM drive you're using) and press Enter.

3. Change directories to the **\i386** directory by typing **cd\i386** and pressing Enter.

4. Type **WINNT.EXE** and press Enter. (If you're installing NT 4.0 on a machine containing an older version of NT, you must use the command **WINNT32.EXE** to use a 32-bit version of the install program.)

5. You'll be prompted to provide the machine with three floppy disks (see Figure 4.1). Mark the disks and refer to the first paragraph in this section to start the installation.

Figure 4.1.
Creating the NT floppy disks.

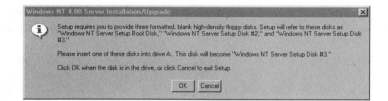

Warning: Performing the installation of NT without creating floppy disks can seem like an awfully convenient installation method if everything goes well. And, for the most part, I'll confess that, when working on projects that include the installation of many NT machines, I perform diskless installations. But I want you to be aware that if you don't have a set of NT boot disks and an emergency repair disk, you are opening yourself up for a long afternoon or evening trying to clean up if something should happen to a boot sequence on your server. Power fluctuations, failing hard drives, ill-behaved code, and many other things can cause your boot sequence to go wrong. Boot disks help to recover from those problems.

Starting the Installation Without Boot Disks

The installation of NT can be started from a command line, as opposed to starting it with boot disks. The differences are primarily based on the source you're starting from and the processor in the server.

Starting the Intel x86 Server Installation

When starting the NT installation on an Intel x86-class server, you use the WINNT.EXE or WINNT32.EXE command. To get to these commands, follow these steps, based on your drive source:

1. Change drives to the drive containing the Windows NT installation files. For example, if the NT installation files are still on the CD-ROM in drive E:, type E: and press Enter.

2. Change directories to the directory containing the Intel x86 install files. For example, if the NT startup files are in the INSTALL directory, type cd\INSTALL and press Enter.

3. Type the appropriate start command for the operating system you're starting from; then press Enter. Windows NT-based starts require that you type WINNT32.EXE. All other command-prompt starts require that you type WINNT.EXE.

Windows 95 CD-ROM Installation

When you install Windows NT 4.0 onto a PC that's booted to the Windows 95 desktop, you may get the impression that you're about to experience a friendly upgrade (see Figure 4.2). You're not.

Figure 4.2.
The Windows NT opening screen in Windows 95.

The installation of Windows NT from the Windows 95 desktop interface is simply a convenient tool for installing Windows NT along with or over the Windows 95 operating system. Although Windows 95 and Windows NT 4.0 now share very similar interfaces, Windows NT is not able to upgrade Windows 95 in the same sense that Windows 95 could upgrade Windows 3.x or that NT 3.5x could upgrade Windows 3.x.

Note: The reason you can't upgrade from Windows 95 to Windows NT is that Windows NT and Windows 95 don't store setup information in text files anymore. All of the more complex setup information is stored in the Registry. Because Windows NT and Windows 95 have Registries that are not compatible (on a binary level), Windows NT can't upgrade a Windows 95 system.

If you install Windows NT on a machine that currently uses Windows 95 as its primary operating system, you'll need to decide whether you'll use NT only from that point forward. If you want to do so, it would be in your best interest to back up your data files and reformat the hard drive. Then install Windows NT from scratch and restore the data files you'll need.

By installing NT alongside an installation of Windows 95, you'll still have to reinstall the applications for NT use. By reformatting the drive and reinstalling the applications, you eliminate a great deal of dead weight in files and directories that were used by Windows 95 only. Your chances of finding all the unused files and directories are very slim (and it's time-consuming).

Note: Dual-boot installation is possible, but not discussed in this book. The dual-boot process isn't a commonly needed form of installation in the server world. Hopefully, your server won't be a Windows 95 workstation by day and an NT server by night. For more information on NT Workstation, see *Peter Norton's Complete Guide to Windows NT 4 Workstation* (1996, Sams Publishing, ISBN 0-672-30901-7).

The Windows NT Setup option that appears in the NT opening screen (refer to Figure 4.2) in Windows 95 or Windows NT 4.0 is an interface to install Windows NT, but not to upgrade any version of Windows. If you click the Setup button on this screen within Windows 95, you'll be installing a dual-boot installation of Windows NT 4.0 that will present a choice of Windows NT or Previous Operating System when you start.

Installing Across the Network

The installation of Windows NT from across a network is just like installing from the CD-ROM at a command prompt. The difference is the preparation. I've already covered why you might want to perform this type of installation. Now let's consider what you must do in order to have access to the files:

1. Share the Windows NT 4.0 CD-ROM across the network.

   or

   Locate a shared network directory to install from. See the earlier section "Network Installation Considerations" for supported network operating systems.

2. From that shared directory, type **XCOPY D:\I386 /s** (where **D** is the CD-ROM drive letter).

3. From the PC to be installed, log onto the server containing the installation files. Change drives to the drive containing the Windows NT installation files. For example, if the NT installation files are on drive **F:**, type **F:** and press Enter.

4. Change directories to the directory containing the Intel x86 install files. For example, if the NT startup files are in the **INSTALL** directory, type **cd\INSTALL** and press Enter.

5. Type the appropriate start command for the operating system you're starting from; then press Enter. Windows NT-based starts require that you type **WINNT32.EXE**. All other command-prompt starts require that you type **WINNT.EXE**.

Switches in the **WINNT.EXE** Command

When running the WINNT.EXE setup of Windows NT Server, you can change the behavior of the installation by typing a particular switch setting after the WINNT.EXE command. The following switches allow you to control the install:

- /O or /OX—Create boot disks only.

   If you place the switch /O after the WINNT.EXE command (WINNT.EXE /O), the Windows NT install will create only the boot disks necessary to install NT with a floppy disk boot.

- /B—Diskless installation.

   Inserting /B after the WINNT.EXE command causes the NT install to skip the creation of boot disks and install the necessary files to install NT directly on the PC from which you're installing.

- /U:*script file name*—Unattended installation or upgrade of previous NT installation.

   The unattended install of Windows NT requires that you not only place the /U switch at the end of the opening installation line followed by :*script file name*. It also requires that you also use the /S to give it a source for the NT setup files. For example, in this command line, UNATTEND is the name of the script file: WINNT.EXE /U:UNATTEND /S (see Figure 4.3). Microsoft provides a preconfigured file for this process that you can edit. It's located in the same directory that you use as an install source and is called UNATTEND.TXT.

   The /U switch can also be used to upgrade previous versions of NT, when you want NT to simply gather the information from the previous version without asking for your input.

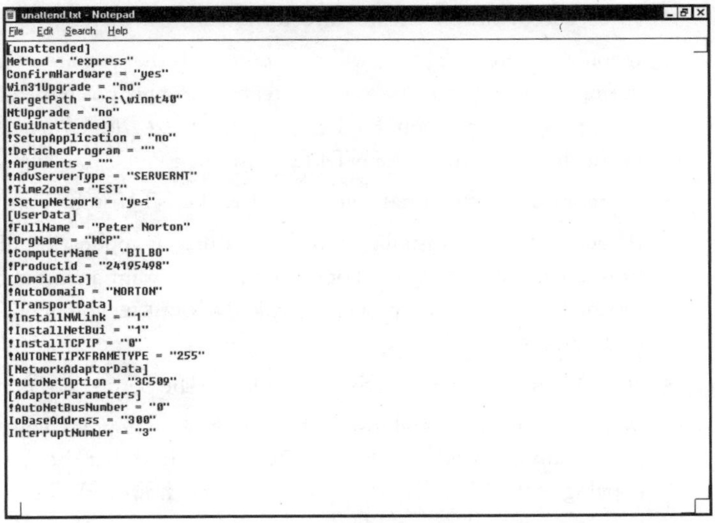

Figure 4.3.

A source file for an
unattended install.

```
unattend.txt - Notepad
File  Edit  Search  Help
[unattended]
Method = "express"
ConfirmHardware = "yes"
Win31Upgrade = "no"
TargetPath = "c:\winnt40"
NtUpgrade = "no"
[GuiUnattended]
!SetupApplication = "no"
!DetachedProgram = ""
!Arguments = ""
!AduServerType = "SERVERNT"
!TimeZone = "EST"
!SetupNetwork = "yes"
[UserData]
!FullName = "Peter Norton"
!OrgName = "MCP"
!ComputerName = "BILBO"
!ProductId = "24195498"
[DomainData]
!AutoDomain = "NORTON"
[TransportData]
!InstallNWLink = "1"
!InstallNetBui = "1"
!InstallTCPIP = "0"
!AUTONETIPXFRAMETYPE = "255"
[NetworkAdaptorData]
!AutoNetOption = "3C509"
[AdaptorParameters]
!AutoNetBusNumber = "0"
IoBaseAddress = "300"
InterruptNumber = "3"
```

- /S[:]*source*—Locates and uses a specific source file.

  This switch specifies the source for the NT setup files. When using features like the unattended install, you must give NT a source to find the files it would normally ask for. By placing /S followed by the exact location of the source files in the WINNT.EXE command line, you give the NT setup a source to find those files without asking (for example, WINNT.EXE /S:\\SERVER1\NTSETUP).

- /X—Skips the creation of boot disks.

  If you don't want to create boot disks during the install, but you'll be using them for the install, use this switch. This is different from the /B switch because you are using the disks, but you just don't want to create them during the install.

- /T:*drive_letter*—Specifies a location for the necessary temporary files created for the NT installation.

- /I:*inf_file*—Specifies a setup information file.

  The setup information file DOSNET.INF is normally used by NT Setup, and it's unnecessary for you to specify a file. But should you want to create a more streamlined version of the file for your installation needs, this switch is necessary. I suggest, though, that this is not a good place to experiment. It's possible to cause problems that you don't see until much later.

- /R:*directory_name*—Creates directories during install.

  If you've created scripts or will run commands that require a directory to be created during the install, this switch will create it. Simply place the directory name in the *directory_name* position. For example, WINNT.EXE /R:NORTON will create a NORTON directory in the directory where the NT files exist.

- /E:*command*—Runs a final command after the NT install.

  If you need an NT installation to run a utility or application file after the installation is finished, use the /E switch. For example, if you want an alarm to go off after the install is finished, and the alarm program is called ALARM.EXE, you might use WINNT.EXE / E:ALARM.EXE.

- /F—Doesn't verify files as they're copied to the Setup boot floppies.

  When running a normal install that builds setup floppies, you may want to speed the process along. By adding the /F switch, you'll find that the system no longer verifies the copying of the files. This is not a wise choice, however. The time saved will be small and the time it costs later could bite pretty hard.

- /C—Skips the free-space check on the Setup boot floppies you provide.

  This is another option to speed the process along when running a normal install that builds setup floppies. When you add the /C switch, the system won't bother to check the disks for the space needed to place the files.

Setup—Beyond WINNT

You have seen several different ways to start the Windows NT Setup. Now we need to explore the path that you'll follow once you've started the setup process.

By starting the setup process with WINNT or WINNT32, you start a program that will create the boot disks necessary to start the machine for setup (see the note on the /B option if you don't want to boot from floppy). It also copies the temporary files necessary to install NT onto the primary hard drive of the machine on which you're installing. You are then requested to restart the machine. Once that's done, all NT installations that aren't automated are basically the same.

The machine will restart from the floppy disks you created in the WINNT setup, unless you chose the /B install method. In either case, once the machine is through the reboot process, you'll be presented with the screen shown in Figure 4.4.

> **Note:** This screen offers you the opportunity to repair a previously installed NT 4.0 installation that has become corrupted, but if you don't create a repair disk during install you won't be able to do the repairs.

Figure 4.4.
The NT Setup opening screen.

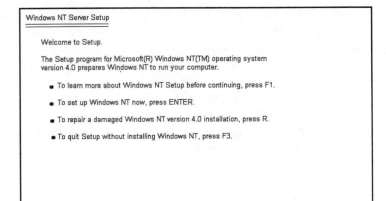

```
Windows NT Server Setup

    Welcome to Setup.

    The Setup program for Microsoft(R) Windows NT(TM) operating system
    version 4.0 prepares Windows NT to run your computer.

        ▪ To learn more about Windows NT Setup before continuing, press F1.

        ▪ To set up Windows NT now, press ENTER.

        ▪ To repair a damaged Windows NT version 4.0 installation, press R.

        ▪ To quit Setup without installing Windows NT, press F3.




ENTER=Continue   R=Repair   F1=Help   F3=Exit
```

This Server Setup screen is the launching point for any Windows installation. Before you press Enter to begin the setup, some items need to be in your possession. It's all stuff we've covered earlier, but now is when you need it.

Here's the install checklist:

- Server name
- User information for the Administrator and initial user accounts (username and password)
- Driver disks for any hardware not specifically listed on the HCL, or updates for those that are supported
- Additional network cards you want to install (beyond the initial card)
- IP information per network card (if used)
- IPX network address per network card (if an IPX/SPX network already exists on that segment)
- Your role in the domain
- Hardware settings such as IRQ, base I/O, DMA, and so on for the hardware that's installed in this PC

At the Server Setup screen, press Enter to proceed with the standard installation. NT will attempt to autodetect a supported mass storage device. If your hard drive controller was on the HCL and drivers for it were available to Microsoft when NT was written, then it will be selected automatically and presented to you as the default choice for NT installation.

If your controller driver isn't available, NT will request that you specify an additional device driver by pressing the S key. (This is also the command to add any additional mass storage controller drivers that you'll need when using NT. As an example, if you want to use a separate controller for external hard drives that aren't listed, now is the time to add those drivers.) After pressing the S key, you'll be instructed to select from a list of available drivers from NT. But the only choice you'll see is Other (Requires Disk Provided by Hardware Manufacturer), as shown in Figure 4.5. If your driver is in the Microsoft HCL, you might try pressing the up-arrow key and looking through the drivers that are listed. Otherwise, select Other. You'll be requested to insert the manufacturer-supplied hardware support disk into drive A: and press Enter.

Figure 4.5.
Specifying a driver.

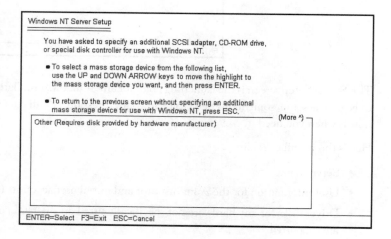

If NT drivers exist on the disk you inserted, they'll be displayed for you to select your particular driver; then press Enter. NT will attempt to load the driver you chose; if it works, you'll return to the drivers list, but this time a driver will be listed. Simply press Enter to continue the install. If no driver is listed, you need to contact your controller manufacturer for help in discovering which driver is correct for your controller.

Peter's Principle: Check the Web Site for Driver Help

When you get into a tough situation with a driver not loading (even though it came with the hardware and says NT), don't feel alone. Many so-called NT drivers are old and untested—even from some reputable companies. The best bet today is to check the company's Web site first. The hardware companies usually have specific areas set aside for drivers and patches for their products and NT. It's a good idea to check with many of these sites even before you do the install—they can sometimes tip you off to a problem before you have it.

Once NT has finished detecting and loading the drivers for your system, it will present one more list of the hardware it has detected. You can change these items, but I suggest that if you're not sure you just leave this list alone. NT has based this list on something during detection that made it believe this is what you have. As an example, don't go looking for a Compaq mouse when Microsoft shows a Microsoft mouse. Microsoft Mouse drivers are often the proper driver for third-party mice. If you approve of the list, press Enter to continue.

Initial Hard Drive Setup and Selection

Once the proper drivers have been selected for the hard drive controllers on your server, you'll be asked to select a drive on which to install NT. Drive selection not only involves choosing the proper drive, but also selecting and managing drive partitions (see Figure 4.6).

Figure 4.6.
Drive selection and management.

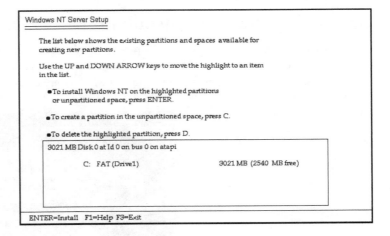

The first item of business in this section of the setup is to make sure that the drive on which you want to install is partitioned and has enough available space to install NT. Remember, you're going to need a minimum of 124MB of partitioned hard drive space to install NT.

Once you've decided on a particular hard drive on which to install NT, follow these steps:

1. If the drive isn't partitioned, you must create a partition. Partitions are created from this interface by selecting the unpartitioned space you want to use and pressing C to create a partition. Then specify the amount of the total space you want in the partition and press Enter.

2. If a partition exists, but you want to reorganize that drive's partitioning scheme, press the *D* key to delete the current partition.

3. Finally, once you have a partitioned space that you want to use, select it and press Enter. Any unformatted space will be formatted, and you'll be asked in which directory you want NT installed. \WINNT is the default.

Your choice of install directory in this case is very important. If you have a previous version of Windows 3.x or Windows 95, you'll be prompted to install Windows NT in that same directory. It's not a prudent idea to install your dedicated Windows NT server in the same directory as any other operating system, and particularly one that it may share files with. Don't install Windows NT Server in the same directory as either of these operating systems.

After pressing Enter once, you'll be asked to confirm your choice. You can escape and choose again or press Enter to install in the directory you've already chosen. NT then proceeds to check your hard drive for corruption. You may be asked for driver disks for these checks, but once the checks are made the NT setup will begin copying files to your hard drive of choice.

Once the files are finished copying, you need to remove any floppy disks from the disk drive and press Enter to restart the computer. That finishes the WINNT portion of the installation.

Setting Up the New Installation

Once you have restarted the machine, you're presented with the graphic interface of Windows (see Figure 4.7). You'll be asked some rudimentary questions, and Windows will walk you through the process of gathering information and setting up networking services.

Figure 4.7.
NT Setup starts its graphical phase.

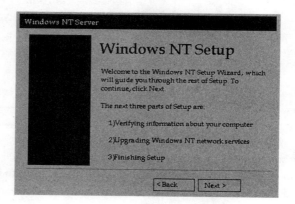

After you enter your name and company name, you'll be asked to provide license information. For more detailed information on licensing, look forward a bit to the section in this chapter called "NT Licensing Options."

Server Name

You'll next be asked for a computer name (server name) that will be used throughout the network for identifying this server machine. The name must be unique and can be up to 15 characters in length. If you don't have a naming convention in your company, now is the time to get one. Server names can be a helpful way of determining location and/or purpose of a server without having to actually go to the server. It can also be a fun way of knowing the relationship between servers.

In some companies, all the servers in a particular department may be named after birds of prey: falcon, eagle, hawk, and so on. In another department, servers are named after characters in *The Hobbit*: Bilbo, Frodo, Gollum, and so on. It isn't boring, and you can tell that the servers are related in some way. If you must be logical and businesslike, you can name the servers by department number, floor, or division. Combinations of useful information like this can be extremely helpful when attempting to track where users should be logged on and where a server fits into the bigger picture.

Initial Identification

"Server type" (see Figure 4.8) is another way of saying "domain role." The choice you make here can be changed, but before you choose you'll want to look at the references to domain role earlier in the chapter and possibly read the Microsoft networking chapters (Chapter 6, "Networking Brief," and Chapter 8, "Microsoft Network Access Concepts Brief").

Figure 4.8.
Server type choices.

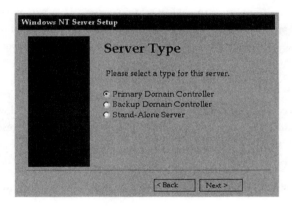

If an NT domain already exists, and you're unsure of this server's role in that domain, choose the Stand-Alone Server option. Servers can be promoted and demoted in the domain roles, but attempting to place a server in a domain role that it doesn't belong in could cause network inconsistencies for others.

Next you'll be asked to provide an administrator password. Obviously, it's extremely important that you remember this password. But it's equally important to note that this may be your only back door into the system if the other admin accounts lose their way or sabotage your system.

At the end of the install process, you'll be asked for the computer name again. This is really your last chance to change the computer name before the computer is fully installed, but it's also when you'll be asked to provide a domain name. Be very careful to make sure that the server is attached to the network physically and the domain name is spelled correctly prior to finishing the install of NT Server. Computer names can be changed, but domain name changes require a great deal of hassle. In a large install, it's nearly impossible.

Emergency Repair Disk

Probably the silliest decision I see administrators make about their networks is not to make an emergency repair disk or to bypass the creation of the initial three disks for NT installation. If you are at this point in the installation and haven't already made the three setup disks, don't fret. You can go back and make those later. The important thing for now is that you should if at all possible make an emergency repair disk now. It will take five minutes to do (even on the Flintstones floppy drive), but it may save you hours of reinstall time later if something gets corrupted.

Selecting Components

The components that you're allowed to select at this point of the installation aren't necessary to the use or functionality of the NT operating system. They can make life easier, however. These choices are all applications that allow you to make use of the server from a user's standpoint. But make no mistake—this is definitely a place to save some hard drive space or a few CPU cycles.

Accessibility Options

The Accessibility components are added to NT and to Windows 95 to allow users with disabilities to make better use of Windows. Sound Sentry, for example, presents a visual cue when the PC would make a sound. These options help the disabled user to use the system without having to feel like he or she isn't getting the whole experience.

These items are some of the options that you can choose to add:

- **Accessories.** These applications help all of us make use of the office without having to leave the PC. Items such as calculators, paint programs, and WordPad allow you to have desktop props that exist on your computer desktop rather than your physical desktop, while screen savers, wallpaper, and clocks make your electronic desktop more usable.

- **Communications.** These tools are really mostly outside of the realm of anything that most people would use from a server-class machine, with one exception. HyperTerminal is a very robust 32-bit terminal emulation package that comes along with NT. This package is helpful in the event that you need to check modems for Remote Access Services (RAS), check serial port connections, or make a bulletin board (BBS) connection to download a patch or driver.

- **Games, Multimedia, and Messaging.** All three of the remaining options are extremely frivolous, and probably have no business on your server. (With the possible exception of games, for the long evenings.)

Initial Network Components

The network is a critical part of an NT Server installation. Unlike its NT Workstation counterpart, NT Server must be connected to a network in some way. Among the initial choices of network participation, you'll find no way to choose "none." You can't even deselect the check box for Wired to the Network (see Figure 4.9).

Figure 4.9.
Selecting your network participation: Yes or Yes?

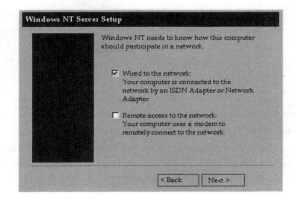

In the first two choices, the important decision is whether you're going to be initially installing Windows NT Remote Access Services (RAS). By selecting RAS, you're opening up an entire line of questions that will help you to ensure that users can later log onto the network through the modems of other communications devices attached to the server.

Internet Information Server

You'll also be asked during the installation if you want to install Internet Information Server (IIS). The name of this product can be deceiving. The product that will be installed is actually a combination of an HTTP server (for the World Wide Web), an FTP server, and a Gopher server. All of these products are services that allow for information distribution over the Internet if you're connected to the greater Internet. But this product is also available to users in-house, through your intranet.

The IIS product is covered in detail in the networking section of this book. But for now, if you don't understand the product, I'd suggest not installing it. The product can be installed very simply later, and it does take up some hard drive space, as well as possibly taking CPU cycles and memory from needed services.

Network Interface Cards (NICs)

The system will autodetect network adapters during the next step in the install. You will initially be presented with a screen that asks you either to allow NT to detect the network adapters in your PC or to select your adapters from a list of available drivers (see Figure 4.10).

Figure 4.10.
Setting up the network adapter.

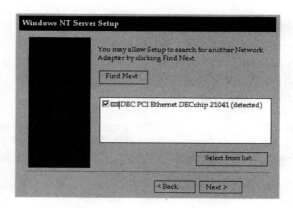

The best bet in this portion of the installation is to allow NT to detect your network card first. If your NIC doesn't appear in the network adapters list, you should click the Select from List button. The list consists of approximately 40 NICs that are supported natively by NT. If you don't find your card listed, insert the NT driver disk provided by the manufacturer of your card into drive A: and select Have Disk. You should now see your card listed.

Choose your card; you should see it listed in the network adapters list. Continue this process until you've added each of the NICs in your PC to the list; then click Next. If you have multiple cards of the same make, you need to add them all by either choosing Find Next for the automatic addition of cards or Select from List to add undetectable cards.

Protocol Choices

The three protocol choices presented during NT install are TCP/IP, IPX/SPX, and NetBEUI. These three protocols should fit almost any networking need you might have, and if you put together your checklist before you started, this should be a rather easy install. If you don't understand network protocols, read the networking section of this book before you proceed. You can certainly weave a tangled web in this area if you're not careful. Networks based on hurried early planning are tough to work with for years to come.

If you'll be using one of the three standard protocols, select the protocol and click Next to proceed. If you need a different protocol, click Select from List and view the list. You can also select from a list of protocols provided on a floppy disk by using the Have Disk option.

Be aware that the protocol choices you make at this point will require user setup during the final stages of the installation. After you've finished telling NT all the pieces you would like to add to the operating system at startup, NT will prompt you for protocol information such as IP address, IPX network address, and domain name server. This information should be in your checklist.

Services

In the NT operating system, *services* are those applications that the operating system runs for the users without user intervention. They might include remote access, name resolution, or even mail services.

Unlike most of the install options, you don't have the ability here to not install certain network services. When the Network Services screen presents itself, removing is not an option. However, if you want to add services, you can use the usual Select from List and Have Disk options.

Date and Time Settings

Setting the date and time screen should really be pretty simple and straightforward, but you need to be aware of the fact that the server can be the central time source for an entire network. By clicking the arrow button beside Greenwich Mean Time, you can see a list of different time zones. Select your time zone and be careful to remove the check mark from the option Automatically Adjust for Daylight Saving Changes if your area doesn't make this change. You'd be amazed how many service calls are made for that reason.

> **Tip:** Even though you might think that you have the date and time right, take a second to look under the Date & Time page on this screen.

Video Adapter Settings

NT should list the video adapter that it believes will be compatible with your current video setup. However, if you have a special adapter, you may have to change the settings.

As you look at the Display Properties screen in NT, you'll notice that you can change many things. During setup, the important setting is Display Type. If you think that you understand this setup based on your experience with Windows 95, you're not completely right, but close.

Windows NT display properties are different because NT takes much deeper control of the hardware. This is because it's built with operating system control in mind—not user hand-holding like Windows 95. During setup you can't change the display controller that NT chooses for you. If NT doesn't find a video adapter that it recognizes, it will choose standard VGA, and you'll need to change your driver post-install.

You can change the presentation settings. NT has a feature that Windows 95 doesn't, making changes to your video mode a more controllable process. This feature is the List All Modes button, which allows the user (depending on the adapter) to list all the supported modes for that video adapter without hunting and pecking.

Once you've changed presentation settings, you'll need to test the settings before proceeding. If you don't choose Test before you choose to proceed, NT will do it for you. The test takes only a few seconds, and again demonstrates that NT deeply controls the video process.

NT Licensing Options

NT licensing follows the same honor system that Microsoft has followed for years. Microsoft is willing to allow the administrator to specify how many licenses he or she has. But make no mistake—this doesn't mean that you have the right to attach as many users as you want to the server. The intent is to give the administrator a convenient way to make use of his or her software.

The license to use Microsoft products refers to the number of users who will be attaching to the server. With many operating systems, this means the number of concurrent users at peak use. In other words, the most users you'll find using the system at any given moment. With Microsoft's licensing scheme, this can be true or not. I'm sorry to say that it really depends on the product you're dealing with. You'll need to read the license that you've purchased.

While you're installing Windows NT, you'll encounter a Choose License Mode screen. This screen allows you to choose one of two methods of validating your license to use the product. You need to be careful which license form you use, because you'll only get one chance to change in the future:

- **Per server.** This licensing method asks you to enter the number of users you want to have access to your server at any given moment. If you have 100 licenses and want to prevent any more than 100 users from logging on at any time, you should choose this method. With this method, it's unnecessary for the administrator to track the number of users on the system in any other way. NT won't allow the number of concurrent users to exceed the number that's entered.

- **Per seat.** When you purchase licenses for Windows NT on a per-seat basis, you are trusted to be in full control of the number of users that you allow to log onto the system. This requires that you run some form of license count application to track the number of users who are accessing the server at any given moment.

Products such as Site Lock by On Technologies or Microsoft SMS allow you to stop users from accessing the server once the license limit has been reached. But it's important to note that your company is legally responsible for making sure that all users are properly licensed.

Migration and Upgrade

If you're installing an NT server in a new environment with no legacy server, this section of the installation chapter is probably not for you. Migration is necessary only if you have a system in place that you want to change to NT. You may want to move on to configuration.

Migration means to move information from one system to another. Hopefully, when you migrate you get to bring a certain amount of your previous system environment with you (see Figure 4.11). NT's migration tools allow for migration from several operating systems of users, groups, files, and security—not just from Microsoft products but from Novell NetWare as well.

Figure 4.11.
The NT Migration facility.

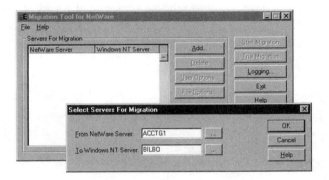

Windows NT 3.5x Server Upgrade

The upgrade of NT Server 3.5x to NT Server 4.0 is simply a matter of running the install of NT Server 4.0 and making the install directory the same for NT 4.0 as it was for 3.51. But making any software or hardware change to your file server always requires that you be very careful, even for a change as simple as this. You are at risk of losing data any time you make an operating system or hardware change. This upgrade is pretty low risk, but there are some things you should be conscious of before you start:

- Have at least two copies of a current backup of the data you can't afford to lose, in the event of a total loss. This includes data files, user and group information, and security considerations.

- Be aware of any driver changes necessary for your hardware. This includes the possible lack of support for your legacy hardware. If you must change hardware, make whatever changes you can prior to the upgrade of the OS. It can be catastrophic to be dealing with an OS upgrade at the same time as a hardware change.

- If the server being upgraded is the primary domain controller (PDC), you'll want to promote another machine to PDC prior to the upgrade. When the upgraded machine has run successfully for a short time, you can promote it back to PDC.

- The operating system upgrade time is not a time to add new protocols or network segments. Get the server running in the capacity in which it was running before, and add new items after the server has run for a short time. Server operating system upgrades make the user population nervous from the start. Any problems in a new protocol or network segment will be seen as a problem with the new operating system and could undermine your efforts considerably. Users have a tendency to panic and start blaming every computer-related problem on the last major change. This can make a great install turn to an operating system reversal (back to the old version) in the wink of a boss' eye.

- If you have installed the preview addition of the Windows 95 shell on your NT server, you need to remove this add-on before you upgrade.

Peter's Principle: Never Change Two System Variables

Server administrators should follow this rule of thumb as often as possible: Never change two variables at once. It just makes for bad science. For example, don't add memory and change a network interface card in one opening of the computer case. If problems arise in conjunction with the change, you could be stuck for finding the answer. In this example, if the PC occasionally locks up during a particular application, you now have two possible culprits.

If your goal is to maintain the same user list and security paradigm from one NT server to another but not replace the old server, you need to consider using a domain model. If you're running your current server security through domain management, by making the new server a member of the same domain you've added that user list to the new server. It's just that simple. For more information on domains, see Part III of this book, "Account and Domain Management."

The NetWare Migration Tool

The tools created by Microsoft for migrating from NetWare to NT are well thought out and feature rich. The fact that Novell has the largest slice of the network operating system market hasn't gone unnoticed by Microsoft. No other operating system made by a manufacturer other than Microsoft has a conversion tool so completely dedicated and maximized for its use. This is very definitely a smart bullet aimed at making NetWare removal from your company as quick and painless as possible. In fact, combined with other products by Microsoft, your clients may not even know that NetWare isn't there.

The Migration Tool for NetWare provides tools for migrating data files, user accounts, groups, and security translations from a NetWare-based server to the NT equivalent. The tools are a migration facility and not an upgrade system. When you're changing from the NetWare server to the NT server, you can't simply run a utility at the NetWare server that will convert it to an NT server. Instead, you must create your NT server on a separate machine and migrate the information.

If you intend to use the same machine as your future NT server that you are currently using as your NetWare server, you have a problem. Your option would appear to be whipping your NetWare server clean of everything, including the operating system, re-creating all your user accounts, groups, and security manually, and then restoring your backup tapes of data to the new installation. The problem with this form of change is that you have no fall-back position should anything go wrong during the installation. Your faithful old server is gone.

A possible solution to this problem is to create a small NT Server machine capable of receiving only the user, group, and security information. Some machine in your office should be able to meet the minimum requirements of being an NT server; it's only for the migration period. Establish this machine as the PDC of your future domain and migrate the users, groups, and security equivalencies to the small NT server. Make sure that you have at least two good backups of the NetWare server data and security. Then proceed to install NT Server on the NetWare server as the BDC of the domain. Last, promote this machine to the PDC, and then you can do as you please with the temporary server.

After installing Windows NT, you'll find the Migration Tool for NetWare in the Administrative Tools menu. Once you start the tool, you'll be asked which servers you want to migrate from and to. When you look at the screen to choose the servers you will migrate, you'll see buttons beside the windows. These browse buttons allow you to select the server of choice.

Now that you've chosen the initial players in the migration, you can choose more servers to migrate to and from. You aren't limited to migrating one server to one server; you can migrate several different NetWare servers to one NT server to consolidate into one "super" server. You can also migrate data from one large NetWare server to several NT servers in order to departmentalize. To add more servers for migration, you need only click the Add button and fill in the blanks. Obviously, the Delete button is to delete a particular migration pair.

Once you've chosen the systems to migrate, you can begin making adjustments to the user information and files that you would like to be migrated.

User Options

The User Options (see Figure 4.12) allow you, first of all, to decide whether you would like to transfer users *at all*. By removing the check mark from the option Transfer Users and Groups, you have effectively made the migration into a file and directory transfer.

Figure 4.12.
User and group options.

Tip: If you're migrating user and security information to servers in a single-domain model, you have to understand that one set of user information is kept in the domain. In this case, transfer only user and security information to the PDC in the domain. It's redundant to migrate this information to a BDC and then realize that the BDC will send it to the PDC.

Mapping Files to Migrate Users and Groups Manually

The next check box in the User and Group Options dialog box is Use Mappings in File. This option gives you manual control over the usernames that will be transferred and what the outcome will be once the transfer has been made. The file that this option is asking for is called a *mapping file*. The file consists of NetWare user and group names and the corresponding NT user or group name to which the information will transfer.

Tip: If you're extremely concerned with password security in the migration, you need to be aware that the only real way to give a specific password to migrated users is to create a mapping file. NetWare security will not allow any migration of passwords—even in its own utilities. But if you use the mapping utility, you can create and edit each username to have a third column that contains the password of the user. It's fairly easy to generate a listing of random numbers and letters for passwords. It's also far more secure than telling everyone that their username is their password. How many people do you think will log on as the CEO that day?

When you select the mapping option and type the name you want your mapping file to have, the next choice is to click the Create button, which sends you to the Mapping File Creation Wizard. This wizard enables you to set the options for the initial creation of the mapping file (see Figure 4.13). The options are pretty straightforward.

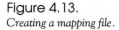

Figure 4.13.
Creating a mapping file.

You can choose to migrate only users or groups or to migrate both. If you choose to migrate users, though, you'll be asked what you want to do about passwords. If you intend to add passwords later, you may want to choose No Password, and then edit the file later to include a comma and a password after each username. It seems to me that if you intend to make everyone's password their username, security is fairly porous.

After making your selections, click OK to create the mapping file. Creating the mapping file is primarily a launching point for obtaining a file that you can edit. The editing of the file once it's created is what makes mapping files so powerful.

In the mapping file, the user and group names from NetWare are listed first, followed by a comma, and then the name as it will appear in Windows NT. In the username area, you'll find a third row for the password (NetWare name, NT name, new password). The file can be edited from any DOS or Windows editor and saved as a text file. It won't be used until you return to the Migration Tool.

Passwords, Usernames, and Group Names Options

Within the pages available in the Users and Groups window are very basic radio button choices. All these pages are used to create a generic scheme for migrating your system to NT.

The Passwords page asks whether you want to create users with no password, make the user's username the password, or give everyone a mutual password. At a minimum, please require each user to change his or her password on first logon, so that if someone breaches security, you'll know when the real user attempts to log on with the universal password. This page alone is enough to encourage you to use a mapping file for migration.

The Usernames page is used primarily to generate switches and errors in the event of duplicate usernames (see Figure 4.14). You can decide to add a prefix to any duplicates (for example, JOHN could become NT_JOHN). You could decide to not add duplicate users and have NT alert you to the fact that users were skipped. You can also decide to copy the user permissions and information to the existing NT user and assume they're the same.

Figure 4.14.
The Usernames page.

The Group Names page is also used to generate switches and errors, but of course it's for group-based migrations. The options are to migrate the groups with a prefix or to simply not migrate it and instead generate an error alerting the administrator that the group was not migrated.

Defaults Options

The Defaults page is used to control the default transfer of account restrictions and administrative rights. When users with supervisor rights are transferred from a NetWare server to an NT server, you need to consider that some users may have supervisor rights that you don't want to have such rights in the new NT environment. If you want users who have supervisor accounts in NetWare to be given the same rights in Windows NT, you don't need to change the Use Supervisor Defaults switch.

The only bad marks I would have to give Microsoft are related to the NetWare Directory Services (NDS). But NT does offer the option of carrying over supervisor-type accounts. If you also check Add Supervisors to the Administrators Group, you'll effectively be making the supervisors on NetWare your administrators in NT. These options are not so scary on a new NT install, but you need to carefully consider the ramifications of making this move in a currently established NT domain.

File Options

The migration of files can be customized and manipulated to allow for placement, file type considerations, and migrating only certain files. By default, all the files and directories (except system and hidden files and directories) will be transferred to the first NTFS drive. By selecting the File Options page, you can change where things will be pointed.

As you open the file options, you'll be presented with a listing of the NetWare volumes to transfer and the NT volumes to which they'll be transferred (see Figure 4.15). NT will transfer the NetWare directories by default to a directory on the NT volume that's named for the NetWare volume it came from. Those directories will then be shared, so that they'll appear to the user as they always did in NetWare. You'll notice in the window that it translates your NetWare volumes into NT UNC share names.

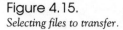

Figure 4.15.
Selecting files to transfer.

Because all the volumes are automatically selected, the options initially presented are modifying or deleting migrating pairs (kind of like lovebirds).

The deletion of volumes to be migrated is pretty straightforward; once you delete one volume, obviously, now you can add a volume.

Modifying the items seems to be mildly more complex, but not much. The reasons for modifying a volume migration range from placing the data on a different drive to wanting to completely revamp the volume-naming scheme. The gist of the modifications is the same either way. Modifying a migrating pair involves selecting the pair by clicking the pair in the File Options window. After selecting them, you need to click Modify to open the Modify Destination window. In the Modify Destination window, you have the option to change the share name that NT will use to publish the directory, and you have the option of changing the directory that will receive the NetWare volume.

Launching the Migration

After you've made the changes to the default migration options, you're ready to launch the actual migration. Make no mistake—migrations can be scary stuff. If you have ever migrated servers with gigabytes of data and large numbers of users, you know that what you plan and what you end up with are often different things. At 5 to 15 megabytes per minute transfer rates, in some cases, that's an awfully long time to wait for failure.

NT migration offers an exceptional tool for avoiding just such a disaster. It's called a *trail migration*. The Trail Migration button enables you to run the migration in a mock fashion and records the events that would have happened in the three log files that NT creates during the migration:

- LOGFILE.LOG—Complete record of the migration.
- SUMMARY.LOG—Statistical summary of the events that occurred.
- ERROR.LOG—Listing of any errors such as conflicts or disk errors.

These files allow you to see that duplications were troublesome, that certain directories couldn't be created, and so on—before you have to ruin a weekend trying to clean up the mess.

> **Note:** Trail migrations take a fraction of the time because they don't do the actual file transfers or create the users. They really only simulate the activity.

After successfully running a trail migration with no errors (or errors that you consider "expectable"), you're ready to launch the migration. Keep in mind that this will take a considerable amount of time. It may not be possible to migrate large servers even in 24 hours, if you take your time and follow the guidelines laid out earlier in this section for any upgrade or migration. User and security migration can go very quickly, but file and directory migration can take as long as one minute for every 5MB—that can be as much as 3½ hours for 1GB.

You also need to take this opportunity to set expectations. If possible, don't promise that this process will occur over a 24-hour period. Allow yourself at least one extra day for a "do over." Many times, you'll think you launched that overnight process and find instead that you had one more key to press before it really launched.

Last of all, don't destroy your old NetWare server until you have had key users log onto the new system and test your game plan. The fact that an administrative account can make it work doesn't prove a thing. Everyday users are what matters, and you may be doing something that they're unaware of or are incapable of doing. You might, for example, be able to access an application and all its data, but you may have excluded that user base from getting there when you established security rules.

Power Considerations

Once a new computer system has been in place for ninety days without failing, there are few things that will fail without outside intervention. We've already discussed hard drive failure and the fact that hard drives are the most vulnerable item in your server, but the most common cause of failure in hard drives and all the other pieces inside your server is abnormal power.

There are very few buildings that maintain a steady flow of clean, noise-free power. Among the few things that can destroy printed circuits and manufactured computer chips are abnormal fluctuations in power and/or heat. The problem that an abnormal fluctuation in power causes is heat or abnormal charge being introduced to things that were created by heat and static electrical charge. Things "pop" or "fry" when the power is too great, and when power is too low the computer's power supply will produce nasty power fluctuations of its own. During low power, your server can literally commit suicide.

Information being stored on a file server is at particular risk during power fluctuation. You must remember that information being written to a file server by users is not all immediately being written to hard drive storage; some of it is being stored in RAM or virtual memory. What happens to the items in RAM when you pull the plug on your server? Right—it goes away. For that reason, any data that is cached or waiting to be written to the hard drive will be lost in the event of a power loss.

Applications that are being run at the server are also of particular interest. Database applications by nature don't deal well with being shut off improperly. The problem is based on the fact that database files share differently than most shared files. Databases share pieces of themselves called *records*, not the whole file. For this reason, if you stop a database without properly shutting down the application, the data becomes fragmented and corrupted. If power is lost, you often lose not only the record that was out, but the entire database.

Hard drive storage also has an extreme aversion to abnormal power. Hard drives depend on power to spin properly, and they spin from the moment the server is powered up to the moment you turn the server off. While they're spinning, they're also moving read heads over and back across the platters that contain your data. If you will, imagine someone passing a wrecking ball over your important information over and over again. Obviously, we want that wrecking ball to have all the power it needs, to not have to take a rest in the middle of our data. For the same reason, it's very important that server-class machines maintain power to the hard drives until all of the data is written and drive activity is finished.

UPS Solutions

There are many different solutions to the power problem, but the one you need is the one that gives you the most control and protection. For NT file servers, the easiest way to control power is with a quality UPS (uninterruptible power supply). A UPS can be nothing more than a car battery in a modified metal box, but you should look for a UPS that will help to solve all the power problems, not just the loss of power.

Here's a UPS checklist:

- The unit should provide enough power storage to maintain power to your server for at least 20 minutes.
- The UPS should be capable of communicating with NT 4.0 to alert it of a power failure.
- Software should be packaged with the UPS to communicate with the NT OS, to request that it shut down in an orderly fashion.
- The UPS software should be able to allow for a variable time between power loss and server shutdown. If the server simply runs until the UPS power is almost gone and then shutdown occurs, you have a quandary when the power comes back up for only a few minutes. The UPS battery is not recharged, but your server is running.
- Power surge protection and voltage regulation should be included in your UPS unit. It's ridiculous to have to plug a surge protector or voltage regulator into your $1,000 UPS, but I've seen it done.

UPS Support in NT

Most UPS units include vendor-supplied software that will allow you to manage the UPS and its relationship with NT. If you don't have that, you probably need to question the quality of the UPS you've purchased. But if you have a unit that doesn't contain software, you can use the software provided by Microsoft with Windows NT. The NT solution to UPS monitoring software is a control panel called UPS (see Figure 4.16). This control panel is more of a security blanket and isn't used often, but it will get the job done.

Figure 4.16.
The UPS control panel.

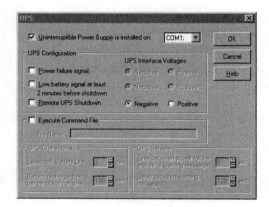

The first consideration that you must make for this control panel to work is that you must have the ability to connect this UPS to your computer through a standard COM port (1–4). The cable used to make this connection can't be a standard serial cable or a null modem cable. You must have the proprietary cable that came with the unit, or, if the unit is standard, you may be able to purchase a UPS cable separately.

Once a connection has been made, you can run the control panel to begin configuration.

Peter's Principle: Don't Run the Server to Death with the UPS

I'm often asked, "How long will this UPS hold the server up?" This is the wrong question. Keep in mind that your goal with a UPS is to protect the data, not to make the server run as long as possible. A good UPS solution will allow the server to run long enough to shut down in an orderly fashion. Trying to make it run to serve some other utility is placing your data at risk.

The control panel settings are described in the following list:

- **Uninterruptible Power Supply Is Installed on**

  This switch is a selection device to tell NT which serial port to listen to for the UPS signal. Possible answers: COM1, COM2, COM3, COM4.

- **Power Failure Signal Positive/Negative**

  This is a simple logic switch that's asking you to specify how your particular UPS sends a power failure signal. This information should be located in your UPS manual. If it isn't, you'll have to call the UPS vendor. If neither is available, you'll most likely not be able to use the UPS. (Power failure signal is why you have the UPS.) *Positive* and *Negative* refer to the signal that will come from the clear to send (CTS) pin on the UPS cable.

- **Low Battery Signal at Least 2 Minutes Before Shutdown**

  Some UPS units can send a signal to identify when the unit is running dangerously low on power. If your UPS does this, you need to alert NT as to whether the data carrier detect (DCD) pin from your UPS will send positive or negative.

- **Remote UPS Shutdown**

  If your UPS can receive a command from the software to shut down the UPS, you can set this switch. The positive or negative signal it's looking for is from the data terminal ready (DTR) pin from the UPS.

- **Execute Command File**

  This check box will allow you to do some housekeeping before you shut down the system. If you check this box, you need to enter the name of a file that you want to have run before the system shutdown. Keep in mind that you'll have only 30 seconds for the tasks to complete.

- **UPS Characteristics/Expected Battery Life**

  This setting is preferable to letting the UPS signal you when the battery is about to die. Set this option to one-fourth of the total battery life of your UPS, if at all possible. This will allow your UPS and server to withstand four separate power failures in succession. The thing to keep in mind is that power seldom fails once and returns to full power for the next few hours (conveniently waiting for your UPS to recharge). More often it will fail and then return to full—and fail at least one more time while maintenance is completed.

- **UPS Characteristics/Battery Recharge Time Per Minute of Run Time**

  You'll need to refer to the manual of the unit for this particular time span variable.

- **Time Between Power Failure and Initial Warning Message**

  This time variable is the time between the moment that the power fails at the wall socket and when you want users alerted that the server has experienced a power failure.

- **Delay Between Warning Messages**

  This time variable is how long you want the server to wait to warn the user again after each warning. Keep in mind that for every new warning, you and the help desk (if you have one) will get a phone call: "The server says we have a problem; that doesn't affect me, does it?"

Advanced Hardware Notes

Hardware problems in the NT installation can usually be traced to a bad or old driver, possibly even a completely unsupported piece of hardware. But for the most part standard hardware is supported by NT. Of course there are a few items that can jump up and bite you, and I've tried to list a few of the more common ones at the end of this installation chapter to give you a starting point for tracking a pesky hardware problem.

Interrupts

When an interface card in a PC wants to address the other pieces of the system, it must first interrupt the processor. The process of interrupting the processor is done through the use of a message called, oddly enough, an *interrupt* (IRQ). It's somewhat like an auction. Because it isn't very efficient to have everyone shouting at once, some auctions give everyone a number. When the bidder wants to get the auctioneer's attention, he displays his number. This gets the auctioneer's attention and submits a bid. In this same fashion, in a PC every I/O device is given an IRQ number. If the device wants to send something to the processor, it interrupts with its own interrupt number.

Many of you may already know this story, but the point of the story is to make you aware that each device has an IRQ number and that they must all be unique. The problem that can haunt you about the IRQ numbering scheme is the need for all these numbers to be unique. Every network card, SCSI controller, video adapter, and mouse port must have a unique number.

Many times, a network installer spends late hours working on a server problem, only to find that the hardware would function fine without IRQ conflicts. Conflicts in interrupts often will appear to be a poorly installed piece of software, because the hardware will function until a certain application or driver is started. The problem actually may be that the application initializes a piece of hardware that steals the IRQ from a functioning piece of hardware.

Some fast facts about interrupts:

- The numbers range from 0 to 15.
- 2 and 9 are the same, so they can't be used together. A brief description of the 2 and 9 relationship is that they're a bridge between ranges of interrupts.

- In EISA machines, more interrupts are made available by allowing each interrupt to be used twice with EISA cards.
- The following interrupts are commonly already in use by system devices. If you have the listed device, chances are that the device IRQ is taken and can't be used by your device:

    0 = System timer

    1 = Keyboard controller

    2 = Many video adapters

    3 = COM2, COM4

    4 = COM1, COM3

    5 = LPT2

    6 = Floppy controller

    7 = LPT1

    8 = Real-time clock

    9 = IRQ2 is the same IRQ

    10 = Available

    11 = Available

    12 = Motherboard mouse port

    13 = Math coprocessor

    14 = Primary IDE controller

    15 = Available or secondary IDE

Summary

This chapter is aimed at making the most of Windows NT from the beginning and not waiting until NT is installed and running before you consider some of the possible pitfalls. Forewarned is forearmed, as they say. In this chapter, we have looked with a jaded eye at the minimum requirements to install NT, and hopefully have seen a more realistic view of what's needed to make NT run as more than the "nightlight" that the minimum requirements would produce.

We looked at the purpose of the HCL and hopefully gained some respect for the fact that it exists to protect you, not just stifle what you're able to purchase. The reality of the HCL is that you can use an unlisted product, but that you should at least deal with manufacturers that are consistently in tune with Microsoft and their direction.

Domain role plays a key part not only in the security of your network, but in the installation of servers throughout your network. It will play a much bigger part in later chapters, and I think that in order to truly understand the installation of the NT product you need to read ahead through Part III to grasp the ramifications of the things you do during installation.

The actual installation of NT can be a very simple task or as complicated as you like, but the key point I hope you take away from this installation chapter is to be prepared. If you don't have all your ducks in a row before you start (drivers, cables, hardware setting, and so on), it will be a very long and obnoxious process. Having the wrong driver can cost you the entire day.

Finally, Microsoft has provided tools for migrating and upgrading to Windows NT 4.0 that make the job fairly easy if you take the time and have the common sense to prepare. The checklist in the "Migration and Upgrade" section of this chapter will help you to avoid ruining a working server in order to move to a new version. Migration and upgrade are processes that should be taken as a very serious threat to a clean-running system. Users are all too willing to pin everything from lost files to bad coffee on a new network operating system and the person who installed it.

5

File System
and Storage
Considerations

Peter Norton™

The Windows NT 4.0 file system involves more than just formatting a hard drive and installing the operating system. If your experience is with personal computers and not server-class machines, you'll learn that the server file system is the basis for all the other systems. If you don't make the proper decisions regarding the server file system, you'll have a difficult time undoing what has been done. Much like the foundation of a building, if you base a server installation on the wrong file system, your only choice may be to reinstall the server entirely.

Windows NT uses the file system to help protect and support the operating system. The file system consists of several basic parts:

- **Hard drives and controllers.** The hardware on which the file system is kept.
- **Partitioning of the hard drive storage.** Allows for separating hard drives just above the hardware level.
- **Volumes and volume names.** Lets the humans interact with the hardware and understand where to access it.

All these pieces require that you understand them and how they can affect your installation. To help you with that understanding, the following major topics are covered in this chapter:

- Hard drive and controller choices
- Selecting a bus
- Intelligent controller tricks
- Hard drive selection
- Disk administration
- Partitioning concepts
- File system formats
- NT Disk Administrator
- Using the FORMAT command
- The distributed file system (DFS)

Hard Drive and Controller Choices

The hard drive and hard drive controller choice you make is comparable to the choice of a house for the three pigs. (The moral of the story being that your house is only as safe as the time and materials you use to build it with.) I remind you of what was said about the importance of your hard drive subsystem in Chapter 4, "Installation Considerations." Simply put, the hard drive subsystem is the most important subsystem in your server in the event of a catastrophe, but it's also the most likely to fail. For that reason, we need to look at some of the possible hardware solutions that can help you get through those catastrophes like a house of bricks.

Taking Control

To communicate with your hard drive, you must have a controller. Many of the choices that are made in the server file system overlook this very important player in the picture. Hard drive controllers ten years ago were just the way that you gained access to the drive. The controller was comparable to the LPT port that gave you access to the printer. Controllers were the interface that the computer used to access the hard drives, and they controlled what was written to the drive. The hard drives did all the storage magic.

Well, hard drive controllers have grown up, and today they're doing a lot of the magic themselves. Different controller types contribute to performance and even protection of data. But, that having been said, what we call "controllers" today are not what we called "controllers" ten years ago.

You'll see as we discuss hard drives and controllers later in this chapter that the controller as it existed ten years ago has moved to the hard drive itself. The logic and circuitry to move the heads and platters actually exist on the hard drive unit. The circuit boards that are commonly called *hard drive controllers* today are not really hard drive controllers in the strict sense.

Controllers today are primarily multifunction hardware-communication controllers. They're capable of communicating with many different types of peripherals. These controllers can control your CD-ROM drives, writeable optical drives, scanners, and many other things. But that's what has made them the survivors.

Of the many different controller types that have come and gone in the last 16 years, two primary types have taken the forefront: SCSI and IDE (or EIDE). Both formats are commonly found in the PC world today, but they've developed definite followings for their distinct talents.

IDE/EIDE

IDE drives appeared on the PC scene on a wide scale eight years ago. Until that time, if you wanted a hard drive in your PC, you had to buy a hard drive controller separately, take up a slot, and have two or three cables running between the controller and the drive. *Integrated drive electronics* (IDE) was introduced in 1989 and actually involves a controller being attached to the hard drive itself. IDE still requires that the hard drive and controller be attached to the computer, but now the IDE hard drive is attached through one cable to the bus or to a bus card.

IDE as we know it today has also grown up. Today you'll most likely find *EIDE* (*enhanced integrated drive electronics*). The enhancement is that it will run more drives from the same controller (four) and is capable of handling larger drives. The original IDE was limited to two drives and a capacity of 500MB.

IDE and EIDE are the most common form of hard drive controller in workstation-class machines for several reasons. Probably the biggest reason is the fact that IDE drives can cost half as much as SCSI drives. IDE drives also don't require the machine manufacturers to supply a complex controller. And probably the biggest shock is that, when compared one on one, an EIDE drive can outperform many SCSI drives. For a single-drive system, it's a good choice.

Manufacturers of drives and drive components often manufacture the same drive component for IDE and SCSI drives. They even attach the IDE controller components to both drives. But to make the SCSI drive do the magic that a SCSI drive must do, the manufacturer will add a *SCSI bus interface controller* (SBIC) *chip*. An example of this process is the Seagate ST-3600A (IDE) and the Seagate ST-3600N (fast SCSI-2). It doesn't take a master of computer science to figure out which of those drives will perform faster. If the SCSI version has to pass through two sets of logic, it's going to pay some penalty.

The breakdown for IDE occurs when you take it to the next level and look at the limitations in a larger installation.

IDE drives do have their own controllers, but the controllers are incapable of working independently of one another and overlapping I/O. In other words, they can't multitask reads and writes to the hard drive. If you're considering a server installation that contains more than one drive, you must take this slowdown into account. The more drives, the more slowdown.

The particular issue arises as numerous people attempt to write to the server at one time. If the hard drives aren't capable of running in tandem, every piece of disk I/O will get caught in a bottleneck, waiting for a hard drive write, while other hard drives may also wait for access to the system.

Tip: Keep in mind that hard drive interfaces that are part of the main system board in your server may cause you more cost or time if they fail. Consider a scenario of your hard drive interface failing and having to replace the entire system board because they're the same. A new hard drive interface could cost $100, but the system board could cost several thousand.

SCSI

SCSI (*small computer systems interface*) *drives* have been around even longer than IDE, but they're really only recently experiencing the boom they deserve. Apple was ahead of the rest of the PC world in adopting the SCSI bus as a method of communicating with peripherals. The rest of the world has caught up with SCSI because of the ease it adds to expandability and the performance that it can add to multiple-drive installations.

It's important to realize that SCSI isn't just a hard drive controlling format. SCSI is actually a communications bus used by many different hardware types. SCSI buses are able to control devices ranging from tape drives and scanners to hard drives. EIDE controllers can control different types of devices as well, but the range of different devices is far greater with SCSI.

SCSI adapters can control up to seven devices (eight, if you include the adapter itself). Each device is given an address that must be unique. The address range is from 0 to 7, but 7 is usually the address reserved for the adapter itself. Much like interrupts in the PC bus world, SCSI addresses allow the different items on the SCSI bus to be uniquely identified.

Note: Some dual-channel SCSI adapters are able to address up to 14 drives. Most of these implementations are proprietary, but it does offer an interesting choice for a large server.

Much like IDE gave way to EIDE, SCSI is giving way to SCSI-2 and the hundreds of variations that it presents. Prior to SCSI-2, IDE was arguably faster even in multiple-drive situations, but SCSI-2 offers a number of new technologies that make it the better choice for multiple-drive systems.

Note: Before any discussion of SCSI-2 features, it's important to note that SCSI-2 is a very loose standard. The list of optional items that make a SCSI bus fit in the description "SCSI-2" is very long, and all a new SCSI item needs to be considered SCSI-2 is one of the items on the list. It's comparable to being able to say that I'm a professional baseball player because I wear a Cincinnati Reds hat.

SCSI-2 options that help your server are described in the following list:

- **Fast SCSI.** High-speed synchronous transfer capability. Fast SCSI can transfer up 10MB per second. Combined with other SCSI-2 standards, it can multiply this rate by four.

- **Wide SCSI.** This is just what it sounds like. Wide SCSI is SCSI over a wider cable, allowing for parallel data transfer. More lanes on the highway allow for more cars to pass down it. The cable that's being used by the industry is really a cable created for the SCSI-3 standard but, simply put, it works now—and allows for fewer cables to achieve the same goal.

- **Command queuing.** In SCSI-1, the SCSI adapter could send only one command at a time to one device at a time. Command queuing in SCSI-2 allows for the adapter to send as many as 256 commands to a single device. It also allows that device to take those commands and release the SCSI bus while it processes them. In SCSI-1, the device was able to receive and process only one command at a time as well. The great value of the SCSI bus is to multitasking operating systems because it allows them to utilize the bus while the device is processing other commands.

You may have heard that certain SCSI installations actually run faster when drives are grouped together, and the more drives you add to the grouping the faster it gets. Well, as hard as this may be to believe, command queuing makes this possible. By allowing the controller to write large amounts of data to each drive and move to the next drive, command queuing allows drives to process data while the controller continues to feed other drives. This is in stark contrast to IDE, which requires that each drive finish writing or reading before the controller can move to the next.

Beyond the Communications Format

The choice of controller goes far beyond which communications format is faster or happens to meet the trend of the future. Controllers are now able to control far more than the transfer of data to the hard drive. When you're installing any server-level peripheral, you should always consider that the peripheral will be involved with an operating system that's able to multitask and a system that will be responsible for responding to multiple users at one time. This is going to require a considerably different set of variables.

Bus Choice

To respond to the multitasking needs of Windows NT Server, each of the interface cards in the system should also be able to multitask. Interface cards that contain their own processors and memory are able to do just that. These cards are called *bus mastering cards* and are found in the PCI, Microchannel (MCA), and EISA worlds. These cards are called *bus mastering* because they can take control of the system bus and handle a certain amount of their own work. This allows the system's processor and memory to be involved in the higher-level tasks and not get tied up in all I/O tasks.

I won't spend a great deal of time here describing the differences between PCI, Microchannel, and EISA. But it's necessary to state that systems that allow you to access one of these bus types are necessary to run your server efficiently.

The *PCI* or *mezzanine bus* has become the most popular of these multitasking and bus mastering systems because of its speed and the fact that it can live peacefully with the other bus types on the same motherboard. The PCI bus is capable of sustaining throughput that's far better than either ISA or EISA. MCA can't exist on the same motherboard as legacy bus types.

You can't just buy a PCI SCSI adapter card for your server without first being aware of the bus types supported. Most server-class systems today support PCI and ISA adapter cards. The server that you purchase should be able to support PCI and ISA, but if the system supports EISA and PCI, that's even better. EISA allows you to install ISA cards, but it's also capable of bus mastering.

Intelligent Controller Tricks

When a controller is capable of controlling its own actions, it becomes possible for the controller to do more than just deliver data to the drives. Many of the controllers manufactured today can control drive relationships, handle fault tolerance, and even monitor drives for future failure.

If any task that normally requires operating-system intervention can be done by the hardware alone, this is going to help the performance of the overall server. The processor is a highly coveted resource in any server system. The object of the intelligent adapter card is to reduce the number of times your adapter must request the processor to get work done. If special considerations can be taken care of by the hard drive controller, that saves CPU and memory for other tasks.

Intelligence in controllers is most often a proprietary attribute, but there are some major categories of intelligence.

Drive Spanning

NT is capable of spanning drive partitions to create the appearance of one drive to the user; this is called *striping*. Intelligent controllers make it possible to tell the controller that multiple drives are to be presented to the operating system as one drive.

The advantage of this type of configuration is that NT isn't responsible for tracking and maintaining these relationships. It doesn't take up the system memory or the CPU cycles that would be necessary to control the flow of data to the drives.

Controller-Based Fault Tolerance and Striping

Fault tolerance for your network server has been the responsibility of the operating system until the last few years. NT has the ability to provide a certain amount of drive fault tolerance through software-controlled drive mirroring or striping with parity. But if you can place the responsibility of fault tolerance on the controller, you'll save CPU and memory for the operating system.

Hardware fault tolerance usually involves some variation of RAID (redundant array of inexpensive disks). RAID is a way of describing hard drive fault tolerance that's being used, and it's important to realize that it isn't a standard. RAID is more of an agreed-upon way of describing how the drives are configured in relationship to each other and where the data is stored.

Remember the *inexpensive* in RAID. The relative expense is up to you. There are six levels of RAID (0 through 5), but for purposes of this discussion I'll cover only the ones that are commonly used by the PC industry. The goal of RAID is twofold: save money and/or protect data. As we go through the different levels of RAID, you'll see that each level does one thing or the other better. At the end of each level, I'll provide a note on the cost versus fault tolerance level.

The fact that RAID is a *de facto* (popular) standard and not a *de jure* (by law) standard makes it possible for different vendors to make up the rules as they go. The basic structure of RAID remains the same from vendor to vendor, but you'll find many different implementations called by the same name.

Common forms of RAID:

- **RAID 0 (Striping).** This process is described in the preceding section. Striping involves configuring the controller to present several hard drives to the server as one drive. No fault tolerance is provided by this form of RAID at all.

Percentage of Storage Lost to Fault Tolerance	Minimum Number of Drives	Fault Tolerance Level
0%	2	None

- **RAID 1 (mirroring/duplexing).** These implementations are sometimes called *drive mirroring* or *duplexing*.

  Drive mirroring involves adding one hard drive for every one hard drive that you want to protect in your system. You then write the same data to both drives or groups of drives. The idea is that in the event of a hard drive failure the system will switch to the other hard drive for data. If all goes smoothly, the users won't know that a drive has failed.

  Duplexing is discussed later in this chapter, but it involves also mirroring the hard drive controllers. Duplexing can only be controlled from software.

  RAID 1 is the most expensive form of RAID because you must completely duplicate the drive space you want protected. The result is a well-protected system, but a loss of half of the disk drive capacity.

Percentage of Storage Lost to Fault Tolerance	Minimum Number of Drives	Fault Tolerance Level
50%	2, in even numbers	Extremely high

- **RAID 4.** This form of fault tolerance is more complicated than simply duplicating disk space. RAID 4 uses a form of fault tolerance that has been used by memory configurations from the beginning of the PC industry, called *parity*.

Note: To understand parity, you must understand that computers use ones (1) and zeros (0) for every communication that they make. Parity memory, for example, uses nine chips to provide memory from eight of those chips. The ninth chip (parity chip) is used to check the accuracy of the information stored on the other eight. Memory parity involves totaling the number of ones and zeros that pass through the parity chip on the way to the remaining memory chips and determining whether the total is odd or even. If the result of the data leaving memory doesn't match what the parity chip saw as the data entered the memory, the parity chip shuts down the PC, because the data is corrupted.

Drive parity is a bit more complicated because the system isn't hoping to stop corrupted data, but to tolerate a fault in a hard drive. Drive parity involves the use of three or more drives in a RAID array. The total number of drives is irrelevant except for the fact that they must be controlled from the same controller and the number must be greater than three.

The drives are split into data and parity drives. All but one of the drives are used as a target for writing data and the single drive left is called the *parity drive* (see Figure 5.1). Data is written to the drives by splitting the data into parts equal to the number of data drives and writing those parts to the data drives.

The parity drive is dedicated to the task of storing a parity algorithm that tracks what was written to the other drives. You could imagine that this drive is an understudy to the part of a hard drive. As the controller writes data to the other hard drives, it continually calculates an algorithm to reconstruct that data in the event of a failure. In very simplistic terms, the parity drive is being told what should be on the drives should they fail.

Should one data drive fail, the parity drive is used to reconstruct data on-the-fly so that users can continue to work. This reconstruction is done by the controller. If a data drive fails, the controller continues to take drive requests and read from the remaining drives. To deliver the data from the failed data drive, the controller uses a parity algorithm and the parity drive to reconstruct the data. If the parity drive fails, data continues to be written to the data drives, but no parity algorithm is figured.

Figure 5.1.
A physical view of RAID 4.

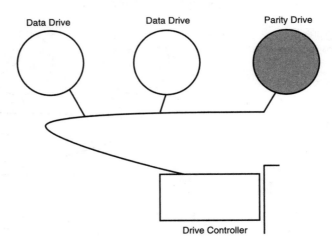

Several things have to be considered when you approach using RAID 4. If a data drive failure occurs, you'll experience up to a 33% reduction in drive speed for data reads. This slowdown is due to the fact that data must be reconstructed every time you read from the array.

RAID 4 is much less expensive then RAID 1 because you only need to use one drive per array. If you're using certain controllers, you can have as many as 14 drives in one array. That allows you to have fault tolerance and only use between 33% and 7% of your total drive capacity for fault tolerance. This is a great number, but if you're only going to use 1GB of storage, the savings become a little more difficult to see.

Percentage of Storage Lost to Fault Tolerance	Minimum Number of Drives	Fault Tolerance Level
7% to 33% (2 channel—SCSI)	3	High

- **RAID 5.** In order to resolve some of the drive latency created when a drive fails in RAID 4, you may want to consider RAID 5. RAID 5 also uses drive parity to maintain drive fault tolerance. But, in RAID 5, all the drives are involved in keeping parity information.

  Just as in RAID 4, you must have at least three drives for a RAID 5 array. But with RAID 5 you divide each drive by the total number of drives and place parity on one section of each drive (see Figure 5.2). For example, if you have five drives in a RAID 5 array, you would use one-fifth of each drive to store the parity algorithm for the other four drives. The remaining drive space is then used for data.

Figure 5.2.
Physical view of RAID 5.

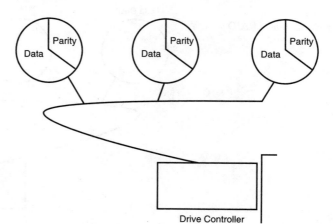

In the event of a failure, RAID 5 behaves in the same way as RAID 4, with one exception. Instead of pulling the parity information from one drive to rebuild the missing data, the array of drives locate the missing information on each other. In an example with four drives, one-fourth of every drive would be dedicated to parity, while three-fourths would be dedicated to data. All the other functions behave the same as RAID 4.

The value of a RAID 5 array over RAID 4 is found when attempting to read information from the drive array during a failure. The disadvantage of a parity-based fault tolerance scheme is the fact that data must be re-created by using an algorithm in reverse of the one written. By spreading parity over all of the drives, the amount of data that must be recovered from a parity algorithm is reduced, although very little.

Percentage of Storage Lost to Fault Tolerance	Minimum Number of Drives	Fault Tolerance Level
7% to 33% (2 channel—SCSI)	3	High

Intelligent controllers can be set to control the particular form of RAID that you'll be using to protect your data or simply to increase your drive space.

As controllers grow in abilities, they are able to add more functionality to what your operating system can already do. Consider that every time you can put the hardware in charge, you can free the operating system to deliver more power to you.

Hard Drives

Choosing a hard drive is often difficult because hard drives have so many variables. Determining the speed, the reliability, and the worth of a drive is comparable to buying a car engine. Often, the engine you buy is the one that happened to come in the car you bought. The fact that the drive comes with the server you purchase doesn't make it a good choice or a bad choice, but it does make it a choice that you have to live with.

I suggest that when you make the choice of server, you include the choice of hard drive. Think of it like buying a truck to haul equipment with, and not a luxury car. When you buy a truck for your place of business, you may consider buying an eight-cylinder engine instead of a six-cylinder; you may even want to consider a diesel engine. But the point is that you would consider such a choice and evaluate the work that must be done with that engine.

The Basics

The basic knowledge of hard drives that's needed to make a good choice has narrowed quite a bit. You really don't need to be aware of the drive interleave, number of cylinders, or seek time. The items that you need to look for are straightforward and should be easy to compare from drive to drive. There are five basic things to look for in a hard drive mechanism:

- **Interface Type.** IDE and SCSI implementations both have strengths, as you saw in the earlier controller discussion. Your choice of hard drive interface must be tied more to the jobs that the server will perform and the controller that will handle that group of tasks better. As you've seen to this point in the chapter, if you choose a hard drive based solely on IDE versus SCSI single-drive performance, you may be wrong.

- **Access Time.** This is the average amount of time it takes the unit to move the drive heads from one cylinder to another during testing. It provides you with an average time to do a single seek. Unlike an interface choice, this is a measure of the hard drive alone and will help you to compare apples to apples when all else matches. Good access times today range from 7.9 to 10ms (milliseconds). Anything slower is just not necessary.

- **Warranty.** Thankfully, hard drives can't measure miles traveled yet. Most hard drives have warranties based on the purchase date. Look for hard drives with at least a three-year warranty—some even have a five-year warranty. When you consider that the average life of a server hard drive is three years, a five-year warranty is a great bet.

- **Size.** The toughest thing for a consultant to tell about your server needs is the hard drive size, because you base your hard drive size on the software you'll be installing and your users' needs. No one can understand your software needs better than you. Before sizing your drive, consider the capacity needs of your users, all your applications, and the operating system. A good rule of thumb for growth is to double that final number. This may seem odd, but my experience has shown that most servers need more hard drive space within one year, even with this rule being followed.

- **Manufacturer.** The one variable that isn't so easy to be knowledgeable of is manufacturer. Sadly, you'll find that this can have as much to do with your success as anything else. The best idea is to stay with a manufacturer that's going to stand behind the product and one that you'll be able to find tomorrow. Very often the manufacturer of the server is a very good choice. If the manufacturer of your server is also the manufacturer of the storage system, you have a short list when it comes time to get help. If the other variables weigh in close to the same, use as few manufacturers as possible.

Tip: When choosing third-party hardware, try to follow this rule of thumb. "If you haven't heard of them before, you may never hear from them again." Don't experiment with server hardware from an unknown source. When push comes to shove, this manufacturer may be your only source for drivers, support, and parts. If you lose those things, you might as well bury your server—no matter how well it ran.

Beyond the Basics

The first choice may well have already been made for you. We just covered the controller and hard drive choices—the two are inseparable. Obviously, if you have a SCSI controller, you need to have SCSI drives, but it goes beyond that. If you have selected an intelligent controller, there may be requirements that the controller must have in a drive in order to do its magic.

Just as intelligent controllers can do tricks, so can intelligent drives. Certain hard drives, when combined with controllers from the same manufacturer, can deliver unique features.

Hot Pluggable Drives

Compaq, Hewlett-Packard, IBM, and many other manufacturers offer hard drives and storage compartments that allow the hard drives to be replaced while the server is actually running. These configurations require that the controller be capable of recognizing that the drive has failed and that it be able to reconstruct the drive when it's replaced. Such configurations are found in RAID implementations ranging from levels 1 to 5.

Early Warning

In the high-end systems offered by the tier-one manufacturers, systems are beginning to be made that are capable of warning an administrator when a failure is about to occur. These manufacturers receive many hard drives that have failed and must diagnose them to find out what went wrong. The logic in these intelligent drives is capable of watching for repeated events that normally precede a hard drive failure. If these drives are in a system capable of interpreting the warnings, many manufacturers are covering the equipment for warranty replacement before you're forced to experience a failure.

These drives don't warn the administrator directly. They communicate with hardware monitoring programs that are able to interpret the signals and send the warning. This type of program is becoming more common and is part of the reason that systems groups that once trusted only the big iron (mainframes) are beginning to put more faith in the PC world.

Drive Self-Maintenance

Many of the hard drives that you purchase have physical defects that are on the drive when they come from the manufacturer. What may shock you is that the manufacturer knows that. When you purchase a hard drive, it may be called a 1GB hard drive, but the actual formatted usable space will vary from drive to drive. This is because the actual usable space—what remains after software scans the surface of the drive and marks the bad spots—is less than the total surface of the drive could deliver. Different drives have different amounts of bad space, so your ending amount of usable space will be different even in drives of the same model and make. With current technology you should only see a slight variance, but the drive should always deliver at least what the manufacturer said it would.

I'm not telling you about hard drive surface errors to scare you, but to let you know that hard drive surface errors are almost always there. Most of these errors can be found and marked up front, but as time goes on more bad places are found or created and must be marked as bad by the operating system. The majority of the time, no data is lost, but from time to time data can be lost and must be restored. Obviously, it would be better to mark these spots before the data is laid down, but the operating system often doesn't have the utility or the time to scan the drive.

Many hard drive and controller manufacturers have developed a plan to bypass this problem. The concept is to have the hard drive and a controller that can scan the drive surface during idle time. If damaged or bad spots are found on the drive, any data is moved to a clean area. The spot is then marked as bad. From that point forward, the drive won't write to that spot again. These schemes are mostly proprietary, but they're worth a look.

The benefit of this is twofold. First, it keeps the data from becoming corrupted. Second, it reduces the operating system and administrator time spent seeking out these bad spots.

Disk Administration

NT Disk Administrator (see Figure 5.3) is the utility that is used to establish how you will make use of your hard drives. But the administration of the storage system is started long before you get to this interface.

Figure 5.3.
Disk Administrator.

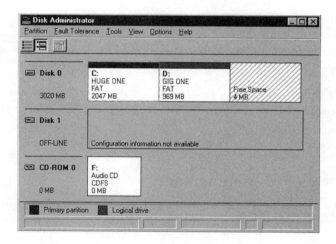

Before you can begin using the Disk Administrator utility, you have to understand a few basic drive configuration concepts and how they apply in NT Server. Before you can use a hard drive in NT you must do the following:

- **Partition the drive.** Set the basic logical division of the physical drives.
- **Format the partitions.** Establish a file system and structure for how to handle data.
- **Create drive volume sets.** Decide on more advanced features of the operating file system.

The following sections provide details on these topics.

Partitioning Concepts

Drive partitioning is not much different in NT than in DOS or Windows 95. If you understand the concept of drive partitioning in those operating systems, you already understand the concept in NT.

Partitioning is done in order to separate the drive into logical usable areas. It's the first level of organization prior to formatting the drive. For any operating system to make use of a hard drive, it must first be partitioned.

Primary versus Extended Partitions

There are two basic types of drive partition that you can create: primary and extended. It's really fairly simple to understand the difference between them.

Primary partitions are the bootable partitions that you create on a bootable hard drive in the system. When you create primary partitions, you're creating partitions that can be set to take the lead position during the starting of the PC and be used to boot the operating system.

Primary partitions can be designated as the "active" partition, and this designation alerts the hardware that this is the portion of the hard drive containing the information needed to boot the operating system (see Figure 5.4). You can designate up to four primary partitions per physical disk. The idea is to allow for different operating systems or boot schemes to coexist. This can be done by setting different primary partitions to active and restarting the system.

Figure 5.4.
Drive partitioning: Primary partitions and active drives.

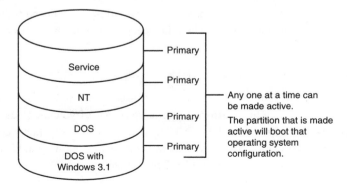

Extended partitions are partitions that consume the remaining free space after primary drives have been established. You can have only one extended partition per physical drive, which makes an extended drive seem very limiting.

The fact of the matter is that with extended partitions you can do a bit of magic that you can't do with a primary partition. Extended partitions in NT can be segmented into numerous logical drives.

Logical drives are logical separations of hard drive space that are represented by a drive letter (see Figure 5.5). They aren't different physical drives, and they aren't separate partitions, but the operating system allows them to behave as if they were different. The idea is to allow the administrator to better segment large drives into manageable space. You must remember that only one extended partition can be created per hard drive. If you are dealing with a 9GB hard drive, that can be very unmanageable.

Figure 5.5.
Drive partitioning: Extended partitions and logical drives.

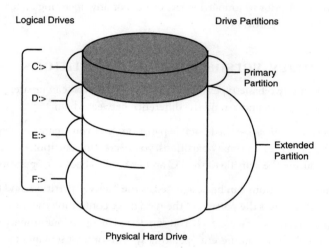

Logical drives are a feature of many operating systems (including NT Server), but they aren't usually supported across operating-system boundaries. So you need to be aware that these drives and their data may not be accessible if the operating system fails to boot.

DOS Considerations

Why concern yourself with the DOS partition? When you install Windows NT Server, it's recommended that your first partition be formatted as a FAT volume. (I know, you've been watching your weight and you would rather not.) The reason for this recommendation is that the FAT format is used for the creation of bootable floppy disks—which most often boot with the DOS operating system. DOS will only recognize a FAT file system.

If your system boot record should fail, it's imperative that you be able to get to the system's hard drive for repairs. If you haven't used a FAT partition to boot your server, you may not be able to access the system at all. If you have used FAT, you may be able to boot from a floppy disk to access the drive. Your only other option will most likely be to reinstall NT on the boot drive and start from scratch.

DOS versions prior to v5.0 are able to recognize only one primary partition—even if the data on other primary partitions is in FAT format, the DOS operating system won't recognize the other drive letters.

DOS-compatible partitions are also necessary for dual-booting the system, but hopefully you won't be dual-booting the file server.

File System Formats

Once the hard drive subsystem has been partitioned for the operating system to use, you can begin to further organize the hard drive by creating formatted volumes. A *volume* is a defined drive space that can be fully prepared by the operating system to contain data. It sounds an awful lot like a partition, but it does have a few distinctions.

Calling a partition a volume is like calling a file drawer a file system. Partitions are used to accommodate volumes. Volumes are more comparable to the file system used by a company to deal with a particular portion of their filing system.

Just as a particular file can consume part of or more than one file drawer, so volumes can take up part of or several partitions (see Figure 5.6). One volume can be spread across several partitions called a *volume set*, and that can be spread over several drives. But, conversely, extended partitions can contain several volumes.

Figure 5.6.
The volume and partition relationship.

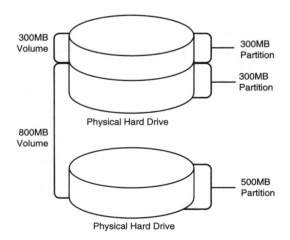

A volume is created by formatting the portion of the hard drive(s) with the file system of your choice. In order to create a volume, you may use several different tools. The tools are the old standby FORMAT command and the NT Disk Administrator. The Disk Administrator is covered fully later in this chapter, but first let's take a closer look at the NT file formats so that you can fully understand what you want to do.

The format that you use to make your hard drive storage space available to the users controls a wide range of items and is far more important than you may realize before you have already installed your server. There are two file system choices in the Windows NT 4.0 operating system: FAT (file allocation table) and NTFS (NT file system). Each has its own strengths, and even though you may think that NTFS would be best in all instances, it isn't.

FAT

FAT format is the default format of hard drive volumes in Windows NT 4.0, just as it has been with every Microsoft operating system for better than a decade. This format is used by many operating systems because of its ease of use, universal acceptance, and the fact that it can be used easily for removable media.

FAT really has two strong uses in the NT Server operating system:

- The first is as a format for the boot partition of your server. Booting to a partition formatted with FAT enables the administrator to have access to the drive in the event of an operating failure to boot. The system should not have any reason to fail to boot from the hard drive, other than the failure of the hardware. But if it does, and your boot drive is formatted with the FAT format, you can access the drive with any DOS 5.0 or higher boot disk.

- The second is the low overhead and efficiency of FAT for small partitions. The FAT format requires less than 1MB for its own use. FAT is also very efficient when using partitions smaller than 200MB.

Before you make use of FAT for the boot partition of your server, you need to be aware of the disadvantages of FAT:

- The biggest disadvantage of FAT is the security issues that you'll have. This file system doesn't support the file or directory security of Windows NT. For that reason, it's possible to subvert the security system of an NT server in those FAT volumes that are shared. FAT is not a good idea for those areas that you intend to share. The security that's available for FAT shares is no more complex than that of Windows for Workgroups. The best security that's available is the file attribute system, and that won't stop even a simple prowler.

- The other disadvantage that you'll find with the FAT format is really related to the fact that it was created to accommodate drives that would reach a maximum size of 10MB. In the bad old days when FAT was created, no one could imagine that we would be using 9GB of hard drive space on a PC. So FAT not only is most efficient in volumes smaller that 200MB, it's just downright inefficient in larger ones.

FAT uses a linked list as a file and directory structure. This means that when a large number of files exist on the drive and files begin to grow, they become fragmented around the drive surface. When the operating system attempts to recover the fragments, this is very inefficient.

Here's a quick list of FAT features:

- Supports 255 characters in long filenames
- Not case-sensitive, and doesn't preserve case
- File sizes can be up to 4GB
- Accessible from NT, DOS, OS/2, and UNIX
- Format overhead of less than 1MB
- Can't use the following characters: " / \ [ ] : ; ¦ = , ^ * ?
- Most efficient with volumes under 200MB

NTFS

Although FAT is the default file system used by NT, NTFS is the *NT file system* by name. The NTFS format was created as a further extension of the OS/2 *high performance file system* (*HPFS*). HPFS and NTFS were created to correct the failings that FAT has in a PC world that needed security and efficiency with large drives.

The NTFS format is capable of handling files of 16 exabytes in size. NTFS was created with large files and filing systems in mind. When you're using large hard drives, directories, and files, the task of managing them can be laborious. NTFS automatically maintains the file system integrity. It automatically logs all the directory and file updates so that it can revert to previously successful file forms.

An exabyte is a very large number. For something that you can better relate to, let's compare it to numbers that you've heard before. An exabyte is 1024 petabytes. A petabyte is 1024 terabytes. A terabyte is 1024 gigabytes. A gigabyte is 1024 megabytes. So, I believe that we can safely say that the 16 exabyte limit is not going to be stretched any time soon.

NTFS supports *hot fix*, a term that should be familiar to NetWare administrators. Hot fix involves a concept that was discussed earlier, in the hard drive and controller section of this chapter. It's a software form of disk maintenance that moves data from a bad spot on the hard drive and to a reserved area that has been deemed to be good. With the software version of hot fix, the operating system monitors data reads and writes, looking for bad sectors of the hard drive. When a bad sector is discovered, the operating system moves the data to a different spot.

Of course, NTFS supports the NT security model. The only way that you can fully implement the NT security model is to install NTFS as the file format on the server volumes you want to share.

Here's a quick list of NTFS features:

- Supports filename and directory name lengths of up to 255 characters
- Not case-sensitive, but does preserve case; if you create the file using capital letters, the characters will be presented that way, but it doesn't affect searching for or using the files
- File size is unlimited, for all practical purposes (16 exabyte limit)
- Accessible from NT, DOS, OS/2, and UNIX
- Can't use the following characters: " / \ : ¦ * ?
- Most efficient format with NT for large volumes over 200MB

HPFS

The high performance file system (HPFS) was created for the OS/2 operating system. It's the predecessor to file systems like NTFS and for that reason was supported in all previous versions of Windows NT Server. But it's not supported by NT Server 4.0.

This shouldn't be a problem for most server installations, unless you're supporting an upgraded OS/2 server that now runs NT and still houses some HPFS drives. If you're upgrading an NT 3.x server, you'll be able to use the drives that you have remaining on the system. But I strongly recommend that you remove HPFS as a drive format.

There really is no nice way of dealing with the legacy HPFS hard drive volumes that you may have. NT Server won't be supporting them natively anymore. I think that most people who have had them around realize that it's past time to convert them. If you're running an OS/2 server from the same machine in a dual-boot installation, you need to consider devoting the server to one operating system or the other, if HPFS means much to you at all. Most of these dual-boot servers are utility players or experimental machines, but they do exist.

To remove HPFS as a file system from the server, you have two choices:

- Format the drive in FAT or NTFS file format.
- Run the NT 3.5x utility CONVERT and convert the drives to NTFS before you install NT 4.0. To do this, run the following command at a command prompt:

  ```
  CONVERT drive: /fs:NTFS
  ```

  where drive equals the drive to be converted.

If you want to preserve the security of the HPFS file system, you have to take more steps. These steps don't apply if you're not running OS/2, but if you are, you'll want to follow these steps before moving to NT:

1. Under OS/2, run `BACKACC.EXE` to convert the security to a file on the same drive.

2. Convert the drive to NTFS under NT 3.5x.

3. Run the `ACLCONV.EXE` utility on the same drive that was converted. This adds the information created in step 1 to the file in NTFS.

NT Disk Administrator

Now that you better understand what partitions and volumes are, you need to know how to create them. The tool used in NT to convert raw hard drive storage area into usable space is NT Disk Administrator. Formatting, creating, and deleting partitions can all be done in this interface.

Disk Administrator gives you a powerful tool and a visual aid to see the current configuration. The tool is used after your initial installation to maintain and update the drive space that remains or is added. The initial partitions and volumes are created during the installation, but everything else is done through Disk Administrator.

Creating a Partition

NT partitions are both made and found. In other words, NT will either create a partition for you if none exists or make use of partitions that already exist. If partitions already exist when you install NT, you'll have the option of using those partitions or starting from scratch. There are two primary tools for creating partitions in NT. One is the installation procedure discussed in Chapter 4; the other is NT Disk Administrator.

Partition decisions need to be made before you start the installation of your server because you can partition the drive during the installation, but this is usually done to start from a clean slate. If partitions already exist, you may use those partitions, but the installation is always a good time to consider what you're going to do with your file system. It's the only time that you'll have the server in a state of readiness for wiping the drives clean.

The following sections contain step-by-step directions for creating a partition.

Creating Primary Partitions

These are the steps for creating a primary partition:

1. Select an area of free space from the disks that are available in Disk Administrator by placing your mouse pointer in the free space and clicking.

2. Choose Partition | Create.

3. You'll be asked how large you want to make the partition. In the dialog box, type in the size partition you want and click OK. Once you click OK, you'll be presented with a new, unformatted partition. (Formatting the partition is covered a bit later, in the volumes section.)

4. If you intend to boot from a particular partition you create, you will want to mark the partition active; choose Partition | Mark Active. Keep in mind that only one primary partition can be active at any given time, and that partition must have the files needed to boot NT if you intend to use NT.

> **Tip:** You can mark different partitions as active as a way of booting another operating system. If you're using the machine for testing or trial purposes, changing the active partition can make a simple way to get a clean boot to other operating systems without involving NT.

5. If you are done with your partitioning, choose Partition | Commit Changes Now. If you have more partitioning work to do, you may proceed, but remember that no new partitions exist until you commit changes. You'll be given a chance to save changes; if you're sure, click Yes.

Creating Extended Partitions

1. Select an area of free space from the disks that are available in Disk Administrator.
2. Choose Partition | Create Extended.
3. You'll be asked how large you want to make the partition. In the dialog box, type in the size of the partition you want and click OK. Keep in mind that you can only have one extended partition per hard drive; if you don't need to put any primary partitions on the drive, use all the available space.

   Once you click OK, you'll be presented with a new, unformatted partition. (Formatting the partition is covered in the next section.)
4. If you're done with your partitioning, choose Partition | Commit Changes Now. If you have more partitioning work to do, you may proceed, but remember that no new partitions exist until you commit changes. You'll be given a chance to save changes; if you're sure, click Yes.

> **Tip:** Partitions can still be created using FDISK, as they were in DOS, but not when you're booted into the NT operating system. NT doesn't support FDISK from the command prompt because FDISK wants access to the hardware, and we know NT doesn't allow that. But if you boot the machine with a DOS disk you can still use FDISK to create a FAT partition. This is only recommended for emergency situations, but if you're familiar with FDISK it can be a help in a pinch.

Creating Volumes

Partitions aren't usable until you format them; by formatting, you create a volume. Formatting is a process that can be handled from the command prompt or from the Disk Administrator. The Disk Administrator allows you to see what you are affecting and to get a complete picture of what drives exist.

Standard Volume Creation

The following steps are to be executed from Disk Administrator on free disk partitions that have been given drive letters:

1. Select a partition.
2. Choose Tools | Format to open the Format dialog box.
3. Choose a file format (FAT or NTFS) and a volume name, and indicate whether you want to use compression. If you believe that you're going to want to use compression, you must use the NTFS file format.

Note: If you're using any form of compression software other than the NT format (NTFS), NT won't support it. For example, if you can dual-boot your server to Windows 95 and you use Windows 95 to compress a hard drive, that drive will be unusable to NT. Compression of files and folders in NT can also cause a mild performance hit, but nothing of major significance.

Tip: Quick format is offered as an option, but unless you're only using FORMAT to erase data I wouldn't recommend this choice. This may be the last chance you have for a while to thoroughly format this partition.

4. Click Start. You'll be warned that you'll be destroying all data on the partition. If this is your intention, click OK.
5. Finally, you will be told that the format is finished and asked to click OK.

You have now created a volume and can begin storing data there.

Volume Sets/NT Striping

If you intend to use partitions in volumes that include more than one partition, you must either create a standard volume set or a volume stripe set. Each has its advantages.

A standard volume set (see Figure 5.7) is a combination of several partitions of any size or location to create one drive letter. A volume set can combine from 2 to 32 unassociated partitions and give you much larger and more usable area.

Earlier I mentioned that it's possible to form RAID implementation with software or hardware. Striping is just that—software RAID that's natively supported by NT.

Both of these methods are controlled in the NT Disk Administrator. But keep in mind that the boot partition can't be part of a volume set of any kind. Also, these special drive configurations aren't supported by other operating systems, so don't create a stripe set if you need access from another operating system in a dual-boot configuration. (Dual-booting the server? Just say no!)

If your goal is just to increase volume space or create a larger volume by combining unused partitions, you're creating a volume set. Volume sets are different from stripe sets because all the sections don't have to match in size. They can be as large or as small as you please, they can be from diverse controller families (SCSI, IDE, and so on)—the fact is that they just need to be available and accessible from NT Disk Administrator.

Figure 5.7.
Volume sets.

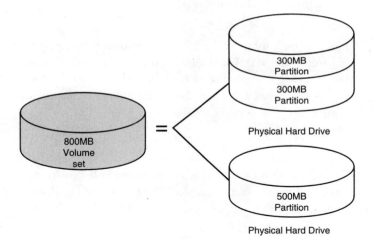

Creating and Extending Volume Sets

To create a volume set, follow these steps:

1. Select the free partitions that you would like to include in the set. To select multiple partitions, hold down the Ctrl key while you select partitions.

2. Choose Partition | Create a Volume Set. You'll see a dialog box that asks what size you want to make the volume. By choosing the total available space and clicking OK, you'll create a volume set with the exact partitions you selected being fully used. If you choose to use anything less than the total partition space, NT will decide for you to use an equal percentage of each partition. This may result in some pretty ridiculous spaces left.

3. Commit the changes and reboot the server.

4. Format the new volume by selecting one section of the volume set and choosing Tools | Format.

Extending an existing partition can be done to any NTFS partition using volume sets. This is accomplished in much the same way that you would create a new volume set:

1. Select an existing NTFS partition that you would like to expand.

2. Hold down the Ctrl key and select the partition you want to use to increase your volume space.

3. Choose Partition | Extend Volume Set.

4. The total size you want is then requested. You can choose from the maximum and minimum. Pick one of these or type a custom size.

Stripe Set Creation

If you can get to several hard drive partitions of equal or approximately equal size, you may want to consider a stripe set. Stripe sets allow for the combination of 2 to 32 volumes, but they also can allow for more speed due to the fact that they stripe the writing of data across numerous drives at one time. Imagine which is faster—writing your name fifteen times on a chalkboard, or five people writing it three times.

Stripe sets are more complex because the partitions need to be of equal size and they must exist on separate hard drives. You don't have to use partitions of the same size, but keep in mind that any of the partitions that aren't of the same size will be lowered to the lowest common denominator. For example, a 100MB partition combined in a stripe set with a 150MB partition would yield a 200MB volume because 100MB is the lowest common size.

To create a stripe set, follow these steps:

1. Select the free partitions that you want to include that come from different hard drives. To select multiple partitions, hold down the Ctrl key while you select partitions.

2. Choose Partition | Create Stripe Set to open a dialog box that asks what size you want to make the volume. By choosing the total available space and clicking OK, you'll create a stripe set with the exact partitions you selected being used to the maximum amount that allows for all of the partitions to be the same size. Like size is achieved by reducing the partitions to the lowest common denominator.

   If you choose to use anything less than the total partition space, NT will decide for you to use an equal size of each partition.

3. Commit the changes and reboot the server.

4. Format the new volume by selecting one section of the volume set and then choosing Tools | Format.

Fault Tolerance Considerations

NT is capable of creating a stripe set that offers RAID implementations. Both RAID 1 and RAID 5 drive sets can be created in Disk Administrator. Make no mistake—hardware RAID is faster, but it's also more expensive. The fact that you can use Disk Administrator to create software-controlled RAID is a significant feature of the NT operating system.

The issues that you must consider when deciding on which form of software RAID to use are the same as those posed by hardware RAID. RAID 1 (mirroring/duplexing) is more expensive but faster than RAID 5 (striping with parity). The fact that the operating system must be involved in the creation and upkeep of the parity algorithm needed by the stripe set with parity is very costly. A failure in a system running software-based RAID 5 can be extremely costly to performance.

Mirroring/Duplexing

I already discussed mirroring in the hardware RAID section, but duplexing is new. Duplexing is a simple variation of RAID 1 that requires that it be controlled by software.

Duplexing involves the addition of one controller, thus mirroring the controllers. The weak link in a drive-mirroring installation is the hard drive controller, because it controls both drives. Duplexing eliminates that link, but the chance of a controller failure is actually no greater than the failure of the computer system board. With that in mind, you must ask yourself how cost-effective it really is. Drive duplexing is also controlled only by software. Hardware controllers can only control the drives attached to themselves.

Creating a duplexed drive set is no different from creating a mirrored set, so the directions for creating them are listed together. Keep in mind that even partitions that already exist can be mirrored to an empty partition. Unlike volume sets or stripe sets, mirrored sets can contain the system partition. This is strongly recommended for mission-critical systems if you can't afford a hardware level of protection.

To create a mirrored/duplexed drive set, follow these steps:

1. From Disk Administrator, select two partitions of the same size or larger. If one partition contains data, you need to select it first; the second drive selected will lose any data that it contains. Hold down the Ctrl key while you select the second partition.
2. Choose Fault Tolerance | Establish Mirror.
3. Commit the changes. If neither of the partitions had been formatted prior to the creation of the mirror set, you'll need to format the drive after committing changes.

Striping with Parity

A stripe set with parity requires that you have at least three or more drives, the same as hardware RAID 5. The reason is that it's software RAID 5. NT is going to create the parity sections of each drive and will figure and maintain the parity algorithm necessary to make it all work.

Creating a stripe set with parity is very much like creating a standard stripe set. The only real difference is the menu selection of Fault Tolerance | Create Stripe Set with Parity:

1. Select the free partitions that you want to include that come from different hard drives. Hold down the Ctrl key while you select partitions.

2. Choose Fault Tolerance | Create Stripe Set with Parity.

3. You'll now be presented with a dialog box that asks what size you want to make the volume. By choosing the total available space and clicking OK, you'll create a stripe set with the exact partitions you selected being used to the maximum amount that allows for all of the partitions to be the same size. Equal size is achieved by reducing the partitions to the lowest common denominator.

   If you choose to use anything less than the total partition space, NT will decide for you to use an equal size of each partition.

4. Commit the changes and reboot the server.

5. Format the new volume by selecting one section of the volume set and choosing Tools | Format.

Using the FORMAT Command

The old DOS-style disk format is still available in a command-line utility from the NT command prompt. This utility allows you to format a drive in a more precise way. Those of us who are used to the old way of doing things don't have to worry—our old command-line friend still exists.

The FORMAT command is also useful for creating batch operations and starting automated installations. If you don't feel comfortable using FORMAT from DOS, use the Disk Administrator. This form of interface is not for the faint of heart. It won't hold your hand through the process.

I list the format parameters in a second, but you should know that you can access this information with the command FORMAT /? at any time.

This is the FORMAT command syntax:

```
FORMAT drive: /variable
```

where *drive:* is equal to the drive letter of the drive that you want to format and */variable* equals any variation that you may want to add to the drive format. The following table describes the variables that can follow the FORMAT command to create different results.

Switch	Description
/FS:*file-system*	Specifies the type of the file system (FAT or NTFS).
/V:*label*	Specifies the volume label.
/Q	Performs a quick format.
/C	Files created on the new volume will be compressed by default.
/A:*size*	Overrides the default allocation unit size. Default settings are strongly recommended for general use. NTFS supports 512, 1024, 2048, 4096, 8192, 16KB, 32KB, and 64KB. FAT supports 8192, 16KB, 32KB, 64KB, 128KB, and 256KB. NTFS compression is not supported for allocation unit sizes above 4096.
/F:*size*	Specifies the size of the floppy disk to format (160KB, 180KB, 320KB, 360KB, 720KB, 1.2MB, 1.44MB, 2.88MB, or 20.8MB).
/T:*tracks*	Specifies the number of tracks per disk side.
/N:*sectors*	Specifies the number of sectors per track.
/1	Formats a single side of a floppy disk.
/4	Formats a 5¼-inch 360KB floppy disk in a high-density drive.
/8	Formats eight sectors per track.

Distributed File System (DFS)

Microsoft has published a unique tool for NT administrators called the *NT Distributed File System* (*DFS*). A distributed file system provides a single tree structure for multiple shared volumes located on different servers on a network. A user accessing a volume on a DFS tree doesn't need to know the name of the server where the volume is actually shared.

With the DFS software, you can create a DFS tree root on any server running Windows NT Server 4.0. Each DFS tree you create is accessible by users of computers running Windows NT Workstation 4.0, Windows NT Server 4.0, or Windows 95.

This section explains what DFS is, why it's useful, and how to create and administer DFS trees on Windows NT Server 4.0.

To download DFS, attach to Microsoft's Web site at the following address:

```
http://www.microsoft.com/ntserver/dfs/dfsdl.htm
```

DFS Trees

As I write this book, DFS is in its infancy, but I suspect that it will be the way that most network operating systems treat their shared volumes in the future. This product is comparable to many of the behaviors of the large host systems that have offered the IS departments of the world a robust and reliable system. Currently DFS is a product that must be downloaded and added to an NT 4.0 server, but in the future it will be part of the operating system itself.

A DFS tree makes network access easier for users, who no longer have to manually locate which server any particular resource is on. After connecting to the root of the DFS tree, they can then browse for and access all resources contained within the tree, no matter which server the resource is physically located on.

With DFS, if a server goes down and you need to replace it, or you need to move a volume from one server to another, you can do so without informing users of the change. Instead, you modify the DFS tree to refer to the new server location for the resource, and users can continue to use the same DFS path to access the volume.

Because you can have multiple DFS trees on your network, you can create a different DFS tree for each type of user on your network. For example, an engineering firm could create one DFS tree containing all the volumes needed by their engineers, another for payroll and benefits people, and so on. Any particular volume can be included in one or more DFS trees, ensuring that every user can access all the resources he or she needs.

With DFS, you can increase data availability and transparently distribute load across multiple servers. This is because multiple servers can serve as duplicate storage points for a single volume.

DFS gives you the flexibility to expand your network as smoothly as possible. When you add disk storage to your network, the physical server on which you add it can be independent of where in the logical name space the new storage is made available.

General Concepts

DFS organizes your shared-file resources into a tree structure (see Figure 5.8). A shared-file resource that's part of a DFS tree can be accessed by either its DFS pathname or its *servername**sharename* path.

Each DFS tree has one *root volume*. The root volume can have one level of volumes, called *leaf volumes*, beneath it. Leaf volumes can be physically located on different servers than the root volume.

The root volume must be hosted on a server running Windows NT Server version 4.0 and the DFS software. Leaf volumes can be hosted on any type of Microsoft server, or any other server software for which a Windows NT-based client is available. This includes any version of Windows NT Server or Windows NT Workstation, NetWare, Windows 95, Windows for Workgroups, LAN Manager, or NFS. (Banyan volumes can't be added to DFS trees, however.)

Figure 5.8.
DFS structure.

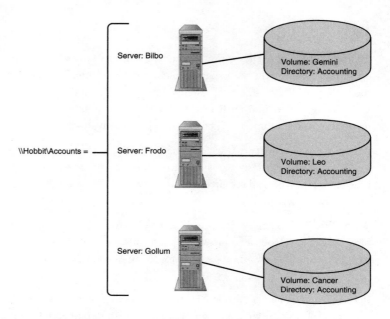

You can have multiple DFS trees on your network. Any shared folder can be a volume in multiple DFS trees. The various folders on a particular server can be made volumes on different DFS trees, but a server can have only one folder that serves as a DFS root.

DFS automatically creates short file and directory names for long names, so that 16-bit applications can use DFS paths to access files.

Nesting DFS Trees

Although each particular DFS tree is limited to two levels of volumes, each volume can contain multiple levels of folders. Additionally, you can create a multilevel tree by nesting DFS trees inside each other. You do this by adding the root volume of one DFS tree as a leaf volume in another DFS tree. Creating a multilevel tree this way is transparent to users; they don't know when they have crossed from one DFS tree to another.

You can also add levels to a DFS tree by using the local storage of the server hosting the root volume. Any files and folders under the DFS root volume will be visible through the DFS tree. In addition, when you add leaf volumes to a DFS tree, you can add them under folders at any level under the DFS volume directory. In the sample in Figure 5.9, `info` is a folder added locally at the server under the folder shared as DFS. The `reports` and `releases` volumes are added under the `info` folder.

Figure 5.9.
Leaf volumes and folders.

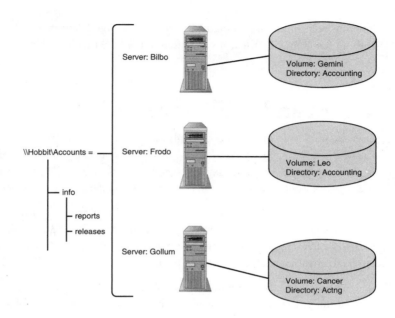

Alternate Paths

Note that some volumes on a DFS tree can use one or more shared folders for storage. If a volume uses more than one shared folder, it has alternate paths. Alternate paths provide load balancing and allow the volume to be accessed even if one of the volume servers goes down. However, the DFS software doesn't replicate information between the two servers; network administrators must ensure that the data on the servers stays synchronized through other means.

Because the DFS software doesn't synchronize alternate paths automatically (without third-party replication software), alternate paths are best suited for read-only volumes, where users won't be adding files or modifying existing files.

Security

The DFS software doesn't add any permissions or security limitations beyond those already assigned to the files or shares themselves. A user can access a volume through the DFS tree as long as the user has permission to access the shared folder directly.

It's not necessary for a user to have permissions for a root volume in order to access leaf volumes. Only administrators can administer a DFS tree.

When you add a leaf volume to a DFS tree, a blank folder is automatically created in the root volume directory. This blank folder serves as a junction point to the leaf volume. DFS prevents you from deleting any of these folders manually. If you use DFS Administrator to remove a volume, the junction point folder is automatically removed. If you delete the DFS software from a root server without first removing the leaf volumes from the DFS tree it hosted, you can then delete the junction point folders manually.

Users and DFS Trees

Users view and access resources through a DFS tree just as they view and access other resources on the network. When browsing a network, a DFS root appears just like a share name of a shared folder in *servername**dfsname* syntax. For example, with the sample DFS tree in Figure 5.8, a user browsing the network would see DFS as a shared directory available under the server (\\Hobbit\Accounts).

Users can browse through a tree transparently, no matter the location of each volume or the file system used for that volume. Users can make connections to and assign local drive letters to the root folder of a DFS tree. Users of Windows NT computers can also make connections and assign drive letters to any folder at any level of a DFS tree.

When a user views the contents of the root volume through its DFS name, he sees the leaf volumes located under that volume, as well as any contents of the shared folder that comprises the root volume.

Users of computers with Windows NT Workstation or Windows NT Server version 4.0 and users of Windows 95 computers that have the DFS client software installed can see and access DFS trees. Older versions of Windows NT and other client operating systems can't see or access DFS trees, but still can use conventional *servername**sharename* syntax to access shared folders included in DFS trees.

Windows 95 DFS clients have some additional limitations that don't apply to Windows NT clients:

- The Windows 95 client can't access non-SMB leaf volumes.
- The Windows 95 client can't use the DNS name space as part of accessing Windows NT shares (for example, DIR \\DFS.Microsoft.Com\Public).

Installing DFS

You must install the DFS server software on any server that will host a root volume of a DFS tree. The DFS software doesn't need to be installed on servers that will host only leaf volumes.

When you download the software from www.microsoft.com, it's automatically installed on the computer you use to download the software. DFS also creates a *systemroot*\system32\dfs folder on that computer that contains all the DFS files.

You can then use this folder to install DFS on other computers in your organization. When you do so, you can connect directly over the network to the *systemroot*\system32\dfs folder on the source server, or you can copy the files from the source server to a single floppy disk and then use the disk for installation. When you install DFS on an additional computer this way, be sure to install by using the files for the correct platform (such as x86, MIPS, PowerPC, or Alpha).

To install DFS after you have downloaded the software, follow these steps:

1. Make a connection to the *systemroot*\system32\dfs folder on the source server, or insert the floppy disk you made into the target server.

2. On the target server, choose Start | Settings | Control Panel.

3. Double-click the Network icon.

4. Click the Services tab, and then click Add.

5. Click Have Disk.

6. Type the path to either the *systemroot*\system32\dfs folder on the target server or to the root of the floppy disk, and then click OK.

7. Click Distributed File System, and then click OK.

8. To host a DFS root volume on this server, select the Host a DFS on Share option.

9. If the folder that will serve as the root exists and is shared, type or select the share name. Or, to use a new share as the root, click New Share and specify the folder.

10. Click OK.

Administering DFS Trees

You administer DFS trees by using the *Dfsadmin* tool. With Dfsadmin, you can add and remove volumes in a DFS tree, modify volumes, create alternate paths to a volume, and view and configure information about the volumes contained in a tree. You can remotely administer any DFS tree on the network for which you have permissions.

Dfsadmin Tool

You can install the Dfsadmin tool on any computer running NT Workstation or Server 4.0. To do so, copy dfsadmin.exe and dfsadmin.hlp from the *systemroot*\system32\dfs folder on a computer that has the DFS software installed to the *systemroot*\system32 folder on the computer you want to use for administration.

Creating a DFS Tree Root

You can create root volumes only on servers that have the DFS software installed. To create them, follow these steps:

1. In Control Panel, double-click the Network icon.
2. Click the Services tab.
3. Double-click Distributed File System.
4. Select the Host a DFS on Share check box.
5. If the folder that will serve as the root exists and is shared, type or select the share name. Or, to use a new share as the root, click New Share and specify the folder.
6. Click OK.

Adding a Volume to a DFS Tree

Any folder you want to add to the DFS tree must already be shared. After the folder is shared, follow these steps to add the folder to the DFS volume:

1. In the Dfsadmin main window, select the volume under which you want the new volume to appear.
2. Choose DFS | Add To DFS.
3. For the option When a User References This Path, type the volume name for the new volume as an extension of a current volume in the tree.
4. For the option Send the User to This Network Path, type the path of the shared folder to add as a volume. (Or use the Browse button to browse the network and select the volume.)
5. Type a comment in the Comment box (optional).
6. Click OK.

Removing a Volume from a DFS Tree

To remove a volume from the DFS tree, follow these steps:

1. In the Dfsadmin main window, select the volume to remove.
2. Choose DFS | Remove from DFS.
3. Click Yes.

Adding Alternate Paths for a Volume

A volume can use one or more shared folders for its storage. If the volume uses more than one, it has alternate paths. When a volume includes alternate paths, user requests to access the volume are distributed among the alternate paths.

The DFS software doesn't ensure that the contents of the alternate paths of a volume are replicated. Network administrators must manually ensure that the alternates stay synchronized.

To add an alternate path for a volume, follow these steps:

1. In the Dfsadmin main window, double-click the volume.
2. Click Add.
3. Click Yes.
4. For the option Send the User to This Network Path, type the path of the shared folder to add as an alternate path for the volume.

To remove an alternate path from a volume, follow these steps:

1. In the Dfsadmin main window, double-click the volume.
2. For the option Send the User to This Network Path, select the network path you want to remove.
3. Click Remove.
4. Click OK.

Saving and Restoring the DFS Structure Table

You can save the current structure of the DFS tree to a file, which you can later reload to restore the DFS volume structure. Note that this saves only the links between volumes, not any volume contents. The save files are server-specific comma-separated files, with a .csv file extension.

To save the current DFS tree structure, follow these steps:

1. Choose DFS | Save As.
2. Type a name for the file in the File Name box, and then click Save.

To restore a previous DFS tree structure, follow these steps:

1. Choose DFS | Load.
2. Select the file to restore, and then click Open.

Filtering the View of Volumes

You can filter the list of volumes shown in the Dfsadmin main window. You can filter volumes by name, comment, and the number of alternate servers that provide storage for the volume.

To filter the list of volumes, follow these steps:

1. Choose View | Filter.
2. Click the filtering option you want, and then click OK.

For more information on any of the filtering options, right-click the option and then select the What's This? option.

Stopping and Starting the DFS Service

DFS is implemented as a service (the Distributed File Service). When DFS is installed on a server, the Distributed File Service is configured to start automatically when the computer starts. You can start and stop the service manually by using either Services in Control Panel or the command line. The commands are net stop dfs and net start dfs.

Administering DFS from the Command Prompt

DFS provides the following commands that you can use from the command prompt:

- dfscmd /map *dfsname**dfsshare**path* *server**share**path* [*comment*]

  Adds the shared folder *server**share**path* as a volume in the specified DFS tree.

- dfscmd /unmap *dfsname**dfsshare**path*

  Removes the volume from the DFS tree.

- dfscmd /add *dfsname**dfsshare**path* *server**share**path*

  Adds *server**share**path* as an alternate path for the specified DFS volume.

- dfscmd /remove *dfsname**dfsshare**path* *server**share**path*

  Removes the specified alternate path from the specified volume.

- dfscmd /view *dfsname**dfsshare* [/partial ¦ /full]

  Displays all the volumes in the DFS tree. Without arguments, only the volume names are displayed. Specifying /partial causes comments for each volume to be displayed. Specifying /full causes the network path of each volume (including all alternate paths) to be displayed.

Summary

I hope that you can see in this chapter that, when dealing with the storage system of your NT server, it's imperative that you consider every variable before setting a decision in action. The decisions that you make are not the kind that you can change lightly.

By looking a little deeper at the hard drive and controller options, it should become obvious to you that it's much more of a decision than it looks like on the surface. You've learned that controllers today aren't really controllers in the old sense, but they're capable of making decisions and protecting your data. Through hardware-based RAID, you can not only protect your data, but save CPU cycles and memory.

Hard drives themselves are the building blocks of your entire file system, and it's important to look at which drives offer the features you find necessary. Remember to look at drive performance and the warranty of the manufacturer of the drive. These factors will ultimately matter even more than the vendor from which you purchased the drive.

Drive partitioning and volume creation are necessary to access the drives that you install, and you've seen the different possibilities for those items. Remember that primary partitions and extended partitions each have their own value, and when to put each to work.

Volumes have several ways of being created and don't have to count on intelligent hardware to protect them. If you're going to use software-based fault tolerance, you need to consider that mirroring and duplexing are fast and efficient, but they can be very expensive in dollars and cents. Parity implementations may be more cost-effective, but the slowdown in your server may cost you more in the long run.

Finally, Microsoft is continuing to move the NT product line ahead by creating new file system features such as DFS. DFS will allow you to keep your clients in touch with their data more reliably and will make better use of the widespread and diverse systems that most large companies have.

6

Networking Brief

Peter Norton™

If you are a veteran Windows NT network administrator, this chapter will probably offer very little to you. But if you are a new administrator or even an administrator for other operating systems, this chapter will help you to understand the basic networking concepts of the Microsoft operating systems. If you are a Novell NetWare administrator, particularly, your understanding of network security may actually be more confusing for you than helpful.

PC networking at its most basic form is the grouping of PCs, peripheral resources, and users into a working unit. This grouping can be viewed from many different angles. The hardware must be connected together, the users must be gathered and managed, and the security model must be assembled. This chapter talks about the basic building blocks for the computer network and discusses Microsoft's networking scheme.

A basic understanding of the hardware and user dynamics will help you in later chapters when references are made to some of these items. By the time you finish this chapter, you will have a basic understanding of how Microsoft approaches network integration and security. All the material in this chapter is covered in later chapters in greater detail, but those chapters assume a certain knowledge of this basic material.

The following topics are covered in this chapter:

- Workgroups
- Domains
- Domain control
- Organizing domains
- Browsing the network
- Network services setup
- Networks (LAN or WAN) versus networks (segmentation)
- The physical topology
- Segmenting the network
- Routing between segments

Microsoft Networking Concepts

Before you can begin creating user accounts, it's necessary to understand how your project fits into the Microsoft networking scheme. Microsoft does a good job of separating account management and services from the actual hardware and communications level. The understanding needed to create and provide services for users can actually be separated from the tasks needed to provide a hardware signal from the server to the users.

There are two major pieces involved in providing account services to users. The first is to create the accounts and the security scheme needed to protect the data. The second is to provide network-based services for those users to access once they have been authenticated. These are separate issues, and we'll explore the basic pieces in this section.

Workgroups and Domains

Microsoft networking really involves two different ways of grouping users: workgroups and domains. These two types of users and resources groupings are divided by the size of the groups you work with and the degree of management that you can use with each of them. The following sections discuss the two groups.

Workgroups

The definition of a workgroup model of managing users and resources is easily remembered by the fact that it's also used in a version of Windows 3.x called *Windows for Workgroups*. Based on that hint, hopefully you understand that the workgroup model (see Figure 6.1) is used for the management and grouping of peer-to-peer or very small network groups.

Figure 6.1.
The workgroup model.

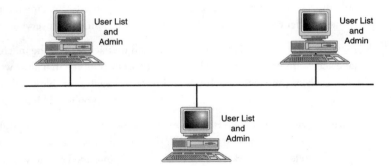

Small networks of users are looking for the ability to share information and peripherals more than they are to protect them. The workgroup model is meant to allow small groups of users to create shared drives and peripherals on their own workstations and share those with others in their network. Workgroups actually make the workstation simultaneously a server and a workstation in the network. Although NT Server is meant for server use, workgroups can be used with an NT Server-based network.

By *server-based*, I mean that the NT machine can run NT Server (the operating system) and still use the workgroup model. The workgroup-based security is not forbidden, but you'll see in the following sections that it's not preferred for NT Server.

The following operating systems can participate in a workgroup:

- Windows NT Server (all versions)
- Windows NT Workstation (all versions)
- Windows 95
- Windows for Workgroups
- Windows 3.x (user only)

Within a workgroup, each workstation contains its own security scheme and administrator. To administer that security scheme, you must be sitting at that machine. Every workstation must create users and groups that are allowed to access the items that will be shared. The decisions that are made for that machine have no effect on the other systems.

Note: Workgroup-type networks have been around for years. They originated in the old NetBIOS networks that were part of the IBM and Microsoft PC network of the early 1980s. Even Novell had its Personal NetWare phase.

This type of system most likely won't be found in a large network, for several reasons. This system doesn't allow you to centrally manage any of its components. Imagine having to go from machine to machine in order to make a change to the security of all of your servers.

The system also requires that you re-create each user account at the machine where you want users to have access. In other words, to have twenty users involved in a large workgroup, you would have to go to each of the server machines and re-create each user. Now let's imagine that you have to make a change to one user each day. That means that you would have to make twenty visits.

The alternative to this system is to have each of the users at those workstations administer the users and shared peripherals at that server. Well, as odd as this may seem, this is really the intent of the workgroup model. The workgroup model was really intended to allow Windows users to share those peripherals at their desk that they would like to share.

Workgroups generally are not the answer for NT Server installations, but instead are a good idea for workstation users. Many administrators feel as if domains and workgroups are mutually exclusive ideas. Workgroups can exist within a domain system. This works well for allowing groups of users to share drives and printers without having to get the entire network involved. Workgroups are easy to install and administer. They also allow the network administrator to be free from worry over small projects like the sharing of a single CD-ROM drive that exists in a group of cubicles.

The important rule of thumb to keep in mind when dealing with workgroups is that they're hard to manage at around ten machines. It could even be said that five machines in a workgroup is when it begins to get difficult. I like to use the air conditioning analogy for deciding when to convert to a domain model instead of a workgroup. If you own a car without air conditioning, it can be comfortable if you're alone. But with each new person in the car it becomes more and more difficult to breathe. You can gauge your need for a change by your own discomfort.

Domain

The domain model allows administrators to manage the network centrally. Domains consist of a shared list of users and groups that are used by all the servers within the domain (see Figure 6.2).

Figure 6.2.
The domain model.

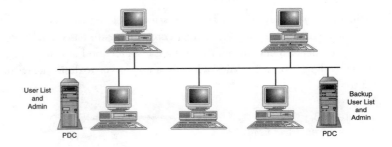

Large groups of users and large network configurations aren't simply concerned with sharing peripherals. They are also concerned with company information being protected and peripherals not being misused. Because of this concern, it's necessary for the administrators to be able to control the amount of access that these users have and to maintain a consistent list of users throughout the network.

Domain Control

In a domain model, each user or group of users is recorded into a shared Security Accounts Manager (SAM) database. This database is kept at a central server called the *primary domain controller* (PDC). All other servers on the network that want to change user information must do so through the PDC. This allows for a consistent security model. But if it ended at that, it could be a bottleneck or even halt the network if the PDC failed.

To allow normal network operations to flow more smoothly and to give user workstations another source for authentication, an alternate plan exists. All account information is kept on the PDC, but the information can also be kept on *backup domain controllers* (BDCs). A BDC is equally capable of authenticating users, but it isn't capable of allowing changes to user and group information.

BDCs receive all of the information they use to authenticate users through an automatic copy from the PDC. The BDC exists only as an alternate site for authenticating users; it doesn't facilitate or store any changes that aren't sent to it by the PDC. The object is to provide some fault tolerance for network login and to spread the load of user authentication.

Once you create a domain, servers in that domain function as either a domain controller of some type or as a simple server. As a rule of thumb, it's good to have at least two BDCs for every PDC that exists on the network. This allows for redundancy and for workflow to continue smoothly.

Organizing Domains

It's of little value to install even small client/server network installations with a workgroup model when you have the option of using a domain. The effort required to create a domain isn't much more than that of a workgroup, but the benefits can save mountains of time.

Domains are generally organized over the same divisions that make sense for other company resources (see Figure 6.3). For example, you might create domains based on departmental lines to allow users in a given department the ability to share resources and a security policy. You might also create domains along geographic lines or locally, allowing you to designate resources to those who are closest to them.

Figure 6.3.
Location versus departmental organization.

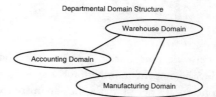

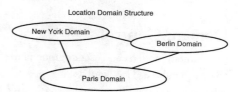

The idea behind organizing your domain structure is to add value to administering each grouping of users. If you have a company that's smaller than 100 users and they're located in the same place, dividing them into multiple domains could provide more work than help. If you have even two small groups of 25 each but they exist in separate cities, on the other hand, there may be benefit to dividing up into two domains.

Domain organization has more to do with common sense than with set rules, but Chapter 9, "Domain Design," covers these concepts extensively.

Browsing the Network

Domains and workgroups are the basic building blocks for the creation and management of users, but to get those users to the resources they're looking for, the users must be able to browse the network. *Browsing* means the ability to see a listing of the items that are available for use on the network. For example, the user might want to use a printer that's shared and would need to see a list of shared printers. That list would be a *browse list* and would be provided by a *browse server*.

In order to provide such lists, Microsoft provides a Browser service in its operating systems that are network-aware. The Browser service keeps a centralized list of servers and shared resources that can be browsed in order to find the resource that the user needs. This is different from other popular operating systems that create unneeded network traffic by advertising the services that they offer—broadcasting a message over the network on a timed basis.

> **Note:** The worst offender in this group is the Macintosh operating system, which continually announces that a resource is available and what items it's sharing. This form of network chatter can bring a large network to its knees. They don't call it "Apple**Talk**" for nothing.

Much like domain controllers, browsing has a hierarchy that it follows to allow users access to the browse list without having to continually depend on one system for browsing information. But unlike domain control, browse lists can be maintained by systems running operating systems other than NT Server.

The following operating systems can participate in browse lists:

- Windows NT Server
- Windows NT Workstation
- Windows 95
- Windows for Workgroups

Browse servers are given roles to play in the continual dance to provide browsing services to users. The idea is to allow users to gain access to the list without having to traverse the network and cause any more traffic than necessary. The roles that they play are browser client, potential browser, master browser, and backup browser (see Figure 6.4).

Figure 6.4.
Browser relationships.

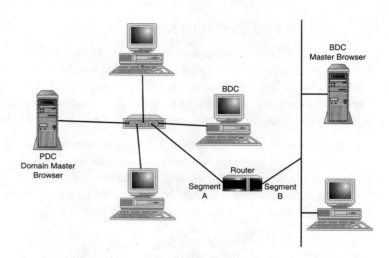

The role that a particular machine plays in the browsing hierarchy is determined by the machines on the network without human intervention, at least initially. The process involves elections that occur when each new machine running the server service is added to the network.

The following list describes the browse roles:

- **Browser client.** Machines that aren't involved in providing any browse services, but use them.

  Potential browser. This machine is a browse client that isn't currently providing browse services, but whose operating system or environment can provide services if instructed to do so by the master browser.

- **Master browser.** Like the PDC, the master browser is the system that collects the lists of available network resources, and maintains and distributes them to a backup browser. Master browsers are elected from among the list of potential browsers that are available when the system running the server service starts up. The elections are based on a set of criteria, but this can be a real issue if the wrong system wins the election.

- **Preferred master browser.** This is a control that the administrator can use to force a particular system as the master browser. ("Hey, this election is fixed!") By designating a preferred master browser, you ensure that when this machine is up it's the master browser. This is done by the machine forcing an election on power-up. If a preferred master browser exists, it will win the election.

- **Backup browser.** Backup browsers are comparable to BDCs in the domain model of security. The backup browser is responsible for distributing the browse list that it is given by the master browser. The backup browser doesn't create browse lists; it simply redistributes them.

When a client system is started in a Microsoft network, it must first find a master browser. The master browser then tells that client where to find a backup browser. The backup browser then will support that client's browsing needs until the client restarts.

Network Services Setup

As you create an NT server, you will actually create user services at the same time. These services involve the basic utilities that users make use of when they are logged into the server. The services range from items that you would take for granted to those that you might find unique. But in order for the users to access that part of the server, a service must exist.

For those brave souls who have already looked at the Control Panel screen, the network services are different from the Services control panel that you see listed in the collection of icons in the Control Panel. Network services involve services that are directly related to assisting users in interacting with the network itself.

The network services are controlled from a subsection of the Network control panel called Services. Here network services can be added or configured (see Figure 6.5). Services can be added by third-party products and generally are not added by the administrator specifically. Software and network applications that are added will install the services they need to allow users to access them.

Figure 6.5.
The Services page in the Network control panel.

Tip: Remember that you can easily gain access to the Network control panel without having to begin at the Start menu and work your way down. Simply right-click the Network Neighborhood icon and choose Properties.

The following list shows example services that exist in NT Server:

- **Workstation service.** The most basic service on the server is actually a service that allows users to log in at the server as a workstation. If you remove this service, you are no longer able to sit down at the server and log in, even as the Administrator account. Removing this service is almost never a good idea.

- **Server service.** Before users can access a file server as a user not seated at the server computer itself, the Server service must be installed and configured. This service is automatically added to your server when you install. Even if you want to stop this activity from occurring, I wouldn't recommend removing this service. There are much easier ways to stop access to the server; the group of subordinate issues that this can cause later are hard to decipher.

- **Computer Browser.** When users in a Microsoft network attempt to find a network resource, they often must access a list of shared components. This list is maintained by certain PCs (not always servers) that hold and distribute the browse list. This service in NT allows this NT server to participate in the browsing process.

- **NetBIOS Interface.** NetBIOS is a throwback to the original form of network name resolution. This service is the interface between the current NT operating system and this form of name resolution. Even if you're using WINS (see the next item) and other name-resolution schemes, it's a good idea to leave this service running. Many legacy systems and software programs require it to interface with the server.

- **Windows Internet Name Service (WINS).** Because the TCP/IP protocol isn't NetBIOS-based, NT offers this service to allow the server to resolve machine names with IP addresses on the network. If you run TCP/IP as the primary protocol on your network, this service is paramount.

- **Microsoft DHCP Server.** When you install TCP/IP as a communications protocol on your network, you can use *dynamic host communications protocol* (*DHCP*) to distribute IP addresses from a master list.

- **Simple TCP/IP Services.** This is the base service required by many of the other TCP/IP services in order to run.

Networks (LAN or WAN) Versus Networks (Segmentation)

In order to build any network properly, it's necessary to understand at least the basic functions to the underlying pieces of the communications network. Everything within your system can be called "the network" and so it can be confusing to try to understand what piece the term *network* refers to.

For the purposes of this chapter, we'll look at the physical network and the protocols related to the different physical schemes. We'll see the differences between the greater network—that is, your *local area network* (LAN) or *wide area network* (WAN)—and the reasons to segment those networks into smaller, more manageable pieces.

Following are some key terms:

- **Local area network (LAN).** Networks completely contained in one building or small campus area.

- **Wide area network (WAN).** Networks that require special long-range communications schemes (frame relay networks, ISDN, leased phone lines, and so on) to make connection. Usually associated with long distances.

- **Network segment (sometimes called a *network*).** A single physical cabling segment containing a common network-level address for use by attached stations.

The Big Picture

Windows NT Server is capable of using an infinite number of physical network schemes and communications protocols. Because of the fact that the operating system separates the functions of application and hardware, the administrator only needs to find a vendor that has written drivers to the NT standard, and that protocol may be used.

The Physical Topology

Computer networks are cabled together physically using many different schemes. The cabling and physical protocol scheme that you use is called the *topology* of the network, and different topologies have limitations and rules that must be followed. These rules and limitations are more controlling than NT itself.

It isn't my intention to completely explain every topology or even fully describe the most popular topologies. But let's take a look at the most popular topologies on a level that will help you to understand why they fit (or may not fit) your need. It helps to understand the topology rules when you're chasing a problem.

There are really only two different topologies that have survived the topology wars over the last 15 years that PCs have been networked. There are hundreds of variations, but really only two different topologies: ring and bus.

Bus Topology

The *bus* (also known as *linear bus*) *topology* that is used by Ethernet and all of its variations is the most popular topology in use today. When Ethernet originated, it was run using coaxial cable in what looked like a single line with termination on each end. This line of coax cable was the Ethernet bus. I say it *looks* like a single line because it's actually a continuous daisy chain of machines (see Figure 6.6) connected by coax cable.

Figure 6.6.
Bus topology as seen in Ethernet.

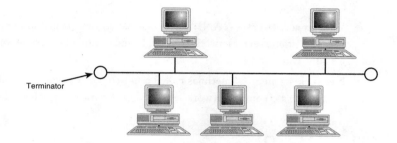

Terminator

The bus topology used today is barely recognizable because it looks very much like the star or "home run" topology. This is because new Ethernet uses a concentrator/repeater that very much resembles (and is often called) a *hub*. These Ethernet installations are installed with twisted-pair cabling running from the PC's NIC to the concentrator. But what you don't see is that fact that the Ethernet bus still exists inside the concentrator (see Figure 6.7).

Figure 6.7.
Concentrator-based bus topology.

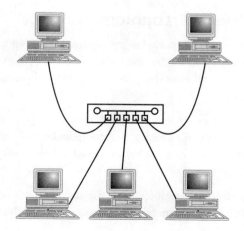

There are limitations that exist for each different form of Ethernet, and there are many different forms of Ethernet. The following table describes the limitations of the most popular forms.

Type of Segment	Speed	Recommended Maximum Number of Concentrators per Segment	Maximum Length of Cable from Source to Node	Cable Type	Maximum Number of Active Users per Segment
10Base2	10MB	N/A	300 meters	Coax	35
10BaseT	10MB	3	100 meters	Category 3-Twisted Pair	35
100BaseT-Class 1	100MB	2	100 meters	Category 5-Twisted Pair	50
100BaseT-Class 2	100MB	5	100 meters	Category 5-Twisted Pair	75

The three terms that are used to name different types of Ethernet topologies have the following meanings:

- **10Base2.** 10-megabit Ethernet across two-conductor wire.
- **10BaseT.** 10-megabit Ethernet across twisted-pair wire.
- **100BaseT.** 100-megabit Ethernet across twisted-pair wire.

Don't take for granted that you can look at the name of an Ethernet topology and determine what it means; they'll throw you a curve. 100BaseVG is another form of 100-megabit Ethernet. VG has nothing to do with the form of cabling; it runs on twisted-pair wire.

Ring Topology

The *ring topology* is used primarily by large firms that have IBM mainframe or minicomputer installations using the *Token Ring* protocol. The topology is popular in those companies because Token Ring was one of only three PC networking topologies supported by IBM for many years. It's called a *ring* because each item on the network is connected to the next, which is connected to the next, and so on until a ring is completed (see Figure 6.8). There are other ring-based communications protocols, but Token Ring has been the prevailing winner.

Much like the bus topology, you wouldn't recognize most ring topology installations as rings. The IBM form of a ring, called *Token Ring*, creates the ring in a concentrated form called a *Multi-Station Access Unit* (*MAU* or *MSAU*). Much like an Ethernet concentrator, these MAUs concentrate the ring into a small box (see Figure 6.9), but the ring does still exist.

Figure 6.8.
Ring topology in its pure form.

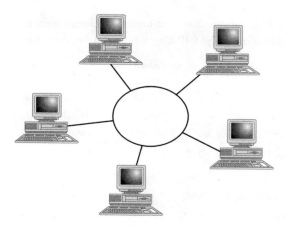

Figure 6.9.
The Token Ring version of the ring topology.

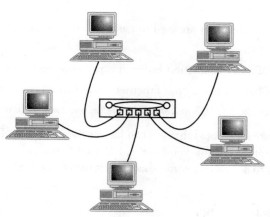

In order to communicate from ring to ring (MAU to MAU), the manufacturer creates ports on the MAU called *Ring In* and *Ring Out*. By simply connecting the Ring In of one MAU to the Ring Out of the other and vice versa, you effectively extend the ring. So even though all of the clients are connected to the MAU through a single line that returns to a central location, you're really involved in a ring.

Token ring exists in two different speeds (4 megabit and 16 megabit) and with many different cabling schemes. The cabling schemes that are possible for Token Ring don't lend themselves to quick and easy tables explaining the limitations and lengths. This is one of the reasons that Ethernet has been the hands-down winner. If you are going to install a Token Ring network, the necessary considerations require a cabling professional with Token Ring experience from day one of the planning.

Segmenting the Network

Each LAN or WAN to which NT is attached will be attached to NT through a *network interface card (NIC)* or cards. When you configure those cards to a cabling plant to communicate with the other PCs attached to that cable, you have attached to a network segment. As Figure 6.10 shows, for example, if you have three Ethernet NICs attached to your NT server, and each of those NICs is attached to a separate cabling plant with other workstations, then you are using three segments.

Figure 6.10.
Network segmentation.

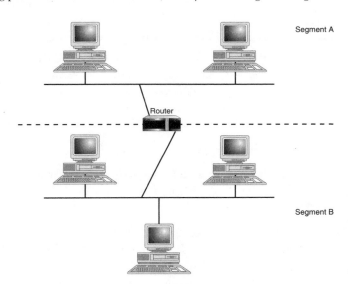

The purpose behind different network segments is to reduce traffic across the network as a whole so that a single segment doesn't become saturated. If you spread the amount of communications across three segments instead of one, you cut down the traffic to one-third of potential. Each network communications protocol requires some cooperation among the workstations, and it becomes like putting people on buses. There is a comfort and workability factor involved. After a certain number of people are on one bus, you need to get another bus.

Further segmentation is necessary whenever your network traffic on a particular cabling segment reaches a saturation point or when you reach the limitations of the protocol or topology you're using. Let's look at a couple of different examples of times that would call for segmentation:

- Example 1: The company has 50 users that occupy a single segment of 10BaseT Ethernet. The users complain that the network has really slowed down in the last few months since the addition of the new design software to the network. The 20 users of the design package are opening very large files and need to store the data on the server for this package.

By adding another NIC to your server and splitting your user base evenly across the separate segments, you'll reduce the load on each segment. You may choose to put all of the Design users on the new segment and to upgrade that segment to 100BaseT, or you could split those users evenly among the two 10BaseT segments. But the idea is to either lighten the load that must be shared by the other users or separate the heavier users.

- Example 2: You're called by a client that's having trouble with network slowdowns that occur only during certain times of the day. The slowdowns seem to be at their worst when people first come in and during times when large projects are due. Upon inspection you find that the client has one Ethernet segment with 150 workstations attached.

Although this may not be the only cause of the problems that this client is having, you can feel safe in recommending that the network be segmented. It's in the best interest of the client to split the network into three segments of 50 workstations each. This will keep the number of active users in the 35 or fewer range for the majority of the time.

Routing Between Segments

Network segments exist on two different levels: the physical and the logical. We've seen the physical segment, but how does the logical exist? How do we create a logical route between the two segments?

Routable network communications protocols require that they be given logical network addresses in order to understand what segment of the physical network they're attached to. Once this address is established, the machines on that network segment will communicate with one another using that network address in combination with a node address to identify themselves. This is a bit like establishing a ZIP code first to establish a general neighborhood, and then a specific address to find the specific home.

If a machine wants to communicate with another machine, it will include information regarding the address of the other machine. Included in that address is the network address and the node address. But in order for a machine to find a machine on a different segment, a device must exist between the two segments that will know the route to the other network address. This piece of equipment is called a *router*. NT is capable of being that router.

By adding a second or third physical segment to an NT server, you have created only the physical connection of the nodes on that segment. On a logical (software) level, the nodes on that segment are now able to see only the other machines on that segment. Within NT, you have the ability to create a logical connection between the NICs contained in that server. This connection isn't made automatically, however. The administrator may not want the two segments to communicate, so you must manually make the changes.

NT has two routable protocols as part of the standard set: IPX/SPX and TCP/IP. Prior to NT 4.0 (or Service Packs for NT 3.51 that came out just before NT 4.0), IPX/SPX was not a routable protocol within NT Server. These protocols and their routings are covered extensively in Chapter 15, "Surviving in a Multi-Protocol World."

Summary

The Microsoft networking scheme is covered in many ways throughout this book, but you should take away from this chapter several key points. Before you can begin understanding the concepts behind how to manage the NT Server network, you have to get this basic knowledge.

The user base can be managed in two fashions, depending mostly on the size and structure of the organization—the workgroup model to manage very small groups of users, and the domain model for groups that require centralized management.

Domains are not just a single entity. They are collections of user accounts, but also a way of connecting those large groups. By gathering certain areas of a company into domains, you are setting up management domains. These are generally organized over the same divisions that make sense for other company resources.

LANs and WANs are not just groups of cable to be thrown together. They require planning and can be responsible for a great deal of the success or failure of the network as a whole. Keep in mind the rule of thumb for network cable planning and the advantages to each of the different topologies when planning your network.

7

Printing

Peter Norton™

NT printing is distinctly different from printing in any other version of Windows. The differences lie in the way that NT communicates with hardware. As you may remember from the chapters on the NT subsystems, NT doesn't allow any software to directly communicate with the hardware, and that alone is enough to make NT printing unique.

But there are many more printing differences between NT and other applications, as will become apparent by the following topics covered in this chapter:

- NT printing concepts
- Printer configuration
- Printer control and troubleshooting

NT Printing Concepts

NT printing begins with some odd concepts. The first and probably the hardest to keep track of is the fact that you don't put paper in a printer. No, printers are not the devices from which you remove hard copy. A *printer* is the name that NT gives to the software device to which applications write. *Print devices* are those hardware items that sit by your computer and put ink or toner on paper (see Figure 7.1). This is an important distinction because throughout this chapter I will be referring to printers and print devices by their NT names.

Figure 7.1.
Printers send to printer devices.

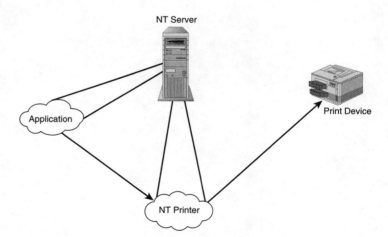

Print devices receive their input from printers and never interface directly with the application in NT. This relationship allows the administrator to monitor and manage the output before it's actually involved with the printer.

Printers can be controlled in ways that actual physical printers (print devices) are not. Jobs can be stopped or delayed. You can give certain printers specific tasks, such as all jobs with a certain priority level. Expensive printers can be assigned for certain users that will make the best use of that equipment.

Printers can be assigned multiple print devices. The concept is called a *printer pool* and it's best done by using multiple printers of the same make and model, but the important factor is that they use the same print driver. Pooling allows for large amounts of data to be printed out more efficiently for large groups. It works very well for groups such as typing pools or publishing departments that require a great deal of output and don't have time to wait.

> **Tip:** If you install a printing pool, try to place the printers in one central location. Pools of printers are more annoying than helpful if your users must find the printer device that they printed from.

Multiple printers can be assigned to one print device. You can configure several printers for a single print device that's capable of multiple behaviors, so as to enjoy maximum flexibility in your printing options. This can also allow for different printing groups to be moved from one printer to another with only a change in the printer, not the physical arrangements.

The entire concept is to allow for maximum flexibility. Users interface with the software-level printers and that's all they really need to worry about. By separating the two pieces, you allow the print jobs to exist without regard for whether the hardware to print on is there. This may seem a bit extreme, but you should see someone's face light up when you assign their printer to a print device that isn't being disassembled by the hardware technician.

Print devices can be connected to NT through either physical connections or network shares from other network entities. This is important because many business printers today are actually able to connect to the network directly and don't depend on the traditional LPT or COM ports.

Connecting to printers that aren't physically attached to the server computer is done in the same way that you attach to drive shares. When you connect to drive shares, you create a mapped drive or a logical drive pointer. When you connect to a printer over the network, you're creating a logical printer port. You do this by using the browse function or by using UNC (`\\server\printer`).

If you have managed printers in a NetWare bindery environment (NetWare versions 3.x or lower), you need to understand the minor distinction between printers and print queues. *Print queues* in older versions of NetWare are both the collection point for print jobs and the controlling software that's used to communicate with the print device. NT and newer versions of NetWare (4.x) separate the spooling (or queuing) of print jobs. In the NT environment, printers actually accept the data and then spool it to the print device. NetWare now has separate printers (software) and print queues, but the jobs are still found at the queue. That really is the distinction—NT print jobs are managed and controlled from the printer. This allows things to be controlled before they leave for the spool.

Printing as we have seen it so far has involved three basic pieces. Applications send print jobs to the printer and the printer sends the print jobs to the print device (see Figure 7.2). It's just that simple, but for those things to occur there's a great deal of work going on underneath. There are actually as many as seven steps:

1. The printer driver is loaded (if necessary) at the client.

2. The application at the client creates a file for output (non-NT clients move to step 5). If the client is NT as well, the GDI (graphics device interface) is used to create this file.

3. The NT client's spooler receives the DDI (device driver interface) journal file that was contained in the GDI in step 3.

4. The NT client's print processor uses the journal to create the print data for the actual print device.

5. Print data is sent to the spooler of the print server.

6. The spooler in the server sends the data to the print monitor, which sends it on the proper destination port (LPT or UNC).

7. The print device is sent the data and the client is sent a message regarding the job's completion.

Figure 7.2.
The printing flow through the NT server.

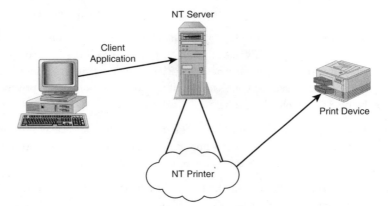

The NT server doesn't just print for applications that exist on the NT server. It must accept print jobs from clients. Clients initially must install the printers on their machines through the use of printer drivers. *Printer drivers* are the hardware-specific pieces of software that the applications will need in order to communicate with the particular printer after the job moves through the print device. The particular type of client that you're using will use printer drivers differently from other clients.

NT clients have many of the same components included in the server, and for that reason I'll cover the print process through that client. But if you're dealing with a client that isn't NT, you'll most likely find that the process begins after the raw data arrives at the server spooler in step 5 of the preceding steps. You can catch up with the process in the long descriptions in four paragraphs.

The data is then sent to the *spooler*. The spooler's initial job in this process is only to gather the data and pass it on to the *print processor*. The print processor sits out of the trail of the print job unless it's needed—sort of "in the pocket of the spooler" to be used in special events. The print processor performs any rendering or processing that it must perform and passes the job back to the spooler. If the data that's sent to the print processor is raw data or text, the processor has no need to further manipulate the data and will send it on. But if the data is application data that requires a specific resolution, font, or driver-specific changes, the processor will make those changes. Once finished, the job is returned to the spooler.

The spooler is more of a waystation or a place for jobs to go to be moved from one task to another. It performs the intermediate tasks between applications and print devices. The spooler keeps directories at the server that house print jobs, and the spooler is responsible for tracking those jobs and their printers, ports, and priority.

If the job is coming from a client and not locally on the server, the job will pass from the spooler on the workstation to the spooler on the server through a special software device called the *print router*. The print router's job is solely to move the print job of one NT machine to a print server that will accept the job into its spooler. Once it arrives at the server, the job is moved to the print monitor.

As you may recall from Chapter 3, "Windows NT Subsystems," not all items can access hardware and hardware devices. The print monitors are that piece of the printing process. Print monitors are responsible for accessing the port, writing to it, and releasing it. The monitor interfaces with the printing device. It tracks problems and make notifications if needed.

Printer Configuration

Managing printers in NT involves the use of a group of control panels, the same as it has in Windows for years. But with Windows NT and Window 95 there's no longer a Print Manager and a Printer control panel. Printers are created, deleted, monitored, and manipulated from one utility. This is not a new feature for NT, but it used to be called the Print Manager. Print Manager in 4.0 is now found in the Control Panel (see Figure 7.3) and behaves more like the Windows 95 utility.

Figure 7.3.
The Printers control panel.

One of the nice additions to NT 4.0 is the fact that you can access the Printers control panel through the Start menu (under Settings) and in the My Computer window.

To call the Printers control panel a single tool that replaces two in standard Windows is really a misrepresentation. When you open the Printers control panel, you're actually looking at a tool that's more like a printer manager that gives you access to the two old utilities.

The Printers control panel presents the icons of printers that already exist and an icon that allows you to create new printers. From this location, you can access all the printers or add a new one, but you haven't reached the utility that makes changes to the printers or monitors their activity. Managing the printers is done by selecting the printer itself. A printer is just like other objects in this new interface; to manipulate its behavior you need to open its properties. If you're an experienced Windows 3.x user, you will feel closer to home once you open the properties of a printer in NT 4.0 or Windows 95. The screen that you see is much more like the control panel screen that you find in those older versions of Windows.

Note: Windows NT 4.0 and Windows 95 aren't exactly the same in regard to printing; as a matter of fact, once you're inside the controls you find them to be quite different. But I mention Windows 95 to point out the "look and feel" similarities. If you're familiar with Windows 95, you should be comfortable.

The printer properties dialog box (see Figure 7.4) is the place where controls are changed for each printer. Changes in the printer port, the printer driver, and even security for each printer are made at this level. In the following sections, we'll look at the different options in depth.

Figure 7.4.
Printer properties.

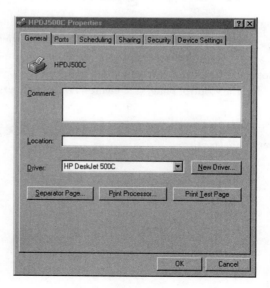

If instead of looking at the properties of a printer you simply double-click the printer object, you'll see the print queue utility (see Figure 7.5). This utility is most closely related to what Windows 3.1 would have called the Print Manager. From this screen, you can see the print jobs that are queued and waiting to be spooled to the print device.

Figure 7.5.
The print queue utility.

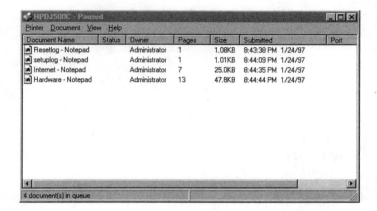

But you don't just see the jobs from this vantage point. This is the screen that you use to stop, start, and even reschedule the jobs that have arrived to be printed (these topics are covered in the later section "Managing Print Queues").

Creating a Printer

Creating printers in NT 4.0 is a relatively simple process, but not quite as simple as the Add Printer icon in the Printers control panel implies (refer to Figure 7.3). By double-clicking the icon, you begin the process, opening the Add Printer Wizard. The Add Printer Wizard initially offers you the choice of creating a local printer or a network printer. The choice that you make here is between the server accessing this print device from a local printer port and accessing it over the network. The choice has nothing to do with sharing it as a network printer.

Local Printer

If you leave the default choice of local printer intact and click Next, you'll be given a choice of the eight locally possible printer ports (see Figure 7.6). You now need to choose one of the standard ports that are listed or create a new port. By selecting a standard port and clicking Next, you'll move to the printer driver choices.

Figure 7.6.
Local port choices.

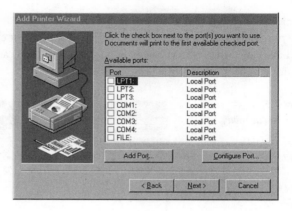

If you choose to add a port, you'll be asked to list the name of the port you want to add. Adding a port isn't done on a whim, so you probably have purchased a proprietary option card that provides extra port options.

If you're using locally attached printers, you can attach only five print devices bearing special hardware (not including files) to the server at any given time. Even though you are given the choice of four COM ports (COM1 through COM4), you must realize that only two standard COM ports can be used at any moment. The reason is that COM1 and COM3 share the same interrupt address, and COM2 and COM4 share the same interrupt address. COM1 and COM3 use IRQ 4, COM2 and COM4 use IRQ 3. So you can't have a printer on both COM1 and COM3 or on COM2 and COM4. The same holds true for anything using standard COM (serial) ports (modems, mice, scanners, and so on). Some special devices can give you COM ports with no standard IRQs, but these devices are not commonly used.

Network Printer

Printers can be created at an NT server (and even shared) that aren't physically attached print devices. The advantage of this setup is that you as an administrator maintain a certain amount of control over the print device, even though it's located elsewhere.

This choice is being used more today for two reasons. One is that printers themselves are becoming network-aware. Hewlett-Packard, Xircom, Intel, and many others have created printers and printer attachments that allow administrators to place printers anywhere on the network independent of a PC. These devices include just enough logic to present themselves as shared printers on the network.

The other reason is the fact that so many user workstation operating systems are now capable of sharing their local printers. This allows the administrator to share printers throughout the company by attaching printers to the workstations. If the workstations are capable of sharing a printer on a Microsoft network, then you can attach to that port through NT.

Given a choice between these two methods of sharing printers, I would personally recommend that you use a print device or printer attachment capable of sharing a print device without using a workstation PC. Users by their very nature are going to cause issues to arise with printers attached to their workstations. And even if the user doesn't cause the printer to have issues, the possible excess work for the user's CPU could cause more grief than help. The advantage of the directly connected printer is that it's not concerned with anything but printing. The other advantage is the fact that the network speed is many times faster than the local ports of the PC.

If when presented with the initial printer screen you choose the network printer and click Next, you're choosing to create a printer at this NT server that is actually a print device physically shared from a location other than this server. The window that opens next will list the printers that are available on the network (see Figure 7.7). This list is actually the same list that you would see in the Network Neighborhood, minus the drives, of course.

Figure 7.7.
Network printers.

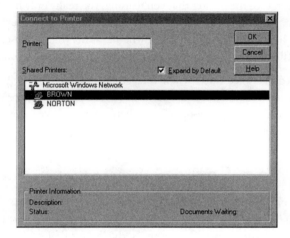

You can traverse the tree inside this window in the same way that you use the Windows Explorer. Once you've found the icon that you want to attach to the printer that you're creating, select it by clicking the icon and then clicking Next. You'll move to the printer driver choices.

Selecting a Driver

Once you've decided how you'll physically attach to the print device, you must select a driver that will make the best use of that device.

Drivers are selected from the next screen (see Figure 7.8). Click the name of the manufacturer of the print device to which you'll be attaching; then click the name of the printer (the Printers box lists printers created by this manufacturer that are natively supported by NT).

Figure 7.8.
Selecting a driver.

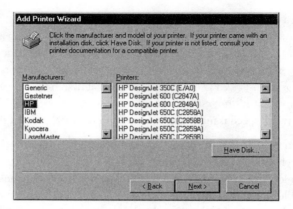

If you don't see the printer that you're using, you really only have two choices. One is to find a print driver on the list that the device *will* respond to. Often a previous generation of the same printer may be listed. Try this driver to see whether it fits your purpose. As often as not, this driver is more compatible with NT than the new one provided by the manufacturer for the new model.

The second choice is to use a manufacturer-provided driver. For this option, click the Have Disk button in the drive selection window. You'll be prompted to provide the location of the driver disk. Once you give the location, NT will then scan the drive for available drivers and will present a list of the drivers.

Peter's Principle: Use Manufacturer-Provided Printer Drivers

A word of advice when using manufacturer-provided printer drivers. If at all possible, call the manufacturer or look on the manufacturer's Internet site before installing the provided driver. Particularly in new printers, the drivers that come with the printer are often quirky and/or don't work at all. If the manufacturer doesn't know of any problems, you might also check the Microsoft Web site for news on that printer.

If a manufacturer provides a separate install or setup program for the printer drivers and software, be careful. These programs are often no help and can hurt. Whenever possible, use the NT-provided method for installing drivers. I continue to be amazed at how many manufacturers' release drivers don't work from day one.

Naming and Sharing Your New Printer

The choices that are left in the printer setup process are choices that will be seen by the rest of the world. You're going to name the printer and decide whether to share it with the rest of the network. Once you've decided on a driver, the next screen gives you an entry box for naming your printer.

Naming printers for sharing purposes is very much like naming a file server or any shared device. If at all possible, follow a consistent naming convention; but with printers, location is probably more important than choosing cute or fun names. For example, you could use a naming convention that would report both a printer type and location—for example, HPLJ4-220c. In this example, you use the first five characters to describe the printer (a Hewlett-Packard LaserJet 4) and the last four to describe the location (suite 220, cubicle C). Just give it some thought up front, or 200 printers later you could be trying to locate "Mollys-favorite-printmonster" on a late night troubleshooting mission.

The next decision is whether you want to make this printer the default printer for this NT workstation. This is strictly a matter of choice, for the moment. You aren't locked into this decision. If you choose Yes, all you're deciding is that the next thing you print from an application on this machine will go to this printer. Once you've made the choice, click Next to open the printer sharing window (see Figure 7.9).

Figure 7.9.
Printer sharing and extra
driver screen.

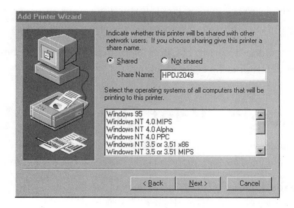

On this screen, you'll indicate whether you want to share the printer, and, if so, whether you'll be providing driver software for the clients that want to use the printer.

To share the printer, you simply select Shared and fill in the name that you want to share the printer with. Hopefully, you've already given some thought to this idea before you reached this position, and this isn't the toughest decision to make. But you should give this some thought.

Note: Printer share-naming conventions can allow you to locate and manage the printers at a later date without having to get a schematic and a compass. One scheme that I'm fond of involves naming the printer with a combination of alpha printer name abbreviation and the phone extension of a close desk (for example, HP4M-1042). You can follow any convention you choose. The point is to not wait until you're installing your 25th shared printer before deciding that this really matters.

Once you've given your share a name, you'll have the choice of loading extra drivers to be associated with this printer. This may seem like a foreign concept if you're used to the conventional network-printing world, but it's a feature of NT. NT will provide drivers to systems that create an initial connection to an NT-shared printer.

If you place a check in the selection beside the operating system, NT will store a copy of the driver for that operating system. When a user creates a printer on her own workstation that's connected through the printer at this NT server, NT will send a copy of the print driver to her workstation. This utility enables you to provide printers to the network without having to manually install the drivers on each workstation that may potentially use the printer. Drivers are only installed on those stations that attach.

By clicking Next, you'll arrive at the final screen in your journey to create a printer. This screen allows you to see whether you've at least completed the rudimentary task of being able to print to the printer you've created. After you click Finish on this print test screen, NT will send a test print-out to the printer you've created. If you don't want to send a print job at the moment, select No. Otherwise, click Next and wait to see if your test page prints.

If the page doesn't print, NT provides a troubleshooting wizard to walk you through various routines to determine the cause of failure.

Managing Print Queues

The management of print queues is really closer to the old Print Manager in Windows than you would believe. The basic concepts are the same but on a grander scale.

To see the different print queues, you first need to access the Printers control panel. Once the control panel is open, you'll see the list of printers that are known to this server. By double-clicking the printer, you can view the jobs that are currently being serviced in that queue.

The options here are pretty straightforward. To manipulate the jobs that are here, you first need to click the job that you want to manipulate. Once you've chosen a job, you have several options:

- **Deleting a job.** You can delete a job by selecting the job and pressing the Delete key. You can also achieve the same effect by choosing Document | Cancel.

Note: A rather annoying problem for those trying to stop a print job is that many printers today have enough memory of their own to hold numerous pages. This often leads to you attempting to stop a print job that's moving at the speed of light into RAM on the printer before it clears the server's spooler. Good luck!

- **Pausing a job.** You can pause the job by selecting the job and choosing Document | Pause Printing. The job will stop printing. Once you've chosen to pause a job, you can restart the job by choosing Document | Resume.

- **Restarting a job.** The Restart choice is like a reset button. Instead of stopping a job halfway through and resuming the job from that point, Restart actually recycles the job from beginning to end. So, if you printed half of the quarterly report on pink paper before you noticed, you can start from scratch.

- **Changing the print order.** You can raise or lower the priority of a print job or print jobs to change the order in which jobs will be printed. Changing a job's priority requires that you look at the job properties—print jobs have properties just like files and directories have properties (see Figure 7.10). You change a print job's properties the same way that you change the properties of a file or directory; right-click the print job and click Properties on the shortcut menu (or just double-click the job).

  Once you've opened the job properties, you'll notice a slide box that can be used to change the priority of this job. Keep in mind that time stops for no man. If you're changing the priority of a job, the jobs that are currently in the queue will continue to print. If you want the job in question to absolutely be the next job out, you need to pause all printing prior to changing priority.

Figure 7.10.
Individual job properties.

- **Scheduling a timed job.** Print jobs can be scheduled to print at a given time to perhaps move a large job to a less busy time that won't interfere with others. Notice the Schedule section at the bottom of Figure 7.10. By choosing Only From and typing in a range of time, you will cause that particular job to print during the next event of that time range.

- **Pausing all printing in the queue.** All printing may need to be stopped due to a malfunction that the server hasn't detected, or simply because you don't want to continue using that particular paper. The way that you stop printing for a particular printer is to open the queue window for that printer (refer to Figure 7.10) and choose Printer | Pause Printing. This will stop all printing until you can make whatever changes you need to make.

Printer Control and Troubleshooting

NT offers the ability to take control of the print devices that your users will be accessing; this control is one of the reasons for NT printers to exist. Simply attaching a print device in the middle of a group of users and allowing them to share it can be done from any number of desktop operating systems. But by using NT printers, you can tie the security and control of those print devices to the domains that you already manage.

Printer security is covered along with the other security topics in later chapters. Chapter 8, "Microsoft Network Access Concepts Brief," discusses security in shared printers.

Printer-specific controls are found in the same place that queue operations are, in the Printers control panel. When you initially begin attempting to control the behavior of specific printers, you can do some printer management by right-clicking the printer icon and selecting options from the shortcut menu (see Figure 7.11). This menu is used the same way that other object menus are used, and the options are pretty self-explanatory. The Properties option gets you to the meat of the Printers control panel. This option can be accessed through the File menu, but it's easier to just access it here.

Figure 7.11.
The printer shortcut menu.

The printer properties dialog box is much like the Windows 3.x printer control panel. The ability to control ports to which you're printing, the driver that's used, and the device settings from this screen are very much like the control panel of old.

Many of the printer properties in this dialog box have already been covered earlier in this chapter, but not all of them.

The General options identify the printer and give it some distinguishing features. Perhaps the most often used function here is the Print Test Page button, which gives the administrator a simple way of testing basic printer functionality. When you click Print Test Page, you'll be prompted for the result of the test print. If you answer that the test page didn't print, you'll be presented with a Windows NT Help window to walk you through solving the problem (see Figure 7.12).

Figure 7.12.
Troubleshooting the printing problem.

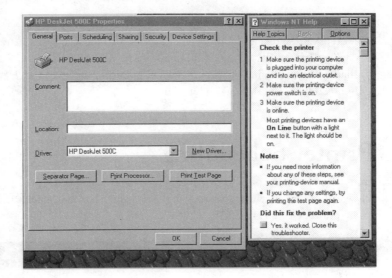

This page also offers the ability to change the driver that's being used by the printer, in the event that a new driver is offered, or to change a driver that isn't working. If you choose to change the driver, you'll be warned that this isn't a temporary choice—the change will be permanent. But the screen involved in changing the driver is simply the print driver screen that was used in the creation of the printer (refer to Figure 7.8).

Ports Options

The Ports page in the printer properties dialog box should be familiar from the creation of the printer. You get a listing of printer ports that are available from general local hardware (not necessarily your hardware), along with a list of any network print shares to which the server is connected. If you want to change the port that the server is currently using, your options are to select from a port that's listed or click the Add Port button.

Choosing to add a port will take you to a new dialog box, asking whether you'll be using a digital network port, a local port, or a PJL language monitor. Adding a local port involves using a device name that NT recognizes as a location that it can send information to, generally not a standard port

(LPT1, COM2). This type of installation is generally used for proprietary port installations that offer extra serial (COM) or parallel (LPT) ports. But it can be used to refer to special DOS device names (such as `LPT1.DOS` or `LPT2.OS2`).

I won't be covering the addition of digital network ports or PJL language monitors here, because they're not part of the Intel class of server I'm writing about.

> **Note:** A PJL language monitor sends printer job language (PJL). Any bidirectional print device that uses PJL can use a PJL language monitor. For example, PJL is the language that implements all the bidirectional communication between an HP LaserJet 5Si (a bidirectional print device) and its print server.

Printer Scheduling

From the Scheduling page in the printer properties dialog box, you can create behaviors that will allow you to control when a printer can be used and what the default priority is for documents sent to the printer (see Figure 7.13).

Figure 7.13.
The Scheduling page in the printer properties dialog box.

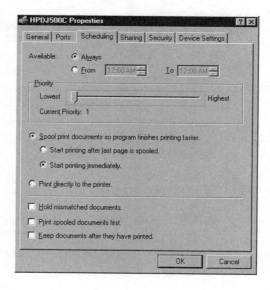

The printer availability settings control when this particular printer is available to the users. It's important to remember that this doesn't mean when the *print device* is available. One of the advantages of this particular option is not only the ability to change the availability of a particular printer, but also to create another printer that's available to a select group of users that will print to the same print device during any time period.

For example, you may want to create a printer that prints for general users on a very expensive, high-output print device only from 12:00 p.m. on, to allow only shipping paperwork to print in the morning (so that delivery drivers can be dispatched before noon).

Priority refers to the default priority level of jobs that come into the print queue. This is of little value to the administrator sitting at the print queue, but users who have enough rights can change priority for individual print jobs. An administrator who wants to level the playing field can change the priority level of a default job to a higher level.

Spooling options are your next choice, but I would strongly recommend that you not change something here without good reason. These options are the kind of options that can drive you mad when you're troubleshooting later. Spooling a document, as you may remember, is the process of preparing a document to be sent to the print device. Once a page is finally spooled, it's ready to be sent to the device itself. The order in which a document is sent to a print device can have an effect on the way that a document is actually printed.

The default spooling order for documents is to begin printing a document the moment the first page has been spooled. This approach allows the sending application to continue without waiting for the document to start printing. This setting for the most part should be left on.

If your user prints a document that continually prints partial pages or odd combinations of pages, you may want to consider choosing one of the other two options. By choosing Start Printing After Last Page Is Spooled, you're holding the application until it has fully released the document, and this will stop the user from accessing the application. But it may be required to get certain graphically-intense documents printed. Print Directly to the Printer may be required in order for certain programs to print, but it's the last resort. If neither of these options helps, consider that perhaps the printer driver for the user application is to blame.

The final choices on the Scheduling page are there primarily to offer management, rather than scheduling:

- By telling the printer to hold mismatched documents, you're really telling the printer that it should only print documents at this printer that match a certain group of device settings.

- Printing spooled documents first can offer some speed enhancement by not making jobs that are ready to print wait for higher-priority jobs that aren't ready.

- The option of keeping documents after they've been printed is (hopefully) a temporary fix that will allow you to continue to print from a queue without having to leave the application running at the client workstation. Some administrators will create printers whose only purpose is to hold documents that are printed over and over again. By holding printed jobs, the printer becomes a document storage-and-recovery device. But it makes a poor substitute for a filing cabinet. My advice would be not to waste memory or storage space on this tool.

Sharing Options

The Sharing options were covered earlier, in the section "Naming and Sharing Your New Printer" (refer to Figure 7.9), but they merit mention here as well. The Sharing page is the place where an administrator can modify the sharing of a printer, add new drivers for the users to download, and change the share name.

Security Options

The Security page (see Figure 7.14) allows an administrator to control specific user behaviors for a printer. Printer security is a little different from that of files and directories, because the utility of the print device hardware can be different for users at different times of day, and departments may be responsible for perishable materials for the print device in their area. For these reasons, printer security is discussed both here and in Chapter 8. Here we cover how it affects printer use; there we cover how it affects overall security, as well as how the greater security scheme affects printing security.

Figure 7.14.
The Security options.

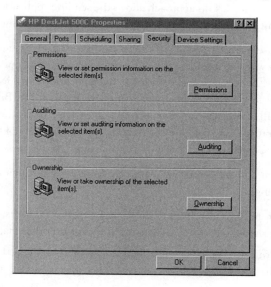

Print Permissions

Print permissions are the controls that you have as an administrator that are user- and group-specific (see Figure 7.15). As you will learn, in NT security it's always best to make changes to users in groups. Even if you must create a group that contains one user, you'll find that later you have saved yourself time and effort in adding users to or removing users from an object.

Figure 7.15.
Printer permission options.

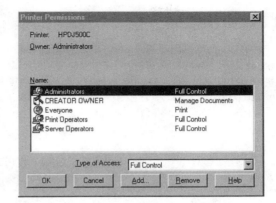

Permissions in printing are very basic. There are four different possible types of printer access:

- **Manage Documents.** This permission grants the recipient the right to change the behavior and properties of the documents to which the user has rights—for example, those documents owned by the user. By default, this permission is granted to the creator of a document.

- **Print.** The print permission is exactly what it sounds like—permission to send a print job to the printer. By default, this permission is given to all users. It's important to note that if you don't remove the group Everyone, all users can print to any printer you create.

- **Full Control.** A user or group that has full access to a printer is effectively given the other permission levels Manage Documents and Print. But they're not restricted to managing the documents they create—they can manage all the documents that are sent to the printer. By default, this permission is given to the Administrators, Print Operators, and Server Operators groups.

- **No Access.** This permission level differs from having no right to use the printer. The unique feature of No Access is that even if a group that the user is part of is given permission to use the printer, a No Access permission for that user (or another group he's part of) will stop him. Twenty Full Access grants won't cancel one No Access, so be very careful in setting this permission level.

Adding users or groups to a printer and removing users or groups from a printer are both very simple. If you click the Add button in the Printer Permissions dialog box, you'll see a list of groups that can be added to the permissions list. If you want to specify a user, click the Show Users button. By selecting a group or user and clicking Add, you have added that group or user. The only thing left to do is to establish the level of permission that you want to grant. By clicking the arrow button next to the Type of Access option, you can select a level of permission. When you're done, click OK to complete the process.

Print Auditing

The options in the Auditing dialog box (see Figure 7.16) suggest that you may be auditing the printer's use in general, and that can be done. But the idea behind this auditing tool is to allow you as an administrator to monitor the use of the printer by certain individuals and groups. This audit can be used for internal charge backs, service tracking, or to place responsibility. Auditing reports to the Event Viewer in NT, and each of the events that you set to be audited will appear as a line in the Event Viewer.

Figure 7.16.
User and group auditing of printer use.

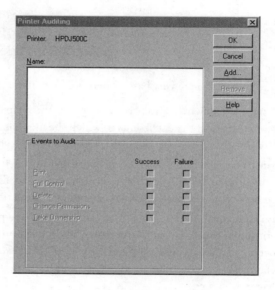

In order to audit, you must first decide on the user or group of users that you want to track. The process is the same as choosing a user or group to grant permissions to; click Add and then select the user or group to monitor. Once you have a user or group, select that user or group in the Auditing dialog box by clicking its listing in the Name box. The events that you can audit will then become enabled and allow you to put check marks in the boxes beside the options.

Ownership

Taking ownership of a printer requires that the user first have Full Control permissions for the printer. The ownership of an object is incredibly big magic in the NT world and ownership is discussed fully elsewhere, but for the purposes of this chapter you just need to know that by taking ownership of a printer, the individual is removing ownership responsibility from the local administrator's group.

Summary

Printing in NT is not simply sending raw data to a piece of hardware that puts ink (or toner) on paper. NT is an advanced operating system that has to not only print for itself, but also be capable of sharing and managing print services for multiple clients. The NT printing process helps to keep this flow smooth and usable.

Printing information is sent to an operating system object called a *printer*, which is not to be confused with a *print device*. The print device is that hardware piece that puts the letters on the paper. Printers are created as network and local objects that allow applications to have a target to which to send printing information.

This chapter covered the creation of both network and local printers, as well as some of the possible problems that might arise. Each function of the creation process and the control panel involved allow you to have better control of the process, so that the users are better served.

III

Account and Domain Management

Peter Norton™

8

Microsoft
Network
Access
Concepts
Brief

Peter Norton™

The purpose of this chapter is to help you understand how Microsoft and specifically NT Server use this security model to help you control your resources. Access to network resources in a Microsoft world isn't necessarily what you are used to as a network administrator if you have some familiarity with the more popular platforms. Frankly, there are pieces of the Microsoft security model that can be maddening if you don't come from a Microsoft world.

If you're looking for a security model to compare the Microsoft model to, it will be a little tough. The Microsoft model doesn't compare well to NetWare, UNIX, or even OS/2. I'm afraid that you're probably going to have to take this framework on its own.

Security Concepts

When you begin to look at a security model, it helps to understand what the initial state of security is in the system before you begin to make changes. As I have dealt with PC network security systems, I've found that there are two basic structures from which a security model can start:

- **Open to Closed.** When a resource is created in this model, the entire user base has some level of access to that resource. The administrator must then close the doors to that resource in the places that he wants closed. The advantage of this form of security model is that it allows for quicker creation of shared devices and less work for the administrator if the system is to be open. The disadvantage is that when a resource is created it is inherently available to all users.

- **Closed to Open.** When a resource is created in this model, the general user population has no access to that resource. For any user without administrator clearance to access the resource, he or she must be given permission to do so. The strength of this model is the complete security that it offers—at no point is the resource exposed to users that the administrator didn't manually facilitate. The disadvantage of this system is that each resource must be handled in order to be delivered to the general user public.

Windows NT Server is more closely related to the Open to Closed model. Each resource that you create in an NT Server model is created as available to the general public. Once you have created the shared resource you can close the door, but the door is created in an open state.

Being inherently open can be a severe weakness in your network if you don't monitor it. When an administrator creates a share on an NTFS-formatted drive, the default permission on that share is Full Control to the group Everyone. Before we've even covered what the group names include and what the permission level Full Control means, it should be obvious that this needs to be changed as soon as possible. If you don't want the general public to have access to this data, you can't forget to change the permissions.

> **Looking Ahead:** Shares and how to create them are covered in later chapters. But you need to understand what a share is in order to grasp the concepts in this chapter. In case you don't already understand the basic idea, here's an explanation.
>
> Generally a share is any resource that is chosen and made available across the network. Shares can be hard drive directories (`c:\`, `c:\ACCNTG`, `d:\SALES\MDWST`), or printers (LPT1, LPT2, or \\SERVER2\HPLJ5). Once you decide to share a device, you give it a share name. For example, if you share the directory `c:\ACCTNG`, you might want to present it to the network as the share name `Accounting`.

By contrast, when an NT server is created, the shares that exist aren't even viewable by the general user population. When the NT Server operating system is installed on a machine, all the drives on that machine are shared, but even the administrators can't see these shares from the network. The type of share that's created is called a *hidden administrative share*. These shares can be attached to, but you have to know that the name exists and you have to have administrative permissions (at least until the administrator changes those permissions). These shares are distinguished by their name. The names given to these shares are followed by a dollar sign (`$`): `C$`, `D$`, and so on.

The point is that NT can wear both sets of stripes—Open to Closed with newly created shares and Closed to Open with the shares that the operating system creates by default.

You need to be most careful about the shares that you create after the system is running. If you've been around the NT operating system for much time at all, you begin to see trends in the administrators of NT networks—you are often able to break the security of these systems based on the lack of knowledge and laziness they may display.

If you're running a system of your own, do the following test to make sure that you haven't left some simple doors unlocked:

1. Log in as the account Guest if you can. Did the account have a password?
2. If you were able to log in as Guest, observe the drives that are automatically mapped for you. If you weren't able to log in as Guest, log in as a user that has the least amount of security clearance you're aware of.
3. Now observe in Explorer (Windows 95 or NT) or File Manager (Windows 3.x) which network shares you can see. Map a drive to them if you can and take a look around.

If you were able to participate in the experiment, I hope that you didn't find any surprises. My experience has been that about 50% of the administrators who run this simple experiment are either surprised or don't know how to give their clients access without unlocking too much.

You may not be ready for this experiment just yet. Your system may not be ready for an audience yet. But if you're moving along with us in the book, try the experiment again when you feel secure, or at least realize that this is the downfall of an Open to Closed system.

Access Control Lists

From the beginning, the NT operating system has been described as an object-based operating system, and the security of the system is no different. Security in NT is centered in the object that's being addressed. All the security for an object is contained in the object. The users and groups that have the right to interact with that object are tracked at that object. This access is kept in an *access control list* (ACL).

This ACL is the master list of users and groups that can access the objects and the specific permissions that they have to that object. Objects such as directories, printers, files, and network shares all are referenced by an ACL. When one process passes a user to a given object, the ACL is checked to see whether the user or a group that the user belongs to can have access to the desired object.

It's a bit like being on the guest list for a large wedding party. When you hit the front door, someone checks to see whether you are on the guest list (ACL). Once you're inside, are you on the bride's list or the groom's list? Now that the ceremony is over, are you on the reception list or are you to be escorted to the door? Wait—I wanted to kiss the bride… (you must be on her ACL).

Which Comes First: Users or Groups?

From a basic level, I suppose that everyone who would read this book has figured out by now that in order to gain access to Windows NT you must have a user account name. But I haven't exactly covered what a username entitles a user to and how it relates to security of NT. How users are gathered and managed has been implied, but not specifically attacked. Before we can go any further, we have to be very specific about users and groups.

Users

Before a user or even some applications can access the NT operating system objects, they must have user accounts. User accounts are a way of differentiating who is in the access control lists of the different objects on the system. By establishing who is in the list, you control who has access to the objects throughout the system.

A user account can be thought of as the smallest unit of measure for NT access. Unlike DOS, Windows 3.1, or even Windows 95, this operating system requires that you have some form of user account to even access the most basic operating system services.

NT creates three accounts by default:

- **Administrator.** This account is created with the sole purpose of installing and managing the system, and has full control of all objects in the system. The account can't be deleted, but it can be renamed.

  This account shouldn't be used to do general day-to-day user tasks for anyone. This promotes security openings and accidental destruction in the system. Renaming this account is recommended, but seldom done. The reason for the recommendation is the fact that users who want to break in will use this account based on the fact that they know it exists. When a hacker attempts to break your security, there are two initial puzzles: account name and password. If you leave the Administrator account intact, half the battle is over. And what a door to open!

- **Guest.** This account is really a holdover from some of the large multiuser host systems. The account is meant as an account to allow for basic public services to be used by a guest for a short period of time.

  You need to be aware that this account is a member of the group Everyone (before we discuss groups). The earlier section "Security Concepts" covered the fact that new shares are open by default to the group Everyone. Guest by default is disabled; it's my suggestion that it stay that way for the same reasons, but not the same threat as Administrator. This account can be renamed, but not deleted.

- **Initial Account.** When you install NT Server, you'll be asked to provide an initial account name. This account is created primarily to give you some other name besides Administrator with which to log into the system. NT has now encouraged you to use an account besides Administrator, but you should be aware that this account has the same rights as the Administrator account. This account can be deleted or renamed.

  If at all possible, you should keep this account or some secondary Administrator account as a back door in case of disaster with the Administrator account. If you lose that administrator password or if someone changes it and leaves, you need to have another way into the management of the system.

Tip: One of the greatest security risks to your system is users leaving the system casually unattended or staying logged into the system when they leave. Users who go to the restroom, snack area, or even go home without logging out don't imagine that they may be blamed for the loss of data or a security issue. But a crook can find access to the system in almost any office with more than 10 employees through simply finding a system unattended (see Figure 8.1). This can be very ugly if the user is a member of the Administrators group. The cure can be as simple as a screen saver that's password-protected and mandatory.

Figure 8.1.
The truly open system (a
Windows 95 desktop with
network shares left un-
attended).

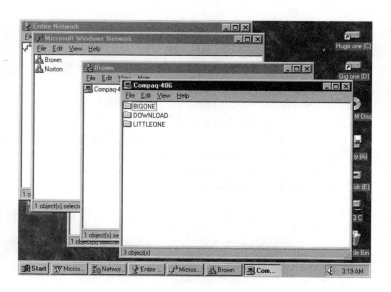

The three accounts just described are created by the operating system to give NT basic accounts so that you can access the system and control it the first time. All other accounts have to be created by an Administrator or Operator account.

User accounts and groups are created for each user who logs into the system (see Figure 8.2), but oddly enough some of the services that run on the PC itself must log into the system with an account in order to function. In fact, any user or application that wants to gain access to the operating system must log in with a user account. An example of this type of account might be an e-mail or database engine that you want to start on the NT server, even if no user logs into the machine.

Figure 8.2.
User Manager being used to
create a user account.

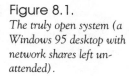

For such applications to have access to operating system resources, they must be given a user account name and a password that they can use (see Figure 8.3). This only strengthens the security model of NT by making some account responsible for every action that isn't part of the basic operating system function.

Figure 8.3.
The account permissions page of the Server service.

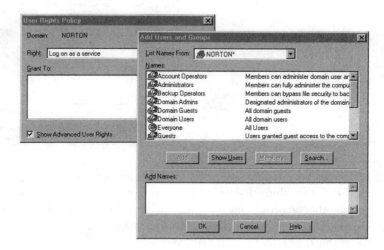

Groups

In order to simplify user management, NT allows administrators to gather users together into groups and assign permissions to those groups. The concept is to avoid redoing the work of modifying access over and over. By creating a group and granting permissions to the group, the administrator is more efficient.

Microsoft is very enthused about the whole group concept; in fact, if you are taking any test regarding the NT operating system, keep in mind that they believe that you almost never assign a right to a user directly. Instead, the Microsoft solution is to assign the user to a group and assign the permissions to the group or add the user to a group that already has the permissions.

This way of doing things can seem a bit uptight, but if you give it some thought it really does save time in the long run. When you assign permissions to groups instead of users, you allow yourself a very simple way to remove the permission from the user—simply remove the user from the group. Conversely, if you want to add new users, you simply have to add them to the groups that meet those users' needs (see Figure 8.4).

Figure 8.4.
User Manager being used to assign a user to a group.

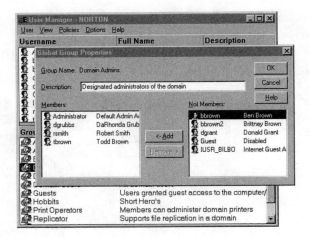

Many administrators believe that by granting permissions to users specifically, they're being more precise. But the thing that you need to consider in the Microsoft plan is that you may later want to give another user that same set of rights or resources. By creating groups and assigning users to the group, you give yourself the edge of being able to better track what a user has permissions for and being able to remove those permissions easily.

NT creates several groups by default and even more groups in the event that you choose to use a domain model for your security scheme. These are the default NT groups:

- Administrators
- Users
- Guests
- Power Users
- Backup Operators
- Account Operators
- Print Operators
- Server Operators
- Replicators
- Domain Admins (if a domain is used)
- Domain Users (if a domain is used)
- Domain Guests (if a domain is used)

Another group is found in the NT permissions screen, but this group isn't a group to which you assign members. The group Everyone is seen in the permissions page (see Figure 8.5). When you create a new share, this is the group that's automatically assigned Full Control of the share. It's important to know that this group exists, because it isn't a group that you make a conscious decision to add users to or to give permissions to. But, again, this can be a back door to allow anyone to come in.

Figure 8.5.
The permissions of a newly created share with the group Everyone.

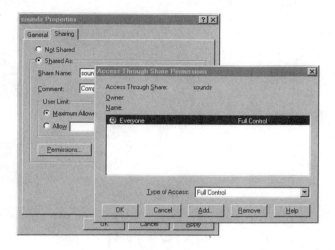

Chapter 10, "User Account Creation and Management," provides details on these groups and their uses in the NT scheme.

Domains, Workgroups, and Expanding the Network

Workgroups and domains as they relate to network access are part of the control that allows NT to be both a local machine operating system and a network operating system. Chapter 6, "Networking Brief," discusses workgroups and domains, and Chapter 9, "Domain Design," discusses the creation and management of domains, but here we'll look at how the choices made with workgroups and domains relate to network access as a whole.

Workgroups, as we have established, are the peer-to-peer solution to network security. Workgroups really have no place in our server-class machines. Workgroup models actually should be used exclusively for the peer-to-peer connections that you might make between client systems. By creating servers that operate in a workgroup mode within your greater network scheme, you are leaving systems outside of the management umbrella.

Domains are necessary to create a complete management picture (see Figure 8.6). Just as groups are collections of users and make it possible to make changes on a larger scale with less work, domains make it possible to manage the network as a whole by grouping all of the pieces into a single manageable environment.

Figure 8.6.
The NT domain hierarchy.

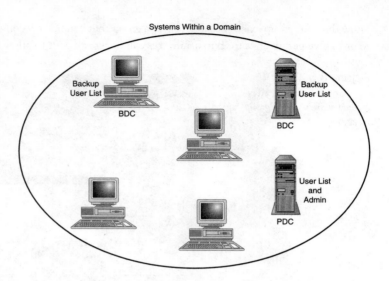

Expanding the Reach

To this point we've discussed domains as single entities—as if once you had created a domain you had defined your network universe. Actually, domains can be thought of as a way of creating a control environment. Numerous domains can be created and connected to each other in what are known as *trusts*.

Trust is both a type of connection that can be made from one domain to another and a description of the relationship. Figure 8.7 shows two domains and an arrow that points from the Brown domain to the domain Norton. The arrow is a common way of signifying that the Brown domain trusts the Norton domain. By trusting the domain Norton, the administrator of the Brown domain is actually opening a one-way relationship that allows the members of the Norton domain to access the resources in the Brown domain.

Figure 8.7.
Trust relationships expanding your network.

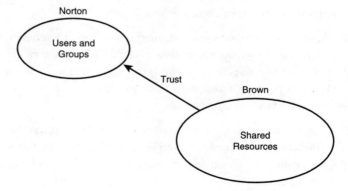

By creating the trust, the members of the Domain Admins, Domain Users, and Domain Guests groups in the Norton domain are also made members of the same groups in the Brown domain. Effectively, the Brown domain has been made part of the available resources for the users in the Norton domain. This type of trust is referred to as a *one-way trust* because the relationship is only open one way.

If you create a trust, the door is open in only one direction unless you manually create a trust in the other direction as well. If both domains have created a trust from one another, that's called a *two-way trust*, as shown in Figure 8.8.

Figure 8.8.
A two-way trust relationship.

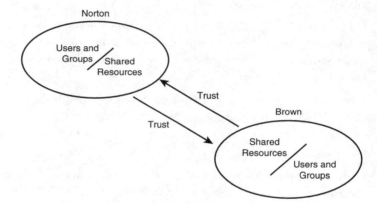

You might think of domain trust relationships as neighbors that live close to one another and trade keys. If Mr. Brown and Mr. Norton live next to one another and Mr. Brown elects to give Mr. Norton a key to his home, Mr. Brown has effectively established a trust with the Norton domain. Mr. Norton can do as he pleases with the Brown domain, but that doesn't mean that Mr. Brown has been given any right to the Norton domain. I suppose the analogy falls apart when you consider that the Brown domain wouldn't change its locks because it got its feelings hurt over the whole lack of trust.

Mr. Norton doesn't have to give Mr. Brown his keys in order to establish the trust from Brown to Norton, but to establish the trust from Norton to Brown he would. If the two neighbors trade keys, a two-way trust has been established.

Trusts are used for many different reasons, but once the trust is established it must be maintained by both domains in order to continue. If the trust is broken on either side, the trust must be reestablished by both domains. You can't simply re-create the trust on the side that broke it.

Trusts can also be used to separate users from resources. If you can imagine creating a domain that is occupied only by servers, printers, and other network resources, then you are imagining a *resource domain*. The purpose of such a domain is to allow administrators to cut down on the number of trusts that must be established between domains and yet give users the access they need to the resources that exist.

Summary

When you move on to other chapters from here, carry with you a few key points about NT that can otherwise really come back to bite you. NT Server is an inherently open system that I believe is built more to share your data than to protect it. The operating system is continuing to grow, but by its very nature it makes sharing items the first priority.

The NT access control list further continues the whole object orientation of the Windows NT operating system and should help you to understand the concept of user accounts and the need to relate even users to an object.

User accounts are the smallest single unit in the NT operating system, but no access to the operating system is going to be gained without one. Even applications that want to run require a user with an account or an account of their own to start. Accounts allow the system to track and control the access to every object on the local and network level.

As you create users and the resources for those users to utilize, keep in mind that the easiest and cleanest way to manage and organize those users is through groups. In the chapters that follow, there are examples of group management that will further help you to see the benefit of grouping users before giving permissions.

Gathering all the pieces together depends on the domain model of security, but keep in mind that the domain doesn't need to be the edge of your universe. These superstructures of NT security can be linked through trusts, and those trusts can be arranged to allow communications on any level that fits your needs.

The next chapter looks specifically at the domain model and how that structure can be used not only to control user access, but also to help divide resources, users, and groups into management subsets.

9

Domain Design

Peter Norton™

Creating, administering, and maintaining a domain can be very simple process if you're dealing with one domain, but the world is seldom so elementary. Because of the ease with which NT Server can be installed, and because we live in a NetWare-dominated world, many NT networks are created independently and then joined.

This chapter looks at some of the ins and outs of domain control and domain communications. We'll spend a great deal of time on connecting domains and what to watch for in those relationships, as well as how to choose the connection that might make the most sense for you. These are some of the concepts that are covered:

- Domain control choices and placement
- Adding a computer to the domain
- Creating or promoting to a PDC
- Domain clients
- Domain synchronization
- Domain replication
- Trust relationship types
- Multiple-domain relationships
- Creating trusts and joining domains
- Removing a trust relationship

Domain Control Choices and Placement

Domain control is carried out through the use of servers in the domain that are called, aptly enough, *domain controllers*. Previous chapters discussed the fact that there are two different forms of domain controller: a single primary domain controller (PDC) and one or more backup domain controllers (BDC). These controllers work together to allow domains to maintain a single unified security model throughout the entire domain.

The purpose of the primary domain controller is to be the single reference for all domain members for changes and master lists of the domain security accounts management (SAM) database. All changes that are made to the SAM must pass through the PDC directly.

The backup domain controllers (BDCs) are responsible for maintaining a copy of the SAM and taking care of client requests so that the workload is spread around. This setup allows users to work without being bogged down waiting in line to speak to the great and powerful PDC for every request. The problem for BDCs in this system is that, if the PDC should fail or be down for service, no changes can be made to the domain security until the PDC returns. This is because the PDC is the only one allowed to process changes to the SAM database.

If you have been with us throughout the book, that much is review. But what we need to cover now is the process of creating a PDC or BDC and the effect that can have on the domain as a whole.

If you're used to other enterprise network operating systems, the problem that you'll run into with the NT operating system is that, should the PDC fail, there's no automatic recovery from that failure. You may be more familiar with an election process in which the enterprise security control is contended for in the event of a failure. With NT, this isn't the case, and you could look at this as either a good or a bad situation.

With the NT plan of action, you must manually promote a BDC to the job of PDC. This allows the administrator to decide which machine is best suited or available to do the job. The problem may be that the administrator is not as aware of the connections and availability as the machines themselves might be. The other problem is that the administrator may not have the time or the inclination to do what could just as easily be automated. But do it he must.

Adding a Computer to the Domain

Computers are added to a domain through two methods. One method, discussed in Chapter 4, "Installation Considerations," is choosing a domain while a computer is being installed (see Figure 9.1). During NT Server installation, you're asked what role the computer will play in the domain. If you're a user with permission to create a computer account in the domain, you can simply do it at the install screen.

Figure 9.1.
Choosing the domain role at installation.

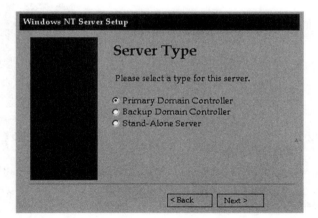

There's another way to make the decision about the computer accounts that will appear in your domain. You can create them in the Server Manager utility. This utility is primarily for managing computer accounts in the domain and the relationships that those computers have to the domain.

Before you install a new NT server in the domain, if you want the PC to already be established in its domain role, you can use Server Manager to create that account in advance ("Welcome, Ms. Server, your reservation has been made"). With the account already created, it's possible to allow some other person to install the server without giving him or her permissions in the domain to create a computer account.

To create a computer account in Server Manager, follow these steps:

1. Open the Server Manager utility in the Administrative Tools (Common) menu.
2. Choose Computer | Add to Domain (see Figure 9.2).
3. Indicate whether you'll be installing a Windows NT workstation or server only, or a Windows NT backup domain controller.
4. Type the name for the computer in the Computer Name text box.
5. Click Add.

Figure 9.2.
Adding a computer to the domain with Server Manager.

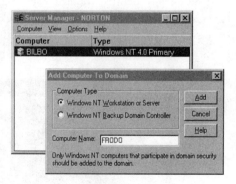

Creating or Promoting to a PDC

PDCs are most often born, not elected. When you initially install the first server in a domain, that server is made the PDC. Why? Well, it's the only one in the domain—no one else is available to take the job.

Every server installation that you do in the domain will ask what role the server will play in the domain. The server can be a PDC, BDC, or server. Creating a BDC in the domain sends a copy of the SAM database to that machine. Whenever a change is made to the PDC, it updates the BDCs to make sure that they're up-to-date.

Should the PDC fail, you have two choices for domain control. You can simply let the domain continue to run as it is until the PDC is returned to working order. Or, if the PDC PC will be unavailable for a longer duration, you can promote a BDC to PDC.

Once the domain is up and running, there may be a machine that's better suited to the job of PDC, based on location in the physical network or the fact that the original server is saturated with other tasks. Again, the plan of action is to promote a BDC to the PDC.

Changing the PDC can be done only by promoting a BDC, and this setup is with good reason. If you were to demote a PDC, the network would momentarily be without a PDC. Instead, by promoting a BDC, you are at the same time demoting a PDC. This allows for complete coverage. (The King is dead; long live the King!)

The promotion of a BDC is done using the Server Manager utility. Follow these steps:

1. Open the Server Manager utility.
2. Select the BDC that you want to promote to PDC.
3. Choose Computer | Promote to Primary Domain Controller.
4. Click Yes when asked to confirm the choice.

Be aware that if you promote a BDC while the PDC is down, the former PDC can't be PDC again until you have manually demoted it while it's online. If you turn the old PDC on while the new PDC is running, the Net Logon service will fail to start until you enter the Server Manager utility and demote the server while it's running.

Warning: Be aware that if you should turn the old PDC on while the new PDC is down or out of communication with the old PDC's segment of the network, you can really wreak havoc on the domain as a whole. You may split loyalties among the BDCs and ruin your SAM database. The problem can be solved simply by turning off the old PDC; then, when communications are reestablished with the new PDC, demoting the old PDC immediately.

Domain Clients

NT domains obviously don't consist only of PDCs. They require clients to be of any value. The following client operating systems and environments, in conjunction with network software, are the pieces necessary to attach a user to the domain:

- Windows NT workstations
- Windows 3.1

- Windows for Workgroups
- Windows 95
- OS/2 workstations
- Workgroup add-on for MS-DOS
- MS-DOS client

Domain Synchronization

From time to time in large domains, you'll find that a user has problems being authenticated in a given section of the network, or that certain groups can't access a new shared resource. This can sometimes be due to the fact that changes in the domain database haven't yet made it to the BDC in the area. The perfect world plan tells us that instantly after a change is made to the SAM database, it's whisked off to the BDCs and all users are able to take advantage of those changes. Well, in some large domains, this can take up to 48 hours to happen.

If you have finished changes to the domain security scheme that you'd like to happen right away, you can force the changes to be synchronized immediately. For example, if you've just created a large number of users for a new department that will report tomorrow, you may want to push that information across to the BDCs today. The synchronization can be done directly to the BDC of choice, or, if you prefer, you can select the PDC and synchronize with all the BDCs.

To synchronize the PDC with all the BDCs, follow these steps:

1. Open the Server Manager utility.
2. Choose Computer | Synchronize the Entire Domain.
3. Choose Yes to confirm.
4. Click OK to finish this process.

If you have a large domain and want to expedite the synchronization of the PDC with a particular BDC, you can be more selective:

1. Open the Server Manager utility.
2. Select the BDC with which you want to synchronize.
3. Choose Computer | Synchronize with Domain Controller.
4. Choose Yes to confirm.

The process of synchronizing can take a considerable amount of time, even if you're manually forcing it. To determine whether the synchronization has actually occurred, you can look in the Event Log; the event will register there (see Figure 9.3).

Figure 9.3.
Event Log registry of the synchronization of the domain.

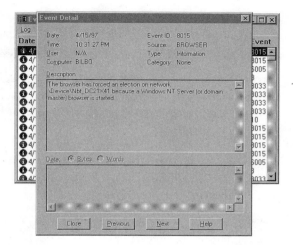

Domain Replication

Replication is a feature of Windows NT domains that enables identical directory structures and files to be maintained on multiple servers and workstations. Replication simplifies the tasks of maintaining identical sets of data, because only a single master copy of the data needs to be maintained. Each computer synchronizes its copy of the data to this master copy.

Replication can be used for load balancing by keeping a copy of the master data on several NT servers. An example is clients that need to access data for lookup purposes on a central NT server. As the number of clients increases, so does the workload on the NT server. One way of distributing the load is to replicate copies of the master database on other NT servers. This allows several NT servers to handle the client requests and distribute the workload.

The computer that has a master copy of the data is called the *export server*. The computers that receive a copy of the master data set, or the computers that synchronize their copies of the data set with the master, are called *import servers*.

The export server must be a Windows NT server. The Windows NT server contains the files and directories to be replicated to the import servers. The import servers can be any of the following:

- Windows NT server
- Windows NT workstation
- LAN Manager server

On LAN Manager server computers, the import directories and files must match the file-naming conventions of the export computers. If the import directory is HPFS, you must ensure that the directory-naming conventions for exported and imported directories on the export and import computers match.

To use replication, you need to have at least one Windows NT server. The data that's replicated can be system-related data such as logon scripts for users, or application-specific data such as a database of employee records, word processing templates, phone lists for vendors, and so on.

Logon scripts for users are maintained in files on NT computers and are not part of the domain accounts databases automatically replicated. So, if you want changes in logon scripts on the PDC to be copied to the BDCs, you must set up replication between the PDC and its BDCs for logon scripts.

When you set up replication, you can specify whether entire subdirectories under a specified directory should be replicated, or only specific files in those subdirectories. Locks can be applied to specific directories in the export and import trees to prevent them from being exported or imported.

This is a list of the default replication directories:

- The default export directory is `%systemroot%\System32\Repl\Export`.
- The default import directory for import computers is `%systemroot%\System32\Repl\Import`.
- The default logon script directory on the PDC is
  `%systemroot%\System32\Repl\Export\Scripts`.
- The default logon script directory on import computers is
  `%systemroot%\System32\Repl\Import\Scripts`.

By keeping the logon script directory (`Scripts`) as a subdirectory of the default export and default import directory, logon script replication is enabled if the default export/import directories are used when replication is enabled.

Only one directory tree can be exported from each export server. If you want to export multiple directories, you should have the directories as part of the same export directory tree structure. The default location for logon scripts therefore is a subdirectory of the default export directory tree.

You can configure replication so that changes in the directory tree are propagated to other import computers immediately or after a two-minute stabilization period.

It's possible to use replication for backing up critical data directory structures on a server. However, you should not use this method as a replacement for normal backup procedures or as a solution to providing near-line backup of user information.

You can set up replication of directories to individual computers in a domain or to an entire domain. By default, the export servers export to the local domain, and the import client computers import from the local domain.

Exporting to an entire domain gives the entire domain access to the replicated directory. Importing to a domain is often more convenient than exporting to individual computers in a domain. You also can replicate data to individual computers in a domain.

If you're exporting to a domain separated by a wide area network (WAN) bridge from the export server, the replication might not work, because broadcast mechanisms are used to initiate the replication of data, and if the bridges are configured to block broadcast packets to minimize broadcast storms, the replication operation won't work.

When exporting data to import computers separated from the export servers across WAN bridges, it's preferable to specify the import computers by name. Similarly, when importing from another domain across a WAN bridge, it's preferable to specify the export server by name rather than specifying the export domain name. Use of explicit names avoids the use of broadcast query packets to discover explicit names of the computers involved in the replication operation.

> **Note:** When exporting data across domains, you must ensure that appropriate trust relationships exist between the domains to permit data flow between domains. The later section "Trust Relationships" discusses implementing trust relationships between domains.

Configuring Replication

Before you can configure replication, you must create a special user account under which the Directory Replicator service will run. You can use any username except the name Replicator, because this is the name of a built-in domain group. Additionally, this special account must have the following properties:

- The password account never expires. This is set by selecting the Password Never Expires option and clearing the User Must Change Password at Next Logon options in the User Manager for Domains.
- The account must be accessible 24 hours a day, seven days a week.
- The account must be a member of all the following domain groups: Backup Operators, Domain Users, and Replicator.
- You must set up the same username and password for the replicator account on both export and import computers.

Next, you need to configure the Directory Replicator service to start automatically and log on under the replicator user account on the export server. This step can be performed by using the Server Manager. Then configure the export server and import servers.

The following procedure outlines setting up the replicator account (see the following sections for more details). Begin by logging on to the domain of the export server, using a domain Administrator equivalent account. Now you need to create the user account with the right properties to be a replicator in the domain. Follow these steps:

1. Start the User Manager for Domains.
2. Choose Users | New User. The New User Property dialog box appears.

3. Enter the property values in the following table:

Property	Value
Username	`ReplicatorAccount` (or any other name)
Full Name	`Replicator Account` (optional)
Description	`Replicator account for replication purposes` (optional)
Password	Suitable password
Confirm Password	Same password as in the Password field

4. In the User Must Change section, deselect Password at Next Logon and select Password Never Expires.

5. Click the Groups button. Notice that the new account is already a member of the Domain Users group. To make the account a member of the Backup Operators and Replicator local groups, select those accounts from the Not Member of list box, and click the Add button.

6. Click OK to save and exit group membership changes.

7. Click the Add button in the New User dialog box to create the replicator account.

8. Close the user creation screen.

9. Close User Manager for Domains.

Follow these steps to add the account to the Directory Replicator service:

1. Select Services from the Control Panel.

2. Highlight the Directory Replicator service and click the Startup button. The Service dialog box for the Directory Replicator service appears, as shown in Figure 9.4.

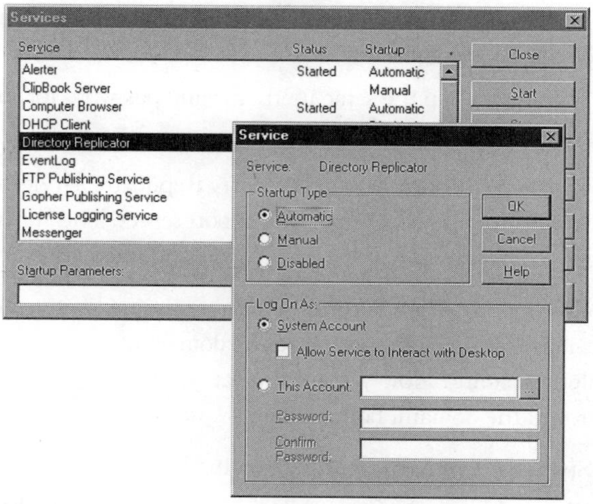

Figure 9.4.
The Services dialog box for the Directory Replicator service.

3. Set the Startup Type to Automatic.

4. Click the browse button to the right of the This Account field. The Add User dialog box appears. Highlight the replicator account that you just created, click the Add button, and then click OK. The replicator account name appears in the This Account field.

5. Enter the password information for the replicator account in the Password and Confirm Password fields.

6. Click OK to save the startup information on the Directory Replicator service.

A message informs you that the selected replicator account has been granted the Log On As A Service right. If the account was not added to the Replicator group, it's added automatically to the Replicator local group.

To start the replication activity, follow these steps:

1. Start the Directory Replicator service by restarting the export server, or clicking the Start button from the Services dialog box.

2. Set up a domain user replicator account on import computers with the same username and password, using the procedure just described.

Configuring the Export Server

On the export server (implemented on a Windows NT server), you can perform the following:

- Identify the export directory tree that will export the data.
- Specify domain names or computer names to which to export data.

Replication is set up from the Directory Replication dialog box. Follow these steps:

1. Start Server Manager from the Administrative Tools folder.

2. Double-click the export server or choose Computer | Properties to open the Properties dialog box for that server.

3. Click the Replication button to open the Directory Replication dialog box (see Figure 9.5).

Note: The To List box is used to list the computers and domains to which you want to export the directory. By default, this list is empty, which indicates that the export server exports to the local domain. If you add any entries in the To List box, the system no longer exports to the local domain. You can add the names of computers and domains to which the directory data will be exported. If you need to include the local domain along with lists of computers and other domains, you must enter the local domain name explicitly.

Figure 9.5.
The Directory Replication dialog box.

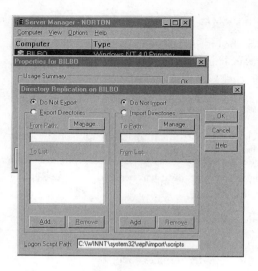

4. Click the Export Directories radio button. The default path is listed: (`%systemroot%\System32\Repl\Export`). If you plan to use a non-default path for importing the data, you need to change the From Path field.

5. Click the Add button under the To List box to add a list of domain or import computers. The Select Domain dialog box appears, which lists the domains. Double-clicking a domain name lists the computers in that domain. You can select any combination of domain names and computer names to export the data to.

If you need to export selected subdirectories in the export path, click the Manage button next to the From Path field. The Manage Exported Directories dialog box opens (see Figure 9.6). You can add a directory to the managed list by clicking the Add button, and you can remove a directory by clicking the Remove button.

Figure 9.6.
The Manage Exported Directories dialog box.

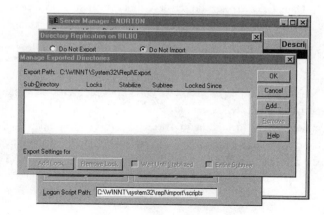

After export directory choices have been made, this dialog box can be used to observe the status and progress of the export:

- Export Path (a display-only field) lists the path to the directory from which subdirectories and files are exported.
- The Sub-Directory column indicates the list of subdirectories exported from the computer. The subdirectories under the Export Path are added to this list automatically, if the subdirectories were created prior to the start of the Directory Replicator service on the export server. You can add subdirectories by clicking the Add button.
- The Locks column indicates the number of locks applied to the subdirectory. A lock prevents a subdirectory export, and you can place more than one lock on a subdirectory. A subdirectory is exported only if no locks are placed on it—that is, the number of locks must be zero. You can add locks by clicking the Add Lock button, temporarily preventing subdirectories from being replicated.
- If the Stabilize column value is set to Yes, it indicates that files and subdirectories in that subdirectory must be stable for at least two minutes before replication can occur. A value of No indicates that changed data will be replicated as soon as it's changed. The default value is No. You can change the setting by selecting the Wait Until Stabilized check box.
- If the Subtree column value is set to Yes, it indicates that the entire subdirectory will be exported. A value of No indicates that only the first-level subdirectory will be exported. The default value is Yes. You can change the setting by selecting the Entire Subtree check box.
- The Locked Since field indicates the date and time that the oldest lock was placed on this directory.

Saving any changes that you have made by clicking the OK button will start the export process for that selection.

Configuring the Import Computer

The import computer can identify the imported directory tree that will receive the replicated data. It can also specify domain names or computer names from which the data will be imported. Replication is set up from the Directory Replication dialog box. You can access this dialog box using one of the following procedures:

- Select the Server icon in Control Panel.
- Start Server Manager from the Administrative Tools folder. Double-click the export server or choose Computer | Properties to open the Properties dialog box for the server.

To configure the import computers, follow these steps:

1. In the Properties dialog box, click the Replication button. The Directory Replication dialog box for the import computer appears.

2. Select the Import Directories radio button. The default path of %systemroot%\System32\Repl\Import is listed. If you plan to use a non-default path for exporting the data, you need to change the To Path field.

3. Click the Add button under the From List box to add a list of domains or import computers. The Select Domain dialog box appears, which lists the domains. Double-clicking a domain name lists the computers in that domain. You can select any combination of domain names and computer names to export the data to.

If you need to import selected subdirectories in the export path, click the Manage button next to the To Path field. The Manage Imported Directories dialog box opens (see Figure 9.7). You can add a directory to the managed list by clicking the Add button, and you can remove a directory by clicking the Remove button.

Figure 9.7.
The Manage Imported Directories dialog box.

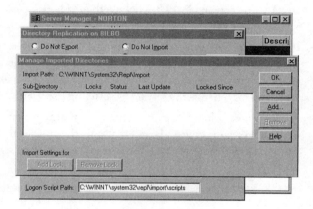

After import directory choices have been made, this dialog box can be used to observe the status and progress of the import:

- Import Path (a display-only field) lists the path to the directory from which subdirectories and files are imported.

- The Sub-Directory column indicates the list of subdirectories imported to the computer. The subdirectories under the Import Path are added to this list automatically, if the subdirectories were created prior to the start of the directory Replication Service on the import computer. You can add subdirectories by clicking the Add button.

- The Locks column indicates the number of locks applied to the subdirectory. A lock prevents a subdirectory import, and you can have more than one lock on a subdirectory. A subdirectory is imported only if no locks are placed on it—that is, the number of locks must be zero. You can add locks by clicking the Add Lock button, and remove locks by clicking the Remove Lock button.

- The Status column indicates the status of the replication. The word OK indicates that the subdirectory is receiving regular updates from the export server, and that the imported data is identical to the exported data. The words No Sync indicate that the subdirectory has received updates but the import data isn't synchronized to the master data. This could occur because of communications failure, open files on export or import computers, export or import server malfunction, or not having enough access permissions at the export or import computer. The words No Master indicate that the import computer is not receiving updates. This may be because the export server isn't running or has stopped sending updates. A blank entry in the Status column indicates that the replication has never occurred to that subdirectory. This can occur due to improper configuration of replication at the export or import computer.

- The Last Update column indicates the date and time that the last update was made to the file in the import subdirectory or its subdirectories.

- The Locked Since field indicates the date and time that the oldest lock was placed on the subdirectory.

Troubleshooting Replication Services

This section is a collection of ideas that may help you to find the reasons that your replication isn't taking place properly. First carefully go through the steps that have been outlined in the preceding sections; then check through this list.

- Has the Directory Replicator service been started on export and import computers?

- Is there a network path between the export and import computers?

- Are the export and import computers able to talk to each other? Try sending messages or using the browser in File Manager to see whether the export/import computers are visible on the network.

- Have you set up the replication account correctly and assigned this account as a member of the User Domains, Backup Operators, and Replicator groups?

- If the export and import servers are in the same domain, are the replication account and password the same on the export and import computers?

- Are there appropriate trust relationships between domains?

- Are files kept open in the export or import directories? This can cause sharing violation errors in the Event Log.

- Are the clocks on the export and import servers approximately synchronized?

- Windows NT doesn't support HPFS extended attributes written to noncontiguous parts of the disk, whereas the OS/2 HPFS implementation does. You might have problems with extended attributes replicated from an HPFS volume on a Windows NT server.

- If you're importing to a LAN Manager server, ensure that no other user is using the replicator account. Directory Replicator service will be suspended temporarily if another user is logged on with the replicator account.

- Does the Replicator group have Change permission to the export/import directories? Is there a bridge between the export and import computers? If so, the replication should be configured to export directly to the import computers.

Trust Relationships

NT domains are not islands; they need to be able to communicate with one another. This communication is done through the use of trusts, as we have established. Trusts are the connections of domains and are capable of establishing that communication in many ways. These relationships can be complicated, and they're very often too complicated. If I were giving Microsoft grades for its operating system, trust relationships is the one place where I would probably give it a C. You need to be very careful about how you make these connections, and the relationships can be almost impossible to maintain once they're up and running.

When a user wants to connect to a resource that exists in a different domain, he must depend on a trust to get that done. But that isn't the only reason for trusts to exist. Many times, domains are created just to gather like users or resources. Creating trusts then becomes a way of gluing together the pieces of the domain model.

It's important to note that the trust relationship is between the domains and not between the users and the domains. Users and resources are contained in the domains, but they aren't the domains themselves. One of the toughest things for NetWare 4.x administrators to understand is the fact that, in NT, a domain being trusted doesn't meant that the users and groups contained in that domain gain any rights. Users must still be given the permissions to the resources that they need to use. This is accomplished by assigning permissions to groups in just the same manner that local and global groups are given permission in a single-domain model. Local groups in a trusting domain can contain domain accounts in the trusted domain. The local group that contains the global accounts in another domain can be given permissions to a resource.

By establishing trusts, an administrator makes it possible to deliver resources to users located in diverse parts of a company, and yet maintains the ability to manage users within domains that better fit the company look or feel. Administrators can centrally manage a large enterprise network, but keep the managed items in smaller, more manageable groups. You can design a network with all user accounts in one domain, for example, and then use trust relationships to give users in the domain access to resources in other domains. This arrangement enables the network administrator to manage the multiple-domain network by using a single domain.

Trust Relationship Types

There are many different models used to connect NT domains, but really only two different trust relationships:

- **One-way trust relationships.** If domain A trusts domain B, then domain B users and groups can be given permissions to resources on the A domain (see Figure 9.8). This in no way gives users in domain A rights to resources in domain B.

- **Two-way trust relationships.** If domain A and domain B trust each other, users and groups from both domains can be given permissions to resources on either domain (see Figure 9.9).

Figure 9.8.
One-way trust.

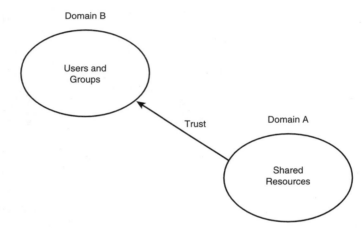

Figure 9.9.
Two-way trust.

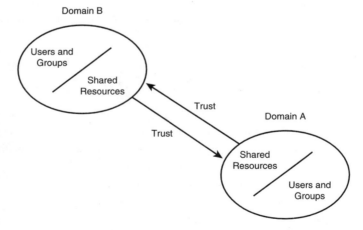

Now to complicate this otherwise simple relationship. Trust relationships don't pass from one domain to another down the line. This means that just because domain A trusts domain B, and domain B trusts domain C, you can't assume that a user from domain A can attach to domain C. Microsoft calls this being *non-transitive*. Each trust must be established individually (see Figure 9.10).

Figure 9.10.
No pass-through of trust is allowed.

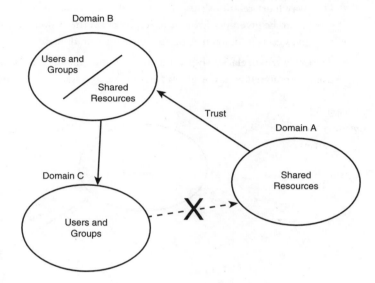

When the trust is established, the value of that trust is based on the placement of the resources to be shared. Just as the file server has value, the domain containing the desired resources has value. Often domains are divided along lines that are completely drawn on the location of resources, and users are placed in domains divided along human resources lines. The trusts must then be drawn along lines that give users rights to the resources in the proper domain.

Pass-Through Validation

Users in a large network are very likely to log on at many points throughout the company. It's even possible to find users logging on in different countries. When a user attempts to log on in a strange office, she should still be able to log onto the network. In order to facilitate this capability, NT uses what's known as *pass-though validation*. The user's request for authentication is passed through to her home domain so that she can be guided home.

Pass-through validation is used in Windows NT domains when a user account must be validated by the local computer, but the computer can't validate the account because it's in another domain. The user account and password information supplied by the user are passed to the Windows NT server that has the user account information to validate the user. The user information then is returned to the computer requesting the validation. The concept is fairly simple to understand if you keep in mind that NT domains that have established trust relationships must keep track of who has permissions to use the resources that they house.

Suppose that Rhonda is sent to the office in the Chicago domain, but her user account is in the New York domain. Rhonda would like to use the computer system at her desk, but she isn't sure that she has the permissions she needs to even get on the network from Chicago. When she asks the local IS group whether she can get an account, she's told no, but she's also told that she doesn't need one.

Figure 9.11 shows what the IS group means when they say that Rhonda doesn't need an account. Because Rhonda's New York domain is trusted by the Chicago domain, she can be validated when she attempts to log on, by virtue of the fact that she's a member of the trusted domain. It is a bit like saying, "Joe sent me."

Figure 9.11.
Rhonda's trail to computer use.

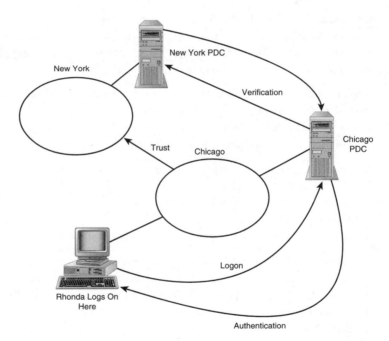

Here's how it works:

1. Rhonda attempts to log onto a workstation in Chicago with the user name RHONDAZ, by changing the standard domain to New York.

2. When the domain initially checks Rhonda's username and password, it sees that she's from the New York domain and asks the New York domain to authenticate her information.

3. The New York domain checks the account information on Rhonda.

4. The New York domain sends back word that Rhonda is a valid user in the New York domain.

5. The Chicago domain then allows Rhonda a valid logon. ("New York sent me!")

These relationships are still dependent on the existing trust relationship, though. In other words, if Tim from the Chicago domain went to the New York domain, he wouldn't be authenticated at a workstation in the New York domain. Because the trust flows only one way, the New York domain doesn't trust users from the Chicago domain. The process also isn't transferable, just like the trust itself. Trusts and transfers are one to one.

Multiple-Domain Relationships

One place where the NT domain and trust model becomes spooky is the relationship of multiple domains. When you're connecting the Chicago and New York domains, the complications are fairly clear and easy to understand. But when you add Muncie, Boston, Belgrade, Stockholm, and so on, the combinations can get incredibly complex and unruly.

The problem lies in the fact that the domain model is a one-to-one relationship. No matter how many domains you connect, you still have only one domain connected to another domain—no more and no less. The number of connections that need to be maintained can be staggering in domain models that contain as few as five or six domains.

If you can, imagine simply connecting the domains that all trust one another in a four-domain grouping (see Figure 9.12). This type of collection of trusts will involve the establishment of 3 trusts from each domain to the others. That's a total of 12 individual (multiple-step) actions that must be taken. If you simply add 1 more domain that must be connected, you add 8 more actions. Add another and add another 10. I think you're seeing the picture.

The idea is not to have you heaving your copy of NT Server into the great abyss, but to warn you that without some thought this can be a very complex can of worms you're opening. The problem can be brought back into perspective if you take a minute to plan. Even though it seems that you would initially want to simply connect all of your domains, there's a smarter way. (Twenty-five domains blindly connected would be 600 actions—run away! run away!)

There are many different ways to build your web of domains. But before you become too creative, there are four basic types of relationships that give you a form to follow:

- Single domain
- Master domain
- Complete trust
- Multiple master

Figure 9.12.
Creating multiple trusts.

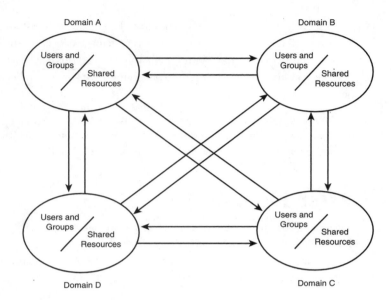

These models don't have to be mutually exclusive, but they give you some frame of reference for how relationships can be better managed.

Of course, the easiest way to avoid all the complexities of a trust relationship is to stay single. (Right, bachelors?) Well, that's possible, but you also need to consider the growing pains that come along with keeping all your eggs in one basket.

If your number of computers and resources is small, lack of complexity is the obvious choice. Users are dealing with a very controllable number of resources. But you need to consider that the network can become resource-bound when the users have so many choices presented to them as the total domain. Viewing the sheer number of resources (drive shares, printers, and so on) can not only confuse the users, but slow the network performance (see Figure 9.13).

Figure 9.13.
Single-domain models—simple, but crowded.

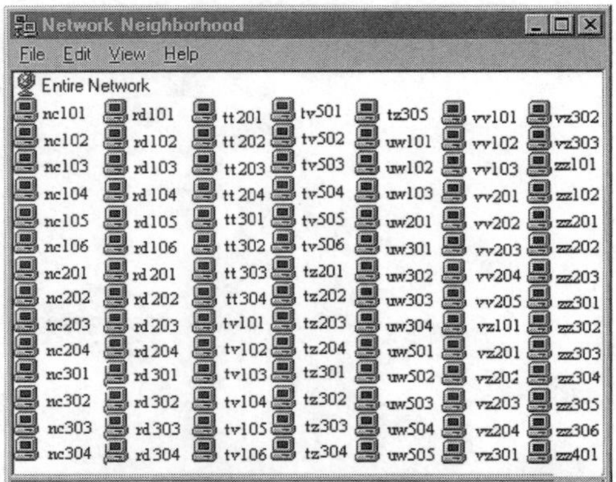

With this model, the users that need to be controlled by the administrator are all contained in one list. With a small number of users, this can be very manageable. But if the number of users begins to exceed your ability to view and control them from one list, this can be a hassle. Not only a hassle to control, but, because NT counts on the domain for workflow, it can begin to slow performance of the network as a whole.

Simply put, if your company needs lie along a single path or in a single location, there's really no reason to divide your resources and users into diverse domains. But if there are location, size, or departmental reasons to divide, a single domain will get cramped.

Master Domains

The idea that feeds the creation of a *master domain* model is the idea that users travel (or get moved around) and resources don't. A master domain model involves the creation of a single domain for user and group accounts (the master domain) and at least one other domain that primarily contains resources (the resource domain). By doing this, the administrator is separating resources and the relationships that users have with them from the domain in which the users exist.

These domain models rarely exist with one resource domain. The idea generally is to separate the resources into manageable units that fit along location or department lines. The master domain is then trusted by all the resource domains, but a real key is that no relationship is created between any of the resource domains (see Figure 9.14). This scheme allows the administrator to assign permissions based on the resource domains to the users, and maintain as few domain trusts as possible.

Figure 9.14.
The master domain model.

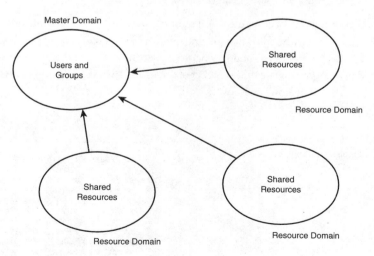

As long as the users log on from a computer in the master domain, they can be authenticated directly from the master domain. If they log on from one of the resource domains, pass-through validation is used to authenticate the user accounts that reside in the master domain. Because all resource domains trust the master domain, users in the master domain can access resources in any domain. For this reason, the master domain can be used for defining the accounts for the IS department of an organization. This enables the IS department to manage the network from a central location. Users with accounts in the trusting domains (resource domains) won't be able to access resources in other domains.

A great advantage of this model is the fact that you can create the resource domains and allow the departmental or local administrators to have accounts that control their own resources, without having to make them administrators in your master domain. This gives departmental or local hardware some autonomy, without giving the key to the whole kingdom to the individual administrators.

To create the permissions needed to access the resources in the resources domain, you can follow these steps for the computer containing the resources:

1. Create a local group on the computer that has the resources that need to be accessed by other users.
2. Create global groups to describe different categories of domain users. Place domain users in their appropriate global groups.
3. Place the global groups in the local group.
4. Give the local group permissions to the local resource.

This method again returns to the basic concept of adding users to the global group and adding global groups to local groups. This allows you as the administrator to more easily track who has rights and to remove those rights without going on a wild goose chase. This becomes more and more important the more complex your domain model becomes.

Groups that should make use of a master domain model are most likely groups that have a small to medium-sized list of users and that must separate resources along some dividing line. Your own interpretation of small to medium-sized may vary. Microsoft says that up to 40,000 users can exist in a master domain model (hey, it's hot in here). I tend to think that more than 1,000 users in a single collection is more than I care to handle.

I like to use the "power steering" analogy for this decision if I must reconsider later. If things are hard to manage and you're experiencing performance issues, you may need to look at separating your users into smaller account domains. This isn't a decision you want to make retroactively. Moving users and reestablishing trusts and permissions can be a complete nightmare.

Peer-to-Peer (Complete Trusts)

The time when NT domain trusts are at their most dangerous is when the domain model is based on numerous peer-to-peer relationships between domains. This type of trust is called a *complete trust* because the peer domains have created a trust relationship with each other. In Figure 9.15, domain A has trusted domain B and domain B has trusted domain A. This is a very simple complete trust.

Figure 9.15.
The complete trust model.

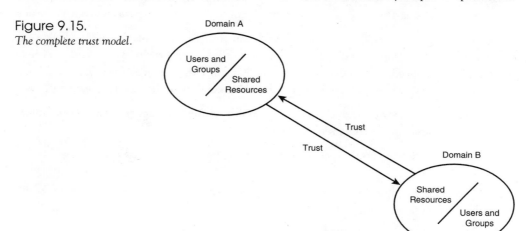

These domain models often grow out of networks that contain several new NT servers. These new NT servers often contain their own domain scheme, because they were created independently. These relationships don't have one domain that's primarily a resource domain or one that contains mainly user accounts. Both domains have created the trust to facilitate the use of each other's resources.

Sadly, many multiple-domain models contain complete trusts. The problem with this model for large domains is the reason that NT domains have gotten a bad name. When the original NT installation arrives, complete trusts often arrive with it. But the complete trust model is the model that will lead you to that tangled web. When they're small, complete trusts are simple to administer. But as they grow, they can become completely unmanageable.

Not only is this type of trust difficult to establish, it's difficult to manage if it grows beyond the small to medium-sized network. Finding the location of user accounts and resources can be very difficult when the management of these items has been lumped into several piles that used to be independent domains. Administrators must administer many domain relationships and many user-to-resource permissions.

The advantage of this type of domain is simply the fact that it's simple in small portions. When two companies merge, for example, this structure makes it easy to simply connect the two domains and make one big happy family. The two groups maintain their independent administration and user structure, but they're connected and can share resources. When connecting fewer than 10 domains, you'll most likely not have trouble administering these relationships, and everyone will be able to access every resource that you would like them to have access to. If you're looking for the most open model possible, this model will give you the most open network.

Multiple Master Trusts

The lines of demarcation are often more complex than simply deciding to have a master domain and several resource domains. Sometimes you have to find a compromise between what makes the most sense logistically and what has to be done politically or departmentally. But you may still have too many resources and users to build a complete trust.

If you need to create separate user account domains based on department or location lines, you may still want to consider creating separate resource domains. When a domain model contains multiple users' domains that are still separated from the resource domains, this is called a *multiple master model*.

The concept is the same as the master domain model, but it leaves you the option of creating separate user (master) domains to divide your users. The multiple master domain model can be used for organizations that have multiple departments. In many such networks, there can be separate IS departments for each department that wants central management of the networks. You can assign a master domain for each department and hardware resources into separate resource domains. You can establish a trust relationship from the resource domains to the department domains. By splitting the network resources into multiple domains, you have the advantage of organizing a large number of resources into manageable units. The master domain for each department is used to provide centralized administration (see Figure 9.16).

Figure 9.16.
A multiple master domain.

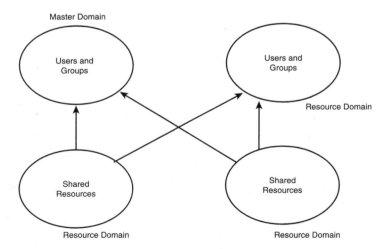

The Admin users for a domain log on from a computer in a master domain. If they have to log on from a trusting domain, they can use pass-through validation to authenticate their user accounts. Because a resource domain trusts at least one of the master domains, users in the trusted master domains (Admin users) can access resources in the resource domain. The master domains can be used for defining the accounts for the IS departments of the divisions in an organization. This method enables the IS departments to manage the networks in each department. Users with accounts in the trusting domains (resource domain) won't be able to access resources in other master domains, and this is usually a requirement for an organization's network security policy.

These models allow the administrators of the network to expand the network easily because they can create new user domains with a small number of trust relationships to create. By creating resources in separate domains, you maintain all the advantages of a master domain model. But by creating divided user domains, you also gain some of the simplicity of the complete trust.

Creating Trusts and Joining Domains

Trust relationships are established using the User Manager for Domains in the Administrative Tools group. To identify a trust relationship, you first must identify a list of all domains that can trust a certain domain.

Building trust relationships is like sharing hard drive space or printing devices. You need to be careful or you could leave the door open for trusts to opened by the wrong people. With each domain that's identified, you must agree on a password (or lack of one) to validate this trust relationship.

Passwords are optional and used only initially to set up the trust relationship. After the trust relationship is set up, the password isn't used for any data flow between the domains.

Next, the administrator of the trusting domain, domain A, specifies the name of domain B as the trusted domain. When the name for domain B is entered, the administrator must specify the password established in the trusted domain for this trust relationship. If the password is correct, a trust relationship is established from domain A to domain B, enabling users in domain B to access resources in domain A.

The list of domains permitted to trust a domain and the associated passwords prevent unauthorized domains from setting up a trust relationship. Because domain B is a trusted domain, a user in domain B can access information in the trusting domain. If the trusting domain is unauthorized, illegal information transfers can occur between the domains. A network administrator, for example, can use the network to transfer sensitive information from domain B to a directory on a computer in the unauthorized domain. In order to access a directory in the unauthorized domain, the rogue network administrator in domain B needs directory permissions to appropriate directories in both domains. This directory permission can be granted for a directory in the unauthorized domain if the administrator has friends in the unauthorized domain.

Consider an example in which domain A is the resource domain (trusting domain), and domain B is the administration domain (trusted domain). The following steps are a guideline on setting up a trust relationship from domain A to domain B:

1. Log on as Administrator domain user for domain B. Domain B is the trusted domain, so you must identify the domains that are permitted to trust domain B.
2. Start the User Manager for Domains for accounts in domain B.
3. Click the Add button next to the Trusting Domains box. The Add Trusting Domain dialog box appears.
4. In this dialog box, use the Trusting Domain field to enter the name of the domain that trusts the domain being administered.
5. Use the Initial Password and Confirm Password fields to specify the password to be used in the establishment of the trust relationship.

Next, you must administer the trusting domain—domain A, in this case—and make the trusted domains known to the trusting domain. You can log on as a domain administrator to domain A and perform the next step. Alternatively, you can select domain A while using the User Manager for Domains and administering domain B, the trusted domain. This approach is more convenient if you're the domain administrator for both domains, because you don't have to log on separately in domain A. Perform the following steps to select a different domain from the User Manager for Domains:

1. In the User Manager for Domains, choose User | Select Domain to open the Select Domain dialog box.
2. Select the trusting domain (domain A) to be administered.
3. Choose Policies | Trust Relationships. The Trust Relationships dialog box for the trusting domain (domain A) appears.
4. Click the Add button next to the Trusted Domains list. The Add Trusted Domain dialog box appears.
5. Enter the name of the trusted domain and the password.

If you entered the trusted domain name and password correctly, the domain appears. If you entered an incorrect domain name, a message appears, telling you that User Manager for Domains was unable to find the domain controller for this domain. If you entered an incorrect password, User Manager for Domains informs you that the password is incorrect.

Removing a Trust Relationship

When removing a trust relationship, you should remove the trust relationships from both sides. The recommended order for removing a trust relationship is as follows:

1. Users in the trusted domain should stop using the resources in the trusting domain.

2. The trusted domain should remove the trusting domain from its Permitted to Trust This Domain list box. You can find this dialog box by choosing Policies | Trust Relationships in the User Manager for Domains.

3. The trusting domain should remove the trusted domains from its Trusted Domains list box.

Keep in mind that once you remove the trust relationship from one side, the relationship is no longer valid on either side. The relationship can't be reestablished, even if the administrator who removed the trust immediately reopens the door. Both sides must close the trust and reopen it.

Summary

Domain design is a relatively easy concept, as long as you're building only one domain. But once the domain structure must reach out to other domains or involve many domains, you're going to have to give serious thought to the process. This is one area of NT Server that has been built with a few dents in the armor.

The first piece of the process involves the planning of the inside of your individual domains. Domain roles must be established for fault tolerance and speed. Clients and resources must be added as well as user roles in the domain. And finally, replication and synchronization of directories will further the fault tolerance.

But once the walls of the single domain will no longer hold the network account structure, you'll be creating trusts between multiple domains. Keep in mind that most often location lines make the best choice for domain boundaries. But, if forced, you can use political or departmental lines. Location offers network bandwidth and resource advantages, if you can use that as a guide.

Trust can be divided again along three major lines: location, resources, and user accounts. The different models—master domain, complete trust, multiple master, and variations—will help you to make an educated choice.

10

User Account Creation and Management

Peter Norton™

There's a big difference between using the tools to create and manage users and understanding the ramifications of the changes you make. Before the next chapter, "The User Manager Tool," which is the nuts and bolts of creating users and groups, this chapter will take a look at the concepts that are needed to use that tool.

User accounts and groups have been discussed as objects to this point; in this chapter, we'll take a look at the specific pieces of those objects and the items that you can control. Here are some of the basic concepts that are covered:

- User accounts
- Naming and password conventions
- Password schemes
- Controlling the user environment
- Groups
- Local versus global groups
- When to create a group
- Assigning permissions using groups and users

User Accounts

Before a user—or even some applications—can access the NT operating system objects, there must be a user account. User accounts are a way of differentiating who is in the ACL of the different objects on the system. This is established to control who has access to the objects throughout the system.

Predefined (Default) Users

When NT Server is installed, there must at least be some usernames available for the operating system even to operate. NT creates three accounts by default:

- **Administrator.** This account is created for the sole purpose of installing and managing the system, and has full control of all objects in the system. The account can't be deleted, but can be renamed.

  This account shouldn't be used to do general day-to-day user tasks for anyone—that promotes security openings and accidental destruction in the system. Renaming this account is recommended, but seldom done. The reason for the recommendation is the fact that users who want to break in will use this account, based on the fact that they know it exists. When a hacker attempts to break your security, there are two initial puzzles: account name and password. If you leave the Administrator account intact, half the battle is over. And what a door to open!

- **Guest.** This account is really a holdover from some of the large multiuser host systems. The account is meant to allow for basic public services to be used by a guest for a short period of time.

  You need to be aware that this account is a member of the group Everyone (before we discuss groups). New shares are open by default to the group Everyone. Guest by default is disabled, and it's my suggestion that it stay that way not for the same reasons, but because of the same threat as the Administrator account. This account can be renamed, but not deleted.

- **Initial account.** When you install NT Server, you'll be asked to provide an initial account name. This account is created primarily to give you another Administrator account with which to log onto the system. NT has now encouraged you to use an account besides Administrator, but you should be aware that this account has the same rights as the Administrator account. This account can be deleted or renamed.

  If at all possible, you should keep this account or some secondary administrator account as a back door in case of disaster with the Administrator account. If you lose that administrator password, or if someone changes it and leaves, you need to have another way into the management of the system.

Naming and Password Conventions

Because the primary reason for user accounts is security, you need to be aware that the usernames and passwords that you choose are the second easiest way to wrongfully gain access to your network. People who want to get around your security system will most often begin by trying to find a system that has been left unattended and logged on, but if that's not available they'll next try to find a combination that will work for them.

Note: Users who try to gain access to your system by trying different security schemes and combinations of accounts are often called *hackers* or *crackers* because they continue to hack away at your system until they get what they want. *Cracker* comes from continually trying to "crack" your security system or application code.

Hackers rely on user error or lack of concern to gain access to the data they want. By observing users over time, they've learned that people will continually repeat the same patterns when establishing usernames and passwords. Your job is to control your system in order to stop the hacker from controlling it for you.

NT Server offers many different controls to stop hackers from making it into your system, but the simplest way to stop a hacker is to control your account naming and password conventions.

Naming Conventions

The usernames that you choose when you begin your network will most likely have to serve your needs as the network grows. Usernames used to be more of a threat to the network as a whole than they are today. One of the most popular methods for hacking into a computer network is to "throw the book at it"—in other words, the hacker will send a list of human names at the system until the system responds.

In many legacy systems, the job could be divided into two different tasks. The first was to send a list of responses to the system's request for a username. When the hacker was asked for a password, he knew that he had found a valid username. In these systems, the request for a valid username and the request for a password were separated. If you responded to the request for a username (see Figure 10.1) with a proper username, you would then be asked to provide a password.

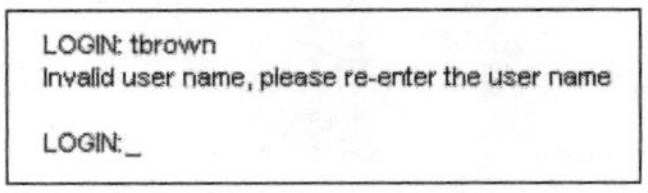

Figure 10.1.
Legacy username request.

```
LOGIN: tbrown
Invalid user name, please re-enter the user name

LOGIN:_
```

NT no longer separates this request, so the job becomes far more difficult. The hacker must now have the combination of both items to gain access. But if users and administrators aren't smart about how they form these combinations, they can still be caught.

NT does have some hard-and-fast rules for usernames that you have to follow when naming users. There are only two, and they aren't that difficult:

- Usernames must not contain any of the following characters:

    :   ;   ¦   =   ,   +   ?   <   >   /   \   [   ]

- Names can contain up to (but no more than) 20 characters

Usernames today are more likely to reflect the fact that our servers and domains exist in a global environment, and these users will need to communicate with each other. It's important in many systems that the users be able to find each other; establishing a naming convention will help users to find one another and communicate.

Note: If your intentions include the use of Microsoft Exchange as an e-mail system, each member of your Exchange user base will have the same e-mail name as his or her NT username.

The naming convention that I most often recommend at client sites and on the Internet is the convention of using the first name initial combined with the first seven letters of the last name—for example, John McFatridge becomes jmcfatri. If there are two users with the same name, you begin either using a number as a last digit or replacing the last digit with a number if the name is less than or equal to the full eight characters—for example, John Smith becomes jsmith2 or John McFatridge becomes jmcfatr2. This combination is used for several reasons:

- The fact that this is the most commonly used convention on the Internet. If you care about following international conventions within your installation, it helps to follow even the user naming convention.

- It becomes easier to manage users based on the fact that you have some starting point for knowing their username. I've worked in environments that used far more complex user-naming conventions, and the amount of work necessary to find the username you want is far more complex than needed or useful.

- The most technical reason is the fact that the name fits in the old filename convention of being no longer than eight characters. When an administrator interacts with users, it's convenient if the username fits well into the rest of the environment.

- Users want to be able to communicate with one another and often will want to assign permissions to their own system resources based on the domain or workgroup of the server. This convention gives them a starting point for knowing who is who.

There are many different possible naming conventions that can be used, but the general idea is to maintain a plan.

Password Schemes

The amount of control that you maintain over the passwords used on your network is up to you. Keep in mind, though, that this is a double-edged sword. Heavy password control is ideal for maintaining a safe and clean network. But if you heavily control the password scheme on your server or domain, you're going to have to devote a great deal of time to managing it. On the other hand, if you let the passwords roam free, you decrease your workload at the expense of your network security. User passwords can be controlled to the point of aggravation, but if you need high-level security this is almost what you want.

Users' passwords can be controlled through NT in the following ways:

- Not allowing the users to change passwords can be the ultimate form of password control. When users select and change their own passwords, they have a tendency to use familiar or easy-to-use words instead of something that's difficult to subvert. If you control the passwords, you can stop this problem before it happens.

  Administrator-assigned passwords have their own pitfalls, of course. When you create and distribute passwords, you first have to commit them to paper. The fact that they're on paper can be a security risk in and of itself. Once the passwords are distributed, you must also consider that a user won't remember the password you give him—so he'll probably write it down. If you're lucky, he won't put it on a "sticky note" on his monitor.

- Forcing periodic password changes can prevent random observation from allowing someone to steal a user's password while she types it. If I watch you type your password enough times, I'll eventually know what it is (I can't help it). A new combination of keys every so many days makes it harder to steal the password by casual observation.

- Enforcing a password length can make it tougher for you to watch someone type the password and steal it. It's more difficult to steal an eight-letter word by observation than a two-letter word.

- Forcing users to use a unique password can prevent users from using only a limited selection of words. If a user uses her dog's name, then her husband's name, and then back to the dog again, it becomes fairly easy to steal over time. If you see R-O-V-E typed enough times, you might be able to get *rover* from the fact that your cube mate's dog is named Rover. (Or was that her husband?)

- Forcing a user to change his password the first time he logs on can prevent even *you* from knowing what his password is. This is often done to allow users to feel safe, by the fact that changes made in their names were done by them. If an administrator wants to change someone's password and work as that user, that's fine, but then the user will know because his password has been changed.

There are many conventions for the creation of passwords, and you're going to have a difficult time enforcing these rules unless you control the passwords. But even if you don't control the passwords of your users, introduce them to some basic guidelines for password creation.

Never use the following words as your password:

- Spouse's or loved one's name
- Pet's name
- Your child's name
- Nickname
- Company name
- Curse word
- Your home phone number or work extension
- Any word viewable from your seat at work

If your password fits into any of those categories, don't feel bad—most do. But do change it soon. These are the most commonly used words and will usually get me into any PC server.

The best password convention that I have found follows this list:

- Longer than 5 characters.
- Contains both alphabetic and numeric characters (for example, 5234DRFE). Alphanumeric passwords don't make sense to someone trying to watch you type them in, and are therefore harder to steal.
- Changed every 30 days.

All of these rules can be enforced by the administrator. You're going to have to maintain the entire password system if you control the word choice itself, though, and you really need to consider the downfalls of that system if you choose it. The biggest real threat to administrator-assigned passwords is the internal threat of users leaving passwords posted or written down.

How Many Hacks Do They Get?

Illegitimate logon attempts can be stopped on many different levels, but if a hacker can continue trying as often as he likes he'll eventually get through. One of the methods used by people trying to gain access to your network is to sit in one place and try combinations of username and password over and over again. If they do this—or they have a computer program that will do it for them—then they may get lucky. NT contains a logon security feature that can help you avoid numerous attempts to get into your system.

Within the user account policies, you'll find that NT allows the administrator to set a limit on the number of times that a user can attempt to log on using the same username and getting the password incorrect (see Figure 10.2).

Figure 10.2.
The Account Policy dialog box.

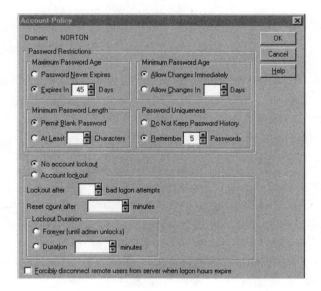

You want to allow users some leeway in this area, just because of human error. NT account policy allows you to do that by letting you choose how many times you'll let the user make a mistake before it locks the account.

NT also allows you to determine how long you want to track those mistakes. In other words, how many times did they try incorrectly in a given period of time? Without setting a given period of time for the incorrect attempts, you would have a large number of users locked out very quickly. Most everyone uses the wrong password once or twice in a day. By week's end, everyone would be locked out of the server.

The recommended policy for these options is to set them to a tolerable number (such as three bad attempts) that doesn't compromise your network. Use common sense. For example, if you set the bad attempt count to three and make the reset time a half hour, you'll discourage a hacker, but you won't anger users. If you set the bad attempt count to three but set the reset count to 24 hours, you'll likely spend a great deal of time unlocking accounts.

User Environment Needs

When users attached to a PC network, the network experience should be as transparent to the user as humanly possible. Ideally, you'd like the user to believe that he's actually not connected to a network at all, but that his computer magically has a connection to the peripherals that he needs to use. Shared printers should just print as if they were connected to the local printer port at his PC. Storage should just be a drive letter, as if it were connected to his PC. His network interface should be no different than simply using the desktop operating system that he already has.

Once a user has gained this access, the next task for the administrator is to control the users who are there, as described in the following section.

Controlling the User Environment

Delivering this type of environment must be accomplished by setting network operating system variables that allow the user to attach to the network as simply as possible, and for the network to set the environment with as little user interaction as possible. Ideally, the user's total responsibility will be to give his username and password at logon, and from that moment on he'll just use the peripherals he needs.

Logon Batch (Script) Files

Just as the AUTOEXEC.BAT is the batch file used to control the environment in the DOS world, Windows NT users can be controlled by using an opening batch file at logon. These batch file are commonly called *logon scripts*, not just in the NT world but in most network operating systems. When a user has successfully logged onto the network, the logon script is a batch file (.BAT or .CMD) that's delivered to the client workstation and automatically run. This batch file can make any environmental change that can be made by you from the command line. It's also able to make certain changes based on Microsoft networking variables.

The idea is to create a batch file that uses NT and DOS operating system commands to create the drives, printer port connections, paths, and so on that users in your domain need to function. Figure 10.3 shows a logon script that creates accessible network drives for the user, sends print jobs addressed to LPT3 to a network printer, and sets the user's COMSPEC to a network drive for programs that require it.

Figure 10.3.
A sample logon script.

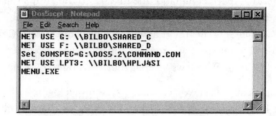

Logon scripts can contain variables, just like batch files, but there are a select set of variables that are available only to logon scripts based on their relationship to the network. By placing a logon script variable in a script, you gain the ability to use network services and utilities. These variables are signified by a percent sign (%) preceding and following the variable in the script. The following list discusses some of these variables and provides an example of a command line for each that you might use in a script:

- *%PROCESSOR_ARCHITECTURE%*. This variable refers to the processor family to which the user's workstation belongs. If the user is at an Alpha-based workstation, this variable would return ALPHA in place of the variable in the script.

  ```
  net use p: \\SERVER_NAME\SHARE_NAME\%PROCESSOR_ARCHITECTURE%
  ```

  This example would allow you to point a user to an executable that would run best on her processor family. If she's sitting at an Intel-family workstation, she would find that she now has a drive p: that points to the INTEL directory.

- *%PROCESSOR_LEVEL%*. This variable refers to the processor classification to which the user's workstation belongs. An Intel 80486 workstation, for example, would return 486 in place of the variable in the script.

  ```
  net use p: \\SERVER_NAME\SHARE_NAME\%PROCESSOR_LEVEL%
  ```

  This example would point the user to a directory based on the fact that this user is in a 486 class of processor. This allows you to house programs that run well on the 486 platform in a separate location. A user sitting at an Intel 80486 workstation would find that he now has a drive p: pointing to a 486 directory.

- *%HOMEDRIVE%*. The drive letter that contains the user's home directory.

- *%HOMEPATH%*. The path to the home directory, without the drive letter.

- *%HOMESHARE%*. The share name of the user's home directory.

- **%OS%**. The operating system running on the current workstation.
- **%USERDOMAIN%**. The domain that contains the user's account information.
- **%USERNAME%**. The user's login name.

Some legacy DOS programs require that they be able to locate COMMAND.COM at all times. The COMSPEC=*drive*:*path* command line in a batch file allows the operating system to point these programs to COMMAND.COM when the program closes. Adding this line will solve the error Unable to locate command interpreter that will lock up some workstations. When setting a COMSPEC for workstations on the network, you must point those users to a version of COMMAND.COM that matches the version of DOS or Windows 95 that they're using to boot up their workstations.

When you create a user, you can assign that user a logon script. The logon script variable is found in the User Environment Profile dialog box (you get there by clicking the Profile button in the User Properties dialog box in User Manager). When you create a new user, the profile presents this dialog box to you and allows you to change the name of the logon script that you use (see Figure 10.4).

Figure 10.4.
The User Environment Profile dialog box.

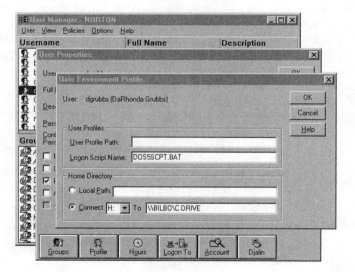

Logon scripts should be stored in the export directory on the server. You don't need to place these scripts on all servers of the domain manually if you place a copy of all the logon scripts in the SYSTEM32\REPL\EXPORT\SCRIPTS directory of the PDC and replication is set to run. By placing these files here, you guarantee that the scripts will be available to the user, no matter where he logs on. The user's script must be made available at the validating server, and replication makes that possible.

Logon Access Capabilities

When you refer to controlling the user environment, a basic piece of that control is controlling where and when a user can even access the network. If left to the user, his environment can cause the administrator problems based on when and how he logs on.

Through a combination of user profiles and user properties, the conscientious administrator can guide users through the use of the network in a controlled way. Users can be forced to log on at particular workstations, during certain times, and from the locations the administrator feels comfortable with. NT has a way to control these variables.

Workstation Restriction

A great problem for network administrators is the user who will log on in different locations and leave those systems logged on. I refer to these users as *social bumblebees* because they flit from one PC to another, logging onto the system and pollinating my network with security risk after security risk. They may also be a problem because they are tying up systems and resources that you don't want them using. Users such as temporary employees, interns, and station-specific workers are not people that you want moving from machine to machine for their network activity.

This point also comes back to the issue of users having access to your system in places and at times over which you have no control. If you feel that a user poses a threat of stealing company information, you may want to limit that user to only certain workstations.

Workstation access can be limited for users in NT. By opening the User Properties dialog box and clicking the Logon To button, you open the Logon Workstation dialog box, in which you can enter the computer names of the computer(s) that the selected user is allowed to log onto (see Figure 10.5).

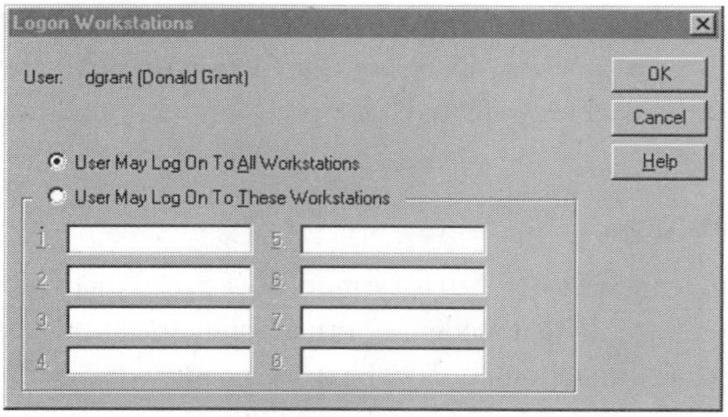

Figure 10.5.
The Logon Workstations dialog box.

Of course, this option depends on the operating system that's on the user's PC to participate in NT network naming schemes. If the machine is a DOS workstation and doesn't report a computer name, the user won't be able to use that PC—but then again, you wouldn't have restricted him or her to a PC with no name.

> **Note:** This feature and many others like it are reasons that many companies have chosen NT Workstation as a corporate standard. NT Workstation doesn't make for a very pleasant home environment because it's very restrictive about hardware calls, but it's great for security issues like this.

Desktop Environment

Windows NT and Windows 95 users can be controlled in ways that users of other operating systems and environments can't, and one of the most powerful ways is the control of the user's desktop environment.

Windows presents the network administrator a unique problem when it comes to controlling the user environment, because Windows by its very nature is an environment based on user individuality and control. But network administrators need to be able to present a unified interface that can be supported by help desk personnel. These two needs fly in the face of one another. NT and 95 offer two features that allow the administrator to control the desktop environment, but can offer the users some individuality. The two features are called *profiles* and *policies*, and are covered in great detail in Chapter 16, "Client Workstation Considerations." But for now, we'll take a brief look at profiles, and how the administrator can point the user account to the profile that is to be used by the user account.

By clicking the Profile button in the User Properties dialog box, you display the User Environment Profile dialog box. In this dialog box is an option to specify the location of the user profile to be used for this particular user (refer to Figure 10.4). Profiles can be individual or mandatory.

RAS Access

Remote Access Service (RAS) is a feature of NT Server that allows users to gain access to your system from the outside world via a modem or other communications device (ISDN, frame relay, and so on). This type of connection needs to be strictly controlled, and we'll review the RAS product in detail later. But, for now, there's control of individual users to consider.

> **Looking Ahead:** RAS is covered in great detail in Chapter 13, "Remote Access Services (RAS)." That chapter covers the facts of authentication and the threat that opening your system to modem access can cause.

Within the User Properties dialog box is a button called Dialin that displays the Dialin Information dialog box. Here administrators can control whether a user account can even make use of RAS (see Figure 10.6). This is a very basic control of whether the user can even gain access through this method. It doesn't control what the user can do once she gains access, but simply the access itself. Settings in this dialog box include control of the basic right to dial into RAS and the possible use of call-back security.

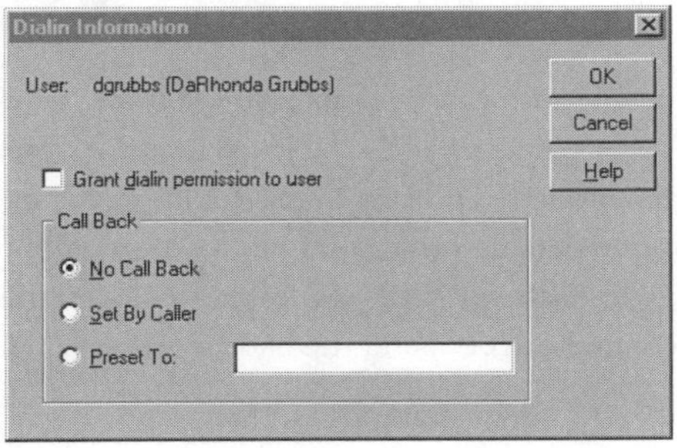

Figure 10.6.
The Dialin Information dialog box.

Dial-back security can be very effective in preventing users from using another user's name and password to gain access to the system. If you set dial-back to call the number from which the authorized user dials, the system will acknowledge that the user has called, but then hang up on the connection and call the user's PC back at the agreed-upon number. By doing this, administrators avoid even the most clever hacker, because the system won't allow real communications until the call back has been made.

Time Restrictions

To gain access to your system without your knowledge, a user may wait to use the system during a time that you aren't around to observe his actions. This gives him time to continue trying an account that isn't his own or possibly remove information from the company without anyone knowing that it has been done. For example, a disgruntled salesperson may want to print a customer list in the evening hours to take with him to a new job. If the system is accessible to his account during his off-hours, the user can log on and take his time printing your accounts list. By restricting the time range during which users can log on, you could lessen the risk of such activity. In the User Properties dialog box in User Manager, click the Hours button to open the Logon Hours dialog box, in which you can adjust the allowable logon times for a specific user (see Figure 10.7).

Figure 10.7.
Using the Logon Hours
dialog box for user control.

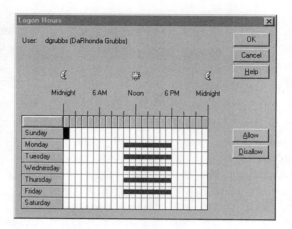

Logon time restrictions can be helpful in many ways—not just security. If you have times on your system that require that users not be logged on, then logon time restrictions can help make it possible to use an automated process to get this done. For example, if you want to create an automated backup of certain data files that must be closed in order to back up, you could use time restrictions. By restricting the users who make use of those files for the hour or so that it takes to back up the files, you'll have complete access, and the backup won't fail due to an inability to access an open file.

Hard Drive Space

NT can't control the amount of disk space that a user can use if the user has enough rights to write to a disk. A particularly wicked way of creating havoc on a system is to start an event that continually takes up more and more disk space. For example, a user who feels that her hard disk data is critical, but who doesn't have a backup system for her machine, may back up her workstation's hard drive(s) to her home drive on the server. That user tells her friend, who tells his secretary, who helps a buddy in Accounting, and you have a mess on your hands.

There are some third-party utilities that you can use to monitor and control this problem. But NT has no facility to do this.

Groups

To simplify user management, NT allows administrators to gather users together into groups and assign permissions to those groups. The concept is to avoid modifying access over and over. By creating a group and granting permissions to the group, the administrator is more efficient.

Microsoft is very enthused about the whole group concept; in fact, if you're taking any test regarding the NT operating system, keep in mind that Microsoft believes that you should almost never assign a right to a user directly. Instead, the Microsoft solution is to assign the user to a group and assign the permissions to the group, or add the user to a group that already has the permissions. That way of doing things can seem a bit uptight, but if you give it some thought it really does save time in the long run. When you assign permissions to groups instead of users, you give yourself a very simple way to remove the permission from the user—simply remove the user from the group. Conversely, if you want to add new users, you simply have to add them to the groups that meet each user's needs.

Many administrators believe that by granting permissions to users specifically, they're being more precise. But the thing that you need to consider in the Microsoft plan is that you may later want to give another user that same set of rights or resources. By creating groups and assigning users to the groups, you give yourself the edge of being able to better track what a user has permissions for, and being able to remove those permissions easily.

Local Versus Global Groups

The groups that are created in the NT world are divided between the machine itself and the network as a whole. This division can be very complex when you're creating administration schemes of your own. The concept that you must keep in mind is that NT is both a workstation and a server operating system. To separately control the functions that occur at the domain level as a whole and at the local level, two types of groups have been created—local and global (see Figure 10.8).

Figure 10.8.
Local groups and global groups, and where you might find them.

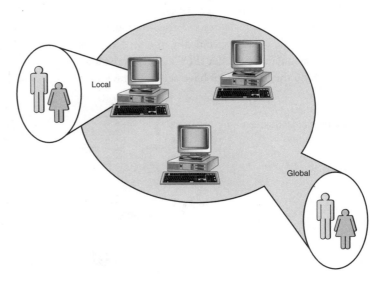

Local groups are created in a machine's local account database for the purpose of managing local resources only. These groups are created to access and manage the local resources and shares. Local groups can contain domain users, local users, and even global groups. If trusts have been established, members (domain groups and domain users) of trusted domains can be added to the local groups (see Figure 10.9).

Figure 10.9.
Creating groups.

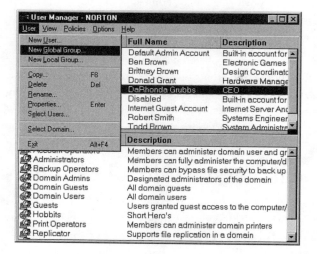

The concept of local groups doesn't disappear when domains enter the picture; local groups still exist in the domain world. The waters get fairly muddy when you consider that NT servers in domains actually have local groups, because you might think that these groups are automatically global groups. Global groups are created specifically in User Manager for Domains. Oddly enough, if the local machine is a domain controller (PDC or BDC), the local database is the domain database (see Figure 10.10). So the local groups have access to the local resources of all of the domain controllers.

Figure 10.10.
Local groups in workstations versus local groups in domains.

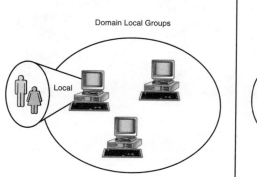

Global groups are created in the domain model and are managed through the different domain controllers discussed earlier. Global groups are used to gather users who are part of the domain. A global group includes only domain users because the entire purpose of a global group is to gather the global users. Local users can't be part of a global group because local users aren't part of a domain model.

The biggest difference in your thinking about these two types of groups is that global and local groups really have two different base purposes. Local groups are intended to gather all user types and user group types to allow administrators to grant them permissions to local resources. Global groups are really more of a user-gathering tool only. If you want to grant user rights, you need to consider which of these two things you're looking to do:

- If you want to manage permissions to a given resource within a domain, you should create a local group. This is because not only can you give permissions to the items in the domain, but you can include groups and users from all domains. The idea is that local groups offer you the flexibility that a global group wouldn't have offered. By creating a global group, you limit yourself to being able to add only members of the same domain as the global group.

- If you want to gather a group of users who are part of a new task force so that you can assign them to different resources across domains (or in a single domain), you should create a global group. The idea is to then make that group part of local groups that already have permissions to the resources that you want this group to access, or directly assign this group the permissions you would like them to have.

Tip: Ideally, you should assign the global group to a local group that has permissions to the resources, but not because assigning the global group directly won't work. It's because you have better ability to remove a group of users without completely destroying all access to the resource.

Predefined (Default) Groups

NT creates several groups by default and even more groups in the event that you choose to use a domain model for your security scheme.

These are the default NT groups:

- **Administrators.** Just as it sounds, the Administrators group is that group that has full access to the entire local system and workgroup. Any user who has been made a member of this group effectively has the same privileges as the Administrator user's account.

- **Users.** Each user account on the NT machine has been automatically made a member of the Users group. This group is the equivalent of "all users" in the NT system. The permissions level granted here consists of those permissions necessary to log onto the system, run applications, and print to printers.

- **Guests.** This predefined group gives a limited amount of access to users who are members. Making a user a member of this group is the same as making him equivalent to the Guest user account. The group doesn't remove rights, but if a user is a member of the group Guests, it's usually to allow him to use basic public services and nothing else.

- **Power Users.** The members of this group are users who don't require that you maintain a close rein or that can even help with the administration of the system without causing damage. Power Users are able to create shares, manage printers, create accounts, and even delete or modify the user accounts that they create. The difference between the Power Users and Administrators groups is that Power Users can't modify or delete the users and resources that already exist. There are also certain privileges set aside for the administrator only.

Note: Operator groups are groups created with the permissions necessary to accomplish just the particular subset of tasks that might be offloaded to a user, relieving the administrator of those responsibilities. The groups Backup Operators, Account Operators, Print Operators, Replicators, and Server Operators are operator groups. They can also be used to allow a user to administer just his own group of users. This type of user is primarily needed for large companies with a national or international campus.

- **Backup Operators.** This operator group is given just the permissions necessary to back up and restore the file system and system structure. These users might be strategically located near the backup, or they might be users who have been given the responsibility of ensuring that the data for a project is safe. The catch is that these rights are available to these users only while they're using the NT Backup program or a comparable third-party package.

- **Account Operators.** This operator group is created with the sole purpose of creating, deleting, and modifying users and groups. You might consider this group to be a human resources group for NT administration (even though non-humans can have accounts). This group is often populated by department managers or departmental IS staff.

  This group can't modify Administrators or Server Operators groups, because they would then be able to have the same powers as those groups, and might as well be given those powers.

- **Print Operators.** Managing printing can require that people who are close to the print device be able to control the printer. Print operators are users who have been given the permissions necessary to control and create printers.

- **Server Operators.** Just like printers, servers may need to be controlled by someone who is close to the server, but who doesn't need to control more than that physical server. In this case, you make that user a member of the group Server Operators for that particular server. This change makes that user able to create and delete shares, manage server drives, back up and restore, and even shut down that server.

    The Server Operator isn't an account that controls users and groups. It isn't able to create or manage accounts at all. Being a member of this group is also not meant to allow a user to manage a server from over the network. Keep in mind that this account is meant for "server" management to help with location issues, not to facilitate account management or remote management.

- **Replicators.** This is a very unique account in that it isn't really meant to be an account for any human being. It's really a group for the account created for the Replicator service. Because the Replicator service is used to replicate information across the network and the system can't log onto the network, a user-style account must be created to make replication possible.

Note: Domain groups are groups created in conjunction with the domain. Groups in conjunction with the security schemes combine to create accounts that can allow different levels of access from the server machine to the network as a whole.

- **Domain Admins.** This global group automatically contains the administrators from the NT servers that have been created in the domain. Effectively, this account is the administrator for the entire domain. Its initial member is the Administrator.

- **Domain Users.** This group is equivalent to the user account in the global or domain model. Its initial member is the Administrator.

- **Domain Guests.** This group is the equivalent of the Guest account in the global domain model. Its initial member is Guest.

NT contains group names that you won't be able to change and won't see presented in any list of users that you can remove or delete. However, you'll be presented with these groups in the permissions screens when you're assigning rights (see Figure 10.11). For that reason, we will call them *hidden* or *administrative groups*.

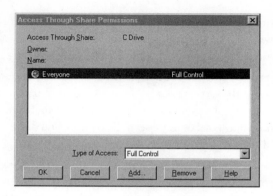

Figure 10.11.
Where did that group come from?

These are the hidden/administrative groups:

- **Everyone.** All users. Any user account that has access to the system from any source.
- **Network.** Any user who can access the system from a network connection.
- **Interactive.** Users logged on to local machine (NT Server PC or NT Workstation PC).
- **System.** The Windows NT operating system itself; for example, server processes that may need to gain access to a share.
- **Creator/Owner.** Any user who can create a directory, printer, or share is considered the creator/owner of the resource.

When to Create a Group

Group creation in the NT environment isn't just to allow you to better organize users, like directories organize files. Groups are the preferred way to manage and control the users' access to resources. The greater question in group creation is when the creation of a new group is needed and what unique qualities that group will need (see Figure 10.12).

Grouping users not only makes it easier to assign permissions—it makes the job of an administrator easier. Following are a few examples of when a group can make the job of the administrator easier and more precise:

- If you want to share a domain resource, you should first consider creating a global group that you can manage and add to. Domain resources can be shared only with global groups and domain users. By adding individual domain users, you're adding to the individual steps that must be made in the creation; worse, you're adding the time required to track who has access to a resource. If you want to remove a department from the permissions of a resource, it's far easier to remove the entire departmental group than to remove all the individual users.

- Printer shares are used to allow users to make use of a particular printing device, but they're also used to prevent users from using it. If you've created a print share for a particularly expensive color printer, the creation of a printer global group and the removal of the group Everyone can selectively allow certain groups of users to gain access. But also, when you want to add a user to the printer, you'll find it easier to add the user to the printer's group than to open the printer's permissions and add the user.

- Companies can create groups that fit job descriptions and then assign to the group the permissions that users in that department need. When a user is moved from one department to another, the administrator simply needs to move the user from one department group to the other.

Figure 10.12.
Creating a group with User Manager.

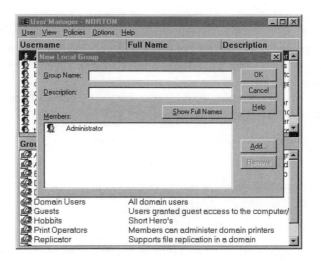

The toughest thing to resist in these situations is the temptation to simply add a user to the list of users and groups that have permissions in a particular resource. When you get a request to add a user to the list of users who are allowed to use the resource, you need to consider the long-term ramifications of having to go back and weed out the individual users from all the resources they have if a change is made.

Assigning Permissions Using Groups and Users

When all is said and done regarding users and groups, what we hope to know is how to assign permissions to the resources and get our clients to the resources conveniently. Chapter 11 deals with the specific use of the User Manager and making permission assignments, but for now let's take a look at some rights scenarios that may fit what you would like to get done. Specifically, let's look at what we should do in relation to users and groups.

Keep in mind as we look at these cases that you may not agree with my solution, but what I want you to do is look at why this solution is chosen. The idea is not to say that this is the only way that it will work, but rather that this is the way that will work using the Microsoft-preferred logic.

Case One

All the data resources for the Accounting department of Water Drop Gum Company exist on the WD-ACCNTG server in the Central domain. The files exist in the \PLATNM directory and the directory has been created. Currently, the ACCNTG local group in the WD-ACCNTG server has been given the rights needed to access the information and has been using it for some time. You've been told to allow the Payroll Management Task Force from the four other divisions to have permissions to the directory. Each division has its own domain (East, West, South, and UPTHERE), as shown in Figure 10.13.

The Task Force consists of the following users:

- Todd in the East domain
- DaRhonda in the South domain
- Ben in the UPTHERE domain
- Brittney in the West domain

What would be the best plan of action to grant these user permissions to the data?

Answer: Before any solution can be effected, the Central domain is going to have to trust the South, East, West, and UPTHERE domains. This will allow the users from those domains to be granted permissions in the Central domain.

Because you're gathering users from diverse domains, you need to make Todd, DaRhonda, Ben, and Brittney members of a local group (see Figure 10.14). If you'll recall, members of a global group can only come from that domain's account database.

Figure 10.13.
Case One.

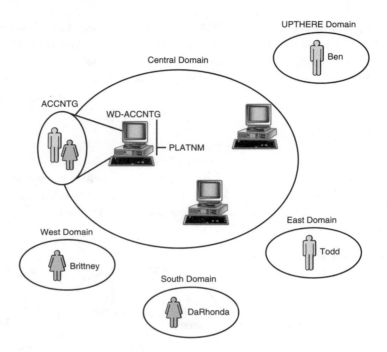

Figure 10.14.
Case One, as seen after my solution.

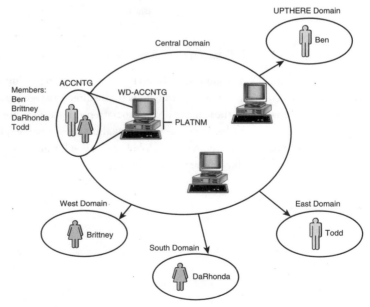

Because the local group ACCTNG is already making use of the data, it would make sense to make these users part of that group. The only other option that you may want to consider is making them a part of a local group that signifies that they're from other domains, and then making that group part of the group ACCTNG. But you can't do that because a local group can't be made part of a local group.

Case Two

As the administrator of two domains (Trucks and Dolls) at Bobo Toys, you've been given the task of giving the vice presidents of the Monster Truck division permissions to the \R-N-D directory on the LAB server in the Dolls domain. There are three vice presidents, and all of them have usernames in the Trucks domain (Donald, Tammy, and Brian). They don't already belong to a common group, global or local (see Figure 10.15).

Figure 10.15.
Case Two.

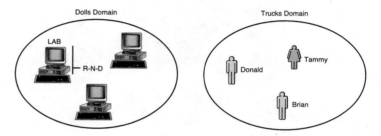

What group type would allow you to manage these users now and in the future?

Answer: By making Don, Tammy, and Brian members of a global group (possibly TRUCK-VP), you create a tool for granting the users permissions to the directory (see Figure 10.16). You also create a tool for future changes to these users along association lines as vice presidents. When the Dolls division gets angry over the breach of security, you also give yourself a quick way to remove all three users. Once you have added them to the global group, you'll want to add that group to a local group on the LAB server that has the proper permissions.

Figure 10.16.
Case Two, my solution.

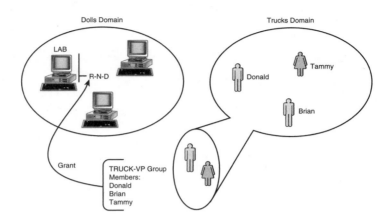

Summary

This chapter covered basics of user management from user accounts to groups and the way they're used to control the network flow.

What you've learned about the user account is the fact that it isn't just for humans, but instead is the basic level of access required even for some programs to gain access to the system. User accounts are created by the system by default to allow administrators to gain access to the system and even to allow guests to make use of the basic operating system functions. But user accounts are also needed by some operating system and application services.

Usernames and passwords not only need to be assigned, but also monitored. Laziness in this area is the primary threat to your security system. By using a naming convention, you can make your network easier to use. By using password schemes to control the passwords used and the changes that must be made, you can keep the target moving so that your security isn't shot down.

Groups can be hard to understand and seem magical. The basic use of NT groups is to gather users together and allow the administrator to make changes to them as a whole. Global and local groups really have two different purposes. Local groups are to gather all user types and user group types, to allow administrators to grant them permissions to local resources. Global groups are really more of a user-gathering tool only.

The next chapter guides you through the use of User Manager for Domains to create and use these pieces.

11

The User Manager Tool

Peter Norton™

By the time you reach this chapter, you should have a good understanding of NT Server's relationship to users and groups. The basic concepts involved in the "why" of creating these items are covered in previous chapters. What's needed now is a detailed view of how to create users and groups and how to use the User Manager for Domains.

User Manager is the name of the tool used in NT workgroups and domains, but there's a distinct difference between User Manager and User Manager for Domains. If you're working from a machine involved in the domain control process (PDC or BDC), you'll be presented with User Manager for Domains. All other NT machines present User Manager, which controls the machine itself and the resources that the machine offers.

The User Manager for Domains (see Figure 11.1) can be found under the Administrative Tools (Common) option in the Start menu.

Figure 11.1.
User Manager for Domains.

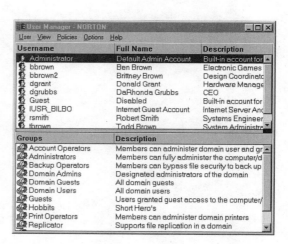

As you cover the "how to" portions in this chapter, you may also want to consult Chapter 9, "Domain Design," and Chapter 10, "User Account Creation and Management," for reference material on the reasons for each choice.

Managing and Creating Users

The most basic use of User Manager is the creation of new users. The following is a step-by-step description of the process:

1. On the User menu, click New User. The New User dialog box appears, as shown in Figure 11.2.

Figure 11.2.
The New User dialog box.

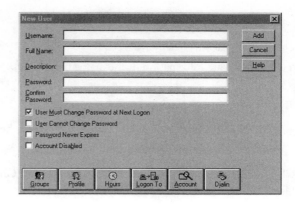

2. In Username, type a user name.

3. In Full Name, type the user's complete name (optional).

4. In Description, type a description of the user or the user account (optional).

5. In both Password and Confirm Password, type a password of up to 14 characters (optional, but recommended).

6. Click to select or clear the check boxes for User Must Change Password at Next Logon, User Cannot Change Password, Password Never Expires, and Account Disabled.

7. To administer a property associated with a button in the New User dialog box, click the button and complete the dialog box that appears; then click OK.

8. Click Add.

If you are creating a number of users, don't close the New User dialog box. Simply repeat these steps. Once you are done, click Cancel. Canceling after already choosing Add won't cancel the new user you have added; it simply closes the New User dialog box.

Copying a User

After you have created a user account, you may decide that the variables that were set for that user are the same as the variables that you would like for a number of new users. Particularly when you are creating the initial user accounts in your domain, you can avoid repeating the same work by copying a user account that you have already created.

As a matter of practice, you may want to create template accounts that fit several descriptions and use those accounts to create users. When you copy a user account, you copy all information from that user except the username, full name, and password. Everything else, even description, is copied.

To copy a user account, follow these steps:

1. On the User menu, click Copy.

2. Type appropriate information in the dialog box:

   - In Username, type a user name.

   - In Full Name, type the user's complete name.

   - In Description, type a description of the user or the user account (optional).

   - In both Password and Confirm Password, type a password of up to 14 characters.

3. Click to select or clear the check boxes for User Must Change Password at Next Logon, User Cannot Change Password, Password Never Expires, and Account Disabled.

4. To administer a property associated with a button in the Copy Of dialog box, click the button and complete the dialog box that appears; then click OK.

5. Click Add.

These steps can be repeated as many times as you like to create a large number of users with the same basic structure. By using this method, you can avoid hours of creation time for departments— or even small groups of users.

Modifying a User Account

Obviously, once user accounts have been created, those accounts will need occasional updates and modification. Modifying a single user account is as simple as or even simpler than the creation of an account. The process involves no more information and requires fewer steps than the creation.

To modify one account, you can follow these steps:

1. In User Manager for Domains, select a user account; then click Properties on the User menu (or simply double-click the account name).

2. In the User Properties dialog box (see Figure 11.3), modify the property or properties that you want to change.

3. Click OK.

To make the same modification to more than one user account, follow these steps:

1. In User Manager for Domains, select two or more user accounts.

2. On the User menu, click Properties.

3. Modify the property or properties that you want to change.

4. Click OK.

When you modify more than one account at one time, you'll be presented only with the options that you can change. This will help to guide you through the process without wasting your time.

Figure 11.3.
The User Properties dialog box for modifying a user.

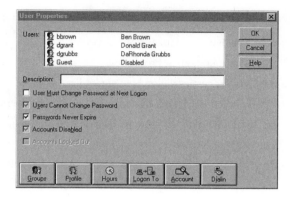

Once you have opened a user account to be modified, you can change many settings beyond those on the initial screen. The Groups, Profile, Hours, Logon To, Account, and Dialin buttons at the bottom of the User Properties dialog box can also be modified. It seems awfully easy to say "modify the items that you want changed," in the earlier steps, but each area has its own steps for modification. The following sections describe each area of potential modification.

Groups

To modify group memberships for a single user, follow these steps:

1. Click Groups in the New User, Copy Of, or User Properties dialog box.

2. Choose the desired option (see Figure 11.4):

    • To add the user account to one or more groups, select one or more groups in Not Member Of, and then click Add.

    • To remove the user account from one or more groups, select one or more groups in Member Of, and then click Remove.

    • To change the user-account primary group, select one global group from Member Of, and then click Set.

Figure 11.4.
Groups Memberships dialog box for a single user.

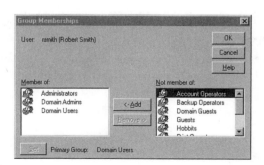

To manage common group memberships for two or more user accounts, follow these steps:

1. In User Manager for Domains, select two or more user accounts.

2. On the User menu, click Properties.

3. In the User Properties dialog box, click Groups.

4. Use the following methods to make the changes you want (see Figure 11.5):

   • To add all the user accounts to one or more groups, select one or more groups in Not All Are Members Of, and then click Add.

   • To remove all the user accounts from one or more groups, select one or more groups in All Are Members Of, and then click Remove.

   • To change the primary group for all the selected user accounts, select one global group from All Are Members Of, and then click Set.

Figure 11.5.
Group memberships with multiple users selected.

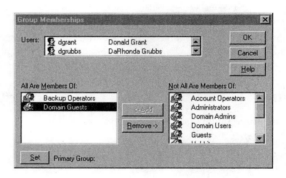

If even one of the selected user accounts is not a member of a particular group, that group is listed in Not All Are Members Of.

Profile

To configure the user-environment profile, follow these steps:

1. Click Profile in the New User, Copy Of, or User Properties dialog box.

2. Choose the desired option(s):

   • To enable the user profile to be roaming or mandatory, create a share on the appropriate server, grant Full Control to Everyone, and type the full path in User Profile Path, such as:

     ```
     \\bilbo\profiles\baginsf
     ```

- To assign a logon script, type the filename in Logon Script Name, such as:

`clerks.cmd`

If the logon script is stored in a subdirectory of the logon script path, precede the filename with that relative path, such as:

`clerks\baginsf.cmd`

- To specify a home directory, click Connect, specify a drive letter, click To, and then type a network path, such as:

`\\bilbo\users\baginsf`

If the specified directory doesn't exist, User Manager for Domains creates it.

In Local Path, you can specify a path to a local directory (for example, `c:\users\baginsf`). Remember, local home directories assigned in domain user accounts are not created automatically; they must be created manually.

- Optionally, substitute `%USERNAME%` for the last subdirectory in the home directory path, such as:

`\\bilbo\users\%username%`

Looking Ahead: User policies are discussed in greater detail in Chapter 16, "Client Workstation Considerations."

Hours

The Hours tab helps to control the user's ability to even get to the system during certain hours of the day. By following these directions, you can direct users to be off of the system during the desired hours:

1. Click Hours in the New User, Copy Of, or User Properties dialog box.
2. In the Logon Hours dialog box (see Figure 11.6), select the hours to be administered:
   - To select one hour, click that hour.
   - To select a block of time, click the beginning hour and drag through the rows and columns to the ending hour.
   - To select an entire day, click that day in the left column. To select one hour for all seven days, click the top of that column.
   - To select the entire week, click the upper-left box (above Sunday).

Figure 11.6.
The Logon Hours dialog box.

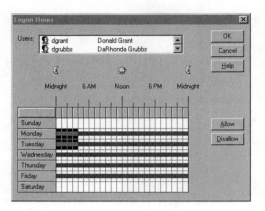

3. To allow connections during the selected hours, click Allow. Or, to deny connections during the selected hours, click Disallow.

4. Repeat steps 2 and 3 as necessary.

The default setting allows users to connect at any time, but you can restrict individual users to certain days and hours. These settings only affect connections to the server; they don't affect a user's ability to use a workstation.

Logon To

The Logon Workstations dialog box is designed to allow the administrator to control the actual computers that the user can log onto (see Figure 11.7). This is highly dependent on the operating system being able to report a NetBIOS name back to NT so that the choices made here apply. If the name isn't NetBIOS-compatible, NT will allow the logon.

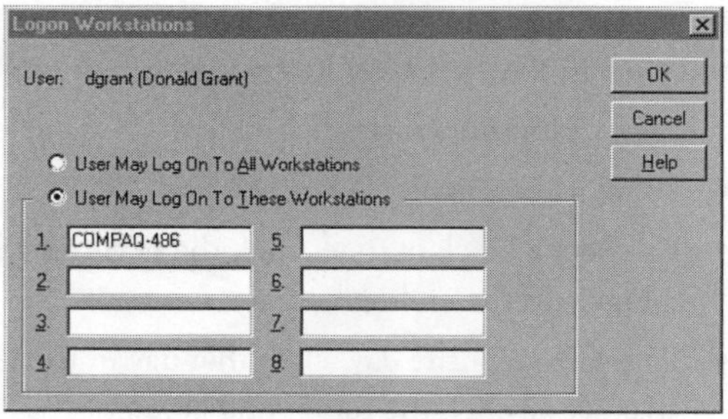

Figure 11.7.
The Logon Workstations dialog box.

This form of control is not the default and requires a great deal of work to control. Following are the steps:

1. Click Logon To in the New User, Copy Of, or User Properties dialog box.
2. Click either User May Log On To All Workstations or User May Log On To These Workstations.
3. If you selected User May Log On To These Workstations in step 2, type a computer name in at least one and up to eight of the numbered boxes.

Account

The Account button is meant to give the administrator control over the existence of the account over time and the relationship it has to the domain (see Figure 11.8). This control allows the administrator to give accounts an expiration date or make decisions about whether the account will exist on a global scale.

Figure 11.8.
The Account Information dialog box.

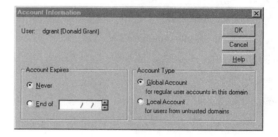

To make changes in the Account Information dialog box, follow these steps:

1. Click Account in the New User, Copy Of, or User Properties dialog box.
2. Under Account Expires, select either Never or End Of.
3. If you selected End Of in step 2, enter an expiration date.
4. Under Account Type, select either Global Account or Local Account.

Most accounts are global accounts. Assign local accounts only when a trust relationship does not exist with the user's home domain.

Deleting and Disabling User Accounts

User accounts can be deleted but, as Chapter 10 discusses, it makes more sense to disable an account before you delete it. The issue is that once the account is gone the relationships and unique properties of that account are gone. The re-creation of that user will never be exactly the same. If you can disable the account, you not only allow yourself to reopen that account for the original user, but you also allow that account to possibly be renamed later for a replacement employee or temporary employee doing that job.

To disable or enable a user account, follow these steps:

1. In the User Manager window, select one or more user accounts.

2. On the User menu, click Properties.

3. To prevent logons to the selected user accounts, select the Accounts Disabled check box. Or, to permit logons to the selected user accounts, clear the Accounts Disabled check box.

Note: The built-in Administrator account cannot be disabled.

To delete one or more user accounts, follow these steps:

1. In the User Manager window, select one or more user accounts.

2. On the User menu, click Delete.

3. If a confirmation message appears, click OK.

4. When the delete message appears, click Yes. Or, if you selected multiple user accounts, click Yes To All.

To rename a user account, follow these steps:

1. In the User Manager for Domains window, select one user account.

2. On the User menu, click Rename.

3. In Change To, type a user name.

To select multiple user accounts, follow these steps:

1. In the User Manager for Domains window, do one of the following:

   • Select the user accounts you want as the initial members of the new group.

   • Select any group to ensure that no user accounts are initially selected.

2. On the User menu, click Select Users.

3. To select the member users of a group, select the group from the list and then click Select.

4. To deselect the member users of a group, select the group from the list, and then click Deselect.

5. Repeat steps 3 and 4 as necessary.

When you finish selecting accounts, you can apply commands on the User menu to those accounts.

Only the user accounts listed in the User Manager for Domains window can be selected or deselected. Although local groups can contain user or group accounts not from the local domain, those accounts are not affected by choices made in the Select Users dialog box.

Some options change when you are using certain RAS connections. When Low Speed Connection is selected as a RAS option, for example, Select Users is unavailable.

> **Tip:** You can hold down Ctrl and then click to select specific user accounts in the User Manager for Domains window, or hold down Shift and click to select a contiguous range of user accounts.

Group Creation and Management

The creation of groups would appear to be a task that's done after the administrator has created the users to put into those groups. But I'd like you to ignore the fact that the discussion of users precedes the discussion of groups in this chapter, and remember that groups are the primary way you will be assigning permissions and control to your users. It's often a better idea to put together a list of categories into which you believe your users will fit and then create those groups before you create your users.

Group creation is done in the User Manager; which type of groups you create is determined by the form of User Manager that you are using, and the choices that you make when you begin to use it. For information on why and when to create each type of group, see Chapter 10.

Global Groups

Global groups, you'll remember, are the groups used to gather user accounts across a single domain. Because global groups exist as part of the domain, they exist only in User Manager for Domains. Keep in mind when you work with global groups that you are primarily grouping users across the domain and that global groups will often be assigned to other local groups.

To Create a New Global Group

To create a global group, follow these steps:

1. In User Manager for Domains, select the user accounts you want as the initial members of the new group, or select any group to ensure that no user accounts are initially selected.

2. On the User menu, click New Global Group. The New Global Group dialog box appears, as shown in Figure 11.9.

Figure 11.9.
*The New Global Group
dialog box, in the selected
users approach.*

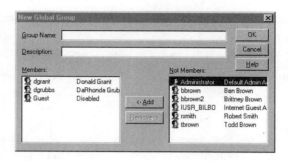

3. In Group Name, type a group name.

4. In Description, type a description.

5. To add members to the new group, select one or more user accounts in Not Members, and then click Add.

6. To remove members from the new group, select one or more user accounts in Members, and then click Remove.

Note: Keep in mind as you create group and user names that they can't be identical. For example, you can't have an Admin user and an Admin global group.

To Make a Copy of an Existing Global Group

Just like copying users, copying global groups can save you work in the early stages of creation and management. Global groups that are copied retain the user list and the description of the group from which they originate. The important difference to note when copying groups is that the permissions and memberships are not copied along with the user list. When you copy a group, it's merely to avoid having to retype the user list.

To copy a group, follow these steps:

1. Open User Manager for Domains and select one global group.

2. On the User menu, click Copy.

3. In Group Name, type a new group name.

4. The remaining portion of the setup process is independent of the copied group and can be changed in the same ways as the original.

Once you have selected the Copy option, you are presented with the new group. Notice that the user list and description are the same as in the creation of the original group (refer to Figure 11.9).

From that point on, you're creating a new group. Take the time to adjust the description of the group to avoid confusion later.

> **Note:** Global groups can't be managed when Low Speed Connection is selected, or when you're administering a computer running Windows NT Workstation or Windows NT Server that is not a domain controller.

Modifying or Deleting Existing Global Groups

Once a group has been created, you can modify it to include the users that you want to possess the properties of that group. To modify a group, follow these steps:

1. In the User Manager for Domains window, select the global group; then click Properties on the User menu.
2. To change the description, type new text in Description.
3. To add members, select one or more user accounts in Not Members, and then click Add.
4. To remove members, select one or more user accounts in Members, and then click Remove.

Before you actually delete any group, consider these issues:

- Deleting a global group removes only the group, not the user accounts that were members of the deleted group.
- A deleted group can't be recovered. If you delete a group and then create another group with the same group name, the new group won't have any of the rights or permissions that were previously granted to the old group.

To delete a global group, follow these steps:

1. In the User Manager for Domains window, select the global group.
2. On the User menu, click Delete.

A global group that is the primary group for one or more user accounts cannot be deleted. Built-in groups also cannot be deleted.

Local Groups

Local groups are those groups that control the permissions and access of the resources located on the local machine. The unique feature of local groups is the ability to contain global groups. When creating local groups, you are adding not only users, but groups as well.

To create a new local group:

1. In the User Manager for Domains window, select the user accounts you want as the initial members of the new group, or select any group to ensure that no user accounts are initially selected.

2. On the User menu, click New Local Group to open the New Local Group dialog box (see Figure 11.10).

Figure 11.10.
Creating a new local group.

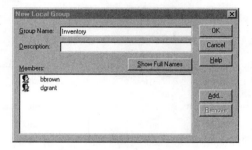

3. In Group Name, type a name for the new group.

4. In Description, type a description for the new group.

5. To add members, click Add and then complete the Add Users and Groups dialog box.

6. To remove members from the new group, select one or more names in Members, and then click Remove.

Copying, Modifying, and Deleting Local Groups

Just as with global groups, local groups can be copied to allow the administrator to avoid doubling the workload—but it's rare to find two local groups that have the same needs. At best, you may find that a new group will be a subset of a previously created group that you can pare down to create the group that you want.

The steps and rules for copying, deleting, and modifying a local group are the same as those for a global group (listed in the preceding section). The only real exceptions, of course, are the selection of a local group to copy. Global groups can't be copied to a local group or vice versa.

Policy Editor Tool

The changes that are made under the Policies menu choice in User Manager apply to the domain or workgroup as a whole. A *policy* implies a change in the way that the system deals with users, groups, and even domain relationships. It may help to consider policies to be the rules that apply to all entities in the NT Server environment—house rules, if you will.

The policies themselves are covered in some detail in Chapters 10 and 16. This chapter looks at how to change the policies.

Account Policy Changes

The Account option on the Policies menu allows the administrator to control basic user account password and account lockout status. As mentioned elsewhere, the administrator may want to control the minimum password length, the unique nature of the passwords used, and so on. Account policies control those issues.

To manage the account policies, follow these steps:

1. On the Policies menu, click Account. The Account Policy dialog box opens, as shown in Figure 11.11.

Figure 11.11.
The Account Policy dialog box.

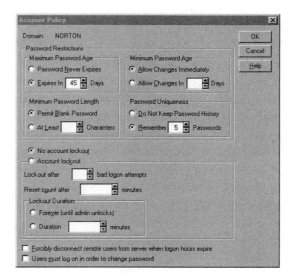

2. Enter the values you want in any of the dialog box sections: Maximum Password Age, Minimum Password Age, Minimum Password Length, and Password Uniqueness; or click Password Never Expires, Allow Changes Immediately, Permit Blank Password, or Do Not Keep Password History.

3. If necessary, select or clear the option Forcibly Disconnect Remote Users from Server When Logon Hours Expire.

4. If necessary, select or clear the Users Must Log On in Order to Change Password check box.

When you are changing account policies, remember the items mentioned in Chapter 10 about not creating work for yourself that you don't want to track later. Once you begin giving users limitations and walls, you may have to keep those walls in repair or help them over the limitations (even if their mistakes cause the problem).

If you select the option Allow Changes Immediately in the Minimum Password Age section, you should also click Do Not Keep Password History in the Password Uniqueness section. If you enter a value under Password Uniqueness, you should also enter a value for Allow Changes in __ Days under Minimum Password Age.

Minimum and maximum values for the various options are as follows:

- 1 to 999 days for Maximum Password Age and Minimum Password Age.
- 1 to 14 characters for Minimum Password Length.
- 1 to 24 passwords for Remember __ Passwords under Password Uniqueness.

User Rights Policy Changes

User rights are quite different from permissions; in the NT world, that distinction can be made in the user rights policies. The rights listed in the User Rights Policy dialog box (see Figure 11.12) are not the ability to access files or directories, but the ability to control different parts of the operating system itself. If you come from a Novell environment, this may be a difficult distinction.

Figure 11.12.
The User Rights Policy
dialog box.

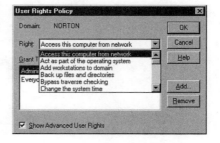

A group may be given the right to back up files and directories, but may not have permissions in many of the directories for basic use. The operating system itself contains user accounts that must be given permission to log onto the system as a service. Both of these examples are system rights examples.

Just as in any permissions example, most often the easiest way to provide rights to a user is to add that user's account to one of the built-in groups that already possesses the needed rights, rather than manage the user rights policy.

To assign system rights, follow these steps:

1. On the Policies menu, click User Rights to open the User Rights Policy dialog box (refer to Figure 11.12).

2. Select a user right from the Right list. The users and groups who currently have that right appear under Grant To.

3. To grant the selected right to additional groups or user accounts, click Add and then complete the Add Users and Groups dialog box.

4. To remove a group or user account from the list, select a name in the Grant To box, and then click Remove.

5. Repeat steps 2 through 4 as necessary.

6. To administer the advanced user rights, select the Show Advanced User Rights check box and repeat steps 2 through 4 as necessary. Advanced rights are primarily used by programmers writing applications for computers running Windows NT Workstation and Windows NT Server.

Audit Policy Changes

If you would like to track the success or failure of your policies or of the user population as a whole to interface with the network, you need some form of tool. The audit policy that is established in User Manager allows the administrator to track login traffic such as successful logins, unsuccessful logins, and frequency of these events.

These events (see Figure 11.13) are tracked system-wide or domain-wide so that the administrator can be aware of security issues arising—before the users become aggravated or the system is subverted.

Figure 11.13.
The Audit Policy dialog box.

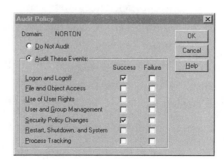

To set the audit policy, follow these steps:

1. On the Policies menu, click Audit. The Audit Policy dialog box opens (refer to Figure 11.13).

2. To record events in the security log, click Audit These Events; to not record any events in the security log, click Do Not Audit.

3. If you selected Audit These Events in step 2, click to select or clear the Success and Failure check boxes for each type of event.

When administering domains, the audit policy affects the security logs of all domain controllers in the domain because they share the same audit policy. When administering a computer running Windows NT Workstation or Windows NT Server that is not a domain, the audit policy affects only the security log of that computer. Entries in a security log can be reviewed using Event Viewer.

Because the security log is limited in size, carefully select which events to log. The maximum size of each computer's security log is defined in Event Viewer.

Domain Trusts

It's important to remember in a domain trust relationship that the relationship requires that an administrator account from both domains be involved in creating the trust. Chapter 9 looks at the significance of domain trust relationships; this section covers the responsibility of both administrators.

To add a trusting domain, follow these steps:

1. If necessary, click Select Domain on the User menu and complete the Select Domain dialog box, specifying the name of the domain that will add to its list of trusting domains.

2. On the Policies menu, click Trust Relationships.

3. Click Add. In Trusting Domain, type the name of the Windows NT Server domain that will trust your domain.

4. Type a password in both Password and Confirm Password.

5. Provide the password to the administrator of the domain that you have added to the Trusting Domains list.

The administrator on the other domain must now complete the following steps to complete the trust:

1. Obtain a password from the administrator of the domain that will be trusted.

2. If necessary, click Select Domain on the User menu and complete the Select Domain dialog box, specifying the name of your domain that will be configured to trust the other domain.

3. On the Policies menu, click Trust Relationships.

4. Click Add. In Trusted Domains, type the name of the Windows NT Server domain that is to be trusted.

5. In Password, type the password required by that domain.

Summary

The purpose of this chapter was to provide you with the nuts and bolts of User Manager from the "how to" standpoint. Hopefully, this chapter has given you a section that you can return to during the conceptual chapters and find the steps to put the concepts in action.

The management and the creation of users can be done in a couple of different ways, but hopefully you have learned that the best idea is to create the groups that you would like to use and manage users with the help of groups. Changes can be made either way, but the things that must be done to user accounts are seldom needed for a single user.

I have covered the fact that user accounts can be controlled down to a detailed set of variables. Profiles can be used to control scripts and desktop behaviors. Hours of use can be controlled from many different angles, and you can even control access from the standpoint of time of day.

You now have a better grasp of the use of local and global groups to control the use of resources on both the network shares and the local machine. Keep in mind when you work with global groups that you are primarily grouping users across the domain and that global groups will often be assigned to other local groups. Local groups are able to contain global groups, and make a great tool.

Once you enter the domain-size grouping, there's the trust to remember. These domain relationships are used to make the connections needed between domains.

IV

Network Services

12

Network Browsing

Peter Norton™

Just like humans browsing for houses or cars, computers must browse the available pathways to find the network resources that they need. The big difference is that computers don't have the ability to arbitrarily go from place to place looking at the choices. Computers remember things better, they process information faster, they even entertain our kids better sometimes—but they can't browse as well as we do.

Network browsing for computers requires that computers be given the job of helping others browse. Computers on the network have roles that they play and areas that they are responsible for. In this chapter, we take a look at how these computers facilitate browsing and what roles they play—the roles that are played in a larger network and the effects that a large network have on the browse scheme.

We also look at the Windows NT approach to protocols that don't usually allow what Microsoft calls *browsing* to function, including WINS (Windows Internet Name Service) and the role that it plays in the browsing of the network.

Here are a few of the things covered:

- Browsing concepts
- Browser server roles
- The election process
- Operating the browser environment
- Synchronizing master browsers
- Multiple-domain and multiple-segment networks
- Browsing multiple-subnet TCP/IP
- Hiding items from the browser

Browsing Concepts

When a user sits down at a PC running Windows 95 and sets out to make use of a network resource, she will first do one of two things. She will either open the Network Neighborhood or she will make use of a network resource that has already been assigned to her through a script or some other environmental control from the administrator. Chapter 10, "User Account Creation and Management," and Chapter 11, "The User Manager Tool," looked at how to set up those environmental controls, but now we'll look at how products and tools like Network Neighborhood can search the network and return a list of network resources that users can use.

Not only Windows 95 users browse the network for resources and servers. Windows, Windows for Workgroups (WfW), Windows NT (all versions), Macintosh, OS/2, and even DOS have the ability to present the user with a list of available resources. The differences in this area really amount to the way that the operating system presents the data to the user. The network browser is doing the real browsing work in an NT network.

The browser service builds a list of the domains and servers that are available on the network. Computers view this list to see which computers they can access. For example, when a user issues a NET VIEW request from a command prompt or chooses Connect Network Drive from an Explorer menu, the Browser service generates the list of domains and servers that are active and available on the network. These lists are generated from browser servers.

Browser Server Roles

Just like domain control, the Browser service requires that some hierarchy be involved in the process of browsing the network. If the network is to maintain a consistent list, one machine needs to be responsible for the master list, but in browsing there are many more players than in the domain-control process. The process of browsing the network is a more rudimentary process, and it requires all PCs to be able to get it done quickly and efficiently. For that reason, there are many browser roles to be played:

- Master browser
- Domain master browser
- Backup browser
- Preferred master browser
- Potential browser

The following sections describe these roles.

Master Browser

The master browser receives announcements from computers within the workgroup or domain and provides a list of domain resources to the backup browsers. Announcements are made by network computers and members of the network segment (subnet) or domain to indicate what the computer's name is and what that computer has to offer. The master browser is responsible for collecting announcements for the entire segment (see Figure 12.1) and providing a list of resources to workstations and backup browsers.

Figure 12.1.
Master browsers are needed for each segment.

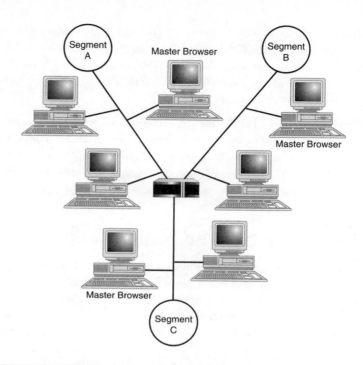

Why (Larger) Networks Need to Be Segmented

When a segment or subnet is mentioned, what's being discussed is the way that the logical and physical network is separated. To maintain an efficient network, administrators separate groups of network nodes into segments on diverse sides of a router. This setup allows network traffic to stay within the section of the physical network containing the resources that the nodes use most often. For example, if two groups of users use different resources but exist on the same busy network cable, you might consider dividing them into two segments and placing a router between them. The router allows cross traffic but leaves local traffic on the proper side.

By physically connecting each group of users on separate sides of the network, you create a dedicated area for the traffic to stay in. It's a bit like creating separate highways for two suburbs that normally travel down the same route. The fact that the different highways exist doesn't stop drivers from traveling to the other suburb, but it allows each group to have less traffic on the trip to and from their destination, instead of sharing.

If you're working with workgroups, you'll find that there's a master browser for each segment of the network. However, if you're dealing with a domain model, there's one master browser for the entire domain (all network segments), known as a *domain master browser*.

Domain Master Browser

In the hierarchy of the network-browsing task, the master browser is closest to the primary domain controller (PDC) of the process. In fact, the domain master browser is always the PDC for the domain. The domain master browser is responsible for keeping the list of network announcements for the entire domain without regard for the segment.

Domains have a unique responsibility for the browsing of the network and a uniquely qualified server for the job of helping users with network browsing. Because all network resources contained within the domain require that the PDC or BDC be involved in the process of authentication, those servers make a good logical choice as well as being required to perform the task of browser control. By combining browser responsibility with domain responsibility, some of the complications are removed for client machines.

This is not to imply that, just because you are running a domain model instead of a workgroup, there will only be one master browser, even if you have numerous subnets (see Figure 12.2). On the contrary, you still will have a master browser for each subnet. The master browsers in a domain are required to report to a domain master browser to allow the domain to perform at optimum.

Figure 12.2.
Domain master with subordinate master browsers.

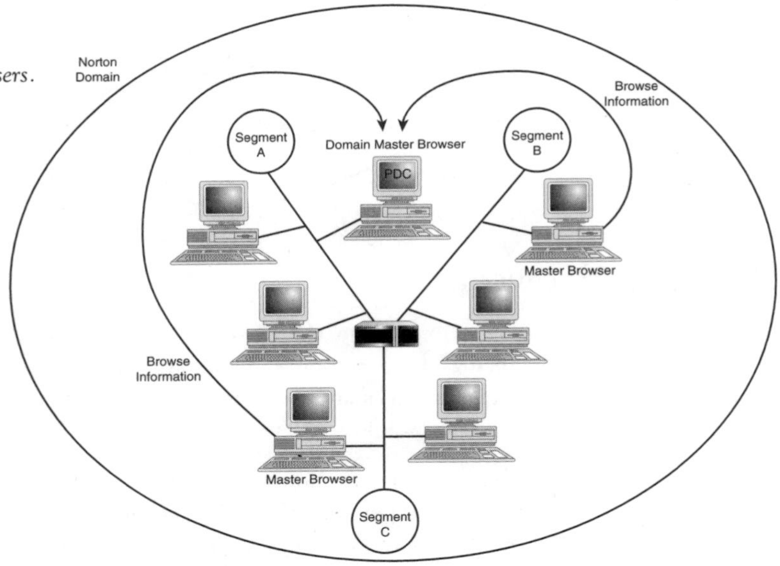

Backup Browser

In much the same way that backup domain controllers allow users to find available authentication easily, the backup browser allows network clients to find resources and servers without waiting for the master browser. Backup browsers are found throughout the network, on all segments and domains.

A backup browser maintains a copy of the browse list and distributes the list to computers in the domain upon request. All Windows NT Server domain controllers are automatically configured as backup browsers (see Figure 12.3). Windows NT Workstation-based and Server-based (non-domain controller) computers have the potential to be backup browsers if there are not already at least three Windows NT Server-based computers performing master browser and backup browser functions for the workgroup or domain.

Figure 12.3.
The backup domain controller's relationship to the domain.

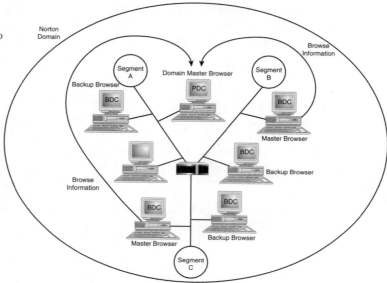

Potential Browser

From the fact that Microsoft network browsing occurs on both workgroups and domains, you can make the assumption that being a browser is not limited to NT servers. Microsoft workgroups exist in many different operating systems, and many of the operating systems that exist in those workgroups are capable of having browse responsibility.

Browse responsibility is given to a computer in the network when the first computer is created in any workgroup or domain. From that point on, the computers in the network continue an ongoing selection process to find the systems best suited to progressing the browsing process.

Initially, as a computer announces its presence on the network, it announces the operating system. In this way, it indicates its ability to participate in the browsing process. If the machine is capable of being elected to master browser or backup browser, the machine is said to be a *potential browser*.

Potential browsers include machines running any of the following operating systems or environments:

- Windows NT Server
- Windows NT Workstation
- Windows for Workgroups
- Windows 95

Preferred Master Browser

Direct human intervention is not needed to determine which server or workstation will be the master browser in a Microsoft network. The nodes on the network make that determination, if they are not otherwise directed. They do so by checking the network for potential browsers and electing the most qualified candidate from among them. The election process is covered shortly, but for now note that the *preferred master browser* is a browser server that has been configured to win browser elections and become the master browser (the fix is in).

The fact that it's a preferred master browser means that you must set the machine to win. It also implies that you aren't working in a domain model, because in a domain model, remember, the PDC must be the master browser.

To specify a computer as a preferred master browser, set the value of the `IsDomainMaster` parameter in the Windows NT Registry to either `True` or `Yes`. (This value will automatically be set to either `False` or `No`, even if the computer is currently the master browser.) This parameter is located in the Registry under the following key (see Figure 12.4):

`\HKEY_LOCAL_MACHINE\SYSTEM\CurrentControlSet\Services\Browser\Parameters`

Figure 12.4.
REGEDIT view of the change.

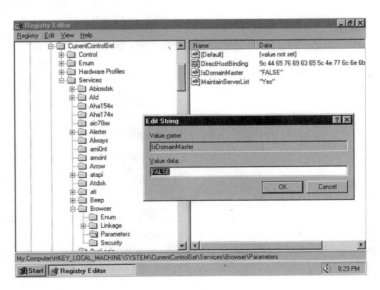

> **Warning:** When you use the program REGEDIT, you're editing the operating system at the Registry level. When making changes to items in the Registry, be *very* careful not to make changes that you're not sure of. This is particularly important when you're dealing with the Registry because you can make changes in the Registry that will permanently damage an NT installation, and require you to completely reinstall.

To make the necessary changes, follow these steps:

1. Start the REGEDIT program by choosing Start | Run, typing **REGEDIT32**, and clicking OK.

2. Once REGEDIT is open, click the plus sign beside each of the following items, in order, to arrive at the desired Registry entry. `HKEY_LOCAL_MACHINE`, `SYSTEM`, `CurrentControlSet`, `Services`, `Browser`, `Parameters`.

3. When you have finally selected the last item on the list in step 2, you'll see the item `IsDomainMaster` in the right pane (refer to Figure 12.4). Double-click `IsDomainMaster` and the dialog box for that item will appear.

4. Type **True** in the Value Data area and click OK.

5. Choose Registry | Exit from the menu.

6. Restart the machine to be certain that the changes take effect.

Election Process

In a master browser election, as in any other type of election, there are criteria that must be met. The master browser is chosen from a domain's servers through an election algorithm. The criteria for electing a master browser are evaluated in the following order:

- If the local computer's operating system criterion is greater than the requester's, the local computer wins. For example, a Windows NT-based computer will win over a Windows for Workgroups-based computer. The rating of each system is based on the operating systems that can be a browser, ranging from Windows NT Server 4.0 down to Windows for Workgroups.

- A higher operating system version number wins the election.

- Of the two, the computer that has been powered-on the longest wins.

- The server with the lowest alphabetical name wins. For example, a server named A will become a master browser over a server named X.

You can fix the election, as mentioned earlier, but barring the presence of a domain controller or a preferred master browser, this is how the network will establish a master browser.

Operating the Browser Environment

The operation of a browser environment is a bit like driving the tour cars at an amusement park. If you want to let the systems do the driving, they certainly will. For the most part, this should be fine. But if you find that you're constantly running into the car in front of you or that your users are becoming lost, you can take control.

There are a great number of operations that occur from the operating-system side that you should understand before you attempt to manipulate the process. The process does work fairly well on its own (keep your hands and feet in the car).

Synchronizing Master Browsers

When dealing with domain browsing, one unique problem is maintaining a consistent browse list on all segments. The domain can have only one domain master browser, but by their very nature domains often span subnets. The rules just say that every subnet must have its own master browser—each subnet *does* have a separate master browser, but the master browsers are not independent.

As mentioned earlier, in order to maintain a consistent browse list across the network subnets in a domain environment, the backup and master browsers must synchronize the browse list with the domain master browser. The process must occur across the subnets and throughout the domain.

It's important to realize that the master browsers in a workgroup environment don't synchronize. Only domains communicate in this way, because they must coordinate the domain over the entire enterprise.

The process runs in the following order:

1. Once every 15 minutes, each master browser sends a synchronized message to the domain master browser. The message it sends is a directed `MasterBrowserAnnouncement` datagram.

2. The master browsers automatically synchronize the browse list with the backup browsers.

Multiple-Domain and Multiple-Segment Networks

When you are dealing with multiple domains and segments in a network scheme, the browsing pot thickens considerably, but Microsoft networking will maintain the browsing. Each local subnet functions as an independent browsing entity with its own master browser and backup browsers because broadcasts, by default, don't pass through routers. Browser elections occur within each subnet.

In Figure 12.5, the domain master browser contains a browse list for all servers registered on subnets ACME, WILY, and RRUNNER.

Figure 12.5.
Subnet elections.

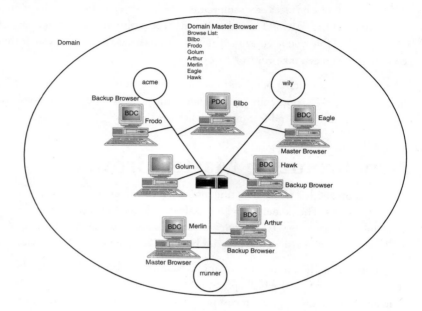

Domain master browsers are responsible for collecting computer name information used in maintaining multiple-segment browse lists of available computers in all domains.

These rules apply to local area networks (LANs) with multiple segments as well as wide area networks (WANs). You need to consider that most WANs consist of a separate segment for the users on each side of the WAN. By virtue of the distance that makes them "wide area" networks, WANs depend on the fact that each subnet will have a master browser. Consider the idea of all segments in a domain having to report to a single master browser across the wide area link—this could have a severe impact on network performance.

Browsing Multiple Domains

In a multiple-domain environment, clients have to be able to get lists of domains and servers within the domain. For clients to be able to access resources on other domains easily, Windows NT provides domain-browsing capabilities. Windows NT adds a new information level to NET VIEW that allows clients to retrieve a list of available domains from the master browser.

After becoming a master browser, a computer broadcasts a DomainAnnouncement every minute for the first 5 minutes. After the first 5 minutes, the master browser makes DomainAnnouncement broadcasts once every 15 minutes.

If a domain has not announced itself for three announcement periods, the domain will be removed from the list of domains. It's possible for a domain to appear in the browse list for up to 45 minutes (3 times 15 minutes) after the domain has gone down.

Although it might seem prudent to be able to change the time intervals at which these announcements are made, it's not possible. (This would be especially nice in a WAN environment, where browse information may not be necessary on a frequent basis and could cause unneeded traffic on an already slow line.)

Announcements

Master browsers receive `DomainAnnouncement` packets from other domains and place the specified domains in the master browser's local browse list. Upon becoming a master browser, a master browser can force domains to announce themselves. However, the master browser does this only if its domain list is empty, such as when a potential browser is promoted to master browser.

A `DomainAnnouncement` packet contains the following information:

- The name of the domain
- The name of the master browser for that domain
- An indication as to whether the browser computer is running Windows NT Workstation or Windows NT Server

If the browser computer is running Windows NT Server, the `DomainAnnouncement` also specifies whether that computer is the domain's PDC.

Failures and Ghosting

When considering the possible failings of a domain model over WANs, you must seriously consider the fact that NT PDCs are the domain master browsers. Because of that relationship, you may lose touch with functioning equipment in your WAN if the PDC fails (see Figure 12.6).

If the domain master browser fails, the master browsers will see only the servers located on the local subnet. This means that all servers that are not on the local subnet will eventually be removed from the browse list.

Because a domain master browser is also a PDC, an administrator can correct the failure by promoting a backup domain controller (BDC) to a PDC. A BDC can perform most PDC network tasks, such as validating logon requests, but it cannot promote itself to a PDC in the event of a PDC failure. The fact that this process is manual is now even a larger failing.

Figure 12.6.
Browser failure can spell big
trouble in a domain
environment.

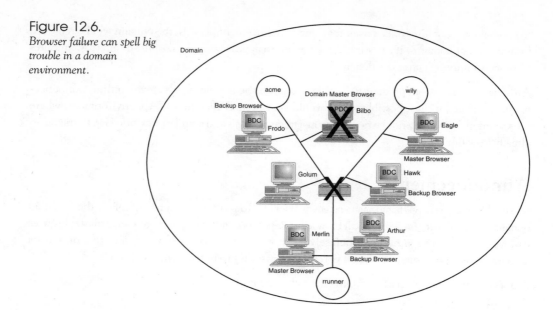

When this event occurs, users who have already gained access to the resources on diverse segments may or may not maintain contact with those resources. Even worse, they may not be warned of the loss of the resource, but it may be gone from their site when they attempt to save data to the lost site.

Browsing Multiple-Subnet TCP/IP

NT browsing and TCP/IP present a problem when combined. The first issue is that TCP/IP is by nature a protocol that communicates with its own naming conventions for its own domains. TCP/IP does not by nature carry NetBIOS naming, which NT browsing depends on.

The second issue is the fact that, for NT browsing to occur, a great deal of broadcasting must also occur. In a TCP/IP subnet in which domains are separated by routers, broadcast problems can arise because IP broadcasts don't pass through routers.

To resolve this issue, Microsoft has gone to great lengths to create both a low-tech and a high-tech solution. The low-tech solution is an LMHOSTS file; the more technical solution is a WINS server.

Tip: If your router can forward NetBIOS name broadcasts, it's not necessary to use the LMHOSTS file or WINS.

The Windows Internet Name Service (WINS)

If you understand the concept of TCP/IP domain naming, the Windows Internet Name Service (WINS) won't seem like any great leap to you. The thing that you must keep in mind, though, is that this type of domain isn't a TCP/IP domain at all. The names that must be managed here are NetBIOS names that are understood by PC networks—Microsoft networks in particular.

In a classic Internet domain model, the name mcp.com would mean nothing to TCP/IP unless you could reach a domain name server on the Internet to translate the name to an IP address such as 102.43.54.34 (the IP address of a host machine). By the same token, a TCP/IP installation of NT WINS resolves NetBIOS names to the IP address of the server for which you are browsing (see Figure 12.7).

Figure 12.7.
WINS browsing.

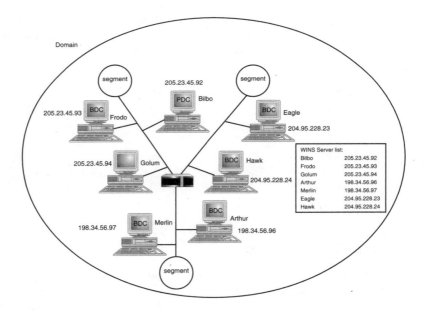

The Windows Internet Name Service resolves NetBIOS names to IP addresses so that datagrams can be sent to the targeted computer. Implementing WINS eliminates the need to configure the LMHOSTS file or to enable UDP port 137 (NetBIOS name service broadcasts—described shortly).

Not all WANs will have problems browsing. Some routers can be configured to forward specific types of broadcasts while filtering out others.

All NetBIOS over TCP/IP (NBT) broadcasts are sent to UDP port 137, which is defined as NBT Name Service. This usage is defined by Request for Comment (RFC) 1001 and 1002 (Internet Specifications). Routers normally filter out these frames because they're sent to the hardware and subnet broadcast addresses. However, some routers allow all frames sent to this particular UDP port (which is used only by NBT) to be forwarded.

As a result, the browser looks like it's on one big subnet. All domains and computers within the subnets will be seen by all systems, including Windows for Workgroups-based computers.

Using WINS requires these conditions:

- WINS must be configured on at least one computer running Windows NT Server with a TCP/IP internetwork.
- Clients must be WINS-enabled. WINS clients can be configured with Windows NT, Windows 95, Windows for Workgroups (running TCP/IP-32), LAN Manager 2.2c client, and Microsoft Network Client software (provided on the Windows NT Server 4.0 CD-ROM).

Non-WINS clients still require the LMHOSTS file to perform WAN browsing, even if WINS has been implemented in the domain.

> **Tip:** If you have Windows for Workgroup clients running Microsoft TCP/IP-32, you must use the modified VREDIR.386 file supplied on the Microsoft Windows NT Server CD-ROM to participate in WAN browsing.

The LMHOSTS File

Again, comparable to the TCP/IP Internet domain world, the LMHOSTS file has a counterpart. In the Internet world, you may be familiar with a static list of hosts available on the IP network that consists of an IP address followed by a domain name (for example, 204.95.229.61 lmbmicro.com). In the TCP/IP world, this file is called a HOSTS *file*. The HOSTS file still works in NT for TCP/IP domains; the difference is that NetBIOS references won't work in this file.

Clients not configured to use WINS require an LMHOSTS file configuration with the IP address and NetBIOS name of the domain controllers (either PDC or BDC) located on other subnets (see Figure 12.8). This is required even if a WINS server has been configured in the domain, because NetBIOS name broadcasts won't go through routers. The LMHOSTS file is located under \winnt_root\SYSTEM32\DRIVERS\ETC and is cached when TCP/IP is initialized.

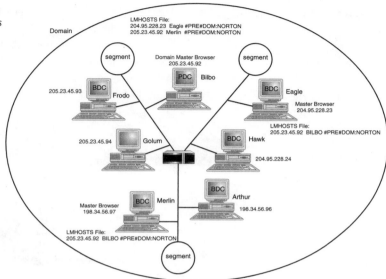

Figure 12.8.
Example of LMHOSTS *files across subnets.*

To implement communication between subnets and the domain master browser, the administrator must configure the LMHOSTS file with the NetBIOS names and IP addresses of all browsers.

To ensure that the master browser for each subnet can access the domain's PDC, the PDC for each domain must exist in the LMHOSTS file on each master browser. The same requirement exists for the BDCs. Each subnet's master browser's LMHOSTS file should contain the following information:

- IP address and NetBIOS name of the preferred master browser
- The domain name preceded by the #PRE#DOM: tags

For example:

```
204.95.120.34 BILBO #PRE#DOM:NORTON
```

Here, 204.95.120.34 is the IP address of the domain master browser in the NORTON domain, and the NetBIOS name of that browser is BILBO.

To guarantee that the PDC can request the local browse list from the subnet's master browser, TCP/IP and all other WAN transports must cache the client's IP address for a period of time.

Hiding Items from the Browser

It's possible to share items in an NT network and not want to have them viewed by all of the users who can browse the network. The problem that must be considered is that it's not possible to hide the server NetBIOS names in the browse list. A point that was made in earlier chapters about administrative shares should be mentioned again when discussing browsing the network. It's possible to hide some shared items from the browsing eyes of users on the network. By adding a dollar sign ($) to the end of any share name, you can create an item that can be attached from any workstation, but the item won't show in a browse list. An example of a hidden share name (Admin$) and the presentation to the client can be seen in Figure 12.9.

Figure 12.9.
Server shares and the user's Explorer window.

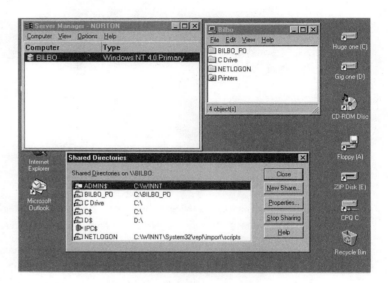

Summary

The concepts behind network browsing are not new, by any means. Two forms that we are concerned with in this chapter are NetBIOS and TCP/IP domains, because they relate to the NT installations that we run today. NT has made a great effort to coexist in both the inter-company and Internet worlds, and network browsing presents some large challenges in that area.

The basic concepts that you need to take with you when dealing with Microsoft network browsing involve the fact that, without network browsing, computers on a greater network have no way of publishing their shared peripherals. Clients and services have no way of finding needed resources.

Unlike NT domain control, NT network browsing does have the redundant features necessary to maintain network browsing in the event of a failure. Elections and preferred master browsers allow the administrator of workgroups and LAN segments to continue in the event of a master browser failure. But within a domain model, browsing can be even less fault-tolerant than domains if the PDC should fail.

Finally, even though TCP/IP provides no smooth transport for NetBIOS, NT has created both the LMHOSTS and WINS solutions to allow the large WAN to maintain a global browse list.

13

Remote Access Services (RAS)

Peter Norton™

The ability to gain access to the company network from a remote site has become a necessity instead of a luxury in recent years. The fact that so many employees have equipment of their own and want to use it to connect to the office network has made it necessary for the network to stretch outside the office walls. Company connections to the Internet and better use of the company network for the distribution of employee information has made the network an indispensable tool from anywhere.

Windows NT has provided a utility for the task of external connections along with the basic operating system through the Remote Access Service (RAS—pronounced *razz*). Windows NT Server and NT Workstation have both been made to be capable of using RAS. Through the RAS connection, NT is capable of creating connections to users in the outside world, other servers, and outside networks. The basic premise is to make the external connection the equivalent of a network interface card (NIC) in the server.

The only difference between NT Server RAS and NT Workstation RAS is the number of connections that are supported in the product. NT Workstation supports only one connection to RAS at any given moment; NT Server supports up to 256 connection to the server through RAS. The reason for this difference is the difference in the need to connect to the product. NT Workstation includes the product simply to allow a user to connect to his workstation from home or any remote site. Server RAS needs to support the entire user base of the network.

The limit is somewhat less when the connections are NetBIOS-based because of the limitations of NetBIOS. NetBIOS only allows one system to have 250 names registered on the network at any given moment.

NT uses RAS not only for connections coming into the server from users wanting to gain access to the network, but also for the ability to connect to other servers or network services. The service comes in two basic flavors: RAS client and RAS server. The RAS client is used by NT to connect to any other RAS server or any server platform that shares protocol support and a SLIP or PPP connection (see Figure 13.1). An example of such a connection would be an Internet service provider. If you keep in mind that RAS is making the modem (or other connection method) into a NIC, it makes the process easier to understand.

Figure 13.1.
RAS client and RAS server relationships to the network.

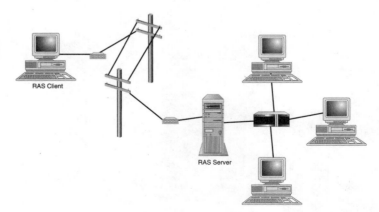

Connection Types and Considerations

RAS connections come in many different varieties beyond the typical dial-in user who needs to use the company network at home. RAS can also be used to connect corporate networks or connect the LAN to a public network such as the Internet; it isn't just a dial-up service.

The breakdown of applications that can be used across RAS is related more to the interfaces that will connect with RAS than with the particular operating system. Once a communications method has been established, any application using the following interfaces will function with the RAS connection:

- **Windows Sockets (WinSock).** Along with the Internet craze came the Windows Socket Services API, a programming interface that allowed application writers to create applications that would use the WinSock connection to communicate across the network.

- **NetBIOS.** The basic network-connection application, created along with the Microsoft and IBM PC networks of old.

- **Mailslots.** The message-delivery system used for announcing and locating network services and resources.

- **Win32 and LANMAN API.** The programming interface used to call the functions of Windows NT, Windows 95, and LAN Manager.

- **Remote Procedure Call (RPC).** This is a device used by some network applications to call on the services of other computers on the network.

- **Named Pipes.** The communications method used to communicate between remote and local processes.

If you are not creating applications (or involved in the selection of those who create your applications), this grocery list could be shortened to say "Most network programs will run fine." Again, the concept is that almost anything that would function through an in-house network connection should work through a RAS connection. If you understand that idea, that should be the last that you have to concern yourself with it.

Dial-Up Networking Considerations

Before planning and installing a RAS server for the public to use for dial-up connections, you need to consider the practicality of such a plan. There are many different ways to connect users to the local LAN—the RAS method is just one of them.

The two basic forms of dial-up networking are

- Remote node
- Remote control

The following sections discuss both forms.

Remote Node

This is the form of dial-up networking that RAS uses to connect your users. The user connects to the system as if the modem he uses in his PC at home is the NIC, and the phone company is really just the network cable connecting his equipment to the wall.

The advantage of a remote node connection is the fact that the remote user is making full use of the PC that he has at his site. The interface is almost like the network interface that he uses in the office, because the relationship between his PC at home and the LAN is basically the same as it is on his office PC. He's simply using a long-distance NIC called a *modem*.

The disadvantage of a remote node connection is the fact that he's using a very slow "NIC" when using a modem for that purpose. Even the slowest local network connections today run at 10,000,000 bits per second (bps)—not including ARCNET and very old Token Ring. Modems today, even on the cutting edge, run at 57,600bps.

What this really boils down to is that users can't run applications that are based on the server from across a remote node connection. For example, if you run a shared installation of Microsoft Excel that's housed on the file server, remote users will need to install Excel on their remote PCs in order to use the product.

Because of this condition, you may want to give users different logon accounts or logon scripts, based on the fact that they're logging on over a RAS connection. This avoids having users start processes that will lock up or severely slow down the remote node connection.

Remote Control

Products such as PC Anywhere, WinGate, and Carbon Copy use remote control connections. The user dials into the company and connects to a machine that's dedicated to her use while she is dialed in (see Figure 13.2). This machine forms a special connection to the PC that has dialed in, allowing the remote user (B) to actually use the PC (A) that's on the LAN site. Once the connection is made between the remote machine (B) and local machine (A), the local machine's screen appears on the remote machine, and the remote keyboard and mouse control the local machine.

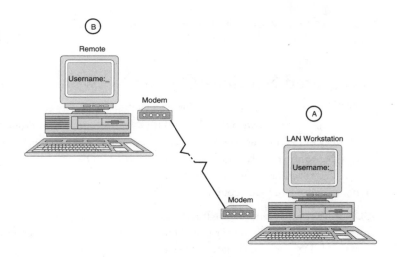

Figure 13.2.
*Remote control of system A
(local) from system B
(remote).*

The advantage of this relationship is that it allows the remote user to achieve LAN speeds while using applications that exist on the LAN. Because the user is actually using a PC that's on the LAN, the response time is equal to that of the LAN. The only information that's being passed between the remote (B) and local (A) machines is the screen, keyboard, and mouse activity.

The disadvantage of this type of relationship is that the user isn't really utilizing the PC resources at her own site. She is also costing the company two PCs per user while she is connected.

Network-to-Network Considerations

Communication between networks, whenever they are not contained in the same campus area or building, are considered to be wide area network (WAN) connections. These connections can also be made with RAS. RAS allows for three types of WAN connections:

- Public switched telephone networks (PSTN)—also known as common phone lines
- Integrated services digital networks (ISDN)
- X.25

The following sections describe these types of connections.

Public Switched Telephone Network (PSTN)

Wide area communications using PSTN or common telephone lines have two great advantages: cost and ease of use. Because common telephone lines have been around for so long and are available in any location, they're extremely cost-effective. No special setup is needed to arrange for the installation of these lines. NT RAS is capable of using practically any phone line that you can speak over.

The later section "Modem and Phone Line Considerations" provides more coverage of phone line choices.

Integrated Services Digital Network (ISDN)

ISDN connections can be thought of as extremely clean modem connections—frankly, because they are. The difference between a PSTN and ISDN connection is the *digital* in the ISDN connection. ISDN line connections use the digital phone network to make connections from 64Kbps to 128Kbps. This is due to the fact that an ISDN connection contains two 64Kbps lines called *B channels* that can be used together or split into different tasks. Some businesses may use the second B channel for digital telephone or video communications.

ISDN RAS connections require ISDN modems on each side and are comparable to a PSTN modem connection. One system must run a client session while the other server runs a RAS server session from that ISDN port. The major drawback is the cost of this type of service. Prices range from $30.00 to $200.00 a month and include a minute-to-minute charge as well.

X.25 Connections

When you hear that X.25 communications can be used to connect networks using RAS, it sounds like we're discussing another form of phone line. Actually, X.25 is a communications protocol standard used with many different types of communication lines. The idea behind X.25 is to create a reliable form of communication based on some less-than-reliable forms of communication. From time to time, this can even include common phone lines.

X.25 involves the way that the equipment speaks rather than the media or language it speaks. An X.25 network is what's called a *packet-switched network*. There are many different ways of communicating data—we could write another book discussing this one—but, simply put, data is sent in packets that can be assembled and disassembled on each end. This is helpful in a less-reliable communications method because, if packets arrive out of order or jumbled, X.25 is capable of reassembling them. The types of lines involved in an X.25 network can be point-to-point like phone lines or through public networks like a frame relay cloud.

A *frame relay cloud* is a shared switch that delivers connectivity through a connection that's more like a party line than a direct connection. It's referred to as a *cloud* because the client system is connected to a system that consists of several possible paths for communication. The exact path isn't always the same and isn't meant to be. The communications may follow several different paths, but it will be delivered. Thus it's a bit like putting the information into a cloud and having faith that it will arrive.

PSTN Protocol Support

ISDN and X.25 connections are given special consideration in a RAS connection. Both ISDN and X.25 are treated as if they're as reliable as an Ethernet connection. NT gives these connections a direct data feed across the WAN as if they were directly connected to the LAN. PSTN connections, on the other hand, require that special protocols be used in order to create a reliable connection.

Two protocols are supported for these connections:

- Serial line Internet protocol (SLIP)
- Point-to-point protocol (PPP)

Both protocols are variations of the original SLIP protocol developed for UNIX systems to use for serial TCP/IP communications. SLIP isn't used as often and has been replaced in most applications by the hybrid PPP. Serial communications protocols allow the operating system to use asynchronous communications (communications through a serial port and an asynchronous modem), as if the modem were a network interface card.

Because PPP is the more complete version of the serial communications protocol, it's the preferred protocol when a choice exists. Because of the rising popularity of the Internet and asynchronous communications, most operating systems offer PPP connectivity as part of the base operating system. PPP isn't limited to the original TCP/IP protocol, however. Current PPP connections to an NT RAS server can support most protocols that are supported by the NT operating system, including TCP/IP, IPX/SPX, NetBEUI, DECnet, and AppleTalk protocols.

Security

Once you open your internal network to the outside world, security becomes a much deeper issue. It's a bit like running a mail-order business versus running a department store. If the front door is open, anyone can at least try to come in. With the mail-order business, no one even knows the door exists.

Beyond the basic security considerations discussed in Chapter 10, "User Account Creation and Management," you must also be aware of the following things:

- Is your data number published? This may sound silly, but many people don't realize that their data line numbers are published as phone numbers for the business along with all the other numbers associated with the business. Unless you specifically request that the number be unpublished, you may get unwanted calls.
- RAS allows you to enable auditing of connections. Do it.

- A RAS server can be configured to call a user back at his location. The caller calls in and identifies himself to the system; the system then hangs up the line and calls the user back at a predetermined number. If all users are called back at designated numbers, it becomes very difficult to gain access, even if you have pirated an account and a password.

- Will RAS users be allowed to access the entire network or just the computer that they dial into? You have the option of stopping RAS users from accessing the network. This strategy allows administrators to make resources available on a particular server without opening the network to security risks.

Installation

The installation of RAS is a bit different from that of other products that you'll install on your NT server. You really need to be prepared before you install the product. (It seems that you should be prepared for any new install, and I don't mean to say that you shouldn't. But RAS needs information that you won't be able to skim over, making changes later.)

Before you start the installation, you need to know the following information:

- System requirements
- RAS communications device you'll be using, and the settings for both sides
- Protocols you want to make available

Requirements

Installing RAS as part of an NT server has specific requirements, just like any other addition to your server. The minimum additional needs for your server are as follows:

- 2MB of hard drive space
- A compatible communications device (see the HCL for compatible devices, or Appendix A, "NT Server 4.0 Hardware Compatibility List")

Protocol Support

The RAS installation supports the following protocols:

- TCP/IP
- IPX
- NetBEUI

If the protocol you want to use for your dial-in clients is already installed on the server machine (as part of LAN-based networking) when you install RAS, support will automatically be added in RAS for that protocol. So, if at all possible, you should install all protocols that you want to use prior to installing RAS on the server.

When you are considering the protocol choices that you will support for RAS, you need to consider the strength of the different protocols and what you are wanting to deliver to your client. Each protocol has its strength.

> **Looking Ahead:** Chapter 15, "Surviving in a Multi-Protocol World," covers each of the
> NT-supported protocols in depth.

TCP/IP

TCP/IP is a very common choice for remote connectivity. The reason for its popularity in this application is the fact that it is necessary for many of the Internet utilities to function. It's also the default choice for protocol for NT. TCP/IP provides a very controlled and logical addressing scheme. It's a routable protocol that allows users to gain access not only to the items in the NT network, but also to the many other sources that supports the TCP/IP suite of protocols.

TCP/IP is a very popular choice—but it's not the only choice. The other protocols have their strengths, and RAS is one place that shows those strengths.

Remote Access Services for NT can control TCP/IP settings for clients in three different ways. During RAS installation, you will see the RAS Server TCP/IP Configuration dialog box shown in Figure 13.3. This dialog box allows the administrator to determine how RAS clients will use TCP/IP upon dial-in.

Figure 13.3.
RAS server TCP/IP
configuration.

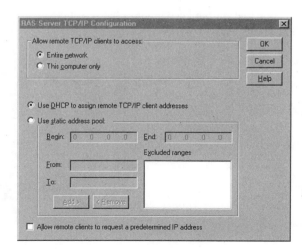

These are the TCP/IP options from which you can choose in the dialog box:

- **Use DHCP to Assign Remote TCP/IP Client Addresses.** This choice refers to allowing a central machine to assign IP addresses for all clients that dial in. (See Chapter 21, "TCP/IP Networking," for more information on DHCP.)

- **Use Static Address Pool.** By selecting this option, you elect to assign IP addresses to the dial-in clients. But with this choice you need to enter the range of addresses that you would like given to the clients as they attach.

- **Allow Remote Clients to Request a Predetermined IP Address.** This choice assumes that all clients that dial in have a valid IP address.

IPX

The IPX protocol is used by a large portion of the networking community because they have NetWare-based network schemes that depend on it for basic use. But the strength of this protocol for RAS is not just the fact that it's popular. If you don't need TCP/IP support for your remote clients to function, IPX makes a strong choice because it's a very easily managed protocol.

IPX doesn't require that the administrator create a separate address for each workstation. IPX uses a combination of the hardware addresses supplied by the users' machines and the network address to dynamically create addresses for all users.

IPX is also a very fast protocol to use over dial-up because of the very nature of the protocol. IPX sends the signal that it has to deliver without regard to its successful delivery, so no signal is wasted on maintaining or tracking packets.

Remote Access Services for NT can control IPX settings for clients in four different ways. During RAS installation, you will see the RAS Server IPX Configuration dialog box shown in Figure 13.4. This dialog box allows the administrator to determine how RAS clients are assigned IPX network numbers upon dial-in. But keep in mind that IPX network numbers are not nearly as important to control as TCP/IP.

Figure 13.4.
RAS server IPX configuration.

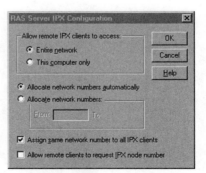

These are the IPX network addressing options from which you can choose in the dialog box:

- **Allocate Network Numbers Automatically.** An IPX network number not currently in use is determined by the RAS server and assigned to the RAS client.

- **Allocate Network Numbers.** Ranges of IPX network numbers can be given to a RAS server for assignment to clients. Allocated IPX address pools are useful if you want to identify RAS clients on the network by number. Provide the beginning network number in the From box. RAS automatically determines the number of available ports and calculates the end number.

- **Assign Same Network Number to All IPX Clients.** Selecting this check box reduces the size of RIP announcements on the network. If this box is selected, only one network number is added to your routing table for all active RAS clients. If this box is not selected, a network number is added to your routing table for each active RAS client.

Looking Ahead: RIP is one protocol used by routers to dynamically exchange routing information. After installing RIP for IP and RIP for IPX, NT will route these protocols and dynamically exchange routing information with other routers running the RIP protocol. This subject is covered in Chapter 15, along with many networking protocol terms used here.

- **Allow Remote Clients to Request IPX Node Number.** Select this check box to allow the remote client to request its own IPX node number, rather than use the node number provided by the RAS server. Clients will rarely make such a request, but if the security of certain applications requires a specific MAC address as part of the node number, they may need it. (See Chapter 15 for info on MAC addresses.) Allowing remote clients to specify their own node numbers is a potential security threat to your network. Choosing its own node number allows a client to impersonate a previously connected client and access network resources accessed by the other client.

NetBEUI

The NetBEUI protocol is really picked on in the world of protocols because it's very simplistic. This protocol doesn't route well and isn't a robust protocol for large networks. But because it's so simple it makes a nice choice for RAS connections that need connectivity only to gain access to file or print resources.

Because NetBEUI is the simplest of the NetBIOS-based protocols, it makes a strong choice for RAS connections. It doesn't concern itself with routing, because it can't route.

Note: An odd behavior of NT and many Microsoft products that's related to NetBEUI is the fact that, if you're having problems with finding (browsing) network resources, installing the NetBEUI protocol on the local or RAS clients may make browsing run smoothly. If you're having browsing issues, you have a greater issue that should be explored, but NetBEUI may get you by in a pinch.

Modem and Phone Line Considerations

There are two basic types of modem that you can order for a RAS installation: asynchronous (for PSTN) and ISDN. The items that you need to consider when installing these products must begin long before you sit down to install your RAS server, as described in the following sections.

PSTN

Public switched telephone networks (PSTN), also known as common phone lines, are going to be used by the majority of the users that you'll encounter. But the considerations that must be made when installing them are anything but easy. The fact that the technology is so old means that there are many options and possible configurations. Let's take a look at some of those considerations.

Phone Lines

When you begin to order phone lines for a PSTN RAS installation, or any asynchronous modem installation, you need to understand what type of line is required. The line that's required for an asynchronous modem isn't special. As a matter of fact, special phone lines are exactly what you *don't* want. When ordering a phone line to use for asynchronous connections, you need a standard voice-grade line.

Tip: Often, you can order the line by telling the phone company that you need a fax line installed. This avoids a great deal of confusion on the front end. Even in 1997, the phone companies in many areas don't understand modem use.

These lines should not be part of any phone system that passes through an in-house switch before the phone company, Centrex system, or any phone system that doesn't allow a standard telephone to operate. These lines often require a special handset to gain connection.

Some Centrex systems allow for a standard (home grade) phone to be plugged in and used—they may even allow for fax transmission. But be aware that because Centrex systems are for voice use only, the fastest asynchronous modem connection that you can achieve through Centrex is 9600bps. If clients are on a Centrex system, they may not even know that the modem line they're using is Centrex—but they'll complain that they're only achieving speeds of 9600bps or less. Some Centrex systems have been set up to perform better—allowing for a common analog phone or modem to connect at speeds up to 28.8 or 33.6. The chances are that the system you install should be investigated before you count on such speeds, however.

Asynchronous Modems

When choosing a modem for home use or to connect your workstation to the Internet, you have a different set of variables to use than with RAS server modems. RAS server modems will receive calls on a regular basis and must be capable of speaking to a larger variety of modems. They also don't have to worry about things like receiving voice calls, or possibly even sending and receiving faxes.

Modem selection can be as complicated as you like, but for the moment let's create a grocery list of important items for a RAS server modem:

- **Speed.** 33.6Kbps or greater speed is a must for RAS connectivity. Because users are counting on this connection as their NIC, you must provide as much speed as possible. A 33.6Kbps modem is also most likely capable of achieving the same speed as the user modem after dial-in.

- **Error correction and compression standards.** As important as the speed of the modem in these installations is the ability of the modem to correct and compress data so that much higher speeds can be achieved. If both 36.6Kbps modems can meet the v.34 standard for compression and error correction, speeds of up to 115Kbps can be achieved.

- **Upgradability.** One of the greatest threats to a modem pool is the fact that the users are constantly appearing with new modems and new standards. The modem pool, on the other hand, must continue to service this user base over enough time to recover from the investment. Some modem manufacturers make it possible to upgrade your modems to the latest set of standards through software downloads and flash ROM chips on the modem. If you are able to do this, you may avoid having to buy new modem equipment for a much greater time span.

- **External versus internal.** External and internal modems are going to perform the job equally well on a daily basis. The issues that you need to concern yourself with are the number of ports that you have available and the serviceability of these modems. For RAS server installations, my preference is external modems. An external modem allows you to change the modem when service is needed without turning off the server. External modems offer control lights on the surface that allow me to see what's happening at the modem level during failed communications. And finally, an external modem can be moved to another configuration if the server is upgraded or if a multi-port serial card is added.

ISDN

Integrated services digital networks (ISDN), oddly enough, should make life a bit easier as far as the number of options is concerned. But you're going to find that the number of new things you have to understand is going to grow here.

ISDN Lines

In the last two years, ISDN lines have become readily available in most metropolitan areas, but you may find that you have trouble getting connected through ISDN. To order an ISDN line, you need to contact your local phone line provider. Yes, the same one that provides your standard voice line.

Microsoft is firmly on the ISDN bandwagon, with a Web site location that will help you gather the phone numbers and/or contacts necessary to get an ISDN line:

```
http://www.microsoft.com/windows/getisdn
```

This site will not only help you understand what ISDN is, but will actually place a request for you with a local provider so that you'll be contacted.

Getting a bad ISDN line is a bit like getting a bad-sounding CD player. It's rare to find that you have a bad line when using ISDN, primarily because the phone companies have hung their hats on ISDN as the solution to all your modem problems. In many areas, the phone company won't help you with a standard phone line connection to a modem if you can use the line for voice communications. Instead, they'll suggest that ISDN is the only supported media for data.

The real issue with ordering an ISDN line is that there are many different types of ISDN connections being offered across the country. It can be like saying, "I want a slice of pizza"—what you get may not even be close to what you anticipated. The best advice is to contact your ISDN modem vendor and get the line-ordering instructions. The phone companies and the modem vendors realize that this is tough, so they're attempting to standardize the process with items like ISDN Ordering Codes (IOC) and EZ-ISDN, which specify a set of parameters.

ISDN Modem Considerations

ISDN modems are sold by most popular modem manufacturers. The variations on the modems are many; ask yourself what you need to get from the modem, or you'll get an elephant gun to go squirrel hunting. Because of the strict definition of ISDN, there aren't as many variations on the ISDN modem that you will need to control. Be aware of these items, though:

- NT RAS compatibility

- U Interface (integrated NT-1 device), a commonly used interface that allows you to connect directly to the ISDN interface

- External versus internal (see the earlier asynchronous modem list)

Server Installation Steps

Before you can install RAS on the NT server, you must first be logged onto the server as an administrator account, and it would be best if you closed all open programs.

You have to restart the server when this process is finished, so performing this process on an active file and print server is not a good idea. Try to install the package either on a dedicated server or during off-hours when the server is not being used. At a minimum, you should back up the server's file structure and warn the users that the server will be inaccessible during the next couple of hours. Warn the users again ahead of time and disconnect the users before starting the install.

Tip: Whenever changes are made to a server that's operational, it's best to assume that the server will not recover. Prepare for disaster before you install anything—not only packages that need a restart, but all software installations and certainly all hardware installations. I've witnessed many thousands of dollars lost due to a brave/foolish administrator's desire to put on just "this one small thing." Just as any surgery can result in death, any server installation can result in a reinstall.

Once you have secured the server, install any modem or X.25 PAD devices that you may have to install in the system.

Note: Packet assemblers/disassemblers (PADs) are comparable to a modem in X.25 networks. X.25 PAD boards can be used in place of modems when provided with a compatible COM driver.

Follow these steps:

1. Open the Network control panel and click the Services tab (see Figure 13.5).

2. Click the Add button to open the Select Network Service dialog box.

3. In the Network Service list, select Remote Access Service (see Figure 13.6); then click OK.

Figure 13.5.
The Network control panel
with the Services tab
selected.

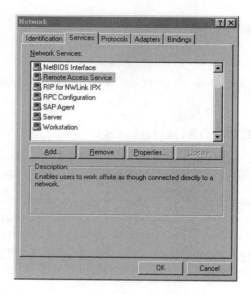

Figure 13.6.
Services available from the
Network control panel.

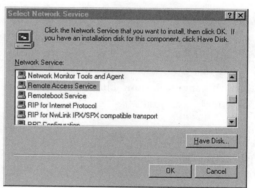

4. You will now be asked to tell NT the source directory for the RAS files. If the drive letter and directory listed are no longer the source of your NT installation files, replace the entry with the proper syntax. Here are a couple of examples:

    ```
    D:\i386
    ```

    ```
    \\resources-server\installs\NT-server\i386
    ```

5. Click Continue. The Add RAS Device dialog box appears.

6. Under the heading RAS Capable Devices, you'll see any modems or X.25 devices installed prior to starting the RAS install. Select the first RAS device you want to add and click OK.

> **Tip:** If you have modems or X.25 PAD devices that you would like to install now, you can choose Install Modem or Install X.25 Pad from this dialog box. However, I would strongly recommend that you install these items *before* you start this process. It will make the RAS installation process flow more smoothly and help you to separate problems into categories.

7. Once you have selected the first device, a Remote Access Setup dialog box appears (see Figure 13.7). If you want to add another device, click Add to reopen the Add RAS Device dialog box from step 6.

Figure 13.7.
The Remote Access Setup dialog box.

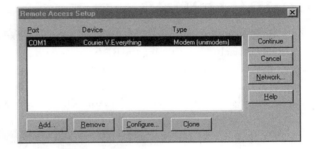

8. You can now configure the devices that have been selected in the Remote Access Setup dialog box:

   • To configure the options for the selected port, click the Configure button. The options are fairly simple: Dial Out Only, Receive Calls Only, Dial Out and Receive Calls. Make a selection and click OK to configure that port.

   • Clicking the Network button allows you to configure the behavior and availability of the RAS network protocols. There are two basic sections: Dial Out Protocols and Server Settings. Server settings options are covered in the earlier "Protocols" section of this chapter. The Dial Out Protocols option simply controls which protocols you'll allow your RAS dial-out client to use.

9. Once you have made the configuration changes you want, click Continue in the Remote Access Setup dialog box.

10. If you have selected to allow IPX to function, you'll be asked whether to propagate certain NetBIOS broadcasts (see Figure 13.8). If you intend to have NWLink clients, click Yes; otherwise, click No (chances are that if you've been given this choice you should choose Yes).

Figure 13.8.
The IPX RIP question.

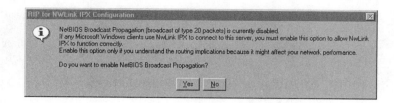

11. The installation is now complete; you must restart the server in order to use RAS.

Administration

The administration of a RAS server can be done from any trusted administrator account in the domain and from any NT machine containing the RAS server service. RAS administration is like administering any resource. The primary controls regard the permissions and activity on the shared ports. This control of the RAS server is done through an application called Remote Access Admin (see Figure 13.9), found in the Start menu under Administrative Tools (common).

Figure 13.9.
Remote Access Admin.

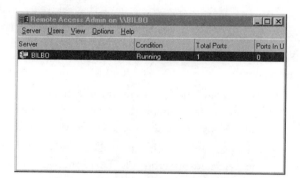

The first choice that you must make to manage a RAS server is which RAS server to manage. This choice is fairly simple if you have only one RAS server—it's the only choice presented when you open the Remote Access Admin application. If you want to manage a different server, choose Server and then Select Domain or Server. A list of domains will be presented, along with the other servers in your current domain. Select the domain or specific servers you want to manage; then simply click OK to complete the change.

COM Port Control

To control the availability and use of the communications ports in the RAS server (see Figure 13.10), you need to choose the Communication Ports option on the Server menu in Remote Access Admin.

Figure 13.10.
The Communication Ports dialog box.

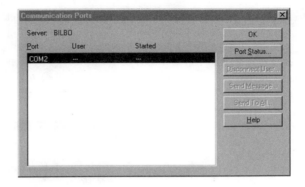

The choices here involve the status and control of the ports that have been installed in the RAS server machine. Choosing the Port Status button allows you to view the current state of the selected port (see Figure 13.11). The port statistics in this dialog box will help you to determine whether the port is functioning.

Figure 13.11.
The Port Status dialog box.

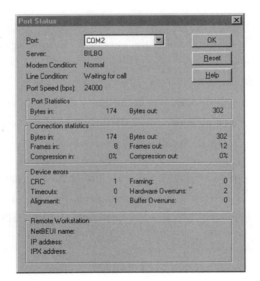

User Control

On the Users menu in the Remote Access Admin application, you'll find simple commands that allow you to control which users can dial in and how users must establish connections. When you consider the idea of restricting dial-in, forcing dial-back, and other security measures, this is the starting point, from a RAS point of view.

The Remote Access Permissions dialog box appears when you select Permissions from the User menu (see Figure 13.12). This section allows the administrator to specify which users are allowed to dial in.

Figure 13.12.
The Remote Access
Permissions dialog box.

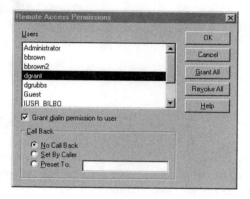

To manage user permissions, follow these steps:

1. In the Remote Access Admin application, choose Users | Permissions.

2. The Users list shows all the users in the domain; select the user whose settings you want to change.

3. Select the option Grant Dialin Permission to User.

4. In the Call Back section of the dialog box, you have one of three choices:

   • No Call Back won't call the user back.

   • Set by Caller allows the user to establish a call back from the RAS server. This choice isn't a security measure, but is most often a cost-saving measure that allows the user to have the server dial back at a chargeable number.

   • Preset To allows the administrator to set a predetermined number from which the user will call. By clicking in Preset To and typing a phone number, you're establishing that every time this user calls in for remote service, he or she will be called back at the specified number.

5. The remaining choices in the dialog box are really two:

   • **Grant All.** This selection is equivalent to clicking each user in the domain or workgroup and choosing to grant dial-in permission to that user. This is not a good idea unless you have considered all the security angles and headaches of allowing everyone to dial in.

   • **Revoke All.** This selection removes the ability to dial in from all users. It makes for a very good method of undoing what was granted by the previous choice.

6. After making the changes you want, click OK and your changes will take effect.

Summary

The Remote Access Service allows NT to open up the server to the world, but it also opens the doors to some unwanted creatures. If you're going to run a RAS server, you need to consider the consequences of the additional security risk.

This chapter has covered many forms of communications that may have been new to you—and some old friends: public switched telephone networks (PSTN), also known as common phone lines; integrated services digital networks (ISDN), for cleaner digital connections from home or small office; an X.25 network that's a form of packet-switched network. Each of these forms of communications has a strength and reason to be chosen over the others.

The installation of the RAS server service is very simple if you take the time to consider the steps before you start—just like the installation of the operating system. Remember the pointers on the purchase of modems and contacting the phone company.

Finally, I hope you've found that RAS administration is very simple. The concerns that you have, once the product is installed, primarily involve whether or not the client can connect. Beyond allowing the connection, the product actually could use a bit more control. But for the moment, that control isn't there. The greatest control you can exhibit is a firm grasp on your NT base security scheme.

14

The Workgroup Post Office

Peter Norton™

Electronic mail (e-mail) has become a staple of our modern business world. Because e-mail is so quick and efficient, it has replaced a great deal of the interoffice paper in major corporations. By creating communications that are written but don't require people to carry them, physically go to them, or even unfold them, we have found an incredible use for the PC.

If your network contains more than 50 users, the choice is no longer *whether* to have e-mail on your system, but which package you will purchase. Many installed networks begin with little or no e-mail. But if e-mail is installed it can (and more often than not does) take over the network. People become dependent on the ability to deliver messages to one another without having to make physical contact or hope that the other person will happen to pick up a piece of paper. Basic e-mail has almost become a right.

With that said, it's hard to imagine that most network operating systems don't contain basic e-mail as part of the system. Mainframe, midrange, and even UNIX-based systems have always had e-mail as part of the operating system. But since Novell cut the free text-based e-mail package from NetWare eight years ago, PC networks haven't really offered a generic e-mail package. Some peer-to-peer systems offered e-mail, but mainstream systems didn't. Many NT Server installers may be surprised to hear that NT Server, NT Workstation, and Windows 95 offer a basic e-mail server package called Workgroup Post Office as part of the operating system.

Note: I am amazed at how few NT administrators even know that this package exists. Because Microsoft currently has two supported commercial e-mail packages, many administrators don't even realize that the package is contained in NT at no extra cost. The fact is that Microsoft doesn't even discuss it in polite company.

Free Mail?

Workgroup Post Office is not a replacement for the commercial e-mail packages. This product is actually a very basic service that allows a small workgroup to exchange basic messaging and scheduling without having to invest in a separate package. Because of the simplistic controls and lack of features, this system isn't meant for large or even medium-sized companies, at least on a company-wide basis.

Windows NT, Windows 95, and even Windows for Workgroups come with e-mail interfaces that allow the user to access any Microsoft Mail-compatible post office. The Exchange client that comes with Windows 95 and now Windows NT addresses this post office as if it were a Microsoft Mail post office. By offering Workgroup Post Office as a basic part of Windows NT Server, NT Workstation, and even Windows 95, Microsoft allows small companies or even groups within large companies to get started down the e-mail road.

> **Note:** Be aware that the Exchange client that comes with Windows 95 and Windows NT isn't the same as the client that comes with Microsoft Exchange. By the time the real Exchange client was released with Microsoft Exchange Server, the Windows 95 client was dated; it wasn't a proper choice to use a full-featured Exchange client. Exchange comes with two proper clients for Exchange: Exchange Client (which looks like the free client) and now Outlook (a full-featured e-mail, scheduling, and task management client).

It's important to note that this package doesn't offer Internet mail capabilities, post office-to-post office communications, or any of the advanced features of the commercial packages such as Microsoft Exchange or Lotus cc:Mail. This isn't supposed to be the package that you use to start an e-mail system and then upgrade at a later date to a larger package. This package doesn't upgrade or grow at all. It's strictly meant as a utility player for small groups.

I wouldn't recommend this form of e-mail post office for more then 25 to 50 users, for many of the same reasons that I wouldn't recommend a workgroup model for large networks of users. The fact that the post office can't be managed or maintained to any depth makes it very difficult to handle the issues that arise for large groups.

Installing a Workgroup Post Office

The installation of a workgroup post office from Windows NT is a relatively simple process. This chapter discusses the NT Server product only, but once again the basic difference is only the number of users that can use the post office. Once you get started, like many Windows NT 4.0 and Windows 95 processes, it's a tour guided by a wizard.

> **Note:** *Wizard* describes the menu-driven applets that Microsoft uses to guide you through the process of creating something new. They are often characterized by the Next buttons that you click to proceed until you hit the Finish button to complete the project.

The process is started from the Windows NT Control Panel (see Figure 14.1).

Figure 14.1.
*NT Control Panel showing
the Microsoft Mail Postoffice
choice.*

Prior to starting the installation process, be aware that you'll need a shared directory to house the post office file. This directory should be large enough to house the e-mail for the entire group. My minimum recommendation is five megabytes per user. All the users you want to have access to e-mail will also need to have Change permissions to this directory.

The directory has to exist before you install the post office. Permissions can exist for everyone else except the creator at any time before the users need access. If you're going to create the directory in Explorer anyway, why not complete the process and give the user permissions during the process?

Follow these steps:

1. Double-click the Microsoft Mail Postoffice icon in the Control Panel to begin the installation. A Microsoft Workgroup Postoffice Admin dialog box appears, prompting you to indicate whether you are managing or creating a new post office.

2. Select the option Create a New Workgroup Post Office and then click Next.

3. You are now prompted to give a file system location for the post office. The response the dialog box is looking for is the name of a drive and a directory, or a share name and possibly a directory (for example, d:\BILBO_PO or \\BILBO\BILBO_PO). Type the location of the post office and click Next (see Figure 14.2).

   Be aware that the post office location needs to be one that can be accessed by all of the users who will be sending and receiving mail. The minimum permission that's needed to use the post office properly is the Change permission.

4. You will now be asked to confirm your directory choice. Click Next if you agree with the directory where the file will be placed. To change the directory, click Back and repeat the preceding step. Note that the filename of the post office is listed on the screen in the selection following the directory.

Figure 14.2.
Specifying the name for the post office.

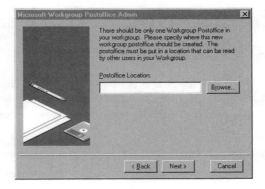

5. The Administrator Account Details dialog box appears (see Figure 14.3). Fill in the information with the details of the e-mail administrator. The only absolutely necessary information is Name, Mailbox, and Password.

Figure 14.3.
Administrator account details.

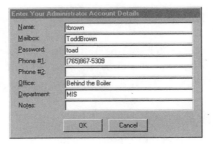

Keep in mind as you create the initial account that these accounts are in no way tied to the NT domain or workgroup user base. These are strictly mail account names. Permissions to access the server and mail directory will have to be given to the user's NT domain or workgroup account.

6. When you are finished filling in the information, click OK.

7. The system will prompt you to remember the name of your post office directory and will remind you to share it. Click OK and then close the Control Panel to finish the post office install.

8. The remainder of the installation is simply to go to Explorer and share the directory that you named as the workgroup post office. If you created and shared the post office before starting the installation, you can proceed to administration.

Remember that only the initial administrator account exists; that's a pretty lonely mail system. The next step is to create other users.

Administering a Workgroup Post Office

Post offices in this utility are very particular about who manages them. Only the creator of the post office can administer it. Even the administrator of the NT workstation can't administer the post office. For this reason, it's very important that you remember the original name and password that you created during installation.

The administration of such a simplistic post office basically involves only the creation and removal of user accounts. All of the administration is done from one interface, other than granting Access permissions to the files.

To administer a workgroup post office, follow these steps:

1. To begin the administrator program, you simply need to open the Microsoft Workgroup Postoffice Admin dialog box again (refer to Figure 14.2). But this time, choose to administer an existing workgroup post office, rather than create a new one.

> **Tip:** Realize that you have this control panel at any NT or Windows 95 workstation. You have the option of administering the post office from anywhere on the network by simply changing this directory entry at the new machine to match the location of the post office share.

2. Confirm the post office directory where the post office exists and click Next.
3. The following screen asks you to enter the mailbox name and password for the administrator (see Figure 14.4). Enter the information and click Next.

Figure 14.4.
Administrator confirmation.

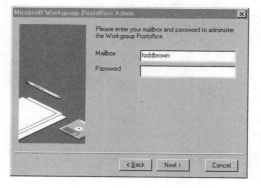

4. The screen that follows is finally the actual administration screen (see Figure 14.5). Once you have opened this tool, you really have three options:

- **Add User.** By choosing Add User, you are requesting to add a new user; you will see the same details screen as when you created the original administrator account (refer to Figure 14.3). The creation process is exactly the same.

- **Remove User.** This option simply removes the e-mail account. Keep in mind that this is a *permanent* removal. All messages will be unrecoverable. Prior to removing an account, it would be best to temporarily rename it until you are sure that the user will no longer need the information.

- **Details.** With this option, you are once again presented with the details screen shown in Figure 14.3, but this time to edit an existing account. All the information can be edited, including the initial (administrator) account.

Figure 14.5.
Manager options.

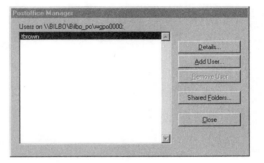

The Shared Folders button on this screen allows you to monitor the progress of the post office in size (see Figure 14.6). It isn't an active monitor—you must view it from this screen. In other words, unless you're in the Postoffice Manager screen, you won't receive warnings about the size of your post office in Event Viewer or any form of pop-up message. So it's important to check this screen on occasion.

Figure 14.6.
Viewing the shared folders.

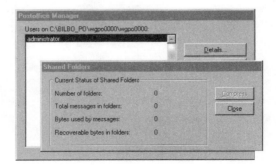

Summary

The purpose of this chapter was to introduce you to a product that few administrators even know exists. It isn't meant to be a replacement for the mainstream e-mail packages; the point of this product is to provide a solution for small or startup groups.

The workgroup post office is incapable of creating gateways between its e-mail system and other post offices. The product is meant for stand-alone use. The product is not capable of allowing a manager to manipulate it or manage its database. It will never get you to the Internet, but that isn't its place.

The tools to manage and install this product couldn't be simpler—if you prepare before you begin the install. About the only hassle occurs if you don't create a directory for the post office prior to the installation.

15

Surviving in a Multi-Protocol World

Peter Norton™

Much of network administration involves the underlying network and the protocols that control it. This chapter takes a look at the protocols supported by NT and the strengths and weaknesses of each. If you don't have some understanding of what a protocol is, this chapter may have something for you—but the primary purpose of this chapter is to help the administrator who must now live in a world that's open to multiple protocols. The chapter starts with a brief description of network protocols, but for a dedicated look at the subject you should consult *Windows NT Server 4 Unleashed, Professional Reference Edition* (Sams Publishing, 1997, ISBN 0-672-31002-3).

The Protocol Basics

When I mention a *communications protocol*, the piece of PC network that I'm referring to is the language that the PCs use to communicate with one another. That's a very simplistic explanation, but the concept fits. PCs, like humans, must speak to one another using rules and a formed language in order to understand each other. The portion of the communications protocol that's controlled by the network operating system is the part that must act as liaison between the hardware (NICs, cables, hubs, and so on) and the portions of the operating system that control the applications.

These protocols contain rules for how communications signals must be formed, how and when communications can occur, and to some degree how to physically lay out the network. A PC protocol can be compared to human protocol. Certain humans have protocol for how they must communicate, and protocol problems can really cause basic problems.

When meeting the Queen of England, protocol demands that you bow or curtsey to her. You are also not to offer your hand or touch her unless she offers first. United States citizens, however, are never to bow or curtsey before any power, and they always offer their hand as a show of trust and friendship. If the Queen of England meets a United States citizen, you have a protocol problem. The rules are different, even though the language is supposed to be the same. Queen's English, right?

Way back in 1993, a network administrator could be very selective about the network protocols that he allowed to roam free across his network. In fact, the decision was often made for him before he even got involved. Until very recently, most PC networks fully functioned with only one protocol:

- Microsoft Windows NT v1.0-v3.1 supported only native logon with NetBEUI.
- Novell NetWare v1.0-v4.1 supported only native user login with IPX/SPX protocol.

The operating systems supported the routing of these foreign protocols, but they didn't support users logging into the system with any protocol other than the "blessed" protocol. System administrators now have to bow to the demands of more knowledgeable users who want to connect to many different systems.

Computer networks have become like an international community of protocols. Because of the demands of mixed environments, support of the Internet, and more complex utilization of PC networks, administrators have to create an open system that will support all of these demands.

The predicament that network administrators have before them is the need to choose the proper mix of protocols to allow communications, but also not clog the network with too much traffic. Computer networks behave like any shared resource; there's a finite amount of utilization that can be attained or sustained.

Imagine the connecting infrastructure of the network as the water pipes that connect a city; only a certain amount of water can pass through the pipes at any given moment. The amount of water that the pipes can accept in a given time is a finite amount. That finite amount of flow, if sustained over a long period of time, will cause problems.

In the same way that the water system has a finite amount of water that can pass through, your network has a finite amount of network traffic that can pass through. This traffic capacity is called the *bandwidth* of the network. Lack of available bandwidth can cause an otherwise efficient network to appear to have problems that it doesn't have, and it can cause problems that are very real.

As a network administrator, the predicament that you have because of these capacity issues is that you must not pollute your bandwidth with too many protocols, but you must also create an open communications environment. Understanding the protocols that are needed and the capacity of the underlying physical network can help you create that environment.

The combination of the network physical layout and the rules used for the computer network are commonly called the *topology*. The topology of the network is really controlled by the base transport protocol that has been selected for the network. Each transport protocol has a specific set of hardware rules that must be followed in order to communicate.

> **Note:** Chapter 6, "Networking Brief," contains a section called "Networks (LAN or WAN) Versus Networks (Segmentation)" that explains the concept of network topology and bandwidth issues. It also covers the topology considerations that you must take into account.

There are two basic transport protocols used today:

- Ethernet
- Token Ring

Next we'll take a look at the higher-level communications.

Supported Protocols in NT 4.0

Once a physical connection has been established through a transport protocol, you must decide what network-level protocol you'll use. Network-level protocols exist at the same level for networks that language exists for humans. Once humans have decided to speak and what medium they will use to speak (phone, written letter, and so on), they must establish a common language. That language for computer communications is called a *network protocol*.

> **Note:** The difference between a topology protocol and a network protocol is explained in depth through the use of the OSI model. This seven-layer model was created by the International Standards Organization (ISO) to give clear definition to the different tasks that must be performed by each part of the network. This model is explained in detail in the book *Absolute Beginner's Guide to Networking, Second Edition* (1995, Sams Publishing, ISBN 0-672-30553-4). If you learn this model, it will help you to understand many of the relationships between protocols.

Like many advanced network operating systems, Windows NT supports almost any protocol that you're willing to introduce it to through proper channels (the Network control panel). The modularity of NT allows the administrator to install services, drivers, and protocols into the system as the networking world grows up around it. NT does, however, have a certain number of protocols that are supported natively without having to add from an outside source.

In the Windows NT installation, you make choices about the network protocols that you will support when NT starts for the first time. Among the protocols that Microsoft includes with NT are the following protocols (see Figure 15.1):

- TCP/IP—Transmission control protocol/Internet protocol
- IPX/SPX—Novell's Internet Packet Exchange/Sequenced Packet Exchange protocol
- NetBEUI—Microsoft NetBIOS protocol
- AppleTalk—Apple Computer protocol
- PPP—Point-to-point protocol
- DLC—Data Link Control from Hewlett-Packard
- Streams—Common transport interface

Figure 15.1.
NT network protocols.

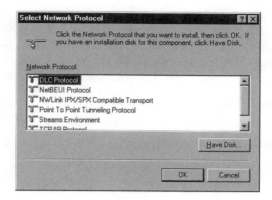

TCP/IP

Did you know that you own a protocol? TCP/IP is a public standard that's owned by the United States government and available for change by anyone. I don't mention this lightly. The United States Department of Defense (DOD) developed the TCP/IP protocol (okay, some universities helped) for communication between sites on the Internet, and for that reason it belongs to the people. The government has established a group called the *IETF* (*Internet Engineering Task Force*) to control the protocol and the direction that it takes.

> **Looking Ahead:** TCP/IP configuration and usage is covered in great depth in Chapter 21, "TCP/IP Networking." That chapter covers TCP/IP from the standpoint that TCP/IP is not just a network protocol, but a suite of tools.

A Public Standard

TCP/IP is a public and open standard, and for that reason has become very popular. Anyone who has a desire to add to the TCP/IP protocol can do so by submitting an *RFC* (*request for change*) to the IETF. Because anyone can contribute to the progress of the protocol, the protocol has a life of its own. This has made it very appealing to networking operating system (NOS) vendors.

One appeal for NOS vendors is that they don't have to control the standard to use it and they don't have to pay anyone else to make use of it. If a vendor wants to add a TCP/IP connection to their operating system, they simply add it. No questions asked and no one to pay. If they want to change the protocol, they simply submit an RFC; if no one complains, it becomes a standard part of TCP/IP.

Note: Another appeal of the protocol is that it doesn't require that they give credit to any competitor in order to use it. If Microsoft uses IPX/SPX, even though Novell has made it a public standard, they are kowtowing to a Novell-developed technology.

The fact that IP is a public standard has made it the most widely used of all network protocols. You can currently communicate with the following list of vendors and operating systems using TCP/IP:

- Microsoft Windows NT (all versions) and Windows 95
- Novell NetWare 4.x
- Banyan Vines
- OS/2 (all versions)
- UNIX (all flavors)
- Digital VMS and Pathworks
- Apple Macintosh OS

The above list of vendors constitutes most of the network connections in the world. That alone speaks volumes for the appeal of the TCP/IP protocol.

Robust and Full-Featured

The UNIX and mainframe host worlds have used the TCP/IP protocol for 20+ years. This protocol and the associated protocols that it contains are robust and easy to use because they've been around for so many years. This is part of the appeal for NOS vendors. As mentioned in Chapter 1, "Windows NT Introduction," Microsoft wanted to make NT an open system that could be accessed from any operating system, and TCP/IP makes that possible.

TCP/IP is really the name given to many different protocols and features that make it a protocol suite. This protocol suite contains a list of protocols that control all facets of network use:

- **TCP.** Transport protocol used for reliable acknowledgment-based communications.
- **IP.** Network protocol used for standard network connectionless communications.

Note: Acknowledgment-based and connectionless communications refers to the fact that protocols will require an acknowledgment of success and will establish a connection prior to sending. TCP requires that each communication have a direct path established and acknowledgment or it will not be considered successful. IP, on the other hand, sends the communications across the network and relinquishes responsibility. The difference is the time and resources required for each style.

- **FTP.** File transfer protocol used to move files reliably across a network.

- **HTTP.** Hypertext transfer protocol used for transfer of hypertext-based documents, allowing for smooth document retrieval. The World Wide Web uses this protocol.

- **Telnet.** Terminal communications protocol that allows the user to establish a terminal connection with a host computer.

- **NFS.** Network file system used to allow the user to attach network drives to her local computer and use those drives in their native environments.

These products offer the ability to make use of a computer network from time-tested, well-known utilities. One of the greatest downfalls of newer protocols is the fact that you may find yourself using that protocol for something for which it either isn't equipped or is rarely used. The TCP/IP suite of protocols offers a way around that issue.

Built to WAN

TCP/IP protocol can be routed through most—if not all—routers. Because this protocol has existed as part of the host-based world for so long, router vendors always include TCP/IP routing as part of their basic package.

TCP/IP was created to communicate across long distances and to deal with adversity. After all, the Department of Defense developed it. The TCP/IP protocol has built-in routing and redundancy to make it possible to communicate over network segments and over large networks.

The Internet is the largest computer network in the world and TCP/IP is the only protocol that's allowed to function across the entire network. This is appealing on many levels, but one of them is the fact that your wide area network (WAN) should be a cakewalk by comparison. It also makes it possible to consider using the world's network as part of your wide area connections.

Addressing

All networks need a way to separate and identify the nodes that exist on that network. Networks can be thought of as any other computer bus—if items on that bus must communicate, there has to be a way of identifying and separating where the communication came from or is going to.

Tip: The term *node* refers to any participating intelligent network entity. There are times when all devices fit the description of the network entity and the term node is used to generically refer to all of them (for example, servers, workstations, printers directly connected to the network).

Network addresses typically have two pieces. The first is a network address to identify the segment of the network that the node came from. The second is the node address, which allows for the identification of the individual machine. It's somewhat like your postal address—containing your city, state, ZIP code, and your street address. The first piece separates items into general areas and the second is more specific.

TCP/IP has built-in network addressing. Each host is given an IP address; these addresses are created and assigned by the administrator of the network and need to be unique for every node.

> **Note:** The term *host* in the TCP/IP world refers to any node on the network that receives an address. The name host makes it appear as if the system is providing services, but that isn't necessarily so.

An IP address consists of four numbers from 0 to 255, separated by a period. For example, `198.78.23.45` is a legal IP address. The full range would be from `0.0.0.0` to `255.255.255.255`.

Based on the class of the address, different sections of the address are the network and node pieces. Chapter 21 covers the details of the scheme, but Figure 15.2 gives you a general idea of how it works.

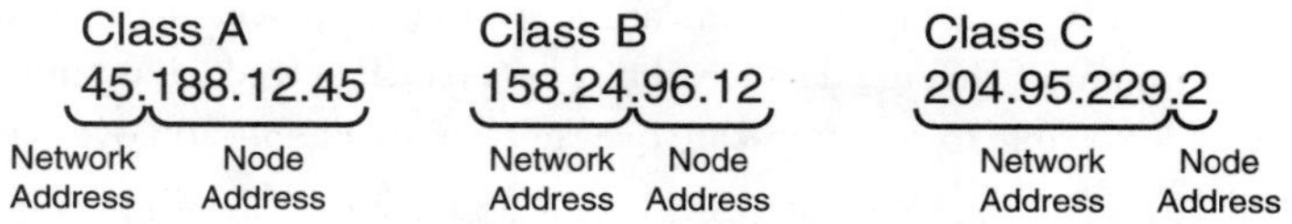

Figure 15.2.
IP address divisions along network and node lines.

Class A	Class B	Class C
45.188.12.45	158.24.96.12	204.95.229.2
Network Address Node Address	Network Address Node Address	Network Address Node Address

Addresses can be created by the administrator from scratch, but if the network will be added to the public Internet, an address range must be applied for from a group called the *Internet Network Information Center* (*InterNIC*). InterNIC is a not-for-profit organization that's in charge of assigning addresses on the Internet so that no one uses that same address twice. By getting a unique address range from InterNIC, the business will then be able to assign a unique address to each of its host machines.

Strengths and Weaknesses

The following list shows the strengths of TCP/IP:

- Large installed base and vendor support
- Time-tested
- Inherently routable
- Built-in WAN through the Internet

This list shows the weaknesses of TCP/IP:

- Network addresses must be added to each node manually (DCHP takes care of this weakness to a great extent, but it also requires more work than other protocols).
- IP routing and segmentation can be complex if the range of addresses that you have is small.
- IP is available to anyone who wants to use it; this can mean that many people know how to break down its security.

IPX/SPX

Unlike TCP/IP, the IPX/SPX protocol suite wasn't born in such a public fashion. IPX/SPX is the creation of Novell Corporation and was originally created for their NetWare product. The IPX/SPX protocol suite was a variation of the Xerox XNS standard originally designed for Ethernet communications among their systems.

A Public Standard

Novell realizes the power of releasing a protocol to the public and did so with the IPX/SPX suite. By releasing it to the public, Novell gains market strength. Other vendors creating ways to connect to their protocol strengthens the Novell position because it makes NetWare ultimately more connectable.

There's a great difference, though, between making a protocol that's free for public use and one protocol that's owned by the public and publicly controlled. Novell has released IPX/SPX to the public to use as they see fit without charge, but the standards for IPX/SPX are ultimately in the hands of Novell. For that reason and others, fewer vendors have created a path for users to gain access to their systems through IPX/SPX.

The following network operating systems provide support for IPX/SPX:

- Novell NetWare (all versions)
- Windows NT v3.5 (Service Packs needed for full support), v4.0
- OS/2 (all versions)
- Apple Macintosh

This is a smaller list than that of TCP/IP, but make no mistake—IPX/SPX is a very well-supported network protocol in the network community. The reasons are different from those of TCP/IP. IPX/SPX is supported very heavily partially because, until very recently, NetWare controlled as much as 70% of the NOS market. A vendor of networking products would be irresponsible to ignore the native protocol of that kind of market. There most definitely is strength in numbers.

Lean and Mean

The appeal of IPX/SPX as a protocol is the fact that the IPX protocol is a very lean and direct method of communicating from node to node.

IPX is to the IPX/SPX protocol suite what IP is to the TCP/IP suite. IPX protocol is a connectionless protocol that simply sends communications packets to the network. The members of the network look at the packets; if the message doesn't have the member's address in the destination, the packet is ignored.

IPX also offers a unique addressing scheme that allows network administrators to not worry about the addressing of every individual node. IPX uses a combination of the network address and the MAC (Media Access Control) address that comes along with most network cards to create a node address (see Figure 15.3).

Note: Network interface card (NIC) manufacturers use a method of uniquely identifying every NIC. The process involves placing a unique address of up to 12 digits electronically on the card. This allows the node containing the card to be identified on the network.

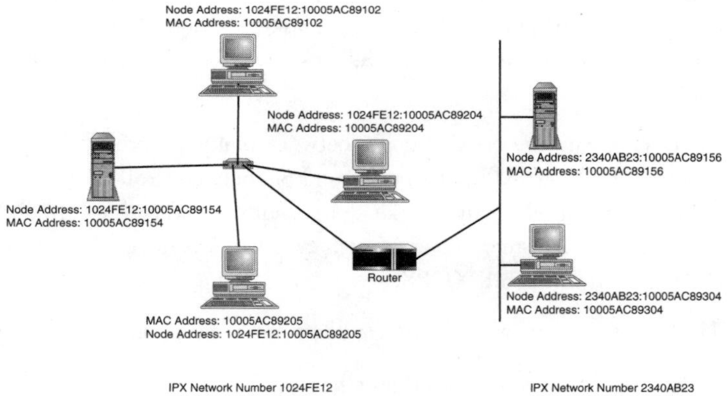

Figure 15.3.
IPX network addressing.

Recently Available for WAN Services

IPX has always been a routable protocol. The routing of IPX is supported in almost all commercial routers. The fact that the protocol has both a network and node address makes it possible to route information between segments. The problem arose in the past when you attempted to route IPX through your NT machine.

The fact that Windows NT would not route IPX made IPX a bad choice of network protocol for wide area networks in the NT world until recently. With the advent of Windows NT 4.0, NT now routes IPX. The lack of this support in earlier versions, along with the huge installed base of NetWare, made the installation of NT in key positions very difficult. But the problem has been solved.

Peter's Principle: Get Service Pack 3

With Service Pack 3 for NT v3.51, you can make legacy versions of NT route IPX.

Strengths and Weaknesses

The strengths of IPX/SPX are indicated in the following list:

- Requires very little network-address planning
- Very fast and efficient standard communications
- Routable

This list shows the weaknesses of IPX:

- Less control over the network-addressing scheme (I know—both a strength and a weakness)
- Not quite as universally accepted as IP, not allowed on the Internet
- Tied to a single vendor

AppleTalk

Windows NT also supports the AppleTalk protocol for use by Macintosh computers and printers. This protocol's only real utility for NT is the fact that it offers this Macintosh connectivity.

Apple Computer developed many things with the Macintosh computer; among them was a networking protocol called AppleTalk. The Macintosh computer was designed with the idea in mind that the computers should do the work and the humans should be helped at every point along the way to get the input to the computers, so that that work could occur. The AppleTalk protocol is an extension of that philosophy.

A Very Noisy Neighbor

Just like the computers that it was designed for, AppleTalk is a unique creation that fits well in a niche market. AppleTalk is an extension of the AppleTalk networking concept that's used by Apple to share computer hard drives, printers, and even modems. The protocol uses broadcasts and "advertisements" to alert the other members of the network that each peripheral and computer exists—thus the expression "Apple talk."

The protocol hasn't been widely used by other computer companies because it's very inefficient. AppleTalk clients can slow a heavily populated network simply because each node and server must send broadcast packets across the network in order to function. The difference between this behavior in AppleTalk and other protocols is that other network protocols use broadcasts as a way of announcing emergencies or occasional announcements of a general nature.

To understand the reason for all this chatter, you must understand the basic connection that's made by a Macintosh computer to the AppleTalk network. When a Macintosh computer attempts to make use of a network resource, it opens a utility called the Chooser (see Figure 15.4).

Figure 15.4.
Macintosh Chooser menu
containing network shares.

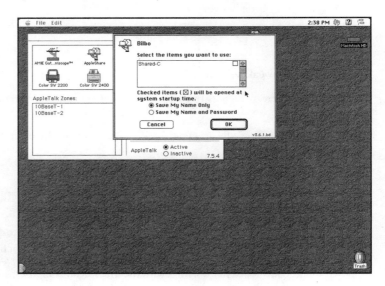

When the Chooser opens, it presents the Macintosh user with a list of resource types (seen on the left side of Figure 15.4) from which to choose. Once that choice has been made, the user will choose from a list of the available resources of that type that exist on the network (the list on the right side of Figure 15.4). By that choice, the resource becomes available for use at that Macintosh.

The process can be more or less complicated than just described, depending on the resource that's being chosen, but the important factor is that the Macintosh depends on this protocol for listings of available resources. The noise that must be made in order to present these lists is considerable and simply makes the protocol weak for large networks.

Addressing Schemes

In the AppleTalk world, addressing is handled in a fashion that resembles IPX/SPX on some levels, but of course with Apple it has its own variations.

AppleTalk networks are given individual numbered addresses per segment, but an AppleTalk network may require a network number range if the network contains more nodes than 253. The reason is that, each time more than 253 nodes are found on the network, a new network number must be used (see Figure 15.5). So, for example, if you have 303 Macintosh computers and printers on the network, you would be required to use a network number of 10–11. This is because 303 is fifty nodes outside of the 253-node limit.

Figure 15.5.
AppleTalk network addressing and zoning scheme.

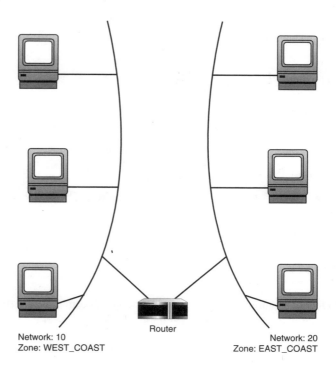

Network: 10
Zone: WEST_COAST

Router

Network: 20
Zone: EAST_COAST

Each workstation on the network is then assigned a node address as they attach to the network, based on a sort of first-come-first-served basis. For example, the third Macintosh to log into a Macintosh network with the number 10 would have an address of 10.3.

To further complicate the networking issue, AppleTalk uses an early form of virtual networking that creates entities called *zones* to identify the items that exist in a particular network range. Because everything in an AppleTalk network has some verbal nomenclature, even network segments become known by a name that can be viewed in the Macintosh Chooser. For example, the network number 10–11 may be known to the user base as the zone "Upstairs."

The advantage of this relationship to network numbers is that it allows Macintosh users to identify and group resources by a network zone. The network resources that are presented to the users appear to be in different "containers," if you will. Notice in Figure 15.4 that there are two zones in the AppleTalk Zones list. When a user initially attempts to find a resource on the network, he can select to choose resources in different zones. By selecting a zone in the zone list, he is presented with the resources available from that zone. If only one zone and network exists in the LAN, the users don't see a zone list.

AppleTalk is routable, and that's done using the zones and different network numbers mentioned.

Strengths and Weaknesses

Strengths of AppleTalk are as follows:

- Allows Macintosh computers to connect to your NT server
- Offers a great deal of help to the clients that use it

These are the weaknesses of AppleTalk:

- Ties up great amounts of network bandwidth by broadcasting necessary information to Macintosh clients
- Only really useful to a select group of users and a proprietary group of computers

PPP

NT offers administrators not only the ability to communicate through in-house cabling, but also the ability to connect using the public telephone networks. This type of communications requires special protocols and applications for what's called *serial communications*.

To make use of public telephone networks, the TCP/IP world developed a protocol known as the *Serial line Internet protocol* (*SLIP*). SLIP isn't used as often these days and has been replaced in most applications by the hybrid PPP.

Serial communications protocols allow the operating system to use asynchronous communications (communications through a serial port and an asynchronous modem), as if the modem were a network interface card. Unlike the other protocols discussed to this point, PPP is more closely related to the pipe mentioned earlier in the chapter. PPP is used as a connection method from point A to point B, not as a language.

Because PPP is the more complete version of the serial communications protocol, it's the preferred protocol when a choice exists. Because of the rising popularity of the Internet and asynchronous communications, most operating systems offer PPP connectivity as part of the base operating system.

PPP is not limited to the original TCP/IP protocol. Current PPP connections to an NT RAS server can support most protocols that are supported by the NT operating system, including TCP/IP, IPX/SPX, NetBEUI, DECnet, and AppleTalk.

NetBEUI

Windows NT and many other Microsoft operating environments have used a protocol called *NetBEUI* for basic network connectivity for years. NetBEUI stands for *NetBIOS extended user interface*, and is an extension of the old Microsoft Network. The concept is to be a simplistic protocol to allow users to communicate between PCs. Something that, back when it was created, would certainly have no need to ever be "robust and full-featured." Oops!

The NetBEUI protocol can't be routed at all because it doesn't have any network numbering scheme or any way of defining separate networks for communications between them. The protocol simply makes use of NetBIOS to connect to the shared network resources on the local network.

The odd thing with this protocol is that, when other protocols have trouble finding network resources on the local network, NetBEUI can often produce them. Windows NT and all other Microsoft products seem to have a cosmic connection to this protocol. The reality of the situation is that human hands don't often ruin the simple nature of the protocol. NetBEUI simply searches for NetBIOS entities and reports them—nothing more and nothing less.

This behavior makes it a good choice for a RAS connection or a small uncomplicated network. The simplicity makes for a very fast communication method.

Strengths and Weaknesses

Strengths of NetBEUI are as follows:

- Speed and efficiency in small one-segment networks
- Good choice for basic network function when troubleshooting, because of its ability to find NetBIOS entities and avoid human "help"

These are the weaknesses of NetBEUI:

- Unable to be routed, which prevents networks larger than one segment
- Not supported by many other vendors

Multi-Protocol Router (MPR)

The Multi-Protocol Router was at one time a separate product offered by Microsoft to allow Windows NT to function as a router solution (see Figure 15.6). The reason for this is that many small to medium-sized companies had a need to segment their networks, but didn't have enough of a need to warrant buying a separate device for routing.

Figure 15.6.
IP routing.

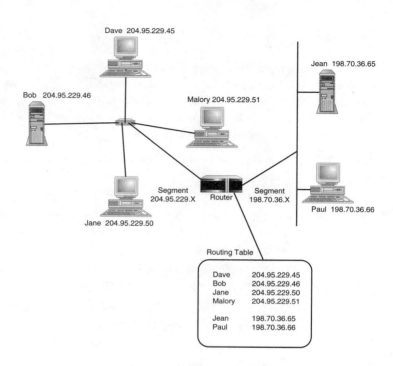

The concept is to allow the administrator to place a second NIC in the server and turn on the routing ability of the server. This allows the server to route packets between the two network segments. Windows NT Server already provides routing support for remote users to a LAN environment and LAN-LAN routing support for AppleTalk networks. With the Windows NT Server MPR service, the LAN-LAN routing support is now enhanced for TCP/IP and IPX/SPX networks. Like other routing solutions, the Windows NT Server MPR service provides a WAN routing solution when used with additional network cards.

Peter's Principle: Add IPX Routing with Service Pack 3

The major drawback for NT prior to including Multi-Protocol Router (MPR) was that it couldn't route the IPX protocol at all. It also wasn't exactly robust about the routing of IP. MPR capability is available as part of NT Server 4.0, but if you do have any NT 3.51 servers you can find the MPR service as part of Service Pack 3. This Service Pack is available at the following address:

```
http://www.microsoft.com/ntserversupport/Default-SL.HTM
```

MPR (Multi-Protocol Router) consists of RIP (routing information protocol) for TCP/IP, BOOTP relay agent for DHCP, and RIP for IPX. RIP is one protocol used by routers to dynamically exchange routing information. After installing RIP for IP and RIP for IPX, NT will route these protocols and dynamically exchange routing information with other routers running the RIP protocol. The BOOTP relay agent allows the NT router to forward DHCP requests to DHCP servers on other segments. This allows one DHCP server to service multiple IP segments.

Routing Information Protocol (RIP)

Routers learn about the network routes that are available in two basic ways. One is to be told directly by the humans, and the other is to find each other on their own. When routers must find each other, they require that they be able to participate in routing information protocol (RIP) traffic on the network.

The routing information protocol is a basic part of both the TCP/IP and IPX/SPX protocol suites and the process is necessary to allow networks to learn about each other's existence.

RIP for IP and IPX can be enabled in the Network control panel, under the Protocols tab. Click the TCP/IP or NWLink Compatible Transport (IPX/SPX) protocol and then click the Routing tab (see Figure 15.7).

Figure 15.7.
The Routing tab in IP presents the same basic screen as in IPX.

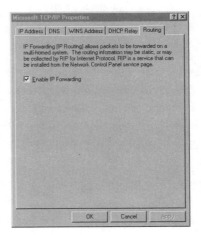

Once you arrive at the Routing tab, simply click the check box Enable IP Forwarding to enable routing. By enabling routing, you have enabled RIP, and the server will be able to route traffic between segments.

Troubleshooting

For more detailed information on IP, look at Chapter 21. For now, here are some ways to determine whether you have set up MPR correctly and whether route information is actually passing through:

- RAS and MPR—RIP broadcasts will *not* be sent out on serial or ISDN interfaces. RIP broadcasts will be sent only on LAN interfaces or cards such as T1 or frame relay that appear to be LAN interfaces to NT.
- Is the default gateway correct on the NT router? Use only one default gateway configured on the appropriate NIC.
- Remember that the default gateway route is used only if there's no other valid route to the destination. Therefore, the default route will be used only for addresses outside of your company or autonomous system. All routes in the company will be learned via RIP.

> **Tip:** To find the IP information that has been set for your workstation, you can use WINIPCFG for Windows 95 or IPCONFIG for Windows NT, depending on the OS running at your workstation. These programs are run from the DOS prompt or the Run command on the Start menu.

- Verify the correct configuration for the client, including IP address, subnet mask, and default gateway.

Ping

The utility called *Ping* is used to determine whether your machine can locate a PC on the network. It's named Ping because it resembles the behavior of a ship that sends out a ping sound and listens for the echo to determine whether another ship or submarine is close. With Ping, your PC sends out a signal toward an address on the IP network to determine whether it is actually connected to the same network—or even if the system exists at the moment. Here's how you use it:

- Ping yourself—This will tell you that TCP is functioning. It does *not* tell you that your NIC is functioning.
- Ping your default gateway or next hop router—This will show that the router is up.
- Ping beyond the next hop router—If a ping fails, what's the response? `Request timed out` can mean that the destination host is down or that there's no route back to you. `Destination Net Unreachable` will show the IP address of the router that tried to route the packet but didn't have a valid route.

Summary

The basic premise behind networking computers is to find a common language and a common medium through which to speak. By looking at the protocols that are supported in NT, we have examined the possibilities in this area. The concept of protocols is not just a single layer of the communications between PCs. Protocols are involved in all of the different levels of PC communications.

The concept of choosing a protocol has only recently been a true choice in NT—which has now gained not only the ability to use the major PC protocols, but also the ability to route them efficiently. NT supports TCP/IP, IPX/SPX, NetBEUI, and even AppleTalk as protocols for communicating. Your job as an administrator is to make a decision about which best fits your needs.

16

Client Workstation Considerations

Peter Norton™

We have spent a great deal of this book covering what a client can do once it becomes connected to the NT network, but we haven't really covered the nuts and bolts of how to get those client workstations connected. NT provides for connectivity by workstations running almost any operating system or hardware platform. This chapter looks at the steps you need to go through to get the major clients connected. These are the major topics covered in this chapter:

- Client services
- Specific client operating system considerations
- Windows NT Workstation clients
- Windows 95 clients
- Profiles and policies for Microsoft 32-bit clients
- DOS and Windows clients
- Windows for Workgroups clients
- Macintosh clients

Client Services Brief

For client workstations to attach to a Microsoft (workgroup or domain-based) network, they need to be equipped with the proper client software. Many of the Microsoft operating systems are delivered with some form of built-in connectivity to Microsoft networks. Windows NT, Windows 95, and Windows for Workgroups (WfW) all have basic Microsoft network connectivity built directly into the system. Even the Macintosh computer line has the basic ability to attach to the NT server, if the server is running Macintosh services.

The purpose behind client software is to give the workstation the ability to generate a call to the network and discover resources. A machine has to have some way of activating a network interface card (NIC), introducing that interface card to the proper communications protocols to speak on the network, and authenticating the user to the domain. In an atmosphere where DOS is the predominant operating system, this can be a bit tougher (see Figure 16.1). But hopefully you have found the virtues of some of the newer operating systems.

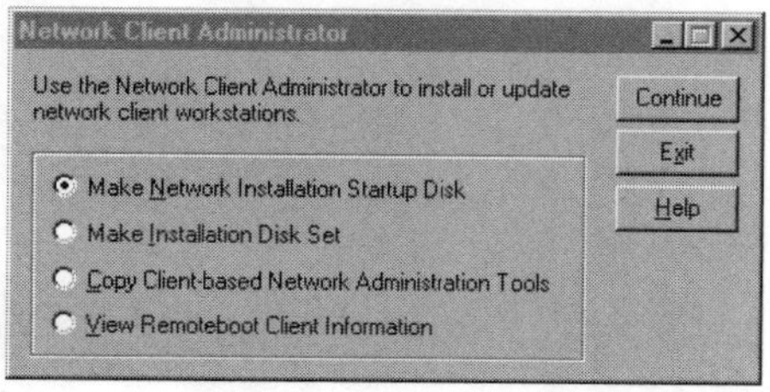

Figure 16.1.
Client activation on the network.

Specific Client Operating System Considerations

Windows NT comes with the software necessary to make the connection between the server and client operating systems that don't have a built-in network client. On the NT CD-ROM, you will find clients for DOS, Windows 3.1, and OS/2.

> **Tip:** You have to question the further progress of these clients—DOS and Windows 3.1x are not being actively progressed by Microsoft. If at all possible, consider upgrading Intel-based clients to Windows 95 or NT Workstation as the workstation OS. Before you consider OS/2 as a desktop operating system, ask a few IBM employees what OS they use.

WfW was the first version of Windows to come equipped to use the network as part of its basic operation, so it was capable of connecting to NT from the beginning. The WfW environment still runs on top of the DOS operating system, but it allows the user to wait to connect to the network until after he has chosen to run Windows. If you must use DOS as your base operating system, WfW is the best option. If you're using Windows for Workgroups, you'll be able to participate in the network, but still maintain the underlying DOS operating system.

Windows NT Workstation and Windows 95 have 32-bit Microsoft network clients as part of the basic network operating system. The fact that these operating systems use networking as part of their basic functionality makes the networking very efficient and easy to use. For that reason, they make the best final choice for Windows NT clients.

Windows NT Workstation Clients

Preparing Windows NT Workstation and Windows NT Server network connectivity is the same process. The installation process for NT connectivity covered in Chapter 4, "Installation Considerations," also applies for Workstation. But there are some items that you should look at, especially for NT clients.

All PCs on your network running the NT operating system should be registered with the Server Manager for Domains. This is so that these PCs can participate in the domain and be authenticated. Items such as domain control, profiles, and browsing count on this registration.

These are the steps to register the NT client PC:

1. In Server Manager, choose Add to Domain from the Computer menu.
2. Type the computer name of the Windows NT Workstation client and click Add.

Windows 95 Clients

Because Windows 95 contains network support as part of the basic operating system, the client for all networking can be installed at any time during or after the operating system is installed. Whether you complete this process during or after installation, Windows 95 makes the process fairly easy. With the combination of Plug and Play NICs and the installation wizards in Windows 95, it's tough to make the process fail.

> **Tip:** When installing hardware or networking items in Windows 95, I've found that it's easier if you don't fight the direction that Windows 95 gives. As an example of what I mean, I have seen times when using the NIC driver that was automatically detected by Windows 95 worked better than the driver provided by the manufacturer.

When installing Windows 95, the operating system automatically makes some choices for you about the network card and networking services that you need. Just like the Windows NT operating system, the Windows 95 networking setup is very modular in nature. As Figure 16.2 shows, the Windows 95 system offers the ability to separate the protocols, logon clients, and hardware into separate tasks. By separating the tasks in this way, Windows NT and Windows 95 allow the user to load one set of tools to obtain all the desired connections.

Figure 16.2.
Network setup is automatically divided into separate components.

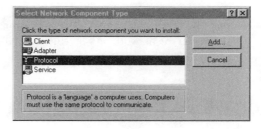

For example, the user may want to connect to the NT network through IPX/SPX protocol, but may also want to connect to the Novell server through the same protocol. By separating the pieces into modular installs, the client finds that he needs to load only the two clients and the one protocol—not a separate occurrence of each protocol for every client.

Peter's Principle: Choose the Frame Type While Installing

When installing the Windows 95 client on a network using IPX/SPX as a protocol, it's often best to click the Advanced tab in IPX/SPX Compatible Protocol Properties and then choose Frame Type. Under the choices on the right, choose a frame type for the entire network (802.2, 802.3, and so on). This is particularly helpful if a NetWare server is running that the Windows 95 client is required to use. Unlike Windows NT, Windows 95 is not good at auto-sensing the frame type of a NetWare network and won't find the network at all if multiple frame types exist on the wire. The default frame type for NetWare 3.12 and higher is 802.2, all else is 802.3.

The choices of when and how to install the Windows 95 client for Microsoft networks can make a great deal of difference in the options presented. The following sections take a look at the differences when starting from scratch by installing networking along with the operating system, versus installing networking after a workstation has existed for a while without it.

Installing Networking from Scratch

By installing networking as part of the initial installation of Windows 95, you'll get a bit of help from Windows 95 regarding the items that it believes exist on your network. If you miss the opportunity to install networking at the time of initially installing Windows 95, you will miss many of the helping hands you get during original install. Once Windows 95 is installed, it's more careful in its discovery and implementation of new networking products.

When you install Windows 95, you are asked whether you would like to install the operating system in a Typical, Portable, Minimal, or Custom style. By making a choice other than Custom, you choose to let Windows 95 make the initial networking choices for you. Windows 95 automatically senses the networking hardware that you have installed, along with the other hardware that Windows 95 is attempting to set up. After the installation is complete, the system will reboot, and you'll be asked to log onto the workstation.

Looking Ahead: If you choose Custom, you'll see the options covered in the following section, so I won't cover that topic here.

The screen you see, oddly enough, will be a Microsoft NetWare logon screen if NetWare servers exist on the network. Microsoft, in its clamor to make Windows 95 a "Better DOS than DOS" and the "Best NetWare Client in the World," made NetWare the automatic choice for default network logon. If no NetWare servers exist, you'll get the Windows 95 logon screen as a second choice. If you want to choose NT domain logon as the default, you'll need to set this up manually.

If you'd like to use a Microsoft networks logon instead of a NetWare logon (and why not?), you can change this setting in the Network control panel.

Tip: For a shortcut to the Network control panel, right-click the Network Neighborhood icon on the desktop. This works for Windows 95 as well as for Windows NT.

Once inside the Network control panel, you'll find an option called Primary Network Logon (see Figure 16.3). By clicking the arrow button associated with this choice, you'll see three possible options. The choice you make here determines which logon screen you get at the opening of the Windows 95 operating system.

Figure 16.3.
The Windows 95 Network control panel.

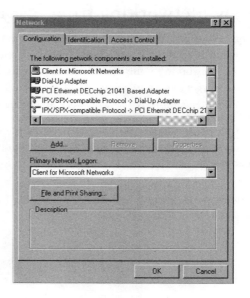

This screen is of less consequence than you might think. Windows NT and Windows 95 use a universal logon when a user sits at a single workstation and logs on. If a user logs on at a NetWare client logon in Windows 95, Windows 95 takes the username and password used and attempts to log onto any remaining clients that are installed. For example, if the workstation has the NetWare client set as the default, but also has the Microsoft client logon installed, Windows 95 uses the username and password initially entered to log onto both systems. If the username and password are the same, the user won't be presented with any further logon screens. On the other hand, if the username and password don't match, Windows 95 simply presents the user with a logon screen for the remaining clients that were not authenticated.

Changing Existing Network Installations (or Building Your Own)

If you have done enough installations of Windows 95 clients in your own network environment, you may have found variables you would like selected that are not being selected by the automatic installation process. You may also find that, once a user workstation has moved, you need to make changes to the initial settings. In either case, you need to be aware of options available for Microsoft networking for this client.

> **Tip:** In this book, I'll primarily cover the items needed to connect systems to Windows 95. Consult *Peter Norton's Complete Guide to Windows 95, 1997 Edition* (1997, Sams Publishing, ISBN 0-672-31040-6), for further exploration of this topic.

In the Network control panel (refer to Figure 16.3), each of the components of Windows 95 networking is separate—as if you could take a piece away and the others would function well without it. Well, if the piece isn't needed for communications, or used by another piece, that's exactly the case.

To connect to an NT server from Windows 95, you need three basic pieces: a client, an adapter, and a protocol.

The client is the piece of the connection that controls the user's interface into the network. It controls the way that you're asked to log onto the network and the way that you'll be allowed to interface with the network once that connection has been made.

> **Tip:** Novell has created an interface for Windows 95 and for Windows NT called *Client 32*. The advantage of the Novell Client 32 is that it delivers the ability to administer the NetWare Directory Services for the workstation that contains it. The problems occur when you discover that some Microsoft applications and connections function more slowly in the Novell client and protocol atmosphere. This doesn't break either company's heart, I'm sure.

To add a client or protocol from the Windows 95 Network control panel, simply click Add. You can choose to add a client, adapter, protocol, or service. If you choose to add a client or protocol, you'll get a selection from which to choose, as shown in Figures 16.4 and 16.5.

Figure 16.4.
Protocol choices.

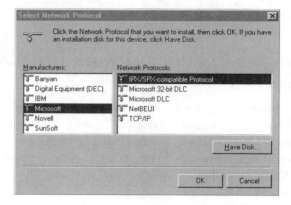

Figure 16.5.
Client choices.

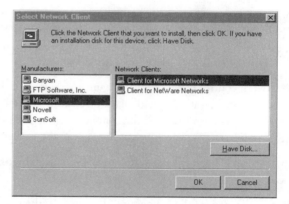

Installing the Protocol

Among the protocol choices you'll find two lists—vendors on the left and protocols on the right. Clicking a vendor opens a list of the protocols provided by that vendor. Clicking the protocol of choice on the right side and choosing OK adds that protocol to the list of protocols that can be used to access the network. But your duties are not done yet.

After you finish selecting all the protocols that you want to use, you must configure those protocols to function within the network framework. When you've finished selecting protocols, choose OK from the Network control panel—you'll be led through several screens that ask you to configure the protocol(s) you added. For example, for the TCP/IP protocol, you'll be asked to provide an address for the PC and a gateway address. If the protocol is simplistic, like IPX/SPX or NetBEUI, you won't be asked to provide further information. After configuring the system, the control panel closes, and you'll be asked to restart the system.

Installing the Client

Like selecting a protocol, when selecting a client you see two lists (vendors and client interfaces). After you select a vendor and a client, you'll be led through the information needed to access the network.

The client that's needed to access the Microsoft domain and workgroup schemes requires that you choose Microsoft from the vendor list and Client for Microsoft Networks from the listed items. Once you have selected these settings and returned to the Network control panel, you need to edit the properties of the client to properly connect to the domain or workgroup.

As you look at the Network control panel with the Client for Microsoft Networks available, you can configure a domain connection and/or a workgroup connection. Keep in mind that those two don't have to be mutually exclusive. You can use a workgroup for peer-to-peer networking and be part of a domain.

When configuring Windows 95 for domain access, follow these steps:

1. Select Client for Microsoft Networks on the Configuration page of the Network control panel (refer to Figure 16.3).
2. Click the Properties button to open the dialog box shown in Figure 16.6.
3. Click in the check box by the option Log on to Windows NT Domain.
4. Type the name of the logon domain for this PC. Click OK.

It's important to note that this doesn't mean that this PC can only log onto the domain that you type into this screen. This choice is only to establish the primary/default domain of the PC. When the client for Microsoft networks is the primary logon for the PC, the user will see a screen that asks for username, password, and domain. If the user would like to change the domain at that moment, she is welcome to do so.

Figure 16.6.
Setting the properties for the Microsoft client.

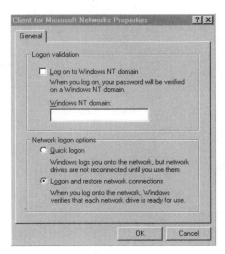

The choices in the Network Logon Options section of the dialog box are not critical to the logon of the user or PC. They're primarily to speed the logon process.

> **Tip:** Client choices are truly more dependent on the third-party networking scheme that you have in place. With Windows 95, the Microsoft networking information can be added into the client properties and will function in the background if you preconfigure them before bootup time. But many network operating systems may require that you use their logon as the primary client.

Installing the Adapter

The adapter is the hardware driver that you use to make your connection to the network. Windows 95 will most often make this selection for you during the installation if the card is already in place before the installation. If you haven't installed a NIC prior to installing Windows 95, the card can be added after the fact.

When using Windows 95, the easiest way to install the driver for a new adapter is to first use the Add New Hardware control panel. The steps vary depending on the NIC that you're installing, so we won't cover installing hardware in another operating system here. The point is that if you use the Add New Hardware control panel to introduce new adapters to the system, you'll find the adapters in the Network control panel when you arrive to install a client or protocol.

Protocols are the languages spoken across the network to make connection. (For more information on protocols, see Chapter 15, "Surviving in a Multi-Protocol World.") The important point to remember about protocols in Windows 95 is that you aren't limited to one protocol. If you use TCP/IP as the primary protocol for connection to NT, that doesn't mean that you can't load the IPX/SPX protocol suite for connection to NetWare.

To configure Windows 95 for workgroup access, follow these steps:

1. In the Network control panel, click the Identification tab.
2. In the Computer Name slot, type the name that will be used by the PC. Descriptions are optional.
3. In the Workgroup slot, type the name of the workgroup in which you would like the PC to participate. Then click OK.

Network Drive Share Usage

Windows 95 clients are capable of responding to NT logon scripts for drive-letter assignments just as Windows 3.x and DOS clients do. If you have many drive assignments or permanent drive assignments to make on a user account basis, this is the preferred method. But Windows 95 clients also have the ability to make use of network drives in two other ways. Drive assignments can be made from the DOS command prompt with the NET USE command, as mentioned elsewhere, but Windows 95 offers a much easier way of accessing network drives and/or creating drive-letter assignments.

First you must realize that Windows 95 and Windows NT are capable of using network entities without assigning a DOS logical pointer, such as C:> or D:>. Windows 95 can use a network resource via the Network Neighborhood or by using a UNC (universal naming convention) assignment, such as \\BILBO\SHARED-C.

Opening the Network Neighborhood icon on the desktop or in the Windows Explorer displays a listing of the network servers for which the user has permissions and a connection. Double-clicking the server icon displays the shares that the user can use. If the user wants to make use of the share, he really has two choices at this point: using the share directly or assigning a drive letter.

To use the share directly, double-click the share and use the share directly from the desktop icon.

To assign a drive letter, follow these steps:

1. Right-click the share and choose Map Network Drive from the shortcut menu. Windows displays a dialog box asking you to specify the drive and whether you want to reconnect at logon, as shown in Figure 16.7.

Figure 16.7.
The dialog box for mapping drives.

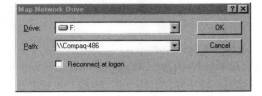

2. The automatic choice in the Drive option is simply the first available drive letter after local and network drive letters have already been assigned. If you want to change the drive letter that has been assigned automatically by Windows NT, click the arrow button and select the desired drive.

3. Click the Reconnect at Logon option if you want Windows 95 to look for this share and reassign that drive letter to the drive if the share is available.

4. Once your choices have been made, click OK. You will be taken to the drive and the Explorer window will be opened for that drive.

Printing Choices

Windows 95 printing is well-suited to the task of network printing. The operating system has built-in features that allow it to attach to network printers and use them from many different clients.

The concept of connecting to network printers through Windows 95 is the same as connecting to drive shares. The network interface can use network shared printers though either a UNC or the Explorer window.

NT uses logon scripts for printer port assignments just as Windows 3.x and DOS clients do. If you have numerous port assignments or permanent port assignments to make on a user-account basis, this is the preferred method.

Port assignments can be made from the DOS command prompt with the NET USE command, as mentioned earlier, but Windows 95 offers a much easier way of using network printers and/or creating printer port assignments.

Again, you need to realize that Windows 95 and Windows NT are capable of using network entities without assigning a DOS logical LPT port, such as LPT1 or LPT2. Windows 95 can use a network resource via the Network Neighborhood or by using a UNC assignment, such as \\BILBO\HP-Deskjet.

Opening the Network Neighborhood icon on the desktop or in the Windows Explorer displays a listing of the network servers for which the user has permissions and a connection. Double-clicking the server icon displays the shared drives and printers that the user can use. If the user wants to make use of the share, he really has two choices at this point: using the share directly or assigning a printer port.

To use the share directly, double-click the share and use the share directly from the desktop icon. Once you have double-clicked the printer share and added the proper driver (if necessary), the printer is listed among the available printers in 32-bit applications capable of using network devices directly (without a printer port assignment).

Note: If the printer you choose hasn't already been used on the PC, you'll be asked to configure the printer drivers for the printer before you're allowed to use it.

To assign a printer port, follow these steps:

1. Right-click the share and choose Capture Printer Port from the shortcut menu. You will then see a dialog box asking which port to assign and whether to reconnect at logon, as shown in Figure 16.8.

Figure 16.8.
The Capture Printer Port dialog box.

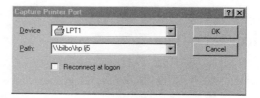

2. The automatic choice in the Device option is simply the first available port after local and network printer ports have already been assigned. If you want to change the port that has been assigned automatically, click the arrow button and select the desired port.

3. Click the Reconnect at Logon option if you want Windows to look for this share and reassign that port to the printer share if the share is available.

4. Once your choices have been made, click OK.

Profiles and Policies for Microsoft 32-Bit Clients

The Microsoft 32-bit operating systems (Windows NT and Windows 95) can be controlled to a much greater degree than the other clients that log on. This is simply because these operating systems have been created from the ground up to attach to and make use of the networked world. By using rules that have been preset for network clients, an administrator can control even the most minute behavior of a client. These preset rules and regulations for client workstation behavior are called *policies* and *profiles*.

Profiles are used to control the look and feel of the workstation when a particular user logs on. Items such as the desktop wallpaper, the applications that are available in menus, and network connections to printers and drives are all controllable through the use of user profiles.

If you have ever logged onto a Windows 95 workstation that has been used by someone else, but used a different username, you have seen profiles in action. The system informs you that you have logged on using a new username, and asks you to confirm your password. What's happening in the background is that Windows 95 is learning who you are and what you want in an operating system—it's beginning to keep a profile on you as a user. Once you're logged on, Windows 95 begins remembering things like what wallpaper you use, what icons you like on the desktop, what network connection you establish. It keeps those settings for you as your profile. That's just one type of profile, called a *local profile*. There are two types of profiles that we'll work with—local profiles and network profiles.

Local profiles control the workstation behavior based on user logon name to the local workstation. The local logon of a user into Windows NT Workstation or Windows 95 is primarily to facilitate this personalizing of the user experience. You as an administrator don't need to create these profiles. They're created for each new user who logs onto the system, and kept in a file named USER.DAT (for Windows 95) or NTUSER.DAT (for Windows NT).

Network profiles are obviously controlled at the network level. The profile in this case is stored on the server or within the domain structure that the user is logging onto. When a user attaches to the domain, her NTUSER.DAT file is sent down to the workstation and the profile is used from there. The point is to allow users to maintain a consistent look and feel from wherever they may attach to the network.

When users log onto different workstations throughout the network, a network profile allows them to have consistent presentations and tool sets to work with. But more importantly, the administrator can use profiles to give a more supportable desktop. If all the workstations on the network present a client with a uniform desktop and uniform set of network resources, it makes the administrator's job much easier.

Before you can manage profiles in the Windows 95 and Windows NT client environment, you must understand that they're not interchangeable. The two profile types are very close and do perform that same basic function, but NT profiles offer more security and control.

These are the differences between Windows NT and Windows 95 profiles:

- Windows 95 is not prepared to use network profiles by default. You must set the operating system to use them.

- Mandatory profiles in Windows 95 require that every user have an individual profile. NT users can all be forced to use the same profile.

- User profiles for Windows 95 users must be stored in the user's home directory.

Creating Network Profiles

When you want to create a profile to be shared by several users, keep in mind that it's no different from creating a profile for yourself when you log onto a particular NT or 95 workstation. When you sit down at a particular workstation and make the changes that you want to make the environment fit your needs, you're changing the profile file (NTUSER.DAT or USER.DAT) for the user you're logged on as. The easiest way to create a profile is to simply create the environment and copy the file containing the profile to the share location. You can make the process more difficult if you like, but it really is no more difficult than that.

The toughest part of the profile distribution process is knowing where to get the file and where to copy it to in order to make it available to your users. Windows 95 and Windows NT have different placement considerations; I'll cover those in the next two sections.

Managing Windows NT Network Profiles

Once you have logged onto a Windows NT workstation or server and have created a functional desktop environment, you're ready to distribute that profile.

The profile that you're using when logged on as an administrator can be copied from the System Properties control panel, under the User Profiles tab. This page provides you with a convenient tool to copy the profile that you are currently using to another location and to assign permissions to the user(s) who will be using the profile. Simply click the Copy To button to open the Copy To dialog box (see Figure 16.9).

Figure 16.9.
The Copy To dialog box.

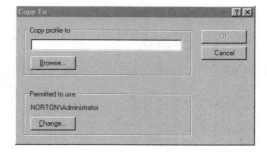

The Copy Profile To field asks where to copy the profile you're currently using. Your choices are to give a destination or to grant permission to the users who will use the copied profile. Typing a destination directory indicates that you want the current profile copied to that location. That's simple enough. But once that's done, you must grant the users who will use the profile permission to use the directory (if they don't already have it). Clicking the Change button in the Permitted to Use section of the dialog box displays a permissions dialog box containing user groups and offering you the opportunity to select individual users (see Figure 16.10). As with any NT permissions screen, you simply need to select the group or user that you want to use the profile and click OK.

Figure 16.10.
Permissions dialog box for profiles.

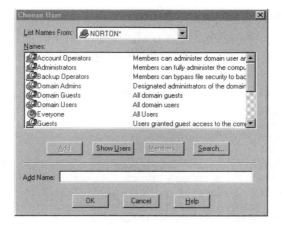

Managing Windows 95 Network Profiles

Windows 95 profiles exist on two different levels, depending on the way that the administrator has set up the operating system. Either the user base all uses the same profile, or each user has an individual profile. Within the Passwords control panel (only Microsoft knows why it's there), you must establish whether to allow for multiple profiles to be used at all. Before you can control your Windows 95 user profiles, you must first change the selection in this control panel.

To allow profile differences in Windows 95, follow these steps:

1. Open the Passwords control panel and click the User Profiles tab, as shown in Figure 16.11.

Figure 16.11.
The User Profiles page.

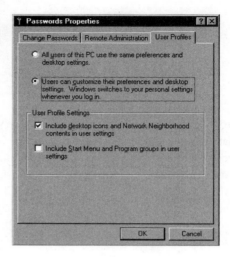

2. Once in this page, you'll see the choice to allow users to customize their desktop settings. By clicking this choice, you have effectively enabled profiles.

3. There are two check boxes at the bottom of the dialog box that should also be checked to allow for full control. Then click OK.

4. Once profiles have been activated for the operating system, you must reboot the system to begin recording separate profiles.

    Now the ability to use profiles in Windows 95 has been established.

The simplest part of profiles for Windows 95 clients is the creation of those profiles. Once you have set the system to use separate profiles, the system begins creating a new profile for each new user who logs onto the system.

Once you log onto a PC and set the desktop and Explorer properties in the desired manner, you'll find profile files in the WINDOWS\PROFILES directory, in directories named after the username, like this:

```
C:\WINDOWS\PROFILES\TBROWN
```

To make the profile available to a user on the network, you'll need to copy the profile to a network share and change the permissions of the directory to allow the user to use the profile.

Assigning Profiles to User Accounts

Once you have copied a profile to the network and made it available to the user base, your next task is to assign profiles to the users that you want to use network-based profiles. Before assigning profiles, you need to decide whether the profile will be mandatory or personal, as described in the following section.

Personal Profiles versus Mandatory Profiles

Personal profiles behave like the local profile in that the user is able to change the desktop and Explorer options and find those changes the next time she logs on. This allows users to have their individual desktop and Explorer settings follow them across the network to any workstation. This is the choice for you if you're looking for individuality and user control.

Mandatory profiles can't be changed by the user and most likely provide the desired effect for network profiles. Users who attach to a mandatory profile can make changes to the desktop and Explorer for the session in which they're participating, but once they log out and back on they find that things have returned to their original state. The point is to give a consistent presentation for every new logon.

The differentiation between these two types of profiles is the file extension for the profile file. Personal files have a .DAT extension; mandatory profiles have a .MAN extension.

The default filename you'll find in the user's profile directory has an extension of .DAT. To change the profile to mandatory, simply change the filename extension to .MAN. Giving the file a .MAN extension effectively makes the profile read-only.

User Assignments of Profiles

Once you have created a profile to be used by a user, the assignment of that profile follows these steps:

1. Open User Manager for Domains.
2. Select a user from the user list and double-click the user icon.
3. Click the Profile button. The User Environment Profile dialog box will appear.
4. Type the path of the profile for this user and click OK.

Tip: Keep in mind that Windows 95 users should use profiles located in their home directories. Mandatory profiles for Windows 95 users must be in their home directory.

Policies

Policies in Windows NT and Windows 95 allow an administrator to control the items to which users have access within the desktop operating system. Controlling a user's access to the network is one level of security, but often the next step is to control the access that the user has to making changes to the operating system that he depends on for daily access. In short, it's a way to stop users from creating mischief or shooting themselves in the foot.

Some examples of the items that you can change:

- The control panels that users can see—or any access to control panels at all.
- Items can be removed from the Start menu—items that allow a client to gain access you don't want, such as Run, Find, and so on.

Because of the differences in the Windows NT and Windows 95 operating systems, there are some differences in the things that can be controlled through policies. But beyond that, this is one place where Windows NT Workstation shines. There are a great number of items that you can control in NT through policies that you can't control in Windows 95. In fact, one of those options is the ability to completely avoid your policies. For the moment, though, we'll start by covering the way you edit policies and put them in action.

To edit the system policies, you must open the Policy Editor found in the Administrative Tools (Common) menu choice. The opening screen for the Policy Editor is blank, as shown in Figure 16.12.

Figure 16.12.
A fresh Policy Editor.

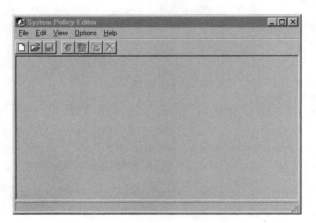

To edit the policies of both Windows NT and Windows 95 users, you need to make sure that you have both the Windows NT and Windows 95 templates loaded before creating a new policy. Choosing Options | Policy Template before opening any policy can do this. Once the template screen is open, make sure that you see the following templates (depending on the operating system that you want to control):

- COMMON.ADM for items that exist in both the Windows NT and Windows 95 environments
- WINNT.ADM for Windows NT-only items
- WINDOWS.ADM for Windows 95-only options

Once you've established that you have the necessary templates, you can proceed with editing the policy choices.

Choosing File | New Policy creates a new policy. You can choose from two icons: Default Computer and Default User. These policies apply to any computer or user that doesn't have a specific policy created for them.

Computer policies apply to any user who logs onto that specific machine in the domain. User and group policies apply to users who attach to the system and the specific things that they're allowed to do.

We won't look at each of the policies that you can change. (There are hundreds.) Instead, I'll encourage you to double-click the Default User and Default Computer icons, and then open some of the Registry choices that are available by clicking the plus (+) that's beside them (see Figure 16.13).

Figure 16.13.
The default user policies.

As you open and look at the user policies, you should see that there are three basic categories of Windows 95, Windows NT, and Common (those without a Windows NT or Windows 95 in front). Drilling down even further, you'll see that there are three general states of control for each option (see Figure 16.14):

- Shaded indicates that no change has been made.
- Clear signifies an explicit right to use that option.
- Checked marks an explicit denial to change or use that item.

Figure 16.14.
*Individual policy item
choices.*

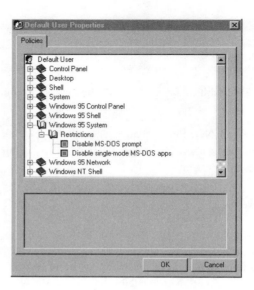

Changing an individual user, group account, or computer requires that you choose Edit followed by Add—and the option of your choice. The options are the same as they were for the default.

Once you've made the changes that you want, simply choose OK at the bottom of the dialog box. Then choose File | Save. Saving the .POL file to the DEFAULT directory of your PDC will enforce the policies domain-wide.

Something to consider when using group and user profiles is the relationship between user and group profiles and which profile will be used. When a user has a specific profile assigned, that's the profile that will be used, but if that user has no specific profile the operating system will look for any applicable group profiles. Multiple group profiles will be run in priority order. After all profiles have run, any computer policies that exist will be applied.

DOS and Windows Clients

It's important to remember when contemplating connecting Windows 3.x to the network that Windows 3.x is not an operating system, but an environment. For that reason, the connection of Windows 3.x and DOS workstations to the network really requires many of the same tools to get the job done.

Installing the DOS Client

The client installation can be run from two different locations. If the client workstation has a CD-ROM, you can use it to run the installation directly from the NT Server CD-ROM in the CLIENTS\MSCLIENTS\NETSETUP directory. You can also create floppy disk sets from the

CLIENTS\MSCLIENTS\DISKS directory. This directory contains two more directories, DISK1 and DISK2; by copying the contents of each directory to its respective floppy disk, you'll have a nice traveling kit to install the NT client.

After choosing a method, follow these steps:

1. Change to the proper directory (CLIENTS\MSCLIENTS\NETSETUP on the CD-ROM, or the root of DISK1 in the floppy disk install), type **SETUP**, and press Enter. Press Enter again for the opening screen.

2. The setup program prompts you for a target directory in which to install its files. By default, the directory name is C:\NET. Press Enter.

3. Next you'll be presented with a list of NIC drivers that are provided by Microsoft, or you can choose the Network Card Not Shown on List Below option. By picking from the listed cards and making your protocol choices, you'll move onto the next selection. If you choose an unlisted card, you'll be expected to provide a driver floppy disk and know in what directory to find the proper driver.

4. The next option is User Name. It's important to note that this isn't the only username that can ever be used at this PC—just the default choice. Type the default username for this workstation and press Enter.

5. You're now given an option to change any of the entries that have been made to this point. If you want to make a change, simply highlight the choice with your up- or down-arrow key; you'll be presented with that option again. If you're satisfied that you have chosen correctly, select The Listed Options Are Correct and press Enter.

6. Next you'll start the process of identifying the PC to a workgroup and/or domain. Select each option and type the proper response. Once you're satisfied that you have chosen correctly, select The Listed Options Are Correct and press Enter.

7. The choices that follow control the way that the client will interface with the network from a logon perspective. Once you're satisfied that you have chosen correctly, select The Listed Options Are Correct and press Enter.

   - Redirector options involve either the full or basic redirector. The only real advantage to the basic redirector is a memory savings of a few kilobytes of RAM. But that's at the cost of Windows 3.x functionality. If you can load the full redirector, I would suggest that you do so.

   - Startup options are the equivalent of deciding how much of the network you would like to load at each reboot of the machine. It doesn't stop you from connecting to a server or domain later, but it does allow you to control *when* you attach. The options are Run Network Client, Run Network Client and Load Pop-Up, and Do Not Run Network Client.

   - Logon validation is simply a question of whether this PC is going to participate in a domain or function solely in a workgroup environment.

8. Finally, you'll see a screen that allows you to review the options that you've chosen. If you're satisfied with your choices, select Network Configuration Is Correct and press Enter. Rebooting the PC allows the changes to take effect.

Using the DOS Client

Once you've installed the DOS client, you really rely on the pop-up menu TSR or the NET USE command to create connections to shared resources on the network. The idea is to create a way for users to control these shares in much the same way that Windows NT and Windows 95 users can use the Explorer and the Network Neighborhood scheme.

The Network Pop-up

The Network pop-up gives users a point-and-shoot type of interface into the network without Windows (see Figure 16.15). The pop-up is loaded with the key combination Ctrl-Alt-N.

Figure 16.15.
The network pop-up.

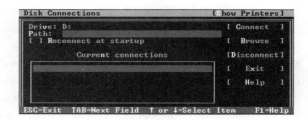

Once started, the interface allows the user to move through a selection of drive shares and printer shares. The first dialog box to appear when using the NET command is Disk Connections, which allows the client to make attachments to shared drives on NT servers and other PCs that have Microsoft drive sharing enabled. Pressing Ctrl-S brings up the Printer Connections dialog box, which allows for redirecting the output of printer ports to network printers. Pressing Ctrl-S again causes the Disk Connections dialog to be redisplayed. Pressing the Esc key causes the NET pop-up box to unload.

The NET Command String Variables

The NET commands are another way of making use of the available resources on the network from a DOS-based client. If you are experienced with the old LAN Manager networks, Windows for Workgroups networks, or even Personal NetWare, NET commands will return as an old friend.

The idea is to type out the command NET followed by a variable that will make the desired resource connection or change. For example, you might use the command NET USE F:\\BILBO\SHARED-C to create a logical drive that points to the shared drive C: on the BILBO server.

The following table lists the NET commands and their uses.

Syntax	Description
NET USE *drive letter*:*server**share_name*	Used where *drive letter* equals the letter you want to represent the shared drive in your environment.
NET USE *printer port*:*server**share_name*	Used where *printer port* equals the printer port (LPT1, LPT2, and so on) to allow DOS applications to use the shared resource.
NET LOGON	Used to start the logon process.
NET LOGOFF	Used to disconnect you from the network.
NET CONFIG	Used to help you discover the configuration of a workstation after the PC has already started.
NET VER	Reports the redirector version.
NET HELP	Displays this list of descriptions.
NET VIEW	Creates a listing of the available servers and shares in the PC's browsing scope.
NET DIAG	Displays diagnostic information about your network connection.

Windows 3.x Connectivity

Remember that, when installing Windows 3.x networking options, you have to first install the DOS full redirector. Once you have completed that task, you can install support for Microsoft networking in Windows. This is done by using the Windows Setup, which can be invoked either through the DOS-based SETUP.EXE command, run from the WINDOWS directory, or from the Windows Setup icon in the Main program group. Choose Microsoft LAN Manager 2.1 Enhanced for the Network (see Figure 16.16).

Figure 16.16.
*The Windows 3.1 Setup
window.*

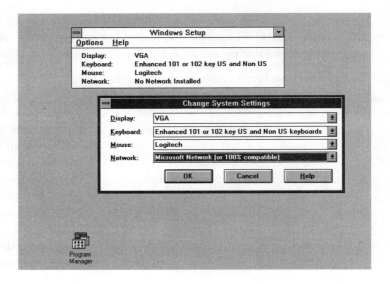

To attach to network drives under Windows 3.x, use the Disk menu in File Manager and choose Network Connections. The Network Connection dialog box will allow you to choose the drive letter to use, but you must manually type the UNC for the share you are connecting to.

The Network Connections dialog box in Print Manager is similar to the drive connections in that you can choose a printer port, but must manually type the UNC for the shared printer name.

Windows for Workgroups Clients

Windows for Workgroups (WfW) is really the first version of Windows that didn't have networking pasted onto it from the operating system below. WfW is capable of generating the activity to make a network connection, even if one wasn't created before entering Windows.

The WfW installation program or the Network Setup program (see Figure 16.17) in the Network program group allows you to install support for Microsoft networking. By double-clicking the Networks icon, another dialog box pops up that allows you to choose Install Microsoft Windows Network.

Clicking the Drivers button allows you to install network interface cards and protocols. Choose from the list of included NIC drivers, or use the driver that came with the client's NIC. Protocols include NetBEUI, which is the default for Microsoft networking on the client side, and NWLink, which is Microsoft's IPX-compatible protocol. The Windows NT Server CD-ROM also includes the 32-bit version of Microsoft's TCP/IP, which is installable through this dialog box by selecting the item Other; when prompted, point to the CLIENTS/TCP32WFW directory on the Windows NT Server CD-ROM.

Figure 16.17.
The Windows for
Workgroups Network Setup
dialog box.

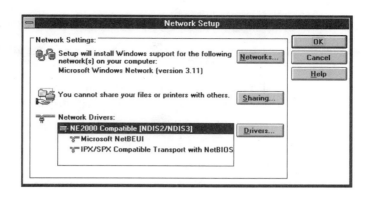

Once the network drivers are configured, Windows for Workgroups needs to be configured to log onto the Windows NT domain. This is done through the Networks icon located in the WfW Control Panel. This dialog box allows the user to change his computer name, include a description, and also change the workgroup.

Attaching to shared resources on the server can be done either through the command line with the NET USE command, or by using File Manager and Print Manager.

Opening the Disk menu in File Manager and choosing Connect Network Drive allows the client to see a list of servers and workstations on the network that have file sharing enabled. The client can then choose an available drive letter and select a share to associate with that drive letter. In Print Manager, you can associate a network printer with a printer port by choosing Printer | Connect Network Printer. The resulting dialog box shows a list of printer ports; if the Browse button is selected or the Always Browse check box is checked, all of the available network printers will be listed.

Macintosh Clients

One of the more difficult explanations that I must give administrators in the field is that the Apple Macintosh computer really doesn't need any special software or client to use an NT Server shared drive. The Macintosh is already equipped to attach to items on an AppleTalk network from day one.

This is really made possible on an NT network by a combination of two key factors. One, already mentioned, is that Macintoshes network at birth. But the second is that the NT server presents itself as a Macintosh when seen on the network by Macintosh clients. If your NT server is running Macintosh Services, the NT server advertises itself across the network as any other Macintosh server or peer.

The necessary pieces for this magic to happen are the following:

- Windows NT Server running Macintosh Services (covered in Chapter 18, "Macintosh Services")
- Macintosh clients running System 6.07 or higher (I strongly recommend System 7.5 or higher, if possible, because of its superior TCP/IP attributes)
- A common cable medium (Ethernet, Token Ring)

Once these criteria have been met, you should be able to use the Macintosh Chooser to simply view the NT server under the Appleshare icon.

Summary

It's the client connectivity that make the network go forward, and it's important to note that you'll probably put together 25 to 100 clients for every server you build. Hopefully, this chapter has given you some direction on the installation and management of those client stations.

The purpose behind client software is to give the workstation the ability to generate a call to the network and discover resources. We've seen that the two generations of Microsoft clients are extraordinarily different in what they offer as a client, and hopefully you've realized how much the 32-bit clients offer you as an administrator.

NT is capable of making resources available to client operating systems and machines including Windows NT, Windows 95, Windows 3.x, Windows for Workgroups, DOS, OS/2, LAN Manager, and even Macintosh. This chapter covered the installation and use of all of the Microsoft clients and the Macintosh client.

Finally, Windows NT has shown that it's clearly the choice when selecting a secure and controlled client for Windows NT Server or any network server. Because of the ability to create solid policies and profiles to control the user environment and lock down those resources, NT is superior to all the other client choices.

In the chapters that follow, we'll look deeper into some of the third-party clients and the NT tricks that you'll need to do to make them connect. But this chapter has laid some groundwork for how we must proceed from the client side.

Peter Norton™

Connectivity in a Heterogeneous World

17

NetWare Connectivity

Peter Norton™

The relationship between Microsoft and Novell has been in various states of flux for years, based on several factors. They've been a bit like strange dance partners that don't want to touch, but are forced by the dance. Not only does the dance require that they touch, but no other partners are really coming to the dance.

A frustration for Novell is that, throughout the existence of the NetWare product, the primary client operating system used by its customers has been made by Microsoft. Novell has always been limited by or driven with the things that it could deliver to its clients by the limits or strengths of the Microsoft operating system of the day. The limits of MS-DOS were so frustrating for Novell that they purchased a DOS version that they could manipulate themselves, called DR-DOS. DR-DOS never really took off, but no one really thought it would. The point was to show the glaring problems in the DOS world. This, of course, strengthened the relationship with Microsoft. ;-)

> **Note:** Norton Utilities was created to fill the holes that existed in the MS-DOS operating system. Many companies made their living from the fact that DOS was not as full-featured as it might have been. But, just like network operating systems, Microsoft does appear to leave room for the industry to make a living around them. If many companies depend on your product to make a living, they'll support you in a fight—a fact that some think Microsoft has lost sight of in recent times.

Microsoft has had the opposite problem to contend with. Over the last 10 years, Microsoft has thrown several network operating systems onto the market (OS/2, LAN Manager, NT 3.0), but none had really taken a swing at Novell. Microsoft still wakes up every day to find that the majority of the Microsoft business clients are connected to a Novell NetWare server. The numbers are changing a bit, and it really depends on who you listen to as to which story you'll get. But I think it's fair to say that NT is taking a much greater share of the NetWare market than DR-DOS took from MS-DOS.

The relationship is full of shots taken at each other, not the least of which is the purchase of WordPerfect and Quattro Pro by Novell to compete with Microsoft even on the productivity suite level.

When all is said and done, the real issue is that we most likely will have to live with both for many years to come. As an administrator of a large network, you'll almost certainly have to manage a relationship between Microsoft and Novell. Whether it's from an NT server to a NetWare server or from a Windows 95 workstation to a NetWare server, you'll most likely have to be involved in this type of relationship.

Estimates have Novell's market share at anywhere from 40% to 60% of the network operating systems (NOSes) installed. This is an important number because, whether you believe that the number is 40, 60, or something else, you have to consider that the closest competitor is not going to replace this product with a great deal of speed.

Market share matters to these NOS manufacturers because the user base depends on other software vendors supporting their NOS choice. If you could prove that NT as NOS would deliver files and printing devices at twice the speed of NetWare, it wouldn't matter that the user's primary accounting package wouldn't run on NT. But if a NOS company has enough market share, the problem solves itself—because software vendors begin to get pressure from a larger client base to make their products work on the new NOS.

Conceptual Differences

NT and NetWare have differences that go beyond the rocky relationship between their creators. Each of the operating systems has basic conceptual differences, as described in the following sections.

Security

To get started in the security area, let's review the security concepts from Chapter 8, "Microsoft Network Access Concepts Brief," because that chapter points out the differences between Windows NT Server and NetWare. When you begin to look at a security model, it helps to understand the initial state of security in the system before you begin to make changes. As I have dealt with PC network security systems, I've found two basic structures from which a security model can start:

- **Open to closed.** When a resource is created in this model, the entire user base has some level of access to that resource. The administrator must then close the doors to that resource in the places that he or she wants closed. The advantage of this form of security model is that it allows for quicker creation of shared devices and less work for the administrator if the system is to be open. The disadvantage is that when a resource is created it is inherently threatened.

- **Closed to open.** When a resource is created in this model, the general user population has no access to that resource. For any user without administrator clearance to access the resource, he or she must be given permission to do so. The strength of this model is the complete security that it offers—at no point is the resource exposed to users that the administrator didn't set up manually. The disadvantage of this system is that each resource must be handled in order to be delivered to the general user public.

Windows NT Server is more closely related to the open-to-closed model. Each resource that you create in an NT Server model is created as available to the general public. Once you have created the shared resource you can close the door, but the door is created in an open state.

Being inherently open can be a severe weakness in your network if you don't monitor it. When an administrator creates a share on an NTFS-formatted drive, the default permission on that share is Full Control to the group Everyone. Before we've even covered what the group names include and what the permission level Full Control means, it should be obvious that this needs to be changed as soon as possible. If you don't want the general public to have access to this data, you can't forget to change the permissions.

NetWare is a closed-to-open system. Shared disk resources in a NetWare environment are created with no access available to the users other than the supervisor or Admin-equivalent accounts. The door can be opened, but it must be opened for each user or group.

The fact that NetWare is inherently closed allows the administrator to relax about the creation of shared directories and volumes. But it also means that you must always be conscious of who has permissions and whether you need to grant those permissions.

Enterprise Account Management (Domains versus Bindery and Directory Services)

These two products have completely different approaches to enterprise account management. By *enterprise account management*, I'm referring to the concept of centrally managing user accounts within an enterprise.

Earlier chapters looked at Windows NT and domains for enterprise account management—the concept of containing the accounts in domains and then creating trusts between those domains, if sharing is necessary between domains.

NetWare uses two different schemes for containing users at the server level: bindery services and NetWare Directory Services (NDS). The scheme is really based on the version of NetWare with which you're interfacing; NetWare 3.x and lower use a bindery database, while NetWare 4.0 and above use NDS. They're also divided along lines of single-server versus enterprise schemes.

Bindery Services

NetWare versions prior to NetWare 4.0 use bindery services to contain user and group accounts along with system information about the items that are being shared with the network. The *bindery* is a collection of files responsible for keeping authentication information for users and groups—much like a domain in NT. All information about the user is kept in this database.

The difference between an NT domain and the bindery of a NetWare 3.x (or lower) server is that the bindery is a per-server item. Unlike an NT domain, the bindery is an item that each server maintains. For a user to access the resources of a bindery-based server, he must have an account on that server.

This is not conducive to an enterprise scheme because it requires the administrator to create and maintain users and groups on all of the servers individually. Imagine a large firm with 50 servers and several thousand users. This poor soul would have to make changes to every server individually when the user permissions need to be changed. The most difficult issue is attempting to maintain a consistent and clean management scheme.

NetWare Directory Services (NDS)

NetWare Directory Services (NDS) is the current form of user account and resource management used in the NetWare world, and frankly the place that NetWare shines the most. NDS compares more closely with the domain model of NT than bindery services. NDS also involves the creation of user accounts in centrally-manageable containers, but there are several twists in the NetWare scheme.

Users in an NDS environment no longer log onto a particular server, but instead log onto the network. Just as in the domain structure, the servers themselves share a list of users, groups, and resources that are controlled and authenticated through that central list.

The difference in the NDS world is that every item in the network is an object contained within a multilayered directory. The objects (users, resources, and containers) are kept within a directory structure that resembles the directory structure found on your hard drive (see Figure 17.1).

Figure 17.1.
Directory structure in a simplistic form.

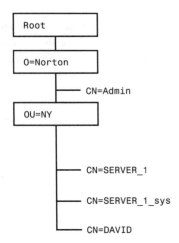

Objects are divided and kept within containers that resemble directories and subdirectories in the DOS world. The concept of a domain still exists in this structure, but is instead called a *container object*. Container objects contain user objects and resource objects, but they can also contain other container objects. The user and resource objects are referred to as *leaf objects* because they cannot contain other objects, just as a tree leaf can grow no limbs or leaves. This structure allows for multiple layers within a single network structure.

There are four object types in the NDS world:

- Root or [root]
- Organization (o)
- Organizational unit (ou)
- Leaf objects or common name (cn)

The root container is comparable to the root directory of a DOS directory structure. The only items that can exist in the root container are organization (O) containers (like directories).

Notice that the term cn is used for a leaf object instead of LO. This is to conform with the international standard for directory services called X.500. The term *common name* fits within that structure, as does the entire NDS structure. But it would have been to simpler to name them *common name* in NetWare.

Note: There's another type of container that we won't cover, called a *country container*. Simply, country containers are a special container for multinational companies, and are rarely used. But they don't really fit in the context of what we're covering—Novell administrators, please forgive the pun (context).

Organizations can contain organizational units (comparable to subdirectories) and leaf objects. If you're creating a small network, such as a single-domain network, this may be the point at which you stop your directory structure. You can add users and shared resources at this level, and there's no reason to add more if you're not faced with security, size, or political reasons.

Organizational units (OU) are simply containers that can exist within containers. They can contain leaf objects and OUs, just like the organizations can (see Figure 17.2).

Figure 17.2.
A sample NDS tree.

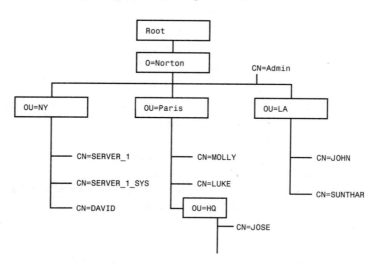

Writing the location of a specific item in an NDS directory tree is much like writing a directory path in a file system, but in reverse. An NDS object's path is referred to as the object's *context*. The context is written in reverse of the way that you think of a file path; you begin at the deepest point in the NDS tree, at the object you are referring to (if you understand Internet domain names, it will make more sense). Here's an example:

`.CN=PNORTON.OU=NORTON.O=SYMANTEC`

In this example, PNORTON is the username. Because a user is a leaf object, the username is referred to as a CN (common name). NORTON refers to an organizational unit (abbreviated OU). Finally, SYMANTEC refers to an organization (abbreviated O). The period separating the pieces is just that—a separator.

The context can be written in an abbreviated fashion to save characters; the abbreviated version wouldn't include the initials to identify what the pieces are:

`.PNORTON.NORTON.SYMANTEC`

The assumption when you use this type of address is that the item farthest to the left is a leaf object and the item on the far right is an organization. Everything between must be an organizational unit.

If you understand the NT world, it may help to consider the idea of domains that can contain not only users and resources, but also other domains. If you make that leap, you can imagine that the domains within the containing domain would be members of the containing domain. The administrator of the containing domain could administer all the domains within it. Permissions could be assigned for users and resources across domains because trusts would be irrelevant to the administrator of the containing domain. Because these "super" administrators can assign permissions across domain lines, they can administer users and resources in the subdomains. That's NDS from an NT perspective.

NDS permissions (or *rights*, as they're called in the NetWare world) are related not only to the user or group but also to the object's place in the directory tree. The objects contained within a container object are given the rights of that container and have Read and Browse rights to everything in the container. This system allows containers to behave not only as domains, but as groups as well. If I wanted to grant all the users in a specific container the right to use a printer in another container, I could simply grant the container the right to use the printer (no trusts, no blips, no errors).

Note: This is obviously a much deeper subject, but since our goal is not to be NDS experts, I'll suggest that you see *NetWare Unleashed, Second Edition* (1995, Sams Publishing, ISBN 0-672-30712-X).

The use of containers doesn't eliminate the need for groups. In fact, Novell and Microsoft do agree on the management of users rights/permissions through the use of groups. It just makes sense to create groups that do what you want, and then assign users. Containers simply add a layer of manageability to the scheme.

Management of containers can be done from any position that the installing administrator sees fit, including assigning an administrator within the container. The scariest part of the NDS world is that an administrator can remove the rights of all other administrators—including administrators of up-line containers, effectively locking the door to the container from the inside. The idea is to be able to create a shared directory structure, but still maintain independent security.

Printing

NetWare printing is more simplistic in its nature than that of NT Server. NetWare functions in more of a store-and-forward mode than NT.

Connectivity to NetWare printers can be made through many different methods. The actions necessary to connect depend on what client you're using.

DOS prompt connection to NetWare printers can be done through two methods:

- Capture. Capture is a command-line tool that functions like a NET USE command when you're connected using the NetWare client. Commands follow the same basic structure as NET USE. For example,

  ```
  Capture l=2 q=HPLJ5 s=Bilbo
  ```

  would be the equivalent of

  ```
  NET USE LPT2 \\Bilbo\hplj5
  ```

- NET USE LPT? \\Server\Share-Name. If you are attached to the network using a Microsoft networking-compatible OS (Windows 95, Windows NT, or Windows for Workgroups), you can use NET USE commands just as you would in an NT environment.

From within the Windows NT or Windows 95 operating system GUI interface, you attach to NetWare printers in the same way that you attach to any other network printer. When using NetWare shared printers, if you have the right driver locally installed at the client, you can use the printer.

NT Connectivity for NetWare

Earlier I mentioned the fact that software vendors would be remiss if they ignored the NOS vendor with the lion's share of the market. Well, Microsoft understands that if they are going to take over Novell's market they must first get in the door. Microsoft's server product offers numerous ways to connect to the NetWare world and make it possible for NetWare users to connect to Microsoft servers without making special arrangements.

To make the job of integrating Windows NT Server and NetWare even easier, Microsoft offers three other utilities that ship with Windows NT Server 4.0:

- Gateway Service for NetWare
- IPX/SPX-compatible protocol
- Migrate NetWare Servers to Windows NT Server

They also offer a product enhancement that can be purchased separately called *File and Print Services for NetWare*.

The following sections describe these utilities.

Gateway Service for NetWare (GSNW)

The Gateway Service for NetWare (GSNW) is a very interesting use of the fact that NT can share pretty much anything to which it has a connection. With this service, that just so happens to include shared drives from NetWare servers. The concept is to allow clients with NT client software installed to access a NetWare share—without requiring access to the NetWare Core Protocol (NCP) found in the NetWare client.

In effect, the NT server accesses the NetWare server as a user account and mounts a shared drive. NT then in turn shares the drive back out to the network. The advantage of this setup is that clients running protocols other than IPX/SPX and NCP are able to access NetWare drives (see Figure 17.3). Now, Novell's client can be made to use other protocols, but if you have users who are already connecting to an NT server with TCP/IP or NetBEUI, this makes it possible to use that connectivity with as little changing of clients as possible.

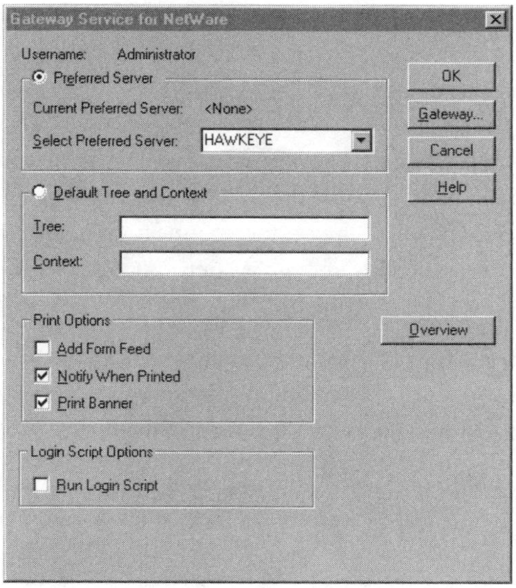

Figure 17.3.
Gateway Service for NetWare gives access to NT users for NetWare resources.

The downside to this relationship is that you're using double the hardware to access a single resource. This isn't meant to replace the purchase of hard drive space on your NT server or avoid paying for NetWare licenses. It's a convenience item to be used in an interim time frame or to get a small number of users across to a resource that they need. The fact is that this can be a very slow connection if it's overused.

> **Note:** Previous versions of this product did not support NDS, but now the product does support NDS, primarily because the client portion of the product now attaches to NDS servers. It allows users to navigate NDS trees through the connection made by the server. Users can even print to NDS-based printers.

Installing Gateway Service for NetWare

The installation of GSNW has three parts:

- Before you can install GSNW, you must lay the proper groundwork at the NetWare server. There must be a service user available for NT to use to access the resources to share, and that user must be a member of the proper groups.

- The second part is the installation of the client portion of GSNW. You must be able to log onto the NetWare server before you can share it with others. GSNW is not only a gateway product—in fact, it can be used as a client for NetWare servers only. Unless you follow the final steps, that's all it's being used for.

- The third piece of the puzzle is to configure the gateway to allow NT users to have access to the NetWare resources. Once the NetWare server is ready to accept a connection and the client has facilitated that connection, you must set up the actual gateway service.

Licensing Considerations

Okay, so the last thing that anyone wants to hear about in the middle of this opening of doors is the legality of it all, but it must be brought up. Licensing of this product is not supported by Novell in a formal sense; if you need support for a connection made in this manner, Novell will most likely not be able to hang up quickly enough. When you know the facts, I don't think you could blame them.

The fact of the matter is that NT is using only one licensed connection at the Novell server to provide this service. If you owned a two-user version of NetWare (given away freely at numerous events) and used this product, you could literally share the NetWare resources with as many clients as the NT server could handle. But that is not legal.

Your responsibility to Novell in this case is to make sure that every user making use of a NetWare resource is licensed by Novell to use the resource—no matter how they get there.

NetWare Preparation

Before the NT server can access the resources that it wants to share, some groundwork must be done at the NetWare server. Following is a grocery list of the items that must be taken care of from the NetWare side before you can use GSNW as a gateway. You can either perform these duties yourself or have them done by the NetWare administrator (if that's a different person):

- A user account must be created that can be used by GSNW. Don't force a periodic password change to this account. Keep in mind that it will be the equivalent of a service account because a server will be attaching, not a human who sees password warnings.

- A group named NTGATEWAY must be created and the user just mentioned must belong to that group.

- The group NTGATEWAY must have the maximum rights to the shared resource that you would like to give to any NT user. This is because the NT server cannot grant to any NT user more rights than the NT server has.

NetWare versions of 4.0 and higher use a portion of the NDS tree for bindery emulation so that a legacy client can make connection. This area is more tolerant of users that log on with no context or the wrong context specified. Creating users and groups in the bindery context is no longer necessary, but if you can create the user in the bindery context, you may lend yourself some fault tolerance in the event of a logon problem.

Installing the Gateway/Client Service

The installation of the gateway/client service is very simple from the NT side. In fact, it's no more difficult than installing a network client on a Windows 95 workstation. Follow these steps:

1. Open the Network control panel and click the Services tab.

2. To add a service, click the Add button. You will see a list of the available services.

3. Click Gateway (and Client) Services for NetWare and then click OK.

4. You will be prompted to locate your NT installation files. Enter the path and click Continue.

5. Once NT has finished copying the files it needs to install the service, you can click Close to finish the installation.

6. You will be prompted to restart the server for the changes to take effect. Click Yes to restart.

Once you have installed the Gateway Service and restarted, you'll be prompted for NetWare preferences for your user account as part of the logon. After you supply your username and password to log onto the NT domain, the GSNW user information screen appears, asking for the following information regarding your NetWare connection (the list is on the next page):

- **Preferred Server.** This is the default server that you will be logged onto when attaching to the network. Type the name of the server that you would prefer to be attached to upon logon.

- **Default Tree.** This refers to the name of the NDS tree that you would like to attach to (provided there's a NetWare 4.x server).

- **Context.** This is the context where the user you will be logging onto the NetWare server exists in the NDS tree. If you fill out this information during logon, it may save you some time later.

The completion of this information is the completion of the client side of the GSNW package. If you were installing the service purely as a client, then you're now finished and able to use the NetWare server from a client standpoint.

Completion of the Gateway Connection

Now the NetWare server is prepared for the gateway to attach and the gateway has the client necessary to make the connection. The remaining task is to configure the gateway to share the resource that you would like to present to your clients.

These are the steps to configure the Gateway Service:

1. Open the GSNW dialog box (refer to Figure 17.3). This initial screen is for configuring the client portion only. If you missed the initial screen, you'll need to fill in this portion and reboot before continuing to step 2.

2. Click the Gateway button. This will open a dialog box for configuring the gateway (see Figure 17.4).

Figure 17.4.
Gateway configuration.

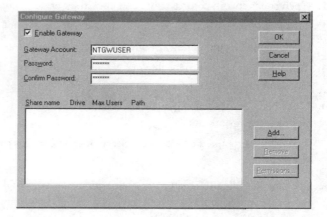

3. Click in the check box in the upper-left corner to enable the gateway. This will open the dialog boxes for the remaining information.

4. Fill the open form with the pertinent information. The Gateway Account is the account that you had created on the NT server. Password and confirmation are for the password assigned to the account.

You are now ready to begin sharing NetWare resources. The first step is to add a share:

1. Click the Add button in the Configure Gateway dialog box to open the New Share dialog box (see Figure 17.5).

Figure 17.5.
The New Share dialog box.

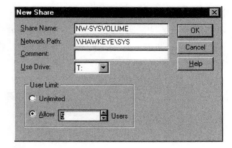

2. In the Share Name field, enter the name of the share as you want it presented to NT users.

3. In the Network Path box, type the UNC path to the drive and directory you want to share. For example, if you want to share the MAILBOX directory from the SYS volume of the server HAWKEYE, type \\HAWKEYE\SYS\MAILBOX.

4. If you want a share comment, fill in the Comment field (optional).

5. The Use Drive field will assign whichever drive letter you choose to the resource you entered in Network Path.

6. Finally, you must decide whether to limit the number of users that you will allow to access this share. The default is not to limit the number of users. If you click the Allow option and enter a number in the box beside it, that number is the maximum number of NT users who can access the NetWare resource at any one time. This option can also help to avoid license violation on the NetWare server.

7. Click OK to create the share.

8. Click OK to close the Configure Gateway dialog box.

9. Click OK to close the control panel.

Once the share is created, you are dealing with an NT share—just as if you had created the share from an NT volume. A Permissions button has been added to the Configure Gateway dialog box (refer to Figure 17.4), but this is more of a reminder and a convenience item than a necessity.

NWLink IPX/SPX-Compatible Protocol

The Windows NT Server network operating system NWLink IPX/SPX-compatible protocol provides NetWare clients access to NT Server-based applications. With the NWLink IPX/SPX-compatible protocol, NetWare clients can access applications such as Microsoft SQL Server databases or Microsoft SNA Server host connectivity, without having to change their client-side software.

NWLink IPX/SPX-compatible protocol can be added through the Network control panel by following these steps:

1. Open the Network control panel.

2. Click the Protocols tab.

3. Click Add, select NWLink IPX/SPX Compatible Transport from the listed protocols, and click OK (see Figure 17.6).

Figure 17.6.
Protocol choices.

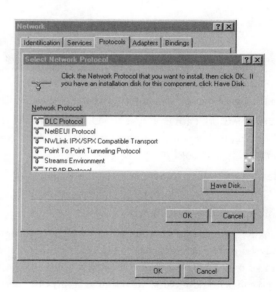

4. You will be prompted to provide the location of the NT installation files. Enter the path of the drive and directory containing the NT install files (for example, `f:\i386`) and click Continue.

5. If you have installed RAS, you'll be prompted for whether you want to install the NWLink IPX/SPX for RAS. Answer as you choose, but realize that you can change this setting later if you like (see Figure 17.7). If you choose to add the protocol to RAS, you'll have to configure RAS.

Figure 17.7.
The RAS option.

6. You should now be returned to the Network control panel. Click Close. The computer will prompt you to restart to finish the installation. Click Yes.

Once you have installed the protocol and the computer has rebooted, you'll need to configure the protocol to function in your NetWare environment. Follow these steps to configure the NWLink IPX/SPX protocol:

1. Open the Network control panel and click the Protocols tab.
2. Choose NWLink IPX/SPX Compatible Transport and click Properties to display the optional items in the IPX/SPX protocol (see Figure 17.8).

Figure 17.8.
NWLink IPX/SPX options.

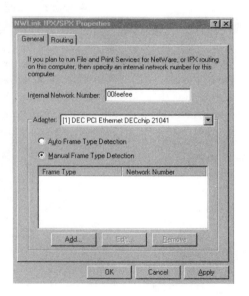

3. The first choice is the Internal Network Number. The internal network number in a Novell network is a unique identifier for servers in a NetWare network. The number can be from one to eight digits in hexadecimal (see the following note on hexadecimal). Enter a number and press the Tab key.

Note: The hexadecimal (hex) numbering scheme is used in the engineering world to expand the possible digits in a number address by including alpha characters, but still avoid confusion. Digits include the following: 0123456789ABCDEF. The idea is to be able to give an address with letters and numbers without the confusion over digits such as lower-case *L* (l) and one (1). It can also add some humor with addresses like C0FFEE or F0B1A.

The options that remain will matter to you only if you have more than one NIC or if you have numerous frame types running on an Ethernet segment. If you're running only one segment that contains only one frame type, you can simply click OK.

Note: Frame types are basically different flavors of Ethernet. When you use the Ethernet protocol, you can build the Ethernet packet of data in many different ways. The way in which you build the packet is called the *frame type*. This matters in the NetWare world because two different frame types are used for IPX/SPX communications on NetWare servers. See Chapter 15, "Surviving in a Multi-Protocol World," for more detail on frames.

If the segment that you're attaching to has more than one frame type running, you may want to consider specifying a frame type for that NIC. NetWare runs two different Ethernet frame types; in order to maintain connectivity to older systems, some NetWare networks will run both frame types across the same segment. When this happens, it can confuse your NT server when it attempts to auto-detect the frame type, and may slow your server startup or make connectivity sluggish.

If you are using IPX/SPX as a protocol choice for an NT-only network, you must establish the frame type and network number in order to seed the network. In other words, auto frame-type detection assumes that a frame type and network number have already been selected by another entity. If they haven't, no frame or network number will be found. In that case, you have to start the IPX/SPX network from scratch.

To select a frame type and establish a network number, follow these directions (the instructions here are a continuation of the preceding steps):

1. Click Manual Frame Type Selection. If more than one NIC is present, you'll need to select the desired NIC in the option above the frame type choice before choosing a frame type.

2. Click Add. You'll get a list of frame types available for your protocol and a network number option.

3. Click the arrow button beside the Frame Type option and select the frame type being used by the NetWare network to which you want to connect (see Figure 17.9).

Figure 17.9.
Frame type selection.

4. In the Network Number box, enter the network number for that segment of the network. This number can be up to an eight-digit hex number and must match any other NICs running on this segment of the network. For example, if a NetWare server on the network is already running an 802.2 frame on this segment with a network address of f2453a23, your 802.2 frame must also have a network number of f2453a23.

If you are operating two or more NICs in the server, you may want activate routing for IPX/SPX. Select the Routing tab in the NWLink IPX/SPX Properties dialog box and click the check box Enable RIP Routing.

Migrating NetWare Servers to Windows NT Server

The Migration Tool for NetWare is covered in detail in Chapter 4, "Installation Considerations," but we'll cover the function of the tool briefly here so that you have some idea why it exists. For details on how to use it, see Chapter 4.

The Migration Tool for NetWare is a utility that automatically ports NetWare 2.x/3.x user accounts, group accounts, security information, logon scripts, administrator accounts, files, directories, file attributes, and file rights to Windows NT Server. In addition, it performs this migration without affecting the NetWare server in any way. As a result, NetWare user services are not interrupted.

The Migration Tool for NetWare offers administrators flexibility in transferring user accounts and data to a Windows NT Server-based computer. The Migration Tool allows the following:

- Migration from a single NetWare server to a single Windows NT Server
- Migration from multiple NetWare servers to a single Windows NT Server
- Other configurations, meaning that administrators can redistribute information across many servers
- A trial migration to identify problems, such as duplicate user accounts, and resolution options before the actual migration is performed
- Availability of all NetWare and Windows NT Server-based services throughout a migration

The Migration Tool for NetWare automatically migrates NetWare user and group accounts, logon scripts, files, directories, security, and permissions to Windows NT Server. It's important to note that if you're going to migrate security, the NT volume needs to be formatted as NTFS in order to transfer the rights to permissions.

File and Print Services for NetWare (FPNW)

File and Print Services for NetWare (FPNW) is a product sold separately by Microsoft to help in the transition from a NetWare world to an NT world. The product gives an NT server the ability to present itself and its resources as a NetWare 3.x server.

This product is really the opposite of the Gateway Service for NetWare in its appeal. This product allows an administrator to let NetWare clients continue using their NetWare client software, but have access to an NT server and its resources. This allows the administrator to slowly convert clients to the Microsoft client at their desktops.

> **Note:** One of the toughest parts of a migration from one NOS to another is the changing of the client connection software, not the server migration. You see, the server migration is all done at one PC, but the clients have many variations—and there are at least "two" clients for every server.

The product installs through the Network control panel just like any other network service.

Microsoft Directory Service Manager for NetWare (DSMN)

Microsoft Directory Service Manager for NetWare (DSMN) sounds like a wondrous revelation that Microsoft has finally released directory services for NT, but that's not the case. This product is an add-on product available through download from Microsoft that allows the administrator to do some cross-product management. With Windows NT Server running DSMN, NetWare administrators can centrally manage their mixed Windows NT and NetWare environments with the Windows NT Domain Manager. DSMN copies the NetWare user accounts to the Windows NT Directory Service and then propagates any changes back to the NetWare server. All this is done without the need to install any software on the NetWare servers.

The drawback is that it will only work in the bindery world. If you are running a 4.x version of NetWare, you must be running bindery emulation, and even then the only users that this product can affect are those users created in the bindery context.

If you have a small number of NetWare 3.x and 2.x servers, this product is a nice tool for migrating from NetWare to NT or to support those legacy products. DSMN simplifies network administration tasks. Administrators can centrally manage their Windows NT Server and NetWare account information, while having to maintain only one user account and associated password for each end user on the network.

DSMN includes the following features:

- A point-and-click interface for propagating user and group accounts from NetWare 2.x/3.x (and 4.x in bindery emulation mode) to Windows NT.
- Account database backup and replication to any location on the network.
- Each user's account name and password are identical on all NetWare and Windows NT servers, so they use the same name and password regardless of where they log on.

The Novell Side of the Story

Novell now offers a Windows NT client for NetWare that includes both a client for NetWare NDS and a package for administering NetWare NDS and NT domains in one admin package. The full product is called the *IntranetWare Client for Windows NT*, and it comes along with NetWare v4.11 and IntranetWare (a variation on the NetWare 4.11 product).

Note: If you already own NetWare 4.1, this product will still work well for you. You can download it from http://www.novell.com. It's huge, though—approximately 8MB.

The Novell Workstation Manager

The Novell Workstation Manager, a component of the IntranetWare Client for Windows NT Workstation, provides a solution to managing the local NT Workstation user accounts through NDS. Using this solution, all user account information, both NDS and NT Workstation, can now be centrally managed through a single administration utility—NetWare Administrator.

With the Novell Workstation Manager, administrators can now create a workstation object within NDS, and then associate users, groups, or organizations within NDS with the workstation object. Upon logon, the IntranetWare Client for Windows NT verifies whether the user is associated with a workstation object in NDS. If the user is associated with an NDS workstation object, the IntranetWare Client for Windows NT Workstation is able to create local user accounts dynamically—administrators don't have to concern themselves with creating the local accounts. Also, customers are not forced into purchasing, installing, and maintaining costly NT Server and domains in order to administer the local NT Workstation user accounts.

The NetWare Administrator for Windows NT

The NetWare Administrator for Windows NT gives network managers a single, centralized point of administration for users and groups in a mixed IntranetWare (or NetWare) and Windows NT domain environment. It allows user information to be created and maintained in NDS and synchronized automatically with the NT domain, simplifying network administration. When user accounts are created or given access to a new application, the network manager can make the users members of the domain for the application server. By using NetWare Administrator for Windows NT to synchronize existing NT domains and workgroups with NDS, network managers can simplify the management of NT users and groups.

Figure 17.10.
NetWare Administrator.

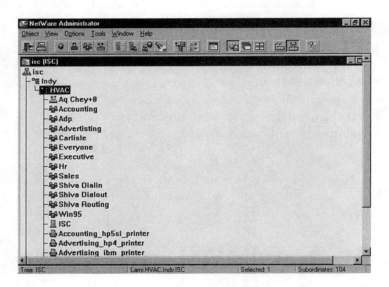

NetWare Administrator for Windows NT gives network managers flexibility in managing users. For example, users who require access only to general applications may be made members of a standard group. When their accounts are established, they are given access rights as "domain users." If the NT Server has been set to allow "domain user" group members the right to access a common area where the applications are located, no additional administration is required. To restrict applications to certain users, the network manager may create a group of selected users to access the more private applications. These predefined NT groups can be given additional rights beyond those of a domain user and may be managed from NDS.

Installing the NetWare Client and Administrator for NT

The latest release of IntranetWare Client for Windows NT includes an updated version of NetWare Administrator, called *NetWare Administrator NT (NWADMNNT)*.

> **Warning:** Before installing this product, consider the fact that this product will replace some rather critical system files. I have personally used the product and have found no major issues, but I wouldn't suggest that you install it on a mission-critical server. This is a workstation product. It will function on an NT server, but if you have NT Server problems, you're now dependent on Novell to help you through them (not good).

To install NetWare Administrator NT, you must have NDS rights to create objects on the directory tree and rights to create files on the SYS:\PUBLIC directory of the server where you are installing NetWare Administrator NT.

These are the steps for installing:

1. Locate the ADMSETUP.EXE icon on the IntranetWare Client for Windows NT CD or in the directory where you have unpacked the downloaded version from the Internet site.

2. Double-click ADMSETUP.EXE.

3. Choose Yes to accept the Novell Terms and Conditions. If you choose No, you won't be able to install the administration utilities.

4. Choose Continue after reading the Administrator Utility title screen.

5. Choose the utilities you want to install by checking the check boxes next to the utilities' names. There are three choices: Novell Application Launcher, NetWare Administrator, and Workstation Manager Administration Module. At minimum, install the Workstation and Administrator pieces.

6. Choose a server from the To Server list.

7. Choose OK. A progress screen appears, with two progress bars. The top bar shows which application is being installed. The bottom bar shows the percentage of files that have been installed. When the files are installed, the Installation Complete dialog box appears.

8. Choose Run NWAdmin to start NetWare Administrator.

   or

   Choose OK to exit the installer without starting NetWare Administrator.

Summary

Microsoft and Novell are not exactly the best of friends at this point in their existence, but neither company is silly enough to leave the client base of the competitor out in the cold.

The conceptual differences today are fairly small in all but the management of an enterprise-network-account scheme, and for the moment I believe that Novell has to be given the nod in this area. But Microsoft has made great strides in keeping the utilities available for the user base to make connections between the two products. NDS and the domain paradigm are barely comparable because of the greater depth of a directory tree. But hopefully you've seen how NDS is used and can gain the help you need for connectivity.

Microsoft has created many products to make this connection possible because they realize how important it is that they be able to get in the door. Gateway Service for NetWare will help you to operate in the transition and allow NT users to still access NetWare resources. NWLink IPX/SPX-compatible protocol is available for protocol-level compatibility, but also to allow NT to use IPX as a central protocol if desired.

File and Print Services for NetWare (FPNW) and Microsoft Directory Service Manager for NetWare (DSMN) are products that are sold separately from NT. These products help the NT administrator to make NT resources available in a NetWare world.

Not only is Microsoft working to make the NetWare connection, Novell is making efforts to stay connected to NT as a client. Products like the Novell Workstation Manager and the NetWare Administrator for Windows NT are being offered to keep the Novell NetWare shops happy.

18

Macintosh Services

Peter Norton™

Among the clients that populate your network you may have many different desktop PC workstations, and among them you may find the Apple Macintosh. The Apple Macintosh (Mac) is very often found in the creative and media departments of large companies because of the great amount of attention and software that has been given to the Mac in this area.

Mac users are often well-versed about why they have the computer that they have and what that computer does for them specifically, unlike many Intel-based PC users. These users aren't just involved in the use of productivity software (spreadsheet, word processing, and so on); they most likely have a very specific need that only Macintosh can deliver. Your challenge is to get them connected to your local or global computing resources.

Windows NT Server integrates with an Apple Macintosh network by adding a service to the operating system. *Services for Macintosh* makes it possible for Intel-based, Alpha-based, and Apple Macintosh clients to share files and printers on the same NT server.

Concepts

Services for Macintosh is simply that—a service that allows Macs to participate in the use of network resources through either their native communications or Microsoft-specific plans.

Windows NT Server Services for Macintosh supports *AppleTalk Filing Protocol* (AFP) versions 2.0 and 2.1. AFP allows the Macintosh to speak natively to the file system of the NT server. The LocalTalk, EtherTalk, TokenTalk, and FDDITalk protocols are variations on the AppleTalk protocol that allow for communications over different networking protocols (EtherTalk=Ethernet, TokenTalk=Token Ring, and so on). In addition, Services for Macintosh supports version 5.2 or later of the LaserWriter printer.

> **Note:** LocalTalk is an old networking topology that was used by Apple to connect the Macintosh systems to one another. The network ran at 256Kbps and was a linear bus topology that worked a bit like 10Base2 (coax) Ethernet. The latest renditions of it are actually called *PhoneNet* and are made by Ferralon.

Support of these native Mac protocols and communications is very important because it allows Macintosh users and systems to play by the rules that they are used to and comfortable with. Comfort and ease of use are even more important with these users, because you as an administrator are dealing with a squeamish audience. These folks have already come to expect Intel-class PCs to fail.

The service includes everything that you will need to manage the Macintosh environment from the NT side. A set of graphical administration tools is fully integrated into Windows NT Server File Manager. An integrated print manager allows the administrator to still use one interface.

> **Note:** You'll see once you install the File Server for Macintosh that an old friend reappears: File Manager. As you read through this chapter, you'll see several references to File Manager; they're not typing mistakes. File Manager is installed again and is the primary access to Macintosh file services.

By nature, Macintosh computers don't print to or see printers that are not PostScript-based. The problem is that very few of them have the ability to advertise over an AppleTalk network. NT Server with the Macintosh service provides a method for advertising that service and allows Mac printing to non-PostScript printers.

The logon process that comes from Apple is not as secure as that provided by Microsoft or Novell, so Microsoft provides some added encryption and security levels.

Macintosh Services

When Services for Macintosh is installed, two services are enabled: *File Server for Macintosh* and *Print Services for Macintosh*. A device, the *AppleTalk protocol*, is also enabled. The services can be controlled through the Control Panel Services application, while the device is controlled through the Control Panel Devices application. By default, the services are started automatically.

AppleShare File Server

The AppleShare File Server service allows you to designate a directory as a Macintosh-accessible volume, ensure that Macintosh filenames are legal NTFS names, and handle permissions.

> **Tip:** File Server for Macintosh should be paused to make changes to the server attributes while currently connected users continue working. No new Macintosh logons can be made while this service is paused. Also, the service should be stopped to change the server name that Macintosh users will see in the Chooser.

Macintosh Print Services

The Macintosh Print Services service, also known as MacPrint, allows network users to send print jobs to a spooler on the computer running Windows NT Server, and they can continue working, rather than waiting for their print jobs to complete.

Tip: MacPrint cannot be paused, and should be stopped when you install another printer driver or configure a printer. It should also be stopped to immediately see the result of deleting, creating, or changing a printer.

AppleTalk Protocol

The AppleTalk protocol is a suite of protocols that Services for Macintosh uses to route information. It works behind the scenes to ensure that computers on the network can talk to one another (see Chapter 15, "Surviving in a Multi-Protocol World," for reference).

Tip: AppleTalk protocol cannot be paused, and should be stopped to change router parameters and the default network zone.

Installing Macintosh Services

The installation requirements and configuration options during and after installation of Services for Macintosh are as follows.

For a Windows NT Server system, in addition to the Windows NT Server requirements, Services for Macintosh also requires the following:

- 2MB of free hard disk space for the Services for Macintosh software.
- An NTFS partition to create directories that can be accessed by Macintosh workstations.

Note: An NTFS partition is necessary to store Macintosh files. If there is no NTFS partition, Services for Macintosh can still be installed, but only print services will be available.

All Macintosh systems that have the ability to use AppleShare (the Apple networking software) can use Windows NT Services for Macintosh (this includes all Macintoshes, except for the Macintosh XL and Macintosh 128K). In addition to using AppleShare, the following are required:

- Version 6.0.8 or later of the Macintosh operating system; System 7.1 is preferred.
- Version 2.0 or later of the AppleTalk filing protocol; v2.1 is preferred.

For a Macintosh client and the NT server to connect, they must share a common communications medium. Macintosh computers have a single port built in for LocalTalk communications. If you want to use this form of network, you need to have a matching NIC for your NT server. The Macintosh can also use Ethernet or Token Ring to communicate, so a NIC can also be added to the Mac to make the connection. The point is to have a commonly shared line of communication, just like an Intel-based PC.

Services for Macintosh is installed from the Network control panel, just like any other network service.

Warning: Be aware before you start this process that Services for Macintosh will require the server to be restarted after the installation in order to function.

The process follows these steps:

1. Open the Network control panel and click the Services tab.
2. Click Add and choose Services for Macintosh from the listed services.
3. Click OK. You'll be prompted for the path of your NT installation files. After typing the path (or if the correct path is already listed), click Continue.

Note: If you don't have an NTFS volume on your server, you'll be prompted and warned that you won't be able to share a volume unless you have that NTFS volume.

4. Close the Network control panel.
5. The Microsoft AppleTalk Protocol Properties will appear for you to configure networking options (see Figure 18.1).

   Your options at this point are to continue setting up the AppleTalk parameters or click OK to restart and configure the options later. The following section describes setting up the AppleTalk network options.

6. After installation, the computer must be restarted for the installation to take effect.

Figure 18.1.
Networking options.

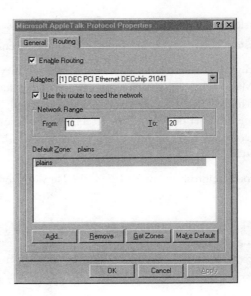

Volume/Shares Creation

On a computer running Windows NT Server, it's possible to share the same directory multiple times with different share names. It's also possible to share a subdirectory of a share with a totally different share name. However, with Services for Macintosh, creating a Macintosh-accessible volume involves slightly different rules:

- It's not possible to configure one directory as multiple volumes. For example, after D:\TEST has been made a Macintosh-accessible volume called TEST, it's impossible to create another Macintosh-accessible volume called TEST2 from the D:\TEST directory.

- It's not possible to nest volumes. For example, if you create a Macintosh-accessible volume called TEST, you won't be able to create volumes for \DOCS, \FILES, or \GAMES if these directories are in the TEST directory tree:

  \TEST\DOCS

  \TEST\FILES

  \TEST\GAMES

  Instead, create individual volumes for the \DOCS, \FILES, and \GAMES directories and don't create the TEST volume at the parent directory level.

- The maximum number of volumes is 255 (this is an AppleTalk limitation). However, the length of the volume names determines the number that can be seen by Macintosh workstations. Volume names can have a maximum of 27 characters. Volume names must all fit in a buffer in order to be displayed; the size of the buffer is determined by an underlying AppleTalk protocol.

To determine the number of Macintosh-accessible volume names that can be displayed, use the following formula, where N is the number of volume names and L is the average length of the volume names (in bytes):

```
N*L< 4624
```

File Considerations

When using Services for Macintosh, there are special file considerations:

- Translating filenames: Files stored on an NTFS partition are translated to 8.3 format.
- Filename appearance: Files appear differently to Macintosh and non-Macintosh users.
- Associating file extensions causes the correct application to launch, whether a Macintosh or non-Macintosh user requests the application.

When a Macintosh file is created on the server, Services for Macintosh ensures that it doesn't contain any characters considered illegal by NTFS. If any illegal characters are found, they're removed before passing the file to NTFS. Any time a filename is longer than a FAT-standard 8.3 filename, NTFS creates a short 8.3 filename for the file.

When using Services for Macintosh, long filenames are translated to 8.3 format in the same manner as any filename translations on NTFS partitions. For the first four files, the operating system substitutes a tilde (~) and a number from 1 to 4, in succession, for everything beyond the sixth character. The tilde is your tip that the name has been truncated.

After the fourth file with an identical name, the naming convention changes: the first two characters are kept, but a hashing algorithm is used to generate a unique alphanumeric name for the next four. It gets complicated and the exact method is not the point. But, simply put, the system begins using alphanumeric character combinations (numbers and letters) to give itself more possibilities (for example, MYOF58~5.DOC, MY6968~5.DOC).

Within a directory that has been both shared and made a Macintosh-accessible volume, the following occurs:

- Non-Macintosh systems accessing the share can see directories and files, which is how everything is actually stored.
- Macintosh workstations can see what appear to be Macintosh files and folders, along with their respective icons.
- When accessing the volume, Macintosh users can create files and folders with Macintosh filenames, which can be 31 characters or less in length, and can contain spaces and other characters. Because Macintosh-accessible volumes are on NTFS partitions, non-Macintosh systems that don't recognize long filenames will see the NTFS-generated 8.3 filename when accessing the shared directory.

- For Macintosh users, if the file has been created by a non-Macintosh system and the filename has more than 31 characters, they will see the NTFS-generated 8.3 filename.

- With extension-type associations, both Macintosh and non-Macintosh versions of applications can easily work on the same data file.

- When a file on the server has an extension associated with a Macintosh file type and file creator, the Macintosh Finder displays the appropriate icon for the file when a Macintosh user looks at the files on the server. In addition, if a Macintosh user chooses the file, the correct application will start and open the file.

- Use the Associate option from the MacFile menu in File Manager to manage file extension associations.

Creating a Macintosh-Accessible Volume

When a Windows NT Server system shares directories, files are placed in the shared directory that other users on the network can access. For a Macintosh user to access the files in the shared directory, the system administrator must designate the shared directory as a Macintosh-accessible volume. Creating a Macintosh-accessible volume is very similar to sharing a directory:

1. In File Manager, select the directory on an NTFS partition to use as a Macintosh volume.
2. From the MacFile menu, choose Create Volume to display the Create Macintosh Accessible Volume dialog box, as shown in Figure 18.2.

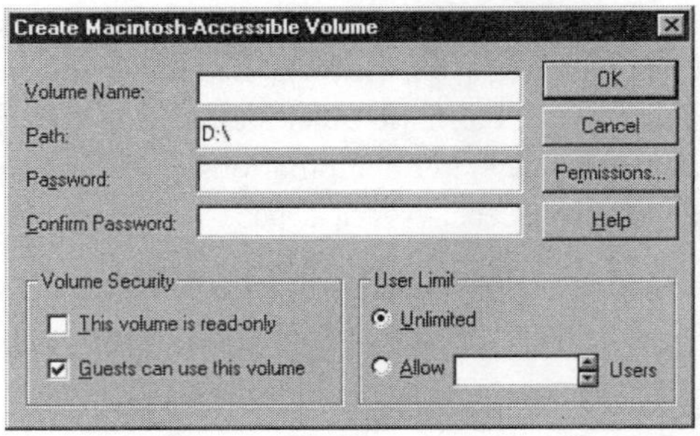

Figure 18.2.
The Create Macintosh-Accessible Volume dialog box.

The main differences between this dialog box and the Share As dialog box, which is used to share a directory, are the fields Password and Confirm Password. If a Macintosh-accessible volume is assigned a password, users connecting from a Macintosh workstation are required to supply the assigned password. The password applies only to Macintosh users accessing the volume. Non-Macintosh users don't have to supply a password when accessing the same directory structure through a share name.

AppleTalk Configuration and Routing Options

The AppleTalk protocol component of Services for Macintosh can be configured through the AppleTalk Protocol Configuration dialog box displayed during the installation of Services for Macintosh. This dialog box allows you to select the *zones* (similar to workgroups) where services will appear, specify the server to act as an AppleTalk router, and choose advanced options for AppleTalk routing.

The configuration options in the AppleTalk Protocol Configuration dialog box are as follows:

- **Network.** The adapter driver that binds the AppleTalk protocol.

- **Zone.** Similar to workgroups, zones are a collection of computers. Macintosh-accessible volumes and Windows NT Server printers appear in zones through the Macintosh Chooser.

- **Enable Routing.** If this box is checked, the computer running Windows NT Server and Services for Macintosh will become an AppleTalk router. This means that if the AppleTalk protocol is bound to more than one network adapter, the computer running Windows NT Server will be seen by Macintoshes connected to all of the bound networks. If this box is not selected, the computer running Windows NT Server will be seen only from the Macintoshes connected to the default network—the one to which the AppleTalk Protocol is bound.

The advanced options are available when the Enable Routing check box is selected in the AppleTalk Configuration dialog box and you click the Advanced button. Advanced options include the following:

- **Networks.** This option allows you to select the appropriate network adapter card for configuration.

- **Seed This Network.** By identifying zones on the network and determining network ranges, this allows a computer running Windows NT Server to initialize network information. This option should be selected only on systems that will be the authority for the zone and network number range for the Macintosh network.

- **Network Range.** Setting the network range is an important part of seeding a network because all AppleTalk networks in an intranet are assigned a range of numbers. Each workstation on the network is identified to the network by one of these numbers, combined with a dynamically assigned AppleTalk-node-identification number. Because of this, no two networks on an intranet should have overlapping ranges.

The allowable values for network range are 1 to 65,279. If you specify a range that overlaps another range, an error message is displayed.

- **Zone Information.** Setting zone information is also part of seeding a network. Through zone information, the current list of zones can be viewed, zones can be added and removed, and the default zone can be set.

  The default zone is the zone in which all AppleTalk devices will appear if a preferred zone has not been specified for them.

Macintosh Printing

Printers in the Mac world have the same network behavior that a Macintosh hard drive does when it's shared. The units advertise themselves across the network in the chatty AppleTalk fashion. Windows NT allows the administrator of the NT network to take advantage of this behavior to either publish AppleTalk printers to the non-Mac clients on the network or to give Mac users the ability to print to NT printers that normally would not advertise for them to use.

The advantage of using AppleTalk-compliant printers for non-AppleTalk clients is that the AppleTalk networking makes the printers easy to find and add to the network printer list. Another advantage is that most of these printers have been created for high-end graphics users and have great print quality.

> **Tip:** Be aware that using AppleTalk-compliant printers for non-AppleTalk clients can be a disadvantage when you find that you have users printing simple text documents to your $25,000 high-end photo imager. This may be a time to finally implement printer security.

Adding an AppleTalk printer to the NT operating system is much like adding any local printer. You will add a port to connect the printer to, because the printer isn't connected directly to the NT machine, but this is the only difference. The following steps lead you up to the point of adding that port (for further instructions on adding a printer in general, see Chapter 7, "Printing"):

1. From the Start menu, choose Settings | Printers.
2. In the Printers control panel, double-click the icon named Add Printer.
3. Choose My Computer to create the printer on this NT machine. Click Next.
4. Click the Add button to add a printer port. A list of port types appears (see Figure 18.3).
5. Click the New Port button to see a choice of AppleTalk zones—as if you were looking at NT domains. Choose the proper zone to locate the printer and double-click that zone. The zone will expand, showing all the available printers in the zone.
6. Select the printer (see Figure 18.4) and click OK. NT will ask if you want to capture the printer; click Yes.

Figure 18.3.
Available printer ports.

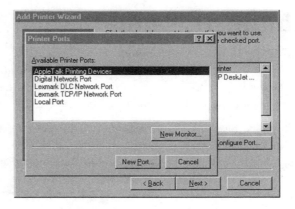

Figure 18.4.
Available AppleTalk printing devices.

From this point forward, you are simply installing a printer. The printer can be shared and/or used locally, but it's now available to the NT operating system.

Macintosh connectivity to the printers available to other NT clients is done for you when you install the Macintosh services. The NT operating system will automatically advertise all the shared printers across the AppleTalk network in the default zone of the server. NT advertises them to the Apple LaserWriter format; when the Mac user opens the Chooser and clicks LaserWriter, she'll see the NT printers as well as all the other AppleTalk printers.

An important point to remember in this situation is that the Macintosh will be printing to these printers as if they were AppleTalk PostScript printers. The Apple LaserWriter printer is a PostScript printer; if you print to a non-PostScript printer with PostScript code, you'll get tons of wasted paper.

Administration

Once you have installed the Macintosh services, you can control the services through use of the MacFile control panel. This control panel should be somewhat familiar to you because it's very much like the Server Properties screen in Server Manager. As a matter of fact, Server Manager has a separate menu choice just for this control panel, called MacFile.

MacFile allows you to observe the active users, the users on certain volumes, and even files—just like Server Manager properties. But the unique feature is the Attributes button that lets you control Macintosh appearance and behavior of your NT server (see Figure 18.5).

Figure 18.5.
MacFile attributes.

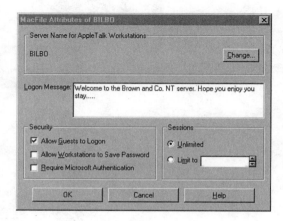

The following list describes the attributes:

- **Server Name.** The name that Macintosh users see when they log on.
- **Logon Message.** A message that Macintosh users see when they log on. Macintosh System 7.1 or later must be running to see this message.
- **Allow Guests to Logon.** Allows users who don't have a user account and password to log on.
- **Allow Workstations to Save Password.** Allows Macintosh users to save their passwords on their workstations, so that they won't always be prompted for the password. However, this will make the Windows NT Server system less secure.
- **Require Microsoft Authentication.** Requires Macintosh users to use Microsoft authentication to log on to the server. This option uses encrypted passwords.
- **Sessions.** The number of Macintosh users that can be connected at one time.

Security

Using Windows NT Server and NTFS, permissions can be placed on shares, directories, and files. Macintosh permissions differ in that they can be set only for folders, not for individual files.

Types of Macintosh Permissions

A Macintosh has three types of file permissions, known as *access privileges*. The following table describes these permissions.

Permission	Description
See Files	Users can see the files in the current folder and read the files.
See Folders	Users can see which folders are contained in the current folder. They can see and open any folders.
Make Changes	Users can modify files, rename files, move files, create new files, and delete existing files.

Macintosh users are given access privileges as members of three different categories:

- **Owner.** By default, the user who created the folder or the user or group account that has been assigned ownership.
- **Group.** Every folder can have one group associated with it, and the permissions apply to members of that group.
- **Everyone.** All users connected to the volume.

When a user at a Macintosh workstation creates a folder on the server, the user's primary group is the group that's associated with the folder. When the owner then gives permissions for the folder to the Group category, it's the owner's primary group that's receiving the permissions.

User Manager for Domains allows an administrator to set a global group as the primary group for a user. The primary group is used for only two things:

- Services for Macintosh
- The Posix subsystem

Using Windows NT, permissions can be assigned separately for each file. The Macintosh doesn't support file-level permissions. Windows NT file-level permissions apply to Macintosh users only if those permissions are more restrictive than permissions assigned to the Macintosh-accessible volume. For example, if a Macintosh user has See Files, See Folders, or Make Changes permissions for a volume, the user can read and make changes to the files in the volume. However, if that user has only Read permission for a particular file in that volume, the user can only read that file.

Services for Macintosh translates permissions so that those set by a non-Macintosh user are translated into the equivalent Macintosh permissions (and vice versa). Permissions are translated based on the following table.

Windows NT Permissions	Equivalent Macintosh Permissions
Read	See Files and See Folders
Write and Delete	Make Changes

In a Macintosh environment, a folder's owner can set Macintosh permissions on a file created in that environment, but only at the folder level.

In a Windows NT environment, a user can set permissions on a file created in a Macintosh environment according to the following rules:

- The folder's owner, an account with the Change Permissions permission, or an administrator can set Windows NT permissions on the directory or files.

- A system administrator can set Macintosh permissions using the MacFile Permissions menu in File Manager.

With Services for Macintosh, network security is enforced in the same way for Macintosh workstations and non-Macintosh workstations.

Services for Macintosh uses the same user accounts database as Windows NT Server. Therefore, if a person using a Macintosh workstation already has an account that can be assigned permissions to a Macintosh-accessible volume on a computer running Windows NT Server and Services for Macintosh, it's not necessary to create another account for that user. It's only necessary to create accounts for Macintosh users who don't already have an account that can be assigned permissions.

Logons

Because the Macintosh logon process uses standard Windows NT user accounts, Macintosh users can log on to the local domain or any trusted domain within the network.

There are three possible ways in which a Macintosh user can log on to a computer running Windows NT Server and Services for Macintosh:

- **As a guest.** Allows logons without requiring a password.

- **As a user with a clear-text password.** Clear-text password protection is part of the AppleShare software on Macintoshes. It doesn't provide any kind of password encryption. Passwords can be no more than eight characters long.

- **As a user with an encrypted password.** The encrypted password can be up to 14 characters long.

Microsoft User Authentication Module (UAM)

Services for Macintosh includes an optional Microsoft authentication component, which is an extension to AppleShare. Microsoft authentication provides a more secure logon session. There are several reasons that Microsoft developed its own User Authentication Module (UAM) instead of using the existing Apple UAM.

The encryption scheme used in the Apple UAM requires that a clear-text password be stored on the server. This is unacceptable in a Windows NT Server environment because of the C2 requirements. The Microsoft UAM uses encrypted passwords.

Microsoft has added support for logging on to trusted domains. Passwords under the Apple UAM have a maximum length of 8 characters; with Microsoft authentication, this increases to 14 characters.

Microsoft authentication can be completely installed on Macintosh workstations over the network. After it's installed, authentication can be required when a Macintosh user connects to a computer running Windows NT Server. If the Macintosh is running System 7.1 or later, and Windows NT Server is configured to require Microsoft authentication, the user can only use Microsoft authentication. Systems prior to System 7.1 have two choices: Microsoft authentication or clear-text passwords.

Summary

Microsoft has added many services for the Macintosh client, realizing that that part of the market will be found in most large firms and many small ones. AppleShare File Server, used for file services, allows the sharing of data. Macintosh Print Services allows for the use of AppleTalk-based printers by NT-, Intel-, and Alpha-based clients, but also can make NT printers available to Macintosh clients.

The installation and setup of Macintosh services is fairly simple, and permissions translate easily. Once the installation is done, creating and sharing volumes is simple, but does involve some new concepts. Keep in mind that you'll once again have to use the old File Manager tool.

NT Services for Macintosh are simple to use because they do a very good job of making both platforms comfortable. The Macintosh user doesn't need to learn the nuances of the Intel/NT world, and the NT administrator is able to simply manage accounts. The product does the work for the humans—imagine that. It seems a bit like a Macintosh idea.

19

UNIX Host to NT Server Connectivity

Peter Norton™

Wherever communications is done, some UNIX system or UNIX-developed protocol is probably involved. UNIX is involved in the majority of enterprise businesses, and most of that involvement is in the routing and generation of network services. It's an incredibly powerful operating system that has been portable, multiprocessing, and 32-bit for many years. So why isn't UNIX the predominant operating system in the world today?

UNIX has had two major problems with market share:

- UNIX has been a cold and unfriendly operating system that appeared to be almost purposefully unintuitive.
- UNIX has lacked a strong voice to market the platform until the last few years.

One of the strengths of the UNIX operating system is also one of the factors that has kept it down. No one company is "the UNIX company." UNIX was created by AT&T's Bell Labs, but it's now being marketed by many different companies. UNIX Systems (once owned by Novell), SCO (Santa Cruz Operation), SGI (Silicon Graphics), UC-Berkeley, and many others have written and/or owned some variation on UNIX. Not to mention XENIX, AIX, Linux, and a multitude of UNIX clones that exist to keep it stirred. For that reason, there has been no real standard-bearer for the UNIX operating system in the PC world.

Sun Microsystems has been sent blazing to the forefront by the force of the Internet. Until recently, the Internet was the sole domain of host systems. But small UNIX hosts (primarily from Sun and SGI) have been the smaller systems in the world of host computers. Along with the boom of the Internet, Sun became the *de facto* standard for Internet service providers (ISPs). But in the meantime, Microsoft has been eating up the PC market and the lion's share of desktop computing.

NT-to-UNIX communications has already been given a tremendous boost by the fact that NT has become so Internet-oriented. The communications methods covered in Chapter 21, "TCP/IP Networking," and Chapter 22, "Internet Information Server," show a great number of ways to communicate between UNIX and NT. But what I believe you'll miss in those chapters is the communications and usage methods that lend themselves to more long-term communications.

By its very nature, UNIX is a tough OS to pin down, but it's always an easy system to communicate with (at least from a host-user point of view). The problem that PC users have with the concept of UNIX communications is that it isn't as friendly to them as the connections being made to a Microsoft or Novell share.

HTTP, FTP, and Gopher all give the feeling of not really being connected in any meaningful way. You attach, get what you want, and move on. Telnet is a connection, but it's no more friendly than a very old version of DOS—and you often might as well be connected to a dumb terminal. No, what the users want from the UNIX world is a connection that gives them a permanent and continuous connection, like an NT share.

Conceptual Differences

When the different operating systems available in the late 1980s for the PC were added up, only one was really powerful enough to offer server-based applications, but that operating system wasn't meant to be used in the server-based file-and-print atmosphere. It also was lacking any usable interface for the common man. That operating system was UNIX. When NT was initially created, one of its primary goals was to match many of the strengths of UNIX, but deliver a more palatable platform.

Windows NT was designed for client/server computing; UNIX was designed for host-based terminal computing. They're two different computing concepts. Windows NT isn't a multiuser operating system in the usual sense of the word. You don't have users with limited-function dumb terminals, dumb-terminal emulators, or X-terminals connecting to a Windows NT-based host. What you do have are users on single-user general purpose workstations (clients) connecting to multiuser general purpose servers, with the processing load shared between both. The distinction between the two environments is subtle, but understanding it is key to understanding Windows NT. Both operating systems obviously have grown a great deal since the late 1980s. But if you read the press for them lately, you'll see that they are again heading in these directions.

UNIX and the companies that support UNIX as a primary platform are moving to what they call a "thin client" model. The concept is to create systems that are thin in the area of local resources, but rich in the way of presentation and network connectivity. In this model, the applications would be delivered through a browser-like interpreter. In effect, the browser would be the "terminal" interface.

One of the hidden powers behind UNIX is the file metaphor. In UNIX, devices such as printers, tape drives, keyboards, and terminal screens all appear as ordinary files to both programmers and regular users. This simplifies many routine tasks, and is a key component in the extensibility of the system. Windows NT capitalizes on this metaphor and expands it, using an object metaphor that's pervasive throughout the architecture of the system. Not only does Windows NT view all the things in the UNIX file metaphor as objects, but so are things such as processes and threads, shared memory segments, and access rights.

Security

The Security Reference Monitor, in conjunction with the Logon Process protected subsystem and the Security protected subsystem, form the security model for Windows NT. In a multitasking operating system, applications share a variety of system resources, including physical memory, I/O devices, files, and directories, as well as the system processor(s). Applications must have proper authorization before being allowed to access any of these system resources, and it's the components of the security model for Windows NT that enforce this policy.

With UNIX, security of this nature usually comes in the form of an add-on such as Kerberos. Kerberos, which gets its name from the three-headed dog that guards the entrance to Hades in Greek mythology, was developed at MIT as part of Project Athena.

The Security Reference Monitor acts as the watchdog, enforcing the access-validation and audit-generation policy defined by the local Security protected subsystem. It provides run-time services to both kernel-mode and user-mode components for validating access to objects, checking for user privileges, and generating audit messages. As with other components in the Windows NT Executive, the Security Reference Monitor runs exclusively in kernel mode.

User Accounts

Both Windows NT and UNIX support groups and user accounts. With groups, you can group together users who have similar jobs and resource needs. Groups make granting rights and resource permissions easier; a single action of giving a right or permission to a group gives that right or permission to all present and future members of that group.

Even though they're conceptually similar, groups within Windows NT are inherently more powerful than groups within UNIX. Windows NT provides a set of built-in groups that gives members rights and abilities to perform various tasks, such as backing up the computers or administering the network printers. Examples of these built-in groups are Administrators, Backup Operators, Print Operators, Power Users, Users, and Guests. It's also possible for the system administrator to define new types of groups, although the built-in groups cover most of the standard combinations of rights and permissions that you would expect to find. User accounts can belong to more than one group at the same time, and share the combined rights and permissions of all of them.

Windows NT offers a set of standard permissions for files and directories in NTFS volumes. These standard permissions offer useful combinations of specific types of access, which are called *individual permissions*. Individual permissions are somewhat analogous to UNIX permissions, and consist of Read (R), Write (W), Execute (X), Delete (D), Change Permissions (P), and Take Ownership (O). These permissions can be specified either directly as individual permissions or indirectly as standard permissions. Examples of standard permissions are Read (RX), Change (RWXD), No Access (None), and Full Control (All). As with the built-in groups, it's possible for the system administrator to create new types of standard permissions, although most of the combinations that you would expect to find are covered in the existing ones.

UNIX supports three sets of file and directory permissions: owner, group, and world. This is the familiar `-rwxrwxrwx` that shows up in the output from the UNIX `ls -al` command. With Windows NT, permissions can be granted to either individual users or to groups. The big difference between Windows NT and UNIX is that, with Windows NT, multiple sets of permissions can be granted to multiple combinations of groups and/or individual users. You are not limited to just three sets.

DNS and WINS

A computer on a network usually has both a name and an address. Take TCP/IP, for example. It requires an IP address and computer name, which are unique identifiers for the specific computer on the network. Computers use the IP addresses to identify each other, but people usually find it easier to work with the computer names. Therefore, a mechanism must be available to convert computer names into their corresponding IP addresses. This mechanism is known as *name resolution*.

A computer running Windows NT can use one or more of the following methods to ensure accurate name resolution in TCP/IP networks:

- Windows Internet Name Service (WINS) is a NetBIOS-over-TCP/IP (NBT) mode of operation, defined in RFC 1001/1002 as p-node.
- Domain Name System (DNS) is defined in RFCs 1034 and 1035.
- A HOSTS file is a flat file used to specify the DNS computer name and IP address mapping.
- An LMHOSTS file is a flat file used to specify the NetBIOS computer name and IP address mapping.

The Windows Internet Name Service provides a dynamic database for registering and querying name-to-IP address mappings in a routed network environment. When a DHCP client moves from one segment to another, the IP address change is automatically updated in the WINS database. As with DHCP, no intervention is required of either the user or the system administrator to update the configuration information.

WINS consists of two components: the WINS server, which handles name queries and registrations, and the client software, which queries for computer name resolution. WINS servers support multiple replication partners in order to provide increased service availability, better fault tolerance, and load balancing. Each WINS server must be configured with at least one other WINS server as its replication partner. These partners can be configured to be either pull partners or push partners, depending on how replications are to be propagated. WINS can also provide name-resolution service to certain non-WINS computers through *proxies*, which are WINS-enabled computers that act as intermediaries between the WINS server and the non-WINS clients.

The Domain Name System (DNS) is a distributed database that provides a hierarchical naming system for identifying hosts on the Internet. A UNIX domain is synonymous with a DNS domain. DNS was developed to solve the problems that arose when the number of hosts on the Internet grew dramatically in the early 1980s. Although DNS might seem similar to WINS, there's a major difference: DNS requires static configuration for computer name-to-IP address mapping, while WINS is dynamic and requires far less administration.

The DNS database is a tree structure called the *domain name space*, where each domain (node in the tree structure) is named and can contain subdomains. The domain name identifies the domain's position relative to its parent domain in the database. A period (.) separates each part of the name. For example, tsunami.microsoft.com could be the name of a computer owned by Microsoft. The root of the DNS database is managed by the Internet Network Information Center (InterNIC). The top-level domains were assigned organizationally and by country. These domain names follow the ISO 3166 standard.

DNS uses a client/server model, where the DNS servers contain information about a portion of the DNS database and make this information available to clients, called *resolvers*, that query the name server across the network. DNS name servers are programs that store information about parts of the domain name space called *zones*. The domain administrator sets up name servers that contain database files, with all the resource records describing all hosts in their zones. DNS resolvers are clients that are trying to use name servers to gain information about the domain name space. Windows NT includes all the resolver functionality necessary for using DNS on the Internet.

NT Connectivity to NFS

Windows NT provides a built-in network file system through its network redirector and server components. Virtually all UNIX implementations provide similar functionality. The three most common UNIX network file systems are

- Network File System (NFS)
- Andrew File System (AFS)
- Remote File Sharing (RFS)

NFS, originally developed by Sun Microsystems, allows directories and files to be shared across a network. It is the *de facto* UNIX standard for network file systems and has been ported to many non-UNIX operating systems as well. Through NFS, users and software can access files located on remote systems as if they were local files. It works transparently through the UNIX hierarchical file system by grafting a branch from the remote file system onto a mount-point or stub of the local file system. Once attached, it appears as just another limb of the tree, and, to either user or software, looks like any other local file.

Just as the network file system for Windows NT has two components, the redirector and the server, so too does NFS with the NFS client and the NFS server. As you would expect, the functionality is similar. The client makes the request and the server services the request. Any given machine can be an NFS client, an NFS server, or both. By now it should come as no surprise that there is third-party software available to turn Windows NT into any combination of NFS client/server. Some of those packages are

- BW-Connect NFS and BW-Connect NFS Server for Windows NT by Beam and Whiteside
- Chameleon 32 NFS by NetManage
- DiskShare for Windows NT by Intergraph

The next-most-popular network file system under UNIX is AFS. Originally developed at Carnegie Mellon University, it is now commercially distributed by Transarc Corporation, which is owned by IBM. AFS has a somewhat different focus from NFS in that it's geared for very large, widely dispersed UNIX networks. There is at least one package available for supporting AFS on Windows NT—PC-Interface (v5.0) from Locus Computing Corp.

RFS, developed by AT&T, has been available under UNIX System V for a number of years. It's not widely used, and, hence, no packages are available for Windows NT.

Several products are available that provide access to Windows-based applications from UNIX. Each of these products has taken a slightly different approach to the solution. They range from emulators with somewhat limited functionality to modified versions of Windows NT with 100% functionality.

An emulator impersonates the real thing. It typically works by providing a pseudo-software library that intercepts the application program's calls and translates them into native-API calls for the machine on which the emulator runs. This library interception/translation can occur in one of two ways. The company that produces the emulator may not have access to the source code for the software library that they want to emulate. In this situation, they simply try to figure out which outputs are produced by various inputs and code for these conditions in their software. This process is known as *reverse engineering*. On the other hand, if the emulator company has access to the library source code, it makes their job much easier, and they can be certain to handle all conditions in their software. In general, this results in a truer emulator.

Windows Interface Source Environment (WISE) is a Microsoft licensing program that enables independent software vendors (ISVs) to integrate their Windows-based applications with UNIX. Microsoft has licensed the Windows source code to MainSoft Corporation, Bristol Technology Inc., Insignia Solutions Inc., and Locus Computing Corporation. The products from MainSoft and Bristol are software development kits; those from Insignia and Locus are emulators.

The WISE emulators enable shrink-wrapped applications for Windows to run unmodified on a wide variety of UNIX systems, such as Solaris, SCO, Open Desktop, and HP-UX. Because they're based on the source code for Windows, the WISE emulators provide much closer compatibility to the real thing. For example, SoftWindows, the WISE emulator from Insignia Solutions, can run virtually any application written for Windows or MS-DOS.

A WISE emulator intercepts and translates API calls from Windows-based applications into API calls for UNIX. In some cases, an additional translation is required at the instruction-set level. All this translation usually results in a sacrifice of execution speed for the application.

Wabi from SunSoft is not a WISE product. It intercepts the output from Windows-based applications and converts it into X. Under Wabi, Windows-based applications look more like X-based applications. Additionally, each application comes up in its own separate X window, resulting in a desktop model very different from that of Windows NT.

Because Wabi is not based on the Windows source code, application compatibility is also an issue. At the time of this writing, there are only 23 Wabi-certified applications. They do, however, cover a good range of business productivity applications, such as Microsoft Word, Microsoft Excel, Microsoft PowerPoint, and Microsoft Access.

Windows Distributed Desktop (WinDD) is not an emulator. It is, however, similar to Wabi and WISE in that it seeks to provide similar functionality. This modified version of Windows NT adds traditional multiuser support, is produced and marketed by Tektronix, and consists of client and server pieces. The WinDD Server software compresses updated screen images and transmits the data over the network. The WinDD client interprets this data and displays the applications. The local client to the WinDD server directs mouse movements and keyboard input. Frequently used images, such as icons, bitmaps, and buttons, are cached in the client's memory, further reducing network traffic and greatly improving the performance of the applications.

WinDD server software can be loaded on a variety of Intel 486 or Pentium-class servers. Tests with a single-processor 90MHz Pentium server and 25 typical users running 32-bit versions of Microsoft Excel and Microsoft Word and a 16-bit version of Microsoft PowerPoint revealed 486DX33-class performance and very low network loading. A typical user was defined as someone who uses one or two applications up to 50% of the time.

Printing in a UNIX World

LPR is one of the network protocols in the TCP/IP protocol suite. It was originally developed as a standard for transmitting print jobs between computers running Berkeley UNIX. The LPR standard is published as Request For Comment (RFC) 1179. Windows NT complies with this standard, as do most implementations of Berkeley UNIX. However, most UNIX System V implementations don't comply with this standard, so in most cases Windows NT will not be able to send print jobs to System V computers or receive print jobs from them. Exceptions are System V computers that are configured to accept BSD jobs; these computers can accept print jobs from Windows NT.

With LPR protocol, a client application on one computer can send a print job to a print spooler service on another computer. The client application is usually named LPR and the service (or daemon) is usually named LPD. Windows NT supplies a command-line application, the `lpr` utility, and it supplies the LPR port print monitor. Both act as clients, sending print jobs to an LPD service running on another computer. Windows NT also supplies an LPD service, so it can receive print jobs sent by LPR clients, including computers running UNIX and others running Windows NT.

Summary

The issues of connectivity between UNIX and Windows NT Server have mostly been solved with protocols that have been brought to us by the Internet. But there are still deeper issues that have to be considered in this relationship. This chapter has introduced you to some of those concepts.

Windows NT was designed for client/server computing; UNIX was designed for host-based terminal computing. They're two different computing concepts.

UNIX relies on DNS for name resolution and NT relies on WINS, but the two are not really the same. DNS requires static configuration for computer name-to-IP addresses mapping, while WINS is dynamic and requires far less administration.

NT and UNIX connectivity on a file-sharing level is going to involve one operating system or the other becoming a client in the world of the other. NT is capable, through third-party software, of becoming an NFS client. UNIX is capable of becoming an NT client and/or NT emulator through third-party software as well.

20

SNA Connectivity with BackOffice

Peter Norton™

With the introduction of the BackOffice suite, Microsoft wants to create an environment where all of the administrator's needs are met. You must understand that a large number of those people to whom Microsoft wants to be all things are MIS managers who are strapped to host system solutions. A large amount of money has been invested in what is sometimes called "heavy metal" among PC engineers.

Host Computing and SNA Basics

The term *heavy metal* refers not to your father's car, but instead to the IBM host machines—mainframes, AS/400(s), and so on. These MIS groups have developed and rely on applications that exist on these machines and are often reluctant to let them go. After all, "If it ain't broke, don't fix it."

Note: These hosts are considered heavy metal because they often take up entire rooms and require special environmental controls. The machines themselves have shrunk along with the PC world, but a small one still can be as big as a washer or dryer.

The International Business Machines Corporation (IBM), which created many of these machines, also created a communications standard called *Systems Network Architecture* (SNA) for communications between these large systems and the many terminals, peripherals, and peer systems that exist on a network. SNA was originally set out as a network standard, but today is used for 3270 terminal emulation, 5250 terminal emulation, APPC, CPI-C, and communications using LUA and involving downstream systems.

The way that users generally communicate with the mainframe or minicomputer is through what's called a *node* or a *data terminal*. These items are also called *"dumb" terminals* because these stations do no processing of their own. A terminal would appear to you as a monitor and keyboard from a personal computer (see Figure 20.1). Terminals really aren't computers at all; instead, they're data-entry points and output points for the host system.

Figure 20.1.
A dumb terminal.

When a terminal is attached to the host, it begins presenting the information that's sent from the host. Generally, the first screen it will present is a logon screen. The host simply listens to the port that the terminal is attached to for input on the keyboard. When data is input on the keyboard, it's processed at the host and the result is posted back at the terminal. So you could think of the data terminal as a porthole to look into the host computer.

In a host/terminal setting, some common relationship issues exist:

- Wherever there's a terminal, there's an opportunity to attach the host. Security and terminal allocation are often random in this atmosphere.

- The interface is not appealing for most users. Terminals usually present a black background with white or green text only.

- Maintaining multiple sessions with the host is either impossible or difficult.

- Terminal users can't simply purchase off-the-shelf software to complete tasks that have a narrow scope. They must wait for the MIS group to either implement or write the application on the host.

All of these issues are partially responsible for the popularity and success of the personal computer, but they haven't eliminated the fact that there are still some tasks that the enterprise or corporation will not trust to the PC. With that in mind, we must find a way to meld these two worlds together and attempt to solve the user's issues while maintaining the connection to the host.

PCs are not incapable of connecting to a host computer. As a matter of fact, PCs can connect to host computers through many different methods, but even if they do connect to the host they're still just terminals. The connection that's made to the host is generally through a card that's placed in the PC—much like a NIC in a LAN installation. But the card is actually a dumb terminal on an interface card. The PC then has terminal emulation software installed, and suddenly you have a $2,000 dumb terminal.

Depending on the emulation package you're using, this is not as bad as it sounds. The advantage that you can gain is that you are now using one machine to do both host and PC work. Because many of these terminal-emulation packages are Windows-based, you often gain the ability to open several terminal sessions at one time. This last item in particular is of great value to users who need to keep several processes running at one time. So our $2,000 terminal isn't sounding so "dumb" anymore.

Another advantage of running terminal emulation at the PC is the added security of the PC platform. If the PC is running NT Workstation and is secured, there's an extra layer between the hacker and the host. Add a "power on" password to the PC, and the road to the host gets even longer. In other words, you no longer have the terminal just sitting there as an open invitation (blinking TRY ME).

The issue that must be addressed with terminal emulation is the fact that if a user's PC is attached to the NT network, she now has multiple cables coming from the back of her PC (one for the PC network and up to two for the host connection). What's needed is a way to combine all the network connections in one cabling scheme and add a layer of security to that network so that we can determine who should have access to the host services.

Microsoft SNA Server is such a product. The purpose of Microsoft SNA Server is to provide host connectivity through a common interface and add manageability to that service. The basic concept involves that host connection being initiated, managed, and distributed by an NT server running the SNA Server service (see Figure 20.2). In an SNA Server installation, the host connection is made to the NT server and the NT server maintains the resources that are made available. The server manages a list of users who are allowed to use those resources, and those users are given host sessions as if they were files or print services or any other NT resource.

The host computer sees the SNA server as a *cluster controller*. The SNA server is granted certain powers by the host to distribute host sessions to the network. The normal job of a cluster controller is to distribute terminal sessions, and terminals are usually directly connected to a controller of some sort. A controller is given a certain range of terminal sessions—logical units (LUs)—that it can distribute; it distributes those sessions on a first-come-first-served basis.

Figure 20.2.
The basic structure of SNA Server.

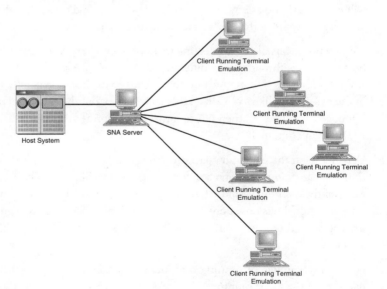

> **Note:** Host sessions may be a foreign idea to you. The idea of connecting to a host computer is the same when attaching through a dumb terminal or a PC emulating a terminal. The only real differences are the fact that the PC can appear to the host as if it were more then one terminal, and the PC has a rich enough user interface to present those multiple sessions in a viewable format.

The advantages of this relationship are several fold:

- The PC workstation no longer needs a special adapter card and it loses the connection of the host cable.
- NT security can be used to manage host sessions as a resource.
- The group responsible for the host now has one physical connection to manage in order to maintain connectivity with all the clients.

Manageable Secure Connectivity

The terminal-to-host relationship still exists today—it's not history. But the way the terminal is manifesting itself is changing. SNA Server has given this old way of attaching to the host a new life. We've discussed the general advantages of the product and why you might want to install it, but now we'll look at some of the specific security advantages that you'll have.

> **Note:** In order to establish good security for SNA servers in a domain, you need to control access to the SNA Server configuration file. To do this, be sure to install the SNA Server software on a Windows NT file system (NTFS) partition. With NTFS, permissions can be assigned on a file-by-file basis; with the file allocation table (FAT) file system or the high-performance file system (HPFS), this is impossible. Installing the SNA Server software on an NTFS partition is especially important with the primary SNA server—the server that contains the main copy of the configuration file (used by all SNA servers in the domain).

The security that's used by SNA Server is just like any service that resides on an NT server; it shares security with the NT operating system. This simplifies the job of the administrator. The resources that can be secured are as follows:

- Who has the right to access a host session
- Number of sessions that a particular user may occupy at a given moment
- How many sessions are available to a given group
- Times that certain host sessions are available

Routing and Distributing Connections

Another advantage of distributing the host sessions of your host through SNA Server is the fact that you're not limited by the physical connections of the traditional SNA world. SNA Server allows the PC administrator to use one connecting point to route and distribute services through one NT Server machine, and distribute those connections to the user base through one network, the PC infrastructure.

SNA Server enables you to establish connections with multiple host or peer computers at the same time, using any combination of the following:

- **802.2.** Token Ring or Ethernet connections via IBM 3x75 front-end processors or 3x74 cluster controllers.
- **Synchronous data link control (SDLC).** Leased or switched telephone line connections.
- **X.25/QLLC.** Public or private packet-switched X.25 connections, using qualified logical link control (QLLC).
- **Distributed function terminal (DFT).** Coaxial or twisted-pair connections using IBM 3x74 cluster controllers.
- **Channel.** Connections that provide direct channel attachment to a mainframe.
- **Twinax.** Twinaxial connections to an AS/400.

You may not understand the connection types that you see listed here, but the point isn't to understand all of them (that's another book). The point is to know that the majority of host connections can be accommodated and distributed. SNA Server supports most communications adapters, cabling, wiring, modems, and controllers.

This is one connection that you're not going to make alone. In order to facilitate this connection, you're going to need a great deal of cooperation from the host computer administration. In order for you to communicate with their machines, they have to let you in, and, frankly, agree that it's a good idea. If the MIS group is unhappy with the idea of making this connection, then it just isn't going to work. It would be like trying to connect a modem without the cooperation of the phone company.

Your position is to get the MIS group involved early and often in the plan. In fact, if you can make it *their* idea, that's a plus. You must understand that you're stealing a bit of their thunder by removing their physical connection to the user. But if you can make it appear that they are looking forward to be more efficient, you will win.

When you're communicating with the MIS group, you'll be depending on them for information like that contained in the following table. This table is a direct excerpt from documentation of the information that you'll need in order to complete an SDLC connection. You would give this table to the host group and ask that they fill in the VTAM portion (host parameters). In the column beside

VTAM is the SNA Server variable that you'll fill in with the information provided by your host counterparts.

> **Tip:** Be prepared for the host group to possibly not fill in all of the lines. Based on how they set up your sessions and security, all of the information may not be needed.

VTAM Parameter	Corresponding SNA Server Parameter	Description
ADDR=	Poll Address (advanced SDLC setting)	A two-digit hexadecimal value that identifies the control unit that the host uses to poll.
IDBLK=	First three digits of local node ID (basic connection setting)	A three-digit hexadecimal value that, together with IDNUM, identifies the SNA Server. The values 000 and FFF cannot be used; these values are reserved.
IDNUM=	Last five digits of local node ID (basic connection setting)	A five-digit hexadecimal value that, together with IDBLK, identifies the SNA Server.
MAXDATA= (in the PU definition for SWPU1)	Max BTU length (advanced SDLC setting)	The maximum length of the basic transmission unit (BTU) sent or received; BTUs are also known as I-frames.
LOCADDR=	LU number	The LU local address at the PU. For independent LUs that communicate with a host, the LOCADDR parameter must be set to zero. For dependent LUs with VTAM, the LOCADDR must be at least 2. Also, for dependent LUs, the LU numbers set in SNA Server must match the LOCADDR values on the host.

If you understand the terms in this table, then you know that you're going to have to depend on the host support group to generate this information before you sit down to use the server. Understand that the host changes function very much like the changes that you make to your NT server. But requesting a host change or information may take literally weeks to facilitate. Not because the host group wants to be hard to get along with, but because they have to bring down the host to generate the changes you're going to be requesting.

SNA Connectivity

The details of your NT-to-SNA connection will have to be worked out with your MIS group. This chapter is obviously not a large enough forum to instruct you about all of the installation; I'll just touch on a few of the different communications methods you may encounter.

SDLC

An SDLC link service enables SNA Server to communicate with host, peer, or downstream computers through full-duplex or half-duplex synchronous modems, over telecommunications lines that are switched (dialed in the standard way) or leased (dedicated). SDLC is IBM's implementation of a bit-oriented serial protocol with a standardized frame reader and block check sequence. SDLC applies to synchronous transmissions; it organizes information in rigidly structured units called *frames*.

X.25

An X.25 link service enables you to connect SNA Server through public or private X.25 packet-switching networks to host, peer, or downstream computers.

DFT

A DFT link service is used to connect SNA Server to host systems, generally over coaxial cables. DFT stands for *distributed function terminal*, a type of terminal supported by IBM 3270 control units, in which some of the terminal's functions are controlled by the terminal and some by the control unit. DFT allows multiple sessions, and connects to host systems (or to peer systems via host systems).

Adapter Support

SNA Server supports the full complement of Windows NT-based adapters. The following is a partial list of adapters supported by SNA Server (other adapters are available from third-party vendors):

- Any Windows NT NDIS-compliant Token Ring or Ethernet device driver, using Windows NT 802.2 DLC transport protocol
- Attachmate SDLC
- Barr Systems T1-SYNC (for SDLC)
- DCA IRMA (for DFT)

- DCA ISCA (for SDLC and X.25)
- Microgate MGx, Microgate DSA, Microgate USA (for SDLC and X.25)
- IBM SDLC
- IBM MCPA
- IBM MPA/A
- IBM DFT
- IBM 3270 Connection A,B
- IBM 3278/9 Advanced Emulation adapter
- Any driver developed through the SNADIS interface

Summary

Finally, this chapter isn't meant to provide you with a step-by-step "how to" for SNA Server, but instead to give you a flavor of what's available for the platform. There are many variables to the general category called SNA, and hopefully this chapter has helped you to see that the SNA world and NT servers can coexist.

SNA Server allows the administrator to distribute IBM mainframe and midrange terminal sessions as a resource. Not only is the system redistributing sessions, but also a shared security with the NT operating system. Connectivity is maintained through standard SNA protocols and connections from SDLC, X.25, and DFT.

VI

TCP/IP and
the Internet

Peter Norton™

21

TCP/IP
Networking

Peter Norton™

In the beginning there was darkness and that darkness covered the whole Earth and… Well, in the beginning there was darkness, but we called it "incompatible networking," and it didn't really cover the Earth—just a very small portion on some government offices and college campuses. But it was changed by the light. We call the light *TCP/IP*.

The original Fathers of the Internet were scientists or programmers and, well, geeks. They were working on computers your pocket watch could outperform, but they needed to share information. The original systems all used their own protocols (languages) and utilities to transfer messages and data.

Because the government was paying most of the researchers anyway, they decided to pay for an open standard (common protocol), hence the birth of TCP/IP (transmission control protocol/Internet protocol).

This chapter covers the following TCP/IP topics:

- TCP/IP basic concepts
- Installing TCP/IP
- Routing and the routing information protocol (RIP)
- Dynamic host configuration protocol (DHCP)
- Windows Internet Name Service (WINS)
- LMHOSTS files
- TCP/IP printing
- Microsoft DNS Server

TCP/IP Concepts Brief

If all the computers in a network are going to communicate, one of the first things that must be established is a way to uniquely number each computer. It's a bit like the trading floor of a large market. For a large group of people to communicate with each other very quickly and all at once, they establish a number for each person. Then the person can be quickly and accurately identified. But in our example, let's imagine that you need to identify billions of people and that you need to also know what company each works for. Well, you could just start at one and give everyone a number. You would need a numbering scheme that would encompass large numbers and would identify two things—company and person.

With computers and Internet protocol (IP) addressing, you have the same puzzle to work out. But instead of company and person, you need to identify the individual computer (called a *host*) and the network segment. The Internet community decided that they would need one number to represent the network portion of the address and another number to represent the host portion of the address. An Internet address is normally represented by four decimal numbers between 0 and 255, separated by periods (for example, `198.23.45.21`). The four numbers represent the 8-bit sections of the IP address, making the entire address 32 bits long. This gives us over 4 billion addresses, which at first sounds like a lot—but so did 640KB of memory.

To understand how many combinations that IP gives you, imagine that it's a lottery. The lottery in Indiana is six numbers of 1 to 49. This is so that the odds are 49 to the sixth power (49 × 49 × 4 9 × 49 × 49 × 49) or a 1 in 13,841,287,201 chance that you will win if you buy a ticket. Yes, that pretty much means that your ticket is useless—fun, but useless. An IP address is 256 to the fourth power combinations (from 0 to 255). That means that there are 4,294,967,296 combinations. So the chances that you will be assigned the same number as someone else are pretty slim. But we're running out of numbers.

> **Tip:** Remember when you're dealing with computers that zero (0) counts as a number—so 0 to 255 is really 256 digits. (Zero counts as a digit.)

The addressing scheme is similar to your home address. If your address were 1777 SOMESTREET you could say your street is SOMESTREET and your house number is 1777. The computer would say if you lived at `172.17.7.7` that your network is `172.17` and your host is `7.7`—well, it would if you used the default subnet mask, but we'll discuss subnets in a minute. First the numbers.

The Numbers

The first issue to address is the numbers. Humans like decimal numbers, and computers like ones and zeros. If you had to represent the address `172.17.7.7` in a preferred human method, it would be a network of 88081 (`172.17`) and a node of `1799` (`7.7`). But the computer would say a network of 10101100000010001 (`172.17`) and a node of 0000011100000111 (`7.7`). As you can see, this is cumbersome and confusing.

> **Tip:** To get the actual host name, you convert the decimal numbers into the binary equivalents so that you can retain their factorial powers; then you combine them and convert back to decimal. I use the scientific mode on the Windows calculator to keep it straight.

The solution was to use something that could easily be converted into the ones and zeros and yet could be understood by humans. This is where octets and decimal numbers come into play. A byte is eight ones and zeros that make up a number between 00000000 (0) and 11111111 (255). Because the Internet addresses were set at 32 bits maximum, that became 4 bytes, or four 8-bit sets. An 8-bit set is called an *octet* (*oct* is the Latin prefix for the number 8, so 8 set = octet—get it?).

Address Classes

There are three standard classes of IP addresses: class A, class B, and class C. If you understand that there are only four octets, the standard A, B, and C classes are simple. In a class A address, the first octet is the network and the last three make up the node number. In a class B address, the first two octets are the network and the last two are the node. In a class C address, the first three octets are the network and the last one is the node.

Let's look at an example. In the following table, the IP address is broken down into network and node addresses.

Class	Original Address	Network Portion	Node Portion
Class A	23.75.85.112	23.	75.85.112
Class B	175.34.114.24	175.34.	114.24
Class C	204.93.229.55	204.93.229.	55

The *subnet mask* tells the computer what part of the address is the network and what part is the node. The standard subnets follow the same pattern as the address class. The class A subnet is 255.0.0.0 or 11111111.0.0.0, class B is 255.255.0.0, and class C is 255.255.255.0. When the computer compares the address against the subnet, it uses the binary representation to separate the network from the node by the ones. The part of the address that lines up with the ones is the network and the part that lines up with the zeros is the node.

TCP/IP is the protocol of the Internet, but when IP networks branch out onto the Internet they need to be sure that the IP addresses they use are unique. In order to manage the IP addresses that are used on the Internet, an independent nonprofit group was formed, called the InterNIC. This group distributes IP addresses and domain names (discussed later). At first, the only way a corporation could get IP addresses was via a large donation to a college of choice, which would in turn give them a segment of their class A network. Now you can request IP addresses from the InterNIC, but they are giving out only class C addresses—and those they give sparingly.

Note: Originally, IP addresses and domain names were free, but in recent years the large number of requests has caused the InterNIC to start charging a small fee for both. Application can be made at www.internic.com.

Installing TCP/IP

When you're installing Windows NT Server, one of the default protocols selected will be TCP/IP. For the purpose of this installation section, we'll describe how to install if you deselected TCP/IP and now want to add it in.

> **Tip:** Many times, I will install using only NetBEUI just to get the server up. This allows me to go back later and set up DHCP, WINS, IP printing, and so on, without needing all my IP information at the start. I realize that this goes against the plan-then-implement approach, but it works better when you are setting up a multihomed server for multiple Web sites and you can't afford the time to set them up right now.

Follow these steps:

1. After you log on as an administrator, open the Control Panel and select Network. The panel opens with Identification as the selected tab.

2. Click the Protocols tab to see which protocols are currently loaded (see Figure 21.1).

3. Click Add to see a list of available included protocols.

4. Select TCP/IP Protocol and then click OK.

Figure 21.1.
The Network control panel, displaying protocols.

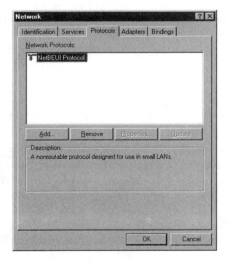

Tip: Windows NT will inform you that it can gather IP information from a *dynamic host configuration protocol* (*DHCP*) *server*, and ask whether you want it to do so. As a rule of thumb, I always assign my server IP manually. If you want the server to act as a WINS or DHCP server, it must be manual, but I have fewer problems when the IP of my servers doesn't change. The last thing you want to find out when the Web servers have been down for an hour is that DHCP reassigned your servers' IP to the CEO's personal system and DNS is sending everyone there for the company home page.

5. NT asks where your installation files are; depending on which installation method you chose, the default points to where NT thinks the files should be. Redirect it to the installation files.

6. Click OK. NT loads the protocol and shows it in the list.

7. At this point, close the control panel.

8. NT asks questions about configuration. The only information you *must* fill in is a valid IP address and subnet mask. You usually will also fill in a default gateway address so that you can access systems on other networks.

9. Reboot for the protocol to finish.

It's very important to choose a valid IP address for your network. If you choose an address that's in use by another system, IP won't start. If you choose an invalid address or subnet, your system will appear to belong to another network, and none of the systems on your network will respond to your system's requests.

Routing

Routing by definition is the passing of information from one segment to another. A router is called a *gateway* in IP terminology, and is the device that sits between two or more network segments with a network card and IP address on each segment. When a host wants to send data to another host that isn't on its segment, it must pass this information to a gateway. The gateway evaluates the destination address and compares it to networks it knows. The gateway then passes the information to the correct host that it can reach, or to the next gateway in the route.

For NT to act as a router, you must have two or more network cards attached to different subnets, and you must enable routing by checking the enable box on the Routing tab of the TCP/IP Properties control panel. You need to reboot for this to take effect.

For the system to route packets, a routing table must be built. The system will add all subnets that it can reach directly from the card configuration. If this system is the only router on the network, this is all you need to do for routing. If this is only one router of many, you'll need to build a table.

> **Tip:** If this is the only internal router, and you're connecting to an outside source such as the Internet or another company, you can set the default gateway address to the address of the other router for the network card that connects to the same subnet as the other router—anything not bound for one of your segments will be sent on the other router.

To build a static table manually, you would use the ROUTE command and specify the ADD option. Type ROUTE /? for exact usage.

> **Tip:** If you forget to include the -P for "permanent," the route will be lost after a reboot.

Routing Information Protocol (RIP)

New to NT 4.0 is the *routing information protocol* (*RIP*). RIP is used to allow routers to pass information to each other about the network segments they're aware of. Without RIP, networks depend on humans to tell them about the networks on each side. But when RIP is initialized on a network router, it begins to send information to and listen to information from other routers about the networks that they know of.

A router broadcasts information about the networks that it's directly connected to and listens for other routers on those segments to do the same. The routers collect information from the other routers they know, add those segments to their list, and rebroadcast the routes they know. This process continues until the network becomes a web of connected routes. "It's a small network, after all."

This whole process allows NT to act as a dynamic router, allowing it to automatically build a routing table from packets and broadcasts it receives. If you are setting up multiple routers or if you are adding into an existing structure where RIP is used, you'll want to add it in. If you're routing only within the subnets you directly attach to, RIP is unnecessary overhead.

Installing RIP for Internet Protocols

To install RIP, follow these steps:

1. Click the Services tab in the Network control panel. This will show you all network services that are currently running.
2. Click Add and select RIP for Internet Protocol, as shown in Figure 21.2.
3. The system asks where the setup files are; type the correct path and select Continue. NT loads the necessary files and returns to the Services page.

4. Close the control panel. The system will check the bindings and prepare to reboot. There are no options to set for RIP; it's dynamic from this point on.

Figure 21.2.
Selecting RIP for IP.

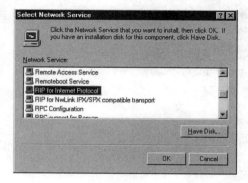

Dynamic Host Configuration Protocol (DHCP)

In the world of TCP/IP, every host address must be unique. Before DHCP, an administrator would create a list of systems and manually assign each machine a valid IP address. The administrator would also manually fill in the name server (DNS or WINS), the timeserver, or any other IP services the user might need access to. DHCP is the answer to the administrative headache of manually assigning the addresses and tracking them so that they remain unique.

Under DHCP, a client broadcasts a request for an address onto his local subnet, and all DHCP servers that receive the request respond with address offers. The client then sends a request to one of the DHCP servers to lease the address that the server offered. Once the server responds with the address lease and configuration information, the client binds the IP address to its card along with any additional information it receives, such as the DNS or WINS address. The client attempts to contact the DHCP server that issued its address when approximately half of the lease period has expired. If it's successful, it resets the lease time to the full lease. If unsuccessful, it goes looking for any DHCP server to renew its address when 87.5% of the lease has expired. If still unsuccessful when the lease ends, it begins the request cycle for a new address again.

Installing DHCP

To install DHCP, follow these steps:

1. Click the Services tab in the Network control panel to see all network services that are currently running.

2. Click Add and select Microsoft DHCP Server in the Select Network Service dialog box, as shown in Figure 21.3.

3. The system asks where the setup files are; type the correct path and select Continue. NT loads the necessary files and prompts you with a warning, as shown in Figure 21.4.

Figure 21.3.
Selecting the DHCP server.

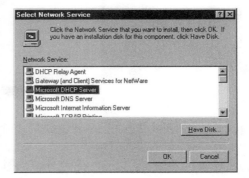

Figure 21.4.
DHCP warning message.

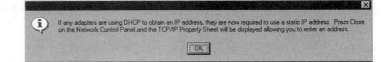

4. If any of your network cards had been set to DHCP for their settings, you now have the opportunity to change them to a static address. Then NT returns to the Services tab.

5. Close the control panel. The system will check the bindings and prepare to reboot; you'll configure DHCP after the reboot.

DHCP Configuration—Scopes

Once the DHCP server is loaded, you need to define a scope. A *scope* specifies what information is given to the client when it requests an IP address; it also determines what addresses are available to be given, depending on what subnet the request came from.

To define a scope, follow these steps:

1. Launch the DHCP Manager. The default location for the manager is as follows:

   `Start\Programs\Administrative Tools\DHCP Manager`

   When you first launch the DHCP Manager, it looks like Figure 21.5.

2. To begin defining a scope, double-click *Local Machine* and then select Scope | Create.

Figure 21.5.
*The default DHCP Manager
screen.*

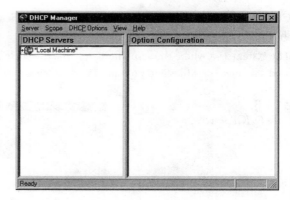

3. The first thing to fill in is the range of IP addresses that this DHCP server will assign using this scope, as well as a valid subnet mask.

   If you have more than one DHCP server, they don't synchronize their databases—you must assign unique scopes on each one, or you'll have problems with duplicate IP addresses.

4. Next, set any excluded addresses. This could be existing UNIX hosts, Windows NT servers, IP printers, or any device that needs a static IP. Then click Add.

Tip: For a class C address, I use an addressing scheme where my servers are in the first five addresses and my routers and hubs are in the last five addresses, unless a server is serving those functions.

5. (Optional) Add a name for the scope and any comments; then click OK (see Figure 21.6).

   The DHCP Manager will tell you The scope must be activated to be used. I recommend waiting until you've set the scope options (see the following steps) before you activate the scope.

6. Now, from the Options menu in the DHCP Manager, add options for the scope. This is where you define the WINS address, DNS, and default gateway for your clients. To begin, select DHCP Options | Scope (see Figure 21.7).

7. Select Router, click Add, and then click Value (see Figure 21.8).

8. Edit the array and add router values, which the clients will use for their default gateway. (If you have more than one to define, put them in the order of preference, selecting Add to enter them.)

Figure 21.6.
Naming the scope.

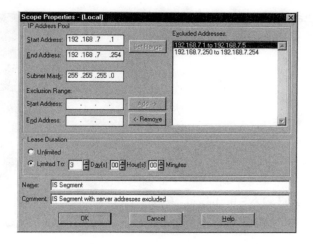

Figure 21.7.
DHCP scope options.

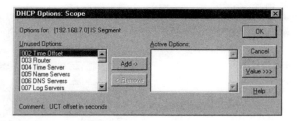

Figure 21.8.
A scope array with values.

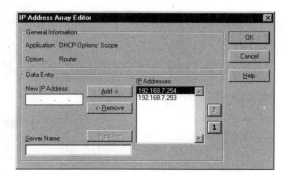

9. Click OK to add the values to the configuration (see Figure 21.9).

Figure 21.9.
The scope with a router array.

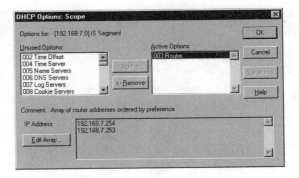

10. Add a DNS in the same fashion (see Figure 21.10).

11. Add the WINS/NBNS server addresses (see Figure 21.11).

Note: NT will remind you to set the name resolution order for the clients.

Figure 21.10.
The scope with DNS array.

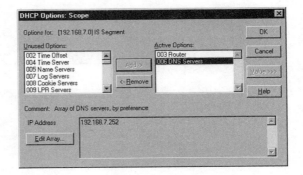

Figure 21.11.
The scope with all options set.

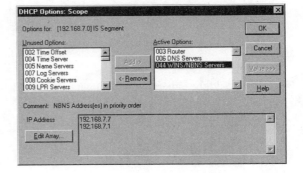

12. The last thing I usually add is the WINS node type (see Figure 21.12). I use H-node (0x8). This keeps broadcasts to a minimum because the client attempts to use the WINS server for name resolution and broadcasts only if a name is unresolved from WINS.

Note: By using the H-node for resolution, if you have a satellite office and the link goes down, you'll broadcast for a BDC on your segment. If you use P-node, there's no name resolution and you won't be able to log on to the domain—even though you can ping the server IP address.

Figure 21.12.
The complete scope.

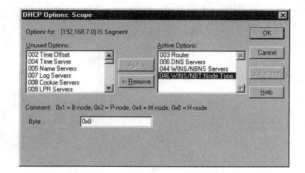

13. The final step is to activate the scope. Choose Scope | Activate in the DHCP Manager. The light turns yellow to indicate that the scope is active.

You have now defined the client defaults for a valid IP, default gateway (router), Microsoft name resolution (WINS), and UNIX domain name resolution (DNS), as shown in Figure 21.13.

Figure 21.13.
DHCP with scope complete.

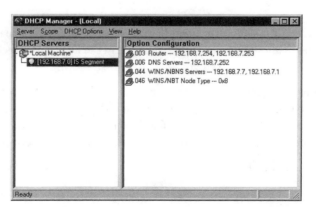

DHCP Management

Once DHCP scopes have been defined, the primary issues in management are verifying that the scopes are unique, monitoring the active leases and available IP addresses, and adding any reserved addresses that you want to name specifically in the DHCP Manager.

To monitor the active leases, choose Scope | Active Leases from the DHCP Manager menu to open the dialog box shown in Figure 21.14.

Figure 21.14.
Displaying the active leases.

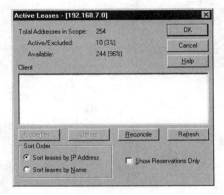

At this point, we only have the excluded addresses for the servers, WINS, DNS, and routers.

Note: If you notice the addresses getting to 10–15% remaining, you'll need to look at breaking the network segment into smaller segments, or you may want to shorten the lease cycle if you have a lot of systems moving around, causing an inflated active count.

Let's add the address of a client that needs a dedicated IP for a specific accounting application. You add reservations by highlighting the scope in the DHCP Manager and choosing Scope | Add Reservations (see Figure 21.15).

In this dialog box, you enter information for the IP address to reserve for this client, as well as a unique identifier. The unique identifier is the hardware MAC address. You can find it by typing NET CONFIG WORKSTATION. It takes the form of a 10-byte hex address such as 0000C03A04BF. You also enter the client's machine name and a comment on what the reservation is for (see Figure 21.16).

After entering this information, look at the active leases to see your reservation (see Figure 21.17).

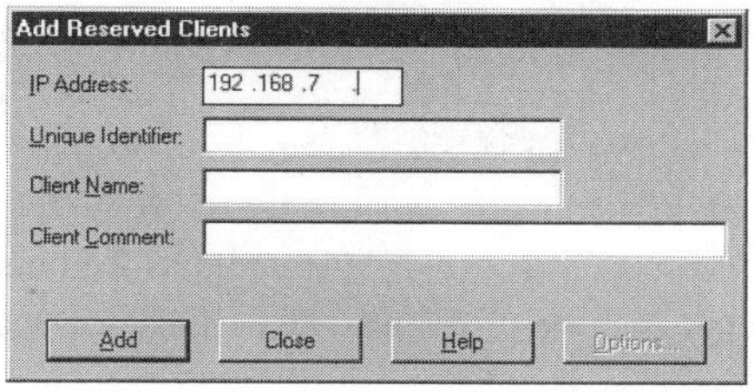

Figure 21.15.
Initial client reservation.

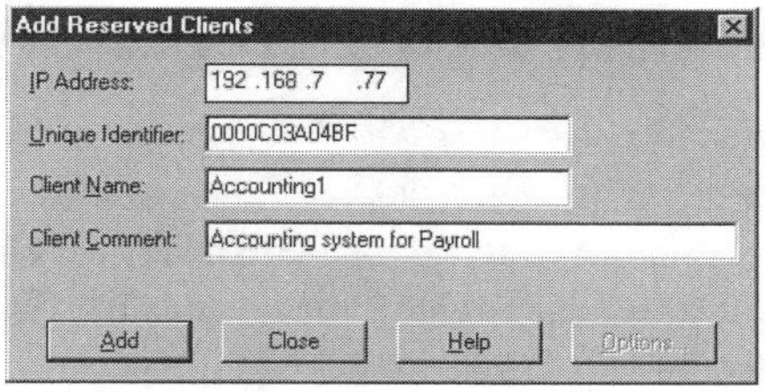

Figure 21.16.
Reservations with data.

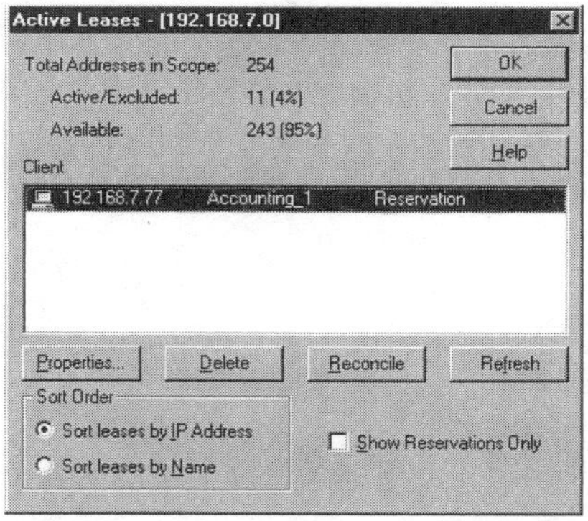

Figure 21.17.
Active leases with reservations.

Windows Internet Name Service (WINS)

WINS is a name service for Microsoft networking. It's also called a *NetBIOS name server* (*NBNS*) because it provides the NetBIOS-to-IP address lookup for Microsoft NetBIOS names. All Microsoft networks that include workgroups or domains use NetBIOS names to communicate. All Microsoft-networked resources, files, and printers are accessed using their NetBIOS names.

Before WINS, broadcasts or the use of an LMHOSTS file supported NetBIOS name registration. The LMHOSTS file follows a format similar to the UNIX HOSTS file, with the addition of special keys for Windows NT domains. Broadcasts worked in small unrouted networks where the additional traffic was not as much of a concern. LMHOSTS files were used in routed networks because most routers are configured not to route broadcasts. A medium-sized network might use both, allowing broadcasts first and then parsing one or more LMHOSTS files for the address before returning an error.

Architecture of Microsoft WINS

WINS is referred to as a *dynamic NetBIOS name server*. The WINS server keeps a database of clients containing the client's name, IP address, LAN Manager service ID, expiration date and time, entry type (dynamic or static), and the version ID. When a client first boots up, it registers itself with the WINS server. If the client attempts to register a NetBIOS name that's already in the database, the WINS server issues a challenge to the original owner. If the owner responds, the client gets a negative response to the registration request, the user gets an error, and network services fail to start. If the original owner doesn't respond, the name is registered with the new owner.

 If you attempt to register a computer with the same name as a workgroup or domain, you should also get an error, because the name already exists on the network. This is why it's a good idea NOT to give your machine or domain the company name. Many people will pick COMPANY for their workgroup name; it can create chaos on your LAN.

Installing WINS

To install WINS, follow these steps:

1. Click the Services tab in the Network control panel to display all network services that are currently running.

2. Click Add and select Windows Internet Name Service, as shown in Figure 21.18.

3. The system asks you where the setup files are; type the correct path and select Continue. NT loads the necessary files and returns to the Services page (see Figure 21.19).

4. Close the control panel. The system checks the bindings and prepares to reboot. We'll configure WINS after the reboot.

Figure 21.18.
Selecting the WINS service.

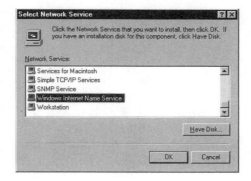

Figure 21.19.
WINS has been added.

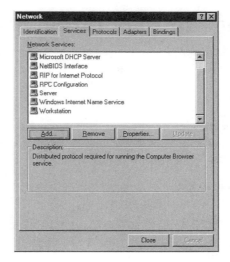

WINS Configuration/Replication

If you're setting up only a small unrouted network of less than 50 users, you need to change the configuration for WINS only if you have non-WINS hosts for which you want to add static addresses, or when you want to back up the database. With only 50 users, a simple reboot brings them all back into the database, so the risk of losing the database is minimal.

If you're configuring WINS for more than 50 users or for a routed network, I recommend setting up a second WINS server. If WINS goes down in a routed network, the broadcast method usually fails, because most routers won't route the broadcasts between subnets. And with more than 50 users, you may not want to walk around rebooting computers.

> **Note:** This is not a hard-and-fast rule. I usually will configure a backup WINS if I have more than one Windows NT server on the network and all clients can reach both—even when the number is as small as 25 clients. I just prefer the security, as name-resolution problems can be a real headache. Also, a WINS server can handle about 1,500 name registrations and 700 queries per minute, so the real issues are the reliability of the servers, load on the servers, and speed of the links. I set up WINS on both ends of a link if the speed is anything less than Ethernet and I have an NT box on both ends. This cuts down on unnecessary traffic across the frame and logon problems if the link is down.

Setting Up Replication

Begin by installing WINS on the second server (see the earlier section "Installing WINS" for details). After both WINS servers are online, you need to set them up to replicate with each other. Replication is set up using push and pull servers.

A *push partner* is a WINS server that sends update notification messages to its defined WINS partners when the changes in its database have reached a certain threshold set by the administrator. A *pull partner* is a WINS server that requests updates from its defined WINS partners at specific times and intervals set by the administrator.

To set up replication, you first need to decide which method you want to use and the replication time and frequency between the servers. WINS replication can be configured by two methods: primary/backup and equal partner.

The *primary/backup* configuration is the most common. One server is referred to as the primary WINS, and all other WINS servers are backup partners in a push/pull configuration (see Figure 21.20). In this configuration, the databases are kept in sync by one system, and the propagation of new machine information to all backups happens quickly. This configuration is also easier to troubleshoot, as there's a focal point for tracking lost machines. You'll generally set up primary and backup WINS servers to be push/pull partners with each other.

The *equal partner* configuration can be useful in a WAN environment where the enterprise is divided into multiple domains that may not have direct roots. The concept is that each server replicates its database with those servers that are closest to it (see Figure 21.21). This would be useful if you have a large site spread across multiple states or countries that have interlining frames but not a direct connection back to a central site. You would configure the WINS to push/pull with whatever other WINS servers your site could connect to in the closest states.

Figure 21.20.
A WINS spoke.

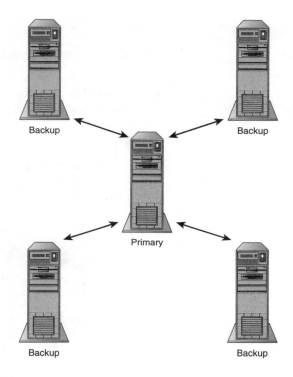

Figure 21.21.
A WINS bus configuration.

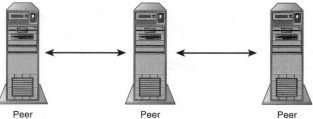

Next you need to decide the default schedule. I usually set the replication for every four hours or 20 updates. This allows the small day-to-day changes to get propagated via the pull set times and the larger migration-like changes to happen via push when you need them.

Setting up replication without setting a schedule is the most-missed piece of a proper configuration. If you don't set the times for pull partners or the count for push partners, the replication never happens. Because most people select Replicate Now after for the initial replication, they never notice this issue. The symptom shows up as domain logon problems and unreachable machines.

To set the default schedule, follow these steps:

1. Open the WINS Manager and select Options | Preferences.

2. Click Partners.

3. Set Start Time to when you want replication to begin, set the time intervals for pull partners, and specify the update count for push partners (see Figure 21.22).

4. Click OK to confirm.

Figure 21.22.
Setting push/pull partner default settings.

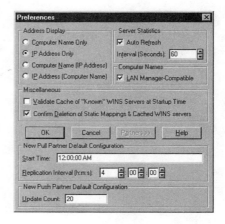

Next you need to add the WINS servers you want to set as replication partners. If you have a single domain, or the account on which you're logged on is an administrator in both domains, the WINS Manager will set up both sides at once. If you don't have administrator access to the other domain, the other administrator will need to configure his or her side to push/pull with yours. This feature prevents a rogue WINS server from being set up to pull your database without your knowledge.

To add WINS servers as replication partners, follow these steps:

1. In the WINS Manager, choose Server | Add WINS Server.

2. Type the IP address of one of the servers you want to add (see Figure 21.23).

   The server is now listed under WINS servers.

3. To set up replication, select the primary server first. Then choose Server | Replication Partners.

4. Select the backup server's IP (see Figure 21.24). Notice that the Replication options are now available.

Figure 21.23.
Adding a WINS server.

Figure 21.24.
Setting up WINS replication partners.

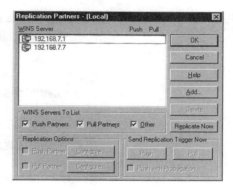

5. Select the Push Partner option and click the Configure button to the right of Push Partner. You'll notice that the default value you set earlier in the preferences is filled in (see Figure 21.25).

6. Select the Pull Partner option and click the Configure button to its right. Notice that the default value you set earlier appears here also (see Figure 21.26).

7. Click OK to set the changes.

Figure 21.25.
Configuring the push partner.

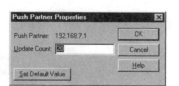

Figure 21.26.
Configuring the pull partner.

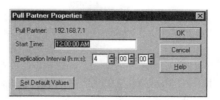

8. Now you can look at your database and verify that you have a replicate from the other server. Select your primary server and choose Mappings | Show Database (see Figure 21.27).

9. Select the other server to display its mapping (see Figure 21.28).

Figure 21.27.
The local WINS database.

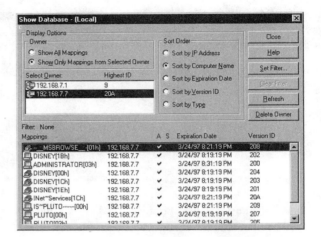

Figure 21.28.
The backup WINS database.

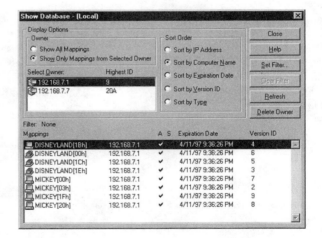

Now that you have replication, it would be good to back up the WINS database. Follow these steps for the manual method:

1. In the WINS Manager, choose Mappings | Backup Database.

2. Select the path where you want the WINS_BAK directory to be created.

3. Click OK. The WINS Manager will tell you when the backup is successfully completed.

You can configure WINS to back up the database automatically whenever the WINS service is stopped. To configure WINS to back up the database, follow these steps:

1. Choose Server | Configuration | Advanced (see Figure 21.29).
2. Type the path where you want WINS to create the `WINS_BAK` directory for backups.
3. Click OK. Now, whenever the service stops, it will back up its database.

Backing up the database is not critical in small networks, as each client will register itself when it comes up and rebuild the database automatically.

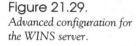

Figure 21.29.
Advanced configuration for the WINS server.

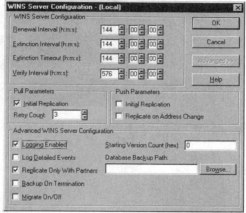

In Figure 21.29, you'll notice a default option to Replicate Only with Partners. You can disable this option on this WINS Server configuration screen, but you need to understand the risks involved—especially if you connect the server to the Internet. Check out `www.microsoft.com/security` for information on how to configure Windows NT as a secure server.

Adding Static Mappings

Adding static mappings allows clients to reach legacy NetBIOS hosts that don't support WINS natively, such as LAN Manager 2.x and Windows NT 3.1. It also allows you to set the IP for static hosts that are critical and won't change.

> **Tip:** I usually add the PDCs and the domain names as static if there's concern with replication happening properly. This usually prevents users from getting the `No logon server available` messages when TCP/IP is the only protocol being used.

Select Mappings | Static Mappings to see all static mappings for this WINS server. Notice that you can add mappings manually or import a list of static mappings from an LMHOSTS file.

Static mappings are *not* replicated between WINS servers, so you need to add static mappings on each server.

When you select Add Mappings from the dialog box, you see five different types of mappings. Figure 21.30 shows both versions of the dialog box—the upper version for unique and group mappings, and the lower one for domain name, Internet group, and multihomed hosts.

Figure 21.30.
Dialog boxes for adding static mappings.

The online Help goes into great detail on NetBIOS-specific names and what each type means. We'll focus on the two most-used types: unique and domain name.

Unique means what you would think: one NetBIOS name mapped to one IP address. These are the normal type. Most things on the network have only one IP address and only one name—your workstation, a server, a printer.

To set up a unique address, fill in the name and the IP address of the host and select Add (see Figure 21.31). When you have finished adding addresses, click Close.

Figure 21.31.
A WINS unique address.

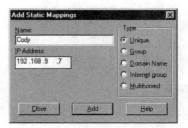

The second common type of mapping is the domain name type. Because Windows NT security relies on the need for someone to authenticate all passwords and communications, you must be able to validate against the domain to share server resources such as file shares and printers.

> **Note:** UNIX services such as FTP, DHCP, and DNS can use the NT security database, but they're not required to do so. They can be set up to allow anonymous access to their resources.

Some of the most annoying problems to track down are the NetBIOS name issues that are domain-name-related. You can ping the server by name, so you either have WINS running or an LMHOSTS file with a good reference. But you can't use any resources unless you also have a domain name. WINS captures the domain name and the machine name when a PDC or BDC updates its entry. The only time I've seen a domain name drop off or not exist is when the server was on another segment and there wasn't a WINS server on that segment. If you want to allow your users to access resources in the other domain and there's no trust (see Chapter 8, "Microsoft Network Access Concepts Brief" for details on trusts), the easiest way to make this work is to define a unique entry for the server and a domain entry for the domain using the server's IP address.

Let's assume for this example that we're trying to log on to the server CODY in the domain PEANUT. The unique address for CODY is already set up (refer to Figure 21.31), so all we need to add is the domain entry.

Select Mappings | Static Mappings from the WINS admin and choose Add Mappings from the dialog box that appears. Select the domain name. The box allows you to add the name of the domain and as many IP addresses as you know. You only need one, but if you're aware of the IP addresses of the other BDCs in the other domain, you can add them in case the server you've set for validation is down. We'll select the PEANUT domain with 192.168.9.7 for the address because that's the address of CODY, the BDC we want to reach, and we know that it can validate the security and get us our data (see Figure 21.32).

Figure 21.32.
The domain entry with the PEANUT domain defined.

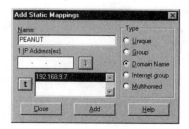

LMHOSTS Files

With the creation of WINS (NBNS) to dynamically keep track of NetBIOS names, the LMHOSTS file has primarily gone the way of the dinosaur, but it still has uses. If you were on a routed TCP/IP network and you wanted to connect to a server across the router in another domain, but they didn't have a WINS server configured on their side, you would have LMHOSTS as your easiest option. With one line of text, you could define the server and the domain, which would allow you to attach to the other server. For instance,

```
192.168.9.7        CODY       #PRE    #DOM:PEANUT
```

would define CODY as a domain server for the PEANUT domain, reachable at IP address 192.168.9.7.

Computers talk in ones and zeros. Computers use numbers like 192.7.7.7 to refer to each other. Humans generally don't refer to a computer by a number. We prefer names like Qwert or Hawk or Indy_1. While we may know what IP address they hold, you wouldn't call the supervisor and ask him to check on 115.213.45.7; you'd ask him to check on Bozo the Web server. Because computers need the numbers to talk and humans need the names, a method had to be developed to keep track of names-to-numbers. LMHOSTS files were the first attempts to organize Microsoft's NetBIOS names into a logical structure. You would enter a name you liked for the computer, and put the name with its IP address in a structure like this:

```
192.168.9.7        CODY
```

In the NetBIOS world, we also have domains that must validate security. If CODY were also a primary or backup domain server in the domain PEANUT, we would add the #DOM: tag to set a security domain reference. CODY would now look like this:

```
192.168.9.7        CODY       #DOM:PEANUT
```

You could log on to the domain PEANUT because the client will ask CODY to validate for the domain.

Another tag you need to know is the #PRE tag. This tells Windows NT to preload the NetBIOS name into the name cache when the server or client comes up. This system cuts down on the need to read the LMHOSTS file every time you need something in the PEANUT domain validated. Here's the final line of the host file:

```
192.168.9.7        CODY       #PRE    #DOM:PEANUT
```

LMHOSTS files can be stored on a central server and referenced from there. You would only need a reference to the server and domain like the previous example, and an #INCLUDE line like this:

```
#INCLUDE \\CODY\public\lmhosts
```

This line points to the LMHOSTS file in the share named PUBLIC on server CODY.

You can even have multiple LMHOSTS files on different servers and set up an alternates list like this:

```
#BEGIN_ALTERNATE
#INCLUDE \\GABRIEL\public\lmhosts
#INCLUDE \\MICHAEL\public\lmhosts
#END_ALTERNATE
```

Note: The LMHOSTS file is discussed in great detail in the sample file LMHOSTS.SAM, which should be in your windows directory.

Note: This is a poor man's method of avoiding the need to update each file on each client manually. This method worked when there were no other options, but we now have WINS (NetBIOS name servers) to dynamically keep track of names.

TCP/IP Printing Concepts

When you want to print a document, you need three basic things: a computer, a printer, and something connecting them. With a stand-alone system, that's easy—your printer is connected to the back of your computer via a printer port. When you say "print," the computer asks the port whether the printer is ready and then sends the data to be printed.

When you add a network to the mix, the computer asks the network client whether the server is ready and then sends the data to the server to be printed. If the printer you're looking for is attached to the back of the server, the printing happens much like it does in stand-alone mode. The server sends the print job to the port attached to the printer. But most printers don't attach to the back of a server. Most modern printers sit alone, with only print-server devices attached to them or installed within them. This setup allows the printers to be in the areas where the users can share them. If all of the printers had to be attached to the server to be used, we'd have some long-walking, frustrated users.

If the printers and the servers are going to communicate, they need a method. The most common methods have been based on IPX (Novell) or DLC (IBM, LAN Manager) for years. The issue now is why you would want another protocol on your wire if you use TCP/IP for everything else—hence, the need for TCP/IP-based printing.

TCP/IP-based printing has existed since the beginning. UNIX users have used TCP/IP-based printing in the form of the LPR and LPD utilities. LPR stands for *line printing remote* (the client), and LPD stands for *line printing daemon* (the server). Microsoft included both LPR and LPD in Windows NT so that you can host LPD printers for UNIX machines and send LPR requests to UNIX hosts and TCP/IP printers.

Most print servers shipping today include the LPD service in their firmware. Once you have set up the print server, you access it from the Windows NT Print Manager much like you would any other printer.

> **Tip:** The configuration of print servers is generally simple, but each manufacturer uses its own software and/or method. Refer to the documentation included with your printer or print server.

Installing Print Services

> **Note:** The first step in installing TCP/IP-based print services is to install TCP/IP. If you haven't already done so, refer to the earlier section "Installing TCP/IP."

To install print services, follow these steps:

1. Bring up the Network control panel and click the Services tab.
2. Click Add and select Microsoft TCP/IP Printing, as shown in Figure 21.33.

   There are no configuration options available within the control panel. All configuration changes are done from the Print Manager and the command-line utilities LPR and LPQ.

3. Close the Network control panel; the computer will reboot.

Figure 21.33.
The Network control panel with TCP/IP printing installed.

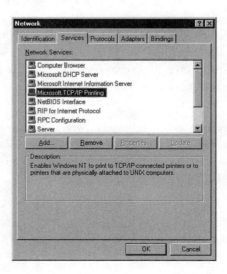

LPR and LPQ Usage

The command-line utilities LPR and LPQ are used primarily to send preprinted jobs to a TCP/IP-based printer (LPR) or to check the status of a job on an LPD printer (LPQ).

Note: Most civilized people will use the Print Manager to submit jobs and check queues, but Microsoft included tools for the technogeek or command-line guru to use.

The help included with the LPR command gives all the information you need to use it. If you type LPR at a Windows NT command prompt, you'll see the screen shown in Figure 21.34.

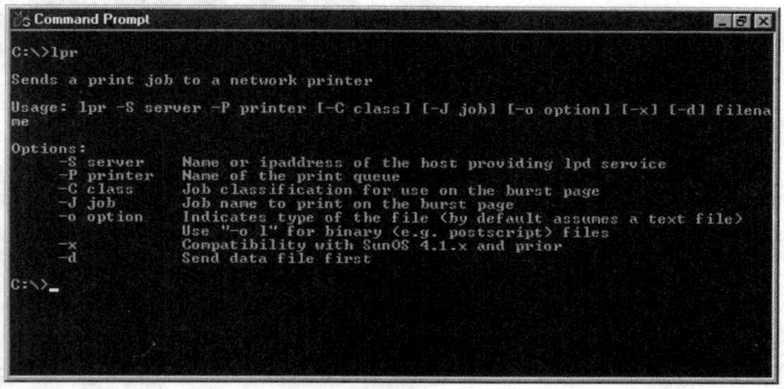

Figure 21.34.
The LPR help screen.

```
Command Prompt                                                    _ 8 X

C:\>lpr

Sends a print job to a network printer

Usage: lpr -S server -P printer [-C class] [-J job] [-o option] [-x] [-d] filena
me

Options:
        -S server      Name or ipaddress of the host providing lpd service
        -P printer     Name of the print queue
        -C class       Job classification for use on the burst page
        -J job         Job name to print on the burst page
        -o option      Indicates type of the file (by default assumes a text file)
                       Use "-o l" for binary (e.g. postscript) files
        -x             Compatibility with SunOS 4.1.x and prior
        -d             Send data file first

C:\>_
```

To use LPR, you first get the information you want printed into a file. If the file is standard text such as help files, you just plug in the server name, queue name, and the name of the printer file, as in the following example:

```
LPR -S unixhost1 -P queue1 -d c:\printout.txt
```

Another use would be printing to a file. Let's say that you have a large 100 ppm printer in the computer room that you use to print manuals. You don't want everyone to be able to send directly to the printer because it will get every e-mail message, spreadsheet, and so on, instead of what you really want. One option is to set up a Windows NT server that has TCP/IP printing enabled and also set up a share for users to save their printouts to. You could run a batch file to send the jobs from that share to the 100 ppm laser, or you could have a print operator manually review the jobs and then send them.

If the information you send is formatted by the printer, such as PostScript printouts, you'll want to add the -o 1 option for binary mode. This will allow the information to be sent to the printer unmodified.

The only thing you can do with the LPQ command is check the status of a remote LPD queue. You can see the help file by typing LPQ at the command prompt, as shown in Figure 21.35. Figure 21.36 shows an example of the status report returned by the LPQ command.

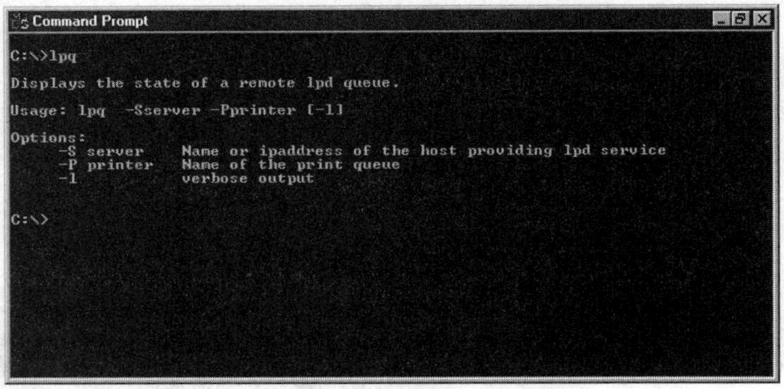

Figure 21.35.
The LPQ help screen.

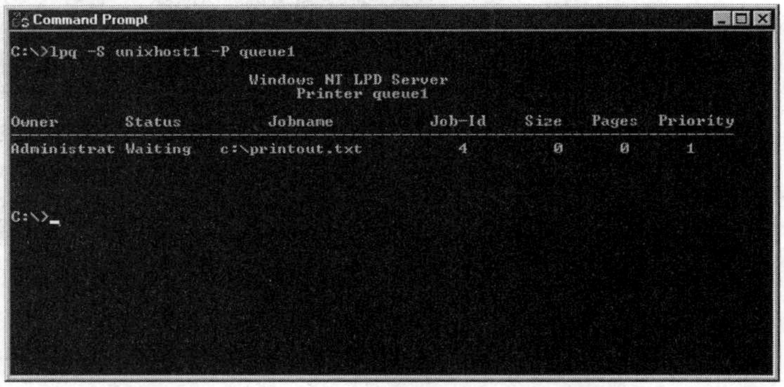

```
Command Prompt

C:\>lpq

Displays the state of a remote lpd queue.

Usage: lpq  -Sserver -Pprinter [-l]

Options:
   -S server     Name or ipaddress of the host providing lpd service
   -P printer    Name of the print queue
   -l            verbose output


C:\>
```

Figure 21.36.
An LPQ example.

```
Command Prompt

C:\>lpq -S unixhost1 -P queue1
                          Windows NT LPD Server
                             Printer queue1

Owner          Status        Jobname         Job-Id    Size   Pages   Priority

Administrat  Waiting      c:\printout.txt        4       0      0        1


C:\>_
```

Print Queue Configuration

The most widely used configuration for TCP/IP printing is the print queue. You usually set up Windows NT to control the print queue for the user, and then Windows NT sends the print jobs to the printer directly, using the LPR function. To configure a printer to act as a queue, you configure the printer driver and point it toward the LPR port. Follow these steps:

1. From the Start menu, choose Settings | Printers.

2. Double-click the icon called Add Printer to open the Add Printer Wizard (see Figure 21.37).

3. The two options are My Computer and Network Print Server. This may seem backward, but because you're setting My Computer to be a network print server, select My Computer.

4. On the next screen, you configure the LPR port. Select Add Port, highlight LPR Port, and select New Port (see Figure 21.38).

Figure 21.37.
The Add Printer Wizard.

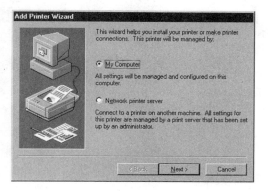

Figure 21.38.
Adding a new port to Windows NT.

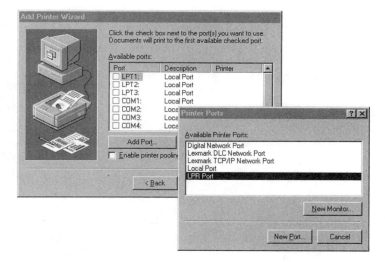

5. Type the host name or the IP address of the device or print server you want to print to. For this example, we'll keep Unixhost1 and Queue1.

6. Click OK. The computer verifies the server and queue you have selected and returns to the Add Printer Wizard. The Available Ports list now shows the port you added; the port is selected (see Figure 21.39).

7. The rest of the printer configuration is normal. Select a printer driver for the printer and set up any defaults in the driver.

Figure 21.39.
The new LPR port.

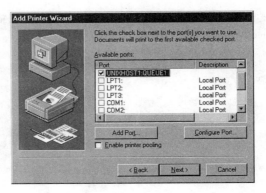

Note: If you were sending the print job to a UNIX host that would format the text, you could select Generic Text Only for the printer; NT would send only basic text to the UNIX host.

Microsoft DNS Server

The DNS Server is to the Internet what the WINS server is to the Microsoft network. DNS has some advantages in that the name space is divided into logical sections that can be managed by different servers. It also has some disadvantages in the fact that it has traditionally been a static address structure that has to be maintained manually. Microsoft is addressing the strengths of both by producing a DNS server that can use a WINS server as a backup method for name resolution, giving you the best of both worlds.

Note: Microsoft is phasing out the WINS servers and phasing in the Active DNS servers. WinNT 5.0 will use DNS for all name resolution, and the DNS will actively manage the name space from the location information of the machine.

The DNS (Domain Names System)

The domain names system (DNS) is sometimes referred to as the BIND (Burkle Internet Naming Daemon) in UNIX systems. DNS offers a hierarchical name service for TCP/IP-based hosts. Like NetBIOS networks (NetBEUI, IPX, and so on), TCP/IP needed some way to make network host addresses more accessible to humans. If I tell you that my IP address is 10.23.223.34, you might remember that until the next sentence, but if I tell you that my DNS is pnorton.mcp.com, that you would remember. DNS gives TCP/IP the naming convention that NetBIOS computer names give to NetBEUI and IPX.

The network administrator configures the DNS with a list of host names and IP addresses. The list by definition is static, and must be updated manually. By using DNS, the user can attach to a friendly name for the system and doesn't need to know the IP address. For example, if you want to connect to the Macmillan Computer Publishing World Wide Web server, you don't type 10.23.223.34 (the IP address); you type in www.mcp.com (the DNS host name).

DNS domains are different from Windows NT domains. NT machines can participate in the DNS domain structure such as www.microsoft.com. This is actually the WWW server in the domain MICROSOFT, which is under the primary domain COM.

Peter's Principle: Use Different Host Names

Because the Internet was originally based on UNIX and other standard TCP/IP-based systems, the use of DNS servers for host name resolution is the *de facto* standard. If you want to attach to a Windows NT server for Web pages, FTP, or just SMTP e-mail, you would only need the host name resolved; this is where DNS comes into play. While people will normally leave their host names the same as their NetBIOS names, they're really different names as far as name resolution is concerned. This is an important fact in that I prefer to have my external host name very different from the internal. This strategy makes it more difficult for an outside user to hack into my Windows NT server, as he would need to know the domain name, a user account, a password, and the correct name for a PDC or BDC.

Installing a DNS Server

To install a DNS server, follow these steps:

1. Open the Network control panel and click the Services tab.
2. Click Add and highlight Microsoft DNS Server, as shown in Figure 21.40.
3. Click OK. Then tell NT where your install files are located. After installing the files, NT returns to the Services tab.
4. Close the Network control panel; the system will reboot.

Figure 21.40.
*Adding the DNS server to
the services list.*

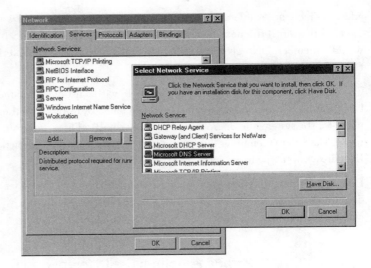

Because DNS is configured using the DNS Manager, there are no changes to be made within the Services tab.

> **Tip:** Because the DNS Server included with Windows NT Server 4.0 is fully RFC-compliant, it creates and uses standard DNS zone files and supports all standard resource record types. Microsoft's DNS also includes two new resource types called *WINS* and *WINS-R*, which allow you to use a WINS server as a dynamic piece of your DNS. This enables the DNS to give accurate data on dynamic hosts that have their IP addresses assigned by DHCP.

The DNS can be configured using standard UNIX RFC text files. If you have an existing DNS server, or if you're more comfortable using the text files for configuration, you'll find Microsoft's DNS comfortable. I personally prefer the graphical approach, and will be focusing on the configuration using the DNS Manager, as described in the following sections.

Initial Configuration

When you initially open the DNS Manager, nothing is listed. You must add your DNS server to the list. To add a DNS server, follow these steps:

1. Choose DNS | New Server from the menu and type the name or IP address of your DNS server.

   You'll notice that the only listing is the cache. If you drill down through the structure, you'll see the Internet root servers—nothing else (see Figure 21.41).

Figure 21.41.
The initial structure with root servers.

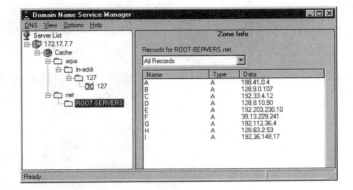

2. To view the automatically created zones, choose Options | Preferences | Show Automatically Created Zones.
3. Refresh the screen by pressing F5. You should now see three reverse-lookup zones. If you double-click these zones, you'll notice that the DNS server automatically created a name server (NS) and Start of Authority (SOA) record for each zone.

At this point, the DNS server could act as a caching server for your internal users reaching the Internet. If the server had a direct connection to the Internet, the user would make a DNS request locally; the DNS server would request the address from one of the root DNS servers and cache the results. This would allow for better response times and less DNS traffic for frequently visited sites.

Setting Up a Primary Zone (Domain)

If you want to provide your own DNS services for the Internet, you need to configure your zone. Because of the hierarchical nature of DNS, you'll connect to the global name space off one of the root servers. For the InterNIC to register a domain name such as `microsoft.com`, you must provide at least two DNS servers that can resolve your names.

A common approach is to have an ISP provide the primary DNS for the domain and for the company registering the name to provide the backup DNS server. This allows you to take your server down for maintenance without wreaking havoc on the Internet while people look for your site.

To create a primary zone or domain, follow these steps:

1. Select your computer name within the DNS Manager.

2. Choose DNS | New Zone. This command starts the Zone Wizard, which will walk you through the creation of your zone.

3. Select Primary for the zone; then click Next.

4. Enter your domain name in the Zone Name dialog box and press Tab. You will notice that the tool fills in the Zone File name with *your domain*.DNS, as shown in Figure 21.42.

Figure 21.42.
Creating a primary zone.

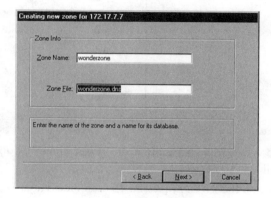

5. Click Next to finish; the Zone Wizard creates the zone. The newly created zone has a name server designation and a Start of Authority, both of which point to your server.

Creating a Zone for Reverse DNS

Many clients attempt to verify that you are who you say you are by reversing the DNS process. If you receive unwanted e-mail from a company and the return address is GET_OVER_IT.COM, for example, you can read the header of the message and find the IP address of the system that sent the message. With the IP address, you can use ping with the -a option and verify who the host really was.

Note: Because most corporate e-mail is sent via firewalls, it's not uncommon for the reverse DNS entry to return a different value, such as Fwall1.company.com. The concern would be when a message comes from IMPORTANT.COM and it originated at MASS-MAIL.ADVERTISE.COM. We would call that *fraud* in other media. ;-)

To create the reverse-lookup zone, you must first do a little work. Follow these steps:

1. You create the zone using the network portions of the IP address, depending on the class. As mentioned earlier, A is the first octet, B is the first two octets, and C is the first three octets. Next you reverse the order of the octets and append them to `.IN-ADDR.ARPA`. The class A of `A.x.x.x` would become `A.IN-ADDR.ARPA`, the class B of `A.B.x.x` would become `B.A.IN-ADDR.ARPA`, and the class C of `A.B.C.x` would become `C.B.A.IN-ADDR.ARPA`. So an address such as `172.17.0.0` (class B) would become `17.172.IN-ADDR.ARPA`.

2. After you determine your zone name, select your computer from the server list in the left panel of DNS Manager. Right-click to bring up the shortcut menu, and select New Zone.

3. Select Primary as the type and click Next.

4. Enter the zone name and press Tab. You'll notice that the zone file is filled in correctly for you, as shown in Figure 21.43.

Figure 21.43.
Setting up the reverse DNS zone.

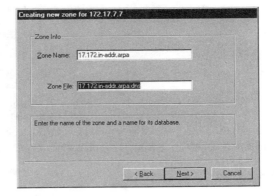

A reverse lookup zone is now listed under your computer for your domain. You'll also notice that the NS and SOA records were automatically created for you, as they were when you created your zone.

Adding Host (A), Mail Exchanger (MX), and Pointer (PTR) Records

To create a host record, follow these steps:

1. In the DNS Manager, select your domain name.

2. Notice the blank space in the right-hand panel. Right-click in the blank area and select New Host from the shortcut menu.

3. Enter the host name and IP address of a host for which you want DNS lookup.

4. Select the Create Associated PTR Record option (see Figure 21.44).

Figure 21.44.
Creating host entries in the domain.

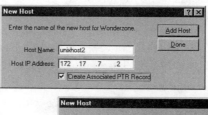
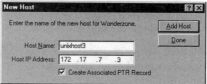

5. Click Add Host to add the entry to your domain.

6. Add any additional hosts and select Done when you are finished.

7. Double-click the Reverse Lookup domain to see the new PTR entries for the hosts you just added.

The other common type of entry is the MX *record*. MX stands for *mail exchanger*. You can have multiple MX records within a domain to allow you to balance the load on multiple incoming machines or to allow for fault tolerance in the case of a failure.

To create the MX record, follow these steps:

1. Right-click the domain name in the left panel of the DNS Manager to open the shortcut menu.

2. Select New Record and highlight MX Record as your record type in the New Record dialog box.

3. Fill in the information for the host name and the fully qualified domain name (FQDN), as shown in Figure 21.45. The host name is optional because it can be derived from the FQDN and the domain entry. The preference number is the key to how the MX record is used in multiple-Mail Exchange sites. The lower the number in the preference, the higher the use.

   The MX entry is now listed in the zone info screen in the right panel of the DNS Manager.

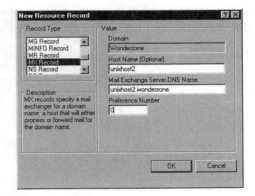

Figure 21.45.
A DNS entry for an MX record.

If you have an e-mail system such as Microsoft Exchange that can handle multiple Internet connectors (SMTP servers) for the same domain, you could configure the DNS to point to the primary connector with a preference of 0 (zero) and the secondary with a preference of 1 (one). Mail would normally come to the primary system and would fail over to the secondary if the primary were down. You could also configure them with the same preference and the load would balance across the two connectors.

Setting Up DNS to Use WINS and WINS-R

Remember that I mentioned earlier that DNS is a static, manually updated name server with no ability to dynamically add hosts? That was before Microsoft added a twist—two new resource records (WINS and WINS-R), which allow a WINS-aware DNS server to use WINS for any addresses it doesn't know about. WINS provides the machine name-to-IP address lookups, and WINS-R provides the reverse DNS lookups for IP address-to-machine name.

To enable WINS lookup, follow these steps:

1. Right-click the domain in the left panel of the DNS Manager and select Properties from the shortcut menu.
2. Click the WINS Lookup tab.
3. Select the Use WINS Resolution check box.
4. Add the IP addresses for your WINS servers and click OK (see Figure 21.46).

Figure 21.46.
Setting up DNS to use WINS.

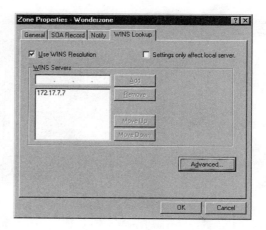

Next you need to set up reverse WINS lookup on your reverse DNS zone. Follow these steps:

1. Right-click the reverse zone lookup domain in the left panel of the DNS Manager and select Properties from the shortcut menu.

2. Click the WINS Reverse Lookup tab.

3. Select the Use WINS Reverse Lookup option (see Figure 21.47).

4. Type in your domain and click OK.

Figure 21.47.
Setting up DNS to use WINS-R.

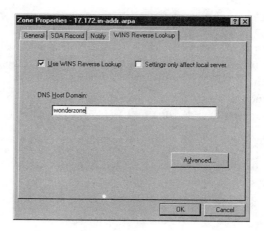

To test the WINS and WINS-R, you want to `ping` a host that you know is on the network in the WINS database but not in the DNS database. When you `ping` by name, you test the WINS lookup; if that works, `ping` the IP address with the -a option. The DNS should WINS-R the host name back to you. You'll notice that the DNS appended the host name you gave it to your domain name (see Figure 21.48).

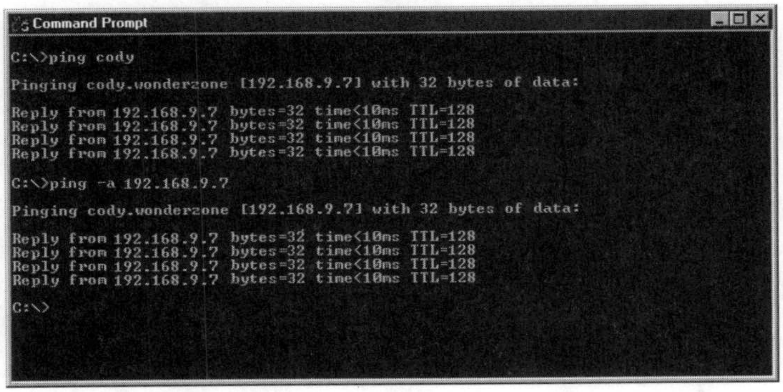

Figure 21.48.
Testing WINS and WINS-R.

Most of the settings for DNS can be configured with the graphical client. If you prefer the old UNIX-style text files, or if you are replacing a UNIX DNS, you can use both.

Summary

In this chapter we've covered the majority of the information you need to properly configure the TCP/IP protocol and the supporting server products (DHCP, WINS, DNS, LPD). With proper implementation, you should have a have a robust scalable infrastructure that will support you well into the next millennium—three to five years.

22

Internet Information Server

Peter Norton™

As I mentioned in the introduction to this book, Windows NT Server had grand aspirations when it was created. Among those aspirations was to be a UNIX rival in many areas. With the introduction of the Internet Information Server (IIS) as a free service contained within the NT operating system, Microsoft has taken a large step toward making the product a major player in the Internet world. NT has begun to replace UNIX as an option for small to medium-sized businesses for their entire Internet presence.

Windows NT isn't as powerful as UNIX at this point in its life cycle, but the items contained in most business Internet sites don't require the underlying strengths of UNIX. NT and IIS offer a set of tools that get the job done well and an interface that doesn't require the company to hire an Internet/UNIX expert. In the same way that NT has infiltrated the network operating system market by being easier to manage than NetWare, it's making inroads into the Internet server market.

It's important to note as you start looking at the usefulness of a product like IIS for your business that it isn't just an Internet tool. This product is really named Internet Information Server as more of a marketing tool than a good description of what it does for you. The tools that are used in the IIS package are equally able to be used as part of your in-house network or intercompany network information distribution plan.

These types of connections are now being called intranets, just as highways that stay inside your state are called *intrastate* highways (versus *interstate*). These Web sites, FTP sites, and so on are becoming popular in companies that may not consider an Internet presence. Even if you can't justify an external Web presence, I think you have to consider the power of HTTP and FTP as intercompany tools.

Following is a list of some of the items covered in this chapter:

- IIS concepts
- HTTP/World Wide Web server
- FTP server
- Gopher server
- Preparing for the IIS installation
- Installation
- Administration and configuration
- Directory rights assignment for secure sites
- Security checklist
- What's included in the IIS v3.0 upgrade?

Concepts

The IIS service contains three major products:

- An HTTP/World Wide Web (WWW) server
- An FTP server
- A Gopher server

The following sections describe each of these products.

HTTP/World Wide Web Server

The HTTP server is responsible for providing the services associated with what you might know as the World Wide Web. *HTTP* stands for *hypertext transfer protocol*. This is the name given to the process because of the use of hyperlinks to transfer users from one Web page to another, moving users from one location to another across the Web.

The technology is not an old one, like much of the Internet. It's a technology developed in the last seven years (1990–1991) and really was created as a way of making the Internet an easier tool to use. I would say that they accomplished what they set out to do. The creation of the HTTP protocol and the invention of Web browsers like Mosaic are responsible for the rest of us diving on to the Internet. In 1988, there were an estimated 235 hosts active on the Internet; by 1994, that number had jumped to 3.2 million. I think the Web affected the Internet.

Note: We won't spend a great deal of time on the history of the process; you can get that information in any of several thousand books on the process, but instead we'll look at how NT can get you involved in using HTTP to publish your information.

If you've never used the World Wide Web, you really need to get some experience as a user before you can begin this chapter. There really is no way to describe the concept better than making use of it. But as someone who has little experience, you may be better able to believe that the process is not magic.

One of the most difficult concepts for users of the World Wide Web to grasp is that it's not magic or tons of complex code that make it work. HTTP is really an elegantly simple process of opening documents from links within other documents. In order to connect from one document to another, the author simply tells a word or graphic in the document that it's a link to open another file. The process is a bit more complex in the underlying code, but with the tools available it doesn't get much tougher than that.

Tip: Most Web documents aren't created today by writing code like a BASIC program, but instead are written in WYSYWIG document-creation applications. These applications function more like a word processor or publishing package and rarely require that you know any HTML to create a page. The HTML code is still being written, but it's being done for you by the application. Applications like Microsoft's FrontPage and Adobe's Site Mill make the document creation process fairly easy.

The text or graphic that's chosen to open the other document is called a *link* because it links the document to another document. The link is really nothing more than a single point that you can click that launches the equivalent of a File | Open command and gives the location of the file. It's much like using Microsoft Word or Excel and choosing File | Open and telling the application to open a file that's at a particular location.

Note: Web documents are called *hypertext markup language* (*HTML*) documents. This is because they're created with a code or language that instructs HTML interpreters called *Web browsers* (for example, Netscape or Microsoft Internet Explorer) on how to present the document. By creating documents with a markup language and reading them through an interpreter, the Web allows many different types of computers to use these documents. All documents use the same language, so now all that's required is an interpreter for each system.

The fact that Web documents are linked in this way isn't important at this point because of the detail in linking, but instead it should help you to understand what your HTTP server will be asked to provide. My point is not to teach you how to create a Web document, but instead give you some idea about what your HTTP server will be serving up.

Web documents are sent from the server to the client workstation. Just like the File | Open scenario, the server and client don't remain actively connected once the file is sent to the client. Imagine that you have opened a Word document from a floppy disk; you don't have to leave the disk in the drive, do you? That's because the floppy disk version of the file and the one that you have loaded into RAM are no longer connected. The same is true of a Web document that has been sent out across the Internet from your HTTP server. The client system requests the file from your HTTP server, and your server sends the file. The connection is severed at that point.

This makes several things possible. Chapter 15, "Surviving in a Multi-Protocol World," discusses bandwidth (traffic) on the network. Well, the Internet is a network, and bandwidth is precious. Sending the document and then disconnecting allows that bandwidth to be freed for other things. This fact also helps to free up the server to move on to the next client request. If instead the server and client needed to maintain a connection for this relationship, it would hold precious bandwidth and tax the server CPU.

The downside of this type of connection is that you aren't maintaining a continuous connection and must reestablish every time you need a service or resource. Although this is less taxing on the host system and the bandwidth, it's more taxing on your system because it must provide all services (memory, CPU, storage, and so on).

A host session that isn't continuously connected also exposes both systems to security risks involved in users stepping in and pretending to be the right recipient of a message or resource. Imagine two people passing a ball back and forth when a third person steps between them and catches the ball. As long as he continues throwing and catching the ball, the other receiver/passer may never know the difference. This is sometimes called a "man in the middle" attack.

FTP Server

FTP stands for *file transfer protocol*. FTP is the protocol used on the Internet any time that you transfer a file to your system, but in today's Web browser world you can access this process through a Web link and may not even know that you've connected to an FTP site.

The concept is to make connection to a host system and copy a file to your system (*download*) or copy a file to the host (*upload*). If you've been using the Internet for fewer than two years, you may have used FTP and not even known it.

When you attach to an FTP site, you're not really connected in the sense that you're connected to a local network host. FTP connections involve a series of messages that are sent between client and host that help facilitate locating the file that you want to get and/or where you want to place a file.

Note: If you'd like to get a look at an FTP site that looks like an FTP site, enter the following information in the location section of your Web browser: `ftp://ftp.microsoft.com` (see Figure 22.1). By using `ftp://` instead of `http://`, you change the protocol that you're using to address the server, and you receive the FTP interface.

Figure 22.1.
The Microsoft FTP site.

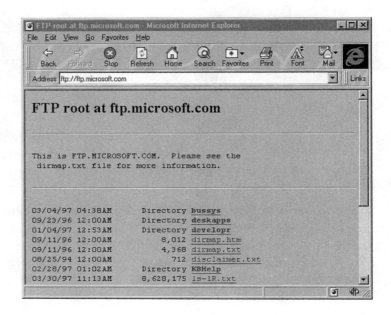

Figure 22.1.
The Microsoft FTP site.

The initial connection to an FTP site involves authenticating your user account much like an NT connection, but once you provide an account name and password (if necessary), you're now on a timer. The FTP server maintains a place for you. If your address continues to communicate within set time parameters, you remain connected. Wait too long and you'll have to establish a place again.

Gopher Server

Gopher is a technology developed at the University of Minnesota (Golden Gophers) to be used for document recovery, and it's really not used much any more. The Gopher protocol was replaced by the HTTP protocol for most applications, and is included in IIS because of legacy demands.

When you look at a Gopher site, you'll see what looks very much like the FTP site (see Figure 22.2). The difference is that a Gopher site is primarily concerned with housing and publishing documents.

When you picture a Gopher site, it may help to picture a library. When you enter the library, you're initially hit with major categories of shelves. As you move closer to the shelves, you begin to see subcategories, book titles, and finally, as you open a specific book, you can view a document.

The experience of opening a Gopher site is to initially see general categories. Once you click a category, you're taken to more and more specific data areas. Eventually the icons change from folders to document icons. These documents can be downloaded or opened directly from the Gopher site.

Figure 22.2.
A Gopher site, seen in a Web browser.

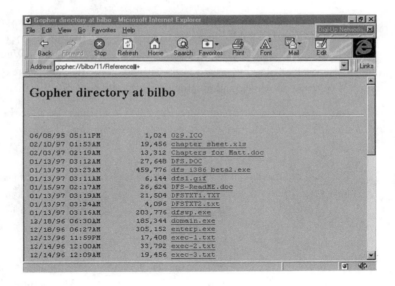

Before Installing Internet Information Server

Before you can begin installing Internet Information Server, there are a few items that must be arranged. We need to cover the needs of the system to be able to handle the addition of the IIS responsibilities, and of course there's the matter of connecting your IIS server to the Internet.

System Requirements

Your system requirements depend greatly on how much you intend to publish through this site. The concept is to treat these products like any other service that runs on the NT platform. It isn't the service that will drain the system so much as the file activity and the disk access.

Microsoft makes no specific recommendation for extra memory or hard drive space, but as a general rule I suggest that you add at least 8MB of RAM when installing this product. That memory is just to cover the additional space for the services that will be running. Beyond that, use the memory calculation chart in Chapter 4, "Installation Considerations," and calculate RAM based on those factors.

Hard drive space is the one piece of this pie that no one can tell you except yourself. The Internet site that you intend to publish is going to be vastly different from that of the next person, but I'll give you this piece of advice. Keep in mind that HTML documents (Web pages), excluding graphics, are simply text files. Even Web pages with color and fluff are just text files. So even a medium-sized Web site with a few small graphics per page will consume less than 100MB.

FTP sites, on the other hand, are fairly easy for you to gauge. Because the purpose of an FTP site is to house files for distribution, you can simply allow that much space.

> **Tip:** The hard drive area that's used for the Internet server should be formatted as NTFS. This isn't a Microsoft requirement, but I recommend that you make it one of yours. Remember that your NT domain security is relying on NTFS security to allow it to function at its fullest.

Since we're going to be using an Internet set of technologies, it stands to reason that you're going to have to install TCP/IP as one of your NT Server protocols. All machines that want to access the site will need to do so via TCP/IP.

TCP/IP decisions should be made for this system long before you arrive at the installation of IIS. These are some of the important items to the install:

- TCP/IP address
- Domain name and domain name server (DNS)
- WINS server

If you're connecting the server to the Internet, a domain name and DNS connection are not optional. You may recall from Chapter 21, "TCP/IP Networking," that the Internet uses DNS as a way of tracking Internet hosts across the giant network. If you don't have a registered IP address and a domain name for your server, you won't be found on the Internet.

Because the IIS v2.0 product comes on the NT CD-ROM, you need the server to have a CD-ROM drive.

Internet Connectivity

Intranet connection to your IIS is pretty easy to figure out, but how are you going to get your server connected to the Internet? Arranging a connection to the Internet for your Internet server is quite a bit different from connecting your individual machine to the Internet to download e-mail or surf the Net. Now you want the Internet to surf you.

Connecting your company or network to the largest computer network in the world really only requires that you find someone who will allow you to attach to their attachment. It's very much like your in-house network. The network that is the Internet is already connected, and you're in need of a place to add another segment (yours).

> **Looking Ahead:** The following chapter takes a look at a product called Proxy Server that has recently been released by Microsoft. This product helps a great deal when trying to manage the connection from the Internet to you.

The process of connecting used to involve finding a willing university—now it's almost solely handled by companies called *Internet service providers* (*ISPs*). An ISP is a company that already has a connection to the Internet and is willing to sell you a connection to their network.

Because you're attaching to the Internet through their network, the ISP has to provide you with a segment of their network, and that often requires that they provide you with the basic IP requirements. In addition to providing your physical Internet connection and IP address (and subnet mask, if appropriate), your ISP can provide many of the Internet services, such as domain name registration, routers, and DNS service.

The physical connection to the ISP will require more bandwidth than that of your dial-up connection for basic services. At a minimum, you'll want users to be able to access your server at better than their modem speed.

The majority of Internet servers are connected to the ISP through what's called a *leased line*. Leased lines are connections made by the local or national phone company that allow for speeds ranging from 56Kbps to 45Mbps. Your choice of speed and type will depend on the amount of traffic that you'll see going to and from your site.

The connection types described in Table 22.1 represent typical levels of service for full Internet connections. The Internet services offered through Internet service providers in other countries may differ significantly. You may observe further differences, depending on the nature of your hardware, the content you make available from your site, and other variables.

Table 22.1. Typical levels of service for full Internet connections.

Type of Connection	Speed in Bits Per Second	Number of Users Expected
Frame relay	56,000	10–20
ISDN	128,000	10–50
T1	1,500,000	100–500
T3	45,000,000	5000+

T1 connectivity can be purchased in fractions instead of the entire 1.5Mbps. The reason is that these T1 connections are actually made of 24 64Kbps lines. So, you can purchase (for example) two 64Kbps lines and have a 128Kbps fractional T1 connection. These connections are a bit less expensive, but the breaking point falls at around four lines. Any fraction greater than four usually isn't a real savings over the entire T1.

The connection that comes into your company from the ISP will most likely terminate (end) at a DSU/CSU and then proceed to a router of some type. Request that your service provider deliver your connection in a manner that makes the connection easiest for you. Most service providers are capable of providing a connection that ends at a router in your building that's capable of being connected to your in-house network (see Figure 22.3).

Figure 22.3.
ISP connection to your local network.

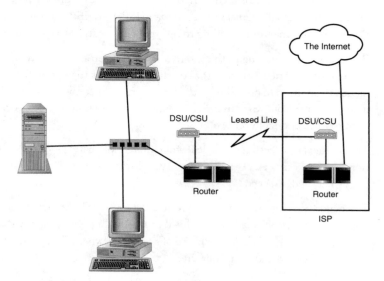

The connection that's delivered should be able to be connected to Ethernet, Token Ring, or an in-house network. The router connection to the phone company connection is best left to your ISP. If the connection down to your in-house network is all arranged and set up by the ISP, when something goes wrong you have a clear path to resolution. Once it's connected, you should be left with no more connection concerns than the TCP/IP needs of that segment of the network.

Peter's Principle: Let the ISP Do the Work

Many ISPs have very good relationships with both the phone company and the InterNIC, and would prefer to be able to make the arrangements for you. I know that this can go against a network engineer's nature, but if you can let them be in charge of everything outside your building, you'll save yourself time and grief in times of trouble. And more often than not, you'll save money as well, based on their connection.

Installing Internet Information Server

The installation of the IIS product is so simple that you actually may have installed it on your server without even knowing it. During the installation of NT Server, you're prompted about whether to install the Internet Information Server. If you answer no during that process, you'll find that an icon is left on your desktop to encourage you to install it later. (Like an odd mint left on your pillow.) There are an almost spooky number of ways to install this product. So many that I really see no reason to list them all.

This install should go fairly quickly. Very little of the site setup is actually done during the installation. The office record for installing the product is 1 minute 50 seconds (my record, but who's bragging?), so it can't be too tough. But be aware that the site is going to come to life as a site that's open to the public.

You don't have to install IIS during the install of NT. In fact, I would encourage you to wait until you have a successful install of NT and a good working relationship with your TCP/IP world before installing IIS. The product isn't difficult to install, but it's best to have your horses ready before you open the door to the barn.

Installation Methods

There are several methods that can be used to install the IIS product. By the time you read this chapter, you may have already installed without even knowing you were involved (during the installation of NT). This section covers the different methods.

To install IIS during the NT install, follow these steps:

1. When prompted, make sure that the Install Microsoft Internet Information Server check box is selected, and click the Next button. The Internet Information Server Setup program begins.

2. Proceed to the next section of this chapter.

For a separate install of IIS, follow these steps:

1. Insert the Windows NT Server compact disc into the CD-ROM drive.

2. In Explorer or at the command prompt, change to the drive containing the CD.

3. Change directories to the `i386\Inetsrv` directory on the CD by typing **CD\i386\Inetsrv** and pressing Enter or by opening the `i386` and then the `Inetsrv` folder.

4. Start the setup from Explorer by double-clicking the file named `INETSTP.EXE`.

5. Proceed to the next section of this chapter.

Installing with the Windows NT Control Panel:

1. Insert the Windows NT Server CD into the CD-ROM drive.

2. Right-click the Network Neighborhood on the desktop and choose Properties from the context menu.

3. In the Network Properties dialog box, click the Services tab.

4. Click the Add button.

5. From the Network Services list, select Microsoft Internet Information Server, and then click OK.

6. In the Installed From box, type the letter of the drive where your compact disc is located (D:, C:, and so on). Click OK.

7. Proceed to the next section of this chapter.

Setup

If you want to just keep pressing the Enter key once you've started IIS setup, you can almost get away with it. The process is really meant to be streamlined. If you just keep pressing Enter, you'll end up with a very public site with all the default choices. You'll also find that you have a record time for installing the product. As neither of those things is the point behind installing IIS—and I don't want my record threatened—let's look at some of the details of the setup. This section walks you through the setup process and gives guidelines for setting up.

Follow these steps:

1. When you start the Setup program, the Microsoft Internet Information Server Welcome dialog box appears. Click OK.

2. All the options in the second dialog box are selected by default except Internet Service Manager (see Figure 22.4). Click OK to install them all. If you don't want to install a particular item, clear the box next to it and then click OK to install the rest.

   These are the options from which you can select:

   • Internet Service Manager installs the administration program for managing the services (not selected by default).

   • World Wide Web Service creates a WWW publishing server.

   • Gopher Service creates a Gopher publishing server.

   • FTP Service creates an FTP publishing server.

   • ODBC Drivers & Administration installs open database connectivity (ODBC) drivers. These are required for logging to ODBC files and for enabling ODBC access through the Internet Database Connector (IDC) from the WWW service (not selected by default).

   • WWW Service Samples installs sample HTML files (not selected by default).

Tip: If you don't understand ODBC as a method of using a database application from other applications, don't leave the ODBC Drivers & Administration option selected. This is a powerful tool, but it's a waste of space if you aren't using it.

Figure 22.4.
Install selections.

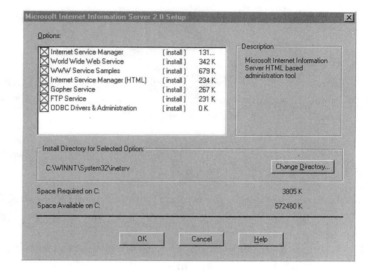

3. Accept the default installation folder (`C:\WINNT\System32\inetsrv`) or click the Change Directory button and enter a new folder.

Tip: If you've installed Internet Information Server, but want to reinstall it into another folder, remove this key from the Registry:

`HKEY_LOCAL_MACHINE\SOFTWARE\Microsoft\INetStp`

If you don't delete this key, the Change Directory button will be dimmed and you won't be able to change the default folder.

4. Click OK. When prompted, click Yes to create the installation folder.
5. The Publishing Directories dialog box appears. Accept the default folders for the publishing services you have installed, or change the folders.
6. Click OK.
7. When prompted to create the service folders (`WWWROOT`, `GOPHROOT`, and `FTPROOT` by default), click Yes.

8. Setup copies all remaining Internet Information Server files.

9. If the ODBC Drivers & Administration option was selected, the Install Drivers dialog box appears.

10. To install a driver, select it from the Available ODBC Drivers list box, and click OK. Setup completes copying files.

11. When the Setup completion dialog box appears, click OK to complete the setup.

Warning: Be aware that you are now open for business. Anything in the chosen published directories is now available to the public. This is an unusual service in the fact that the moment you finish installing, it's running. Really, you don't have to restart. When the install is finished, you can test the site.

Test Your Installation

You can test your installation by using Internet Explorer to view the files in your home directory.

To test a Web server connected to the Internet, follow these steps:

1. Ensure that your Web server has HTML files in the WWWROOT folder. The Setup program has most likely installed these files.

2. Start Internet Explorer on a computer that has an active connection to the Internet. This computer can be the computer you're testing, although using a different computer is recommended.

3. Type in the URL for the home directory of your new Web server. The URL will be http:// followed by the name of your Web server, followed by the path of the file you want to view. (Notice the forward slash marks.) For example, if your server is registered in DNS as www.company.com and you want to view the file Homepage.htm in the root of the home directory, in the Address box you would type the following:

   http://www.company.com/homepage.htm

4. Press Enter. The home page should appear on the screen.

To test a Web server on your intranet, follow these steps:

1. Start Internet Explorer.

2. The URL will be http:// followed by the IP address of your server, followed by the path of the file you want to view. (Notice the forward slash marks.) For example, if your Web server has the IP address 204.95.229.61 and you want to view the file Homepage.htm in the root of the home directory, in the Address box you would type the following:

   http://204.95.229.61/homepage.htm

3. Press Enter. The home page should appear on the screen.

Administration and Configuration

Once the IIS product is installed, the real work begins. Unlike most NT services, IIS is installed and running the moment that Setup finishes, so it's not difficult to make it function. The issue is making sure that it's running in the secure and controlled fashion that you may require.

If your requirements are to have a public Web site or public FTP site, your work is done, for the most part, when the Setup program is finished. IIS starts for the first time with the items in the service directories published. But you don't have to leave things in that state. There's a great deal of control that can be exercised with this product.

Common Controls

The most basic controls for IIS are located in the menu item Start | Programs | Microsoft Internet Server (Common), as shown in Figure 22.5. In that menu, you'll find the Internet Service Manager option.

Figure 22.5.
The Start menu for IIS.

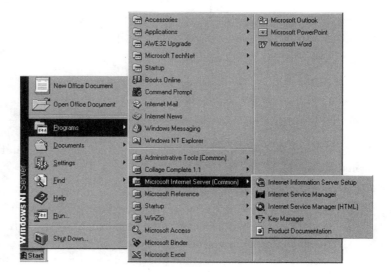

Once you've opened the Internet Service Manager, you will find that you have a very straight-forward and easy-to-understand control application.

Basic Service Control

The controls found in the Internet Service Manager are meant to move the basic administration of the published services into a common interface that doesn't require even NT knowledge to manipulate. The staff involved in publishing the material can control the system on a basic level—without having to call in an engineer.

The Dashboard

Microsoft seems to realize that they're dealing with a different crowd when publishing to the public than when networking the company, but that this product must serve the needs of groups that do both. This is not at all to imply that the group creating the material to be published isn't technically capable or that engineers aren't capable of creating marketing material (look at UNIX!). The point is that this interface must be more universal.

The initial controls in the Internet Service Manager interface involve the running or stopping of the Internet services (see Figure 22.6). Normally, NT services are started and stopped in the control panel called Services, and these can be as well. But the Internet Service Manager offers a common interface for many tasks of this sort.

Figure 22.6.
The Internet Service Manager.

List Internet Servers button —

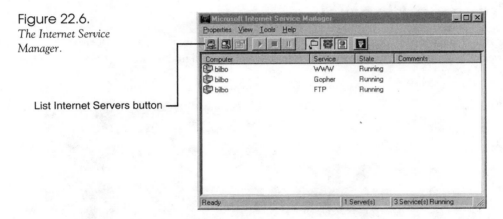

Notice that the interface includes three important columns of data in the server area (below the icon toolbar):

- The Computer column is a tip-off that you can control any computers that are running IIS from this one interface. If you click the List Internet Servers button, the system will search for all IIS servers in the domain. All the computers listed here have an IIS service running. The initial state of this column is to include only the local server, but once you've run the search the servers that are found will appear each time you start the Internet Service Manager.

- The second column (Service) simply refers to which service is being observed on that line.

- The third column (State) holds an indication of whether the service is running or stopped.

Services are stopped and started in this manager through a simple metaphor. You may notice the VCR-style buttons (in the center grouping of the toolbar) that become usable when you select a server and service in the list. These buttons behave in the same way that your VCR buttons do when you select a specific server and service, as shown in the following table.

Button	Description
▶	Starts a service that has been stopped.
■	Stops a started service.
‖	Pauses a service.

The idea is to allow users with little or no understanding of Internet servers—or any servers, for that matter—to control the Internet presence. But then you must ask yourself how many VCRs in the world are still flashing 12:00. This metaphor really only helps if you notice that the third column is displaying the fact that the service is running.

Three other buttons in the toolbar are responsible for finding, selecting, and showing the properties of Internet servers, as described in the following table.

Button	Description
🖳	Finds a specific Internet server. If the server isn't in your network segment, you may have to provide the specific domain name of the host. If you click this button, you'll be prompted for that. Once the server is listed, it won't disappear until Internet Service Manager fails to contact it.
🔍	Looks for a server. Internet Service Manager will search for other IIS servers that exist within its reach.
📝	Lists the properties of the selected server and service in the window below the toolbar. You can also list the properties of a service by double-clicking the icon for the server running the service.

The final set of buttons simply turn on and turn off the view of certain services, as described in the following table.

Button	Description
🗂	If you click this button with your server running, the Internet Service Manager no longer presents that FTP server service. It isn't meant to turn the service off or on, but merely to filter the service from your site.

Button	Description
![Gopher icon]	If you click this button with your server running, the Internet Service Manager no longer presents that Gopher server service. It isn't meant to turn the service off or on, but merely to filter the service from your site.
![WWW icon]	If you click this button with your server running, the Internet Service Manager no longer presents that WWW server service. It isn't meant to turn the service off or on, but merely to filter the service from your site.
![Key icon]	The picture on this button is actually a gold fist holding a key, and knowing that fact will help you to understand what the icon is for. IIS Security, which we'll cover shortly, has a concept called Secure Sockets. In order to create a Secure Sockets connection, the server must create a key pair and distribute a key to be used by client browsers. The key allows the server and client to establish a very secure connection. This button is used to launch the management of these connections and keys.

Anonymous Users

Setup automatically creates an anonymous account called IUSR_*computername* (where *computername* is the name of the NT Server machine). This account has a randomly generated password and privileges to log on locally. On domain controllers, this account is added to the domain database. This process is fully automatic. After installation is complete, you can change the username and password for this account from the Service dialog box in Internet Service Manager, as long as the new username and password match the username and password in the Windows NT User Manager.

If you change the anonymous username account (IUSR_*computername*) in the Windows NT User Manager for Domains, copy the IUSR_*computername* account and then give it a new name and password, rather than creating an entirely new account. By copying the IUSR_*computername* account, you're sure to carry over all the privileges and user rights granted to that account. Then change the anonymous username and password in the Internet Service Manager, making sure that it's exactly the same as the new username and password created in the User Manager for Domains.

The WWW, FTP, and Gopher services use the IUSR_*computername* user account by default when anonymous access is allowed. To set the rights for IUSR_*computername*, use User Manager. To set file permissions on NTFS drives for IUSR_*computername*, use the Windows NT Explorer. To change the account used for anonymous logons for any of the Internet services, choose Properties | Service Properties in Internet Service Manager.

Logging Options

IIS is capable of tracking the users that attach and use your Internet server with relative ease. It will log the connections made, even if you don't specifically request it. The logging that's done is handled on an individual basis for each service that's running (FTP, WWW, Gopher), and will be done even if you don't set up the process.

Keeping logs of the activity on your Internet server is only important to the humans. The server doesn't require that you read these logs; in fact, it will only slow the server to do it. So you really need to look at this page for each of the services that you're running on your server. Take a moment and review the options that you would like utilized (see Figure 22.7).

Figure 22.7.
The logging page in the properties of a WWW server.

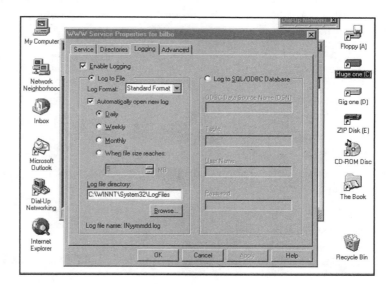

As you look at the logging screen, the first option that you'll notice is the ability to enable logging. You can turn off logging by simply deselecting this option. But before you disable logging, consider the benefits of using it:

- Logging activity on the site can be the only true justification for maintaining a site.
- Logging the activity can be used as justification to potential advertising clients of the site.
- Should security problems arise, traffic logs may be the first line of defense.

Tip: If you've been running the IIS system for some time and have noticed that you're running short of disk space, you may want to look into the log files of the Internet site. These files are usually not large at all, but a year's worth of logs can build up. Relieving this logjam is relatively simple to do. Because IIS doesn't depend on these files to function, you can simply erase the file, and IIS will rebuild the log. If you're using log files, they'll be dated, and it's easy to determine the age based on the filename.

If the choice is made to leave logging enabled then you are presented with a choice of logging methods—logging to file or logging to a SQL/ODBC database.

File Logging

Logging to a file means that IIS will be writing to a text file for the log. This choice enables the administrator to have the system create text-based files and store them in a given directory. The default file is a daily log that records the IP address of a visitor, the time and date of her visit, and any files that she observed while she was at the site.

The selections on the logging page are based primarily on when and how the logging file will be written (see Figure 22.8):

- **Log Format.** Choose either Standard Format or National Center for Supercomputing Applications (NCSA) Format.
- **Automatically Open New Log.** Select this option to generate new logs at the specified interval. If this option is deselected, the same log file will grow indefinitely.
- **Log File Directory.** Shows the path to the directory containing all log files. To change directories, click Browse and select a different directory.
- **Log File Name.** Names the log file. Lowercase letters `yy` will be replaced with the year, `mm` with the month, and `dd` with the day.

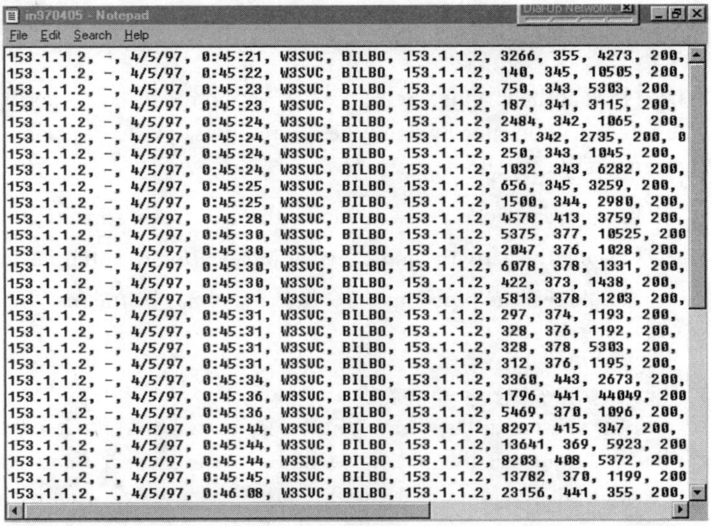
```
in970405 - Notepad
File Edit Search Help
153.1.1.2, -, 4/5/97, 0:45:21, W3SVC, BILBO, 153.1.1.2, 3266, 355, 4273, 200,
153.1.1.2, -, 4/5/97, 0:45:22, W3SVC, BILBO, 153.1.1.2, 140, 345, 10505, 200,
153.1.1.2, -, 4/5/97, 0:45:23, W3SVC, BILBO, 153.1.1.2, 750, 343, 5303, 200,
153.1.1.2, -, 4/5/97, 0:45:23, W3SVC, BILBO, 153.1.1.2, 187, 341, 3115, 200,
153.1.1.2, -, 4/5/97, 0:45:24, W3SVC, BILBO, 153.1.1.2, 2484, 342, 1065, 200,
153.1.1.2, -, 4/5/97, 0:45:24, W3SVC, BILBO, 153.1.1.2, 31, 342, 2735, 200, 0
153.1.1.2, -, 4/5/97, 0:45:24, W3SVC, BILBO, 153.1.1.2, 250, 343, 1045, 200,
153.1.1.2, -, 4/5/97, 0:45:24, W3SVC, BILBO, 153.1.1.2, 1032, 343, 6282, 200,
153.1.1.2, -, 4/5/97, 0:45:25, W3SVC, BILBO, 153.1.1.2, 656, 345, 3259, 200,
153.1.1.2, -, 4/5/97, 0:45:25, W3SVC, BILBO, 153.1.1.2, 1500, 344, 2980, 200,
153.1.1.2, -, 4/5/97, 0:45:28, W3SVC, BILBO, 153.1.1.2, 4578, 413, 3759, 200,
153.1.1.2, -, 4/5/97, 0:45:30, W3SVC, BILBO, 153.1.1.2, 5375, 377, 10525, 200
153.1.1.2, -, 4/5/97, 0:45:30, W3SVC, BILBO, 153.1.1.2, 2047, 376, 1028, 200,
153.1.1.2, -, 4/5/97, 0:45:30, W3SVC, BILBO, 153.1.1.2, 6078, 378, 1331, 200,
153.1.1.2, -, 4/5/97, 0:45:30, W3SVC, BILBO, 153.1.1.2, 422, 373, 1438, 200,
153.1.1.2, -, 4/5/97, 0:45:31, W3SVC, BILBO, 153.1.1.2, 5813, 378, 1203, 200,
153.1.1.2, -, 4/5/97, 0:45:31, W3SVC, BILBO, 153.1.1.2, 297, 374, 1193, 200,
153.1.1.2, -, 4/5/97, 0:45:31, W3SVC, BILBO, 153.1.1.2, 328, 376, 1192, 200,
153.1.1.2, -, 4/5/97, 0:45:31, W3SVC, BILBO, 153.1.1.2, 328, 378, 5303, 200,
153.1.1.2, -, 4/5/97, 0:45:31, W3SVC, BILBO, 153.1.1.2, 312, 376, 1195, 200,
153.1.1.2, -, 4/5/97, 0:45:34, W3SVC, BILBO, 153.1.1.2, 3360, 443, 2673, 200,
153.1.1.2, -, 4/5/97, 0:45:36, W3SVC, BILBO, 153.1.1.2, 1796, 441, 44049, 200
153.1.1.2, -, 4/5/97, 0:45:36, W3SVC, BILBO, 153.1.1.2, 5469, 370, 1096, 200,
153.1.1.2, -, 4/5/97, 0:45:44, W3SVC, BILBO, 153.1.1.2, 8297, 415, 347, 200,
153.1.1.2, -, 4/5/97, 0:45:44, W3SVC, BILBO, 153.1.1.2, 13641, 369, 5923, 200
153.1.1.2, -, 4/5/97, 0:45:44, W3SVC, BILBO, 153.1.1.2, 8203, 408, 5372, 200,
153.1.1.2, -, 4/5/97, 0:45:45, W3SVC, BILBO, 153.1.1.2, 13782, 370, 1199, 200
153.1.1.2, -, 4/5/97, 0:46:08, W3SVC, BILBO, 153.1.1.2, 23156, 441, 355, 200,
```

Figure 22.8.
A sample log file.

Database Logging

If you log to an ODBC data source, you must specify the ODBC data source name (DSN), table, and valid username and password to the database.

Choose to log to any ODBC data source. Specify the data source name, table name (not the filename of the table), and a username and password that's valid for the computer on which the database resides. You must also use the ODBC applet in the Control Panel to create a system data source.

Directory Management and Virtual Servers

As the administrator of an Internet presence as well as a network, you'll find that there are times when you won't fit into the one server/one Web presence plan:

- You may run out of disk space and want to be able to put information on another server. But you would like to publish all the information from one domain name or address. Do you have to publish two different sites to publish information on two different servers?

- You might want to publish two different Web sites, but believe that your one Web server has enough power to handle the traffic involved in both. Do you have to buy another server?

The answer to both questions is no. The NT operating system and the IIS service allow administrators to accomplish these things through the use of virtual servers and multiple IP addresses.

Multiple IP Address Review

Chapter 21 looks at the fact that the Windows NT operating system will allow administrators to add more than one IP address to a single network interface card (NIC). This allows the server to respond to more than one IP address and thus more than one domain name. For example, the NIC in slot 4 of your server could have the IP addresses `202.95.229.61` and `202.95.229.62`. The DNS server will have different entries for each IP address.

These might be the DNS entries:

```
202.95.229.62    www.homeshow.com

202.95.229.61    www.tools.com
```

The result is that users who want to view either of these Web sites will be delivered to the same PC by the DNS server.

The problem arrives when you have site services that aren't intelligent. If you think one step further in this example, you'll realize that if you don't direct users to different places once they get to your server, you really didn't accomplish much.

Once the users arrive at the server, ideally you'd like to be able to deliver them to a different site on your server, based on the IP address they're looking for. This is made possible by using virtual servers and directory control.

Virtual Servers and Directories

Before you can understand the virtual server concept, you must first understand how the IIS services treat requests for a service on your server. If a user requests a Web page from your server, for example, he'll most likely put in the domain name of your Web server (`http://www.tools.com`) and will possibly add the name of a specific page he wants to see (`http://www.tools.com/hammers.htm`).

When the user attaches to your site, you obviously don't want him accessing the root directory of your server. One of the tasks handled by IIS is the redirection of users to the directories that hold the items for their consumption—and not give them free rein on your server or network.

Virtual server and directory setup, in combination with possible multiple IP addresses, allow both of the examples that started this section. Virtual server configuration is a feature of IIS that allows the administrator to point the user at different resources, based on the IP address and extended directory that he requested.

When you open the properties for a given service, you'll find a page called *Directories* (see Figure 22.9). The Directories page is the tool used to give direction to users that approach your site looking to a resource that doesn't necessarily live in the basic root directory of your server. When you first look at this page, you'll see that the installation of the product has already assigned a virtual directory to the basic service.

Figure 22.9.
The Directories page.

The directory C:\InetPub\wwwroot in the figure has been assigned as the <Home> directory for that service. The *home directory* of a service is the directory that will appear to be the root directory of that service, as far as the outside world is concerned. These are called *virtual directories* because the directory path entered and used by the client is not the true physical directory location. You as the administrator use the Directories page to give the clients direction.

The directory listing in the middle of the page is a list of the virtual directories and servers that have already been created and started. The Directory column simply tells the system which resource to use. The Alias column tells you the directory extension that users must use to access the resource listed in the Directory column. The Address column reports the IP address that any virtual servers (extra IP addresses and domain names) are also reporting.

Once you realize that the server is capable of delivering users to a given directory on the IIS server, then you can understand the concept of *directory browsing*. The Directory Browsing Allowed check box prompts you as to whether to allow users to view the contents of this resource in a list or as you would in the Windows Explorer. Directory browsing is used by the HTTP server to allow users the ability to view your site and move freely throughout the site without having to be guided by hyperlinks and navigation bars.

Creating a virtual directory is very simple and is basically the same process in each of the services. The steps for creation are listed here:

1. Open the IIS Service Manager and double-click the service that will be using the virtual directory.
2. Click the Directories tab.
3. Click the Add button.
4. In the Directory entry, type the directory path of the resource that you want to share, or click Browse and locate the directory.

Tip: Keep in mind when entering a path for a directory that you aren't limited to the local server. You can create a virtual directory from any drive resource that the NT server can access.

5. Next you'll be presented with a choice of making this directory the home directory of the service or making it a virtual (extended) directory from the site.

   By clicking the Home Directory button, you're electing to make this virtual directory the <Home> (default) of that service (for example, c:\winnt\inetpub\wwwroot is equal to http://www.tools.com).

By clicking the Virtual Directory button, you create a directory that must be entered at the end of the site's domain name in order to be accessed. If you choose Virtual Directory, you must enter a name for that directory to respond to (for example, the directory named `c:\winnt\inetpub\wwwroot\homeshow` is equal to `http://www.tools.com/homeshow`).

6. Click OK twice to complete the process.

There are other options that exist in the WWW, FTP, and Gopher service choices, as covered in the following sections.

Advanced

The Advanced page in any of the IIS services is used to create roadblocks for users. There are two types of roadblocks that can be created; the purposes are to protect the server from users who are causing trouble for the site, or to keep the service from becoming a drain on the network.

Access Control

The access control portion of the Advanced tab allows you to control which IP addresses are accepted or denied access to your system. If you choose to grant access to all users by default, you can then specify the computers to be denied access.

This is the point in your site management where the log files can really help you to understand what's happening if you have a performance problem or a security issue. By observing the log files, you can see which IP addresses have accessed given resources and how often those resources have been accessed.

For example, if you find that a given IP address is accessing your site several hundred times an hour and accessing the same document, you may have a troublemaker who wants to cause performance problems for you. You can prevent the computer at that IP address from connecting to your site by adding that IP address to the list of prevented addresses. You could also decide to deny access to all users by default, and then specify which computers are allowed access.

What you're about to read may sound backward, but if you pay close attention to the buttons you'll notice that what you're doing is determining the default state for the service. Once that's done, you're deciding who doesn't get default treatment: "Everybody can come in, except you guys." To deny access, select the Granted Access button and click Add; to grant access, select the Denied Access button and click Add. IP addresses or ranges of addresses are then done by clicking the Add button from the Advanced tab and entering the addresses you want to allow or deny. It is just that simple, but it is a very powerful tool.

Bandwidth Limitations

Bandwidth control is something that's rarely used by any service because the administrator rarely understands the complete bandwidth picture. But you can control your Internet services by limiting the network bandwidth allowed for all the Internet services on the server. Set the maximum kilobytes of outbound traffic permitted on this computer.

By changing the number on the Advanced page, in the section called Limit Network Use by All Internet Services on This Computer, you're really limiting the amount of bandwidth that can be taken at any given moment. The problem with this is that you may be preventing users from gaining access to needed bandwidth at times when there may not be any competition for that space.

Limiting Connections

A possible alternative way to control the bandwidth and server drag is to limit the number of users who can be attached to the service at any given moment. It's important to realize that the users who are attached to your system at any given moment are all sharing the bandwidth and disk resource delivery power of your server. If you limit the number of users, in effect you're ensuring that users who do attach are more likely to have usable resources.

The maximum number of users is set on the Service page of any service property screen. The number is fairly simple to change; simply click the Connected box and enter a number.

FTP Site

FTP sites run as a TCP protocol on your server, and they have unique needs for the users they serve, just as WWW and Gopher do. FTP requires that you take a moment and consider who your audience is, so that you can make the files available and usable without breaching your own security in the process.

Messages and Control from the Outside

The first thing to keep in mind with an FTP site is that filenames and locations are very difficult to understand from the outside in. Just because your directory structure makes sense to you, that doesn't mean that I could figure out what you mean.

When a user enters your FTP site, she is looking for any clue about what's located in that site and how she can get to those files. There are two common methods for getting users to the place where they want to be (listed on the next page):

- **Message screen.** The IIS FTP site offers a Message page that enables you to type a message to be presented to users as they log on to the site (see Figure 22.10). These messages do little good if the user is using a command-line FTP client, but are most helpful for users making use of a Web browser or more elaborate FTP client.

Figure 22.10.
An FTP message as seen from a browser.

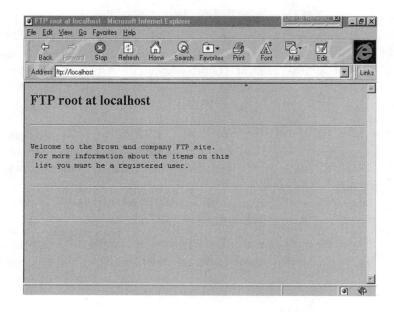

- INDEX **file.** In FTP sites, you'll commonly find a file called INDEX or INDEX.TXT that lists all the files available to the public on the site. It may even list whom to contact to gain access to other areas. There's no particular format that this file must follow; it's more of a "message in a bottle" that's there for the user to use for guidance when she arrives. To use this method, simply create a text file that contains your listing and place the file in the FTP Home directory.

> **Tip:** If the index of the items in your site is too long, you may want to create an INDEX file that points the user to another file with a full listing, but requests that she download the file and read it offline.

Virtual Directory Differences

The virtual directory options that are available in the FTP area are different because you can run an FTP site that allows users to write to the site. You can't write to a WWW or Gopher site, so you don't have the Access section as part of the Directory page.

The options in this section are pretty self-explanatory. If you want users to be able to download files from the site, you need to have the Read option checked on this page. If you want users to be able to write to the server, you need to select the Write option. The Read option is checked by default; it makes a pretty silly FTP site to leave this option unchecked.

World Wide Web Site

The WWW service is the primary reason that most companies will begin using IIS. This service gives you the ability to provide clear and easy-to-use information over the World Wide Web and the intracompany Web (intranet).

In the WWW service, Microsoft makes a nice combination of an easy-to-use interface and a fairly powerful server system.

Password Acceptance

The opening page of the WWW service is the Service page, just as it is for the other services, but there are a few important differences in this service.

An important difference here is the presence of a section called Password Authentication. Password options in this section refer to the fact that you can run secure Web sites from this product. In the sections that follow, we'll look at the NT security options that are necessary to make a site secure, but the first step is here in this section of the Web control (see Figure 22.11).

Figure 22.11.
The Service page.

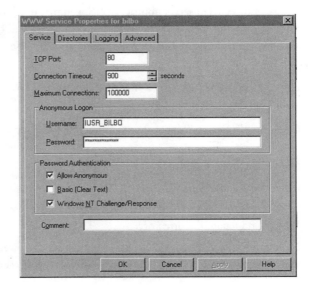

The options here consist of forms of authentication and just how secure you want your site to be.

By allowing anonymous users to access your site, you agree to be a public site and open your root Web site to any user in the TCP/IP environment that you're part of. If that TCP/IP environment is the Internet, your site is open to the world. This doesn't mean that you open the entire server to the world, but until you make changes to NT security, you open the WWWROOT directory. The anonymous user isn't given permissions to any directory outside the originally installed home directory. That is, unless the administrator grants that permission.

When a user attempts to access a restricted Web page or directory on an IIS server, he's challenged for a username and password. There are many different ways to send usernames and passwords across the Internet; the first two choices in this section cover the ways that you would like to accept this information.

If the user isn't using Internet Explorer as an interface, he won't be able to support some of the encryption forms used by NT across the Internet. Think of items like secure logon and remote administration of IIS as examples of things you may need to do. So you're going to need to allow clear text usernames and passwords if you're using a different browser externally. This is done by selecting the Basic (Clear Text) option on the Service page.

If you want those users capable of using NT-encrypted usernames and passwords to be able to do so, you'll need to select the Windows NT Challenge/Response option.

Virtual Server Application

To make use of the virtual server abilities of IIS, you first need to make arrangements with the administrator of your DNS server. Make sure that your server will be sent users looking for all the IP addresses for which your server has been configured. Once those changes have been made, the hardest part of the process is over.

The following steps give your server direction about where to send the users when they arrive. To create a virtual server response, follow these steps:

1. Open the IIS Service Manager and double-click the service that will be using the virtual directory.

2. Click the Directories tab.

3. Click the Add button.

4. In the Directory entry, type the directory path of the resource that you want to use, or click Browse and locate the directory.

5. Next you'll be presented with a choice of making this directory the home directory of the service or making it a virtual (extended) directory from the site.

By clicking the Home Directory button, you're electing to make this virtual directory the `<Home>` (default) of that service (for example, `c:\winnt\inetpub\wwwroot` is equal to `http://www.tools.com`).

By clicking the Virtual Directory button, you create a directory that must be entered at the end of the site's domain name in order to be accessed. If you choose Virtual Directory, you must enter a name for that directory to respond to (for example, entering the name `c:\winnt\inetpub\wwwroot\homeshow` is equal to `http://www.tools.com/homeshow`).

6. Click the check box for Virtual Server and enter the IP address of the Web site that you'll be presenting from the virtual server.

7. Click OK twice to complete the process.

Once you have completed this process, any traffic that comes to the server for that address will be given the information in that directory.

Default First Page Choice

When you type in the URL of your favorite Web site, you most likely don't enter the name of the file used for their opening page. With that in mind, how do you get to the opening page?

Most Web servers are given a variable that says, "If someone attaches to the site but doesn't ask for a specific page, give him this default page." The default page for most Web sites is named `INDEX.HTM` or `DEFAULT.HTM`.

Tip: Some sites use the extension `.HTML` instead of `.HTM`. This is supported in NT IIS, but typically NT servers use the three-character extension for better legacy client support.

IIS allows you to decide whether you want to support a default document, and if so, which file it will be. This is done on the Directories page of the WWW service. To enable a default page, simply select the Enable Default Document option and enter the name of the default document you want to use. The document must exist in the home directory of all the Web servers (virtual and otherwise) that exist at this site. And the choice you make here applies to all Web sites supported on this server.

Peter's Principle: Create a Message Page for Your Site

A trick that can be helpful concerning default pages is to create a pass-over Web page as the default. The idea is to create a default page that automatically passes the user on to another page. By creating such a page, you give yourself a page to leave messages on or stop the user at before he actually arrives at your site. For example, if you decide to create a page to announce a big sale, you could copy that page to the name of your default page, and it would be the first thing the clients see. But you didn't have to destroy your normal opening page to get the notice posted. The HTML coding to do this can be found in even a simple HTML guide such as *Web Publishing with HTML in a Week* (1995, Sams Publishing, ISBN 0-672-30667-0).

Directory Rights Assignment for Secure Sites

IIS takes advantage of the NT security scheme on the most simplistic level. To gain access to any directory on the server, a user must be authenticated. It doesn't matter whether that user is coming from a workstation using Word on the local network or via Internet from Japan.

The anonymous user account is used by Web users and is given permissions to read from the home directory and all its subdirectories. But you can remove those rights and even split them in the same way that you can for any other NT user.

The biggest surprise for administrators when creating user permissions and users to access resources is the fact that the user accounts must have permission to log on locally. The easiest way to do this is to create local groups that can access the items that you want to publish, and assign the Web users to those groups.

Security Checklist

Microsoft provides these suggestions as a security checklist:

- Do not give the `IUSR_computername` account, the Guests group, or the Everyone group any right other than Log on Locally or Access the Computer from This Network.

- Make sure that all user accounts on the system, especially those with administrative rights, have difficult-to-guess passwords. In particular, select a good administrator password (a long, mixed-case, alphanumeric password is best) and set the appropriate account policies. Passwords can be set by using User Manager, or by typing at the system logon prompt.

- Make sure that you specify how quickly account passwords expire (which forces users to change passwords regularly), and set other policies such as how many bad logon attempts will be tolerated before locking a user out. Use these policies to prevent exhaustive or random password attacks, especially on accounts with administrative access. You can set these policies by using User Manager.

- Limit the membership of the Administrator group to trusted individuals.

- If you use the predefined Windows NT user accounts Interactive and Network for access control, make sure that files in your Web site are accessible to these user accounts. For a file to be accessed by anonymous client requests or client requests using basic authentication, the requested file must be accessible by the Interactive user. For a file to be accessible by a client request that uses Windows NT Challenge/Response authentication protocol, the file must be accessible by the Network user.

- Be aware that directory browsing is not a good idea because of security reasons. The less a hacker knows about the structure of your system, the harder it is too break.

What's Included in the IIS v3.0 Upgrade?

You may have seen the IIS v3.0 upgrade on the Internet and in magazine articles and wondered what the difference was between it and what comes with NT Server 4.0. I wondered the same thing as I began to write this book and v3.0 was introduced. The version of IIS covered in this chapter is v2.0, but then again, so is the version of Web Server in the v3.0 IIS.

The odd thing about the v3.0 upgrade of IIS is that it really isn't an upgrade to the base product at all. The upgrade is actually a list of products that upgrade the functionality of the base product you already received with NT Server 4.0. The products included are as follows:

- Active Server Pages
- Microsoft Index Server
- Microsoft NetShow
- Microsoft FrontPage 97 Server Extensions
- Crystal Reports

Active Server Pages

Active Server Pages (ASP) is an open, compile-free application environment in which you can combine HTML pages, scripts, and ActiveX server components to create powerful Web-based business solutions.

ASP is integrated into Windows NT Server, so it knows when a file has changed. A changed script is automatically compiled the next time it's requested. This means that when developing scripts and applications, you can save the page and immediately preview it in your browser.

ASP provides the flexibility of CGI programs and scripts, without the significant performance tradeoff. Unlike CGI, Active Server Pages runs in-process with the server, and is multithreaded and optimized to handle large numbers of users. ASP doesn't require developers to learn a new environment. It combines the ease of HTML with familiar tools such as Visual Basic Scripting (VBScript) and ActiveX server components. For experienced Web developers, Active Server Pages also supports any scripting language and components written in any language, including Java.

ASP supports ActiveX scripting, allowing virtually any scripting engine to be used. Native support is provided for Visual Basic Scripting Editions and Microsoft JScript. It allows Web developers to write scripts that are executed on either the server or the client.

ActiveX components, formerly known as *OLE automation servers*, are components (or objects) that you can access from a Web page or other application to reuse packaged functionality someone else programmed. IIS 3.0 ships with a core set of components, including an Ad Rotator, browser capabilities, the Active Database Object (ADO), and more.

Scripting is how Active Server Pages uses ActiveX server components. For example, to retrieve records from a database, a script passes the request to the Active Database Object that contains the logic to talk to the database. Another script then retrieves the result from the ADO component and displays it on the HTML page.

ActiveX server components support the Microsoft *component object model* (COM), and can be written in virtually any programming language, including Visual Basic, C++, COBOL, and Java.

The Active Database Object provides easy access to any ODBC-compatible data source, including Microsoft Access, Microsoft SQL Server, and other popular databases from Oracle, Informix, and Sybase.

About Microsoft Index Server

Microsoft Index Server is the search engine integrated with Microsoft Internet Information Server and the Windows NT Server 4.0 operating system. Once installed, it automatically builds an index of your Web server that can be searched easily from any Web browser with the sample query forms.

When Index Server is first started, it builds an index of all virtual roots and subdirectories on your Web server. The administrator can choose directories and file types that shouldn't be indexed. The content index is updated automatically whenever a file is added, deleted, or changed on the server. Users always have access to the most up-to-date information on the server.

Index Server uses Windows NT Server security. When users perform a search, they're only shown results for documents they have permission to see. This is unlike other Web search engines that show users every file on the server.

Index Server is able to index documents on any file system accessible to Windows NT Server. This includes Novell NetWare and UNIX servers. Index Server takes special advantage of the Windows NT Server operating system environment. It's designed to operate with low overhead on a multi-purpose server, and to scale up to very powerful servers and very large numbers of documents.

Because businesses are using their intranets for sharing much more than HTML documents, Index Server enables full-text searching of HTML, text, and Microsoft Office documents.

Through the open IFilter interface, Index Server can be extended by third parties to index and search any other document type. An IFilter reads the target file and extracts text to be indexed. Index Server indexes both the full-text contents and properties of documents, such as author, file size, and date of last update. Any custom properties set in documents as properties or HTML "meta" tags are available for searching.

The indexing process works behind the scenes and requires no user input, while minimizing demands on system resources. Any corruption of the master index—from a power failure—for example, is automatically corrected.

Microsoft NetShow

Microsoft NetShow is the streaming media server for Internet Information Server. It provides a standards-based, information-sharing platform that delivers live and on-demand content for enhanced communications over the Web.

NetShow includes two features:

- NetShow On-Demand allows users to stream audio, illustrated audio, and video over networks.
- NetShow Live enables users to multicast audio over their corporate networks.

Microsoft NetShow 1.0 is the only multimedia platform tightly integrated with the Internet Information Server (IIS) and Microsoft Windows NT Server operating system platform. By optimizing around the Windows NT Server platform, Microsoft NetShow delivers high performance, excellent security, and ease of management.

Microsoft NetShow uses two key technologies to enhance a user's networked multimedia experience, while reducing the impact on the network's throughput:

- **Streaming.** Normally, when accessing networked multimedia content, a user has to wait for the entire file to be transferred before she can use the information. Streaming allows her to see or hear the information as it arrives without having to wait.
- **Multicasting.** IP multicasting is an open, standards-based way to distribute identical information to many users simultaneously. This contrasts with regular TCP/IP (IP unicast) where the same information can be sent to many clients, but the sender must transmit an individual copy to each user.

Because NetShow adds streaming and multicasting to the Internet Information Server/Windows NT Server platform, you can deliver solutions using all these technologies from one platform.

NetShow has been optimized to take advantage of the high scalability of Windows NT Server, providing a low entry point and small increments to a high-performance system, making it highly suited to organizational growth patterns. The NetShow Server provides better capacity and efficiency to accommodate a broader range of streaming needs. For example, the server has the ability to simultaneously stream multimedia content files at low bit rates, such as at 14.4Kbps, as well as high bit rates—even as high as 6Mbps.

NetShow uses ASF to archive multimedia content before streaming it. With ASF files, you can deliver multimedia content, such as synchronized images and audio, audio only, or video, at various rates over the Internet or an intranet. You can also open Web pages, deliver scripting commands, and create an entire user experience. Markers can be inserted into the stream to allow users to "fast forward" directly and quickly to a point of interest. ASF files can be created from a variety of sources, including video, images, audio PowerPoint presentations, and URLs.

The NetShow open architecture allows third parties to use NetShow to enhance their products. By exposing both client-side and server-side APIs, NetShow allows tools vendors, for example, to offer fully interoperable products to take advantage of illustrated audio or multicasting. Because NetShow supports Windows standard ACM/VCM codecs (audio/video compression modules), users can take advantage of the latest and most sophisticated innovations as they become available.

NetShow comes with simple starter tools that enable corporate content developers to stream illustrated audio. Files in WAV, AVI, QuickTime, PowerPoint, JPEG, GIF, and URL formats can all be used to generate illustrated audio. You can also leverage all the existing multimedia authoring tools to get your content ready to stream!

Microsoft FrontPage 97 Server Extensions

FrontPage Server Extensions are a collection of server components and APIs that make it easier to build and manage Web sites. The FrontPage 97 client application provides a visual HTML and site management environment, allowing anyone to set up an intranet or Internet site. FrontPage 97 automatically detects an IIS setup on the machine and installs the appropriate FrontPage 97 Server Extensions for IIS. FrontPage also checks for proper IIS setup on the machine.

The FrontPage 97 Server Extensions for IIS are now ISAPI applications rather than CGI, resulting in significant performance improvements. (Native Alpha and PowerPC versions are unavailable, but will be available for FrontPage 97 users.)

FrontPage 97 provides Secure Sockets layer (SSL) support to talk to the secure port on IIS (which requires Service Pack 2). It automatically integrates the FrontPage WebBot search component with the index server (if it's installed). The new FrontPage 97 Insert Script command lets you create Active Server Pages, and the FrontPage Explorer Tools | Permissions dialog box has been redesigned to work like the Windows NT security interface.

Crystal Reports for Internet Information Server

One of the items that has been severely lacking in the IIS product—and any of the NT Web Server packages, for that matter—is a good reporting tool. Microsoft has shored up its SMS product by providing some Crystal Reports prefabricated reports and has decided that it made sense here as well. Following is a list of a few of the Crystal Report features:

- Easy Select Records query interface, plus a powerful Formula Editor
- A drill-down search dialog that allows you to search the reports in a hierarchical top-down fashion
- Cross-tab reports
- Export to other analysis tools (many export formats are supported)
- Save data with the report for after-the-fact analysis
- Integrated e-mail capability (VIM and MAPI)
- Send reports with saved data for distributed analysis

Report engine capabilities:

- Two-pass reporting
- Sorting on groups, unlimited sorting
- Heterogeneous data sources (link various types of databases in one report)
- Formula language with more than 140 functions and operators
- Extensible Formula Language (user-defined DLL functions)

Crystal Reports is particularly useful to Windows NT administrators because it can integrate with any of the ODBC-compliant Microsoft database products, such as Access and SQL Server.

Summary

Microsoft really shines with the inclusion of Internet Information Server in the basic services. Hopefully, you've seen in this chapter an easy-to-use product that allows you to integrate the NT security model with an interface that's simple to use.

The product is put together to allow you not just to have a Web presence, but to cover the FTP and Gopher needs of your clients. This allows you not just to distribute pages of information, but also to serve files.

The products that are included in this package are installed easily, and Microsoft has done everything in their power to make sure that you install and use them. They provide a method of installing it from the initial install of NT Server, as well as providing an icon to install it later in the life of the server. And when the products are installed, they provide a simple VCR-like interface for the management of basic services on the system.

By providing common controls among the services, these products allow an administrator to jump from one product to the other, and bring a very usable skill set. Creating new shares, establishing security, and even logging of activity is almost identical in all three services.

Be aware, though, that there's already an update to this product (v3.0)—but this product update is geared mainly to the developer market. If you're a programmer or application provider, I think you'll be quite happy with the new additions.

23

Other Internet Services for NT 4.0

Peter Norton™

Windows NT has become a strong and viable platform for the Internet and Internet services. Part of the reason for that is the fact that Microsoft continues to produce a strong set of services that make it possible for administrators who don't spend every waking moment on the Internet to use powerful tools on it.

This chapter is meant to give you a brief understanding of a few of these products:

- Microsoft Proxy Server
- Microsoft Exchange Server
- FrontPage Web Creator and Manager

Microsoft Proxy Server

Microsoft Proxy Server as a product is new to the Microsoft product line. It has an approach that's a bit of a dual-edged sword. The proxy server actually provides a cushion between the Internet that you want your people to have access to and the Internet that you want to protect your company from. The product has the benefit of both speeding your users' access to the Internet resources they want and protecting your company. The idea behind the proxy server (see Figure 23.1) is to provide a single point of contact that can provide access and stop inbound traffic.

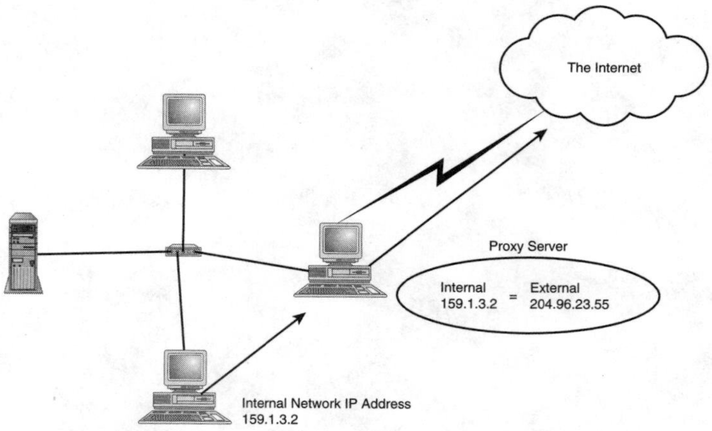

Figure 23.1.
The proxy server concept.

The proxy server is actually providing equal parts facility and security. The basic concept is to provide one controlled connection to the Internet for a given number of users or a company. This connection is capable of providing a viable IP address to any authorized internal machine to gain access to the Internet.

While the connection is being used, all communication is actually being provided through the proxy server. Every document that's being opened can be preserved at the proxy server for a given period of time for faster access later—just like cache for a hard drive. For example, if a user accesses his own home page, you can bet that he'll go back to that page. If he does so within a given period of time, the proxy server will simply serve him the information from cache.

Security is provided by the system in two ways. First is the fact that, as an administrator, you have the ability to control the sites that the users can visit by providing a list of forbidden sites. The list is at the administrator's discretion. But it's difficult to stop users from finding undesirable content to look at. The feature really just keeps good people within the boundaries of good taste—or off your competitor's Human Resources page.

The second security aspect is the fact that Proxy Server operates as a sort of gatekeeper for the IP used to and from the Internet. The best way to think of it is to think of a proxy server that gives users a valid IP address just before they leave the internal network. This valid IP address is to be used only while they're out on the Internet, and no one can access the machine from the outside by reversing that number. The Auto Dial tool in Microsoft Proxy Server automatically connects to your Internet service provider (ISP) whenever a user needs information not already stored in the local cache. When the desired information is retrieved from the ISP and stored, Auto Dial disconnects from your ISP, which can save online costs.

Proxy Server's support of open standards makes for easier integration:

- It supports the HTTP, FTP, and Gopher protocols, providing access to a wide range of browsers and Internet applications.
- It supports the Secure Sockets Layer (SSL) for secure data communication through data encryption and decryption.
- It includes WinSock Proxy, which supports Windows Sockets version 1.1-compatible applications running on a private network—including LDAP, IRC, SMTP, Microsoft SQL Server, RealAudio, and VDOLive—without any modification.

Following are the system requirements beyond the NT minimums:

- 15MB of available hard disk space
- 16MB of RAM

Software:

- Microsoft Windows NT Server v4.0
- Microsoft Internet Information Server v2.0 (included with Windows NT Server 4.0)
- Windows NT Server 4.0 Service Pack 2, available at http://www.microsoft.com

Microsoft Exchange Server

Over the last two years the way that business thinks of and uses e-mail has changed radically. One of the reasons for that change has been the hype and delivered product that's called Microsoft Exchange Server. Exchange Server and products like it have begun to make us believe that we should have one piece of software that will handle all of our business communications. Intraoffice and external communications don't require multiple platforms.

There's a critical need within today's organizations for individuals and groups to be able to quickly access information and easily communicate and collaborate with one another. As a result, organizations are turning to the Internet and corporate intranets. To support customers making this move, Microsoft Exchange Server uses Internet standards and supports existing electronic mail and groupware standards to give rich messaging and collaboration solutions to business.

Originally thought of as just a powerful e-mail and scheduling platform, Exchange has become a complete person-to-person communications package. Using Microsoft Exchange Server, you can set up discussion groups and knowledge bases that are accessible to anyone, anywhere for easy collaboration. You can schedule meetings with virtual team members across your organization and reserve resources such as conference rooms. And you can assign and manage tasks among team members regardless of their location.

You can also set up knowledge bases and list servers that are easily accessible to your business partners and customers. You can create and publish "white pages" of names, e-mail addresses, and phone numbers for efficient collaboration between your partners and your organization. And you can make information on Microsoft Exchange Server accessible by a Web browser for dynamic, efficient information sharing.

Microsoft Exchange Server is built to support Internet standards including SMTP, POP3, NNTP, LDAP, HTTP, HTML, SSL, and existing messaging and collaboration standards, including X.400, X.500, and MAPI. The point is to allow the user base to communicate and collaborate with anyone, anywhere, using e-mail, Internet news and discussion groups, or the World Wide Web.

With the Microsoft Exchange Web client, you can access your Microsoft Exchange mailbox, discussion groups, and more using any Web browser.

The Exchange product was built on the client/server model of storing and controlling the data centrally. This model makes it possible to have better control of the information and it allows the client system freedom to attach from anywhere to receive that information. The fact that the information is centrally managed and stored makes it possible to share e-mail, scheduling, and collaboration tools all in one place. The products are designed from the ground up to work together with the NT Server operating system, making it quick and easy to access and share information.

The information can be managed with customizable server-based rules to process incoming messages automatically, even when users are out of the office. Filters and views help you manage information more efficiently. Integration with the Windows NT Server operating system makes it easy to administer your entire Microsoft Exchange Server environment from a single location.

Technical Features

From the technical standpoint, Microsoft has done its homework with this product. In fact, there are features included in this product that I wish could be quickly included in the operating system. Exchange is very dependent on the fact that it's able to communicate with almost any form of e-mail made over any communications protocol short of Vulcan (for extraterrestrials).

The goal is not to speak all forms of e-mail, but to find some common protocol. Following is a list of all the standards that Exchange will use to make connection:

- SMTP for Internet e-mail
- POP3 for Internet e-mail
- MAPI for Microsoft Mail and cc:Mail connectivity
- MIME for e-mail attachments
- LDAP for directory access
- Native X.400 Message Transfer Agent conforming to the CCITT 1984 and 1988 standards
- NNTP for Internet news and discussion groups

For clients to make connection to the system, users can even use a Web browser as a client. This is all supported through the use of connectivity to the Internet Information Server WWW Service (HTTP) and the ongoing creation of HTML documents.

Client Features

The concept that seems to be guiding Microsoft on this product, from a client perspective, is "any client, anywhere." The list of clients is really endless if you're looking to send and receive e-mail. If you're using Windows 95 or Windows NT, you will of course have the most functional client, but with this product almost anyone can play. You can access information through Microsoft Exchange Server using the Microsoft Exchange client, Microsoft Outlook 97, a Web browser, an Internet mail reader or news reader, or an LDAP client.

Exchange 5.0 provides two distinct clients with the product: the Exchange client (see Figure 23.2) and Outlook (see Figure 23.3).

Figure 23.2.
The Exchange client.

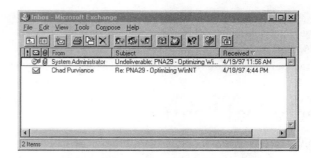

Figure 23.3.
Outlook view of the calendar and task list.

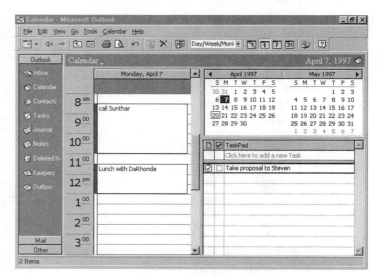

These clients come with the product and have different audiences. The Exchange client is provided for Windows 3.1, Windows 95, Windows NT, and the Macintosh computer lines. It's meant to give you an e-mail interface that interacts with the Exchange server, and has been around since the initial introduction of Exchange.

Warning: You may be confused when you read that Exchange comes with a client application for Windows 95 and NT Workstation, because you've already received a client called Exchange that came with those desktops. You need to be aware that the client that you see already installed there isn't the same as the one that comes with Exchange Server, and shouldn't be used as a replacement for it. If you're going to attach a Windows 95 or NT PC to an Exchange server, you need to install the client that's delivered with the Exchange product.

Outlook 97, which also comes with the Office 97 product, provides integrated messaging, scheduling, and task management on your desktop and enables you to create and use instant groupware. The Outlook client is the glue that pulls this product into a complete solution for companies that have made the leap to Windows 95 and NT 4.0 as primary operating systems.

Outlook provides e-mail, scheduling, task management, journalizing, and contact management, all in one product. Exchange Server makes itself the central repository for the information, but Outlook makes it possible for the users not only to create the information, but also to interact with each other as a group. The Outlook e-mail interface is very close to the old Exchange interface that many of you have already experienced as the free e-mail in Windows 95. But it has the added value of the contact lists and task management of Outlook.

You are still able to use the Exchange client for e-mail editing, but if you have the full Office 97 product you can use Word instead. If you are using Word 97, you can use Rich Text formatting and editing, including drag-and-drop and in-place editing.

Both the Exchange client and Outlook allow the user to establish server-based rules for processing mail, whether you're connected to the server or offline. These rules allow you to establish automated e-mail and scheduling behaviors based on vacation times, unwanted e-mail senders, situational needs. For example, if you have received a number of unwanted messages titled `Knucklehead Club Meeting`, you can set an automatic response to express appreciation for being included, but regretfully being unable to attend.

The Exchange clients offer the ability to create personal folders that allow the users to keep both local and/or server-based copies of the e-mail, schedules, and so on. The idea is to set your server-based versions to interact with and/or synchronize with the local versions. This allows the user to leave the office and still interact with e-mail offline.

Exchange clients will automatically convert any URL (`http://www.MCP.com`, `ftp://ftp.microsoft.com`, and so on) that's placed in a document into a link that can be used from that spot (see Figure 23.4). This feature allows users to make the Internet the carrier of information that they would like to reference. You could think of it like being able to stick the encyclopedia page in your old high school term paper.

With both Exchange and Outlook, views make it possible for you to sort and manage documents as if you were using the Explorer paradigm. You can sort messages in the viewer by clicking the column heading that you would like to sort by. You can create folders that allow you to move and/or copy documents to save or distribute. The idea is to allow the documents that are used as e-mail to become an "easy to control and use" part of your work life.

Another basic fact of the e-mail and messaging world is that we're all beginning to collect more than one source for e-mail messages. I have three e-mail addresses and really only want one. But in today's computer environment, it's very difficult to avoid having multiple addresses. Exchange and Outlook offer the ability to use one inbox for numerous e-mail resources.

Figure 23.4.
*Link from inside an
Exchange document.*

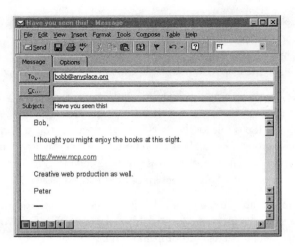

If you look at the Services dialog box in Exchange, you'll see that the inbox actually is just a collective for all the e-mail resources you depend on. This is being called the *universal Inbox* (see Figure 23.5).

Figure 23.5.
The Services dialog box.

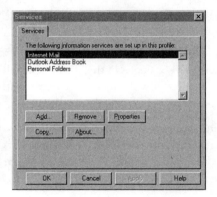

The Outlook client can really be thought of as a product that facilitates the collaboration of many of the tools that you have already been using with the Exchange client, Schedule+, and even Office 95 (or earlier versions). In fact, Outlook can use its own scheduling and contact management or it can use the Schedule+ program. It can use its own e-mail post office file or it can use the Exchange file that you've been using. In fact, you can still use both products separately, because they share the post office file.

Other Clients for Exchange 5.0

Exchange Server can be set up to allow the client types for the associated information types shown in the following table.

Type of Information	Possible Clients
E-mail	Exchange Client, Outlook, Web browser, SNMP clients (Eudora, Netscape Navigator, and so on), Microsoft Mail clients, MAPI-compliant clients (cc:Mail, Microsoft Mail, and so on)
Scheduling	Schedule+, Outlook, Web browser
Contact management	Schedule+, Outlook, Web browser
Task Management	Schedule+, Outlook, Microsoft Team Manager 97, Microsoft Project

Server Administration

Exchange Server administration has been simplified by the fact that user and password management has been tied to the management of the NT operating system. Once the Exchange product has been installed, each of the users on the server has an account in the Exchange world as well. The coordination of these two account lists makes it easier to track who should or should not have accounts, security level, and grouping of mailings by logical categories. It just makes sense to incorporate these functions to allow the administrator to have a single interface.

The integration with Windows NT Server administration tools includes the Performance Monitor, the event log, and backup utilities. Every incorporation into the day-to-day regulation and monitoring of the server helps keep the administrator interested in actively managing the messaging system. All too often these systems get launched and then ignored until the system is creeping along and out of sorts.

One of the biggest downfalls of e-mail systems that don't use a client/server model is that they store messages inefficiently. Exchange uses the fact that users attach to a central resource to more efficiently store and distribute messages on the server. If the same message is sent to several users, for example, only one copy of that message is kept at the server. This reduces the amount of space necessary to house the post office.

The administrator can also limit the amount of mail that can be stored in several ways. The amount of time that mail can be kept (mail aging) can be enforced. But the amount of mail that's stored per user can also be regulated. The fact that the NT Server and Exchange monitoring system can be integrated also makes it possible to track these events along with the standard NT maintenance.

Connection Beyond Exchange Walls

The Exchange client can connect the clients to many different e-mail services, but the Exchange server can also be connected to many different services.

Exchange uses modular connection to the outside world through what are known as *connectors*. A connector is used to connect to any external source. It can be used to connect to other Exchange servers or to other mail systems, such as Microsoft Mail Server, X.400, Lotus cc:Mail, SMTP, All-In-1, and PROFS.

The modularity found in Exchange is much like the modularity in the operating system. The communications to and from external e-mail sources are separate from the task of moving internal mail. In order to connect a source into the Exchange flow, you simply need to add the module for that connection.

If your desire is to move from your current e-mail system to Exchange, you'll find the process to be fairly simple. The biggest leap to be aware of is that you'll need to have an NT server running on the network. Exchange Server won't run on any platform other than NT Server. The clients don't have to connect to an NT server for their primary logon, but the Server service must be running on an NT server version 3.51 or greater. The next section covers the required pieces of that server and the clients.

Migration has been addressed very well for this product. Built-in utilities are available for migrating data from Microsoft Mail Server for PC networks and AppleTalk networks, Lotus cc:Mail, Netscape Collabra, Novell GroupWise, DEC All-In-1, Verimation Memo, PROFS, and other systems.

When installing a new e-mail system in a business that already contains a working e-mail system, it's always best to let the systems coexist until you reach a comfort zone. Exchange's ability to connect to many of these systems offers a unique opportunity to connect the new and old systems and gradually move users.

I've found that if you can connect Exchange to the old system, you'll have the ability to move users in small, manageable groups. If you move a user to the new system, he'll still have the ability to connect to the old system through the Exchange connector. By keeping a complete mailing list in both systems, you allow yourself time to wean users from one system to another.

Requirements

Server requirements above and beyond those for NT are as follows:

- 24MB of RAM; 32MB recommended
- 250MB of available hard disk space; 500MB recommended

Tip: Keep in mind when you are planning hard drive space that users today are sending not only text, but also file attachments. A more realistic number for hard drive space might include around 5–10MB for users to store messages.

- Microsoft Windows NT Server v3.51 or later
- CD-ROM drive

Note: Windows NT Server v4.0 with Service Pack 2 (SP2) and Microsoft Internet Information Server v3.0 are required to use ActiveServer components, which enable access to mailboxes, discussion groups, and the directory on Microsoft Exchange Server via any Web browser.

Client requirements:

- The Exchange client

For Microsoft Windows 95, Windows v3.1, and Windows for Workgroups v3.11:

- 8MB of RAM; 12MB recommended (with Forms Designer, 12MB of RAM; 16MB recommended)
- 12–22MB of available hard disk space

For Microsoft Windows NT Workstation v3.51 or later on Intel-based systems:

- 16MB of RAM; 20MB recommended (with Forms Designer, 20MB of RAM; 24MB recommended)
- 12–22MB of available hard disk space

For Apple Macintosh System 7 or later with a 68030, 68040, or PowerMac processor:

- 12MB of RAM; 16MB recommended
- 20MB of available hard disk space

Tip: Be aware that there's a different version of the client for the PowerMac, and that you'll have to use that version. The standard version can cause pretty severe problems, even with the system software.

Microsoft Outlook 97:

- Personal or multimedia computer with a 486 or higher processor
- Microsoft Windows 95 operating system or Microsoft Windows NT Workstation v3.51 (with Service Pack 5)
- 8MB of RAM for use on Windows 95; 16MB of RAM for use on Windows NT Workstation
- 26–46MB hard disk space required; 31MB required for typical installation, depending on configuration

FrontPage

The World Wide Web as a medium for publishing is very young technology. A short time ago, the creation of documents to be published and the management of those documents was archaic. Web documents were created in the same way that programs are created. The actual text was combined with coding in the *hypertext markup language* (*HTML*), as shown in Figure 23.6, to create a page that could be read by HTML interpreters called *Web browsers*. FrontPage and products like it have come along to allows users to create without becoming programmers.

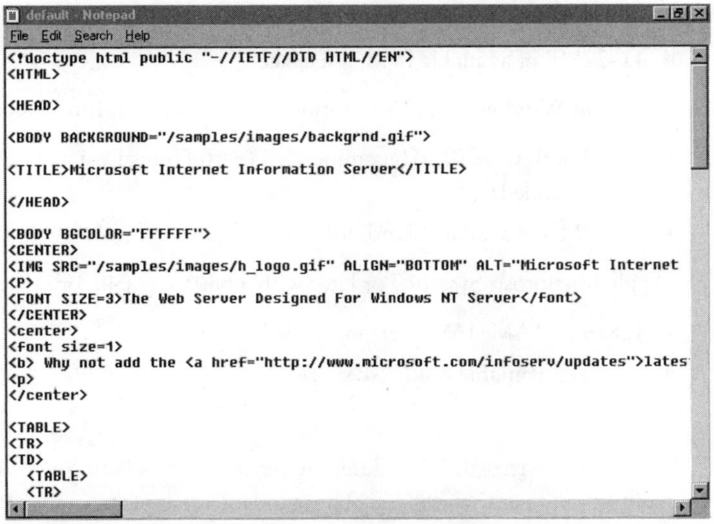


```
<!doctype html public "-//IETF//DTD HTML//EN">
<HTML>

<HEAD>

<BODY BACKGROUND="/samples/images/backgrnd.gif">

<TITLE>Microsoft Internet Information Server</TITLE>

</HEAD>

<BODY BGCOLOR="FFFFFF">
<CENTER>
<IMG SRC="/samples/images/h_logo.gif" ALIGN="BOTTOM" ALT="Microsoft Internet
<P>
<FONT SIZE=3>The Web Server Designed For Windows NT Server</font>
</CENTER>
<center>
<font size=1>
<b> Why not add the <a href="http://www.microsoft.com/infoserv/updates">lates
<p>
</center>

<TABLE>
<TR>
<TD>
  <TABLE>
  <TR>
```

Figure 23.6.
A raw HTML document.

The problem that was being experienced on the Web was that the technicians who could write code were creating the company Web presentations—not the creative and marketing people who *should* be doing it.

Windows NT comes with a product called *FrontPage* to make the creation and management of your Web presence easier. FrontPage makes the creation of HTML documents as simple as the creation of word processing documents. And with the effort that it would take to learn a publishing program, users can learn how to create powerful Web presentations.

FrontPage consists of three products:

- FrontPage Explorer
- FrontPage Editor
- Personal Web Server

Warning: Be very careful when installing the FrontPage 97 product that ships separately from NT, if you install it on an NT server or workstation. Both operating systems have HTTP servers of their own, and the Personal Web Server that comes with FrontPage can corrupt the installations of these products. Don't install Personal Web Server alongside these products.

FrontPage is not just a Web page creation utility; it's also a very powerful site-management tool. When Web pages are created, they most likely have some connection to other Web pages. The relationship between pages within a particular Web site is difficult to manage if you're trying to track it on paper or in your head. FrontPage Explorer allows you not only to access the pages but also to see the relationship that each page has to the others.

FrontPage Editor

The FrontPage Editor is the portion of the package that will appear to you at first to be nothing more than Microsoft Word on steroids. But this package underneath is a very powerful HTML editor. Once you have created a Web site in the FrontPage Explorer, you'll then want to populate that site with pages, and the Editor is the tool that will help you create them.

This product initially will present you with a choice of a template, just like Word. But the choices here include formatted pages. FrontPage wizards make creating new pages or entire Web sites easy. Just answer a few questions, and wizards do the rest for you. The Import Wizard makes it easy to import existing files or entire folders of information into your FrontPage Web sites, and FrontPage includes templates to let you generate Web sites or pages from predefined formats. Then just replace the content with your own words, images, and ideas.

In order to be sure that your pages will appear properly in the Web browser of your choice, FrontPage allows you to edit HTML code directly in the FrontPage Editor and preview your Web pages in any browser installed on your PC—without leaving FrontPage.

The package also includes Microsoft Image Composer, which enables you to create graphics for your Web pages and includes thousands of image samples to help you get started. Use a variety of clip art backgrounds, buttons, lines, and images to increase the graphical appeal of your Web site.

FrontPage Explorer

Building and managing Web sites with graphical tools in the FrontPage Explorer makes the life of a Webmaster much easier . Select the Link view (see Figure 23.7) for hierarchical and link displays of all paths to and from your Web pages, or use the Summary view to display your entire Web site directory structure.

Figure 23.7.
The Link view of FrontPage Explorer.

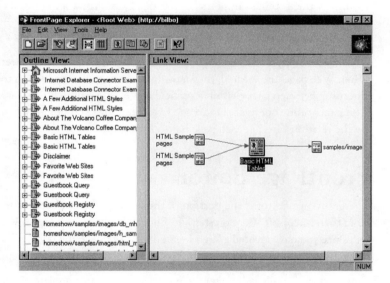

The Folder view provides a directory of your Web site and a sortable list of the properties for each file, making it easy to manage your Web site content more effectively (see Figure 23.8).

Once you're finished, you can verify all the links. This feature automatically verifies that all hyperlinks are valid—even those pointing to files outside your Web site. And when you correct a broken hyperlink in one location, FrontPage automatically corrects all through the site.

Figure 23.8.
The Folder view of the Web site.

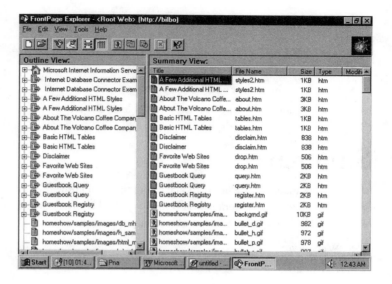

Advanced Scripting and Database Support

Although you probably won't be using them on the first day, FrontPage offers advanced tools to connect to the features that experienced Webmasters require to make their sites function.

Database connectivity is supported through ODBC-compliant databases, so you can create Web pages from database queries, giving you easy access to the information you need. This feature allows Windows NT as a server to show its strength and the Webmaster to use that strength to connect the Web to industry-standard applications. Thousands of database resources have been maintained in ODBC-compliant database applications. Applications such as Access, FoxPro, and Microsoft SQL can all be made available to Web users through this interface.

Support for script usage on the Web is an even more complex layer of Web publishing, but FrontPage supports numerous script formats. ActiveX control and Java applet support give users the ability to develop powerful Web applications in an intuitive WYSIWYG environment. VBScript and JavaScript authoring support allow you to add custom scripts to your Web pages with ease.

On the other hand, if you don't understand advanced HTML concepts or scripting, you are not left out of many of the more powerful Web tools. FrontPage contains items called *Bots* (short for *robot*) that allow authors to choose tasks they want performed and paste them into their Web pages. By pasting a Bot into your Web page, you have effectively pasted the advanced behavior without having to write a script or advanced HTML code.

These are the tasks that can be performed by Bots:

- Including content from other Web pages
- Time-stamping Web pages
- Searching the text of your entire Web site
- Inserting an automatically changing Table of Contents

Summary

Microsoft has made a huge effort to make sure that you know they care about being your Internet choice. If that wasn't apparent to you before, it should be after reading this chapter. They have sent along with NT the ability to host an Internet presence, including:

- Web server
- FTP site
- Gopher site

And now they offer the tools—Proxy Server to manage the connection of your users to the Internet; Exchange Server to communicate in e-mail, NNTP (news server), and active Web communications.

Microsoft has done a very good job of not only offering these products, but connecting them to the operating system as a whole. The Internet Information Server (IIS) was obviously just the start of a number of products that Microsoft intended to bring to the table. By introducing products that connect companies in all of the major Internet communications categories (e-mail, NNTP, HTTP, FTP, Gopher, proxy, security), they have truly positioned themselves as the leader. Because of integrated security, you can keep your learning curve to a minimum and your required work manageable.

24

Point-to-Point Tunneling Protocol (PPTP)

Peter Norton™

The concept of office workers working outside of the office has never been so real as it is right now. But just because we aren't in the office proper doesn't mean that we don't need office resources or information. In other words, we need the network. The solution to this problem can be found in one of thousands of different new technologies that allow users to connect to the network from outside.

Most of the solutions involve the company having to build the infrastructure necessary to allow users to dial in and make a modem connection of some sort directly to the network. This can be cost-prohibitive and can create many different security risks, as described in Chapter 13, "Remote Access Services (RAS)." The fact is that there's no greater threat to any fort than the gate. If you're creating gates into your site, you're creating threats. The ideal situation would use network-style connections that aren't as open to the public dial-in world, but that would still allow your users to connect with their industry-standard modems.

Microsoft has created a form of communications that will allow you to make use of public networks in a private way. The idea is to attach your network to a public network, but provide a private protocol that will communicate private resources only to those using that protocol. The protocol is called *Point-to-point tunneling protocol* (*PPTP*), and the entire concept is called *virtual private networks* (*VPNs*).

PPTP Concepts

The complete purpose of VPN is to create a secure method of making use of public networks for private use. By using the PPTP protocol, VPN creates a network over the Internet that's electronically a separate network. Remote users just dial into the local number of an Internet service provider and securely tunnel into their corporate network.

But PPTP doesn't have to be used only with dial-up connections. The protocol can also be used in larger public networks like V.34 and ISDN dial-up. And corporations can use a PPTP-enabled VPN over IP backbones to outsource dial-up access to their corporate networks in a manner that's cost-effective, protocol-independent, secure, and that requires no changes to their existing network addressing.

> **Note:** Microsoft is working with the PPTP Forum, a group of leading companies including Ascend Communications, 3Com/Primary Access, ECI/Telematics, and US Robotics, to support PPTP as an open industry standard. PPTP is also attracting extensive third-party support.

Make the Internet Your Own WAN

VPN is integrated into the NT Server 4.0 and NT Workstation 4.0 operating systems, providing the tunneling solution for remote access at no extra cost. Eventually, Microsoft will also provide PPTP support for Windows 95.

Using VPN to turn the vast reach of the Internet into your own virtual private network can bring significant economic benefits. In addition to saving the costs of leased lines and long-distance dialing, businesses can escape the cost of purchasing and managing redundant banks of modems and specialized software. VPN allows the same equipment used for Internet access to be used for providing remote access.

The transition for remote users is as simple as a few clicks of the mouse, as VPN is smoothly integrated into the same Windows dial-up commands that users might already be using.

All of this makes Microsoft's multi-protocol VPN an easy way for businesses to securely and economically extend their private networks across the Internet to remote users.

Virtual Private Networks

A virtual private network can be described as the ability to "tunnel" through the Internet or other public network in a manner that provides the same security and other features formerly available only on private networks. It allows a user working at home or on the road to connect to a remote corporate server using the bandwidth provided by the public network. VPN allows a corporation to connect with branch offices or with other companies while maintaining a secure PPTP connection.

From the perspective of the user, the nature of the physical network being tunneled through is irrelevant, because it looks as if the information is being sent over a dedicated private network.

From a more technical perspective, a VPN tunnel involves encapsulating data within IP packets that can transport information that wouldn't otherwise conform to Internet addressing standards. The result is that remote users become virtual nodes on the network they have tunneled into.

A user on a RAS client machine with a PPTP driver as its WAN driver will be able to access resources across the Internet on a remote LAN through a Windows NT RAS server, via tunneled and encrypted PPP packets. (RAS supports bulk data encryption using RSA RC4 and a 40-bit session key negotiated at PPP connect time between the RAS client and the NT RAS server.)

Something that must be considered is the fact that you're adding a surrounding layer to the performance of your network. This performance hit is fairly minimal, though. Consider that the packet is being surrounded only by packets to carry it through to a server on the other end.

The performance hit may be steeper, depending on how you're using PPTP. If you're using it as a single-connection tool for RAS, you'll see minimal effect on speed. This is because the server and client are involved in a fairly slow connection and the bottleneck is the connection itself. If you're using PPTP as a WAN for many users, you may see as much as a 25% reduction in performance for the server to open the packets of many users.

The PPTP-based solution will also enable the Internet to become a backbone for carrying IPX as well as NetBEUI remote access traffic, so a solution isn't tied to IP LANs only.

Beyond the Internet

While the most important focus for VPN is to provide a secure way to extend private network access through the Internet, it can also work in virtually any type of network over which IP packets can be sent, including X.25 and frame relay networks.

VPN allows the Internet to be treated as if it were a telephone network being used to reach the network that the user wants to be on. Companies taking advantage of VPN will be in a position to offer users what the telephone companies might call *IP dial tone*, meaning very high speed PC access from the home. By default, the transport mechanism will be IP. So users can make use of the giant telecommunications networks, tunneling through to get to wherever they want to go. That same tunnel might also go through the Internet, but the pathway would be transparent to the user.

Microsoft is working with telephone and cable companies to create high-speed, dedicated links between a home PC and company networks taking advantage of the existing telephone or cable wiring to the home. Because PPTP isn't bandwidth-constrained, it can work with the underlying communications services, whether that is standard analog phone lines, ISDN, or even ADSL and cable modems. That's because PPTP makes use of PPP transport.

Phone companies can use a device called an *asynchronous digital subscriber line* (*ADSL*) modem, which would be installed both at the central office and the customer's home. It would not interfere with regular phone service, but would multiplex data traffic onto the same line. Using an IP connection, caching Internet servers could be installed at the central office to provide a connection to the Internet, CD-ROM servers, or other system resources. Users could then connect to either the Internet or a private network. PPTP would allow users to tunnel through the service provider's bank of servers and through the different address types. A router at the central office could be connected to the Internet so that users could reach distant corporate networks. Or the corporate network could be directly attached, permitting direct access.

Combining PPTP and TCP/IP

The PPTP protocol is built on the well-established Internet communications protocols of PPP (point-to-point protocol), and TCP/IP (transmission control protocol/Internet protocol). PPP is multi-protocol, offers authentication, and also offers methods of privacy and compression of data. IP is routable and has an Internet infrastructure. PPTP allows a PPP session to be tunneled through an existing IP connection, no matter how it was set up. An existing connection can be treated as if it were a telephone line, so a private network can run over a public one.

Tunneling is achieved because PPTP provides encapsulation, wrapping packets of information (which can be IP, IPX, or NetBEUI) within IP packets for transmission through the Internet. Upon receipt, the external IP packets are stripped away, exposing the original packets for delivery. Encapsulation allows the transport of packets that wouldn't otherwise conform to Internet addressing standards.

A rough analogy would be someone in a branch office addressing an interoffice mail envelope to "Bill Smith, Marketing," and then dropping it into the U.S. mail, hoping it would be delivered to Bill Smith in the home office. PPTP encapsulation essentially wraps the interoffice mail envelope into a standardized envelope carrying the home office's exact (DNS) address. Once it arrives at the home office, the standardized envelope is removed, and the original interoffice envelope's addressing is sufficient for final delivery. Of course, PPTP does more than simply deliver messages. Once a PPTP link has been established, it provides its user with a virtual node on the corporate LAN or WAN.

These are the pieces of the packet:

```
Media    IP    GRE    PPP    PPP    Payload
```

PPTP uses an enhanced *generic routing encapsulation* (GRE) protocol in transporting PPP packets. Encryption is used for encapsulated data, and an authentication protocol is used to verify that users are who they claim to be before being granted access.

PPTP tunneling makes use of two basic packet types: data packets and control packets. *Control packets* are used strictly for status inquiry and signaling information, and are transmitted and received over a TCP connection. When a link has been established between an NT server and a *front-end processor* (FEP), they will use a single TCP connection for the control channel. *Data packets* contain the user data that must be sent to or received from the LAN or WAN. Data packets are PPP packets encapsulated using the Internet GRE protocol Version 2 (GRE V2).

When two machines want to talk to each other, they ask for permission to send IP traffic, establishing the compression scheme and encapsulation method to be used. This "handshaking" is used to make sure that the machines know how to talk to each other.

During transmission, data can be divided into small IP packets, framed with a PPP header, and sent across the network, with PPP providing serialization to detect whether a packet is lost.

Coordination of data transmission is enhanced with the PPTP protocol, which performs the following tasks:

- Queries the status of communications servers
- Provides in-band management

- Allocates channels and places outgoing calls
- Notifies Windows NT Server of incoming calls
- Transmits and receives user data with bidirectional flow control
- Notifies Windows NT Server of disconnected calls

This tight coordination of packet flow assures data integrity while making the most efficient use of network bandwidth.

Security

VPN uses Windows NT RAS security. Businesses can ensure secure communication between remote users and the private network using Windows NT RAS encryption and authentication protocols. Windows NT RAS supports *password authentication protection* (PAP), the more sophisticated *challenge handshake authentication protocol* (CHAP), a special Microsoft adaptation called MS-CHAP, as well as RSA RC4 and DES encryption technologies.

Authentication and Encryption

Clients have their accounts validated against the Windows NT user database, and only those with valid permissions are allowed to connect. The keys used to encrypt data are derived from the users' credentials, and are not transferred on the wire. When authentication is completed, the user's identity is verified, and the authentication key is used for encryption. Windows NT 4.0 uses 40-bit RC4 encryption. For the United States and Canada, Microsoft will provide an optional add-on pack for 128-bit encryption, which provides security so tight that exporting it elsewhere is prohibited today by U.S. law.

Filtering

An important security feature is PPTP filtering. An administrator can decide to allow only PPTP-enabled users to connect to the corporate network from the Internet. Filtering out non-PPTP packets avoids the risk of somebody attacking the corporate net through the PPTP gateway server.

Front-End Processors

PPTP is designed to allow front-end processors (FEPs) to be connected with Windows NT servers so that clients that call into the FEP have transparent access to the server's network. This means that the client won't notice whether it's going straight to the server or to an FEP that's tunneling through the server. Because Microsoft VPN provides transparent access to a PPP client, it can work with UNIX and a large number of Win16, DOS, Macintosh, and other clients.

Telephone companies can operate FEPs, because FEPs don't allow access to the data being exchanged between the client and server. The FEP is just a pass-through, which lacks the intelligence to look at information that's being passed through it. From a security standpoint, this means that a company won't lose control of who gets access to its network. The privacy of the data is maintained. This is very important for companies that outsource dial-up access, because they need their data to be secure.

Another important point is to keep control of who has access to the server on the server itself, rather than on the FEP. The FEP doesn't authenticate the clients calling in—the server itself does. It looks at their identity and establishes the tunnel to the server. Because the FEP has a passive role, security is tight.

Microsoft VPN

Microsoft virtual private networks have been designed to make their implementation easy for network administrators. Some of the benefits:

- Enables installation of PPTP on either the client or ISP
- Supports all major network protocols
- Allows existing network addresses to be used
- Allows existing communications gear to be used
- Provides flow control
- Uses open industry standards
- Ships with Windows NT Server and Windows NT Workstation
- Provides value-added opportunity for ISPs

All of this combines to make Microsoft VPN the economical, easy-to-implement, and secure way to use the vast Internet infrastructure in creating your own virtual private networks.

Once PPTP has been installed on the Microsoft NT Server end, tunneling access can be achieved either through a PPTP-enabled client or through a PPTP-enabled Internet service provider (ISP) point-of-presence (POP) server.

This flexibility means that a person with a PPTP-enabled laptop or home computer could make secure tunneled connections with her company's NT Server network, even if using an ISP that isn't PPTP-enabled. Similarly, a user without a PPTP-enabled computer could make a secure tunneled connection if her ISP has upgraded its network to support PPTP on its servers. This provides ISPs with the ability to provide value-added services to users who want to take advantage of PPTP communication but haven't installed it on their own computers.

PPTP can also be used for a remote client that's using a non-telephone connection such as an Ethernet card connected to a frame relay service with a direct connection into an Internet carrier. As long as both the remote client PC and the server have been upgraded to support PPTP, the user can benefit from secure PPTP connections.

Internet service providers can provide their customers with full multi-protocol VPN capability with an easy software upgrade for their existing remote access servers. Ascend, 3Com, ECI Telematics, and US Robotics are including PPTP support in their existing products as a software upgrade.

Again, end users can install PPTP on their PCs and use essentially any Internet service provider. A software upgrade to the client PC and organization's server will enable the secure tunnel through any Internet POP, even if the ISP hasn't upgraded its infrastructure to support PPTP.

Protocol Support

VPN supports all major networks, including TCP/IP, IPX/SPX, and NetBEUI. Multi-protocol VPN enables remote end-users to access heterogeneous networks across the Internet.

Microsoft VPN allows a user to dial in with an analog modem, an ISDN connection, an X.25 device, or other connection through a POP, which would ideally be local, thereby avoiding long-distance telephone charges. VPN can go through any type of network, including Windows NT remote access server, IPX-based Novell NetWare, and NetBEUI environments. Because VPN supports multiple protocols, users can retain the benefits of PPTP when on different networks.

VPN requires no change to existing network addressing schemes. This is helpful to companies that have deployed internal networks using an arbitrary device-numbering scheme that doesn't conform to the standard *Internet Assigned Numbers Authority (IANA)* approach. Once a user registers his domain name, the DNS can resolve the common name used in the address.

This ability to handle nonconforming addresses can be a huge benefit for LAN administrators, saving them from having to re-address each device on their network just to enable remote access. Because PPTP uses encapsulation, which hides nonstandard addresses, VPNs allow companies to use nonstandard IP and IPX addresses.

VPN allows companies to leverage their existing communications links and services. Rather than add an entire bank of new modem gear or other equipment to allow remote access to its networks, a company can make use of its existing links to the Internet. By eliminating the need for custom hardware and software, Microsoft VPN also saves companies in staffing and training costs that would otherwise be needed to support custom proprietary solutions.

Microsoft has included a new flow-control protocol as part of PPTP. Flow control sits between the client and the server on the data path. Without flow control, a client could continue sending packets to an overloaded server that was unable to handle them. Performance would be slowed as packets were sent several times before they got through. Flow control allows the server to tell the client to stop, and to start again when resources are available. Flow control also reduces network congestion by eliminating the need to resend packets.

VPN is now an IETF Internet Draft Standard. PPTP enjoys broad and growing industry support, and has been embraced by several leading remote access vendors, ISPs, and vendors of other related products.

Because PPTP is an open standard, it isn't specific to Windows-based systems, and can be deployed throughout a heterogeneous environment. Any PPP client machine (including UNIX and Macintosh), server type, or other remote access system can make use of PPTP.

> **Note:** To encourage PPTP implementation on other platforms, Microsoft has published sample source code, downloadable from the Web (`ftp://ftp.microsoft.com/developer/drg/pptp/src`).

Because it's based on Windows NT Server, Microsoft VPN provides all the benefits of Windows NT. Windows NT is open, reliable, and robust; supports multithreading and multitasking; is secure and scalable; and has complete integration with Microsoft BackOffice, the integrated family of server applications for the Internet and intranet. These attributes make Windows NT an excellent platform for value-added development of communications applications, such as routing and telephony, in addition to remote access.

VPN on Windows NT

Setting up VPN on Windows NT Server 4.0 is easy. VPN can be considered just a special case or use of Remote Access Services (RAS), an important feature set already built in to Windows NT. As a result, setting up a VPN using PPTP involves many of the same steps that an IS administrator would go through to set up a server to accept dial-up networking connections via RAS.

After setting up the wide area network (WAN) card, the IS administrator would then select the protocol or protocols to be used with RAS—IP, IPX, and/or NetBEUI. PPTP is now another protocol that can be selected (see Figure 24.1) and installed in the same way in which these other protocols are enabled. IS administrators already familiar with RAS setup will find the few screens and dialog boxes used to set up and use PPTP quite familiar.

The IS administrator retains control of who gets access to the corporate network with Microsoft's VPN, even if the company has outsourced its VPN service to a third party. That's because user profiles are still retained on the Windows NT Server so it can be quickly updated by the IS administrator, to reflect employee changes and so on.

Figure 24.1.
PPTP setup in the WAN selection.

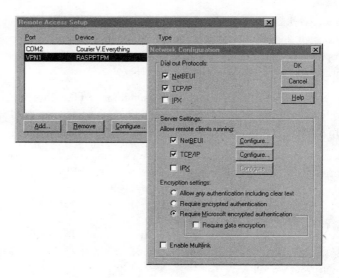

As an added measure of security when using VPN, the IS manager can have the server apply a filter to allow only PPTP-based users access to the corporate network, as shown in the next section.

VPN on the Client

VPN setup and use on the client is also easy. As noted, when PPTP support is provided by an ISP, no change in setup is required to the client PC. The VPN support happens transparently to the user in this situation (see Figure 24.2).

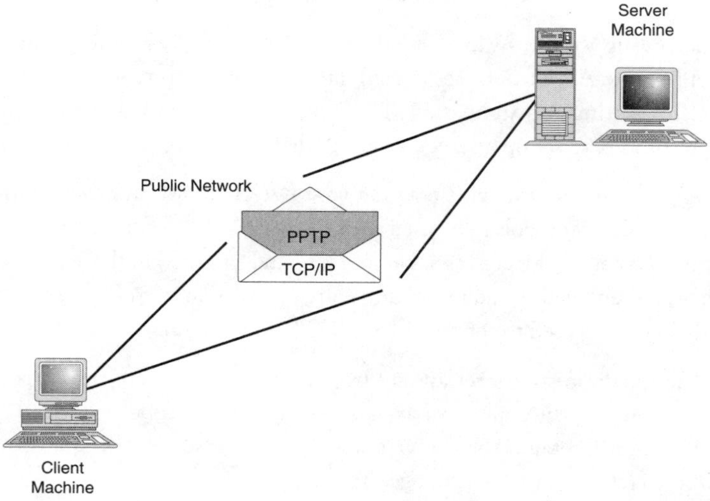

Figure 24.2.
The RAS dial-up sequence.

VPN service can also be enabled on the client PC, allowing the user to connect to the corporate network via any ISP—even ISPs that don't provide PPTP support in their POP. In this case, the client PC must have the PPTP protocol installed, in much the same manner as on the server machine. Again, PPTP is treated just like IP, IPX, or other selectable protocols.

Once PPTP is installed on the client PC, the user then creates a RAS Phonebook entry for the VPN connection. This entry looks like any other Phonebook entry, with two exceptions: There's an IP address where a phone number would usually appear, and the Dial Using pull-down list includes a PPTP option. This VPN Phonebook entry is activated after the user has connected to the ISP, so it's a two-step process. To further simplify use, both the ISP connection and the VPN connection can be set up and activated from one easy auto-dial Phonebook entry.

Setting up a client PC to enable it to use VPN service is straightforward, as Figure 24.3 indicates. PPTP has already been installed on this machine; when a new RAS Phonebook entry is created, a PPTP option is available in the Dial Using pull-down list.

Figure 24.3.
Setting up a client PC to enable it to use VPN.

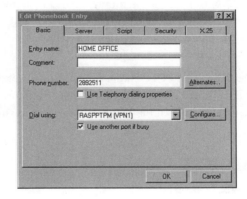

Once this Phonebook entry has been set up, the user can simply double-click the Phonebook Entry icon to automatically dial into the PPTP-supported server via any ISP.

NT RAS Enhancements

The Windows NT platform provides powerful administration tools for LAN managers, ISPs, and other Net professionals. For Windows NT Server 4.0 and Windows NT Workstation 4.0, Microsoft has made several specific enhancements to RAS, including the addition of PPTP support. This is a brief summary of other enhancements to RAS (in addition to PPTP) that are included in Windows NT Server 4.0 and Windows NT Workstation 4.0:

- **PPP multi-link.** Provides the ability to aggregate two or more physical connections to form one larger logical connection, improving bandwidth and throughput for remote connections. Software tools have also been added to facilitate ease of use.

- **Auto dial.** Makes it easier and faster for remote users to connect to their corporate networks.
- **Logon dial.** Automatically connects the remote user to the corporate intranet when the PC is turned on, if this option is activated.
- **Re-startable File Copy (RFC).** Addresses the problem of having to dial in and start over if an interruption occurs while downloading a huge file off a server to a remote PC. RFC allows the transfer to continue where it left off, once the connection has been reestablished.
- **RAS API enhancements.** Gives third-party companies more options to create value, via their own custom solutions and applications or utilities based on RAS.

Providing Cisco L2F Compatibility

In the June 1996 IETF meeting in Montreal, the PPP Extensions working group agreed to the PPTP Forum proposal, which included converging PPTP and Cisco's Layer 2 Forwarding approach to tunneling. Like Microsoft, Cisco has developed its own protocol for virtual private networks. Cisco's product is called Layer 2 Forwarding.

Microsoft and the other PPTP Forum companies are working to provide mutual compatibility between PPTP and Cisco's Layer 2 Forwarding (L2F) tunneling protocol. This is good news for users because, regardless of which tunneling protocol they use initially, the other will be supported.

Summary

The use of Microsoft PPTP is significant because it allows businesses to let third-party companies deal with the complications of maintaining a modem pool and nationwide network. But it will also allow them to make use of that power. The Internet is often accused of being a Toyland that serves to steal employees from productive work instead of providing information, but this product will truly add some value.

Microsoft has based the protocol on industry standards, which should help to make sure that this process will survive the long haul. It's also able to transport almost any industry standard protocol, so it isn't going to dictate changing your whole protocol scheme. And finally, it will transport across both standard phone technologies and more advanced media such as ISDN or ADSL modems.

Built-in security should be adequate to calm those afraid of using the Internet as a private road. But, for those who are still afraid, the supervisor can enable the filtering ability of allowing only PPTP users in. They also might utilize a front-end processor or other security provided by an ISP.

Currently, PPTP is available only for Windows NT clients, but hopefully it will appear for Windows 95 soon. All information points to it being available by the time this book is published.

VII

Server
Administration

25

Server
Management

Peter Norton™

Server management is a short term for a voluminous and far-ranging task. I suppose you could say that server management is the task of keeping the thing running, and that is no small task indeed.

The network administrator is supposed to be the know-all, be-all expert that everyone turns to when the slightest hiccup occurs in their own little personal computing environment. As such, the network administrator has to balance many tasks at once. In addition, the business world is moving to squeeze more blood out of the turnip than ever before. In my own area of responsibility, I have seen the transition from 2 mainframes to 120 separate workstations and servers, while still doing essentially the same tasks and with the same number of people. So how do we survive? The answer to that question is twofold: training and tools.

It's the tools part that I want to discuss in this chapter. Not *all* of the tools—because this chapter would take up the whole book if I tried to capture all the great utilities and wizards that Microsoft and other third-party developers have provided to support Microsoft Windows NT Server 4.0.

The server management areas I want to bring to light in this chapter are

- The Server Manager and some of its many features
- The Event Viewer—a window on what's happening in NT
- The Remoteboot Service—how to keep your operating systems close to the server
- Remote administration—how to do your job from somewhere else
- The Registry—how to really get yourself in trouble if you aren't careful

That's a lot to cover in one chapter, so let me warn you that this chapter is an overview that's intended to prepare you for the details elsewhere in this book.

The Server Manager Utility

Server Manager is a tool you can use to manage domains and computers. Yes, I know that Windows NT comes complete with the DNS Manager for Domains and DNS, the User Manager for the "people side" of the picture, and a dozen more managers for specific areas of the operating system and the network. What Server Manager does for you is to centralize control and allow you to

- Select a domain, workgroup, or computer to be administered.
- Manage a computer. For a selected computer, you can view a list of connected users, view shared and open resources, manage directory replication, manage the list of administrative alert recipients, manage services and shared directories, and send messages to connected users.
- Manage a domain. When administering a domain, you can promote a backup domain controller to become the primary domain controller, synchronize servers with the primary domain controller, and add computers to and remove computers from the domain.

You will recognize that some of the capabilities offered by Server Manager are also provided by the Services and Server options in the Control Panel of every Windows NT computer. However, Server Manager can manage both local and remote computers, while the Control Panel functions affect only the local computer.

Who Can Use Server Manager?

To use Server Manager for administering a domain and its servers, you must be logged on to a user account that is a member of the Administrators, Domain Admins, or Server Operators group for that domain. Members of the Account Operators group can also use Server Manager, but only to add computers to the domain. Server Manager is a powerful utility. If you meet the permissions required for management of a local server, you can manage that same machine from anywhere in the networked world that allows you access to that machine.

To use Server Manager to administer a Windows NT Workstation computer or a server that isn't a domain controller, you must be logged onto a user account that is a member of the Administrators or Power Users group for that computer.

The Server Manager Window

When Server Manager is first started, it displays your logon domain. The Server Manager title bar shows the domain name, and the body of the Server Manager window lists the computers of that domain. You can select a computer from this list, and then manage the selected computer by using commands from the Computer menu. Figure 25.1 shows the Server Manager window.

Figure 25.1.
The Server Manager in Windows NT Server 4.0.

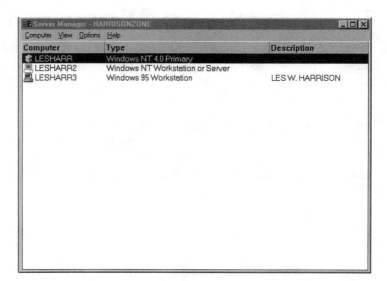

The Server Manager window lists the computers of the domain selected for administration (the domain name is displayed in the Server Manager title bar). This list contains computers that are members of the domain, plus computers that the Computer Browser service reports as active in the domain. This is the default display for Server Manager. The Server Manager list can also contain servers running Windows NT Server, Windows NT Workstation computers that are running the Server service, and Microsoft LAN Manager servers. Windows 3.1, Windows for Workgroups, and Windows 95 machines will also appear in the Server Manager, although you won't be able to perform administration functions on them.

When a Windows NT workgroup is selected for administration, the computers of that workgroup are listed. When an individual computer is selected for administration, only that computer is listed. You can also filter the list of computers, using commands from the View menu.

Selecting a Domain

The logon domain is displayed when you start Server Manager. That's the domain that you logged onto when you began to use the machine. You can use the Select Domain command to display a different domain, a Windows NT workgroup, or an individual computer.

If the domain, workgroup, or computer you have specified communicates with your computer over a low-speed connection, select the Low Speed Connection option. "Low speed" is a subjective term, and you'll use it depending on how irritating the delay in loading the data becomes. I generally use Server Manager with a 28.8 modem over the Internet and the response is fast enough to leave Low Speed deselected.

Displaying Servers, Workstations, or Both

By default, the list of computers in the Server Manager window includes both servers and workstations. Optionally, you can filter the list and display only one of those types. Computers that have accounts but are not active in a PDC's domain will appear grayed out. You can still select a grayed-out computer and manage the machine.

By default, the list of computers displayed in the Server Manager window contains those computers that are members of the domain, plus those computers that are listed by the Browser service as active in the domain. Optionally, you can filter the list to display only those computers that are members of the domain. This will be Windows NT computers and LAN Manager 2.x servers.

Managing Server Properties

Server Manager has three primary classes of management functions: Server Properties, Shared Directories, and Services. To manage server properties, follow these steps:

1. In the Server Manager window, double-click the computer name.

   The Properties dialog box appears, displaying a summary of connections and resource usage (see Figure 25.2).

2. To change the computer description, type new text in the Description box.

3. To administer a property associated with one of the buttons at the bottom of the Properties dialog box, click the button and complete the dialog box for that property.

Figure 25.2.
The Server Properties dialog box in Server Manager.

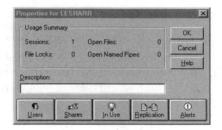

User Sessions

The User Sessions selection provides a list of the users currently connected to the server. You can view the resources opened by a user by first clicking the Users button in the Server Properties dialog box and then selecting the user name in the Connected Users box. You can exercise your incredible administrative privileges and disconnect a user from this same screen. Simply select the user name from the Connected Users box and then click the Disconnect button. To disconnect all users, click the Disconnect All button.

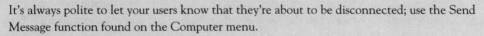

Peter's Principle: Show Respect for Your Users

It's always polite to let your users know that they're about to be disconnected; use the Send Message function found on the Computer menu.

Shared Resources

You can use the Shared Resources dialog box to view the shared resources available on the computer, and the users connected over the network to a selected shared resource. You can share directories or manage shared directories by using the Shared Directories command from Server Manager.

To view a list of the computer's shared resources:

1. In the Server Manager window, double-click the computer name.
2. In the Properties dialog box, click the Shares button.

   The Shared Resources dialog box appears. The Share Name box lists the shared resources available on the computer.

3. To view the users connected to a shared resource, select a share name from the Share Name box.

Again, you can disconnect one user from all shared resources by selecting the user name from the Connected Users box and then clicking the Disconnect button. To disconnect all users from all shared resources, click the Disconnect All button. Remember to be polite and send that message ahead of time. Good relationships will come in handy when your systems are misbehaving.

Resources in Use

Sharing resources is what networking is all about. You can view a list of the computer's open shared resources by double-clicking the computer name in the Server Manager window and clicking the In Use button in the Properties dialog box.

As with the functions already described, you can close an open resource by selecting that resource from the list and clicking the Close Resource button. To close all open resources, click the Close All Resources button. Again, warn connected users before closing resources.

Directory Replication

Server Manager plays an important role in directory replication. *Directory replication* is the duplication of a master set of directories from a server (called an *export server*) to specified servers or workstations (called *import computers*) in the same or other domains. If you're running a tight-budget operation (and who isn't these days?), you can use directory replication to provide a fair amount of backup for a critical operation or set of data. While this isn't the same as a RAID installation, it does keep a current copy on another disk, in the same or another server, at all times. A machine running Windows NT Server can be an export server, an import computer, or both. A workstation can only be an import computer. Once replication is set up, replication occurs each time a change is made to one of the files in a directory set for export. Figure 25.3 shows the Directory Replication dialog box in Server Manager.

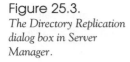

Figure 25.3.

The Directory Replication dialog box in Server Manager.

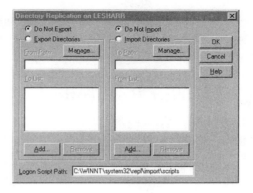

Directory Replicator Service

Before replication can occur, an appropriate logon account must be assigned to the Directory Replicator service of each computer that will participate in replication. To do this, use User Manager for Domains to create a domain user account that the Directory Replicator service will use to log on. This account must have the Password Never Expires option selected, all logon hours allowed, and membership in the domain's Backup Operators group.

Use Server Manager to configure the Directory Replicator service for each computer that will participate in replication to start up automatically, and to log on using the user account just described.

Managing Import Replication

Any Windows NT computer can be set up as a replication import computer. First, you have to establish a logon account and assign it to the Directory Replicator service. When this has been done, follow these steps:

1. In the Server Manager window, double-click the appropriate computer name.

2. In the Properties dialog box, click the Replication button.

3. In the Directory Replication dialog box, select Import Directories.

4. To import subdirectories from a domain or export server, click the Add button under Import Directories and then complete the Select Domain dialog box that appears. The domain name or computer name is added to the From List.

    If it isn't already running, the system will start the Directory Replicator service.

If you want to stop importing subdirectories from an export server or domain, select the domain name or computer name in the From List and then click the Remove button.

You can view a list of the subdirectories that have been imported to this computer or manage locks on those imported subdirectories. To do this, click the Manage button under Import Directories and then complete the dialog box that appears.

Managing Export Replication

Only machines running Windows NT Server can be set up as replication export servers. You first need to establish a logon account in User Manager and assign it to the Directory Replicator service. Once that is done, follow these steps:

1. Use Explorer to create the subdirectories that will be exported. These must be sub-directories of the replication From Path.

2. In the Server Manager window, double-click the computer name of the replication export server.

3. In the Properties dialog box, click the Replication button.

4. In the Directory Replication dialog box, select the Export Directories option.

To export subdirectories to a domain or computer:

1. Click the Add button under Export Directories.

2. Complete the Select Domain dialog box that appears. The domain name or computer name is added to the To list.

If you want, you can stop exporting subdirectories to a domain or computer. This is done by select-ing the domain or computer from the To List that appears under the Export Directories selection, and then clicking the Remove button.

To manage locks, stabilization, and subtree replication for the subdirectories exported from this computer, click the Manage button under Export Directories and then complete the dialog box that appears.

Once you have initialized a directory replication, you'll notice a new special share called `REPL$ share`. If it isn't already running, the system starts the Directory Replicator service.

Setting the Logon Script Path

You can establish a *logon script* file that will run each time a user logs on. It can be a batch file (`.BAT` or `.CMD` filename extension) or an executable program (`.EXE` filename extension). A *logon script path* is the local path to the directory where logon scripts are kept. A good place might be in `<systemroot>\winnt\profiles\userscripts`, or something like that.

When you establish a logon script and link it with a user, the system will locate the logon script by combining the local logon script path specified in Server Manager with a filename (and optionally a relative path) specified in User Manager.

One of the nice things about the Directory Replicator service is that you can establish a master site or server for all of your managerial tasks such as logon scripts. Because logon scripts might be modified more frequently than many other services, you don't want to be trucking all over the place looking for that elusive script file. For a domain, master copies of every logon script should be stored under one replication export directory of one domain controller—either the primary domain controller or a backup. Copies of these master logon scripts should be replicated to the other servers of the domain. Then, for every other domain controller, the path to imported logon scripts must be entered in the Logon Script Path box in the Directory Replication dialog box.

> **Tip:** While you can define the logon script path for the exporting machine, for computers running Windows NT Workstation the logon script path cannot be changed from the default `<systemroot>\SYSTEM32\REPL\IMPORT\SCRIPTS`.

Managing Administrative Alerts

Administrative alerts are generated by the system, and relate to server and resource use. They warn about security and access problems, user session problems, server shutdown because of power loss when the UPS service is available, and printer problems. You can establish which users and computers are notified when administrative alerts occur at a selected computer. You can set these up in Server Manager; double-click the computer name and click the Alerts button in the Properties dialog box.

> **Tip:** As an administrator, you should seek methods of enhancing your own survival. One technique is known as *management by exception*. Of course, being proactive can prevent many problems from ever occurring in the first place. Some balance of proactive and exceptional management is needed. One exceptional management trick is to use administrative alerts.

To add a user or computer to the list of alert recipients, type the user name or computer name in the New Computer or User name box and then click the Add button.

To remove a user or computer from the list of alert recipients, select the user name or computer name from the Send Administrative Alerts To box, and then click the Remove button.

Starting and Stopping Services

You can use Server Manager to manage the services. Use the Services dialog box to start, stop, pause, or continue each of the services available on the selected computer, and to pass startup parameters to the service.

Warning: Because stopping the Server service disconnects all remote connected users, warn users before stopping that service. Also, once the Server service is stopped, that computer can no longer be remotely administered, and its Server service must be restarted locally.

Event Viewer

Event Viewer gives you a management tool to monitor events in your system. You can use Event Viewer to view and manage system, security, and application event logs and to archive event logs. Because event logging starts automatically when you run Windows NT, it begins to capture anomalies as soon as it becomes functional.

This tool is one of the real strengths of NT versus any of the other network operating systems. Event Viewer gives the administrator a way to pinpoint the issues that are causing a server or network to slow or fail, without having to buy a separate product. The toughest problems to conquer as an administrator are intermittent problems or problems that happen only when you leave. If only you could have someone sit and watch the system for you and see when the problem occurs... well, Event Viewer gives you that helper to track events that occur in the server while you're gone. It tracks not just problems on the surface, but also events that you can't see.

Event Viewer is very flexible in that it allows you to sort your data by source, user, category, computer, event ID, or type. You can archive the logs or save them in formats that allow you to manipulate the data in other programs. You can also open an event log on other computers where you are assigned adequate privileges. Figure 25.4 shows the three primary views in Event Viewer: System, Security, and Applications.

Figure 25.4.
The three primary views in Event Viewer.

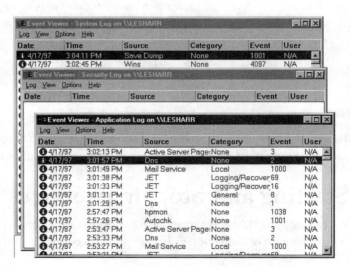

System Log

The system log records events logged by the Windows NT system components. For example, the failure of a driver or other system component to load during startup is recorded in the system log. Because it also logs successful system events, you'll have plenty to review after only a few minutes of operation and setup. Following is a detailed example of an event that was recorded in the system log:

```
SAM failed to start the TCP/IP or SPX/IPX listening thread
```

Security Log

The security log records security events. This helps track changes to the security system and identify any possible security breaches. Think of it as a night watchman with no bullets in his gun. This tool doesn't enforce security policy, but tracks security events. For example, attempts to log onto the system may be recorded in the security log, depending on the audit settings in User Manager.

> **Note:** You can view the security log only if you are an Administrator for a computer.

While Event Viewer automatically shows the events that occur with applications and the system, you must enable auditing for the security events to be captured. To do this, choose Audit from the Policies menu in User Manager. To control the auditing of file and directory access, choose Auditing from the Security menu in File Manager.

The Audit Policy dialog box provides check boxes for the following event types:

- Logon and logoff
- File and object access
- Use of user rights
- User and group management
- Security policy changes
- Restart, shutdown, and system events
- Process tracking

Each of these types can be individually selected or deselected for capture by the Event Viewer. Following is a detailed example from the security log:

```
A new process has been created:
New Process ID:   4290468000
Image File Name:  eventvwr.exe
Creator Process ID: 4290433888
User Name:     Administrator
Domain:        LESHARR4
Logon ID:      (0x0,0x1F60)
```

Application Log

The application log records events logged by applications. For example, a database application might record a file error in the application log. As I was writing this chapter with Microsoft Office 97, I experienced a fault that recorded the following detailed example in Event Viewer's application log:

```
The application, WinWord.DBG, generated an application error
The error occurred on 4/15/1997 @ 13:24:56.219
The exception generated was c0000005 at
address  306c361c (_MsoPvFree)
```

Event-Logging Options

You can define the maximum log size for each type of log and also specify whether the events are overwritten or stored by going to Log Settings under the Log menu. In the Change Settings For box in the Event Settings dialog box, select the type of log for which you want to specify settings. In the Maximum Log Size box, specify the size of the log in kilobytes. Select an Event Log Wrapping option to define how the events are retained for the selected log.

Sorting Events

The events displayed in Event Viewer are listed in sequence by date and time of occurrence. You can specify the order, depending on whether you want to show newest or oldest events first. The default listing order is from newest to oldest. You can archive the events by selecting Save As on the Log menu. This allows you to save the file as pure text, the proprietary event file format, or as a comma-delimited (CSV) file that can be opened in a spreadsheet program such as Excel.

Filtering Events

When you first start Event Viewer, all events recorded in the selected log are displayed. Filtering has no effect on an archived log file because the unfiltered log is saved. If you want to filter events, choose Filter Events from the View menu. In the Filter dialog box, specify the characteristics that qualify an event for display in Event Viewer.

Searching for Events

You can search for specific events that match the type, source, or category that you define. For example, you can search for all error events related to a specific source. Your search choices remain in the Find dialog box throughout the current session. The default settings are restored the next time you start Event Viewer.

Tip: After you define the search criteria, you can press F3 to find the next matching event without displaying the Find dialog box.

Viewing Event Details

For many events, you can view more information than is displayed in Event Viewer. This information is generated by the application that was the source of the event record. However, not all sources or events generate event details.

The event description is saved in all archived logs. The event binary data is saved if you archive a log in log-file format, but is discarded if you archive it in text or comma-delimited text format.

Archiving Event Logs

You can archive an event log in log-file format so that you can later reopen it in Event Viewer. Or the log can be saved in text format or comma-delimited text format so that you can use the information in other applications.

When you archive a log file, the entire log is saved, regardless of filtering options. For a log saved in a text or comma-delimited text file, event records are saved in the current sort order, and the binary data for each event record is discarded.

Viewing a Log Archived in Log-File Format

You can view an archived file in Event Viewer only if the log is saved in log-file format. You cannot choose the Refresh or Clear All Events commands to update the display or to clear an archived log. To remove an archived log file, you must delete the file in Explorer.

Searching a Log for Specific Information

The Event Viewer will capture more detail than you will ever want or hopefully need to look at. You can save a lot of time if you know about what you are looking for, even if it's just the period during which an occurrence is felt to have been logged. You can search for specific events that match the type, source, or category that you define. For example, you can search for all error events related to a specific source.

Your search choices remain in the Find dialog box throughout the current session. The default settings are restored the next time you start Event Viewer.

To search for specific kinds of events in a log, follow these steps:

1. From the View menu, choose Find.
2. In the Find dialog box, select any of the types of events you want to find.
3. Specify any other source, category, event ID, computer, and user events you want to find.
4. In the Description box, type text that matches any portion of the event record description.
5. To specify the direction of the search, select the Up or Down option.

This setup will allow you to get as much or as little output from the log as you like. The following sections provide definitions of the key data elements in the Find dialog box.

Event ID

Shows a specific event number to identify the event. The Event ID helps product support representatives track events in the system.

View From

Click the Events On button to view events that occur after a specific date and time. The default value is the date of the first event in the log file.

View Through

Click the Events On button to view events that occur up to and including a specific date and time. The default value is the date of the last event in the log file.

Information

Select this check box to view events logged by successful operations of major server services. For example, when a database program loads successfully, it may log an information event.

Warning

Select this check box to view events that are not necessarily significant but that may cause future problems. For example, a warning event might be logged when disk space is low.

Error

Select this check box to view significant problems, such as a loss of data or loss of functions. For example, an error event might be logged if a service was not loaded during Windows NT startup.

Success Audit

Select this check box to view audited security access attempts that were successful. For example, a user's successful attempt to log onto the system might be logged as a success audit event.

Failure Audit

Select this check box to view audited security access attempts that failed. For example, if a user tries and fails to access a network drive, the attempt might be logged as a failure audit event.

Source

This is the software that logged the event, which can be either an application name or a component of the system or an application, such as a driver name. For example, `Elinkii` indicates the Etherlink II driver.

User

This field indicates the specific user that matches an actual user name, and is not case-sensitive.

Category

This is a classification of the event as defined by the source. For example, the security event categories are Logon and Logoff, Policy Change, Privilege Use, System Event, Object Access, Detailed Tracking, and Account Management.

Computer

This field is a specific computer that matches an actual computer name where the event occurs, and is not case-sensitive.

Type

This is a classification of the event by Windows NT, such as error, warning, information, success audit, or failure audit.

Description

Type text that matches any portion of an event record description (the text string that appears in the Event Detail dialog box). You can search for any portion of an event record description. The complete text is not required.

Direction

To specify the direction of the search, select the Up or Down option. The search direction is independent of the sort order checked on the View menu.

Event

In Windows NT, an *event* is any significant occurrence in the system or in an application that requires notifying users. For critical events such as a full server or an interrupted power supply, you may see a message on-screen. For many other events that don't require immediate attention, Windows NT adds information to an event log file to provide information without disturbing your usual work. This event-logging service starts automatically each time you start Windows NT.

Filter

Use the Filter dialog box to define the date range, type of events, source, and category of events displayed for the current log. Your choices for filtering are used throughout the current Event Viewer session. When filtering is on, a check mark appears by the Filter command on the View menu and (Filtered) appears in the title bar.

Event Detail

Use the Event Detail dialog box to view additional information about a selected event. This dialog box appears when you select an event in the Event Viewer window and then choose the Detail command from the View menu.

The information displayed at the top of this dialog box is the same information that's presented in the Event Viewer main window. All event information is saved if you archive a log in log-file format (*.EVT). The event data is discarded if you archive the file in any text format (*.TXT).

This is just an overview of the Event Viewer utility in Windows NT 4.0. The Event Viewer is a great utility to use for managing your servers because it quietly sits there and logs masses of information. The real key to success with Event Viewer is to judiciously select what you want to record and how much you want to keep. This is something that you, the administrator, must custom-tailor for each application of NT Server.

Remoteboot Service

Remoteboot Service is included in this chapter on server management because using Remoteboot is really a methodology for centralizing the management of a network environment. Remoteboot uses a *remote program load* (*RPL*) read-only memory (ROM) chip on the network adapter cards in machines with no floppy or hard disk drives. These machines are called *diskless workstations*. The RPL ROM causes the CPU in the diskless workstations to download the operating system boot block from a server into the diskless workstation's memory. This boot block is the code that loads the remainder of the operating system and boots the workstation as if it were booting from its own disk drive.

In this section, I'll provide an overview of the Remoteboot service. If you're going to establish Remoteboot on your network, I suggest that you spend the time to research Remoteboot thoroughly by examining details contained in the Microsoft NT Server Resource Kit or in the online Microsoft Knowledge Base on the Internet. You can find details concerning Remoteboot on the Internet at the Microsoft Support Web site at `http://www.microsoft.com/support/`.

> **Warning:** Remoteboot is not simple to install. Once the first machine is successfully communicating with the server, the remaining machines are somewhat easier. The Remoteboot service must be carefully installed or the workstations will be unable to boot successfully.

The Remoteboot Process

The Windows NT Remoteboot service supports computers running MS-DOS, Windows 3.1, and Windows 95 (clients).

> **Note:** Remoteboot does not support the Windows for Workgroups product.

Each of these clients has a network adapter with a remote program load (RPL) ROM chip that retrieves startup and configuration software from the server when the client starts. Figure 25.5 shows a possible configuration of Remoteboot clients and servers.

Figure 25.5.
The Remoteboot process.

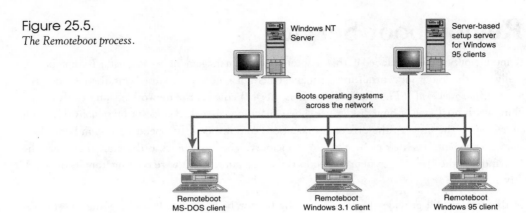

How Remoteboot Works

The Remoteboot service works by providing two kinds of resources on the server:

- A *boot block*, which contains all the information needed to start the client when it boots
- The Remoteboot *profile*, which defines the operating system environment of the client after it boots

The boot block and Remoteboot profile are sent across the network to the requesting client when the client is initialized by the user.

When a Remoteboot client is powered up, the network adapter is initialized and broadcasts a frame of data called a *FIND boot request*. The Remoteboot service on the server receives the FIND request, which contains the client's network adapter ID. The network adapter ID establishes the address of the client so the server will know which machine to communicate with.

The Remoteboot service checks the Remoteboot database on the server to see whether a *workstation record* (a Remoteboot database entry) already exists with this adapter ID. If it doesn't, the Remoteboot service records this adapter ID but doesn't boot the client. To boot the client, the administrator must convert this adapter ID record to a workstation record using Remoteboot Manager. If a workstation record exists with this adapter ID, the Remoteboot service sends a *FOUND frame* containing the server's adapter ID to the RPL ROM on the client. This is called a *boot acknowledgment*.

The RPL ROM accepts the first FOUND frame it receives (it may receive more than one if several servers are running the Remoteboot service), and returns the *SEND.FILE.REQUEST frame* to the adapter ID of the server that sent the first FOUND frame.

When the Remoteboot service receives the SEND.FILE.REQUEST frame, it then uses *FILE.DATA.RESPONSE frames* to send a boot block to the RPL ROM. The workstation record in the Remoteboot database specifies which boot block to send (either MS-DOS or Windows 3.1). When the RPL ROM receives the last FILE.DATA.RESPONSE frame, it transfers execution to the entry point of the boot block.

The RPL ROM boots the operating system specified by the boot block as appropriate for the client. For a client running MS-DOS or Windows 3.1, this completes the basic boot process. For a client intended to run Windows 95, the boot process continues. The client is now running Windows 95 real mode, using files on the Remoteboot server. To complete the boot to Windows 95, the client does the following:

- Creates a RAM disk. A *RAM disk* is an area of the computer's RAM memory set aside to operate as if it were a disk drive.

- Copies Windows 95 real-mode files from the Remoteboot server to the RAM disk.

- Loads the Windows 95 real-mode network drivers and establishes a connection to a *server-based setup* (SBS) *server*. The SBS server can be the same computer as the Remoteboot server. For Windows NT Remoteboot, the SBS server provides the Windows 95 files that the client uses to complete the Windows 95 boot process.

- Connects to a server that has a machine directory with files specific to this client.

Why Use Remoteboot?

The Remoteboot service promotes the use of diskless clients by eliminating the need for a hard disk on each client. This has several advantages:

- Increased network security by using clients that don't have disk drives that can be used to illegally copy data and to introduce viruses

- Greater control over the distribution of information and software resources

- Ease of centrally updating software

- Reduced cost in buying and maintaining client computers

Using the Remoteboot service has advantages for clients with hard disks as well:

- Easy upgrading of software and operating systems on many clients

- Greater flexibility in standardizing clients while allowing custom configurations

In general, the Remoteboot service offers greater control to the network administrator, and we all know how much network administrators like to be in control.

Disk Space Requirements

The first step in preparing to use the Remoteboot service is to ensure that the server has enough disk space for the files needed by the remote clients. Use the values in Table 25.1 as a guideline.

Table 25.1. Remoteboot disk space requirements.

Component	Disk Space Required
Microsoft Network Client version 2.2 for MS-DOS (LAN Manager version 2.2)—required for all client configurations	5.1MB
MS-DOS 3.30	0.7MB
MS-DOS 4.01	1.5MB
MS-DOS 5.00	2.8MB
MS-DOS 6.x	5.9MB
Windows 3.1	12.4MB
Windows 95	2.0MB

Use this table to calculate the amount of disk space you need on the Remoteboot server. For example, to install the Remoteboot service for a configuration of clients running MS-DOS 6.22, some with Windows 3.1, you need 23.4MB of disk space, broken down as follows:

- 5.1MB for the Network Client 2.2 for MS-DOS files
- 5.9MB for the MS-DOS 6.22 files
- 12.4MB for the Windows 3.1 files

In addition, you need room for personal copies of Remoteboot profiles (if needed) and for directories for each client, where people store their own data. The amount of space to allot per client is up to you. You can also define a separate server (or servers) to contain machine directories for Windows 95 clients, to distribute the load of storing client-specific data. Each Windows 95 client needs its own machine directory with a minimum of 8MB of disk space—more if users install additional software.

Windows 95 Remoteboot clients require 8MB of RAM and must be 386-based or higher. The server you use as an SBS server requires 90MB of disk space to store Windows 95 files.

Network Adapters Supported by Remoteboot

The next step to setting up Remoteboot is to install the RPL ROMs in the network adapters in the diskless workstations. There are specific network adapters that are supported by the Remoteboot service for Windows 95, Windows 3.1, and MS-DOS on the client (for the latest list, see `<systemroot>\Rpl\Readme.txt`, which will be installed when you establish Remoteboot service on your server).

Only the ISA versions of these network adapter cards are supported for Windows 95 Remoteboot clients. Note especially that the Remoteboot service does not support PCI, Token Ring, or PNP adapters for Windows 95 Remoteboot clients.

Most network adapters work best with the Remoteboot service when using their default settings. However, in case you need to modify these default settings in the `Protocol.ini` files, these files are located in `<systemroot>\Rpl\Bblock\Netbeui\adapter\Protocol.ini`, where *adapter* is the name of the particular network adapter. For example, a Windows 95 client can have conflicts with interrupt 3 (IRQ3) for the network adapter.

Installing Remoteboot Service on the Remoteboot Server

Next you will need to install the Remoteboot service on the server, unless you had the forethought to do it when you initially built the server. You'll need to have on hand the Windows NT Server compact disc. You'll also need original product disks for any operating system that you want the Remoteboot clients to run, such as MS-DOS or Windows 95 disks.

There are three special considerations for the Remoteboot service:

- The server's computer name must not have spaces in it.
- It is strongly recommended that you install Remoteboot files on a disk partition formatted with NTFS so that permissions are correctly set. Users will be able to read and write their own files in the Remoteboot directory but not write to shared files or system configuration files. Also, the FAT file system doesn't support more than approximately 100 Remoteboot clients.
- Install the *data link control* (*DLC*) and NetBEUI protocols and ensure that clients can communicate with the server by using these protocols. You won't be able to install the Remoteboot service until you have installed the DLC protocol.

The general Remoteboot installation process is as follows:

1. Install the Remoteboot service on the Remoteboot server. When this is done, you'll have a directory in `<systemroot>\RPL\` that will contain all of the Remoteboot initialization and information files.

   or

   Convert an existing Microsoft LAN Manager for OS/2 Remoteboot installation to run on Windows NT Server, and then install the Remoteboot service.

   Note that Windows NT Server doesn't support remote booting of OS/2 clients, Windows for Workgroups clients, Windows NT Workstation clients, or Windows NT Server clients.

2. Install MS-DOS and/or Windows 3.1 operating system files on the Remoteboot server. If you're converting from LAN Manager Remoteboot, this step may not be necessary.

3. If you will have Windows 95 Remoteboot clients, install Windows 95 real-mode files on the Remoteboot server.

4. Start the Remoteboot service.

5. Check the installation for errors, including checking the Event Viewer log.

6. Create profiles (defining the working environment shared by one or more clients).

7. If you will have Windows 95 Remoteboot clients, install a server-based setup (SBS) server. This can be the same computer as the Remoteboot server or a separate server on the network. The SBS server must run the NetBEUI protocol.

8. If you will have Windows 95 Remoteboot clients, create a location for machine directories. This can be on the same computer as the Remoteboot server or SBS server, or a separate server on the network. The server containing machine directories must run the NetBEUI protocol.

Remember, these steps are very high-level generalizations of a large amount of detail that is required to correctly establish clients for the Remoteboot service.

Using Remoteboot Manager

When you use Remoteboot Manager for the first time, you must decide which profiles you need. A *profile* is the working environment shared by one or more clients. It consists of the operating system, the client computer and architecture type, the network adapter type, and all the other information needed to boot a client.

Remoteboot profiles are completely different from user profiles, which are used elsewhere in Windows NT Server. To establish and name profiles, you choose from a list of configurations. A *configuration* is actually a template profile; a profile is created as a copy of one of the base configurations. Generally, you can find a configuration for any profile you want to create. Once the profiles are defined, it's easy to add clients. Figure 25.6 shows the opening screen for the Remoteboot Manager.

Clients use profiles in one of two ways: sharing a profile or using a personal copy of a profile. The profile is the same in either case; the difference is in how the client uses it.

Figure 25.6.
The Remoteboot Manager in Windows NT Server.

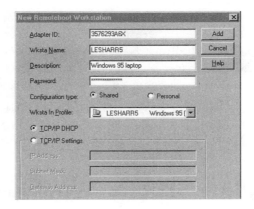

A profile can be shared by a group of similar client computers that use the same startup information. (All of the clients have the same `Config.sys`, `Lanman.ini`, and other configuration files, and those files are read-only.) For example, you may want to have a common profile that's shared by Accounting, and another profile for Sales and Marketing. Or you may want to create a profile shared by all Windows 3.1 users. Keep in mind, however, that the client computer architecture must be similar enough that the clients can share startup files. Clients that share profiles get their environment from a `<systemroot>\Rpl\Rplfiles\Profiles\profile` directory (where `profile` is the name of the profile).

Sharing profiles is not practical in all cases. For example, a client may need customized system configuration files (such as `Config.sys`). In this case, the client should use a personal copy of a profile. Changes to the startup information affect only the individual client. Clients that have a personal copy of a profile get their environment from a `<systemroot>\Rpl\Rplfiles\Machines\cname\profile\Profile` directory (where `cname` is the computer name and `profile` is the name of the profile). Users can edit any of the files in that directory, such as `Config.sys`.

Managing Remoteboot Clients

When you have installed the Remoteboot service and the MS-DOS operating system files and have defined some profiles, you can use Remoteboot Manager to manage the Remoteboot clients. You must boot at least one client on MS-DOS before you can install Windows 3.1 or Windows 95 Remoteboot clients.

When a user starts a Remoteboot client, what appears as the client's drive C: is actually mapped to various locations on servers, such as a personal directory on a separate server. For an MS-DOS or a Windows 3.1 client, the Remoteboot server maps directories and files from various locations to the virtual C: drive using a *file index table* (FIT) *file*. If the Remoteboot client has a hard disk, the hard disk appears as drive D:. Floppy disk drives keep their original drive letters.

Before a client with a hard disk can be booted remotely, its hard disk must be properly configured for the Remoteboot service. This does not prevent users from accessing the hard disk after the client is booted.

Installing SBS for Windows 95 Clients

To support Windows 95 Remoteboot clients, you must install *server-based setup* (SBS) on a server, install the first Windows 95 client, and then install subsequent clients.

For greater technical detail about SBS servers, see the Microsoft Windows 95 Resource Kit. When you set up an SBS server, you can use the server for Remoteboot and for other purposes described in the Resource Kit.

You'll need a Windows 95 installation compact disc (not floppies) and a Windows 95 client computer.

To Install an SBS Server

On the server that will contain SBS files, you must create a shared directory with 90MB of space available. The shared directory can have any name. As you share the directory, you will need to assign read-only permission for regular users and full access for administrators.

Installing the First Windows 95 Client

Installing the first Windows 95 client requires booting that client first to MS-DOS 6.2x, running Windows 95 Setup on the client, and then copying selected files from the client's machine directory to the Remoteboot server. Once you have installed this first client, you can easily install subsequent clients by using SBS to make a modified copy of the original machine directory, without having to run Windows 95 Setup again.

Each Remoteboot client has a *machine directory*—a directory on a server that contains client-specific configuration information and data.

Installing Subsequent Windows 95 Clients

Once you have installed a single client, additional clients of the same type are much easier to install. These additional clients don't have to be exactly the same as the first, but they must use the same type of network adapter and the same adapter settings (IRQ, I/O address, and so on).

If you need to install a Windows 95 client that has different configuration settings, you must treat the installation as a fresh installation; see the preceding section for details.

What You See on a Windows 95 Client

When you boot the client, a Remoteboot logon prompt appears:

```
Type Remoteboot username, or press enter if it is <workstation>:
```

This prompt asks for the account name and password associated with the client computer itself, not for your own user account name and password.

Windows 95 then prompts you twice for your username and password—once from a command prompt and again in a dialog box. At both of these prompts, enter your user account name and password.

After Windows 95 has started, drive C: is unassigned; it was assigned during the Remoteboot process and is no longer needed. Each local hard drive partition takes another drive letter after C: (for example, D: and E: for two partitions). One more drive letter was used as a RAM drive during the Windows 95 boot process; you can now use it as a RAM drive for your own purposes. Two more drive letters, usually the next two drive letters in sequence, are mapped to the SBS server and to the shared directory containing the client's machine directory. When setting up the client, you choose exactly which two drive letters to map, and they'll always be the same for this client. Don't unmap or remap these drives elsewhere.

For example, if you have a local hard drive with one partition, C: is unmapped, D: is the local hard drive, E: is a RAM drive, F: is mapped to the SBS server, and G: is mapped to the shared directory containing the client's machine directory.

Remoteboot with Windows 3.1

You can install Windows 3.1 in similar client environments simply by creating a profile for Windows 3.1 users and installing the Windows 3.1 environment in the profile. In this way, you can add as many new clients as you need without having to install the Windows 3.1 environment with each new addition. Keep in mind, however, that all the clients sharing the profile must be similar enough to share the same startup information.

If the clients aren't similar, you create personal copies of profiles. If Windows 3.1 is already installed for a profile and you create a new personal copy of that profile, the Windows 3.1 installation is part of the new copy, and you don't have to reinstall it. If you have established a personal copy of a profile and later want to add Windows 3.1, you must add it separately for that personal copy of the profile, or delete the personal copy of the profile and create a new one from a profile that has Windows 3.1 installed.

You can see from these generalized steps that the Remoteboot installation process is complex. Once completed, however, you will have a solid networking environment, and one that users cannot easily corrupt with bit-twiddling in configuration files. With the operating system installed safely on the central Remoteboot server, you should have very little ongoing maintenance in the Remoteboot environment. After all, reducing maintenance effort is the ultimate goal for any administrator.

Remote Administration

Getting the job done with less effort (and hopefully while working comfortably in a quiet, remote location away from the noise and chill of the computer room) is a great objective to put high on your priority list. The key to survival in the system administration business is to seek methods to do the job with less effort and more speed. The successful system administrator is capable of demonstrating that fewer—not more—people are required when the job is done correctly. Having this particular quality makes any administrator highly employable.

Microsoft has included two suites of tools for you to use when you are working away from the immediate vicinity of your servers. These tools allow you to perform administrative functions from remote locations with Windows 95 or Windows NT Workstation 4.0, although the tool suite for Windows 95 is somewhat limited in scope, as you will see in the following details.

Windows NT Workstation Administrative Tools

The Windows NT Server tools for 32-bit Windows-based clients allow a Windows NT Workstation computer to administer a Windows NT Server domain. The tools for 32-bit Windows-based clients include the following utilities: DHCP Manager, WINS Manager, User Manager for Domains, User Profile Editor, Remote Access Administrator, Remoteboot Manager, and Server Manager. Once installed, these administrative tools function exactly as they do on a Windows NT Server computer.

Windows 95 Administrative Tools

Windows NT Server tools also enable you to use a computer running Windows 95 to administer servers running Microsoft File and Print Services for NetWare and Microsoft Windows NT Server. Windows NT Server tools include Event Viewer, Server Manager, User Manager, and extensions to Windows 95 Explorer. You can use these extensions to edit security properties of printers and NTFS file objects on computers running Windows NT, and to administer File and Print Services for NetWare and NetWare-enabled users.

Installing Client-Based Administrative Tools

Installing the client-based server tools is a relatively simple procedure. First you share the directory on the Windows NT server where the tools are located. You can either share the server tools directory on the Windows NT Server CD-ROM, or use Network Client Administrator to copy and share the files on the server's hard disk. Then, from the client, you connect to the share and run the appropriate setup program.

Network Client Administrator

One method of sharing the server tools files is to copy them from the Windows NT Server CD-ROM to a directory on the server's hard disk and then share the directory. To simplify this operation, you can use Network Client Administrator. This multipurpose tool, located in the Administrative Tools group, allows an administrator to work with clients.

Network Client Administrator has four main areas:

- Make network installation startup disks to download either Windows for Workgroups 3.11 or Microsoft Network Client 3.0 software.
- Make installation disk sets for client software.
- Copy client-based network administration tools to a server and share them.
- View Remoteboot client information.

To copy and share the client-based tools, use Network Client Administrator and select Copy Client-Based Network Administration Tools. Specify a path to the server tools files. Choose to either share those files or copy them to a new directory, and then share that directory.

After sharing the client-based network administration tools on your Windows NT Server computer, you are ready to install the tools on your Windows-based client computer.

Installing Tools in Windows NT Workstation 4.0

To install the tool set for Workstation, connect to the shared directory where the server tools are located. From the WINNT directory of the share, run the SETUP.BAT file.

The SETUP.BAT file determines the architecture of your client computer and then copies the appropriate programs, along with their associated support and help files, to the client computer's <systemroot>\SYSTEM32 directory. SETUP.BAT doesn't create a program group or add the program icons to any group; you must add them manually—which, in my opinion, is a real shortcoming from

Microsoft. In fact, you may find it necessary to print the contents of SETUP.BAT and copy the files manually. I have had this experience with this batch file; it seems to be caused by non-Intel processor IDs.

Installing Client-Based Tools on Windows 95

To install Windows NT Server tools on a computer running Windows 95, follow these steps:

1. Confirm that your boot drive has at least 3MB of free disk space.

2. Choose Start | Settings | Control Panel.

3. Double-click the Add/Remove Programs icon.

4. Click the Windows Setup tab, and then click Have Disk.

5. In the Copy Manufacturer's Files From box, type the name of the Win95 directory (local, CD-ROM, or network drive) that contains the client-based network administration tools files (there must be a Srvtools.inf file in this directory), and then click OK.

6. Click Windows NT Server Tools, and click Install. Windows NT Server tools are installed in a \Srvtools folder on the computer's boot drive.

7. Manually adjust the AUTOEXEC.BAT file to include C:\Srvtools in the PATH command (if drive C: is the boot drive). For example, if you boot from drive C:, append \srvtools to the line that starts with PATH.

When you install Windows NT Server tools, the installation program performs these actions:

- Copies the Windows NT Server tools files to C:\Srvtools (if C: is the boot drive).

- Adds Windows NT Server Tools to the Start | Programs menu.

- Adds extensions to Windows Explorer that enable you to change security settings when viewing an NTFS drive or a print queue on a computer running Windows NT.

Verifying Your Password for Windows NT Server Tools

When you use the Windows NT Server tools on a client computer running Windows 95, a message appears at times, asking you to log on or enter your password. When you run the Windows NT versions of server tools on a computer running Windows NT, you don't need to supply your password separately. These password prompts ensure that you have administrative privileges for the server you administer.

Establishing Trust Relationships

When you use the Windows NT Server tools, you can create trust relationships between domains, but you can't verify them. Be careful to enter correct passwords for the trust relationships.

Logging On Before Using Windows NT Server Tools

If you aren't logged on and you start any of the Windows NT Server tools, you'll get a message saying that the computer isn't logged on to the network. First log onto the network and then run any of the Windows NT Server tools.

Using Client-Based Administration Tools

You'll find the tools in Windows 95 operate similarly to the NT Server tools, only they're limited to the three provided and the networking limitations of Windows 95. The tools installed in Windows NT Workstation are identical to the NT Server tool set and provide the network connectivity and security features that only a robust product such as Workstation provides.

In the next section of this chapter, I'll discuss the use of the Registry Editor to perform remote Registry administration.

The Registry

In Windows NT, like its junior sibling Windows 95, configuration information is centrally stored in a single database called the *Registry*. The Registry replaces the `.ini`, `.sys`, and `.com` configuration files used in Windows and Microsoft LAN Manager.

The Registry is very scary territory for many of us because a false move in the Registry can cause the server or an important service to fail terminally. I normally believe that the best way to learn is to dive in and try it, but not here on a live server. If you need to modify the Registry, take your time and watch your step. Think of this as sort of brain surgery on your server. Because the Registry controls the underlying behavior of the operating system, one false move could literally lose the patient (forcing a reinstall).

This section of the chapter provides an overview of Registry structure, describes how Windows NT components use the Registry, provides an overview of the Registry Editor and Windows NT Diagnostics, and describes how `.ini` files are mapped to the Registry.

There are many very thick books that cover the Registry in detail. I show the more generic portions of the Registry structure and hierarchy in this chapter. You can find more detailed information about the Registry and specific Registry keys in the Windows NT Server Resource Kit, v4.0.

Registry Hierarchy

The Registry is just a database organized in a hierarchical structure. One of my cohorts recently remarked that the Registry is not all that mysterious, once you understand the concepts behind it. The Registry is composed of subtrees and their keys, hives, and value entries. A key can also contain additional *subkeys*.

The Registry subtrees are divided into per-computer and per-user databases. The per-computer information includes information about hardware and software installed on the specific computer. The per-user information includes the information in user profiles, such as desktop settings, individual preferences for certain software, and personal printer and network settings. Figure 25.7 shows the subtrees in the Windows NT Registry.

Figure 25.7.
The subtrees in the Windows NT Registry.

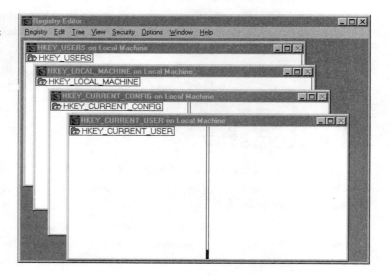

The following are the identities and definitions for the Registry subtrees:

- HKEY_LOCAL_MACHINE contains information about the local computer system, including hardware and operating system data such as bus type, system memory, device drivers, and startup control data.

- HKEY_CLASSES_ROOT contains object linking and embedding (OLE) and file-class association data (equivalent to the Registry in Windows for MS-DOS).

- HKEY_CURRENT_USER contains the user profile for the user who is currently logged on, including environment variables, desktop settings, network connections, printers, and application preferences.

- HKEY_USERS contains all actively loaded user profiles, including HKEY_CURRENT_USER (which always refers to a child of HKEY_USERS) and the default profile. Users who are accessing a server remotely don't have profiles under this key on the server; their profiles are loaded into the Registry on their own computers.

- HKEY_CURRENT_CONFIG contains information about the hardware profile used by the local computer system at startup. This information is used to configure settings such as the device drivers to load and the display resolution to use.

Each root key name begins with HKEY_ to indicate to software developers that this is a *handle* that can be used by a program. A handle is a value used to uniquely identify a resource so that a program can access it.

Hives and Files

The Registry subtree is divided into parts called *hives*. A hive is a discrete body of keys, subkeys, and values that is rooted at the top of the Registry hierarchy. A hive is backed up by a single file and a .log file that are in the <*systemroot*>\system32\config or <*systemroot*>\profiles*username* folder. By default, most hive files (Default, Sam, Security, Software, and System) are stored in the <*systemroot*>\system32\config folder. The Ntuser.dat and Ntuser.dat.log files are stored in the <*systemroot*>\profiles*username* folder. The <*systemroot*>\profiles folder contains the user profile for each user of the computer. Figure 25.8 shows the Registry Editor with the hives and files displayed. Table 25.2 describes the standard hives for Windows NT.

Figure 25.8.
*Hives and files shown with
the Registry Editor.*

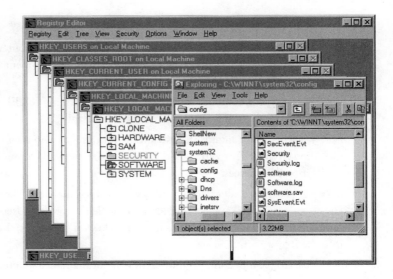

Table 25.2. Standard hives for Windows NT.

Registry Hive	Filename
HKEY_LOCAL_MACHINE\SAM	Sam and Sam.log
HKEY_LOCAL_MACHINE\SECURITY	Security and Security.log
HKEY_LOCAL_MACHINE\SOFTWARE	Software and Software.log
HKEY_LOCAL_MACHINE\SYSTEM	System and System.log
HKEY_CURRENT_USER	Ntuser.dat and Ntuser.dat.log
HKEY_USERS\.DEFAULT	Default and Default.log

Value Entries in the Registry Keys

Each Registry key can also contain data items called *value entries*. You can compare keys to directories, and value entries to files. A value entry has three parts: the name of the value, the data type of the value, and the value itself, which can be data of any length. The three parts of value entries always appear in the order shown in Figure 25.9.

Data types, such as REG_SZ or REG_EXPAND_SZ, describe the format of the data, which can be up to 1MB. Data types from 0 to 0x7fffffff are reserved for definition by the system, and applications are encouraged to use these types. Data types from 0x80000000 to 0xffffffff are reserved for use by applications.

Figure 25.9.
The order of Registry entries.

The following are the data types currently defined and used by the system:

- **REG_BINARY**. Binary data. Most hardware component information is stored as binary data and can be displayed in the Registry Editor in hexadecimal format or via the Windows NT Diagnostics program (`WINMSD.EXE`) in an easy-to-read format. For example:

  `Component Information : REG_BINARY : 00 00 00...`

- **REG_DWORD**. Data represented by a number that is 4 bytes long. Many parameters for device drivers and services are this type and can be displayed in the Registry Editor in binary, hexadecimal, or decimal format. For example, entries for service error controls are of this type:

  `ErrorControl : REG_DWORD : 0x1`

- **REG_EXPAND_SZ**. An expandable data string, which is text that contains a variable to be replaced when called by an application. For example, for the following value, the string `<systemroot>` will be replaced by the actual location of the directory containing the Windows NT system files:

  `File : REG_EXPAND_SZ : <systemroot>\file.exe`

- **REG_MULTI_SZ**. A multiple string. Values that contain lists or multiple values in human-readable text are usually of this type. Entries are separated by NULL characters. For example, the following value entry specifies the binding rules for a network transport:

  `bindable : REG_MULTI_SZ : dlcDriver non 50`

- **REG_SZ**. A sequence of characters representing human-readable text. For example, a component's description is usually of this type:

  `DisplayName : REG_SZ : Messenger`

How the Registry Is Used

The Registry provides a central location for all those pesky `.ini` files you used to have to hunt all over the Windows 3.x environment to locate. Although the Registry looks different, the same information is all in there somewhere, and sometimes it's a bit of a task to locate it.

Figure 25.10 shows how various Windows NT components and applications use the Registry.

Figure 25.10.
How components and
applications use the Registry.

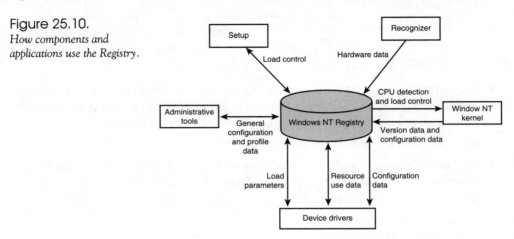

Each major operation performed in regard to the Registry is described in the following list:

- **Setup.** Both the Windows NT Setup program and other setup programs (for applications or hardware) add configuration data to the Registry. For example, new information is added whenever you install a new SCSI adapter or change the settings for your display. Setup also reads information from the Registry to determine whether the prerequisite components have been installed.

- **Recognizer.** Each time you start a computer running Windows NT, the hardware recognizer places hardware configuration data in the Registry. This data includes a list of hardware detected in your system. On x86-based computers, hardware detection is done by the hardware recognizer (`Ntdetect.com`) and the Windows NT kernel (`Ntoskrnl.exe`) programs. On RISC-based computers, this information is extracted from the ARC firmware.

- **Windows NT kernel.** During system startup, the Windows NT kernel extracts information from the Registry such as which device drivers to load and their load order. The `Ntoskrnl.exe` program also passes information about itself (such as its version number) to the Registry.

- **Device drivers.** Device drivers send and receive load parameters and configuration data from the Registry. This data is similar to what you might find on the `DEVICE=` lines in the `Config.sys` file in the MS-DOS operating system. A device driver must report system resources that it uses (such as hardware interrupts and DMA channels) so that the system can add this information to the Registry. Applications and device drivers can access this Registry information to provide users with smart installation and configuration programs.

- **Administrative tools.** The options and administrative tools in Windows NT, such as those provided in Control Panel and in the Administrative Tools (Common) folder, enable you to modify configuration data indirectly.

Registry contents can be directly viewed, modified, or both using one of the following tools:

- The Registry Editor is helpful for viewing and occasionally making detailed changes to the system configuration.
- The System Policy Editor enables you to view and modify certain Registry keys. The System Policy Editor also displays the data in a much more user-friendly manner than the Registry Editor.
- The Windows NT Diagnostics program (`Winmsd.exe`) also provides a view of configuration information stored in the Registry. Windows NT Diagnostics can read and display Registry data about the system resources used by drivers.

The Registry Editor

When you install Windows NT, the system configures Registry values for the local hardware and software on the machine. There are many entries in the GUI environment for which no method exists to adjust or tweak the system. In this case, adjustments to system configuration or operation must be made by directly editing the configuration database with the Registry Editor.

The full path name for the Registry Editor is `<systemroot>\system32\regedt32.exe`. The Registry Editor is not loaded as an icon at installation. Note that there is another file in the `<systemroot>` directory, called `REGEDT.EXE`, that exists for compatibility with Windows 95 applications. You should not use `REGEDT.EXE` to access the Registry in Windows NT, as it is reported to cause corruption of the Registry.

Local or Remote Registry Administration

With the Registry Editor, you can load either the local or a remote Registry. You must have a valid username and necessary rights and permissions on the target system. When the database is in place, you can display, add, modify, and delete keys and values in the database, protect keys with an ACL, modify user profiles, and audit the success or failure of access to selected keys.

Peter's Principle: Back Up Before Working with the Registry

Before doing any Registry modifications, always back up your Registry and critical system files. Also make sure that you have an emergency repair disk on hand to rescue your system from any Registry-tweaking mishaps. If you have a good set of backup files, you can restore damaged or missing Registry hives.

Running the Registry Editor Program

The Registry Editor program does not appear in a Program Manager group after installing Windows NT, but it is installed automatically.

Run the REGEDT32.EXE file from Explorer or type **start regedt32** at the command prompt and press Enter. As shown in Figure 25.11, the local Registry Editor windows appear, each of which bears the name of a predefined key. Also notice in this figure that a key from another machine has been added to the view, demonstrating the remote-Registry editing capabilities of the editor.

Figure 25.11.
The Registry Editor in Windows NT 4.0.

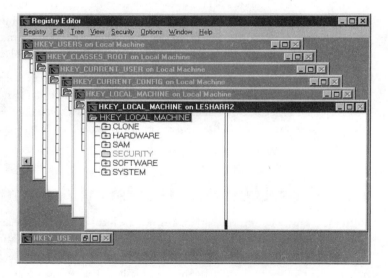

Your ability to make changes to the Registry using the Registry Editor depends on your access privileges. In general, you can make the same kinds of changes in the Registry Editor as your privileges allow for the Control Panel or other administrative tools.

> **Tip:** You can explore the Registry without fear of accidentally destroying it. From the Options menu in the Registry Editor, choose the Read Only Mode command. This command protects the Registry contents while you explore its structure and become familiar with the entries.

Altering Registry Data

Within the Registry, you can alter the value entries for a selected key or assign new value entries to keys. This section describes how to find keys and edit, add, or delete keys and value entries.

Always use the administrative tools such as Control Panel and User Manager to make configuration changes, rather than using the Registry Editor.

To search for a key in the Registry Editor, follow these steps:

1. Choose View | Find Key.
2. In the Find What box of the Find Key dialog box, type the name of the key that you want to find.
3. If you want to restrict the scope of the search or define the search direction, select the Match Whole Word Only box, the Match Case option, and/or Up or Down in the Direction box.
4. Click the Find button.
5. To see the next occurrence of the key name you specified, click the Find Next button.

Because key names aren't unique, it's a good idea to search for additional occurrences of a specific key name, to be sure that you find the key you want. Some key names include spaces (such as `Session Manager`); others use hyphens (such as `Ntfs-rec`) or a continuous string (such as `EventLog`).

To edit any value, double-click the value entry in the right pane of the Registry Editor window.

> **Tip:** If you want to add a key to a system temporarily, use the Restore Volatile command. If you use this command, the Registry makes a volatile copy, which disappears when the system is restarted.

Remote Registry Administration

In the same way that you can use Event Viewer or User Manager to view details on another computer, you can use the Registry Editor to view and change the contents of another computer's Registry if the server services on the remote computer are running.

This capacity to view a computer's configuration remotely allows you, as a system administrator, to examine a user's startup parameters, desktop configuration, and other parameters. Therefore, you can provide troubleshooting or other support assistance over the telephone while you view settings on the other computer from your own workstation.

Auto Refresh is not available when you are viewing the Registry from a remote computer. If Auto Refresh is on, manual refresh is disabled. Therefore, when you open a remote Registry, the Registry Editor checks to see if Auto Refresh has been enabled; if it has been, it's reset to manual refresh while you're connected.

To view the Registry for a remote computer, follow these steps:

1. From the Registry menu, choose the Select Computer command and then select or type the name of the computer whose Registry you want to access (refer to Figure 25.11).

   or

   Double-click the name of a computer in the Select Computer list. Under a Windows NT server, the first name in this list represents the name of a domain. If no computer name appears after this domain name, double-click the domain name to view a list of the computers in that domain.

   Two Registry windows appear for the remote computer: one for HKEY_USERS and one for HKEY_LOCAL_MACHINE.

2. You can view or modify the information on keys for the remote computer if the access controls defined for the keys allow you to perform such operations. If you are logged on as a member of the Administrators group, you can perform actions on all keys.

Restoring Hives from Backup Files

To restore a damaged Windows NT system, you first must restore the basic operating system installation. You have two options for restoring the operating system:

- You can use the emergency repair disk to restore your system to the state it was in just after installation (consult Chapter 28, "Recovering from a Disaster," for details).

- You can run Windows NT Setup again. You end up with a system that starts the computer but lacks changes made since you first set it up. You can recover most of those changes by copying files from backups.

Restoring the operating system does not complete the job of restoring the Registry. Registry hive files are protected while Windows NT is running, so you can't copy those files back onto your system. What you can do, however, is restore the Registry after the system is up and stable. The way this is done depends on how you backed up your system (you did back it up, didn't you?):

- For tape backups, you can use the Windows NT Restore program to restore the Registry. Then restart the computer. Start the computer using an alternate instance of the operating system (or using MS-DOS if the system files are on a FAT partition). Copy the files back to the *<systemroot>*\system32\config directory. Then restart the computer, using the regular operating system.
- Use the REPAIR.EXE program from the Windows NT Resource Toolkit.
- Use the REGREST.EXE program from the Windows NT Resource Toolkit. The REGREST.EXE program performs a ReplaceKey operation, which swaps backup files for the default files that the Emergency Repair or Windows NT Setup programs installed, and saves the default files under other filenames. Restart the computer after running the REGREST.EXE program to see the restored Registry.

Protecting the Registry

You can see how important the Registry is, how it affects your Windows NT system, and how important it is to keep the Registry intact. You will need to plan strategies for protecting the Registry for each of your server or workstation installations. Following are some general ideas for protecting Registry files under most conditions:

- Changing the permissions to limit access to a Registry key can have severe consequences. Be careful not to set No Access permissions on a key that the Network control panel application needs for configuration; doing so causes the application to fail.
- At a minimum, ensure that administrators and the system have full access to the key so that the system starts and the Registry key can be repaired by an administrator.
- Because assigning permissions on specific keys can have drastic consequences, you should reserve this action for keys that you add to accommodate custom applications or other custom settings. After you change permissions on a Registry key, be sure to turn on auditing in User Manager and then test the system extensively through a variety of activities while logged on under different user and administrative accounts. You should also audit the key for failed access attempts.

In the Registry Editor, the commands on the Security menu for assigning permission and ownership of keys work the same as similar commands in File Manager for assigning access rights for files and directories.

Like the other short overviews in this chapter, this part on the Registry falls miles short of telling the whole story. I highly recommend that you spend some time studying the Registry before you start dinking around with it. Take it from one who has had plenty of painful experience, you can give yourself a hemorrhage when you try to reboot a server with a freshly modified Registry and all you get is the Blue Screen of Death. If you are not familiar with that term, fire up your Registry Editor, change a few variables here and there, and reboot. I think you will get the point.

Summary

In this chapter I've discussed the Server Manager Utility in NT 4.0 and how it's used to manage the NT servers and workstations in the realm of authority for the logged-on user. Details of user sessions, shared resources, directory replication, managing administrative alerts, and other fine points were included.

A resource often overlooked on the misbehaving server or workstation is the Event Viewer. This window into the reporting functions of Windows NT 4.0 provides the administrator with the details needed to understand what happened during and following abnormal events and the return to normal. It also shows the normal running events of the operating system, applications, and security.

I delved into a feature of NT called Remoteboot—rarely used, but a tool of importance in an environment that's relatively static or one that is to be a minimal budget operation. Remoteboot is an excellent environment to limit the administrative load, making it attractive for the small enterprise that will use occasional services from an outside administrator.

One of the most important NT 4.0 features, Remote Administration, was also presented. This allows the administrator to be in many places without leaving his own location. I discussed the utilities that Network Client Administrator installs on other Windows NT and Windows 95 machines, and some of their operating characteristics.

Wrapping up this chapter was a discussion of the Registry hierarchy, hives and files, and the Registry Editor. Some of the details for performing local and remote Registry administration were developed, along with methods of restoring and protecting the Registry.

I've tried to cover a lot of ground here in a short space, but I've also tried to leave you with one underlying theme: Make life easier on yourself and learn how to administer your systems without running all over the place and getting in a huff. So few of us take the time to learn our computer tools—and I'm a great example. I recently overheard someone say, "Well, I guess it's time to get out the book."

How often have I sat down at a new operating system or even a desktop product and started poking its insides just to see what happened? Does that sound familiar to you? Well, the truth is that you and I probably won't change. All administrators—at least the good ones—poke and prod to find out what the "undocumented features" are.

I suggest that you back up your systems, put procedures in place before you need them, run a neat and tight ship from a remote vantage point, and you'll find yourself with more time to be proactive instead of always being reactive.

26

Optimizing and Tuning Performance

Peter Norton™

Isn't it amazing how one day your network is fast enough to handle all your users and applications, and the next day it's slow as a snail? It's almost as if someone has sabotaged your network while you weren't looking.

Because every piece of your hardware has performance limitations, locating bottlenecks and squeezing every ounce of performance from your systems will be a constant trial. Adding equipment to the network will just move the bottleneck to the next smallest path. But maintaining a constant tab on performance will help you in tuning your network and optimizing performance.

Since you're reading this chapter, you probably *are* the type of person who likes to squeeze as much out of his or her system as possible, or you may be having some problems with the performance of your NT system and are looking for a solution. Windows NT is such a large operating system that it's often difficult to find where a problem may be hiding. By using the tools that you have available with NT, you can solve most of your performance problems in a relatively short time frame. There are many performance issues you'll need to look at to determine where your problem in performance lies. In this chapter, I'll describe some of the processes that NT uses to help optimize the system, talk about some problems that affect performance, and give you suggestions on how to correct the problems.

Automatic Optimization?

In the early days of NT, it was believed that you could simply install NT, install your applications, and let it run—that NT could "automatically" optimize itself. This belief is correct to a point. NT is able to dynamically allocate processor resources and memory, but NT can't dynamically adjust for an increase in users or applications. It requires someone to monitor and correct performance problems that arise. Monitoring the performance of an NT system is probably one of the most important tasks for a network administrator. If performance slows, the users will let you know—and quickly. There are methods of monitoring your system to give you pre-failure notification.

Pre-failure notification is very important. No one likes to troubleshoot a problem with users breathing down her neck. With pre-failure notification, you can analyze events that could be building up to a failure or performance problem, and correct the problem; the users won't have any idea what's going on. The system will run better, downtime will be minimized, and you'll look better in the eyes of your bosses. Third-party utilities are available that are designed for pre-failure notification, with all the neat features such as notification through pager or e-mail. But for someone on a tighter budget, cheaper utilities are available through third parties or within NT that can help you keep your systems running with optimal performance.

Some of the performance problems that you run into can result from a number of causes, including disk fragmentation; multiple processors, processes, and threads; and disk requests. The following sections describe these issues.

Avoid Fragmentation

A short while ago it was being claimed that, by using an NTFS partition, you would avoid fragmentation and have quicker disk access. Although NTFS partitions have several advantages over other file systems, keeping a disk defragmented isn't one of them.

Why is fragmentation such a drain on performance? After a while, files become broken into different pieces so that they can fit into the empty sectors on a disk. This is efficient for preserving disk space but can decrease your disk-access speed. When a file is broken into several pieces and written into empty sectors scattered on the disk, the disk heads must search for all of those pieces and put them together before the file can be used again. The heads will constantly move around the disk, retrieving each section of the file. This takes more time than if the file were written in contiguous sectors. To help you understand this better, imagine listening to a music CD where each song was scattered across many different tracks on the CD. The laser would have to move back and forth constantly, trying to piece the song together. There would be pauses between each piece of the song that was not contiguous to the preceding piece. It would be difficult to understand the music.

Since it has been proven that disks running under NT can become fragmented, several software vendors have released defragmenting utilities. Among those are the Norton Utilities for NT and Executive Software's DiskKeeper. Norton Utilities information can be found at `http://www.symantec.com`, and DiskKeeper information and sample download can be found at `http://www.execsoft.com`. Executive Software also has an excellent whitepaper available for viewing or downloading that discusses the effects of fragmentation on an NTFS partition.

But what if you don't have such utilities? There's a simple trick that you can use to defragment your hard drives. (This trick works only with NTFS partitions.) To defragment an NTFS partition, you can back up and restore the partition, using any backup utility. The biggest drawback to this trick is that you can never tell how fragmented your hard drives really are, so you won't know how often you'll need to back up and restore.

Warning: Before trying this trick, please ensure that you have a reliable backup.

Prioritizing Processes and Threads

Before I get into how threads and processes can be prioritized to increase performance, let me provide a quick rundown on threading and the Windows NT kernel.

Any task being performed by NT is classified as a *process*. Processes include verifying users, reading from disk or from RAM, or opening a file. When you think about it, NT is constantly executing processes. A process consists of a virtual address space, a list of resources owned by the process, and one or more threads.

A thread is a part of a process. Each scheduled event is an execution of a thread. Each process must contain at least one thread. A more detailed definition of a thread is an entity that executes the program code and is dispatched by the kernel to run on an available processor.

The kernel component of Windows NT is responsible for scheduling and assigning tasks to the computer hardware. The kernel controls two classes of objects: dispatcher and control objects. A *dispatcher object* is used for synchronization and dispatching, and a *control object* is used for controlling kernel operation. Because a thread is dispatched by the kernel, it's a dispatcher object.

The kernel sends threads to the first available processor for execution. Each thread is given a priority level. There are 32 priority levels, which are divided into two classes—real-time and variable. The *real-time class* has priority levels of 16 to 31 and the *variable class* has priority levels of 0 to 15. Of course, the higher the number, the higher the priority. A thread with a higher priority supersedes lower-priority threads; the dispatcher will stop a thread if it's being processed when a higher-priority thread arrives. This is called *preemptive scheduling*.

The dispatcher uses three criteria for scheduling a thread:

- Priority of the thread
- Set of processors that the thread can run
- Time expiration allocated to the thread

As mentioned earlier, there are 32 priority levels, divided into real-time and variable priority levels. The real-time priority levels are available only to Windows NT kernel processes. Applications can't be assigned a real-time priority level. The variable priority class is used by applications. The default starting priority level is 7, but that level can be dynamically adjusted by the dispatcher by up to two levels, to optimize response time. This is done under the following conditions:

- Threads have just come out of a voluntary wait state.
- Threads waiting to receive user input are given a boost of two when input is supplied.
- Compute-bound threads are lowered.
- All threads receive periodic priority boosts to make sure that the lower-priority threads don't wait too long.

You can control the priority of a thread using one of two methods—the START command or the Task Manager. The START command is used to start applications at different priority levels. This command is a command-line utility with the following syntax:

```
START ["title"] [/Dpath] [/I] [/MIN] [/MAX] [/SEPARATE ¦ /SHARED] [/LOW ¦ /NORMAL ¦ /HIGH
¦ /REALTIME] [/WAIT] [/B] [command] [parameters]
```

Table 26.1 describes the switches for the START command.

Table 26.1. START command switches.

Switch	Description
"title"	Title displayed in the window's title bar
/D*path*	Starting directory
/I	New environment will be the original environment and not the current one
/MIN	Start window minimized
/MAX	Start window maximized
/SEPARATE	Start 16-bit program in separate memory space
/SHARED	Start 16-bit program in shared memory space
/LOW	Start program in the IDLE priority class
/NORMAL	Start program in the NORMAL priority class
/HIGH	Start program in the HIGH priority class
/REALTIME	Start program in the REALTIME priority class
/WAIT	Start program and wait for it to terminate
/B	Start program without creating a new window; must break program using Ctrl+Break
command	Determines whether the window will remain after the command has run or will run as a windowed application or a console application
parameters	Parameters passed to *command*

Remember that the START command can only be used to set the priority at the time of execution. To change the priority of a process after it has been executed, use Task Manager (see Figure 26.1). Follow these steps:

1. Right-click an empty space in the Taskbar. There you'll see a pop-up menu with Task Manager as a selection. Click the Task Manager selection.
2. Click the Processes tab.
3. Right-click a process to bring up the context menu for that process.
4. Select Set Priority.
5. Select the appropriate priority level. Windows NT displays the warning shown in Figure 26.2.
6. Click Yes.

Figure 26.1.
The Task Manager.

Figure 26.2.
Priority warning for processes.

Warning: Microsoft didn't include this warning just to make you click an extra button. You need to have a full understanding of the processes that you're going to modify. Their meaning isn't always spelled out, and you must understand everything the process is doing before making a change.

There's even more that you can do with Task Manager if you have a multiprocessor system. *Processor affinity* is a method of assigning a thread to specific processors. In doing so, you must remember that you can easily affect the entire system performance. Change the affinity only if you fully understand the results. You can get to the Processor Affinity dialog box by right-clicking a process and choosing the Set Affinity option. Figure 26.3 shows the Processor Affinity dialog box.

Figure 26.3.
The Processor Affinity dialog box.

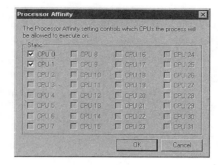

Multiprocessing and Performance

Most system administrators add processors to help speed up their systems and keep the performance level equal to today's applications. What most don't know, however, is how Windows NT uses that additional processor.

With multiple processors, Windows NT distributes tasks to any available processor. The CPU load is then evenly distributed among multiple processors. This process is called *symmetrical multiprocessing* (SMP). The threads being executed can run on any available processor. The dispatcher (discussed in the preceding section) uses the virtual processor interface provided by the hardware abstraction layer (HAL) to synchronize activity among the processors. The kernel can run simultaneously on all processors and synchronize access to critical memory regions. SMP systems increase system efficiency and avoid underuse of CPUs.

Another form of multiprocessing is not currently supported by NT: *asymmetrical multiprocessing* (AMP). Each processor in an AMP is used to run specific tasks, whereas in an SMP system the tasks are evenly divided among available processors. AMP systems are easier to build and design than SMP systems, but the performance gained from SMP is far greater. Figure 26.4 shows a comparison between SMP and AMP systems.

An important thing to remember is that only Windows NT programs are designed to take advantage of multiple processors. Even if the program is written using the Win32 API, it must have multithreading hooks in the API. This doesn't mean that overall system performance won't improve, but an application may not run as smoothly. An example is that you may have to wait for an application to finish printing before regaining control of the application.

Figure 26.4.
SMP versus AMP systems.

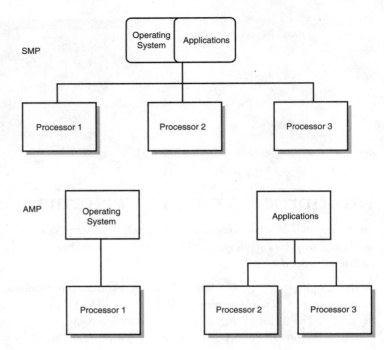

There's a workaround if you're lucky enough to have one CPU per application. NT can route the application to an idle CPU, which would execute the application more quickly than if the application threads were split among multiple processors. Splitting the threads among multiple processors could still place the thread in a wait state because of other tasks waiting to be executed.

Disk Performance and Reliability

Windows NT does an excellent job of managing the performance of the disk subsystem. It does this by *caching* requests to the disk subsystem. Caching is a method of handling requests to improve performance, and is handled within the I/O architecture through the Cache Manager. Instead of reading or writing directly to the disk, frequently used files are kept in the cache in memory. Because those files are kept in memory, the access time is greatly reduced.

The Cache Manager works closely with virtual memory management. As files are needed out of cache, Cache Manager pulls the information from memory and places it in the virtual address space of the process. The cache can also be dynamically increased and decreased, depending on the amount of available RAM.

Cache Manager can use two services to improve file system performance: lazy write or lazy commit. *Lazy write*, used with FAT partitions, is the ability to record changes in file structure in cache. When the load on the CPU decreases, the Cache Manager writes the changes to disk. *Lazy commit* is used on NTFS partitions and is similar to lazy write. Lazy commit holds the change in cache and writes to the file system as a background process. Both services offer a small level of protection for the data that is in cache. The utility used to recover data under lazy write is the chkdsk command. We all know from working with DOS that chkdsk is not the greatest utility for recovery. Lazy commit uses a different method of error control. If the computer system fails before a commit can be logged, NTFS rechecks the transaction to determine whether it was successful. If NTFS can't ensure that a disk transaction was completed successfully, it backs out of the transaction, leaving no incomplete modifications. NTFS checks the status of the cache periodically and marks it as a checkpoint in a log. If the system crashes, the system knows to go back to that checkpoint in the log to begin recovery.

There are three steps (passes) that NT uses for file system recovery under NTFS: an analysis pass, a redo pass, and an undo pass. If a system crash occurs, NTFS begins the *analysis pass*. During this pass, NTFS analyzes the amount of damage and determines which clusters need to be updated. Information on the clusters is obtained from the log just discussed. The *redo pass* performs all the transactions that were logged from the last checkpoint. The *undo pass* then backs out of any incomplete transactions.

Stripe Sets and Virtual Memory Pagefiles

Stripe sets and virtual memory pagefiles both can easily affect the performance of your system.

To improve the performance of your disk subsystem, you can implement a number of different solutions—external or internal RAID, buying faster disks, or using the built-in RAID capabilities of NT. One of the options you have with the NT RAID solution is stripe sets with no parity. (Stripe sets with parity is available only at RAID Level 5, which NT does not support by itself.) A *stripe set* can dramatically improve the performance of your disk subsystem, by using free space on a number of disks to create one large volume. The data that is to be written to disk is broken into several pieces and *striped* across a number of drives. Because each drive operates independently, this process happens almost simultaneously and gives the appearance of writing the data to all drives at the same time. The speed is achieved because the data is written in parallel to each drive.

If an array consists of three disks, operating in a stripe set, data will be transferred in one-third the time it would take to write to a single disk. If the array has five disks, it would transfer data in one-fifth the time. The more drives, the quicker your access. Figure 26.5 shows a diagram explaining disk striping.

Figure 26.5.
Disk striping.

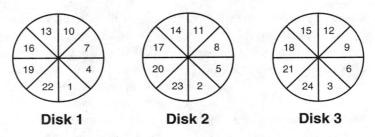

Disk 1   **Disk 2**   **Disk 3**

Disk striping is also known as *RAID level 0*. This is the lowest level of RAID and doesn't provide any reliability or error checking in case of failure. Although you'll gain speed, you may want to reconsider implementing stripe sets. A failure on any of the disks in the stripe set will cause you to lose all your data. Although, if you have slow disk access, a reliable backup procedure may be all the security you need.

Optimizing Virtual Memory Pages

Did you know that Windows NT can address up to 4GB of memory? Most people don't. Most people also don't have 4GB of physical memory in their systems, although it would be nice. Windows NT uses a mechanism called *virtual memory* to run applications that might require more physical memory than the system has.

When I talked about processes earlier in this chapter, I mentioned that each process manages its own resources. One of those resources is memory. Each process views memory based on 32-bit addresses. The largest size of a process address space is 2^{32} or 4GB, the same as the maximum level in Windows NT! The first 2GB of the virtual address space is reserved for user programs and the remaining 2GB is used for system storage.

When the physical memory on a system becomes full, the system can transfer some of the memory contents to disk through a process called *disk swapping*. When or if the contents of memory are needed again, the system brings the data from disk back into memory. The *Virtual Memory Manager* (VMM) handles this transfer. The VMM maps the virtual address spaces to the physical pages in the system's memory. If physical memory is full and additional pages are needed, the VMM moves the least-recently-used pages to disk. Figure 26.6 shows this process.

Figure 26.6.
The Virtual Memory Manager and disk swapping.

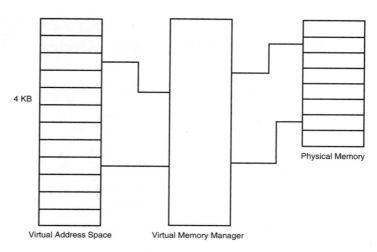

4 KB

Physical Memory

Virtual Address Space   Virtual Memory Manager

Windows NT is very efficient in its use of physical and virtual memory. The VMM manages pages in 4KB blocks. Using fixed-size pages helps to eliminate fragmented system memory. Windows NT uses an automatic optimization scheme to handle fragmented memory and therefore no additional configuration is needed.

When a program references a page that isn't in physical memory but on a disk, the Virtual Memory Manager pulls the information from the PAGEFILE.SYS file. Windows NT allows you to configure the location and size of the PAGEFILE.SYS. You can control the location and size or even delete the PAGEFILE.SYS while Windows NT is running. If the PAGEFILE.SYS is deleted, it will automatically be re-created the next time Windows NT is started.

The virtual memory space limit is determined by the amount of physical memory. To determine the maximum size to which the PAGEFILE.SYS can grow, simply add your physical memory to the maximum PAGEFILE.SYS size that was originally set. For example, if your Windows NT computer has 256MB of physical memory and a maximum 300MB PAGEFILE.SYS, your virtual address space can't exceed 556MB.

To make changes to the PAGEFILE.SYS file, follow these steps:

1. Select the System icon in the Control Panel to open the System Properties dialog box.

2. Click the Performance tab.

3. Click the Change button in the Virtual Memory section. The Virtual Memory dialog box appears, as shown in Figure 26.7.

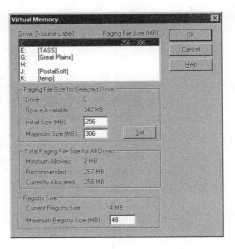

Figure 26.7.
*The Virtual Memory
dialog box.*

4. Set the Initial Size and Maximum Size fields as necessary. You should always at least set the Initial Size to the recommended value.

5. Click OK.

If your system has multiple drives, you should set the page file on a drive other than the one that has the system files. In Windows NT, the system files are accessed quite frequently, resulting in slower paging. You should see less disk thrashing and overall better system performance with the page file on a separate drive. You can see another performance gain if your system is equipped with multiple controllers for your disk system; set one controller to handle one disk and the other controller to handle the other disk, thereby splitting the access time between the two controllers.

Peter's Principle: Split the Page File Between Multiple Physical Drives

A method that is helpful when you have one controller is to split the page file between multiple physical drives. Concurrent swapping can take place, greatly reducing the overhead and resulting in better response times.

Performance Monitor

The ultimate tool for monitoring the performance of your Windows NT system is the NT Performance Monitor. Performance Monitor is an application that allows you to graph, log, report, and set alerts to monitor virtually hundreds of counters that can affect the performance of your NT systems. This tool is the real-time counterpart to Event Viewer, mentioned in Chapter 25, "Server

Management." Now, instead of having to check with the night watchman after a failure has occurred, you have a friend that can point at a particular problem or a component that's stepping outside the lines.

This tool is also more granular, and for that reason makes a good tool for watching a chain of events once you know that a problem is regularly happening. If a problem has occurred or a bottleneck is suspected, you can now monitor the events down to the microscopic level. You could think of Performance Monitor's relationship to Event Viewer like that of a general practice physician to a surgeon. Event Viewer scans the daily events, but Performance Monitor opens up the individual systems and tracks deeper issues.

Using Performance Monitor, you can perform the following tasks:

- Monitor real-time performance
- Identify bottlenecks
- Monitor remote Windows NT computers
- Determine system capacity
- Provide alert notification
- Keep a performance history

An important feature that I want to stress is the ability to monitor the performance of any other Windows NT system connected to the network. This can be helpful if you're monitoring a server in another room. By setting alerts, you can be notified when there's a potential problem with the server. Remember the earlier mention of pre-failure notification? This is a perfect example.

Before you begin to place applications on your system, you should establish a baseline for monitoring. This will allow you to track trends in performance and quickly pick up on any potential problem. To create a baseline, monitor your system over the course of a few hours to a full day and keep a log of activity. After adding an application, rerun the baseline to determine the overhead that the application places on the system. Continue this strategy until all applications and users are on the system. You'll then have an excellent baseline to monitor against.

Objects and Object Counters

Performance Monitor can track counters for many different Windows NT objects. All resources under Windows NT are described as objects; objects are functional subsystems in NT such as memory and physical disks. Each object type can also have multiple occurrences. For example, if you have a multiprocessor system, each processor is an occurrence of the processor object. Table 26.2 lists some of the object types that you can monitor with Performance Monitor.

Table 26.2. Objects monitored by Performance Monitor.

Object	Monitors
Browser	Browsing functions on NT computers, such as browser announcements and elections.
Cache	Utilization of the disk cache.
LogicalDisk	Logical disks.
Memory	Memory usage and virtual memory.
Objects	Usage of objects. Can be used to determine unnecessary objects.
PagingFile	Paging file activity.
PhysicalDisk	Physical disks that contain the logical disks.
Process	Processes.
Processor	Processor activity on each processor.
Redirector	Redirecting activities.
Server	Server processes.
System	All processors in a system.
Threads	Threads in the system.

Each object listed in Table 26.2 has several counters that you can track. Some of those objects have several counters for each occurrence in the system, meaning that you can virtually keep track of hundreds of counters. But remember that the more counters you add, the greater the effect on the performance of the system. Because Performance Monitor is an application, it also adds a small amount of drain on the system.

Other counters are available, depending on the services and applications you've installed. For example, if you have RAS or SQL Server installed, each of those applications adds its performance counters into Performance Monitor.

If you want to monitor physical or logical disk counters, you need to run the diskperf command. This is the syntax:

```
diskperf -y
```

The only problem with diskperf is that it won't be active until the next time the system is rebooted. It's a good idea to set this up prior to adding users. The reason Microsoft doesn't include it by default is that it has a small effect on the system performance. The faster the processor, though, the less the effect.

Charts

Charts are the most visually appealing screens within Performance Monitor. When you open Performance Monitor, a chart screen is what first greets you. The chart screen allows you to watch Performance Monitor in real time and see how your system is running. A good use for the chart screen is testing the effect that something may have on your system. An easy example is to quickly move your mouse around the screen and see how it affects the processor or memory. This experiment works best with slower machines. But you can't do the experiment unless you know how to create a chart. The following section provides the details.

Creating a Chart

When you first open Performance Monitor, the chart screen appears empty, as in Figure 26.8.

Figure 26.8.
The main Performance Monitor chart screen.

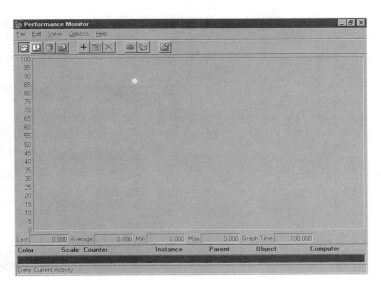

To begin monitoring your network or system, you need to add parameters to monitor. Follow these steps:

1. Choose Edit | Add to Chart. This action opens the Add to Chart dialog box (see Figure 26.9). You can also use the plus sign on the toolbar to get to this dialog box.

Figure 26.9.
The Add to Chart dialog box.

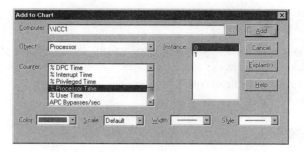

2. In the Computer field, specify the computer you want to monitor. You can select any NT system on the network; the default setting monitors the local system.

3. In the Object field, select the object that you want to monitor.

4. In the Counter list box, indicate which counters to monitor for each selected object. Sometimes the counter names don't make much sense. For an explanation of the counter that's highlighted in the Counter list, click the Explain button. Figure 26.10 shows the Explain option being used to explain the % Privileged Time counter.

Figure 26.10.
The explanation for the % Privileged Time counter is shown in the bottom of the dialog box.

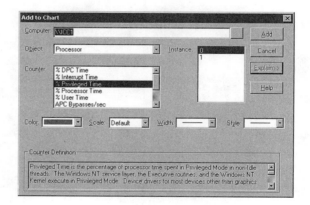

5. Use the Color, Scale, Width, and Style fields to customize how you want the counter information to be displayed.

   The most notable of these settings is the Scale option. Different counters are measured at different levels; the Scale option allows you to choose the value by which the counter information will be multiplied. This option is used so that values plotted between 0 and 100 in the counter can easily be viewed in the chart. An example is the Processor: Interrupts/sec counter, which is normally in the range of 120 to 1000. The default scale for this counter is 0.1. If you multiply the counter range by the default scale, the counter will usually appear in the 12.0 to 100 range.

The default setting is usually the easiest to work with; if you use the default setting for every counter it makes it easier to view the information on the chart screen, although there may be instances when you'll want to adjust the scale.

6. In the Instance field, select which instance of the counter to monitor. If you have multiple network cards or multiple processors, each card or each processor will have an instance number.

7. After you've specified the parameters to monitor, click the Add button.

8. Continue adding counters by repeating steps 1 through 7. When you're finished adding counters, click the Done button.

Figure 26.11 shows several counters in a real-time chart. Notice the multiple instances of processors.

Figure 26.11.
Real-time chart of several counters.

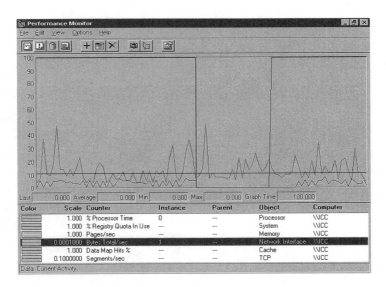

Interpreting Charts

The chart in Figure 26.11 (shown above) looks like a lot of lines with some confusing information at the bottom, but it's really not that bad. In fact, Performance Monitor charts are very easy to read.

The Performance Monitor chart always displays values between 0 and 100. This can be seen on the right side of the Performance Monitor chart screen. For each counter, the chart displays these values:

- **Last.** The value of the counter over the last second.
- **Average.** A running average of the selected counter at the bottom of the chart window.

- **Minimum and Maximum.** The lowest and highest values the selected counter has achieved.

- **Graph Time.** The time it takes to complete plotting a chart.

The maximum, minimum, and average are calculated using only the values currently shown on the chart.

> **Tip:** In Figure 26.11, Bytes Total/sec is selected. To make it easier to view the information for Bytes Total/sec in the chart window, you can select the counter at the bottom, as in Figure 26.8, and press the Backspace key. When you do this, the counter in the chart window turns white, making it easy to distinguish among the different counters.

Viewing Real-Time Activity

Now that you understand the chart-creation process and how to read the chart, you need to know why you would want to monitor activity in real time.

Earlier I mentioned an experiment that you can run to see how just moving a mouse would affect performance. This is an important experiment. Viewing real-time data can be helpful when you're testing system resources, installing a new application, or are just bored and enjoy watching different colored lines on a screen. But like the mouse experiment, when you make a change to the system, it will more than likely affect performance. Viewing real-time data allows you to immediately recognize the change in performance and be able to act on it. The important thing to remember is never to make more than one change at a time. Ease into changes gradually. Because one change can affect the performance of another, gradual steps pay off when performance problems arise.

To view real-time data, all you have to do is add the counters you want to monitor (for details, see the earlier section "Creating a Chart"). As you add counters, they immediately begin to track and appear behind the Add to Chart dialog box. After you're done selecting all the counters you want to monitor, click the Done button, sit back, and watch.

I encourage people who are new to Performance Monitor to watch real-time monitoring and use it to learn how to track and indicate trends and to become familiar with the chart screen.

Using the Alert View

The alert view can help you keep a close eye on several counters, with small overhead. As you can see in Figure 26.12, the alert view is similar to every other view in Performance Monitor except for the Alert Interval dialog box.

Figure 26.12.
The alert view screen.

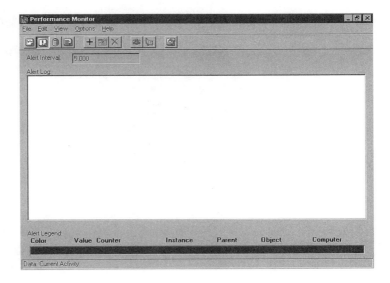

Adding counters here is much the same as adding counters in the chart or report view except for a couple of unique features. For each counter for which you want an alert, you need to set the threshold value. You do this in the Add to Alert dialog box, as shown in Figure 26.13.

Figure 26.13.
The Add to Alert dialog box.

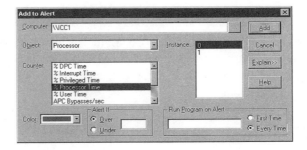

The threshold value is set in the Alert If box. Notice that you can select either over or under a certain value. For most counters, you'll be concerned only with going over your threshold setting; for counters such as Memory: Available Bytes, however, you'll want to know when you go under the threshold. For example, I used the Processor: % Processor Time counter. In the Alert If box, I selected to be notified if the counter ever goes over 20%. This is not a realistic setting, but will work well for this example. I also used current activity data, but could use data from a log file just as easily. Figure 26.14 shows the alert view screen with several alerts that were triggered.

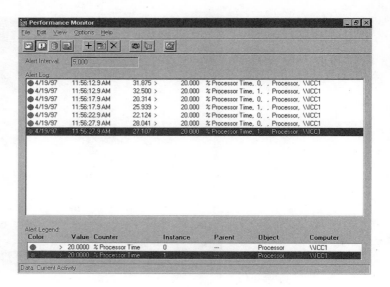

Figure 26.14.
*Alert view with several alerts
triggered.*

The information in this figure is really easy to understand. The colored circle tells you which counter the alert relates to in the legend. You also see the time of the occurrence, the value of the occurrence, and whether the value was less than or greater than the threshold value. The next set of information gives you the same information that's in the legend: counter, instance, parent, object, and computer. This is nice to have in the alert log window, because you can hide the legend using Ctrl+G if you need more room to view alerts.

Here comes the pre-failure notification again! The alert function of Performance Monitor allows you to set the alerts to send a network message to a chosen person or location on the network. If you choose to send alert messages to a person, the alert will be sent to the first Windows NT computer the user is logged onto.

Peter's Principle: Keep Yourself Notified of Alerts

A more convenient method would be to choose an arbitrary name such as "alert" to assign the alerts to. Whichever computer you're using, issue the following at the command prompt and all alerts will be sent to that computer:

```
net name alert
```

Every time an alert is triggered, a new pop-up box appears. This can get to be a hassle, because each box has to be closed manually. You don't want to use this function if your thresholds are set at a low level, such as in the preceding example. Establish your thresholds by using the baseline information you created earlier. Determine an acceptable level of performance and set your thresholds there.

The alert view is an excellent way to keep a handle on the performance of your systems. Alerts give you first notification that you may have a performance problem.

Reports and Logs

You have several counters selected, but it would be a waste of your time to sit and watch lines move across the screen. Fortunately, Performance Monitor allows you to log real-time activity that you can then use to create reports, view in the chart screen, or run against alert settings.

Follow these steps to log real-time information for any of the counters you want to monitor:

1. From the Performance Monitor menu, choose Options | Data From. The Data From dialog box appears, as shown in Figure 26.15.

2. Choose Current Activity and click OK.

3. In Performance Monitor, choose View | Log. A blank log screen should appear.

4. From the Log screen, choose Edit | Add to Log. The Add to Log dialog box opens, as shown in Figure 26.16.

Figure 26.15.
The Data From dialog box.

Figure 26.16.
The Add to Log dialog box.

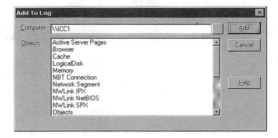

5. In the Objects list, select any of objects you want to monitor. You can select multiple objects by Ctrl+clicking.

6. Click Add when you're finished. Your screen should look similar to the one in Figure 26.17.

Figure 26.17.
Objects added to the log.

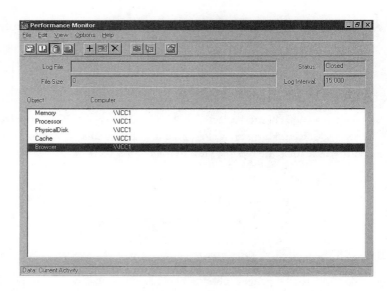

Note: Notice that you're not selecting any counters. Whenever you create a log of objects, every counter related to the selected objects is logged. You can filter through the logged counters at a later time.

7. Choose Options | Log. The Log Options dialog box appears (see Figure 26.18). Within the Log Options dialog box, you can enter the log file name and directory and set the update interval. By default, the interval is set to 15 seconds.

Figure 26.18.
The Log Options dialog box.

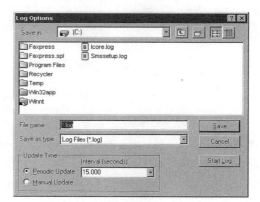

Note: The number of objects selected and the interval period affect the size of the log file. The more objects you select and the shorter the interval, the larger the log file. It's advisable to place the log file on a drive that has plenty of available space. If you're monitoring disk performance, it's advisable to place the log file on a disk that isn't being monitored or doesn't contain the system files.

8. Click the Start Log button to begin logging.

You can run the log for as long as you like. Stopping the log is a simple process. To stop the log and display the data, follow these steps:

1. From the Log screen, choose Options | Log. Click the Stop Log button.
2. Choose View | Chart.
3. Choose Options | Data From (refer to Figure 26.15).
4. Click the Log File button, locate the log file that you just created, and click OK.
5. Choose Edit | Add to Chart. The Add to Chart dialog box opens (refer to Figure 26.9).

Note: You can only select from the objects that you added to the log file from the Objects list. If you forgot to include an object, you have to start the logging process over.

6. Select the counters you want to view and click the Add button. After you've selected all the counters, click the Done button. You'll see a screen similar to the one in Figure 26.19.

Figure 26.19.
The chart screen from a log file.

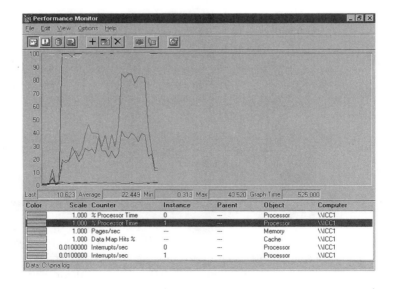

In Figure 26.19, the information isn't displayed in real time; it's displayed over the period of time that you logged the information. In other words, the information displayed is from the time you started the log to the time you stopped the log.

Placing log data into a chart isn't the only way to view the data. You can also run the log against alert thresholds and view the information in a report, as described in the next section.

Report View

Performance Monitor's report view enables you to view information either from a log or in real time. Report view is handy to use to look at information from several counters on one screen. To get to the report view, choose View | Report.

You can select multiple counters and instances for a report, just as you can for a log or a chart. With the report view, you can either monitor the activity in real time or pull information from a log. If you choose to report information in real time, the only option you have is the time interval, which by default is set to five seconds. This is a good amount of time because it allows you to read the values before they're updated. If five seconds is too long, you should probably be logging the information or using the chart view.

After selecting some counters and instances, you'll have a screen similar to the one in Figure 26.20. I populated this screen with information from the log in the preceding section.

Figure 26.20.
A report view with counter information displayed.

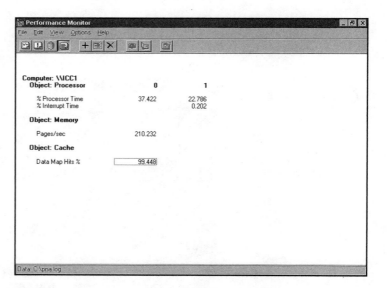

Not bad, is it? Using reports can give you all the information you need in an easy-to-read format. There are a couple of items I want to point out about Figure 26.20. If you look at the Processor information, you'll notice two columns with 0 and 1 above them. The 0 and 1 represent the instance of the processor. This shows that I monitored the activity of two processors on a multiprocessor system.

You can use the information in the report view by exporting it to a spreadsheet package and create some nice graphs that track counter activity over a period of time.

> **Tip:** A nice utility comes with the Windows NT Server Resource Kit, called *PerfLog*. PerfLog logs activity from counters to tab- or comma-separated text files. This makes it easier to import the counter data into a spreadsheet!

Logging Processor Activity

Windows NT is very dependent on the processor. Other network operating systems such as Novell NetWare are not as dependent. There are times when the bottleneck in your system is actually the processor. If you're running processor-intensive applications such as SQL Server, you'll definitely want to look at upgrading the system's processor, adding a second processor, or switching to a RISC system.

You can use Performance Monitor to help you decide when to improve your processing power. A good way of doing this is to log the performance of the processor(s) over a period of time. The following section describes some of the specific counters that you'll want to monitor and tells you what to look for.

There are many counters that are available for you to use to monitor the performance of your processor(s), as described in Table 26.3.

Table 26.3. Processor object counters.

Counter	Description
Processor: % Privileged Time	Percentage of processor time spent in privileged mode in non-idle threads.
Processor: % Processor Time	Percentage of elapsed time that the processor is busy executing a non-idle thread.
Processor: % User Time	Percentage of processor time spent in user mode in non-idle threads.
Processor: Interrupts/sec	Number of device interrupts the processor is experiencing.
System: % Total Processor Time	Monitors multiple processors.
System: Processor Queue Length	Determines the number of threads contending for the processor.

Processor: % Privileged Time

The Processor: % Privileged Time counter deals with a protection mechanism called *privileged mode*. Privileged mode is used by applications when the application needs Windows NT do some of the work for it. The application accomplishes this by calling a system routine. The system routine begins in user mode, moves to privileged mode, performs the operation, and slides back to user mode. What Processor: % Privileged Time tells you is how much the operating system is being used by applications.

Processor: % Processor Time

Processor: % Processor Time is probably one of the most-used counters. It measures the amount of time that the processor is being used to execute a non-idle thread.

> **Tip:** There could be times when you're measuring Processor: % Processor Time and it shows minimal usage, but tasks are still being completed. This doesn't necessarily show an efficient processor. There could be a bottleneck somewhere else that's preventing the flow of threads to the processor.

Processor: % User Time

Processor: % User Time is the opposite of privileged time. *User mode* is another protection mechanism that's the opposite of privileged mode. When an application is in user mode, the application can't access peripherals directly and read or change data maintained by the operating system. This way, NT protects one application from corrupting data needed by another application. When Processor: % User Time is up, Processor: % Privileged Time is down. If you added the two, it would equal the total processor time being used!

Processor: Interrupts/sec

Processor: Interrupts/sec tells how many device interrupts the processor experiences. Each time a device completes a task or requires some attention, it issues an interrupt to the processor. During an interrupt, normal thread operation is suspended. Windows NT is capable of handling thousands of interrupts per second.

System: % Total Processor Time

System: % Total Processor Time measures the amount of time that all processors in the system are busy executing non-idle threads. This is a much better counter to use in a multiprocessor environment than Processor: % Processor Time.

System: Processor Queue Length

System: Processor Queue Length is a difficult counter to work with. It always measures zero (0) unless you've selected a thread to monitor with it. This counter is great to use on an application server to measure the performance of any application. Of course, the higher the Processor Queue Length, the less optimized the application is. If you're a software developer for Windows NT, this counter will prove to be your most valuable—you just need to develop the performance counters!

That's a pretty good size chunk of information to absorb about processor monitoring. You need to remember that other objects can also have an effect on your processor(s). Just because your processor utilization is low, that doesn't mean that the system is performing well. Bottlenecks can exist anywhere and can take some time to find.

Disks

As mentioned earlier, before you can track any logical or physical disk, you must run the `diskperf` command. After running `diskperf`, you must then reboot the machine.

But why would you care about monitoring disk performance? Monitoring logical or physical disks will give you indication of how clogged the disk subsystem may be, and you'll be able to isolate the potential bottlenecks with a minimum of effort. Table 26.4 describes some of the counters that will help you to do this.

Table 26.4. Physical and logical disk counters.

Counter	Description
Disk Bytes/sec	Indicates disk throughput. If this value is below 20KB/sec, the disk is being accessed inefficiently.
Avg. Disk sec/transfer	Tells you the average time a disk takes to fulfill its request. A value greater than 0.3 seconds indicates problems or fragmentation.
Disk Queue Length	The number of requests waiting in a queue. Indicates whether the disk controller could be a bottleneck.

These counters usually will suffice to tell you if you have a problem with the disk subsystem. There are many more counters that are available for monitoring disk performance. The additional counters add up to equal one of the above. For example, Disk Read Bytes/sec and Disk Write Bytes/sec add up to Disk Bytes/sec.

Note: The LogicalDisk counter also exists for the PhysicalDisk object.

If you think you've discovered a disk bottleneck, one of the first things you need to check is whether it's really more memory that you need. Shortness of memory is reflected in slower performance from the disk.

Some other things to look at include your controller card and bus architecture. Check your controller card to determine what bit transfer rate it has. Most newer cards have a 32-bit transfer rate or higher. Avoid using a card with built-in cache. You'll be better off using the money saved to buy more memory for your system, because NT uses an adaptive cache system. The bus architecture can play a big role in I/O performance. PCI buses are quicker than EISA or ISA. Even though changing the bus requires changing your motherboard, it may be time to upgrade that old system.

Summary

This chapter talked about methods that NT uses to self-optimize, including the Virtual Memory Manager, Cache Manager, automatic prioritization of processes and threads, and processor affinity. Because these are done behind the scenes, most people don't know about them. They're designed to work without intervention and should only be modified by someone very knowledgeable.

The second part of the chapter introduced Performance Monitor. Performance Monitor is a built-in application of Windows NT that's used to measure the performance of your system through objects and counters. Performance Monitor is a powerful tool and should be used in all network environments.

27

Peter Norton™

This chapter will try to impress upon you one of the most important lessons you will learn about modern computing. When you look at your server and consider what you would save from it in the event of a problem, the answer would have to be the data. A scary problem is that the data is being stored on the most common piece of a PC to fail—the hard drive.

In any machine (bikes, televisions, lawnmowers), the likeliest item to fail is the one with moving parts. In your server, the only parts that move without human intervention are the fans and hard drives. Hard drives spin constantly, from the time the server is turned on until it's shut down. Just like miniature record players, they spin to allow the arms of the reading device (the head) to have instant access. So that puts you "behind the eight ball." The most important piece to you is the most likely to fail. You must find a way to protect your data.

In the traditional client/server model becoming so popular in local area networks (LANs), there are usually client computers that users work on to perform their daily tasks, and one or more file servers that offer programs and data storage to the clients. If this is the case in your office, making sure that the file servers get all their data disks backed up to an offline medium (such as magnetic tape) on a regular basis is very important. Other forms of offline backup are coming into use now, such as re-cordable CD-ROM devices, as well as newer re-recordable CD-ROM devices. For the most part, however, unless you have archival material that needs to have a very long shelf life, your most cost-effective medium to be used for backup purposes will be magnetic tape.

Most businesses need to keep only enough data on backup tapes to give them a secure feeling that, no matter what, they can recover from a major catastrophic failure of their computer system (or network). The network administrator who doesn't have a disaster recovery plan (covered thoroughly in Chapter 28, "Recovering from a Disaster") is not doing his or her job to its best. Data is important. System disks and application disks that contain installed programs are important.

Although you could probably recover easily from losing a client's computer due to hardware or software failure, replacing the data files and reinstalling programs on a file server can become more time-consuming and can put more clients out of service while they wait for the server to be fixed.

Just put yourself in this place: You've just come into work after a fun weekend (your in-laws just left after a two-week stay). Would you rather spend the next few days (or longer, depending on your situation) reinstalling software and configuring it for each client? Or would you rather spend a few hours restoring a few disks and repairing the Registry on your NT servers?

Warning: Most users have been confident using utilities to recover deleted files that have been around for years for the FAT (file allocation table) disk system. Indeed, the capability was later added to MS-DOS and Windows operating systems. Note that in Windows NT, however, this capability doesn't exist from a client standpoint! If you delete a file as a client, you delete it forever! NT 4.0 did add the Recycle Bin for server-based deletions, but not for network users.

This chapter discusses the basics involved in using the NT Backup program as well as two other third-party programs. Topics covered include the following:

- Scheduling unattended backups to run at convenient times
- Creating a batch file to run multiple NT Backup commands
- Command-line syntax for NT Backup
- Using third-party backup programs
- Selecting files and directories to back up

The NT Backup Utility

Many third-party utilities have been created to back up the NT server and its data, but the NT operating system also delivers a built-in backup utility called NT Backup. The NTBACKUP.EXE program will more than suffice for the needs of a small LAN. You can use the utility to make local backups of all disks on a computer or to make backups of disks that are on other computers in your NT network. Using an emergency repair disk (discussed in Chapter 28), you can even use the NT Backup program to completely restore a crashed system disk or to restore a system to a new set of hardware components.

There are a few caveats that you might find when using the NT version of Backup:

- To make backup copies of the Registry files and the event logging (system error) files, you must do a local backup. The NT Backup program can't back up these files from remote computers.
- Network bandwidth can be consumed dramatically on small LANs if you're using a few servers to back up many client computers.
- You can password-protect tapes made using NT Backup. However, the actual data on the backup tapes doesn't get encrypted. Therefore, it's possible for third-party applications and hackers to access the data on your backup tapes, even though they are password-protected. Physical security is always important when storing sensitive material.

If your network is very small, such as is found in a small business—perhaps an insurance agency or doctor's office—then you can probably get by using a single server with a high-capacity tape drive to perform backup functions for all clients during an off-hours backup schedule.

You can use the emergency repair disk (ERD) and other disaster-recovery mechanisms described in the next chapter to more fully protect the data in a small network.

You can find the NT Backup utility under the Administrative Tools menu (Start | Programs | Administrative Tools | NT Backup). You can also use the command-line interface to use the Backup program (NTBACKUP) from the command prompt. Either way, the utility can be used to back up and restore files.

Figure 27.1 shows the opening window of the GUI version of the NT Backup utility, with the Drives window open. You can see on the left side of the window an expandable hierarchical directory structure that you can double-click to expand or compress. Using this window, you can select the drives, directories or individual files to back up to tape.

Figure 27.1.
The Drives window of the NT Backup utility is where you can select the drives, directories, and/or individual files to be backed up.

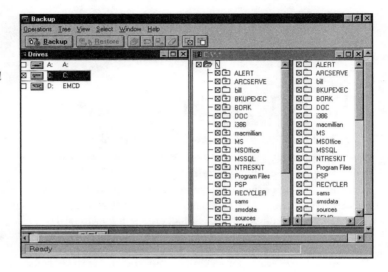

Notice that there is a series of check boxes in the window. Each drive, directory, and file has a check box beside it. You can use them in combinations to select the files you want to put on tape:

- If you select the check box next to a drive letter, all files and directories on the drive are checked automatically. In addition to using this check box to select all files for backup, you can use this feature to check all files and then go back to uncheck directories or files you want to leave off the backup set. This can come in handy when you have directories of information that rarely changes. For example, code libraries and documentation directories rarely change unless you update a compiler or other similar product. You could keep a separate tape of these types of directories and back up this data only when it changes. The rest of the time, you could simply uncheck these types of directories to save time during your regular backup.

- You can use the directory check boxes in a manner similar to the drive check boxes. If you select the check box for a directory, all files in the directory are checked automatically. If you want, you can then uncheck the check boxes for any individual files in the directory you don't want to back up. You can also use the directory check boxes to deselect directories that were selected by a drive check box.

- Use the check boxes for each individual file to select only a small number of files to put on tape, or to deselect files that were automatically selected by checking drive or directory check boxes.

Backing Up with NT Backup

After you've selected the drives, directories, and/or files you want to put on tape, you can then click the Backup button near the top of the Backup utility window. The Backup Information dialog box appears. Here you can configure parameters that relate to the backup tape and the type of backup (normal full backup, incremental, and so on). You can also designate the path for a log file, if you want to produce one, as well as other information.

The following dialog box fields will already be filled in:

- **Current Tape.** The current labeled tape that's in your tape drive.
- **Creation Date.** The date the current tape was formatted and used.
- **Owner.** If an owner was assigned to this tape, the username of that user will appear here.

You can't change these fields from this dialog box. They are properties of the tape you have placed into the drive. The fields you can configure in the Backup Information dialog box are as follows:

- **Operation.** Select either an Append or Replace operation. If you choose the Replace option, all data on the tape will be replaced by the new backup sets you are about to create. If you choose the Append option, the Backup program will advance past all other backup sets on the tape drive until it comes to free space where it can append your new sets.
- **Tape Name.** If you're appending to a tape, you can't change this field; the tape already has a name and some data stored on it. If you're creating a new tape, however (using the Replace option), you can change the tape name with this option. By default, it usually shows the date on which the tape was created, but you can make the text more meaningful so that it will help you in the future when trying to locate data.
- **Verify After Backup.** When you write data to a tape, you can never be sure that the data was correctly written until you read it back and compare it to the original data. Most modern tape drives have error-correcting mechanisms built in; but there's no substitute for doing a disk-to-tape comparison when you have critical data that you simply can't afford to lose. If you use this option, the backup and verify procedure will take longer than a normal backup procedure, but if time permits, the safety factor can outweigh all others.
- **Backup Registry.** If you're performing a backup on a local system disk, this option will be available. If not, it will be grayed out. Remember, you can only back up the Registry and system event log files locally. If you're backing up a system disk for a network client, you won't be able to back up these files.

Tip: Always back up the Registry when you do a local backup. You can never be sure whether it has been modified (by someone else in a large shop) or has become corrupted.

- **Restrict Access to Owner or Administrator.** This option can help you make sure that no user other than the owner or the system's administrator can access the data on the tape using the NT Backup program. Again, remember that the actual data on the tape is not encrypted, so third-party utilities can be used to get at the data. Always physically protect your backup tape.

  A tape that has already been used as a backup will have an owner, so you can't use this feature unless you're erasing the tape and starting new (using the Replace option, for example). A tape can't have two owners.

- **Hardware Compression.** Some backup programs can perform a great deal of software compression on the data before it's put on tape. Some models of tape drives can perform hardware compression before writing the data to the tape drive. If you choose to use hardware compression, you should use this check box. It will be grayed out if your drive doesn't support this feature, or if you're appending to a tape that already has compressed data on it—perhaps from another type of drive or software program.

- **Backup Set Information.** For each drive you decide to back up, you can enter information in the Backup Set Information box. You can select the type of backup (normal, incremental, and so on, described later in this chapter), and use the Description field to give a meaningful name to the backup set.

- **Log Information.** If you want to get a log file of some or all operations performed by the NT Backup program, you can use the fields in this box. If you want, simply select the default directory displayed in the Log File box, which is C:\WINNT\BACKUP.LOG.

Tip: The directory \WINNT would be the actual directory in which you installed your original Windows NT operating system. If you aren't sure which directory is the root system directory for your computer, you can use the SET command to find out what directory is stored in the %SystemRoot% environment variable, to determine whether \WINNT is the correct directory for your implementation. The following command output from the SET command shows a list of variables that you can use for paths and in batch files:

```
COMPUTERNAME=WRC3OES_JCOPENH
ComSpec=C:\WINDOWS\system32\cmd.exe
HOMEDRIVE=I:
HOMEPATH=\TOgletre
HOMESHARE=\\SRELTIS_RPDC\HOME
OS=Windows_NT
Os2LibPath=C:\WINDOWS\system32\os2\dll;
Path=C:\WINDOWS\system32;C:\WINDOWS;C:\DOS;
c:\keaterm;
PROCESSOR_ARCHITECTURE=x86
PROCESSOR_IDENTIFIER=x86 Family 5 Model 2 Stepping 6, GenuineIntel
PROCESSOR_LEVEL=5
PROCESSOR_REVISION=0206
PROMPT=$P$G
```

```
SystemRoot=C:\WINDOWS
SystemDrive=C:
TEMP=C:\temp
tmp=C:\temp
USERDOMAIN=ONO
USERNAME=togletre
windir=C:\WINDOWS
```

In this printout, you can see that the *SystemRoot* variable in this case (shown here in boldface) points to the C:\WINDOWS directory. This is probably because this was a system upgraded from a previous Windows 3.x or Windows 95 installation, and the older directory was used to preserve programs and attributes for the upgraded system. The point is, always check the variables to be sure that you know what system directory you are working with. When using a variable to substitute in a path or other dialog box, use the percent characters (*%variable%*) to cause the value of the variable to be used in the expression, instead of the text of the variable itself.

Finally, in the Backup Log section you can choose to log all file details, summary details only, or not log at all. Keep in mind that the summary details will usually suffice if you're currently having no problems with backups/restores. If you're having missing files or other problems, temporarily turn on the full details option and read through the log files that are created, to further troubleshoot the problems. The full details option can quickly fill your disk with data and slow down or even halt your system when disk space runs out. You might solve this problem by purging previous log files or putting previous log files out to tape and then purging them.

Tip: In fast-paced, intense organizations, there may be a mission-critical reason to be able to quickly locate a file. Some government contracts require that you keep detailed, printed, full copies of backup logs. Check with the security or contract officers at your organization to determine your company's needs.

When you're finished configuring backup parameters in the Backup Status dialog box, you can click the OK button to start the backup procedure.

Tip: Some tapes (such as those using the DC-2000 and DC-6000 cartridge format) require that you format the tape before you can use it. Other tape formats (most 4mm and 8mm tape drives) don't need to be formatted. Be sure to thoroughly examine the documentation that comes with your tape drive to determine the proper actions to take and the capacity of the drive you've selected.

Attended Operations

The preceding section covered the basics for setting up the configuration for the type of backup you want to perform. You can choose to perform the backup (or restore) using the GUI NT Backup utility and watch the progress of the backup procedure. This can be efficient when you're using the utility to back up or restore a small number of files and are waiting on them to complete.

When you click the OK button in the Backup Information dialog box, the Backup Status dialog box appears so that you can watch the progress of the files as they're being put on tape.

The statistical fields in the Backup Status dialog box include

- **Directories.** The number of directories that have been processed.
- **Files.** The number of files processed.
- **Bytes.** The total number of bytes processed.
- **Elapsed Time.** The time since the backup started.
- **Corrupt Files.** Files that are corrupt and were not backed up.
- **Skipped Files.** For example, the pagefile (`pagefile.sys`) can't be backed up.

The Summary field at the bottom of the Backup Status dialog box shows the current tape function procedure (rewinding tape, and so on) and the current files being put on tape.

At any time, you can use the Abort button in this dialog box to stop the backup. You might want to do this, for example, if you suddenly realize that you've chosen the wrong drive or files to back up!

You can use the Tapes option on the Window menu to view the Backup [Tapes] window. Here you'll see listed any tape currently inserted into a drive along with the names of the backup sets and the type of backup.

Command-Line Backup

If you only want to put a few files on tape (for example, for sending to a vendor for diagnosis), using the manual method described previously is the way to go. It's simple to copy the files to a temporary directory and select that directory for backup, using the options you want.

> **Note:** Using the GUI version of NT Backup, you can select individual files. If you decide to use the command-line version, however, you can only back up entire drives or directories. You can't select individual files. Additionally, you must learn the command syntax, which can seem complicated to a new user.

The full syntax of the command-line version of NT Backup is as follows:

```
C:> NTBACKUP operation path [options]
```

Table 27.1 describes the options you can specify.

Table 27.1. Options for the **NTBACKUP** command.

Parameter/Switch	Description
operation	The function you want the NT Backup program to perform. The only valid operations at this time are BACKUP and EJECT. Hopefully, in future versions Microsoft will allow you to use the command-line version of NT Backup to perform restores also.
path	The path of the files you want to put on tape in your backup set.
/a	The append switch. If you use this switch, the new backup set you're creating will be appended to the end of the tape where free space still exists. If you don't use this switch, the tape will be erased and the current contents will be lost!
	If you're going to be doing incremental backups to a single tape during the week, you'll need to use this switch to keep from overwriting the previous night's incremental backup.
/v	The verify flag. If you use this switch, after the backup has been performed the tape will be rewound and read for comparison to the actual data on the disk. This way, you gain a little more confidence that you have a good backup. The drawback is that backups take twice as long, because the tape must be rewound and read again.
/r	Restricts access to the tape (from the Windows NT operating system) to Administrators and Backup Operators groups or the owner of the tape.
/d	Appends a descriptive text string to the backup set to make it easier for you to remember what it contains. You should place the text you want to use after the /d switch and a space, in quotes (" "). Here's an example: `NTBACKUP D:\SUPPORT\ /d "Backup of Support Directory" [options]`
/b	If you're making a backup of the system disk on a local tape drive, this switch will cause the Registry and Event Log files to be backed up. A most important switch.
/hc:on and /hc:off	Turn hardware compression on and off (if your tape drive supports this feature).

continues

Table 27.1. continued

Parameter/Switch	Description
/t	Defines the type of backup that is to be performed. The NTBACKUP program is able to produce full backups and different types of incremental backups (see Chapter 28 for a full explanation and for strategies in designing your backup plans). Another important switch you'll probably use a lot. These are the valid options you can use with this parameter: • normal • incremental • daily • copy • differential
/l	Specifies the log file, if you want to use one, for the backup procedure. Similar to the /d (description) qualifier, you use the /l switch followed by a space and then the path and filename for the log file, placed within quotes.
/e	Tells the NT Backup program to write only exceptions to the log file. Otherwise, you can see the actual names of all files that were backed up to the backup set on tape.
/tape:	Indicates the tape drive to use. Because large servers can have more than one tape drive, they're numbered sequentially from 0 to 9. If you have only one tape drive on your server, this switch is unnecessary. Otherwise, after the /tape: qualifier, enter a number from 0 to 9.

Tip: You're in a hurry. You don't have this book handy. You can't remember the exact syntax for the NTBACKUP command. Simply type **NTBACKUP/?** to bring up the help file, showing the syntax described briefly.

Using NT Scheduler to Back Up with NT Backup

You can also use the NT Scheduler service (executed using the AT command at the command prompt) to back up. The Scheduler service is the procedure that runs tasks as background processes without user intervention. If you create a batch file that contains all the commands necessary to create the backups needed for your system, you can place these commands into a batch file. Then you can schedule the batch file to run during a time that most users are off the system, thus eliminating or minimizing the time the backup interferes with users' work.

The Scheduler service usually runs under the local system account. If you want to use the Scheduler service to back up files that are on other systems, follow these steps:

1. Create a new account (you can't modify the local system account using the User Manager for Domains).

2. Grant the right to the Scheduler service's account.

3. Log on via the network.

4. Place the new account in the Backup Operators group.

> **Warning:** You may have to start the Schedule service manually from the Service control panel, unless you change the Startup setting to Automatic.

Creating a Backup Batch File

To run the commands needed to back up your system(s), you need to create a batch file to hold the commands that will be executed by the Scheduler service. You can use the `Edit` command at the command prompt—or any other ASCII text editor you're familiar with—to create the file. Following is an example of a simple batch file that will invoke the `NTBACKUP` program to back up the local `C:` drive:

```
ECHO ON
    REM         Nightly Backup of System Disk
    REM
NTBACKUP BACKUP C: /t NORMAL /b /v /r /tape:0
```

This simple batch file will back up drive `C:` and the Registry files (with the `/b` switch), verify the backup (`/v`), and restrict the access to the owner or an administrator (`/r`).

You could substitute the following version if you want to back up more than one drive at the same time:

```
NTBACKUP BACKUP C: D: /t NORMAL /b /v /r /tape:0
```

In both cases, the `/tape:0` qualifier is not required, but is shown for completeness. In this new version of the command line, you see that more than one drive is specified. Both will be backed up to the tape drive and both will be verified.

You could also use two separate lines to back up each drive. However, in such a case, be sure to use the /a (append) switch on the lines following the first NTBACKUP command, so that subsequent backups don't overwrite previous backups! For example:

```
NTBACKUP BACKUP C:\ACCOUNTING /t NORMAL /l "c:\backup\accounting.bck"
    NTBACKUP BACKUP D: /t NORMAL /a
```

After you have designed your batch command file, you can submit it to run at a designated time on one or more days by using the Scheduler service.

> **Tip:** If you're going to back up file shares on remote systems, you need to make the explicit connection from within the batch file you create:
>
> ```
> NET USE X: \\server\sharename
> ```
>
> In this example, you would then back up drive X: using the regular NTBACKUP syntax.

Submitting a Backup Batch File to the Scheduler Service

The Scheduler Service can be run from the command prompt using a rather simple syntax. If you have the Windows NT Server Resource Kit, you can also use the GUI version that you'll find there to schedule jobs to run. Here's a simple example of submitting a backup batch file to run at a user-selected time:

```
C:> AT 17:00 /EVERY:M,T,W,Th,F,Sa,Su "C:\BACKUP_FULL.BAT"
```

This command will set up the file BACKUP_FULL.BAT to run every night at 17:00 (5:00 p.m. for the nonmilitary out there).

One mistake you might make is to write a complex batch file that performs a full backup on one night (such as Friday) and then performs incremental backups on other nights. It's much easier to simply write two separate batch files, one called FULL_BACKUP.BAT and one called INCREMENTAL_BACKUP.BAT, and use the Scheduler service to run them on the days they need to run. This way, other operators or administrators will be able to quickly tell what's running when they're monitoring the system. You also avoid the possibility that code changes in a complex batch file can break the entire thing and then nothing gets backed up (until the operator checks the log files, of course).

The syntax for the AT command is as follows:

```
AT [\\computername] [ [id] [/DELETE] ¦ /DELETE [/YES]]
AT [\\computername] time [/INTERACTIVE]
    [ /EVERY:date[,...] ¦ /NEXT:date[,...]] "command"
```

The first line in the AT syntax shows the command being used to delete one or more scheduled commands on the computer. The second line shows the syntax needed to actually schedule jobs for running at a later time.

Table 27.2 describes the options you can specify when scheduling or canceling jobs.

Table 27.2. Options for the AT command.

Parameter/Switch	Description
computername	The name of a remote computer, if you're executing the scheduled command on a computer other than the local computer. This is an optional parameter.
id	A batch identification number that's assigned to the scheduled event.
/DELETE	Cancels a scheduled command. If you don't use the id switch with /DELETE, all scheduled commands are canceled.
/YES	Suppresses a confirmation when you cancel all jobs.
time	The time of the day at which the command will run.
/INTERACTIVE	If you use this switch, the command or program executed will be able to interact with the desktop of the user currently logged into the computer.
/EVERY:date[,...]	Runs the command on the specified day(s) of the week or month. If you don't specify a date, the current day of the month is assumed.
/NEXT:date[,...]	Same as the /EVERY: qualifier, but the job runs on the next date for the day you specify. If no day is specified, the next time the current day occurs the command will run.
command	This is either a single command (or executable program name) that is to be run at the scheduled time, or the name of a batch file that contains a list of commands to run.

If you want to see if any jobs are currently waiting to be started by the Schedule service, you can enter the AT command by itself with no parameters.

The Schedule service can be used to schedule more than just backup commands. You can use it to run other programs, batch files, and so on.

Restoring

You use the GUI version of the NT Backup program to restore files. You can use the Window menu to view the Tapes window; you can also tile or cascade the Drives and Tapes windows if you want to see both.

> **Tip:** Don't make the first time you try a restore procedure also be the day you discover that your server hard drive has failed. During a disaster is not the time to find that the tape has not been functioning or that you haven't been capturing the data you need. Once your tape drive is installed, take the time to do a small backup and a test restore. If it fails then, you can simply correct the issue. If it fails after your hard drive, you may have to fix your employment problem.

For the tape currently inserted into the tape drive, you'll see a listing of the backup sets stored on the tape. Selecting files and directories to restore is similar to selecting files and directories to back up. The single check box beside each tape backup set can be selected to restore the entire backup set. Or you can click the plus (+) and minus (–) icons in the listing to expand or contract the listing so that you can choose individual files or directories.

When you're finished selecting, use the Restore button at the top of the window to begin the restore process.

Just as there was a Backup Information dialog box, there's also a Restore Information dialog box. Here you can view information about the tape, just like in the Backup dialog box. The Restore field, however, allows you to designate the path to which the files will be restored.

You can also elect to restore the local Registry files and to verify the restore by rereading the files after the restore has been completed. One important check box in this dialog box is the Restore File Permissions option. If you're trying to get at files from a user whose account no longer exists on the system, don't select this box, because the user's security identifier will no longer exist.

With the Restore To option, you can restore files into other directories or drives, instead of the default drive/directory from which the files were backed up.

Supported Tape Drives

Before purchasing any backup tape drive to use with a Windows NT computer, you need to be absolutely sure that the device will work with the NT operating system. NT isn't as forgiving as the Windows 95 plug-and-play mechanisms. You can visit the Microsoft home page or the home page of the company that manufactured a particular component of your computer to see whether a new driver is available for downloading. However, if you first check the Hardware Compatibility List (HCL) maintained at the Microsoft Web site, you might save yourself a lot of grief. You can get the latest copy of the HCL from Microsoft at www.microsoft.com. A certain number of items from this list are included in Appendix A, "NT Server 4.0 Hardware Compatibility List," but not a complete list. This is a living document; it changes constantly.

If you don't find your tape drive on this list, you should consult the vendor. Most computer hardware vendors now have home pages on the Internet from which you can download the most up-to-date drivers for their products.

> **Warning:** If you're upgrading, note that many IS departments use a portable external tape backup unit for grunt work. The only externals supported in NT are SCSI externals; there's no workaround for parallel port externals.

Third-Party Programs That Work

If you operate in a more complex environment with many servers and clients, you may want to choose a third-party backup program that's more full-featured than the NT Backup program. Many good programs exist for Windows NT. Two of them are discussed in the following sections.

Seagate's Backup Executive for NT

Seagate's *Backup Exec* software is a 32-bit program that can be used to back up either single or multiple computers in your network. Although the product can be used with autoloader tape drives, and can be used to back up not only Windows NT computers, but also NetWare and Macintosh computers, some of the functionality must be purchased separately from the main product.

Compared to the NT Backup program built in to Windows NT, Seagate's Backup Exec allows you to merely point and click to schedule the backups you want to perform. You don't have to learn a complicated command-line syntax or use the Scheduler service. Another feature you'll find very helpful in a larger network is that Backup Exec can use multiple tape drives simultaneously, thus increasing the throughput of backups when you have many computers from which to save data. Backup Exec also includes software compression and fully supports the Microsoft tape format (MTF), ensuring that the tapes you make can be read by other computers that run only NT Backup.

Backup Exec for Windows NT comes in three different formats, depending on the needs of your network:

- Enterprise Edition
- Single-Server Edition
- Workstation Edition

The Enterprise Edition gives you the most functionality, including the ability to monitor jobs running on other servers that are executing Backup Exec. The Workstation version is the most limited, designed for use in making backups of the local workstation only. The functions discussed in this chapter apply to all versions unless otherwise noted.

Install Briefing

Installing Backup Exec is a simple thing to do. Simply enter the SETUP.EXE command from the source CD-ROM. The program will prompt you with several dialog boxes to enter the information necessary for the installation and you can then begin to configure the types of backups you want to perform.

The first dialog box (shown in Figure 27.2) gives you the option of installing the program in the language of your choice, so long as that choice is English, Spanish, German, or French.

Figure 27.2.
The Backup Exec Setup program allows you to choose the language for the program during the initial installation process.

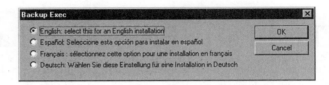

The next dialog box asks which functions you want to install. You can choose a complete installation (the Backup Server button), or you can choose to install just selected components of the full product (see Figure 27.3).

Figure 27.3.
You can choose to install the entire product or just selected components from this dialog box.

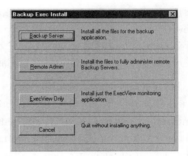

As you might expect, the next dialog box (shown in Figure 27.4) asks you to input the serial number for the product you've just purchased. If you downloaded an evaluation copy from Seagate, leave this field blank and simply click OK. If not, enter the serial number that came with the package and click OK. Note that, if you're using an evaluation copy, you won't be able to use it after 60 days!

Figure 27.4.
Enter the product serial number in this box. Leave this blank if you're using an evaluation copy.

The Specific Directory dialog box pops up next (see Figure 27.5), where you can specify a drive and directory path for the product installation. The default directory is `C:\BKUPEXEX\NT`. To change the drive or directory path, simply click in the field and enter the new destination.

Figure 27.5.

You can accept the default installation directory or you can edit the field to install the product to a different location.

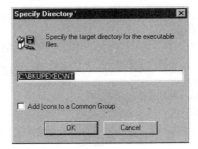

The next dialog box the Setup program uses is the Service Account dialog box (see Figure 27.6). Here you can select the domain or local directory security database from which to choose a user account (use the From box to choose the security database). Then enter a username in the User box. Finally, enter a password for the user account. If you enter an account name that doesn't exist in the security database you selected, the account will be created by the setup program (provided that the account from which you're installing has the appropriate rights to perform this function).

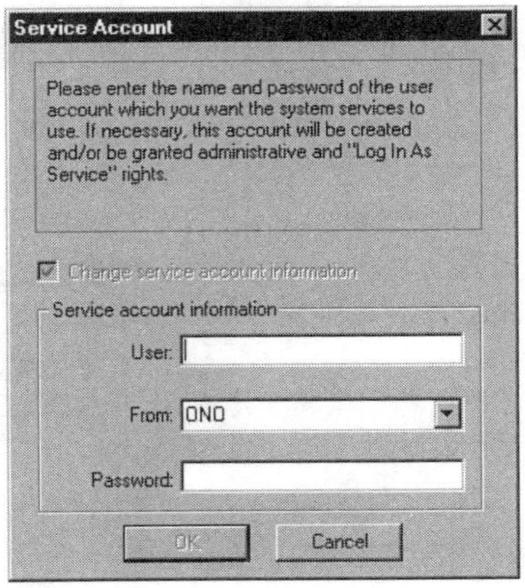

Figure 27.6.

You can enter an existing account or a new account to be created by the setup program. The account will be used as the service account for Backup Exec.

If the setup program has to create the account, it will warn you that the new account will be granted the right "Logon as a Service," among other administrative rights necessary for the Backup Exec services to function.

The setup program prompts you to enter the name of an existing Backup Exec server on your network if this isn't the first installation. This is so that the new installation can download data from the original Backup Exec server. If this is your first installation of Backup Exec, leave this field blank and click OK.

Finally, you'll see the familiar Copying Files to Disk dialog box, showing the percentage of files left to be copied. When all the files have been placed in their correct directories, the dialog box will indicate `Installation Complete`. You also get another dialog box asking whether you want to read the release notes. If you haven't yet read through these, you should take the time to do it.

Attended Operation

Before you can use Backup Exec to put files on tape, you must first create a selection list. You have to choose the disk drives, directories, or files to be backed up. If you're using the Enterprise version, you also can select to back up other computers.

Creating a Selection List

Creating a selection list is a simple matter of pointing and clicking. You bring up the Backup Exec program by selecting it from the Start menu: Start | Programs | Backup Exec | Backup Exec. Figure 27.7 shows the opening window of the program, with the Backup Selections window shown.

Tip: The following figures show an evaluation copy of the Backup Exec program. Before you invest a lot of money in a good backup program, you should consider evaluating several competing packages first. This chapter discusses just two of the more popular programs available; if you surf the Net, you'll find many vendors that encourage you to download a demonstration copy or documentation for their program. Be a wise shopper and use the Internet to try before you buy!

Figure 27.7.
From the Backup Selections window, you can choose the computers, directories, and/ or files for your selection list.

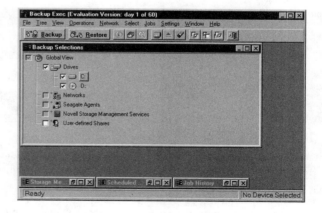

This window shows the drives for the current computer expanded, so that you can select one or all. To select all drives for a particular client computer, you only have to select the Drives check box. Otherwise, double-click the Drives icon (or the word Drives next to it) in the display to show the individual drives on the computer. You can then select individual drives with their corresponding check boxes.

In a manner similar to that for selecting individual drives, you can continue to expand the file hierarchy to show directories and individual files. You can select or deselect them using the same techniques. In other words, if you select a few files in a subdirectory, the subdirectory check box is filled in with a gray check mark. If you deselect this subdirectory check box, all the files you selected in the subdirectory become deselected also.

You can expand the other items in the list, such as Seagate Agents, to see whether there are available other computers (or others running agents) that you can add to your selection list.

Note: When you click a Drives icon in the listing, the program verifies that the drives under this icon are available for backup purposes. If you have a drive (such as a CD-ROM) that's empty, an error message is generated (see Figure 27.8), telling you that the problem drive won't be included in the backup selection.

Figure 27.8.

If a drive is found that can't be backed up (here a floppy drive with no floppy inserted), you get an error message telling you that the drive won't be selected.

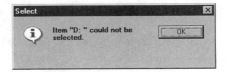

Remember that the listing you see in this window is hierarchical and the check boxes operate in that manner. If you choose to expand a disk drive (see Figure 27.9) and select an assortment of files to back up, a light gray check mark is placed in the drive letter's check box to indicate that some—but not all—of the files on the disk have been selected. If you click this light gray check mark in the drive letter check box to remove it, this will automatically deselect all the files you just selected individually for that drive!

Figure 27.9.
If you choose only some of the files on a disk, the check box for the disk itself receives a light gray check mark.

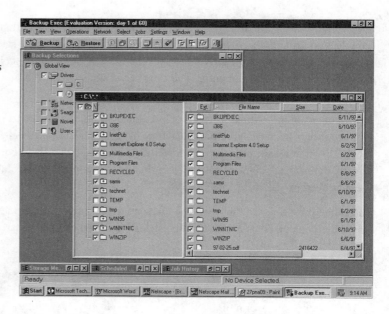

When you're finished selecting the objects you want to include in this selection list, open the Select menu at the top of the window. This menu has several important items:

- **Check.** This command attempts to browse the computer network of computers you have selected and to check the drives associated with them. If you're selecting network clients and don't have permission to access the drive for backup purposes, a dialog box appears, allowing you to enter a new name and password to use for access.

- **Uncheck.** This option performs the same function as the Check option, but removes the check marks from the selected objects.

- **Advanced.** This command brings up a dialog box (shown in Figure 27.10) that you can use to filter the types of files and directories that you want to back up. You can choose by date and other properties.

Figure 27.10.
You can use the Advanced Backup File Selection dialog box to refine your selection of the files you want to put in the backup set.

- **Save Selections.** After you've selected the directories or files you want to include in a backup set, use this option to give the list of files a selection name that you can later use to recall the same selection of files or to create a job that will perform the backup on a periodic basis. Selecting this item brings up the Save Selections dialog box. Here you can choose to use an existing name (in which case, your new selections replace the old ones that were represented by that name) or you can enter a new name. Figure 27.11 shows that I've entered the new name **Computer 2 selection**.

Figure 27.11.
You can give a new name to the selection list you've just created.

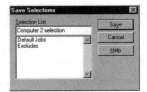

- **Use Selections.** This option allows you to select a previous set of saved selections. If you created a selection by using the Save Selection menu option, the new entry shows up here (see Figure 27.12).

Figure 27.12.
The Use Selections dialog box shows the currently saved selection lists.

- **Delete Selections.** Use this option to delete a selection set you previously saved. You'll get a dialog box similar to the Use Selections dialog box, but you'll be able to use it to delete individual selections.
- **Edit Selections.** From this option, you get the Edit Selection List dialog box, which is a little more functional than the other dialog boxes presented by this menu system. Figure 27.13 shows the dialog box with **Computer 2 selection** in the drop-down list. In the Selection Rules section, you can see the directories and files selected for backup. Use the buttons on the right to edit, delete, or insert a new line. Select the entry you want to edit in the Selections Rules box and click one of the editing buttons.

Figure 27.13.
The Edit Selection List dialog box allows you to modify a selection list created previously.

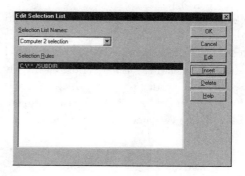

Scheduling Automated Backups

Backup Exec uses the concept of a job for scheduling purposes. You must first create the job, telling it the selection list to process, and then schedule when the job will run.

Creating Jobs

The first step in creating a job is to create a selection list of files that the job will process, as covered earlier. To create a job, choose Jobs | Setup. You'll notice that the Setup menu includes three other selections of predefined jobs you can also use. You can even edit these predefined jobs if you want to change their properties.

After you select the Setup option, Backup Exec posts the Jobs - Setup dialog box shown in Figure 27.14. Here you can select a job (from the defaults shown in this figure) or use the Create button to create a new job.

Figure 27.14.
You can choose to edit an existing job or use the Create button to create a new backup job.

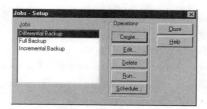

The Create a New Job dialog box (see Figure 27.15) allows you to give the job a name (which will then appear in the other job dialog boxes), select the type of operation, and list the backup selections you've previously created.

Figure 27.15.

The Create a New Job dialog box allows you to associate a name with a selection list you created to make a new job.

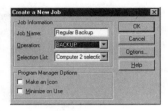

To create a new job, follow these steps:

1. Fill in a unique name that describes the job in the Job Name box.

2. Use the Operation drop-down list to select one of the following operations that the Backup Exec program can perform:

   - BACKUP
   - ARCHIVE
   - RESTORE
   - VERIFY
   - CATALOG
   - RETENSION
   - FORMAT
   - ERASE
   - EJECT

3. You previously created a selection list of files to be backed up. Use the Selection List option to find the name of your list and select it.

4. If you choose, use the Make an Icon check box if you want a desktop icon for this backup job, and use the Minimize on Use check box if you don't want to see the backup in progress while it's working.

5. Click OK and your new job is finished.

You'll notice in the Jobs dialog box that you have a button labeled Run. You can use this button to run the job at this time, or use the Schedule button to set up a schedule for when you want this particular job to be executed. Figure 27.16 shows the Schedule a Job dialog box, in which you click the Add button to add a time for the job to run (see Figure 27.17).

Figure 27.16.
The Schedule a Job dialog box allows you to add new times for the particular job to run and shows all currently scheduled times at which the job is set up to run.

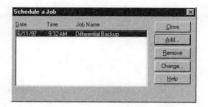

Figure 27.17.
You can select the job and then use a combination of selections to decide when you want it to run.

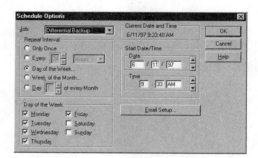

In the Schedule Options dialog box, notice that you don't have to schedule a job to run at the same time every day. You can specify days of the week, start date and time, week of the month, and so on. This flexible scheduling allows you to create complex jobs for departments in your company that need special backups other than the regular nightly backups.

Another handy feature of the Schedule Options dialog box is that you can configure an e-mail account to which notification can be sent when a job completes, along with other requested log file information. Click the Email Setup button to get to the Email Confirmation Setup dialog box (see Figure 27.18).

Figure 27.18.
You can set up e-mail notification for jobs by using this dialog box.

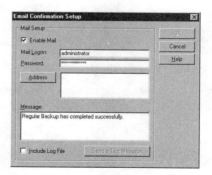

In this dialog box, you must enter a valid username and password for a mailbox on the local server. You can use the Message text box to provide explanatory text about the type of backup, to remind you when you get the message. Finally, you can use the Include Log File check box to have a copy of the backup's log file e-mailed along with the message, so that the user can review the log without having to try to find it.

You can restore files as simply as you back them up. Use the Restore button or choose Operations | Restore in the main Backup Exec window. Instead of selecting files to back up, you can select files from a catalog of the tape that you want to restore.

Cheyenne's ARCserve for NT

Another excellent product on the market you can use for backing up your data is Cheyenne's ARCserve for NT. This program is similar to the Backup Exec program in that it allows you to select files or objects from a directory tree and you can schedule jobs to run unattended.

Install Briefing

Installing ARCserve for Windows NT is a simple process. The setup program first prompts you to specify the type of installation—full or custom (see Figure 27.19). You can also use this dialog box to uninstall the product, if that ever becomes necessary.

Figure 27.19.
You can choose to install the full product or use the Custom Setup button to select only the components you want to install.

Notice the comment in the Setup dialog box about open files. If you're installing a new product, you should always close all other programs to be sure that nothing will conflict with the installation process. Of course, if it does conflict, you can always reinstall. But why not use precaution as the first step and further ensure a successful installation?

If you click the Custom button in the Setup dialog box, you'll be prompted for the components to install (see Figure 27.20). You might choose this option, for example, if you already installed the full product set on a central server and just need to install the backup program or the server administration program on another computer.

Figure 27.20.
You can choose among the different components to install if you use the Custom button from the Setup main dialog box.

The next dialog box is the Software License Agreement dialog box. Be sure to read the terms carefully. Although many users take licensing issues nonchalantly, this can be a costly issue for a large business. And there's always the ethical issue: Someone wrote the program and deserves to be paid, just like you do at your job!

The next dialog box asks you to enter your name and, optionally, a company name. After you click the Continue button, you'll get a confirmation dialog box. Click OK or use the Back button if you need to make corrections.

Next you'll have to supply a directory path to which you want the program files installed. By default, the Setup dialog box lists the directory for the components you chose to install (see Figure 27.21). You can use the Directory button to change to a different path. Figure 27.22 shows the dialog box you use to change the installation directory. Here you can select the disk drive and then enter any directory path you want. The total disk space available is displayed to help you in making your decision.

Figure 27.21.
You can choose the default location for installation of the program files or use the Directory buttons to change to a different path.

Figure 27.22.
When you click the Directory button, this dialog box appears so that you can change the installation path.

If the directory you specified doesn't exist, you'll be prompted before the Setup program will create them. Click OK for this dialog box. Finally, the Setup program will begin copying files from the source disk to the path you supplied. After the copying is complete, you'll be prompted to enter the username and password for an account to be used as the ARCserve system account (see Figure 27.23).

Figure 27.23.
Enter the account username and password to be used for the ARCserve system account.

The last two dialog boxes are simple ones. The first (shown in Figure 27.24) asks whether you want to have the ARCserve services started automatically when the system boots. If you're installing ARCserve on a server that will be used primarily to perform regular backups, you should most likely select this feature. If you're using a computer that has limited memory and will be used only to back up its own disks, you might want to start the services manually when needed. Indeed, when you start the ARCserve Manager program, the necessary services will be started for you. The last dialog box is the Setup Complete dialog box, which you can use to exit the Setup program.

Figure 27.24.
You can choose to have the ARCserve services started automatically when the system is booted.

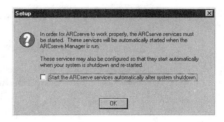

Attended Operation

After installation, there will be a program group in the Start | Programs menu called ARCserve for Windows NT. Under this option, you'll find entries for the help file, release notes, and the setup program. You'll also find an entry for the ARCserve Manager, which is the program that you can use to perform actual backups. Figure 27.25 shows the Quick Access dialog box that pops up when you first start the manager program.

To perform a backup operation, click the Backup button. The Backup Window appears and shows a directory of the objects that you can back up. There are three tabs: Source, Destination, and Schedule. The Source page is shown in Figure 27.26, with several objects expanded.

Figure 27.25.
The Quick Access dialog box allows you to perform the major functions of the ARCserve Manager program.

Figure 27.26.
You can back up the local computer, other computers on the network, and even the Registry files from the Backup window.

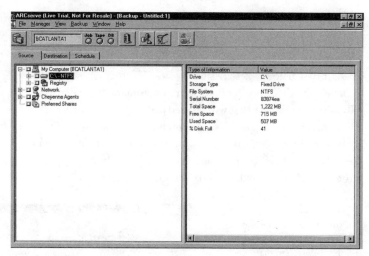

Each object has a check box associated with it. Select the check box to select all the child objects associated with the object (directories, files) or, as with the Backup Exec program, you can expand a branch to select individual objects. Clearing a check box also automatically clears the check boxes beneath it in the hierarchy.

Notice also in this window that the right-hand pane gives information about the object you select. In Figure 27.26, an NTFS-formatted drive is selected. In the right-hand pane, you can see details about the selected drive. If you select a directory or a file, you can see the dates and other file attributes associated with the object. If you select the local computer (at the top of the hierarchy), you can see information such as the CPU type and the amount of total and free memory.

After you select the files you want to back up, you can use the Destination page to select the tape drive. On most PCs, you have only one tape drive from which to choose; however, the program provides for the capability of using more.

To perform the backup immediately, you can either choose Backup | Run | Schedule from the menu or click the traffic-light icon.

Scheduling Automated Backups

You can use the Schedule page to set the backup job to run immediately or according to a schedule you specify. You can choose to create a custom schedule, where you have a variety of options for scheduling the dates and times that backups will be performed. You can also use a rotation scheme on this page to use a rotation schedule such as the *grandfather-father-son* (GFS) scheme that's practically a standard in the business world.

Using the GFS Backup Rotation Scheme

The GFS method involves keeping a set of tapes for daily, weekly, and monthly backups. Usually a full backup is performed once a week, and for the remainder of the week incremental backups are performed. This way, if you need to restore a few files, you only need to use the most recent incremental tape on which they were stored. Of course, if the files hadn't been modified, you would go back to the full backup tape to restore them. This method is described in detail in Chapter 28.

To perform a full restore of a disk, you would have to first restore the full backup tape set and then, in order, the incremental save sets. The disadvantage of this method is that performing a full restore can take longer than if you performed a full backup each night and had to use only one tape for the restore. However, using the GFS method has the advantage of reducing the number of tapes you need and reducing significantly the amount of time needed for a nightly backup.

You also create a monthly full backup under the GFS method. This backup is usually scheduled according to business functions. For example, rather than simply choosing the last day of the month to perform the monthly backup, you might want to do it on the fifth of each month instead, after your accounting department has closed out the previous month's books. This way, you would have a complete end-of-month snapshot of your accounting data (or other data that's regularly condensed) to which you could easily return, should a quick report be needed.

How long should you keep the tapes? That depends on your needs. Usually you can recycle the daily incremental tapes after six days. This is because on the seventh day you perform the full backup and have a complete image of the disk on tape. The same goes with the weekly backups: You can recycle them after the monthly backup has been performed. It's highly recommended that you keep the monthly backup tapes for at least a year. You might want to keep them longer if they contain valuable historical data. For example, some government contracts require long-term storage of accounting information.

Figure 27.27 shows the Schedule page with the Repeat Method drop-down list expanded. You can schedule a backup to occur at any of the following times:

- Once—At the start time and date you specify.

- Every—If you select this option, another set of drop-down lists appears, where you can select the number of minutes, hours, days, weeks, or months for the schedule.

- Day(s) of Week—Similar to the Every menu selection, this selection brings up check boxes for each day of the week, from which you can select.

- Week(s) of Month—This option gives you the option of choosing the first, second, third, fourth, or last week of the month, and also the day of the week on which you want the backup to occur.

- Day of Month—Here you can select numerically the day of the month on which you want the backup to occur.

- Custom—This selection gives you the ability to create a unique schedule. Figure 27.28 shows the Schedule page with the Custom option selected.

Figure 27.27.
You can customize your backup schedule by using the Schedule page.

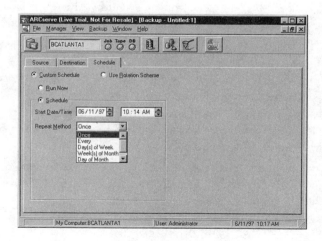

Figure 27.28.
Using the Custom repeat method, you can select the interval and also set days to be excluded from the backup schedule.

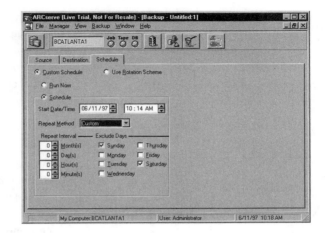

As an alternative to using a custom schedule, you can select the Use Rotation Scheme option on the Schedule page to use a built-in rotation schedule. Figure 27.29 shows the Scheme Name drop-down list expanded to show some of the different schedules you can use.

Figure 27.29.
The Use Rotation Scheme selection on the Schedule page allows you to select from a variety of methods for allocating tapes and performing backups.

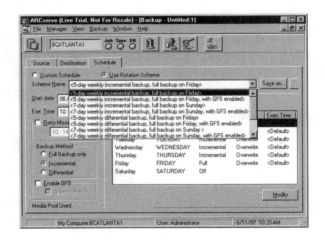

As the figure shows, you can choose from a variety of rotation schedules, depending on your needs. If you perform no work on your computer during the weekend, there's no reason to perform a backup on Saturday or Sunday. Here you can select a schedule that includes or excludes those days. You can specify the day on which you want the full backup performed.

After you select a scheme, you can see in the lower-right section of the window the days on which the backups will be performed and the type of backup. If you want, you can use the Modify button to change any entry in this box. If you decide to make changes, you can then save the new rotation scheme under a name you choose, by using the Save As button. A dialog box will appear in which you can enter the new name. After that, the new schedule will be available for selecting from the Scheme Name menu. Likewise, you can use the Remove button to remove a scheme from the list.

Summary

Performing regular backups of your computers is the most efficient method to ensure quick recoverability in case of a major or minor disaster. This chapter covered the built-in backup program that comes with Windows NT and how to use it via either the command line or the GUI interface. Seagate's Backup application and Cheyenne's ARCserve programs were also covered to show that, depending on your needs, you may need more functionality than what you get with NT Backup. The NT Scheduler service can be used to schedule batch files that contain backup commands if you want to use NT Backup for unattended backups. The two third-party applications include the scheduling function as part of their program.

Even if you have a total hardware failure, you can always restore your data and system information to a different computer and continue to work. Because performing a backup is usually a daily chore, some people can eventually take it for granted. If this happens to you, just remember that the one time you forget to make a backup just might be the time a disaster strikes. It takes so little time to set up a backup procedure, using NT Backup or one of the third-party products discussed in this chapter.

Now that you have a firm grasp on how to prepare for a disaster, it's time to stroll into the next chapter and learn what to do when (not if) a disaster occurs.

28

Recovering from a Disaster

Peter Norton™

Chapter 27, "Server Backup," discusses the importance of making regular backups of your computer's disk drives. In the event of catastrophic hardware failure, you can recover quickly by simply restoring your backup sets to a new Windows NT computer, and by making sure that you have a good backup of the Registry files. In the case of accidental deletion of data files or important system files, recovery may consist of simply restoring the missing files. If you're stuck with a system that won't boot because the initial boot and loader program files are corrupted, you can use a floppy disk to perform the minimal startup.

This chapter emphasizes proactive policies and procedures that you can use to minimize loss due to hardware or software failure. (In other words, be prepared!) Different types of backup schemes are explored along with hardware and software data-mirroring techniques.

This chapter covers the following topics:

- Developing a workable disaster plan
- Data recovery
- How to create a startup floppy disk
- Hardware fail over options
- Disaster recovery planning software
- Using the Windows NT Diagnostics utility

Have a Plan, Work the Plan

When performing everyday tasks of a repetitive nature, most users eventually get to the point where having to read directions when performing actions on the computer is no longer necessary. However, when something goes wrong and quick decisions need to be made, you'll find it extremely helpful to have a plan laid out in advance to handle the situation.

Of course, you can't just sit down and write plans for every situation that can come up. It's not easy to predict the future. But you can design plans for specific situations that are most likely to happen. For example, every business should be prepared for a total restoration of the computing system and the user data, should a major catastrophe strike. If your office burns down tomorrow night, do you have a plan in place to quickly relocate to a new location, set up new hardware, and then restore the data?

Users sometimes delete files unintentionally. Sometimes they do it on purpose. Either way, do you have a plan to regularly back up your files often enough that you can restore a file if it's missing?

A good idea in any computer network environment is to keep a log book of problems that you encounter. You can later refer to this diary to update your procedures and policies. Another good idea is to document the hardware and software components for each computer in the network. Over a period of years, as you replace computers, you are likely to end up with different configurations—even different brands of hardware. Keeping a detailed document for each computer that lists the hardware components (and related data, such as device interrupts, type of CPU, and so on) can also be helpful in recovering from a problem.

Looking Ahead: Check out Chapter 29, "Systems Management Server (SMS)," for an enterprise software solution to inventory.

Consider having a procedures manual that documents everything from ordinary simple procedures (such as adding users to the system or restoring files from backup tapes) to detailed plans for every situation you can imagine that would prevent your users from accessing the network, the computer, or their own data.

Checklists are a good idea to use for emergency plans. As the user performs each step in the procedure, he or she could sign the checklist. Using this technique forces you to slow down and think about each step before continuing. In an emergency, careful thought is extremely important!

Assigning Responsibilities and Staff

One person simply can't do it all in today's computer environment. There are so many different types of hardware, software, programming languages, and so on that unless you're running only a simple application (such as word processing), you'll probably find it advantageous to assign specific responsibilities to selected persons.

For example, performing daily backups (if you haven't already automated the procedure) is a simple procedure that you can train almost anyone to do. Restoring files is another matter. When you restore files, you must be sure to use the correct syntax (if using a command-line-based backup program) or make the right selections (if using a GUI application). Restoring a directory is very different from restoring a single file. Restoring an entire disk is very different from restoring a single directory.

Because many good backup plans involve using full and incremental backup procedures, another thing that the user who performs a restore must possess is knowledge of what's on the daily and weekly tapes. If you don't know where the correct version of the file is located, you won't be able to find it and restore it.

For this reason, you might want to have a user in your organization who is the contact person for restoring files. By having one person perform the function (and keep records of backup/restore activities), you greatly reduce the possibility of making a mistake. Also, with one person assigned this task, he or she will gain experience over time and become better at the job, again reducing your exposure to problematic situations.

A good system administrator doesn't try to do it all. You have to delegate tasks. If you have programmers, you might want to consider having team leaders to head programming projects. In a very large organization, consider having a computer or network SWAT team especially trained in disaster recovery for all nodes in the network. This could be something as simple as a well-qualified help desk that could prompt users to perform the corrective actions, or it could be individuals who "fly to the rescue" when problems arise.

If you use written plans and procedures for all the tasks that are performed on your computer or network, you'll also protect yourself from the "brain drain" syndrome. You have a good user who works for a few years and learns a lot. When that user is offered a large raise to go to another company, how do you replace him? You hire another employee and use the written plans and procedures to bring him or her up to speed.

Delegate tasks. Keep written job descriptions, procedures, policies and disaster recovery plans. Every hour you spend on anticipating the worst and having a plan for it will probably reduce your time of recovery by a much larger amount of time.

Physical Considerations

In addition to protecting your data and providing for detailed recovery procedures, you should also pay close attention to the physical aspects of your computers. If you have file servers that contain sensitive information, or that are critical to your operations, you should really give some thought as to where you place them. A locked computer room has been the traditional method used in the mainframe and minicomputer market. If you have a group of mission-critical servers replacing older, larger machines, think about keeping the computer room intact. It cost a heck of a lot to build in the first place and it can now function to store servers, hardware not in use, documentation, and other important physical pieces of your network.

> **Tip:** One often overlooked aspect of the locked-room approach is the ceiling. It does no good to lock the door if anyone can climb over the wall through the ceiling.

Documentation

In many cases, the documentation you use for computer applications now comes on the distribution media, usually CD-ROMs. However, you should consider having a safe place to keep at least one copy of documentation for each product you use. If you lease computers, you should check your lease to see whether you're required to return the printed documentation and distribution disks when the computers go off lease.

Again, if you use a locked-room approach, you can store not just servers that are currently functioning on the network, but also documentation and source CDs. How many times have you had to go looking for that one book that you need, and can't find a copy? Whose desk is it on? Or did a user take it home and forget to bring it back? You should plan to store at least one copy of all documentation in a safe place. For disaster recovery purposes, it may be necessary in case of a severe problem. If you can't get your programs restored from magnetic tape (and, incidentally, restore the correct configuration options to the Registry), you'll have to resort to using the original documentation and source disks.

Off-Site Materials Storage

Planning for the worst should include off-site storage of everything you can think of that would be required to restore the system. Sending weekly backups off site, for example, is an often-used method for minimizing the amount of data lost during a bad hardware failure (or a fire, flood, or other natural disaster). There are even companies that will provide this service for you. Couriers will pick up and deliver your backup media to you on a scheduled basis.

> **Tip:** If you can't convince management that off-site storage isn't just a good idea, but a necessary one, you might resort to the cheapest method of off-site storage: Take the tapes home with you and store them under your bed! Although not a perfect solution (and some businesses may not want their data stored in this manner), it's at least a last-ditch effort that may pay off when problems arise.
>
> A locked waterproof fire safe is also a good idea. A good one will stand up to most things except robbery.

Do You Have a Hot Site?

Once again, in planning for a really bad disaster, you should consider what would happen if your business premises were rendered unusable. Can you quickly find another location, locate the required new hardware, and restore your system to at least minimal functionality?

A *hot site* is nothing more than a location prepared *in advance* to be activated in case of a major disaster. There are vendors who will provide this service to you for a monthly charge (sort of like insurance—you pay and pay and when you finally need it, it was worth all the money).

If your business is sufficiently large, you could set up a functional computer system at more than one office location, plan for extra capacity, and effectively provide yourself with a cheap version of a hot site. Because Windows NT allows items such as the security database and the WINS database to be replicated throughout the organization, you could take advantage of these features to keep your network running at other sites should one fail. By providing for extra capacity (computers, desk space, and so on) at each site, you effectively have several hot sites that can serve each other in a disaster.

You can also use this multiple-location technique for off-site storage of backup tapes and documentation. Instead of renting space from a vendor, you can rotate backup tapes and other data to different offices on a regular basis.

Data Recovery

So far, this chapter has emphasized the need to be prepared for a disaster and to formalize policies and procedures so that they can be ready for users when harm comes your way. When you start thinking about recovering data, though, the discussion has to get a little more technical.

Windows NT provides many different solutions for saving and restoring data. If you plan carefully, you can with ease reinstall a system on a new computer when one finally bites the dust. Using the techniques discussed in the following sections, you can provide for recovery of data in almost any situation.

Creating and Using an Emergency Repair Disk (ERD)

When you first install Windows NT on a computer, the installation setup program will prompt you to create an *emergency repair disk* (*ERD*) when the installation is complete. Do it! The ERD is simply a floppy disk that contains important Registry files and system files:

- `Autoexec.nt`   This file is used to initialize the MS-DOS environment.
- `Config.nt`   Another file used in initializing the MS-DOS environment.
- `Default._`   A compressed copy of the `HKEY_USERS\DEFAULT` Registry key.
- `Ntuser.da_`   A compressed version of the file `%SYSTEMROOT%\Profiles\Default user\Ntuser.dat`.
- `Sam._`   A compressed version of the Registry key `HKEY_LOCAL_MACHINE\SAM`. This key stores user security information. A very important file.
- `Security._`   The Registry key `HKEY_LOCAL_MACHINE\SECURITY`, compressed.
- `Setup.log`   A copy of a log file that contains information about files that were installed during the Setup process, along with cyclic redundancy check (CRC) values. The Repair process uses this to confirm whether files are corrupted.

- `Software._`   Another compressed file, containing the Registry key `HKEY_LOCAL_MACHINE\SOFTWARE`.

- `System._`   A compressed file containing the Registry Key `HKEY_LOCAL_MACHINE\SYSTEM`.

Creating and Updating the Emergency Repair Disk

Whenever you make software or hardware configuration changes to the computer, add users to the security database, or install new programs, you should create a new ERD by using the `RDISK.EXE` program. If you didn't create an ERD during the original installation, you should use this program immediately to create an ERD. Make it a rule of thumb in your organization to always have an updated ERD for every computer in the network. You can use the ERD to repair corrupted Registry files and restore the system to usability.

`RDISK.EXE` is used not only to create a floppy disk ERD, but also to update configuration information in the directory `%SYSTEMROOT%\Repair`.

`RDISK.EXE` is a program that you run at the command prompt (or, as some still call it, the DOS window). Choose Start | Programs | MS-DOS Command Prompt; at the command prompt, simply enter **RDISK.EXE**. The Repair Disk Utility dialog box pops up, as shown in Figure 28.1.

Figure 28.1.
The Emergency Repair Utility dialog box allows you to update information in the `\Repair` *directory or to create an emergency repair disk.*

Warning: You cannot use a floppy disk that was formatted using the MS-DOS system `FORMAT /S` command. MS-DOS places the files `IO.SYS` and `MSDOS.SYS` (or `IBMBIO.SYS` and `IBMDOS.SYS` if the PC is manufactured by IBM) on the floppy disk when you format it with the system option. Windows NT uses a different bootstrap program. You must use the `FORMAT` command from the command prompt (while running Windows NT) or by using the Windows NT Explorer to format the disk.

Warning: You can run the RDISK program by double-clicking the file in the Windows NT Explorer. However, the RDISK utility won't update the Default._, Sam._, or Security._ files unless you run it from the command prompt, using the /s qualifier. You can also choose Start | Run and enter the command (RDISK.EXE /s). The important thing to remember is that when you double-click the file in Explorer you don't have the opportunity to supply any command-line qualifiers.

The utility creates the ERD by copying files from the %SYSTEMROOT%\Repair directory to the floppy disk. Notice in Figure 28.1 that there's also a selection called Update Repair Info. Use this any time you make changes to the system, to make sure that the information stored in the \Repair directory is an up-to-date copy of the %SYSTEMROOT%\Config directory.

To create a new ERD, use the Create Repair Disk button.

Warning: It's important to realize that, although this disk is called the emergency repair disk, *it is not a complete solution for restoring a trashed system.* The ERD can do nothing to restore user data files and programs if those files are corrupted. You must use a backup tape to restore those types of files, and then use the ERD to restore the correct configuration for these programs to the appropriate Registry files.

Using the Emergency Repair Disk

To use the ERD, you run the same Setup disks that you used to install Windows NT initially (use the command WINNT32 /O to re-create these three disks if you can't locate the original copies). You'll have to insert the first Setup floppy disk and then the second before a menu will appear. Along with the regular installation options, you'll see a Repair option. After selecting the Repair option, you'll be presented with another menu containing the following choices:

- Inspect Registry files
- Inspect startup environment
- Verify Windows NT system files
- Inspect boot sector

Tip: NT 4.0 allows you to boot from the ATAPI CD-ROM if your system BIOS supports this feature. It's a great workaround and you're not required to keep up with those floppies (which sometimes go bad when you need them).

You can select one or more options (or all options) and then select Continue (Perform Selected Tasks) from the menu.

If you choose the Inspect Registry Files option, the Setup program will give you a list of the Registry files that it's able to restore. You can select to restore one or more of the files. You aren't required to restore them all.

If you selected Inspect Startup Environment, the Setup program will check to see whether the Windows NT system files are the correct versions. If any of the files are corrupted or not present, they'll be copied from the Windows NT source CD. During this inspection, Setup will also create a `Boot.ini` file if it doesn't exist, and will insert into an existing `Boot.ini` file an entry for Windows NT if it's not present. On RISC systems (such as Digital's Alpha system), information necessary for startup is stored in NVRAM (non-volatile RAM) and the Setup program corrects the information stored there.

If you choose the option to verify Windows NT system files, the Setup program will use the CRC information located in the `Setup._` file to determine whether any of the system files are corrupted. The `NTLDR` and `Ntoskrnl` files are also checked. These files are necessary to perform the initial boot process of Windows NT. Files that are found to be corrupted or missing (as compared to the listing in the `Setup._` file) can be replaced as the Setup program notifies you of each file.

If you choose the Inspect Boot Sector selection, the partition boot sector on the system partition is checked to be sure that it references the `NTLDR` program.

After performing the selected functions, Setup will prompt you to enter the third Setup disk. After it has completed copying files needed from this disk, the program will ask you to insert the ERD. When the repair process is finished, you'll be instructed to remove the floppy disk and reboot the computer before the repairs will take effect.

How to Create a Startup Floppy Disk

Creating a bootable floppy disk for an MS-DOS computer is an easy chore. You simply use the `FORMAT/S` command to format the floppy and then copy the necessary system files from the system disk to the floppy disk. Windows NT is a much more complex operating system and as such requires a much larger number of files during the boot process to configure software and load the correct files and drivers into memory.

It would be impossible to put all the files required to completely boot Windows NT on a single floppy disk. However, it's possible to create a disk that might be able to kick-start the boot process. This startup floppy would have to contain enough files to get the boot process started, with the remaining startup initialization coming from files stored on the disk. Obviously, the start disk won't be able to boot the computer in all emergencies. It's used when the computer is unbootable because of corruption of the first few programs that are used in the boot process.

To create a startup disk, first use the FORMAT A: command at the command prompt. The FORMAT command copies the partition boot sector to the floppy disk. After you format the disk, you'll have to copy files from the hard disk to the floppy disk. However, before you can copy most of these files, you must change the attributes assigned to the files. If the files have the System or Hidden attribute set, you won't be able to see them using the DIR command and you won't be able to copy them.

To change the attributes on a file, you can use the ATTRIB command at the command prompt (using the -s and -h command-line qualifiers to remove the attributes), or you can use Explorer. To use Explorer to reset the attributes (by changing the properties associated with a file), follow these steps:

1. Choose View | Options.

2. On the View page, select the Show All Files option.

3. Click the filename that you want to copy.

4. Choose File | Properties to see the Attributes box on the General page (shown in Figure 28.2). Here you can use the check boxes to set or remove an attribute from a file.

Figure 28.2.
The Properties dialog box allows you to change the attributes of a file.

5. For purposes of copying the files to the startup floppy disk, deselect the Read Only, System, and Hidden attributes.

6. Repeat this procedure for each of the files to be copied.

If your hardware is an Intel-based computer, the files to be copied are as follows:

- NTLDR
- Boot.ini
- Ntdetect.com
- Bootsect.dos
- Ntbootdd.sys

The `Ntbootdd.sys` file is required only if you have SCSI drives on your computer. This file is actually just a copy of the device driver used by Windows NT to communicate with the disk. You can copy the file from the root directory (`%SYSTEMROOT%`), or you can copy the driver file from the NT source CD (or a manufacturer's updated copy of the driver) to the floppy disk and then rename it to `Ntbootdd.sys`.

> **Tip:** To determine which file is used as the SCSI driver on your computer, use the Registry Editor (`REGEDT32.EXE`) to view the Registry key that has the following designation: `HKEY_LOCAL_MACHINE\HARDWARE\DeviceMap\Scsi`. However, because it's always possible to erroneously corrupt the Registry by using this editor (a powerful tool) you can always find out the name of the driver file by viewing the properties for the disk device. In the Windows NT Control Panel, select the SCSI Adapters applet and click Properties on the Devices page. Finally, click the Driver tab to view the driver's filename.

If you're using a RISC-based system, the files to copy are different. For these systems, you must first create a directory on the floppy disk that matches the system folder tree. Unless you've changed the default, this would be the `Os\Winnt40` directory. Then, after making sure that the attributes have been cleared (as described earlier), you should copy the following files to the startup disk:

- `Osloader.exe`
- `Hal.dll`
- `*.pal` (if the computer uses the Digital Alpha RISC chip)

You should also create a path in NVRAM that points to the floppy disk, to take care of problems you might encounter if the system partition becomes corrupted. To create a new boot selection on a RISC computer, follow these steps:

1. Restart the computer.
2. When the boot menu appears, select the Supplementary Menu option.
3. Select the Setup the System option from the supplementary menu. The Setup menu will appear.
4. Select Manage Boot Selection.
5. From the Boot Selections menu, select Add a Boot Selection.
6. The program will then prompt you for the information needed to create a selection in the boot menu that points to the floppy disk. Depending on the actual hardware involved (Alpha, MIPS, or PowerPC), the dialog box will be similar, but different.
7. Use the New System Partition selection when prompted for a boot partition.
8. When asked for the location of the system partition, select Floppy Disk. Also, when prompted for the drive number of the floppy disk, enter `0` (zero).

9. You'll be prompted to enter the directory and filename of the `osloader` program. Enter `\os\Winnt40\osloader.exe` for this item.

10. Next, the program will ask you whether the operation system files are on the same partition as the `osloader`. Because you're going to put the `osloader` program on the floppy disk, answer No to this question.

11. Enter the location and type of media for the operating system partition—SCSI hard disk, floppy disk, or CD-ROM. If you select the SCSI option, you'll be prompted to enter the SCSI bus number (usually 0), SCSI ID (can be from 0 to 6, but usually is ID 2), and the partition number.

12. Next you'll be prompted to enter the location of the system root directory (usually `\Winnt40`, unless you chose a different directory name during the initial installation), and a name for this selection. You can put in any name you want, but it would be best to use something indicating that this is a boot option for the startup disk. In an emergency situation, it's much easier to be confident about what you're doing if you can quickly determine which boot selection to take.

13. The last question inquires whether you want to start the debugger when the system is booted using this partition. Answer No to this question.

14. When you finish entering the required information, the Boot Selections menu will reappear. Click the Setup menu; then select Supplementary Menu and finally Save Changes.

To use your RISC system startup floppy disk, start the computer in the normal manner. When the boot menu appears, select the option Boot an Alternate Operating System. Another menu will appear, from which you should select the entry you created for the floppy disk.

Repairing Registry Files Without an Emergency Repair Disk

As noted earlier in this chapter, important Registry files are copied to the ERD. If by some chance you were careless and forgot to maintain an updated copy of the ERD, you can use the Disk Administrator or the Registry Editor to save and restore copies of the `HKEY_LOCAL_MACHINE\SYSTEM` key, and you can use the Registry Editor to save and restore copies of the `HKEY_LOCAL_MACHINE\DISK` key.

To save a copy of the `\SYSTEM` key by using the Disk Administrator, follow these steps:

1. Run the Disk Administrator utility (Start | Programs | Administrative Tools | Disk Administrator).

2. Choose Partition | Configuration | Save.

3. Insert a floppy disk into the floppy drive on which the files will be stored. You'll usually need around 512KB of storage space.

4. Click OK to finish the process.

To use the Registry Editor to save the SYSTEM key, follow these steps:

1. Start the Registry Editor (run REGEDT32.EXE at the command prompt).

2. Use the mouse to locate and click the key HKEY_LOCAL_MACHINE\SYSTEM.

3. Choose Registry | Save Key. Enter the path to the floppy disk and directory, if necessary.

To save a copy of the DISK subkey by using the Registry Editor, follow these steps:

1. Start the Registry Editor (run REGEDT32.EXE at the command prompt).

2. Use the mouse to locate and click the subkey HKEY_LOCAL_MACHINE\SYSTEM\DISK.

3. Choose Registry | Save Key. Enter the path to the floppy disk and directory, if necessary.

Should you ever need to restore these keys, you can do so by following the procedure for using the emergency repair disk (discussed earlier). If you don't have this disk, and have saved the keys using the Registry Editor and/or the Disk Administrator, the restore process is different.

To restore the SYSTEM key by using the Disk Administrator, follow these steps:

1. Run the Disk Administrator utility (Start | Programs | Administrative Tools | Disk Administrator).

2. Choose Partition | Configuration | Restore. A warning dialog box will remind you that you're about to overwrite an existing system file. If you're not sure about what you're doing, STOP!

3. Insert the floppy disk on which you saved the key.

4. Click OK. The information will be copied from the floppy disk to the hard drive and the system will then be rebooted so that the new Registry files can take effect.

To restore the DISK subkey by using the Registry Editor, follow these steps:

1. Start the Registry Editor (run REGEDT32.EXE at the command prompt).

2. Use the mouse to locate and click the key HKEY_LOCAL_MACHINE\SYSTEM\DISK.

3. Choose Registry | Restore. You'll be prompted to enter the path to the backup copy of the key.

4. Click OK.

5. Exit the Registry Editor and reboot the computer.

Note: If you have purchased a copy of the Windows NT Workstation (or Server) 4.0 Resource Kit, you can use the utility `Regback.exe` to save Registry files and the `Regrest.exe` program to restore Registry files.

Backup Operations

Chapter 27 covers the use of the NT Backup utility and two third-party products. No matter which program you decide to use, it's important to remember that backups will do you no good if they don't contain recent versions of the data files. If you simply perform a full backup of the system and data disks on a weekly basis, you must be prepared to accept the loss of a week's worth of data if your system crashes on the last day before the next full backup.

In many cases, it's just as easy to perform a full backup every night. If each computer in your network has a tape drive of sufficient storage capacity, you simply perform a full backup every night and allow the users to be responsible for their own data. However, using a central server to manage backups for many client computers can be beneficial for many reasons. First, you have control over the physical backup media. If a user forgets to put a tape in the drive, there will be no backup. If you have a person assigned to the responsibility of changing backup media on a central server (or several servers, if necessary), you have only one point of failure to contend with. The backup operator could also be assigned the responsibility of checking log files, making sure that files get backed up, and keeping a log of problems.

Network bandwidth can be consumed quickly if you have a lot of client machines backing up their data to a central server. There is a mechanism, however, that you can use to minimize the amount of data that has to be backed up each night. This is the incremental backup. The Windows NT Backup utility provides for five specific types of backups. The most often used types are

- Full backup
- Incremental backup
- Differential backup

The following sections discuss the specifics of each type of backup procedure and the advantages and disadvantages of each type.

Full Backup

This is the slowest but most comprehensive type of backup you can perform. *Every file* on the source disk is copied to tape by the backup program. If you're using the Windows NT Backup program, this type of backup is called a *normal backup*, though on most third-party utilities this is typically called a *full backup*.

> **Warning:** A full backup doesn't necessarily back up every single file on a disk. Most programs don't back up files that are open. For example, if you have a SQL database, you should produce a dump of the database and then back up the dump, not the database files.

Each file on the disk has certain attributes associated with it. There are bits set aside to indicate that a file is read-only or a system file, for example. Another bit, the archive bit, is used to determine when a file has been successfully backed up. When a backup program runs, it resets this bit to indicate that the file has been saved offline. When a user modifies a file, the bit is set to indicate that it has been changed since it was last backed up and therefore is a candidate for selection by the next backup program to run.

Because the normal (full) backup copies all files on the disk to the backup medium, it also clears the archive bit for all files on the source disk.

Incremental Backup

This type of backup looks at the archive bits associated with files and selects to back up only those that have been modified since the last backup. It doesn't matter whether the last backup was a full or an incremental backup. You can combine a full backup done on a regular basis with incremental backups scheduled between full backups to effectively cut down a large amount of tapes needed to store the data. Using an incremental backup with a full backup also cuts down on the time required to back up a system, because it doesn't back up files that haven't been modified.

If you have to restore more than a single file, and use a combination of full and incremental backups, you may have to use more than one tape to perform the restore. You would have to restore first from the full backup and then, in order of their creation, the incremental backups. If you only have to restore a few files, you can simply use the log files (if you decide to use this feature) to locate the most recent copy of the file(s) and do the restore from just the incremental (or full) tape.

Although this method is much faster than using a full backup each night, the restoration process can possibly take much longer than using a full backup. You should decide which is more important to your operations. If you have the time and the storage tapes—and, of course, sufficient network bandwidth—you should use a full backup each night, because this is the simplest and fastest type of backup set from which to restore multiple files or the entire disk.

Like the full backup method, the incremental backup method also clears the archive bit to indicate that a file has been saved offline.

Differential Backup

The differential backup method is similar to the incremental backup method in that it doesn't back up every file on the disk. It backs up only the files that have been modified. However, this type of backup differs from the incremental backup in a very significant way.

Each time you perform a differential backup, all the files that have been modified since the last full backup will be put on tape. For each day that goes by, the backup process will potentially have to put more files on tape—all the files it backed up the night before and those that were changed on the current day.

You might describe this type of backup as a "growing incremental" backup.

The major advantage this method has over the incremental backup method is that, if used in conjunction with a full backup, you only have to use the last full backup tape and the latest differential tape to perform a full restore. This method takes longer each day to perform the differential backup than the incremental backup, but makes complete restoration much faster than using the full and incremental backup types together.

A Time-Tested Backup Plan: Grandfather, Father, Son

As mentioned in Chapter 27, the Grandfather, Father, Son (GFS) method of tape rotation is one of the most popular methods in use today. The name comes from the fact that you're using a family of tapes that's progressively aged and stored to allow you to recover from data disaster over a great span of time. Properly implemented, the GFS plan can allow you to recover data that's years old.

The basic idea is a backup plan that maintains data for each day of the week (five or seven, depending on your need), weekly tapes (usually four), and monthly tapes. If you execute the plan properly, you can recover data from one to seven days old, two to four weeks old, and as many months back as you store monthly tapes. Many companies use this plan to store data for years.

Here's how the plan works, specifically:

- You need five to eight tapes the first month, depending on your scheme, and you only need to replace one tape per month for as long as you want to be able to recover data.
- Daily backups—(Monday through Thursday). The idea behind daily tapes is to allow you to recover data from one to five days old.

    Full backup method: You need a tape for every day of the week, Monday through Thursday (Fridays will be weeklies). Mark each tape with the day of the week (Monday, Tuesday, Wednesday, or Thursday) and on the corresponding day perform a full backup to the tape. Remove the tape from the server site and store it in a safe place while other tapes are being used.

    Incremental or differential backup method: You need one tape that will be marked Daily. Each day, Monday through Thursday, perform your backup to this tape. Remove this tape from the server site on days when the weekly backup is being performed.

- Weekly backups—(Friday). The idea of the weekly backup is to provide you with the ability to recover data from one to four weeks old.

  You need four Friday tapes (Friday-1, Friday-2, Friday-3, and Friday-4). Mark the tapes with the corresponding day and perform a full backup on that day. On the first Friday use Friday-1, on the second Friday use Friday-2, and so on. Remove the tape on Monday and move the tape off-site.

- Monthly backups—(January, February, and so on). The idea of the monthly backup is to allow you to recover data from as many months back as you chose to store. Keep in mind that software corruption can show up months after it occurs. If you're simply restoring one week of data or day-old data, you may not solve your problem.

  You need to mark each month's tape with the month (January, June, and so on). On the last Friday of each month, perform your usual full backup, but use the monthly tape instead of a Friday tape. Some months will require an extra tape and some won't. But always use a separate tape for each new month you plan to store. Using a Friday tape will cause you to overwrite a Friday and thus lose that restore possibility.

If you look carefully at the plan as it's laid out, you'll see that you can now find a tape for the last five days, the last four weeks, and for as many months as you have chosen to keep them. Removing the tape to an off-site location is crucial to disaster recovery because, if a site disaster should occur, you don't want to lose the tape that you depend on for recovery.

You can carry out this method for as many months or years as you like. I've seen plans that span seven years for tax record recovery. But the point is to have the data available. Often the recovery of data has nothing to do with hard drive loss. You may find data corruption, and this will allow you to recover data from a safe time and place.

Choosing to Do a Full Backup

If you have only a few computers to back up each night, and you have the time to perform a full backup, a full backup is perhaps the best route to follow. The GFS method is an excellent solution for a large network where network bandwidth is at a premium and local tape drives for each computer are not cost-prohibitive.

However, if you have a small number of computers, each with their own tape drive (in order to back up the local Registry), performing a full backup each night is a better solution because it makes restoring files much easier. Also, in the event that you need to perform massive file restores after a disaster, having a local tape drive and only one backup tape set to restore can buy you the time to deal with other problems.

Hardware Fail Over Options

In some business situations, downtime is unacceptable. A disk failure on a major network server can put many users out of work for the hours it takes to replace or restore the disk. For these situations, you should consider using a hardware-based mechanism in order to strive for that 100% up time.

There are two basic types of hardware failures you can provide for:

- Disk drive failure
- Total computer system failure

Windows NT provides for a concept of mirroring information on more than one disk. The *RAID* (*redundant array of inexpensive disks*) strategy comes in several flavors (and they aren't necessarily cheap anymore):

- Windows NT provides for *disk striping*, which consists of storing data in blocks across more than one disk. While throughput is increased using this method (because each disk drive can be reading information at the same time), no provision is made for fault tolerance. This is called *RAID level 0*.
- *Disk mirroring/duplexing* (*RAID level 1*) uses a combination of disk striping and disk mirroring. Microsoft has chosen to implement this feature using only the mirroring part. In disk mirroring, data is written to two separate disks, which are effectively mirror images of each other. Fault tolerance is provided because if one disk fails, the other can be used to continue operations while the reason for the disk failure is diagnosed and fixed.

Warning: To make the most of disk duplexing, you should attach each disk to a separate controller. Otherwise, a single controller failure could render both disks unavailable, thus defeating the purpose of disk duplexing.

To set up your system to use disk mirroring, you need two disks instead of one for each data disk you'll use. To set up a Windows NT computer for disk mirroring, you have to log on as a user with Administrator-level privileges. Establishing a mirrored set of drives is done using the Disk Administrator utility (located in the Administrative Tools folder).

To construct a mirror set, follow these steps:

1. Run the Disk Administrator utility.
2. Click the disk partition you want to mirror.
3. While holding down the Ctrl key, click a partition on another disk that you will use to mirror the first disk partition. Logically, the second partition must be *at least* as large as the first partition. It can actually be larger, but the space will be wasted.

4. Choose Fault Tolerance | Establish Mirror.

5. Click OK when a confirmation dialog box asks if you really want to do this.

6. Exit the Disk Administrator utility (choose Partition | Exit). A dialog box warns you that you have to reboot the computer before the changes will take effect. Click the YES button.

7. One last confirmation dialog box will ask if you really want to update the disk configuration. Click OK. The system will then be restarted automatically. Unlike some utilities in Windows NT, this one doesn't give you the choice of continuing or restarting. The system must be restarted at this time for the changes to take effect.

   After the system reboots, a copying process will begin and the mirrored set will be unavailable until this completes. Instead of each partition having its own drive letter, the two mirrored partitions will now share the same drive letter.

Tip: As discussed earlier in this chapter, you should *always* update your emergency repair disk after a hardware configuration change. After the disk mirroring process has finished copying and the drive is available, you should update your ERD. The original ERD will not suffice to reconstruct the data on the mirrored partitions.

You can also use the Disk Administrator utility to extend the disk striping method to include fault tolerance (*RAID level 5*), called *parity disk striping* in Windows NT. In this implementation, the data is still stored across an array of disks (a minimum of three disks) and additionally a parity byte is calculated and stored along with data and used to reconstruct corrupted blocks, using the parity stripe and a logical XOR operation.

Note: You can't use parity disk striping for the system disk or the boot disk.

To construct a striped set with parity, you use the Disk Administrator. Follow these steps:

1. Select a section of *free space* on the first disk by holding down the Ctrl key and clicking the space.

2. While holding down the Ctrl key, click free space on two other drives. Remember that you have to have at least three disk drives to implement parity disk striping.

3. Choose Fault Tolerance | Create Stripe Set with Parity.

4. The Disk Administrator program will display the minimum and maximum size that you can make the stripe set. Because the data is not mirrored, but merely written to more than one disk, and because the parity stripe must also be written, you can effectively have less space to store data (space is taken up by the parity stripe). Select a size that suits your needs. The Disk Administrator will then create equal-sized unformatted partitions on the three disks.

5. Exit the Disk Administrator. Answer Yes when prompted to save the configuration data. You'll also be prompted to reboot the computer before the changes take effect.

After you reboot, you have a stripe set with unformatted space. You should use the Disk Administrator to format the partitions you have just created:

1. Click any partition that's part of the stripe set. All the remaining partitions will also be selected automatically.

2. Choose Tools | Format. Select the type of disk format (NTFS or FAT) and format the disk.

After you exit the Disk Administrator, the stripe set will be available for use. You don't have to reboot the computer again.

Although Windows NT provides fault tolerance mechanisms that you can use to protect your data, you might find that these software implementations don't provide the level of safety you need. You can find on the market today a variety of products that allow you to do disk duplexing and disk striping, using hardware controllers that are independent of and generally invisible to the operating system. Since the hardware actually controls what the operating system sees, hardware solutions can enable you to boot from a striped or duplexed disk set almost any time. If you use the NT software solutions, the striping and duplexing software *are not present at boot time*.

Another advantage you gain by implementing hardware fail over techniques for your disks is that the work involved in writing to the set of disks is done by the controller. The computer's CPU is not taxed by the additional work; thus, users won't suffer from performance degradation.

Online Recovery Server

Although the RAID solutions just discussed can help you to recover from disk failures, they can't help you recover from a crashed computer. The concept of *clustering computers* (pioneered by Digital) can be defined as a collection of individual computers that work together to act like a single system. Client computers can access data stored on disks that are available to all members of the cluster. This type of technology helps prevent a single computer crash from causing downtime. If a computer that's a member of a cluster crashes, the user can simply log on again (to another member of the cluster) and continue working.

A combination of clustering and disk mirroring can provide a very secure environment for maintaining your system's integrity and availability. In addition to providing high availability, the clustering concept also embraces scalability. Scalability implies the ability to add more computers to the cluster as your capacity needs increase.

The Wolfpack clustering software currently under development by Microsoft and other vendors will provide these features and more, as clustering technology for Windows NT becomes more popular. At this time, however, there are third-party vendors who can provide some of the capabilities of clustering technology for a modest price.

One of the early entrants into this field is Octopus Technologies, Inc. Its Octopus software provides for mirroring disks on one computer to another standby computer. The computers can be separated by a LAN or WAN and still provide these capabilities. In addition, you can configure the product to perform an automatic fail over in case the main server goes down.

Using Octopus fail over technology has another advantage that's very useful. If configured properly, the backup computer can change its computer name to that of the failed computer. It will then stop and restart its services, and clients that were connected to the failed server can be reconnected automatically.

For details, visit the Octopus Technologies, Inc. Web page and request the demonstration CD. The address is `http:\\www.octopustech.com`.

If you're using Windows NT as an Internet server for the World Wide Web, Octopus can give you a very high availability advantage from both its ability to mirror data to different computer systems (as opposed to different disks on the same system) and to literally take over the identity of a failed server.

Hardware-Controlled RAID

Windows NT can implement RAID solutions in software. Earlier, this chapter covered using the Disk Administrator to create stripe sets with parity and to establish mirrored disks. Using this type of RAID implementation requires that the operating system calculate the parity stripe values.

If you want to implement RAID solutions in your system and relieve the CPU of the extra processing, you can use a hardware-based solution. In a hardware-based RAID implementation, the operating system writes the file to the controller, which performs the job of calculating the parity stripe values and writing the files to disks. This is transparent to the operating system.

Another advantage that hardware RAID implementations have over software versions is the ability to use RAID on the system or boot disk. Because the controllers provide the RAID capability, the operating system can boot even if a mirrored disk fails. The controller simply hides this fact and delivers the data to the CPU so that it can boot. When you use a software implementation, the computer must first boot the operating system and then start the RAID software. This is the reason you can't perform software RAID on the boot or system disk under Windows NT.

Disaster Recovery Planning Software

Planning strategies for recovering from disasters is becoming more important every day to modern business. In some writings, you even see it called *business contingency planning*. The importance of disaster recovery planning has led to the development of software applications to assist you in the process.

Using a software package to assist you in planning for disaster recovery for your business can be a good investment. You don't have to "reinvent the wheel," so to speak. Software applications will help you assess the risks to which your network is exposed and come up with solutions to correct the problem.

You can use any good search engine on the Internet to locate a number of diverse companies that offer software for this type of service.

Using the Windows NT Diagnostics Utility

The Windows NT Diagnostics utility is located in the Administrative Tools menu. With this program, you can examine or print information about the computer's hardware components, services, and device drivers. Printed copies of the output of this utility can be a lifesaver if you're trying to resolve device conflicts and other system problems. Figure 28.3 shows the Windows NT Diagnostics dialog box with the Version page selected. You can choose from several pages to view different categories of information:

- Version—Operating system version and some hardware information (such as the CPU type).

- System—Information about the CPU as well as the type of HAL (hardware abstraction layer).

- Display—Video display and its associated device driver.

- Drives—Information about all disks recognized by the operating system, including partition information. You can also view information about network shares to which you're connected.

- Memory—Data concerning the actual physical memory details about the pagefile.

- Services—More information about services and devices than you can see using the Control Panel's Services and Devices applet.

- Resources—IRQ and I/O channel information, memory addresses, and DMA channels.

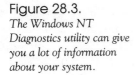

Figure 28.3.
The Windows NT Diagnostics utility can give you a lot of information about your system.

Summary

The best way to survive a disaster is to prepare for it ahead of time. Keeping an updated book of procedures and policies and keeping users trained to perform specific tasks is a way of keeping available the knowledge you'll need when trouble strikes. The failure of a single computer node in a network has the potential of putting many users out of productive work for hours or longer. The need to understand the topology of your network and to try to lessen the chances of having single points of failure is becoming more important as computers and networks become more complex.

Some of the important topics that were covered in this chapter include keeping good backups of your system and Registry files. You also must be prepared (with a plan) to cope with a disaster, should you be so unfortunate as to have one. By keeping written procedures and by training employees to do specific, well-defined jobs, you can make your computer network secure from not only catastrophic failures, but also loss of employees (brain drain). Written procedures allow another person to step in during an emergency, when the employee who would normally do the job is not present (such as at night).

Protecting your data doesn't necessarily mean just keeping good backup copies. Downtime costs money also. By implementing hardware or software disk fail-safe mechanisms, you can shield your users from a lot of downtime that can result from disk failures. You can buy yourself the time needed to repair problems later, while keeping your users online and working.

Lastly, one very important point that was made in this chapter—and needs to be made over and over—is that you should *always* have an updated version of the Emergency Repair Disk and the NT Setup disks to prepare for total system failure. With a good backup set, you can move your system to new hardware should the failure be that bad.

Devise a reasonable schedule for backups that takes into account what you can and can't live without. If you have needs of absolute 100% up time, you can use mirroring and clustering techniques to try to achieve this goal. If you keep copies of important Registry files stored in a safe place, you can reduce the time it takes to recover a computer after a major failure.

Be prepared. Plan ahead.

29

Systems
Management
Server
(SMS)

Peter Norton ™

One of the greatest challenges facing support professionals today is the basics: How many Pentiums do we have? How much RAM do the Pentiums have? Who has Office 97 loaded and who still has Office 95? Who's running a beta copy of Netscape and who's using Internet Explorer? What version of Explorer are they using? Do we have as many licenses for Doom as our network analysts are using? If we were audited today, what would they find? How can we improve support, but not increase the support resources? Just what did we buy last year?

These are the question that *Systems Management Server* (SMS) is very good at answering. SMS is a front-end package to populate a Microsoft SQL database affectionately known as *SMSDB*. The database contains almost every hardware and software thing you could want to know about a machine, from the IP address to the IRQ usage. The SMS client (the piece that does the work) gathers the information from the PC when you log on to the network, and stores it where the SMS services can act on it. You control how often the hardware and software inventories are taken, how often you run a software audit, or even what package is to be installed.

Note: You use software inventory to check for programs you want to monitor closely. Typically, you set software inventory to perform daily, inventorying only 5–20 packages. Each software package you inventory adds about 1 second to the SMS logon script. If you inventory too many, you'll find that your SMS script runs too long and your users complain.

You use audit packages for the once-a-month or once-a-quarter check of everything on the machine. At last count, SMS would recognize about 7,500 packages by name and audit them. An audit takes from two to five minutes to run, depending on the hard drive size and the speed of the machine.

What SMS is, in a nutshell:

- Hardware and software inventory
- Remote control and diagnostics
- Software distribution with server-load balancing
- Applications sharing with load balancing
- Scalability to support any size organization
- One-tool overview of your organization's machines

What SMS is not, in a nutshell:

- Instant gratification (most requests must wait for a logon)
- Software automation (just because you can distribute, that doesn't mean you can automate)

- The very best of all possible tools (for example, there are faster remote-access packages)
- The tool to allow *one* engineer to replace the five you have busting their chops on the help desk

One thing to understand about the SMS world is that it takes time. With our "I want it NOW!" mentality, it's not uncommon to tell the manager on Friday that you've just installed SMS, and have her ask for either a complete listing of all hardware and software in the company or for a new software package to be installed—by Monday. While SMS can do both, it takes time for all the machines to be inventoried, or to tweak a package so it can be distributed automatically to the users. You must do your research and testing before you unleash SMS on your world.

This chapter discusses the following topics:

- Installing SQL v6.5 and SMS v1.2
- Setting up SQL Server to back up SMS databases
- Setting up the SMS clients
- Remote diagnostics and remote control
- Creating distribution packages
- The Network Monitor

Pre-Installation Checklist

The following items are essential to running SMS:

- A Windows NT v3.51 or v4.0 server installed as a PDC or BDC
- An administrative logon
- An NTFS partition with at least 1 gigabyte of free disk space
- 64MB RAM—96MB if SQL is on the same box
- A second NTFS drive for SQL database and logs, with at least 250MB free disk space

Tip: For a server, I recommend a minimum of a Pentium 166—with the Pentium Pro 200 preferred and needed if you also run SQL on the same box. You'll also want RAID 5 for fault tolerance and performance, because SMS is *extremely* disk I/O intensive.

While it's possible to put SQL Server on the same drive as SMS, putting the database on a different drive makes a considerable performance difference unless you have a RAID set for both.

Preparing the Windows NT Server

> **Warning:** Before you begin installing the server, I recommend that you review the *Concepts and Planning* manual included with the package. I don't normally push the included docs, but once you set up the site, you can only change some items with a reinstall.

Because SQL Server is critical to the operation of SMS, it's important to decide whether you'll be installing SMS and SQL Server on the same machine or on separate machines. If the only reason you have SQL is for SMS, I recommend using the same machine. The actual SQL load of SMS on the server is minimal, so they'll coexist well. However, if you're using SQL for some heavy client/server operations, or you have an existing SQL server with backup schemes and administration already in place, I recommend that you dedicate a machine to SQL and add the SMS database to the dedicated machine.

> **Note:** For this installation, we install SQL on the same box, installing SQL as if it's only going to service SMS. I cover only the basics of what an SMS administrator would need to know to keep up the site.

Creating the Service Account

Because SMS is a server-based process that must access other services on the network, it's important to create a logon account for the services to use. This account must have a password that doesn't expire, and it must be a member of the Domain Admins group. For this reason, I recommend using a password that's as secure as possible. Something like moLpi$7639 would be good because it mixes case and uses alphabetic, numeric, and non-alphanumeric characters together. I wouldn't recommend using this particular one, of course, because 30,000 people have read it now, but a similar one would work. Although the Administrator account meets this requirement, you should change the Administrator password regularly, and you don't want SMS stopping because you changed its logon.

I like to create one service account and use it with all of the services that need network access. From User Manager for Domains, follow these steps:

1. Select New User to set up the service account.
2. Set the Username to **SERVICE**.
3. Set the description to **ACCOUNT USED FOR SERVICES**.
4. Set the password to something cryptic.

5. Deselect the option User Must Change Password at Next Logon.

6. Select the options User Cannot Change Password and Password Never Expires.

7. Put the account in the Administrators and the Domain Admins groups.

8. Click Add.

9. Highlight the SERVICE account and choose Policies | User Rights.

10. Select the Show Advanced Rights option and scroll down to Log On as a Service.

11. Click Add, click Show Users, and select the SERVICE account.

12. Click Add and then click OK.

Note: You also need to set up the SQL logon for SMS. The method used will depend on the type of security you implement with SQL Server. For this example, we use the default logon of SA with a blank password. If you need more information, refer to the security section of the Microsoft SQL Server documentation.

Installing SQL Version 6.5

To install SQL 6.5, you must first log on to the server, using the new service account. Follow these steps:

1. Insert the SQL Server 6.5 CD-ROM.

2. Change to the directory for your processor type (I386, Alpha, and so on).

3. Run SETUP.EXE.

4. Click Continue. Enter your company information and click Continue twice.

5. Select the option Install SQL Server and then click Continue.

6. Select your licensing mode and click Continue.

Note: You need only one SQL client license for SMS because SMS will technically own all the database connections; as such, your SMS client license covers the SQL usage. I would recommend purchasing a few licenses for your developers and report generators, however, because legally you need a license to connect directly to the SQL database and pull your reports.

7. Specify where you want the database files and click Continue. The default size for the MASTER device should be 25MB. SMS doesn't store its data in the MASTER database, so you don't need to increase the size (see Figure 29.1).

Note: In SQL terminology, the *device* is the file that holds *databases*. You set aside space in the device and later populate the device with databases and log files.

Figure 29.1.
Creating the MASTER device.

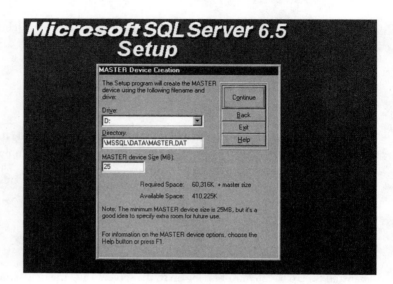

8. Decide where you want the SQL books and click Continue.

Note: Select both of the Auto-Start boxes for SQL Server and SQL Executive. If you don't select Auto-Start for the services, SQL Server won't be running after you reboot, and you can't do anything in SMS without SQL Server running. ;-)

9. Enter the logon information for your service account and click Continue.

10. Get some coffee while the installer copies the files and sets up the initial configuration—it will take about 15 minutes on a fast machine!

11. When the installation is finished, click the Exit to NT button.

12. You need to start the SQL server before you can install SMS. To start the services, click the SQL Service Manager. Start the MSSQLServer and the SQLExecutive services.

At this point, SQL Server is installed and configured with the basics you'll need for SMS. After you install SMS, you'll set up SQL backups for your SMS database.

Installing SMS Version 1.2

To install SMS Version 1.2, follow these steps:

1. Insert the SMS 1.2 CD-ROM. If you're running Windows NT v4.0, the Install screen will appear; if you're running NT v3.51, use the command File | Run | x:\SETUP.EXE (replace x with the drive letter of your CD-ROM drive).

2. Select the Install SMS 1.2 icon. Continue through the initial screens until you reach the Installation Options dialog box (see Figure 29.2).

Figure 29.2.
The SMS 1.2 Installation Options dialog box.

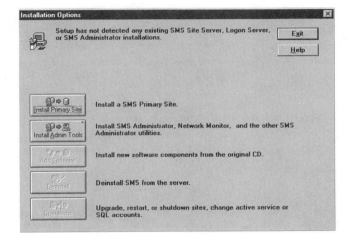

3. Because you're installing your primary site, click the top button, Install Primary Site. (If you wanted to install only the administrator tools on your NT workstation or another server, you would choose the second button.)

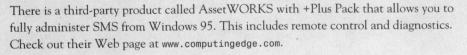

Peter's Principle: Try AssetWORKS for Win95

There is a third-party product called AssetWORKS with +Plus Pack that allows you to fully administer SMS from Windows 95. This includes remote control and diagnostics. Check out their Web page at www.computingedge.com.

4. Agree to the licensing and click Continue on the next screen.

5. Verify the path to your NTFS partition and select Continue.

6. The next screen that appears is the Setup Install Options dialog box, which should have the correct default options. If you need to add anything, click the Custom button to display the Software Installation Options dialog box shown in Figure 29.3.

Figure 29.3.
Changing the client options.

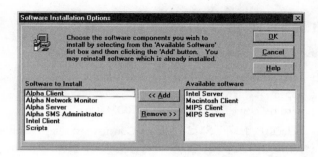

Note: This is also where you would add support for the Macintosh clients. SMS only supports inventory and package distribution on the Macintosh. If you need to add Macintosh support, refer to the SMS installation manual, as you'll need to set up additional items within NT Server and SMS.

7. After you have set or verified the options, click Continue. The SQL Server logon screen appears. If you have changed the SA password, type it in. If you haven't, leave the password blank, as this is the default. SMS has already set the database name as well as the database and log devices.

Note: A *device* in SQL Server is a just a file. For example, if you want to create a 20MB database, you must first set up a device that's at least 20MB in size. I recommend creating a second device for the transaction log that's roughly twenty percent of the size of the database. Because SMS is installing on the SQL server, it will create the default 45MB database devices and 15MB log device.

8. When you click Continue, SMS opens a SQL connection and verifies some settings before creating the database for you. Because SMS needs 20 user connections and the default is 15, you'll get an error message. Set the count to 25 in the dialog box that pops up and click Continue.

9. The Primary Site Configuration Information dialog box appears, as shown in Figure 29.4. Fill in the site code, site name, and service account information. Select the Automatically Detect All Logon Servers option.

Figure 29.4.
The Primary Site Configuration Information dialog box.

> **Warning:** If you're in a NetWare environment or you're setting up a test environment, leave the Automatically Detect All Logon Servers box unchecked and proceed as normal. This keeps SMS from grabbing all the Novell servers anywhere on the LAN/WAN and putting them into one big site. It also allows you to test SMS without taking up processor and disk space on logon servers until you're ready for rollout.

10. Click Continue. SMS will set up the site, create your database in SQL Server, and copy the SMS files to the appropriate places. Setup will pause for you to install the Network Monitor agent. The agent allows you to use SMS to monitor the network on a packet-by-packet basis. I recommend canceling this process and installing the agent and application on your administrating workstation, so you aren't loading down the server doing network diagnostics.

11. The last dialog box says that the install is complete. Click OK.

> **Note:** Windows NT Server v4.0 comes with a light version of Network Monitor and a full version of the Agent. Using the light version of Network Monitor on a server will only let you monitor traffic to and from that server, as it won't put the network card into promiscuous mode. If you use the full version of Network Monitor that comes with SMS to connect to the server, you can use the server as a remote monitor, and it will collect every packet on its segment.

Note: If you have a portable with a good network card, Network Monitor can be a very effective network sniffer. You can get a lot of good diagnostics on your LAN with the monitor, even if you can't decode Ethernet packets.

You will notice the SMS installer is still running. You could install the Crystal Reports or view the release before closing, but I like to do those functions from my workstation.

Now that SMS is running, you'll notice services and directories appearing on the logon servers as SMS assimilates your network. Can you say "BORG"?

On a logon server, SMS will take approximately 25MB of space from the drive with the most free space to set up its files. If you also want to use the server for packages, you'll need substantially more space.

Looking Ahead: Later in this chapter, I cover the space needs for packages, while discussing software distribution and load balancing.

Setting Up SMS Database Backups

Daily backups of your SMS data are generally not critical. If you lost a day or even a week of data, SMS would re-create most of it at the next logon. The issue is not wanting to lose a month or all of the inventory data and asset tracking because you just never backed it up.

You can use whatever Windows NT backup solution you want to back up your NT installation, but if you don't set the SQL server to dump a copy of the database into a dump file, you'll never get a good backup. The problem is caused by open files, which you can't back up. There are creative solutions that monitor the open files and then back them up when they close, but they'll never get your SMS database—because it never closes.

Note: I have yet to see an SMS installation that was actually getting a good backup. Many sites use ARCserve or Arcadia, but they don't buy the SQL Server module, which would allow them to back up the databases while they're running. They think they're backing up the data; they only realize the truth after a crash.

To set up SMS database backups, you must configure the SQL Enterprise Manager to manage your SQL server. Follow these steps:

1. Launch the SQL Enterprise Manager by choosing Start | Programs | SQL Enterprise Manager.

2. Type the name of your server in the Register Server box and select Register.

   You can now see your SQL server listed in the SQL Enterprise Manager. The expanded view should look like Figure 29.5.

Figure 29.5.
SQL Enterprise Manager.

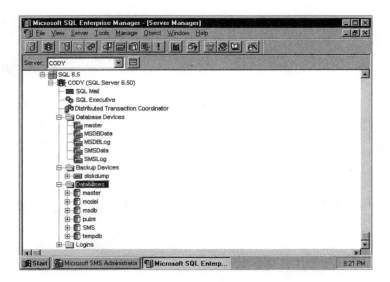

3. We're interested in the backup devices and the databases. Choose Tools | Database Backup and Restore to open the Database Backup/Restore dialog box.

4. In the Database Backup section of the dialog box, select SMS. In the Options section, select the options Initialize Device and No Expiration Date.

5. Click the New button in the Backup Devices section to open the New Backup Device dialog box (see Figure 29.6).

6. Give the device a name (such as SMS) and click Create.

7. Now you need to schedule the backup for a repeating interval. Click Schedule and click OK in the Volume Label dialog box. In the Schedule Backup dialog box (see Figure 29.7), select the Recurring option and click the Change button. Set your backup to occur daily, every 1 day, 1 hour before the rest of the backups, and No End Date.

Figure 29.6.
Creating the backup device.

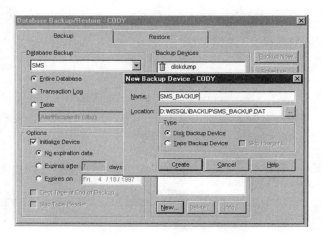

Tip: I set my schedule for once a night, at about an hour before the standard backup runs, so I know the database dump will have occurred and the dump file will be closed so the backup can pick it up.

Figure 29.7.
Scheduling a backup.

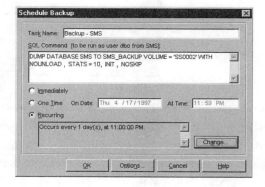

8. Click OK twice and close the Database Backup/Restore dialog box.

If you check under Server | Scheduled Tasks, you'll now see Backup - SMS listed as repeating at the time you requested.

Note: SQL Executive must be running for your scheduled tasks to be completed. If you aren't doing anything scheduled, and you aren't using mail notification or any of the other automated tools, you could stop the SQL Executive (SQLEXEC.EXE) to save about 4MB of memory.

This would be a good time to change the SA password to something else. If you expand the Logins section in the SQL Enterprise Manager and double-click the SA logon, you'll see the password box. After you verify the new password, it's changed in the database. Because SMS relies on the SQL account, you need to run SMS Setup again and click the Operations button in the Installation Options dialog box, and then use the SMS Database icon in the Operations dialog box to put in the new password. SMS will stop the services and restart them, using the new security. Close Setup and you're done.

Administration with SMS

SMS is an extremely versatile package. On the following pages, we can only touch on the administrative functions that are most critical. For a good reference to overall SMS administration, check out the latest edition of *Microsoft BackOffice 2 Administrator's Survival Guide, Second Edition* from Sams Publishing (1996, ISBN 0-672-30977-7).

To begin our SMS session, we must first launch the SMS Administrator (SMS Admin) and log on to the SMS database in SQL Server. Click the SMS Administrator icon to start the SMS Admin tool. You'll see the default logon screen where you log onto SQL Server, as shown in Figure 29.8.

Figure 29.8.
The SMS Administrator Logon screen.

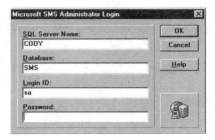

After you log on, you'll get a dialog box asking which windows you want open. I always select Sites, Packages, and Jobs. These are the three windows from which you'll do most of your work.

If you double-click the site name and then the domain, you'll see the machines in the site. Initially, the only machine SMS is aware of is itself. As the logon servers are finished and the cycles run through their paces, you'll see servers pop up under the SMS server, and the SMSID should increment. The SMSID is assigned by SMS to each machine as it shows up in the database. It's a unique entry formed from the three-character site code and a sequential five-digit number.

To see more information on a system broken down in a logical fashion, double-click the computer name (see Figure 29.9). In this example, notice that my SystemRole is listed as server, and my SystemType is listed as an Alpha-based PC. As you select the various icons on the left side of the window, you'll see lots of data on virtually every aspect of your system—from the operating system build number to the network card's hardware address.

Figure 29.9.
Properties of the server.

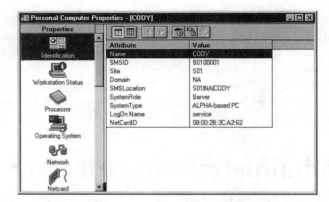

If you scroll to the bottom of the list, you'll notice that all the administrator tools you need for the Windows NT server are listed, including Help Desk (remote diagnostics). This feature allows you to do all your administrative tasks from one tool. This is where the benefits of combining so many functions and tools into one package really shine.

Setting Up the SMS Client

The SMS client installation is the piece that loads the hardware and software inventory pieces as well as the remote diagnostic pieces onto the workstations.

The quickest way to get machines into the database is to run the SMSRUN.BAT file manually from \\SERVER\SMSSHR. This will allow you to get the SMS client installed on your workstation without modifying the logon scripts either manually or automatically via SMS.

If you're using a client other than Windows NT, you need to reboot and run the .BAT file a second time to finish the install. If you're running NT, it will install and start the services automatically.

If you want SMS to automatically add the RUNSMS.BAT file to the logon script of your users, use the site properties. In the SMS Admin tool, highlight your site and choose File | Properties. You're now staring at the control panel for SMS. If you click the Clients button, you'll see what options are available.

The first thing to notice is that all options are grayed out and the Current Properties option is selected at the top. Because SMS is not real-time for most operations, we'll propose a change. If you select Proposed Properties, you can now modify the settings (see Figure 29.10).

Figure 29.10.
Client configuration screen.

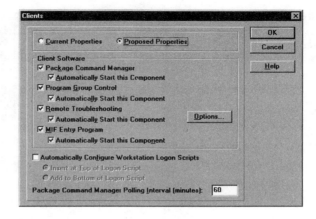

You'll notice that, by default, all options are enabled and turned on. If you don't plan to use SMS for packages or remote diagnostics, you can turn off some of these features. I recommend *only* starting the Package Command Manager automatically, unless I've sent a package that will need the other pieces. Windows NT will start the services no matter what you say in the autostart box.

If you select Automatically Configure Workstation Logon Scripts, SMS will add SMSLS.BAT to the top or bottom of your logon script. If you don't have a logon script defined, SMS will just set the script to SMSLS.BAT.

Remote Diagnostics and Control

By default, the Remote Control Service loads but has all rights set to NONE. Unless you change the options, you'll see the Administrator tool connect to the workstation, but all your options will be grayed out. The workaround for a Windows NT server or workstation is to modify the SMS.INI file on the root of the user's boot drive and change the Allows from NO to YES. The easiest way to do that is to use Notepad to modify the SMS.INI file on the machine you want to control. For example, you could use a command like this to attach to the Administrative share for the primary hard drive (see Figure 29.11):

```
NOTEPAD.EXE \\GABRIEL\C$\SMS.INI
```

You will notice a [Sight] section near the bottom of the INI file. On Windows NT, we want to modify only the first five settings and the signal variable. Set the first five to Yes, leave Visible Signal at Yes, and turn off the audible signal and the permissions. This setup allows you to do whatever you need to do on the server from your desk and still gives a roving administrator a clue as to what you're doing. For the changes to take effect, you must stop and restart the Remote Control service, using the Server Manager (which you can get to using the SMS Admin tool from the bottom icon in the Personal Computers Properties dialog box for the system you just modified, as shown in Figure 29.12).

Figure 29.11.
Modifying the SMS.INI
*file—here you see the default
version and the modified
version.*

Default Settings   Modified Settings

Figure 29.12.
*Restarting the Remote
Control service.*

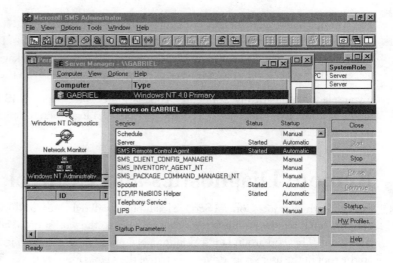

Now, if you select the Help Desk icon in the Properties window, the option icons are enabled, and you can select Remote Control. In Figure 29.13, you see the screen of the computer on which I'm writing this chapter in the Quick Windows Viewer, which pops up over the SMS Admin console. I could have finished the chapter from my server, as I had complete control of my workstation.

Performance in the Remote Control Service is relative. It's not as fast as sitting at the user's desk and working, but it's much faster than walking to the user's desk and working. I have used this feature to control a server in Sydney, Australia, from my NT workstation in Indianapolis across a 56KB frame relay; although it was painfully slow, I was done in about 15 minutes, and it saved $3,000 in flights and two days' downtime.

Figure 29.13.
Remote control of another machine from the Administrator tool.

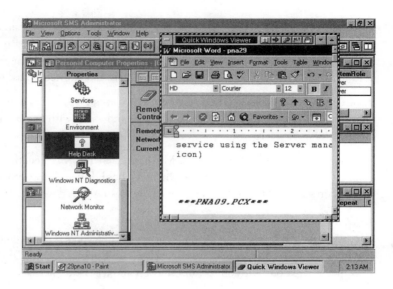

Creating MIF (Management Information Format) Files

MIF is a standard way of storing computer component information in a text file to be used by other programs. It was originally developed to standardize the way collected data was listed so that the collected data could be used by many different inventory packages. SMS uses the MIF files to store information about hardware and software changes that are collected by the SMS services on the logon. MIF files can also be used to survey the user community for information. An example would be the default User Information MIF (UINFO.XNF) that SMS sends to every client upon installation. If the user fills in the information and saves, it will be added to the database and viewable from the Admin tool (see Figure 29.14).

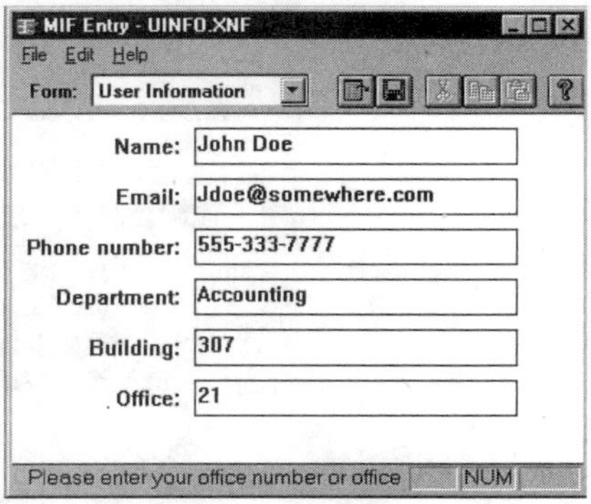

Figure 29.14.
The User Information MIF.

You'll notice this MIF is very basic—it uses only the text boxes. You can also use list boxes, which allow you to give the users a set of choices for the main items. If you create a survey on service levels, for example, you might want to provide options for the answers and leave a comment section at the bottom for the personal touch. This way, your data is standardized in case the boss asks for feedback.

If you open the file `\MS\SMS\noidmifs\UINFO.MIF`, you can view the actual MIF file. Notice that they follow a basic format of `Name`, `ID`, `Type`, `Storage`, and *value* with `begin` and `end` statements around each section.

You can create your own MIFs with the MIF Form Generator. You get them to the client by copying them to the `\MS\SMS\BIN` directory on the user's hard drive. (This is usually `C:\MS\SMS\BIN`, but it depends on where SMS chose to put the client files.)

> **Note:** The MIF entry screen will pop up every time you log on if you leave the Automatically Start This Component box checked in the Clients section of the site properties. This is the very reason I turn off the autostart on all pieces but Package Command Manager.

Packages

The heart of SMS is inventory, but the most common reason people buy the product is for the package distribution. A *package* is anything you want to distribute to your clients, such as applications or data files. A package is also anything you want to run against a client machine, such as a software audit or virus scan. A package can be thought of as the "thing" to be done, while the job is the actual work being done.

The example package is an installation for Internet Explorer. It's one of the common "Install on workstation" type of apps (see Figure 29.15).

Figure 29.15.
An example installation package.

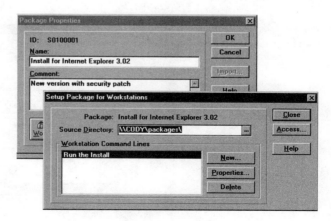

Warning: When you create the actual Run command, you must verify that you can get directly to the executable by selecting the three dots. If you must click into a directory to get to the file, SMS will read the root directory as the beginning of the source, and if that's the root of the package share, it will attempt to compress all your installs and send it as a package. I did this once and it took six hours and an incident to Microsoft Tech Support to get the server back from the 480MB package it was trying to send to my five distribution servers.

Installation Automation

If you have almost any product from Microsoft, you'll find built in an automated installation and quiet mode (an installation that runs and shows nothing on the screen while it runs). Few other software manufacturers seem to care about how easy it is to install their package on a thousand machines in a week. To install most other packages, you either have the end user walk through the standard install screens, or you get really creative with RegEdit and XCOPY.

Tip: If you need to automate the install and uninstall of a package, check out WinInstall (now owned by Seagate Software) at http://www.seagatesoftware.com. It's a great package for creating automated installations, and it even creates the hooks for SMS to deploy and monitor the packages.

Before you create packages for distribution, it's important to understand a few processes. You need to create a storage area big enough to hold the source files you want to use for the install. You also need at least 60% more space to store the compressed image of those source files, and an equal space for the actual distribution point for the package. In English, this means that if you want to distribute a 300MB package, you need 300MB + 180MB + 300MB = 780MB of space to create this package.

While the SMS server is also a distribution server by default, technically the SMS server is only responsible for the compressed package. The source files could be on any server and the distribution files will reside on all the distribution servers.

With regard to distribution servers, the best structure of your site will depend on how you use SMS. If you only send a few packages to a handful of people on a limited scale, it's safe to use the SMS server as the only distribution server. However, if you want to use SMS to distribute Office 97 and Internet Explorer to all 3,500 users over the weekend, you'll want to set up all or most of your logon servers as distribution servers and remove the SMS server as a distribution server.

Tip: If you're using the SMS server as your only distribution server, you can make this more manageable by creating a share for the packages and creating a batch file to attach to the share and run the install. You create your package with the batch file as the source, and it's the only piece that gets compressed and moved. This technique also works well for network-shared packages that must be in a certain location to run.

On whatever server you select as the keeper of your source install files, I recommend creating a package directory and sharing it. This will give you a central place for all your application installs and a known share to which your support team can connect to install apps manually. It's very common to have the same installation files on two or more servers because a central place was not created.

Jobs

Jobs are the pieces that do the work in SMS. If you create a package to do a software audit, nothing will happen until you create a job to send it to the users. There are basically three types of jobs in SMS. The first and most common job type is the Run Command on Workstation (I'll get to the other types in a second). The Run Command on Workstation is what you use to launch an install, run a virus scanner, copy a batch of files from a server to the client (see Figure 29.16). These are the types of jobs you'll use for 90% of your packages.

Figure 29.16.
The Run Command on Workstation job details.

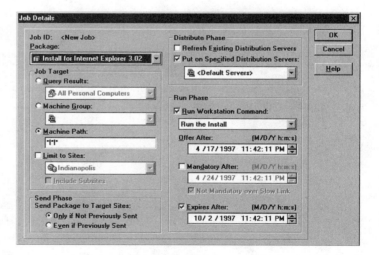

The Job Details dialog box reveals the heart of the configuration. This is where you select which package to run and which machines to run it on. You also configure what steps to perform during the send, distribute, and run phases of the job. It's very important to verify which command will be run during the run phase, because many packages can install in different modes or even uninstall applications. You would have a very bad day if you uninstalled 1,500 copies of Office instead of upgrading them!

The second type of job is the Share Package on Server (see Figure 29.17). This is the job that sends the client pieces for an application that runs from the server. It was once very popular to load all the applications on the server and only a small stub on the client. The problem with that scheme is that, if you have a large group of people using an application from the same server, it will slow down as more people use it. The solution was the shared application model via SMS.

Figure 29.17.
A Share Package on Server job.

SMS installs a stub on the client; when the user asks for the application, the stub looks for the first distribution server to respond to its request, and gets its shared programs from that server. Using the logic that the server with the lightest load will respond first, this will effectively balance the load across all the distribution servers.

The final type of job is the Remove Package from Server job. This job does exactly what it says. It removes the distribution files from all distribution servers—or only those servers you select (see Figure 29.18). This job is used to remove both the server-based distribution files and the Run on Workstation-based distribution files.

Figure 29.18.
A Remove Package from Server job.

> **Note:** The Remove Package from Server job is not an uninstall for the client software installed by a Run Command on Workstation job (like installing Microsoft Office on the user's hard drive). It will leave the client pieces unaffected .

What Do You Have and Where Is It?

The one thing we all want to know is, "Where is my stuff?" SMS will pull more information about your client machines than you will want or need to look at. The big issue is still how to view what you have. The SMS Administrator tool allows you to do queries against the data for everything from machine type to network card address to software packages by name and/or version. This is great for those quick questions like "How many copies of Excel do we have?" or "Do all the machines have 150MB free for the new upgrade?"

The first thing you must do before you can get at the SMS data from an external tool is to run the little utility called *SMS SQL View Generator*. This tool creates database views on which you can query.

For the more elaborate reports, you can use the free copy of Crystal Reports (see Figure 29.19). Although the full version includes a lot of BackOffice templates and will run against virtually any database, the included copy will give you 90% of what you need for management. It even includes a publish-to-Web option so you can post the data to your intranet and everyone can see the results of the last audit for Doom.

Figure 29.19.
A canned Crystal Report of computer services by domain.

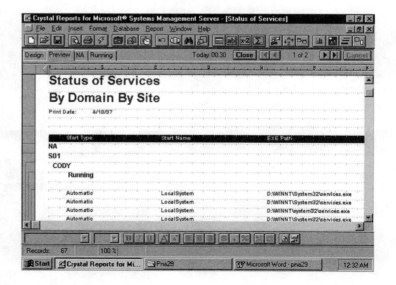

One approach for getting to the data is an Access database used as a front-end tool to query the tables in SQL Server. The linked tables allow the help desk to pull up canned reports on the user you're talking with, and Access populates the machine and user data from SMS into the call-tracking system, so the manual step is removed.

Because the back end of SMS is a SQL server, the choice of reporting tools is virtually endless. If you have a SQL database tool you like and it's ODBC-compliant, you can create or incorporate SMS into any reports you need.

The Network Monitor

The Network Monitor is a very powerful tool that can be used to monitor all traffic on a network segment. The tool can actually be used to monitor an entire network structure by loading the remote agent on one computer on each segment. This would allow you to sample the network traffic going to or from any computer on your network.

At its core, the Network Monitor is a packet sniffer or packet decoder. You can break a packet down to its smallest pieces with this tool. Much of the tool will go unused as you rarely are decoding packet-by-packet, but it's nice to have the capability.

Used for Security Breach

In the hands of a guru, the Network Monitor could be used to resolve passwords by decoding the packets and reassembling them (see Figure 29.20). While this won't affect Windows NT with its native encrypted logons, Novell NetWare 3.x and most UNIX services (FTP, Telnet, SMTP) send their passwords in clear text.

For this example, I attempted to FTP to the server CODY:

```
USERNAME: service
32 Character PASSWORD: secret-password-dont-tell-$12345
```

A 32-character password with a blend of numbers, letters, and symbols is considered secure. Because FTP isn't encrypting, however, it won't matter how long you make the password—it can be compromised.

In the figure, notice USER service five lines from the top and PASS secret-password-dont-tell-$12345 fourteen lines from the top. This was not echoed to my screen, but it was captured in plain text. If you're doing password-protected logons into an FTP server, you should not use the same credentials on your internal network.

Figure 29.20.
A Network Monitor decode with the password compromised.

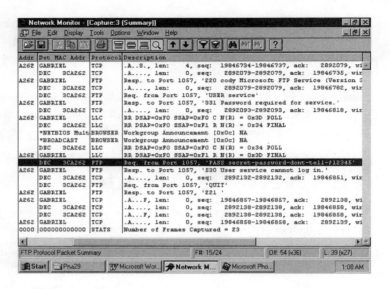

Used to Diagnose a Problem

One function I use the Network Monitor for is basic traffic patterns. With a little effort, you can watch the number of bad packets and broadcasts to see the basic health of the network. I've also found that many of the packets are in plain English and you can read the file names to see what was the last file accessed before a crash.

> **Note:** I had a customer whose system would crash when she opened a certain application. After extensive work with her client, we started monitoring her network traffic. Upon examining the network, we noticed that her machine would request a .WAV file from the network shortly after she launched the application and immediately before it crashed. The .WAV no longer existed, and her client couldn't handle the File not found error.

In the example in Figure 29.21, I attempted to open a file that doesn't exist. Windows NT responded with an error message, as it should have, but the trace also caught the name and displayed it for us. This also works well for that customer who forgets to mention that he gets an error message when he tries to open a document.

Figure 29.21.
Diagnosing a File not found *error*.

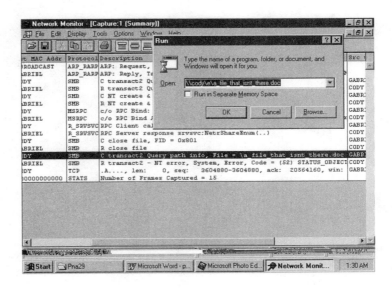

Summary

As you can see, SMS provides access to inventory, remote control and diagnostics, software distribution, application sharing, and even network monitoring—all from one administrative tool.

Over the next twelve months, we'll see Microsoft blend more and more of the administration and control of the entire organization into the SMS Admin to give support professionals an even better administration tool. But by then SMS Admin will be called a "Snap-in" to the "Microsoft Management Console (MMC)." For more information on MMC, check out http://www.microsoft.com/ management.

Peter Norton™

VIII

Appendixes

A

NT Server 4.0 Hardware Compatibility List

Peter Norton™

Chapter 4 mentions that, when most network operating systems talk about a list of compatible hardware, the list is more a list of suggestions. When Microsoft says that they won't support any hardware not found on the HCL, I've found that they're not making a lame suggestion. The Windows NT HCL is a compilation of computers and system hardware that have been extensively tested with Windows NT for stability and compatibility. It's the guide used by Microsoft Product Support to determine whether a computer is supported for use with the Windows NT operating system.

If at all possible, I would suggest that you use only hardware on the HCL or that the vender of the hardware be willing to stand firmly behind the hardware. Obviously, all of the hardware on the market that supports Windows NT 4.0 is not listed in the HCL. Perfectly good hardware is created every day; for that matter, by the time someone gets through testing, the hardware may be obsolete.

My suggestion is that you stay with a vendor who has typically been approved on the HCL. These vendors will typically be willing and able to support you in your time of need, even if their product isn't on the list. If these vendors report that the product will work, it will—or they'll know how to help.

Because of the constantly changing nature of such a list, the easiest way to keep track of the HCL is through the World Wide Web. The Web site that Microsoft has established for finding HCL information is at the following site:

`http://www.microsoft.com/`

But this appendix lists several popular peripherals that may help you through in a pinch. We've chosen hard drives, LAN adapters, WAN adapters, UPS, and tape drives. You can find a living version of this document on the Web site just mentioned.

LAN Cards (NICs)

Hardware Vendor	Device Bus	Device Name
3Com	ISA	3C503 EtherLink II (Coax & TP)
3Com	ISA	3C503/16 EtherLink II/16 (Coax & TP)
3Com	ISA	3C507 EtherLink 16 (Coax & TP)
3Com	ISA	3C508 Etherlink OEM Adapter
3Com	ISA	3C509 EtherLink III Parallel Tasking Adapter
3Com	ISA	3C509B EtherLink III Parallel Tasking Adapter
3Com	MCA	3C523 EtherLink/MC (Coax & TP)
3Com	MCA	3C527 EtherLink/MC 32 Bus Mastering Adapter

Hardware Vendor	Device Bus	Device Name
3Com	MCA	3C529 EtherLink III Parallel Tasking Adapter
3Com	EISA	3C579 EtherLink III Parallel Tasking Adapter
3Com	PCMCIA	3C589 Etherlink III PCMCIA Ethernet Adapter
3Com	PCMCIA	3C589B Etherlink III PCMCIA Ethernet Adapter
3Com	PCMCIA	3C589C EtherLink III PCMCIA
3Com	PCMCIA	3C589C Etherlink III PCMCIA Ethernet Adapter
3Com	PCI	3C590 EtherLink III PCI Bus-Master Adapter
3Com	EISA	3C592 EtherLink III EISA Bus-Master Adapter
3Com	EISA	3C592-C Etherlink III (Rev 6B)
3Com	EISA	3C592-TPO Etherlink III (REV 2B)
3Com	PCI	3C595-TX Faster Etherlink PCI
3Com	EISA	3C597 EtherLink III EISA Bus-Master Adapter
3Com	ISA	3C619 TokenLink III
3Com	EISA	3C770 FDDILink-F for Optical, UTP & STP
3Com	PCI	3C905 Fast EtherLink XL Adapter
3Com	EISA	EtherLink III EISA 10/100BASE-T (3C597-TX)
3Com	PCI	Fast EtherLink 10/100Base-T4 PCI (3C595-T4)
Accton Technology	ISA	EN166X MPXII Ethernet Adapter
Accton Technology	PCMCIA	EN2216 PCMCIA Ethernet Adapter
Allied Telesyn	ISA	AT-1500 PnP
Allied Telesyn	PCI	AT-2450
Allied Telesyn	PCI	AT-2560 Series PCI/100 Ethernet
Allied Telesyn	ISA	AT1700 Series Ethernet Adapter
Allied Telesyn	MCA	AT1720 Series Ethernet Adapter
Allied Telesyn	PCI	AT2450 Ethernet Adapter
Allied Telesyn	PCI	AT2560 Series PCI/100 Ethernet Adapter
AMD	EMBEDDED	PCnet Family Adapters

continues

Hardware Vendor	Device Bus	Device Name
AMD	VLB	PCnet-32 VL Ethernet Adapter
AMD	ISA	PCnet-ISA+ Ethernet Adapter
AMD	PCI	PCnet-PCI Ethernet Adapter
Andrew	ISA	ISA IIA Adapter
Cabletron	ISA	E21XX Ethernet DNI
Cabletron	ISA	E22XX Ethernet DNI
Cabletron	ISA	F3015 FDDI Adapter
Cabletron	MCA	F30XX FDDI Adapter
Cabletron	EISA	F70XX FDDI Adapter
Cabletron	ISA	T20XX 16/4 Token Ring DNI
Cogent Data Technologies	PCI	eMASTER+ 960 PCI Ethernet Adapter
Compaq	EISA	32-Bit Dualspeed Token Ring Controller
Compaq	EISA	32-Bit Netflex Controller
Compaq	EISA	32-Bit Netflex Controller with Token Ring Module
Compaq	ISA	Ethernet 16TP Controller
Compaq	PCMCIA	Ethernet LAN Card
Compaq	EMBEDDED	Integrated Netelligent
Compaq	EMBEDDED	Integrated NetFlex-3
Compaq	PCI	Netelligent 10 T PCI UTP Adapter
Compaq	PCI	Netelligent 10/100 TX PCI UTP Adapter
Compaq	EISA	NetFlex-2 DualPort ENET Controller
Compaq	EISA	NetFlex-2 DualPort TR Controller
Compaq	EISA	NetFlex-2 ENET-TR Controller
Compaq	EISA	NetFlex-2 TR Controller
Compaq	EISA	NetFlex-3/E
Compaq	PCI	NetFlex-3/P
Compaq	PCI	TC4048 Token Ring PCI Controller
Compex	ISA	ENET16-COMBO/VP PnP Ethernet Adapter
COPS	ISA	LTI ISA
D-Link	ISA	DE-220 ISA Ethernet Adapter
D-Link	PCI	DE-530CT+

Hardware Vendor	Device Bus	Device Name
D-Link	PCMCIA	DE-650 PCMCIA Ethernet Adapter
D-Link	PCMCIA	DE-650CT PCMCIA Ethernet
D-Link	PCMCIA	DE-660T
D-Link	PCI	ProFast Ethernet Adapter
DayStar	ISA	Digital LocalTalk Adapter
DCA	ISA/MCA	IRMAtrac 16/4 Convertible Token Ring Adapter
Digital Equipment	EMBEDDED	DC21040 PCI Ethernet Controller
Digital Equipment	ISA	DE100 EtherWORKS LC
Digital Equipment	ISA	DE101 EtherWORKS LC/TP
Digital Equipment	ISA	DE200 EtherWORKS Turbo
Digital Equipment	ISA	DE201 EtherWORKS Turbo/TP
Digital Equipment	ISA	DE202 EtherWORKS Turbo TP/BNC
Digital Equipment	EISA	DE422 EtherWORKS EISA TP/BNC
Digital Equipment	PCI	DE434 PCI Ethernet Adapter
Digital Equipment	PCI	DE435 PCI Ethernet Adapter
Digital Equipment	PCI	DE450-CA Etherworks Turbo PCI
Digital Equipment	PCI	DE500 Fast Ethernet Adapter
Digital Equipment	PCI	EtherWorks Turbo PCI 10 (DE450)
Digital Equipment	PCI	Fast EtherWorks PCI 10/100 (DE500-AA)
Digital Equipment	PCI	Fast EtherWorks PCI 10/100 (DE500-XA)
Digital Equipment	EISA	FDDIcontroller/EISA(incl. CDDI)
Digital Equipment	PCI	FDDIcontroller/PCI(incl. CDDI)
Fujitsu	ISA	FMV-183
Fujitsu	ISA	FMV-184
Fujitsu	ISA	ICL EtherTeam ISA Ethernet Network Adapter
Fujitsu	PCI	ICL EtherTeam PCI Ethernet Network Adapter
Grey Cell Systems	PCMCIA	2200 Series Ethernet Card
Hewlett-Packard	PCI	10/100TX PCI Ethernet Adapter
Hewlett-Packard	ISA	HP 27245A PC LAN Adapter/8 TP

continues

Hardware Vendor	Device Bus	Device Name
Hewlett-Packard	MCA	HP 27246A MC LAN Adapter/16 TP
Hewlett-Packard	ISA	HP 27247A PC LAN Adapter/16 TP
Hewlett-Packard	ISA	HP 27247B PC LAN Adapter/16 TP Plus
Hewlett-Packard	ISA	HP 27250 PC LAN Adapter/8 TL
Hewlett-Packard	ISA	HP 27252A PC LAN Adapter/16 TL Plus
Hewlett-Packard	ISA	HP J2573A 10/100VG ISA LAN Adapter
Hewlett-Packard	EISA	HP J2577A 10/100VG EISA LAN Adapter
Hewlett-Packard	PCI	HP J2585A 10/100VG Selectable PC LAN
Hewlett-Packard	PCI	J2585B DeskDirect 10/100 PCI LAN Adapter
Hewlett-Packard	PCI	J2970A DeskDirect 10BaseT/2 PCI LAN Adapter
Hewlett-Packard	PCI	J2973A DeskDirect 10BaseT PCI LAN Adapter
IBM	PCI	100/10 PCI Ethernet Adapter
IBM	ISA	16/4 Token Ring II ISA Adapter
IBM	ISA	16/4 Token Ring ISA-16 Adapter
IBM	ISA	Auto 16/4 ISA Token Ring Adapter
IBM	MCA	Auto LANStreamer MC 32 Adapter
IBM	PCMCIA	Etherjet PC Card
IBM	MCA	Ethernet Quad PeerMaster Adapter
IBM	MCA	EtherStreamer MC 32 Adapter
IBM	ISA	ISA Ethernet Adapter
IBM	MCA	LAN Adapter/A for Ethernet
IBM	MCA	LANStreamer MC 32 Adapter
IBM	PCI	LANStreamer PCI Token Ring Adapter
IBM	PCI	PCI Ethernet Adapter (P13H9237)
IBM	PCI	PCI Token Ring (41H8900)
IBM	PCMCIA	PCMCIA Ethernet Adapter II
IBM	MCA	Token Ring Adapter /A (4 Mbps)
IBM	ISA	Token Ring Adapter 16/4
IBM	MCA	Token Ring Adapter 16/4 /A
IBM	PCMCIA	Token Ring Auto 16/4 Credit Card Adapter

Hardware Vendor	Device Bus	Device Name
ICL	ISA	EtherTeam16i Combo Adapter
ICL	ISA	EtherTeam16i Duo Adapter
ICL	ISA	EtherTeam16i TP Adapter
ICL	EISA	EtherTeam32 EISA Adapter
Intel	PCI	EtherExpress (TM) PRO/100B PCI
Intel	MCA	EtherExpress 16 MCA
Intel	ISA	EtherExpress 16 PCLA8110
Intel	ISA	EtherExpress 16C PCLA8100
Intel	ISA	EtherExpress 16TP PCLA8120
Intel	EISA	EtherExpress Flash32 EISA LAN Adapter
Intel	ISA	EtherExpress FlashC PCLA8105
Intel	ISA	EtherExpress PRO/10 ISA
Intel	PCI	EtherExpress PRO/10 PCI LAN Adapter
Intel	ISA	EtherExpress PRO/10+ ISA
Intel	PCI	EtherExpress PRO/100B PCI LAN Adapter
Intel	EISA	TokenExpress EISA 16/4
Intel	EISA	TokenExpress EISA/32
Intel	ISA	TokenExpress ISA/16S
Intel	MCA	TokenExpress MCA 16/4
Intel	ISA	TokenExpress(TM) ISA 16/p LAN (PCLA8130B)
Kingston Technology Corporation	PCMCIA	EtherRx PCMCIA Adapter
LinkSys	PCMCIA	EC2T PCMCIA Ethernet Adapter
Linksys	ISA	Ether16 LAN Card
Linksys	PCI	EtherPCI LAN Card
Madge	ISA	Blue+ Token Ring Adapter
Madge	ISA	Smart 16 Ringnode
Madge	ISA	Smart 16/4 AT Plus Ringnode
Madge	ISA	Smart 16/4 AT Plus Ringnode (Rev 2)
Madge	ISA	Smart 16/4 AT Ringnode

continues

Hardware Vendor	Device Bus	Device Name
Madge	EISA	Smart 16/4 EISA Ringnode
Madge	ISA	Smart 16/4 ISA Client Plus
Madge	ISA	Smart 16/4 ISA Client Ringnode
Madge	ISA	Smart 16/4 ISA PnP Ringnode
Madge	MCA	Smart 16/4 MC Ringnode
Madge	MCA	Smart 16/4 MC32 Ringnode
Madge	ISA	Smart 16/4 PC Ringnode
Madge	PCI	Smart 16/4 PCI Ringnode
Madge	PCI	Smart 16/4 PCI Ringnode (Rev 3)
Madge	PCMCIA	Smart 16/4 PCMCIA Ringnode Token Ring Adapter
Megahertz	PCMCIA	CC10BT/2 Ethernet PCMCIA Adapter
Megahertz	PCMCIA	CCEM3288 Ethernet+Modem PCMCIA Adapter
Megahertz	PCMCIA	XJEM3288 Ethernet+Modem PCMCIA Adapter
Microdyne	PCI	NE 10/100 PCI Fast Ethernet
Microdyne	ISA	NE10/100 ISA FAST Ethernet Adapter
Microdyne	PCI	NE100 PCI Adapter
National Semiconductor	EMBEDDED	DP83932 (SONIC)
National Semiconductor	PCMCIA	InfoMover NE4100 PCMCIA Ethernet Adapter
NCR	ISA	StarLAN 16/4 Token Ring NAU
NCR	MCA	StarLAN 16/4 Token Ring NAU
NCR	ISA	WaveLAN/AT
NCR	MCA	WaveLAN/MC
Network Peripherals	ISA	NP-AT FDDI
Network Peripherals	EISA	NP-EISA/S FDDI
Network Peripherals	MCA	NP-MCA/S FDDI
Network Peripherals	PCI	NuCard PCI FDDI
NoteWorthy	PCMCIA	Ethernet PCMCIA Adapter II (10Base2)
NoteWorthy	PCMCIA	Ethernet PCMCIA Adapter II (10BaseT)
Novell/Eagle Technology	ISA	NE1000

Hardware Vendor	Device Bus	Device Name
Novell/Eagle Technology	ISA	NE2000
Novell/Eagle Technology	EISA	NE3200
Olicom	PCMCIA	Ethernet GoCard
Olicom	ISA	Ethernet ISA 10/100 Adapter (OC-2375)
Olicom	ISA	Ethernet ISA/IV Adapter (OC-2173)
Olicom	ISA	Ethernet ISA/IV Adapter, OC-2173
Olicom	PCI	Ethernet PCI/II 10 Adapter ,OC-2185
Olicom	PCI	Ethernet PCI/II 10 T (OC-2185)
Olicom	PCI	Ethernet PCI/II 10/100 Adapter (OC-2325)
Olicom	PCI	Ethernet PCI/II 10/100, OC-2325
Olicom	PCMCIA	GoCard ET/Modem 288
Olicom	PCMCIA	GoCard TR 16/4
Olicom	PCMCIA	GoCard TR/Modem 144
Olicom	ISA	ISA 16/4 Token Ring, OC-3118
Olicom	ISA	OC-3118 ISA 16/4 Token Ring
Olicom	PCI	PCI 16/4 Token Ring, OC-3136
Olicom	PCI	Token Ring PCI/II DC-3137
Olicom	EISA	Token-Ring,PowerMAC EISA SRV, OC-3135
Olicom	EISA	Token-Ring,PowerMAC EISA WS, OC-3133
Olicom	ISA	Token-Ring,PowerMAC ISA WS, OC-3117
Olicom	MCA	Token-Ring,PowerMAC MCA WS, OC-3129
Ositech	PCMCIA	Jack of Diamonds Adapter
Ositech	PCMCIA	Jack of Diamonds Trumpcard PCMCIA
Proteon	ISA	ProNET 4/16 p1390 Token Ring Adapter
Proteon	ISA	ProNET 4/16 p1392 Token Ring Adapter
Proteon	ISA	ProNET 4/16 p1392plus Token Ring Adapter
Proteon	MCA	ProNET 4/16 p1892 Token Ring Adapter
Proteon	MCA	ProNET 4/16 p1892plus Token Ring Adapter
Proteon	EISA	ProNET 4/16 p1990 Token Ring Adapter
Proteon	EISA	ProNET 4/16 p1990plus Token Ring Adapter
Racal Guardata	EISA	InterLan ES3210

continues

Hardware Vendor	Device Bus	Device Name
Racal Guardata	ISA	InterLan XLerator/EB/NI6510 Adapter
Realtek	PCI	RTL8029 PCI Ethernet Adapter
RNS	PCI	2200 PCI FDDI LAN Controller
RNS	PCI	2200 Series PCI Bus FDDI
SMC	PCI	8432 EtherPower with ROM socket
SMC	PCI	9332BDT EtherPower 10/100
Socket Communications	PCMCIA	Socket EA PCMCIA (NE2000 Compatible)
Standard Microsystems	ISA	8013EBT EtherCard PLUS16
Standard Microsystems	ISA	8013EP EtherCard PLUS Elite16
Standard Microsystems	MCA	8013EP/A EtherCard PLUS Elite/A
Standard Microsystems	ISA	8013EPC EtherCard PLUS Elite16
Standard Microsystems	ISA	8013EW EtherCard PLUS EliteCombo
Standard Microsystems	ISA	8013EWC EtherCard PLUS EliteCombo
Standard Microsystems	ISA	8013W EtherCard PLUS Elite16T
Standard Microsystems	ISA	8013WB EtherCard PLUS
Standard Microsystems	ISA	8013WC EtherCard PLUS Elite16T
Standard Microsystems	MCA	8013WP/A EtherCard PLUS Elite10T/A
Standard Microsystems	ISA	8216C EtherCard Elite Ultra
Standard Microsystems	EISA	8232 EtherCard Elite 32 Ultra
Standard Microsystems	ISA	8416 Ultra PnP
Standard Microsystems	PCI	8432BT EtherPower PCI LAN Adapter
Standard Microsystems	PCI	8432T EtherPower PCI LAN Adapter
Standard Microsystems	PCI	8434 EtherPower2 PCI Adapter
Standard Microsystems	PCI	9332DST EtherPower 10/100 PCI LAN Adapter
SVEC	ISA	FD0421P EtherPlug-ISA Adapter
SVEC	PCI	FDO455P EtherBoard-PCI Adapter
SysKonnect	ISA	SK-51xx ISA-bus FDDI Adapter
SysKonnect	MCA	SK-52xx MCA-bus FDDI Adapter
SysKonnect	EISA	SK-53xx EISA-bus FDDI Adapter
SysKonnect	PCI	SK-NET FDDI PCI
SysKonnect	PCI	SK-NET FDDI PCI Adapter

Hardware Vendor	Device Bus	Device Name
SysKonnect	ISA	SK-NET Flash (Coax and TP)
SysKonnect	ISA	SK-NET G16 Ethernet Adapter (/TP)
SysKonnect	EISA	SK-NET G32+ EISA Ethernet Adapter
SysKonnect	PCI	SK-NET Token Ring PCI Adapter
SysKonnect	ISA	SK-NET TR4/16+ Token Ring Adapter
TDK	PCMCIA	PCMCIA Ethernet LAN
TDK	PCMCIA	PCMCIA Ethernet LAN
Texas Instruments	PCI	ThunderLAN-based Ethernet
Thomas-Conrad	MCA	TC4046 MCA Token Ring Adapter
Tulip	ISA	Computer NCC-16 PNP Adapter
Ungermann-Bass	ISA	NIUpc
Ungermann-Bass	ISA	NIUpc/EOTP
Ungermann-Bass	MCA	NIUps/EOTP
Xircom	PCMCIA	Corporate Series CreditCard Ethernet
Xircom	PCMCIA	Corporate Series CreditCard Ethernet IIps
Xircom	PCMCIA	Credit Card Ethernet Adapter CE3-10/100
Xircom	PCMCIA	CreditCard Token Ring IIps
Xircom	PARALLEL	Pocket Ethernet II Adapter
Xircom	PARALLEL	Pocket Ethernet III Adapter

WAN Adapters

Hardware Vendor	Device Bus	Device Name
Digi International	ISA	SyncPort
Digi International	PCI	SyncPort PCI
Eicon Technology	ISA	DualPort Network Adapter/PC 2MB
Eicon Technology	ISA	EiconCard C21 (WAN)
Eicon Technology	ISA	EiconCard HSI/PC 1MB
Eicon Technology	ISA	EiconCard S51/S50 (WAN)
Eicon Technology	ISA	MultiPort Network Adapter/PC 2MB

continues

Hardware Vendor	Device Bus	Device Name
MicroGate	ISA	MicroGate SyncLink WAN Adapter
Niwot	ISA	Niwot Networks NiRAS AT/SD
U.S. Robotics/Megahertz	ISA	Allegra 56k Frame Relay Adapter
U.S. Robotics/Megahertz	ISA	Allegra T1 Frame Relay Adapter

SCSI Controllers

Hardware Vendor	Device Bus	Device Name
Adaptec	ISA-16	AHA-1510
Adaptec	ISA-16	AHA-1510A
Adaptec	ISA-16	AHA-1510B
Adaptec	ISA-16	AHA-1520
Adaptec	ISA-16	AHA-1520A
Adaptec	ISA-16	AHA-1520B
Adaptec	ISA-16	AHA-1522
Adaptec	ISA-16	AHA-1522A
Adaptec	ISA-16	AHA-1522B
Adaptec	ISA-16	AHA-1530P
Adaptec	ISA-16	AHA-1532P
Adaptec	ISA-16	AHA-1535
Adaptec	ISA-16	AHA-1535A
Adaptec	ISA-16	AHA-1540B
Adaptec	ISA-16	AHA-1540C
Adaptec	ISA-16	AHA-1540CF
Adaptec	ISA-16	AHA-1540CP
Adaptec	ISA-16	AHA-1542B
Adaptec	ISA-16	AHA-1542C
Adaptec	ISA-16	AHA-1542CF
Adaptec	ISA-16	AHA-1542CP
Adaptec	MCA	AHA-1640
Adaptec	EISA	AHA-1740

Hardware Vendor	Device Bus	Device Name
Adaptec	EISA	AHA-1740A
Adaptec	EISA	AHA-1742
Adaptec	EISA	AHA-1742A
Adaptec	EISA	AHA-2740
Adaptec	EISA	AHA-2740A
Adaptec	EISA	AHA-2740AT
Adaptec	EISA	AHA-2740W
Adaptec	EISA	AHA-2742
Adaptec	EISA	AHA-2742A
Adaptec	EISA	AHA-2742AT
Adaptec	EISA	AHA-2742W
Adaptec	VLB	AHA-2840
Adaptec	VLB	AHA-2840A
Adaptec	VLB	AHA-2842
Adaptec	VLB	AHA-2842A
Adaptec	PCI	AHA-2905
Adaptec	PCI	AHA-2910
Adaptec	PCI	AHA-2910A
Adaptec	PCI	AHA-2920
Adaptec	PCI	AHA-2920A
Adaptec	PCI	AHA-2940
Adaptec	PCI	AHA-2940AU
Adaptec	PCI	AHA-2940U
Adaptec	PCI	AHA-2940UW
Adaptec	PCI	AHA-2940W
Adaptec	PCI	AHA-3940
Adaptec	PCI	AHA-3940U
Adaptec	PCI	AHA-3940UW
Adaptec	PCI	AHA-3940UWD
Adaptec	PCI	AHA-3940W
Adaptec	EMBEDDED	AIC-7770

continues

Hardware Vendor	Device Bus	Device Name
Adaptec	ISA-16	AVA-1502AP
Adaptec	ISA-16	AVA-1502E
Adaptec	ISA-16	AVA-1505
Adaptec	ISA-16	AVA-1515
Adaptec	VLB	AVA-2825
Adaptec	N/A	BusLogic 958D
Adaptec	PCMCIA	SlimSCSI
Always	ISA-16	IN-2000
AMD	EMBEDDED	PC-NET SCSI
AMIscsi	EISA	Series 441
AMIscsi	EISA	Series 48
BusLogic	VLB	BT-445C
BusLogic	VLB	BT-445S
BusLogic	ISA-16	BT-542B
BusLogic	ISA-16	BT-545C
BusLogic	ISA-16	BT-545S
BusLogic	MCA	BT-640A
BusLogic	MCA	BT-646S
BusLogic	EISA	BT-742A
BusLogic	EISA	BT-747C
BusLogic	EISA	BT-747S
BusLogic	EISA	BT-757C
BusLogic	PCI	BT-946C
BusLogic	PCI	BT-948
BusLogic	PCI	BT-956C
BusLogic	PCI	BT-958
BusLogic	PCI	FlashPoint DL (BT-932)
BusLogic	PCI	FlashPoint LT (BT-930)
BusLogic	PCI	FlashPoint LW (BT-950)
Compaq	EMBEDDED	32-Bit Fast-Wide SCSI-2/E Controller
Compaq	EMBEDDED	32-Bit Fast-Wide SCSI-2/P Controller
Compaq	EISA	Fast SCSI-2 Controller

Hardware Vendor	Device Bus	Device Name
Data Technology	EISA	3290
Digital Equipment	EISA	KZESC-AA (SWIKX-BA) EISA BackPlane RAID 1-CHANNEL
Digital Equipment	EISA	KZESC-BA (SWIKX-BB) EISA BackPlane RAID 3-CHANNEL
Digital Equipment	PCI	KZPAA-AA PCI-SCSI Host Bus Adapter
Digital Equipment	PCI	KZPSA Differential SCSI Adapter
Digital Equipment	PCI	KZPSC-AA (SWIXK-CA) PCI BackPlane RAID 1-CHANNEL
Digital Equipment	PCI	KZPSC-BA (SWIXK-CB) PCI BackPlane RAID 3-CHANNEL
Digital Equipment	PCI	KZPSM SCSI/Ethernet Controller
DPT	ISA-16	SmartCache III (PM2021 with cache)
DPT	ISA-16	SmartCache III (PM2021)
DPT	EISA	SmartCache III (PM2022 with cache)
DPT	EISA	SmartCache III (PM2022)
DPT	PCI	SmartCache III (PM2024 with cache)
DPT	PCI	SmartCache III (PM2024)
DPT	EISA	SmartCache III (PM2122 with cache)
DPT	EISA	SmartCache III (PM2122)
DPT	PCI	SmartCache III (PM2124 with cache)
DPT	PCI	SmartCache III (PM2124)
DPT	PCI	SmartCache III (PM2124W with cache)
DPT	PCI	SmartCache III (PM2124W)
DPT	ISA-16	SmartCache IV (PM2041FW with cache)
DPT	ISA-16	SmartCache IV (PM2041FW)
DPT	ISA-16	SmartCache IV (PM2041W with cache)
DPT	ISA-16	SmartCache IV (PM2041W)
DPT	EISA	SmartCache IV (PM2042FW with cache)
DPT	EISA	SmartCache IV (PM2042FW)
DPT	EISA	SmartCache IV (PM2042W with cache)
DPT	EISA	SmartCache IV (PM2042W)

continues

Hardware Vendor	Device Bus	Device Name
DPT	PCI	SmartCache IV (PM2044W with cache)
DPT	PCI	SmartCache IV (PM2044W)
DPT	EISA	SmartCache IV (PM2142FW with cache)
DPT	EISA	SmartCache IV (PM2142FW)
DPT	EISA	SmartCache IV (PM2142W with cache)
DPT	EISA	SmartCache IV (PM2142W)
DPT	PCI	SmartCache IV (PM2144W with cache)
DPT	PCI	SmartCache IV (PM2144W)
DPT	ISA-16	SmartCache Plus (PM2011b with cache)
DPT	ISA-16	SmartCache Plus (PM2011b)
DPT	EISA	SmartCache Plus (PM2012b with cache)
DPT	EISA	SmartCache Plus (PM2012b)
DPT	PCI	SmartRAID (PM3021)
DPT	EISA	SmartRAID (PM3222)
DPT	PCI	SmartRAID (PM3224)
DPT	PCI	SmartRAID (PM3224W)
DPT	PCI	SmartRAID IV (PM3334W)
Future Domain	MCA	MCS-600
Future Domain	MCA	MCS-700
Future Domain	PCMCIA	SCSI2Go
Future Domain	ISA-16	TMC-1610m
Future Domain	ISA-16	TMC-1610mer
Future Domain	ISA-16	TMC-1610mex
Future Domain	ISA-16	TMC-1650
Future Domain	ISA-16	TMC-1660
Future Domain	ISA-16	TMC-1670
Future Domain	ISA-16	TMC-1680
Future Domain	PCI	TMC-3260
Future Domain	EISA	TMC-7000EX
Future Domain	ISA-8	TMC-845
Future Domain	ISA-8	TMC-850
Future Domain	ISA-8	TMC-850M(ER)

Hardware Vendor	Device Bus	Device Name
Future Domain	ISA-8	TMC-860
Future Domain	ISA-8	TMC-860M
Future Domain	ISA-16	TMC-885
Future Domain	ISA-16	TMC-885M
IBM	MCA	PS/2 Microchannel SCSI Host Adapter
IBM	MCA	PS/2 Microchannel SCSI Host Adapter (with cache)
Initio	ISA-16	INI-6102
Initio	PCI	INI-9100
Initio	PCI	INI-9100 PCI-SCSI Bus Master Host Adapter
Initio	PCI	INI-9100W
Initio	PCI	INI-9100W PCI SCSI BUS Master Host Adapter
Iomega	ISA-16	Zip Zoom
Maynard	ISA-16	16-bit SCSI Adapter
MediaVision	ISA-16	Pro Audio Spectrum-16
Mylex	EISA	DAC960-3 Channel
Mylex	EISA	DAC960-E
Mylex	PCI	DAC960-P
Mylex	PCI	DAC960-PD
Mylex	PCI	DAC960-PL
NCR	MCA	53C700 SCSI Adapter
NCR	EMBEDDED	53C700 SCSI Adapter
NCR	EISA	53C710 SCSI Adapter
NCR	EMBEDDED	53C810 SCSI Controller
NCR	EMBEDDED	53C90 SCSI Controller
NCR	EMBEDDED	53C94 SCSI Controller
NCR	PCI	8100S PCI Host Adapter Board
NCR	PCI	8150S PCI Host Adapter Board
Olivetti	EISA	ESC-1
Olivetti	EISA	ESC-2
QLogic	PCI	Fast!SCSI IQ PCI

continues

Hardware Vendor	Device Bus	Device Name
Trantor	ISA-8	T-128
Trantor	ISA-8	T-130B
UltraStor	ISA-16	14f
UltraStor	EISA	24f
UltraStor	EISA	24fa
UltraStor	VLB	34f

Hard Drives

Hardware Vendor	Device Bus	Device Name
Box Hill	SCSI	ModBox 5000 10DS
Box Hill	SCSI	ModBox 5000 44DS
Conner Peripherals	IDE	CFA1275A
Conner Peripherals	IDE	CFS1621A
Fujitsu	IDE	M1606TA
Fujitsu	IDE	M1612TA
Fujitsu	IDE	M1614TA
Fujitsu	IDE	M1623TAU
Fujitsu	IDE	M1624TAU
Fujitsu	IDE	M1636TAU
Fujitsu	IDE	M1638TAW
Fujitsu	IDE	M2713TAM Fixed Disk Drive
Fujitsu	IDE	M2714TAM Fixed Disk Drive
Fujitsu	IDE	M2722TAM
Fujitsu	IDE	M2723TAM
Fujitsu	IDE	M2724TAM
Hewlett-Packard	IDE	HP 2.0GB Hard Disk, C5283A
Hewlett-Packard	IDE	HP SureStore Hard Disk 2000V, C5436A
Hewlett-Packard	IDE	SureStore Hard Disk 2000A, C5273A
Hewlett-Packard	IDE	SureStore Hard Disk 2000V, C5436A
IBM	PCMCIA	105 PCMCIA Hard Disk (Model 8105PA)

Hardware Vendor	Device Bus	Device Name
IBM	IDE	TravelStar 3LP (DMCA-21080)
IBM	IDE	TravelStar 3LP (DMCA-21440)
IBM	IDE	UltraStar ES (DORS-32160)
IBM	SCSI	UltraStar ES (DORS-32160)
Integral Peripherals	PCMCIA	Viper 105
Integral Peripherals	PCMCIA	Viper 260
Kingston Technology	PCMCIA	DataPak 170
Kingston Technology	PCMCIA	DataPak 260
Kingston Technology	PCMCIA	DataPak 340
Maxtor	IDE	71626AP
Maxtor	IDE	71670AP
Maxtor	IDE	72004AP
Maxtor	IDE	7245AT
Maxtor	IDE	7425AV
Maxtor	IDE	7540AV
Maxtor	IDE	7850AV
Maxtor	PCMCIA	MobileMax 105
Maxtor	PCMCIA	MobileMax 131
MiniStore	PCMCIA	131 (Model MP260P3)
Noteworthy	PCMCIA	260 PC Card Hard Disk Drive
Quantum	IDE	Bigfoot 1280A
Quantum	SCSI	Capella VP31110
Quantum	SCSI	Fireball 2110S
Quantum	SCSI	Fireball 3200S
Quantum	IDE	Fireball 540A
Quantum	IDE	Fireball 640A
Quantum	SCSI	Fireball II 640S
Quantum	IDE	Fireball TM1080AT
Quantum	IDE	Fireball TM2110AT
Quantum	SCSI	Trailblazer 420S
Quantum	SCSI	Trailblazer 840S

continues

Hardware Vendor	Device Bus	Device Name
Quantum	SCSI	XP31070
Quantum	SCSI	XP32150
Quantum	SCSI	XP34300
Seagate Technology	SCSI	ST15150N Baracuda 4LP
Seagate Technology	IDE	ST31220A
Seagate Technology	IDE	ST31270A Medalist 1270
Seagate Technology	SCSI	ST32430N
Seagate Technology	SCSI	ST32550N Baracuda 2LP
Seagate Technology	IDE	ST3630A
Seagate Technology	IDE	ST3660A
Seagate Technology	IDE	ST51080A
Seagate Technology	SCSI	ST51080N Decathlon
Seagate Technology	IDE	ST51270A
Simple Technology	PCMCIA	DATACARD 260MB
Western Digital	IDE	AC2850F
Western Digital	IDE	AC31000F

UPS

Hardware Vendor	Device Name
American Power Conversion	Back-UPS 1250
American Power Conversion	Back-UPS 400
American Power Conversion	Back-UPS 450
American Power Conversion	Back-UPS 600
American Power Conversion	Back-UPS 900
American Power Conversion	Matrix-UPS 3000
American Power Conversion	Matrix-UPS 5000
American Power Conversion	Smart-UPS 1000
American Power Conversion	Smart-UPS 1000I
American Power Conversion	Smart-UPS 1000RM
American Power Conversion	Smart-UPS 1000RMI

Hardware Vendor	Device Name
American Power Conversion	Smart-UPS 1000XL
American Power Conversion	Smart-UPS 1000XLI
American Power Conversion	Smart-UPS 1250
American Power Conversion	Smart-UPS 1250RM
American Power Conversion	Smart-UPS 1400
American Power Conversion	Smart-UPS 1400I
American Power Conversion	Smart-UPS 1400RM
American Power Conversion	Smart-UPS 1400RMI
American Power Conversion	Smart-UPS 2000
American Power Conversion	Smart-UPS 2000RM
American Power Conversion	Smart-UPS 2200
American Power Conversion	Smart-UPS 2200I
American Power Conversion	Smart-UPS 2200RM
American Power Conversion	Smart-UPS 2200RMI
American Power Conversion	Smart-UPS 2200XL
American Power Conversion	Smart-UPS 2200XLI
American Power Conversion	Smart-UPS 250
American Power Conversion	Smart-UPS 250I
American Power Conversion	Smart-UPS 3000
American Power Conversion	Smart-UPS 3000I
American Power Conversion	Smart-UPS 3000RM
American Power Conversion	Smart-UPS 400
American Power Conversion	Smart-UPS 400I
American Power Conversion	Smart-UPS 450
American Power Conversion	Smart-UPS 600
American Power Conversion	Smart-UPS 600RM
American Power Conversion	Smart-UPS 600XL
American Power Conversion	Smart-UPS 700
American Power Conversion	Smart-UPS 700I
American Power Conversion	Smart-UPS 700RM
American Power Conversion	Smart-UPS 700RMI

continues

Hardware Vendor	Device Name
American Power Conversion	Smart-UPS 700XL
American Power Conversion	Smart-UPS 700XLI
American Power Conversion	Smart-UPS 900
American Power Conversion	Smart-UPS 900XL
American Power Conversion	Smart-UPS VS1000
American Power Conversion	Smart-UPS VS1000I
American Power Conversion	Smart-UPS VS1400
American Power Conversion	Smart-UPS VS1400I
American Power Conversion	Smart-UPS VS420
American Power Conversion	Smart-UPS VS420I
American Power Conversion	Smart-UPS VS650
American Power Conversion	Smart-UPS VS650I
Best Power Technology	FERRUPS FE1.15KVA
Best Power Technology	FERRUPS FE1.4KVA
Best Power Technology	FERRUPS FE1.8KVA
Best Power Technology	FERRUPS FE10KVA
Best Power Technology	FERRUPS FE12.5KVA
Best Power Technology	FERRUPS FE18KVA
Best Power Technology	FERRUPS FE2.1KVA
Best Power Technology	FERRUPS FE3.1KVA
Best Power Technology	FERRUPS FE4.3KVA
Best Power Technology	FERRUPS FE5.3KVA
Best Power Technology	FERRUPS FE500VA
Best Power Technology	FERRUPS FE700VA
Best Power Technology	FERRUPS FE7KVA
Best Power Technology	FERRUPS FE850VA
Best Power Technology	Fortress LI 1.3KB/D
Best Power Technology	Fortress LI 1.7KF/FX
Best Power Technology	Fortress LI 1.7KG/GX
Best Power Technology	Fortress LI 1.7KJX
Best Power Technology	Fortress LI 1020B/D
Best Power Technology	Fortress LI 1420B/D

Hardware Vendor	Device Name
Best Power Technology	Fortress LI 2.5KP/PX
Best Power Technology	Fortress LI 2KF/G/H/J
Best Power Technology	Fortress LI 360B/D
Best Power Technology	Fortress LI 3KL/LX
Best Power Technology	Fortress LI 3KN/NX
Best Power Technology	Fortress LI 3KQ/QX
Best Power Technology	Fortress LI 3KR/RX
Best Power Technology	Fortress LI 3KS
Best Power Technology	Fortress LI 3KS/SX
Best Power Technology	Fortress LI 460B/D
Best Power Technology	Fortress LI 660B/D
Best Power Technology	Fortress LI 950B/D
ViewSonic	Opti-UPS 1000E
ViewSonic	Opti-UPS 1400E
ViewSonic	Opti-UPS 280E
ViewSonic	Opti-UPS 420E
ViewSonic	Opti-UPS 650E

Tape Drives

Hardware Vendor	Device Bus	Device Name
Archive	SCSI	2000DAT (EAX4350)
Archive	SCSI	2150/2250
Archive	SCSI	2525
Archive	SCSI	2750
Archive	SCSI	2800
Archive	SCSI	4000DAT (4324NP)
Archive	SCSI	4000DAT (4352XP)
Archive	SCSI	4356XP
Archive	N/A	51250Q (SuperHornet)

continues

Hardware Vendor	Device Bus	Device Name
Archive	SCSI	Archive 4326NP
Archive	SCSI	Archive 4326RP
Bull	SCSI	EXB-8505XL
Bull	SCSI	TDC4222
Colorado	N/A	Jumbo 120
Colorado	N/A	Jumbo 250
Compaq	SCSI	4/16 Gigabyte TurboDAT
Compaq	SCSI	TurboDAT Autoloader
Conner Peripherals	ISA-8	2Mbps Controller
Conner Peripherals	SCSI	4326NP
Conner Peripherals	SCSI	4326RP
Conner Peripherals	SCSI	4356XP
Conner Peripherals	SCSI	CTD2004H-S
Conner Peripherals	SCSI	CTD2004R-S
Conner Peripherals	SCSI	CTD4004H-S
Conner Peripherals	SCSI	CTD4004R-S
Conner Peripherals	SCSI	CTD8000E-S
Conner Peripherals	SCSI	CTD8000H-S
Conner Peripherals	SCSI	CTD8000R-S
Conner Peripherals	N/A	CTM1360
Conner Peripherals	IDE	CTM4000
Conner Peripherals	N/A	CTM420
Conner Peripherals	N/A	CTM700
Conner Peripherals	SCSI	CTMS 3200
Conner Peripherals	N/A	CTT3200
Conner Peripherals	N/A	CTT800
Conner Peripherals	IDE	CTT8000-A
Conner Peripherals	SCSI	CTT8000R-S
Conner Peripherals	N/A	TapeStor 1360/1700
Conner Peripherals	N/A	TapeStor 3200
Conner Peripherals	N/A	TapeStor 420
Conner Peripherals	N/A	TapeStor 700/850

Hardware Vendor	Device Bus	Device Name
Conner Peripherals	N/A	TapeStor 800
Digital Equipment	SCSI	DLT2000
Digital Equipment	SCSI	TLZ06
Digital Equipment	SCSI	TLZ07
Digital Equipment	SCSI	TLZ09
Digital Equipment	SCSI	TLZ7L-DA
Digital Equipment	SCSI	TZ-88
Digital Equipment	SCSI	TZ-88N
Digital Equipment	SCSI	TZ86
Digital Equipment	SCSI	TZ87
Digital Equipment	SCSI	TZK10
Digital Equipment	SCSI	TZK11
Digital Equipment	SCSI	TZK12
Exabyte	SCSI	2501
Exabyte	SCSI	4200
Exabyte	SCSI	4200c
Exabyte	SCSI	EXB-8200
Exabyte	SCSI	EXB-8200ST
Exabyte	SCSI	EXB-8205
Exabyte	SCSI	EXB-8205ST
Exabyte	SCSI	EXB-8500
Exabyte	SCSI	EXB-8500c
Exabyte	SCSI	EXB-8500cST
Exabyte	SCSI	EXB-8500ST
Exabyte	SCSI	EXB-8505
Exabyte	SCSI	EXB-8505ST
Exabyte	SCSI	EXB-8505XL
Hewlett-Packard	SCSI	35470a
Hewlett-Packard	SCSI	35480a
Hewlett-Packard	SCSI	C1503a
Hewlett-Packard	SCSI	C1504a

continues

Hardware Vendor	Device Bus	Device Name
Hewlett-Packard	SCSI	C1533-00100
Hewlett-Packard	SCSI	C1533a
Hewlett-Packard	SCSI	C1534-00100
Hewlett-Packard	SCSI	C1534a
Hewlett-Packard	SCSI	C1536-00100
Hewlett-Packard	SCSI	C1536a
Hewlett-Packard	SCSI	C2224c
Hewlett-Packard	SCSI	C2225b
Hewlett-Packard	ISA-16	Colorado FC-10 (1Mbps)
Hewlett-Packard	ISA-16	Colorado FC-20 (2Mbps)
Hewlett-Packard	N/A	Colorado Jumbo 1400
Hewlett-Packard	N/A	Colorado Jumbo 350
Hewlett-Packard	N/A	Colorado Jumbo 700
Hewlett-Packard	N/A	Colorado T1000
Hewlett-Packard	SCSI	Colorado T4000s
Hewlett-Packard	FLOPPY	HP Colorado T3000 Tape Drive
Hewlett-Packard	SCSI	JetStore 2000
Hewlett-Packard	SCSI	JetStore 2000e
Hewlett-Packard	SCSI	JetStore 2000i
Hewlett-Packard	SCSI	JetStore 5000
Hewlett-Packard	SCSI	JetStore 5000e
Hewlett-Packard	SCSI	JetStore 5000i
Hewlett-Packard	SCSI	JetStore 6000e
Hewlett-Packard	SCSI	JetStore 6000i
Hewlett-Packard	SCSI	SureStore 2000e
Hewlett-Packard	SCSI	SureStore 2000i
Hewlett-Packard	SCSI	SureStore 5000e
Hewlett-Packard	SCSI	SureStore 5000eU
Hewlett-Packard	SCSI	SureStore 5000i
Hewlett-Packard	SCSI	SureStore 6000e
Hewlett-Packard	SCSI	SureStore 6000eU
Hewlett-Packard	SCSI	SureStore 6000i
IBM	SCSI	2.0GB 4mm DAT 3440 001

Hardware Vendor	Device Bus	Device Name
IBM	SCSI	2.0GB 4mm Tape Drive Option
IBM	SCSI	3445 Model 001 5.0GB 8mm
IBM	SCSI	3450 1.2GB Tape Drive
IBM	SCSI	3532-023 8mm Tape Drive
IBM	SCSI	4/10GB 4mm DAT Drive
IBM	SCSI	5.0GB 8mm Tape Drive Option
Iomega	N/A	Ditto Easy 3200
Iomega	N/A	Ditto Easy 800
Iomega	N/A	Tape 250
Maynard	SCSI	1350Q
Maynard	SCSI	525Q
Quantum	SCSI	DLT 4000
Seagate Technology	ISA-8	2Mbps Controller
Seagate Technology	SCSI	4320RT
Seagate Technology	SCSI	4324RP
Seagate Technology	SCSI	4326NP
Seagate Technology	SCSI	4326RP
Seagate Technology	SCSI	4356XP
Seagate Technology	SCSI	CTD2004H-S
Seagate Technology	SCSI	CTD2004R-S
Seagate Technology	SCSI	CTD4004H-S
Seagate Technology	SCSI	CTD4004R-S
Seagate Technology	SCSI	CTD8000E-S
Seagate Technology	SCSI	CTD8000H-S
Seagate Technology	SCSI	CTD8000R-S
Seagate Technology	N/A	CTM1360
Seagate Technology	IDE	CTM4000
Seagate Technology	N/A	CTM420
Seagate Technology	N/A	CTM700
Seagate Technology	SCSI	CTMS 3200
Seagate Technology	N/A	CTT3200
Seagate Technology	N/A	CTT800

continues

Hardware Vendor	Device Bus	Device Name
Seagate Technology	IDE	CTT8000-A
Seagate Technology	SCSI	CTT8000R-S
Seagate Technology	N/A	TapeStor 1360/1700
Seagate Technology	N/A	TapeStor 3200
Seagate Technology	N/A	TapeStor 420
Seagate Technology	N/A	TapeStor 700/850
Seagate Technology	N/A	TapeStor 800
Sony	SCSI	SDT 2000
Sony	SCSI	SDT 4000
Sony	SCSI	SDT 5000
Sony	SCSI	SDT 5200
Sony	SCSI	SDT 7000
Tandberg Data	SCSI	3660
Tandberg Data	SCSI	3820
Tandberg Data	SCSI	4120
Tandberg Data	SCSI	4220
Tandberg Data	SCSI	4222
Tandberg Data	SCSI	Panther Mini 4600
Tandberg Data	SCSI	TDC 3520
Tandberg Data	SCSI	TDC 3720
Tecmar	SCSI	DATaVault 2000
Tecmar	SCSI	QICVault 2400ex
Tecmar	SCSI	QICVault 4000ex
Tecmar	SCSI	QICVault 720ex
Tecmar	SCSI	QT-525ES
WangDAT	SCSI	Model 1300XL
WangDAT	SCSI	Model 3100
WangDAT	SCSI	Model 3400DX
WangTek	N/A	3080
Wangtek	SCSI	51000ES
Wangtek	SCSI	5150ES
Wangtek	SCSI	5525ES

B

Troubleshooting/ Error List

Peter Norton™

There are literally thousands of error messages and probable causes for those messages in any operating system. Microsoft's reference for Windows NT includes more than 700 pages of messages and possible answers to those messages. This is not to pick on Microsoft, but only to illustrate that if an error message doesn't exactly seem like English, you must consider the sheer volume of messages that a operating system company must catalog for you.

Chances are that if you've come to this appendix you have an error of some sort in your life right now. I certainly hope not, but if so, you're looking for some answers. Well, as I mentioned, there are many possible answers, so what I concentrate on here is giving you some of the more common issues and pointing you to places to find others. The areas covered here are the most common areas for being stopped or left without communications. (If you're completely stopped or unable to communicate, you won't be checking the Internet for answers any time soon.)

This appendix looks at

- Service packs
- Common RAS errors
- Common STOP errors

Service Packs

Service packs are used by Microsoft to distribute updates to software packages that have already been released. Service packs keep the product current, and extend and update your computer's functionality so you'll never have to worry about becoming out-of-date. Service packs include updates, system administration tools, drivers, and additional components. All are conveniently bundled for easy downloading.

Windows NT 4.0 (Server and Workstation), by the release of this book, have already been updated twice; the current service pack is called Service Pack 2. This service pack is essential to being able to add any services from Microsoft that are released after it.

Peter's Principle: Get in the Support Call Fast Lane

When calling for vendor support, it's very important that you have all the patches and/or updates already loaded. This is not to save the support staff time, but instead to help you get answers. When a phone support person answers the call, he has been given a certain amount of time to spend with each client. So support staff will often weed out callers as soon as the call begins by asking whether you have the current patches. If not, you'll be sent to get them. Waiting for a half hour on the phone only to be sent away can be heartbreaking.

The service pack can be ordered on CD-ROM or downloaded from the Web at http://www.microsoft.com/ntserver. The CD-ROM version is available alone or on the Microsoft TechNet CD subscription service.

> **Tip:** The Microsoft TechNet CD subscription service is a monthly service offered by Microsoft that allows the user to keep current versions of the Microsoft Knowledge Base and Microsoft service packs. It can be quite valuable to anyone who does frequent support work.

In addition to various fixes for Windows NT 4.0, the downloadable version of Service Pack 2 includes the following:

- Hooks for Microsoft Transaction Server
- Hooks for routing
- Hooks for clustering
- New DHCP Superscope feature
- Strong password filtering
- Scheduling tool for Autocheck on NTFS partitions
- 128-bit RAS encryption (North American version only)
- Enhancements to NetBIOS over TCP/IP (NetBT)
- New Win32 APIs that increase the performance of Microsoft SQL Server

In addition to various fixes for Windows NT 4.0 and the items just listed, the CD-ROM version of Service Pack 2 includes the following:

- Internet Information Server 3.0, which includes the following:
  - Active Server Pages
  - Microsoft Index Server 1.1
  - Microsoft NetShow Live and On-Demand Server
  - Microsoft FrontPage 97 Server Extensions for IIS
  - Crystal Reports
- Internet Explorer 3.01
- Microsoft FrontPage 97—installs only on Windows NT Server

> **Tip:** Many of the troubleshooting messages that are known to Microsoft can be easily researched through a Web site that Microsoft publishes called the "Trouble Shooter" at

`http://www.microsoft.com/support/tshooters.htm`. This site walks you through an issue step by step—not only for Windows NT, but for Windows 95 and Office products as well.

Common RAS Problems

Modem connectivity has become the lifeline of many network administrators in recent years. In fact, many of us couldn't get through the day without making some sort of modem connection. Because RAS is the modem facility that your NT server will use, this section covers some common RAS issues that you may encounter, as well as some of the solutions.

Each problem follows a format of announcing the problem followed by steps that you might take to solve the problem.

Cannot Connect After Dialing with RAS

You may need to disable software compression for this connection. To do so, use the following steps:

1. In Dial-Up Networking, click the appropriate phone book entry.
2. Click More, and then click Edit Entry and Modem Properties.
3. On the Server tab, clear the Enable Software Compression check box.

692 Error in RAS

When you attempt to dial with Dial-Up Networking, the following error message may appear:

```
Error 692: Hardware failure in port or attached device
```

If you receive this or another error message, the modem is not working properly.

Dial-Up Networking Error 633

If you have upgraded from Windows NT v3.51 and you are running a program that monitors the phone line (for example, a fax program), you may receive an error message similar to the following message that indicates that the port is busy when trying to dial out with Dial-Up Networking:

```
Error 633: The port is already in use or is not configured for Remote Access dial out
```

If RAS was installed in Windows NT 3.51 prior to the upgrade, the kernel-mode telephony driver that's used in Windows NT 3.51 is retained and RAS uses non-Unimodem drivers. If another program (for example, a fax program) uses the Unimodem driver and is set to answer automatically, that program will cause TAPI 2.0 to control the communications port. The result is that the communications port is not available to the non-Unimodem version of RAS.

To resolve this problem, remove the non-Unimodem driver and replace it with one supplied with Windows NT 4.0. Follow these steps:

1. In Control Panel, double-click the Network icon.

2. Click the Services tab.

3. Click Remote Access Service, and then click Properties.

4. If the type of modem listed indicates that the kernel-mode TAPI driver is still being used [that is, it lists the type as Modem (modem.inf)], click the port and then click Remove.

5. Click Add to add the Unimodem driver (the driver that's supplied by Windows NT 4.0) for the port.

6. Click Continue, and restart your computer when prompted to do so.

Dial-Up Networking Error 640

If the telephone line is unusually noisy, you may receive an error message such as this:

```
Error 640: A NetBIOS error has occurred.
```

This message indicates that the modems may not be able to negotiate a connection at a higher speed. Try setting the modem speed on the client computer down to a lower speed such as 9600bps by using the following steps:

1. In Dial-Up Networking, click the appropriate phone book entry.

2. Click More, and then click Edit Entry and Modem Properties.

3. Click Configure for the modem, and then click 9600 in the Initial Speed box.

If your modem is able to connect to the RAS server at a lower speed, try the following steps to attempt to connect at higher speeds:

1. Check the Windows NT Hardware Compatibility List to ensure that your modem is supported.

2. Try to call another modem to see whether you can connect at a higher speed.

3. Call the RAS server administrator to determine what type of modem is being used. Some modems may have compatibility issues that may affect the connection speed.

4. Ensure that your modem is not configured in Windows NT for a slower speed.

Use the following steps to determine the speed for which your modem is configured in Windows NT:

1. In Control Panel, double-click the Modems icon.
2. Click the modem you're using, and then click Properties. The maximum speed is displayed on the Properties tab.

STOP Error Messages

This section focuses on troubleshooting kernel-mode STOP error messages (blue screens). This type of screen is sometimes referred to as a *Blue Screen of Death* (BSD) because it's one of the few times that NT really stops cold.

Once a STOP error has been encountered, it's not something that you can ignore. A STOP error usually indicates that the server has encountered a corrupt piece of code within its own set of instructions or software. It's rare to find an NT server at a BSD after it's up and running—it's more common to have these screens occur during startup. But don't think it can never happen.

When a blue screen appears, don't panic. There are some very definite steps that need to be followed, but first of all don't just turn off the machine. The first step is going to be gathering information; if you turn off the machine you may never see the original offending error again.

Steps for Kernel-Mode STOP Screens

Step 1: Gather information.

Gather the following information from the system:

- The top four lines of the STOP screen. Generally, the information you need will look something like the following:

```
STOP 0x0000000A(0x0000000B, 0x00000002, 0x00000000, 0xFE34C882
IRQL_NOT_LESS_OR_EQUAL
ADDRESS 0xFE34C882 has base at 0xFE000000: NTOSKRNL.EXE
```

- Full hardware information, including the following:
  - System information (BIOS, CMOS settings, and so forth)
  - All controllers/adapters installed and their BIOS versions
- The version of Windows NT installed, and any service packs, SSDs, hotfixes, and third-party drivers installed.
- When the STOP screen occurs and how frequently it occurs. If possible, get answers to the following questions:
  - What has changed since the last good start of the server?
  - Does the STOP always occur when you perform a certain operation?
  - If it appears to be random, how often does it occur?

> **Tip:** Most computer problems occur after some change has been made. Random failure is very rare. So track any changes that are made to your system. NO CHANGE IS MINOR TO YOUR SERVER OR NETWORK.

Step 2: Determine whether the problem is a known issue with a hotfix or workaround.

The next step is to search the Microsoft Knowledge Base and other resources to see whether this particular STOP screen is a known issue with a hotfix or workaround. Try the following keyword searches in the Microsoft Knowledge Base:

- Search the word STOP, the STOP code, and the program modules named in the top four lines of the STOP screen as one string. In the previous example, you would search on the keywords STOP 0x0000000A NTOSKRNL.EXE.

- If this search doesn't turn up anything, search on just the STOP code to see whether there are any general troubleshooting articles on the subject. Be warned—for some common STOPs, this will turn up a large list.

Once you get the results of each search back, check through the list for an article where the symptoms appear to match the problem as closely as possible, and apply any fixes or workarounds listed in that article.

Step 3: Determine whether the problem is caused by hardware.

A STOP screen can easily be caused by a hardware failure, an out-of-date BIOS, or a hardware configuration issue, even when the system and components are on the Hardware Compatibility List (HCL). The following indications frequently point to a failure or problem in hardware:

- The system has been working fine until now and suddenly fails when a specific operation is performed. An example of this would be a daily backup that has worked until now but is suddenly failing with a kernel STOP. In these cases, any hardware systems involved are suspect and should be checked out and, if possible, swapped for different ones as a test.

- A new piece of hardware was added, and a STOP screen appeared during system restart or when the new hardware was used. This definitely points to the new hardware, even if that hardware is on the HCL. Investigate the possibility of bad hardware, an old BIOS that needs to be updated, conflicting settings (IRQ, I/O address, and so forth), or just an incorrect configuration. Another possibility is that an updated driver is needed to fix the problem.

- Keep in mind that a STOP that occurs only when a certain operation is carried out (such as booting the system, copying a file, or doing a backup) but doesn't happen every time is probably a software problem. A problem in software will generally occur every time a certain operation or set of operations is carried out, where a hardware problem can show up at random times. While randomness isn't always a sign of hardware problems, it is suspect;

you should carry out normal hardware troubleshooting in these cases—checking for an outdated or problem BIOS, checking for interrupt or I/O conflicts, and swapping out any components that appear to be related to the problem.

Even if you don't find any of these indications, verify that the problem isn't hardware-related by doing the following:

1. Check BIOS versions on the motherboard, as well as the SCSI controller and any other controller.
2. Look for IRQ, I/O address, and DMA conflicts.
3. Verify that all hardware is configured correctly, especially SCSI devices.

Step 4: Troubleshoot well-known STOP codes.

You may not find an article with a specific workaround or solution; however, there are a number of STOP error messages that have common causes:

- STOP 0x0000000A IRQL_NOT_LESS_OR_EQUAL
- STOP 0x0000001E KMODE_EXCEPTION_NOT_HANDLED
- STOP 0x00000024 NTFS_FILE_SYSTEM
- STOP 0x0000002E DATA_BUS_ERROR
- STOP 0x0000003E MULTIPROCESSOR_CONFIGURATION_NOT_SUPPORTED
- STOP 0x00000058 FTDISK_INTERNAL_ERROR
- STOP 0x00000077 KERNEL_STACK_INPAGE_ERROR
- STOP 0x00000079 MISMATCHED_HAL
- STOP 0x0000007B INACCESSIBLE_BOOT_DEVICE
- STOP 0x0000007F UNEXPECTED_KERNEL_MODE_TRAP
- STOP 0x0000008B MBR_CHECKSUM_MISMATCH
- STOP 0xC0000218 STATUS_CANNOT_LOAD_REGISTRY_FILE
- STOP 0xC000021A STATUS_SYSTEM_PROCESS_TERMINATED
- STOP 0xC0000221 STATUS_IMAGE_CHECKSUM_MISMATCH

A detailed description of each of these errors along with possible solutions is included in the next section of this appendix, "STOP Error Solutions."

Step 5: Determine whether the problem is caused by non-HCL hardware.

If the system is not on the HCL or if non-HCL components such as the hard disk drive controller, network card, or video appear to be involved in the problem, Microsoft may not be able to fully support and diagnose the problem.

Appendix A of this book contains a number of the commonly supported hardware items from the HCL. However, if you don't find a particular item in that list, you can find the complete HCL at this Microsoft Web site:

```
http://www.microsoft.com/NTSERVER/HCL/hclintro.htm
```

STOP Error Solutions

Following are each of the errors from Step 4 of troubleshooting STOP errors (see the preceding section), but now listed with possible solutions:

STOP 0x0000000A IRQL_NOT_LESS_OR_EQUAL

One of the most common kernel STOP messages, a STOP 0x0000000A indicates that a kernel-mode process attempted to access and address a memory address it didn't have permission to access. The most common cause of this STOP is a bad pointer, which in turn is caused by a software bug, memory corruption, or bad values returned by hardware queries.

In general, the only way to determine the specific cause of a STOP 0xA is by using the debugger; however, the STOP screen itself can frequently give you clues to the cause. For more information on interpreting the STOP screen and determining the cause of a STOP 0xA, see the following Microsoft Knowledge Base article:

```
Q130802 General Information on STOP 0x0000000A
```

You can also search the Microsoft Knowledge Base on the STOP code; this may turn up a hotfix or workaround if this is a known issue.

STOP 0x0000001E KMODE_EXCEPTION_NOT_HANDLED

A STOP 0x000000001E is probably the second most common STOP error message under Windows NT. This message indicates that an error condition was detected by the kernel and Windows NT was unable to continue running because of this error condition. The types of problems that can cause this STOP error message are very similar to the problems that cause a STOP 0x0000000A, including bad pointers, invalid addresses, and other types of access violations.

The top four lines of a STOP 0x1E will generally appear as follows:

```
STOP: 0x0000001E (0xAAAAAAAA,0xBBBBBBBB,0xCCCCCCCC,0xDDDDDDDD)
KMODE_EXCEPTION_NOT_HANDLED AAAAAAAA from BBBBBBBB (CCCCCCCC,DDDDDDDD)
Address BBBBBBBB has base at XXXXXXXX - MODULE1.SYS
Address CCCCCCCC has base at YYYYYYYY - MODULE2.SYS
```

In the top line, the four hexadecimal parameters after the STOP code have the following meanings:

- 0xAAAAAAAA is a code identifying the exception that was not handled.
- 0xBBBBBBBB is the address at which the exception occurred.
- 0xCCCCCCCC is the first parameter of the exception; sometimes this is another address in code.
- 0xDDDDDDDD is the second parameter of the exception, which can vary in meaning.

Interpreting the Parameters

The first parameter is a Windows NT error code; these codes are defined in the file Ntstatus.h, which can also be found in the Software Developer's Kit (SDK). This parameter tells you the type of error. The second parameter is also important in that it tells you in what code module the error occurred. This can frequently point to an individual driver or piece of hardware that is at fault, which will generally be listed on the third line of the STOP screen. The last two parameters vary depending on the exception that has occurred; you'll generally find a description of the parameters included with the name of the error code in Ntstatus.h. If no parameters are associated with the error code, the last two hexadecimal numbers are 0x00000000.

For example, consider the following STOP error message:

```
STOP: 0x0000001E (0xC0000005, 0xFCA733B9, 0x00000000, 0x00000000)
KMODE_EXCEPTION_NOT_HANDLED 0xC0000005 from 0xFCA733B9 (0x0, 0x0)
Address FCA733B9 has base at FCA70000 - SRV.SYS
```

An access violation (0xC0000005) occurred in module Srv.sys, which is the kernel-mode server service. There were no parameters associated with this error code.

Troubleshooting the STOP

When trying to determine the cause of this STOP, check the following:

- Search the Microsoft Knowledge Base on the STOP code, the error code, and the module in which the violation occurred. This may turn up a hotfix or workaround, if this is a known issue. For example, a search of the Microsoft Knowledge Base on the words STOP and Services for Macintosh could turn up the following article:

  Q135667 STOP 1E When Using File Manager and Services for Macintosh (SFM)

- Look up the error code in Ntstatus.h and search the Microsoft Knowledge Base on the text of the error (for example, access violation) and the module in which it occurred.
- If the module in question is a third-party driver, contact the manufacturer of the third-party driver for help.

If your Knowledge Base searches don't turn up anything, and no third-party driver or hardware is indicated by the STOP screen, a debug will be necessary to determine whether the problem is caused by hardware or software.

STOP 0x00000024 NTFS_FILE_SYSTEM

Although not as common as some other STOP codes, STOP 0x00000024 is specifically tied to error conditions and traps in the Windows NT file system (NTFS) driver. A STOP in the NTFS is unlikely to be caused by hardware problems, although that's a possibility.

STOP 0x0000002E DATA_BUS_ERROR

A STOP 0x0000002E indicates that a parity error in system memory has been detected. This STOP is almost always caused by a hardware problem, such as a configuration issue, bad hardware, or incompatible hardware. The exception to this is when a device driver has accessed an address in the 0x8XXXXXXX range that doesn't exist (that is, it doesn't have a physical address mapping).

The parameters of a STOP 0x2E appear as follows:

```
STOP: 0x0000002E (0xAAAAAAAA,0xBBBBBBBB,0xCCCCCCCC,0xDDDDDDDD)
```

These parameters have the following meanings:

- 0xAAAAAAAA is the virtual address that caused the fault.
- 0xBBBBBBBB is the physical address that caused the fault.
- 0xCCCCCCCC is the processor status register.
- 0xDDDDDDDD is the faulting instruction register.

Troubleshooting the STOP

The most common cause of this STOP is a hardware problem. However, without performing a debug, it can be difficult to be sure whether the cause is hardware or a faulty driver. The following guidelines can help:

- If the system has been up and running for some time and the STOP suddenly occurred, bad hardware is the likely suspect.
- If the STOP occurred after installing a new or updated device driver, the driver is suspect and should be removed or replaced. If the STOP occurs during boot, this may require installing a separate copy of Windows NT in order to rename or replace the driver file.
- If a new piece of hardware was added, the hardware may be suspect and should be removed to see whether the problem still occurs.

- If the problem appears on a freshly installed system, check the following things to see whether they need to be updated:
  - Firmware on RISC systems
  - BIOS revisions on motherboard
  - BIOS revisions on SCSI controller or network cards

STOP 0x0000003E MULTIPROCESSOR_CONFIGURATION_NOT_SUPPORTED

A STOP 0x0000003E indicates that a system has multiple processors that are asymmetric in relation to one another. To be symmetric, all processors must be of the same type and level. For example, trying to mix a Pentium-level processor with an 80486 causes this bug check. Additionally, on x86 systems, either all processors should have floating-point capabilities, or none should.

Also, Windows NT 3.5 and greater no longer support 386 multiprocessor computers. You'll get this bug check if you somehow install a Windows NT 3.5 or later multiprocessor build on a multiprocessor 386 computer. This STOP doesn't indicate a mismatch between the hardware abstraction layer (HAL) and kernel; that mismatch results in a STOP 0x00000079.

This STOP is always caused by hardware incompatibilities or misconfiguration and should be dealt with accordingly.

STOP 0x00000058 FTDISK_INTERNAL_ERROR

A STOP 0x00000058 occurs when your boot or system partition is mirrored and the image on the mirror drive is more up-to-date than the image on the primary.

This situation can occur when you have booted off the mirrored partition while the primary partition was offline and then the primary is brought back online. For more information on recovering from this error, see the following article in the Microsoft Knowledge Base:

```
Q128630 How to Recover From a STOP 0x00000058 FTDISK_INTERNAL_ERROR
```

STOP 0x00000077 KERNEL_STACK_INPAGE_ERROR and ...

Both a STOP 0x77 and a 0x7A indicate that Windows NT attempted to read in a page of kernel data from the paging file and was unable to do so. Both of these STOPs are frequently caused by hardware problems, although in a few rare situations they could also be the result of a software failure. For more information on troubleshooting a STOP 0x77 or 0x7A, see the following Microsoft Knowledge Base article:

```
Q130801 Common Causes of STOP Messages 0x00000077 and 0x0000007A
```

STOP 0x00000079 MISMATCHED_HAL

This is not a common STOP error message; a STOP 0x00000079 has a very specific cause. It indicates that you are using a single-processor hardware abstraction layer (HAL) with the multiprocessor kernel, or vice versa. It can also indicate that one of those two files is out-of-date (for example, the HAL is designed for Windows NT 3.5 and the kernel is from Windows NT 3.51). In any case, you need to determine which HAL and which kernel (Ntoskrnl.exe or Ntkrnlmp.exe) to use, and replace the incorrect file with the correct one.

The kernel file will always be Ntoskrnl.exe for single-processor systems or Ntkrnlmp.exe for multi-processor systems. Once Windows NT has been installed, the file will be renamed to Ntoskrnl.exe regardless of which type of system.

The HAL file will also always be renamed Hal.dll after installation, but there are several possible HALs on the installation media. The default HAL for single-processor x86 systems is Hal.dll; the default HAL for multiprocessor x86 systems is Halmps.dll. There is no default HAL for RISC systems; each type of RISC system has its own HAL. For more information on the different HAL files, see the Windows NT 3.51 Resource Kit Update. In the update to the kernel messaging chapter is a complete list of all HALs shipped with Windows NT 3.51 for all platforms, including the filename on the installation media as well as the size of the file once decompressed, so you can determine which file has actually been installed on the system.

STOP 0x0000007B INACCESSIBLE_BOOT_DEVICE

Another very common STOP, a 0x0000007B indicates that during boot process Windows NT lost access to the boot drive for some reason. This STOP always occurs while booting the system and cannot be debugged, as it generally occurs before the operating system has loaded the debugger.

Troubleshooting the STOP

You can almost always resolve a STOP 0x7B without calling Microsoft Support by first checking for the following causes:

- **Master boot record (MBR) and boot sector viruses.** Even on an NTFS partition, it's possible to contract an MBR or boot sector virus if the system has been booted recently from an infected floppy disk. An MBR or boot sector virus will frequently result in a STOP 0x7B. To check for viruses, boot from a floppy disk that has already been virus-checked and run an up-to-date antivirus utility. It may also be possible to boot by creating an NTFS boot floppy disk (also called an *FT boot disk*) that's clean of all viruses. This will bypass the boot sector on the hard drive and prevent the virus from loading. At this point, your system won't be clean, but you'll be able to run one of the antivirus programs designed for Windows NT.

- **Incorrect device driver installed.** Windows NT generally starts its boot by using INT 13 to access the hard drive; however, during the load of the operating system, it will load a device driver for the drive controller. If the device driver is incorrect, out-of-date, or corrupted in some way, a STOP 0x7B will result.

- **Incompatible, incorrectly configured, or corrupted hardware.** A common cause of a STOP 0x7B is a drive controller or drive that's incompatible, incorrectly configured, or has simply developed problems. Check out the following things:

  - Verify that the drive and controller are on the Windows NT hardware compatibility list (HCL). Please note that most SCSI and EIDE drives are compatible with Windows NT, even if they're not listed on the HCL.

  - For a SCSI controller, check the firmware revision on the controller, make sure that the SCSI bus is correctly terminated, and verify that the cabling is good. It may not hurt to swap out the cable, just in case.

  - If possible, try swapping out the drive controller, cabling, or even drives.

STOP 0x0000007F UNEXPECTED_KERNEL_MODE_TRAP

A STOP 0x0000007F occurs on systems with Intel x86-based processors and indicates that an unexpected failure condition has been signaled by the processor. This STOP error message indicates that a failure has occurred at the processor level; therefore, this STOP message is almost always caused by hardware problems, except in rare cases.

STOP 0x0000008B MBR_CHECKSUM_MISMATCH

A STOP 0x0000008B error message indicates that the checksum of the master boot record (MBR) found during boot did not match the checksum passed in by the loader. This almost always indicates an MBR virus. If possible, run an antivirus program to clean the system. Alternatively, booting from an MS-DOS floppy disk and running FDISK /MBR might also clean out the MBR.

Search the Microsoft Knowledge Base on the STOP code in which the violation occurred. This may turn up a hotfix or workaround, if this is a known issue.

STOP 0xC0000218 STATUS_CANNOT_LOAD_REGISTRY_FILE

This STOP error message indicates that a Registry file failed to load during startup. The most likely cause is that the Registry file is corrupt or missing. Either use the emergency repair disk or reinstall and restore from a backup; this will usually correct the problem.

Another frequent cause of this error message is physical disk corruption, generally a bad sector in one of the Registry files. In this case, it will probably require a low-level format of the drive, followed by reinstalling and restoring from a backup. If access to the drive is required before the low-level format, a second installation of Windows NT on an alternate drive will generally work.

STOP 0xC000021a
STATUS_SYSTEM_PROCESS_TERMINATED

This STOP error message indicates that either Winlogon or CSRSS (Win32 API support) quit unexpectedly. The exit code gives further information. Usually the exit code is c0000005, meaning that an unhandled exception caused Winlogon or CSRSS to stop. There isn't much you can do unless this becomes a persistent problem. For information on exit codes, see the file Ntstatus.h. Because Windows NT can't run without Winlogon or CSRSS, this is one of the few situations where a user mode service can bring down the system.

This STOP error message can't be debugged because the actual error occurred in a user mode process. The first step in troubleshooting this STOP is to gather information on when it occurred, and then search the Microsoft Knowledge Base on the keyword 0xC000021A, the module that the violation occurred in, Winlogon or CSRSS, and the exit code.

If that doesn't turn up any likely hits, the system needs to be configured for a user mode debug so that the user mode process can be debugged when the true error occurs. If the STOP error message is occurring during startup, and occurs every startup, you will need to get the system into a startup state. Try the following:

- Click the Last Known Good Configuration option during startup.
- Run an emergency repair on the system.
- If the problem occurred after adding a driver, adding a piece of hardware, or making a change in the system, try backing out the change.
- Search the Microsoft Knowledge Base on STOP 0xC000021A. For example, a search on STOP 0x00000021A could turn up this article:

  Q139274 Updated System Environment Variables Result in STOP 0x0000021a

STOP 0xC0000221
STATUS_IMAGE_CHECKSUM_MISMATCH

A STOP 0xC0000221 error message indicates that a driver is corrupt, or that a corrupt system DLL was detected. Windows NT does its best to verify the integrity of drivers and important system DLLs; if they're corrupt, Windows NT returns a STOP error message with the name of the corrupt file. This prevents the system from stopping when corruption occurs later.

To correct this problem, try the following techniques:

- Run an emergency repair, and select the option to repair system files.
- Run an in-place upgrade; that is, an upgrade on top of the existing copy of Windows NT. This preserves all Registry settings and configuration information, but replaces all system files.
- If a specific file was identified as corrupted in the STOP screen, try replacing that individual file by hand. If the system partition is FAT, boot from an MS-DOS floppy disk and replace the file by hand; if it's NTFS, you need to install a second copy of Windows NT in another directory and then replace the file by hand.
- If all else fails, try reinstalling and restoring from a backup.
- Search the Microsoft Knowledge Base on STOP 0xC0000221 and any keywords describing the circumstances under which the STOP occurred; there are many articles on specific causes of this STOP error message.

For Further Information

The problems covered here are only a fraction of the error codes. But, hopefully, they're enough to cover the issues that will most commonly occur.

For more information on possible error codes that you will encounter, check these sources:

- Sams titles that cover the full list of error codes; for example, *Windows NT Troubleshooting & Configuration*.
- The Microsoft Knowledge Base Web site:

  http://www.microsoft.com/ntserver
- The Microsoft Windows NT Resource Kit.

  There are separate kits for NT 3.51 and NT 4.0, but to have a complete reference you must have both. The NT 3.51 kit contains a full reference to the error codes, but the NT 4.0 kit contains only an update for the new version.

C

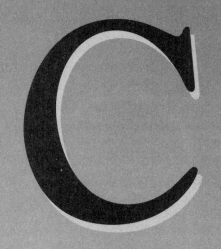

IP Decimal/
Binary/
Hexadecimal
Conversion
Table

Peter Norton™

IP subnet masks have always been a nightmare to calculate in your head because you must be able to see the relationship between the binary octets and the decimal or hexadecimal number that you mask. Hopefully, this chart will help you to see the relationships and equivalence.

As covered in Chapter 21, "TCP/IP Networking," the subnet mask is used in TCP/IP addressing to let the system know what portion of the IP address is the network address and what portion is the node address. I won't cover this topic again here, but I'll help you find the proper number for splitting those subnet masks into smaller pieces.

If you want to split a subnet into even sections such as 255.255.0.0 or 255.255.255.0, it's fairly simple to see which octets make up the network and host addresses. But what if you need to split a network into an even smaller subset—say, for example, leaving seven available node addresses per network? Then you need a mask that leaves only seven bits open.

By looking at the following table, you can see that 7 is represented in binary as 00000111. That means that I need a final subnet number that leaves those last three digits available: 11111000. When you look at it in binary, that makes sense. But what's the decimal number that I can write down? Look at the table—it's 248.

Decimal Number	Binary Equivalent	Hexadecimal
0	00000000	00
1	00000001	01
2	00000010	02
3	00000011	03
4	00000100	04
5	00000101	05
6	00000110	06
7	00000111	07
8	00001000	08
9	00001001	09
10	00001010	0A
11	00001011	0B
12	00001100	0C
13	00001101	0D
14	00001110	0E
15	00001111	0F
16	00010000	10
17	00010001	11

Decimal Number	Binary Equivalent	Hexadecimal
18	00010010	12
19	00010011	13
20	00010100	14
21	00010101	15
22	00010110	16
23	00010111	17
24	00011000	18
25	00011001	19
26	00011010	1A
27	00011011	1B
28	00011100	1C
29	00011101	1D
30	00011110	1E
31	00011111	1F
32	00100000	20
33	00100001	21
34	00100010	22
35	00100011	23
36	00100100	24
37	00100101	25
38	00100110	26
39	00100111	27
40	00101000	28
41	00101001	29
42	00101010	2A
43	00101011	2B
44	00101100	2C
45	00101101	2D
46	00101110	2E
47	00101111	2F
48	00110000	30

continues

Decimal Number	Binary Equivalent	Hexadecimal
49	00110001	31
50	00110010	32
51	00110011	33
52	00110100	34
53	00110101	35
54	00110110	36
55	00110111	37
56	00111000	38
57	00111001	39
58	00111010	3A
59	00111011	3B
60	00111100	3C
61	00111101	3D
62	00111110	3E
63	00111111	3F
64	01000000	40
65	01000001	41
66	01000010	42
67	01000011	43
68	01000100	44
69	01000101	45
70	01000110	46
71	01000111	47
72	01001000	48
73	01001001	49
74	01001010	4A
75	01001011	4B
76	01001100	4C
77	01001101	4D
78	01001110	4E
79	01001111	4F
80	01010000	50

Decimal Number	Binary Equivalent	Hexadecimal
81	01010001	51
82	01010010	52
83	01010011	53
84	01010100	54
85	01010101	55
86	01010110	56
87	01010111	57
88	01011000	58
89	01011001	59
90	01011010	5A
91	01011011	5B
92	01011100	5C
93	01011101	5D
94	01011110	5E
95	01011111	5F
96	01100000	60
97	01100001	61
98	01100010	62
99	01100011	63
100	01100100	64
101	01100101	65
102	01100110	66
103	01100111	67
104	01101000	68
105	01101001	69
106	01101010	6A
107	01101011	6B
108	01101100	6C
109	01101101	6D
110	01101110	6E
111	01101111	6F
112	01110000	70

continues

Decimal Number	Binary Equivalent	Hexadecimal
113	01110001	71
114	01110010	72
115	01110011	73
116	01110100	74
117	01110101	75
118	01110110	76
119	01110111	77
120	01111000	78
121	01111001	79
122	01111010	7A
123	01111011	7B
124	01111100	7C
125	01111101	7D
126	01111110	7E
127	01111111	7F
128	10000000	80
129	10000001	81
130	10000010	82
131	10000011	83
132	10000100	84
133	10000101	85
134	10000110	86
135	10000111	87
136	10001000	88
137	10001001	89
138	10001010	8A
139	10001011	8B
140	10001100	8C
141	10001101	8D
142	10001110	8E
143	10001111	8F
144	10010000	90

Decimal Number	Binary Equivalent	Hexadecimal
145	10010001	91
146	10010010	92
147	10010011	93
148	10010100	94
149	10010101	95
150	10010110	96
151	10010111	97
152	10011000	98
153	10011001	99
154	10011010	9A
155	10011011	9B
156	10011100	9C
157	10011101	9D
158	10011110	9E
159	10011111	9F
160	10100000	A0
161	10100001	A1
162	10100010	A2
163	10100011	A3
164	10100100	A4
165	10100101	A5
166	10100110	A6
167	10100111	A7
168	10101000	A8
169	10101001	A9
170	10101010	AA
171	10101011	AB
172	10101100	AC
173	10101101	AD
174	10101110	AE
175	10101111	AF
176	10110000	B0

continues

Decimal Number	Binary Equivalent	Hexadecimal
177	10110001	B1
178	10110010	B2
179	10110011	B3
180	10110100	B4
181	10110101	B5
182	10110110	B6
183	10110111	B7
184	10111000	B8
185	10111001	B9
186	10111010	BA
187	10111011	BB
188	10111100	BC
189	10111101	BD
190	10111110	BE
191	10111111	BF
192	11000000	C0
193	11000001	C1
194	11000010	C2
195	11000011	C3
196	11000100	C4
197	11000101	C5
198	11000110	C6
199	11000111	C7
200	11001000	C8
201	11001001	C9
202	11001010	CA
203	11001011	CB
204	11001100	CC
205	11001101	CD
206	11001110	CE
207	11001111	CF
208	11010000	D0

Decimal Number	Binary Equivalent	Hexadecimal
209	11010001	D1
210	11010010	D2
211	11010011	D3
212	11010100	D4
213	11010101	D5
214	11010110	D6
215	11010111	D7
216	11011000	D8
217	11011001	D9
218	11011010	DA
219	11011011	DB
220	11011100	DC
221	11011101	DD
222	11011110	DE
223	11011111	DF
224	11100000	E0
225	11100001	E1
226	11100010	E2
227	11100011	E3
228	11100100	E4
229	11100101	E5
230	11100110	E6
231	11100111	E7
232	11101000	E8
233	11101001	E9
234	11101010	EA
235	11101011	EB
236	11101100	EC
237	11101101	ED
238	11101110	EE
239	11101111	EF
240	11110000	F0

continues

Decimal Number	Binary Equivalent	Hexadecimal
241	11110001	F1
242	11110010	F2
243	11110011	F3
244	11110100	F4
245	11110101	F5
246	11110110	F6
247	11110111	F7
248	11111000	F8
249	11111001	F9
250	11111010	FA
251	11111011	FB
252	11111100	FC
253	11111101	FD
254	11111110	FE
255	11111111	FF

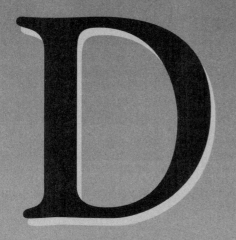

D

Available Software Developer's Kits (SDK)

Peter Norton™

This is a list of some of the SDKs available from different Microsoft development groups. One of the goals of the Platforms SDK is to simplify this process for developers. If you want to start building applications for one of these technologies, you can use the online documentation on the Platforms SDK Web site at the following address:

`http://www.microsoft.com/msdn/sdk`

You can download whichever pieces you need from the following list found at this Web site:

> **Note:** Most of these SDKs require the Win32 SDK from MSDN or included with your compiler. MSDN is the Microsoft Developer's Network; you can find information about it on the Internet at `http://www.microsoft.com/MSDN`.

- ActiveX SDK for the PC—The Microsoft ActiveX SDK includes a variety of technologies from Microsoft that facilitate development of Internet applications and content.

- ActiveX SDK for the Mac—This SDK covers Microsoft's native Macintosh implementation of ActiveX controls.

- NetMeeting SDK—An overview and a downloadable copy of the NetMeeting SDK, which allows you to add conferencing support to your Web pages and applications.

- Java JDK—Lets you develop applets that conform to the Core API for the Java Programming Language, create applets that run in Java-enabled browsers, and develop Java applications. Included are the Java Compiler, Language Runtime, Debugger, and Applet Viewer. Version 1.1.1, March 1997. File size 7.9MB. Released by Sun Microsystems.

- Microsoft SDK for Java—Enables you to write Java applications and applets based upon both the Java language spec and the Microsoft virtual machine for Java Version 1.5, February 1997. File size 6.4MB. Documentation package 2.4MB. Registration form. Released by Microsoft. Evaluation copy.

- Design-time Controls SDK—This SDK will help you create Design-time controls that can simplify complex HTML authoring tasks.

- DirectX SDK—DirectX development involves the direct manipulation of user machines through the use of applets written and interpreted through a Web browser.

- OLE-DS SDK Beta—Create directory management applications using high-level tools such as Visual Basic, Java, or C/C++ without having to worry about the underlying differences between the different name spaces.

Glossary

Peter Norton™

Symbols

10Base2—10 megabit Ethernet across two-conductor wire.

10BaseT—10 megabit Ethernet across twisted-pair wire.

100BaseT (or 100baseTX)—100 megabit Ethernet across twisted-pair wire.

100BaseFX—100 megabit Ethernet across fiber optic.

A

access right—The permission granted to a process to manipulate a particular object in a particular way (for example, by calling a service). Different object types support different access rights.

Administrative wizards—Found in the Administrative Tools. The idea is to be guided step by step through the process of creating NT objects.

AFS—See *Andrew File System*.

alphanumeric mode—See *character-based*.

Andrew File System (AFS)—A file system created and originally developed at Carnegie Mellon University, it's now commercially distributed by Transarc Corporation, which is owned by IBM. A rival Internet file system to NFS.

API—See *application programming interface*.

AppleTalk—Protocol developed by Apple Computer for communications between the Macintosh computer system and other computers or peripherals.

application programming interface (API)—A set of routines that an application program uses to request and carry out lower-level services performed by the operating system.

ASCII—See *text file*.

asynchronous I/O—A method that many of the processes in Windows NT use to optimize their performance. When an application initiates an I/O operation, the I/O Manager accepts the request but doesn't block the application's execution while the I/O operation is being performed. Instead, the application is allowed to continue doing work. Most I/O devices are very slow in comparison to a computer's processor, so an application can do a lot of work while waiting for an I/O operation to complete. See also *synchronous I/O*.

audit policy—Defines the type of security events that are logged for a domain or for an individual computer; determines what Windows NT will do when the security log becomes full.

auditing—Detecting and recording security-related events, particularly any attempts to create, access, or delete objects. Windows NT uses the security ID (SID) to record which process performed the action.

authentication—A security step performed by the remote access server (RAS) before logon validation, to verify that the user has permission for remote access. See also *validation*.

B

batch program—An ASCII (unformatted text) file that contains one or more commands in the command language for Windows NT. A batch program's filename has a .BAT or .CMD extension. When you type the filename at the command prompt, the commands are processed sequentially.

backup domain controller (BDC)—Backup facility and alternate site for the domain database. The BDC exists only as an alternate site for authenticating a user; it doesn't facilitate or store any changes that aren't sent to it by the PDC.

battery backup—See *uninterruptible power supply*.

BDC—See *backup domain controller*.

Browser Service—Keeps a centralized list of servers and shared resources that can be browsed in order to facilitate users and other nodes finding the resource on the network.

C

C2 (C2 Orange Book)—C2 Orange Book Certification means that according to the United States government this operating system meets the criteria set forth by the National Computer Security Center (NCSC). The color of the "Orange Book" is simply a division of the separate levels of the certification.

character-based—A mode of operation in which all information is displayed as text characters. This is the mode in which DOS-based and OS/2 v1.2 applications are displayed under Windows NT. Also called *character mode*, *alphanumeric mode*, or *text mode*.

character mode—See *character-based*.

client—A computer that accesses shared network resources provided by another computer (called a *server*). For the X Window system of UNIX, the client/server relationship is reversed. Under the X Window system, this client definition becomes the server definition. See also *server*.

computer name—A unique name of up to 15 uppercase characters that identifies a computer to the network. The name can't be the same as any other computer or domain name in the network, and it can't contain spaces.

control panel—An application that enables the user to change the behavior of system objects. Items such as printers, network access, and system services are controlled from these applications by making changes in the way in which the operating system interfaces with the object.

D

data link control (DLC)—A protocol interface device driver in Windows NT, traditionally used to provide connectivity to IBM mainframes and also used to provide connectivity to local area network printers directly attached to the network.

default profile —See *system default profile, user default profile.*

demand paging—A method by which data is moved in pages from physical memory to a temporary paging file on disk. As a process needs the data, it's paged back into physical memory.

desktop—The primary interface between the user and the operating system. A frame that allows the user to interact with tools that Windows provides.

device—A generic term for a computer subsystem such as a printer, serial port, or disk drive. A device frequently requires its own controlling software called a *device driver.*

device driver—A software component that allows the computer to transmit and receive information to and from a specific device. For example, a printer driver translates computer data into a form understood by a particular printer. Although a device may be installed on your system, Windows NT can't recognize the device until you've installed and configured the appropriate driver.

DFS—See *distributed file system.*

distributed file system (DFS)—Provides a single tree structure for multiple shared volumes located on different servers on a network.

directory services—The defining element of distributed computing, and, ultimately, a logical name space capable of including all system resources regardless of type. The goal is a blending in which the directory and the network become synonymous.

disk caching—A method used by a file system to improve performance. Instead of reading and writing directly to the disk, frequently used files are temporarily stored in a cache in memory, and reads and writes to those files are performed in memory. Reading and writing to memory is much faster than reading and writing to disk.

distributed application—An application that has two parts—a front end to run on the client computer and a back end to run on the server. In distributed computing, the goal is to divide the computing task into two sections. The front end requires minimal resources and runs on the client's workstation. The back end requires large amounts of data, number crunching, or specialized hardware, and runs on the server. Recently, there has been much discussion in the industry about a three-tier model for distributed computing. That model separates the business logic contained in both sides of the two-tier model into a third, distinct layer. The business logic layer sits between the front-end user interface layer and the back-end database layer. It typically resides on a server platform that may or may not be the same as the one the database is on. The three-tier model arose as a solution to the limits faced by software developers trying to express complex business logic with the two-tier model.

DLC—See *data link control.*

DLL—See *dynamic link library.*

domain—For Windows NT Server, a networked set of workstations and servers that share a Security Accounts Manager (SAM) database and that can be administered as a group. A user with an account in a particular network domain can log onto and access his or her account from any system in the domain. See also *SAM database.*

domain controller—For a Windows NT Server domain, the server that authenticates domain logons and maintains the security policy and the master database for a domain. Both servers and domain controllers are capable of validating a user's logon; however, password changes must be made by contacting the domain controller. See also *server.*

domain database—See *SAM database.*

domain name—The name by which a Windows NT domain is known to the network.

domain name service (DNS)—A hierarchical name service for TCP/IP hosts (sometimes referred to as the *BIND service* in BSD UNIX). The network administrator configures the DNS with a list of hostnames and IP addresses, allowing users of workstations configured to query the DNS to specify the remote systems by hostnames rather than IP addresses. DNS domains should not be confused with Windows NT domains.

DOS-based application—An application that is designed to run with DOS and therefore may not be able to take full advantage of all of the features of Windows NT.

duplexing—Mirroring with the addition of one controller, thus mirroring the controllers. The weak link in a drive-mirroring installation is the hard drive controller because it controls both drives. Duplexing eliminates that link.

DSNW (Directory Services for NetWare)—With this service, the administrator can create and manage users from the NT directory structure and have them automatically propagated to the NetWare servers in the network. Not related to NetWare NDS (NetWare Directory Services).

dynamic link library (DLL)—An application programming interface (API) routine that user-mode applications access through ordinary procedure calls. The code for the API routine isn't included in the user's executable image. Instead, the operating system automatically modifies the executable image to point to DLL procedures at run time.

E

EIDE—see *Enhanced Integrated Drive Electronics*.

Enhanced Integrated Drive Electronics (EIDE)—The enhancement is that it will run more drives (four) from the same controller and is capable of handling larger drives. The original IDE was limited to two drives and a capacity of 500MB. See also *Integrated Drive Electronics*.

environment subsystems—User-mode protected servers that run and support programs from different operating system environments. Examples of these subsystems are the Win32 subsystem, the Posix subsystem, and the OS/2 subsystem. See also *integral subsystem*.

environment variable—A string consisting of environment information, such as a drive, path, or filename, associated with a symbolic name that can be used by Windows NT. You use the System option in Control Panel or the SET command to define environment variables.

event—Any significant occurrence in the system or in an application that requires users to be notified or an entry to be added to a log.

event log—Service that records events in the system, security, and application logs.

Event Viewer—A tool that reads the log files from specific servers. By looking at the log files, the administrator get a more detailed view of the events and is then able to form a plan of action.

Executive module—The kernel-mode module that provides basic operating system services to the environment subsystems. It includes several components; each manages a particular set of system services. One component, the Security Reference Monitor, works together with the protected subsystems to provide a pervasive security model for the system.

Explorer—File and resource interface that manifests itself as part of the Windows NT 4.0 and Windows 95 desktop. A version of the old Windows 3.x File Manager that has been expanded to include object management for the operating system.

extended partitions—Partitions that consume the remaining free space after primary drives have been established. You can have only one extended partition per physical drive. Extended partitions in NT can be segmented into numerous logical drives.

F

FAT file system—A file system based on a file allocation table maintained by the operating system to keep track of the status of various segments of disk space used for file storage.

fault tolerance—The ability of a computer and an operating system to respond gracefully to catastrophic events such as power outage or hardware failure. Usually, fault tolerance implies the ability to either continue the system's operation without loss of data or to shut the system down and restart it, recovering all processing that was in progress when the fault occurred.

file sharing—The ability of Windows NT Workstation or Windows NT Server to share part (or all) of its local file system(s) with remote computers.

file system—In an operating system, the overall structure in which files are named, stored, and organized.

flat file—See *text file*.

FPNW (File and Print Services for NetWare)—A product that makes the Windows NT server emulate a Novell NetWare 3.12 server so that it can participate in file and printer services in the NetWare environment.

FTP service—File transfer protocol service, which offers file transfer services to remote systems supporting this protocol. FTP supports a host of commands allowing bidirectional transfer of binary and ASCII files between systems.

fully qualified domain name (FQDN)—In TCP/IP, hostnames with their domain names appended to them. For example, a host with hostname `tsunami` and domain name `microsoft.com` has an FQDN of `tsunami.microsoft.com`.

G

Gateway Service for NetWare (GSNW)—This NT service is used by the NT server to allow any user of the Microsoft Client for NT to pass through the NT server and use NetWare server services.

global account—For Windows NT Server, a normal user account in a user's home domain. If there are multiple domains in the network, it's best if each user in the network has only one user account, in only one domain, and each user's access to other domains is accomplished through the establishment of domain trust relationships.

group—In User Manager, an account containing other accounts called *members*. The permissions and rights granted to a group are also provided to its members, making groups a convenient way to grant common capabilities to collections of user accounts.

GSNW—See *Gateway Service for NetWare*.

H

hardware abstraction layer (HAL)—Virtualizes hardware interfaces, making the hardware dependencies transparent to the rest of the operating system. This allows Windows NT to be portable from one hardware platform to another.

high performance file system (HPFS)—Created for the OS/2 operating system, this file system is the predecessor to file systems such as NTFS, and for that reason was supported in all previous versions of Windows NT Server. But NT Server 4.0 doesn't support it.

home directory—A directory that's accessible to the user and contains files and programs for that user. A home directory can be assigned to an individual user or can be shared by many users.

host table—The HOSTS or LMHOSTS file that contains lists of known IP addresses.

hostname—A TCP/IP command that returns the local workstation's hostname, used for authentication by TCP/IP utilities. This value is the workstation's computer name by default, but it can be changed.

HPFS—See *high performance file system*.

I

IDE—See *Integrated Drive Electronics*.

IIS—See *Internet Information Server*.

integral subsystem—A subsystem such as the Security subsystem that affects the entire Windows NT operating system. See also *environment subsystems*.

Integrated Drive Electronics (IDE)—Introduced in 1989, involves a controller being attached to the hard drive itself.

Internet Information Server (IIS)—Product that comes as part of the Windows NT Server 4.0 package. Internet Information Server contains three products: FTP service, Gopher service, and an HTTP (World Wide Web) server. IIS integrates all three services into one shared management interface that allows the administrator to control them.

interprocess communication (IPC)—The exchange of data between one thread or process and another, either within the same computer or across a network. Common IPC mechanisms include pipes, named pipes, semaphores, shared memory, queues, signals, mailboxes, and sockets.

interrupt—When an interface card in a PC wants to address the other pieces of the system, it must first interrupt the processor. The process of interrupting the processor is done through the use of a message called an interrupt or *IRQ*.

I/O Manager—Defines an orderly framework within which I/O requests are delivered to file systems and device drivers. The I/O Manager doesn't actually manage I/O processing. Its job is to create an IRP that represents each I/O operation, pass the IRP to the correct driver, and dispose of the packet when the I/O operation is complete.

IPX (Internet Packet Exchange)—Novell's connectionless datagram-based protocol for general communications. Part of the IPX/SPX protocol suite that is the Novell default protocol. See also *NWLink IPX/SPX protocol*.

IRQ—See *interrupt*.

K

kernel—The portion of Windows NT that manages the processor.

kernel module—The core of the layered architecture of Windows NT that manages the most basic operations of Windows NT. The kernel is responsible for thread dispatching, multiprocessor synchronization, hardware exception handling, and the implementation of low-level, hardware-dependent functions.

L

LAN—See *local area network*.

LLC—Logical link control, in the data-link layer of the networking model.

local area network (LAN)—A network of computers and peripherals that usually spans a single building or small campus area.

local printer—A printer that's directly connected to one of the ports on a computer.

local procedure call (LPC)—An optimized message-passing facility that allows one thread or process to communicate with another thread or process on the same computer. The Windows NT protected subsystems use LPC to communicate with each other and with their client processes. LPC is a variation of the remote procedure call (RPC) facility, optimized for local use. Compare with *remote procedure call*.

local procedure call facility—Processes running in the different application subsystems must communicate with one another in order to accomplish anything. For processes in the local machine to communicate with one another, they must use the local procedure call facility.

locale—The national and cultural environment in which a system or program is running. The locale determines the language used for messages and menus, the sorting order of strings, the keyboard layout, and date- and time-formatting conventions.

logon authentication—Refers to the validation of a user either locally or in a domain. At logon time, the user specifies his or her name, password, and the intended logon domain. The workstation then contacts the domain controllers for the domains, which verify the user's logon credentials.

LPC—See *local procedure call.*

M

MAC (media access control)—Part of the data-link layer of the networking model.

mandatory user profile—For Windows NT Server, a user profile created by an administrator and assigned to one or more users. A mandatory user profile can't be changed by the user and remains the same from one logon session to the next. See also *personal user profile, user profile.*

mirroring (RAID 1)—A form of drive fault tolerance that involves adding one hard drive for every one hard drive that you want to protect in your system. You then write the same data to both drives or groups of drives. In the event of a hard drive failure, the system will switch to the other hard drive for data.

N

named pipe—An interprocess communication mechanism that allows one process to send data to another local or remote process. Windows NT named pipes are not the same as UNIX named pipes.

NBF transport protocol (NetBEUI Frame protocol)—A descendant of the NetBEUI protocol, which is a transport layer protocol, not the programming interface NetBIOS.

NDIS—See *network driver interface specification.*

NetBEUI transport—NetBEUI (network basic input/output system) extended user interface. The primary local area network transport protocol in Windows NT.

NetBIOS interface—A programming interface that allows I/O requests to be sent to and received from a remote computer. It hides networking hardware for applications.

NetWare—32-bit network operating system produced by Novell Corporation of Provo, Utah, and the primary competitor of Windows NT Server.

network device driver—Software that coordinates communication between the network adapter card and the computer's hardware and other software, controlling the physical function of the network adapter cards.

network driver interface specification (NDIS)—An interface in Windows NT for network card drivers that provides transport independence, because all transport drivers call the NDIS interface to access network cards.

network file system (NFS)—Originally developed by Sun Microsystems, allows directories and files to be shared across a network. It is the *de facto* UNIX standard for network file systems and has been ported to many non-UNIX operating systems as well.

network interface card (NIC)—Adapter card added to the computer to provide access to the local area network (LAN).

network operating system (NOS)—Any operating system whose primary function is to provide network services and resources to client machines.

NIC—See *network interface card.*

NOS—See *network operating system.*

NFS—See *network file system.*

NTFS (Windows NT file system)—An advanced file system designed for use specifically with the Windows NT operating system. NTFS supports file-system recovery and extremely large storage media, in addition to other advantages. It also supports object-oriented applications by treating all files as objects with user-defined and system-defined attributes.

NT Performance Monitor—See *Performance Monitor.*

NWLink IPX/SPX protocol—An IPX/SPX protocol that allows Windows NT Server services to be seen by Novell clients. It also allows the NT communications to be routed by NetWare servers that run only the IPX/SPX protocol.

O

object linking and embedding—See OLE.

Object Manager—Responsible for making sure that the objects needed to complete a task are available to the processes that need them. It tracks the objects that are needed for each process and also manages the objects throughout their life spans.

object menu—Drop-down menu that appears when you right-click a desktop or Explorer object in the Windows NT 4.0 or Windows 95 operating system.

object type—Includes a system-defined data type, a list of operations that can be performed upon it (such as wait, create, or cancel), and a set of object attributes. Object Manager is the part of the Windows NT Executive that provides uniform rules for retention, naming, and security of objects.

OLE (object linking and embedding)—A way to transfer and share information between applications.

Orange Book—See C2 *(C2 Orange Book)*.

OS/2—Operating system created as a joint project by IBM and Microsoft in the late 1980s as a solution for the new class of processors (80286 and 80386).

P

packet—A unit of information transmitted as a whole from one device to another on a network.

page—A fixed-size block in memory.

partition—A portion of a physical disk that functions like a physically separate unit.

PDC—See *primary domain controller*.

Performance Monitor (NT Performance Monitor)—A graphical tool that allows you to log what's happening now and to track what has happened over a given span of time. The tool does this through graph and logs of both an immediate and time-lapsed nature.

permission—A rule associated with an object (usually a directory, file, or printer) in order to regulate which users can have access to the object and in what manner. See also *right*.

personal user profile—For Windows NT Server, a user profile created by an administrator and assigned to one user. A personal user profile retains changes the user makes to the per-user settings of Windows NT and reimplements the newest settings each time the user logs on at any Windows NT Workstation. See also *mandatory user profile, user profile*.

port—A connection or socket used to connect a device to a computer, such as a printer, monitor, or modem. Information is sent from the computer to the device through a cable.

portability—Refers to Windows NT's ability to run on both CISC and RISC processors. CISC includes computers running Intel 80386 or higher processors. RISC includes computers with MIPS R4000 or Digital Alpha AXP processors.

Posix—A format for UNIX applications that's used in many government installations. Microsoft has made a great effort to make NT accessible to large companies and government contracts.

primary domain controller (PDC)—Central server controlling the domain database in an NT domain.

primary partition—The bootable partitions that you create on a bootable hard drive in the system. Partitions that can be set to take the lead position during the starting of the PC and that can be used to boot the operating system.

print device—Refers to the actual hardware device that produces printed output.

printer—In Windows NT, refers to the software interface between the application and the print device.

print processor—A dynamic link library that interprets data types. It receives information from the spooler and sends the interpreted information to the graphics engine.

privilege—See *right*.

Process Manager—Responsible for the creation of processes and threads, and for moving them on the microkernel.

protocol—A set of rules and conventions by which two computers pass messages across a network. Networking software usually implements multiple levels of protocols layered one on top of another.

provider—The component that allows a computer running Windows NT to communicate with the network. Windows NT includes a provider for the Windows NT-based network; other providers are supplied by the alternate networks' vendors.

R

RAID (redundant array of inexpensive drives)—A way of describing hard drive fault tolerance that's being used. RAID is more of an agreed-upon way of describing how the drives are configured in relationship to each other and where the data is stored. There are six levels of RAID (0–5). The goal of RAID is twofold: Save money and/or protect data.

redirector—Networking software that accepts I/O requests for remote files, named pipes, or mail slots and then sends (*redirects*) them to a network service on another computer. Redirectors are implemented as file system drivers in Windows NT.

remote administration—Administration of one computer by an administrator located at another computer and connected to the first computer across the network.

remote file sharing (RFS)—Developed by AT&T, this protocol has been available under UNIX System V for a number of years. It's not widely used; hence, no packages are available for Windows NT.

remote procedure call (RPC)—A message-passing facility that allows a distributed application to call services available on various computers in a network. Used during remote administration of computers. RPC provides a procedural view rather than a transport-centered view of networked operations. Compare with *local procedure call*.

resource—Any part of a computer system or a network, such as a disk drive or memory, that can be allotted to a program or a process while it's running.

RFS—See *remote file sharing*.

right—Authorizes a user to perform certain actions on the system. Rights apply to the system as a whole and are different from *permissions*, which apply to specific objects. (Sometimes called a *privilege*.)

RISC-based computer—A computer based on a RISC (reduced instruction set) microprocessor, such as a Digital Alpha AXP, MIPS R4000, or IBM/Motorola PowerPC. Compare with *x86-based computer*.

router—A network-level device used to allow communication between different network segments. An example of such a connection is an internal network connected to the Internet.

RPC—See *remote procedure call*.

S

SAM—See *Security Accounts Manager*.

SAM database—The database of security information that includes user account names and passwords and the settings of the security policies.

Scalability—Scalability depends on the overall architecture of the entire application server. The three critical components of a scalable system are operating system, application software, and hardware. No one element by itself is sufficient to guarantee scalability. High-performance server hardware is designed to scale to multiple processors, providing specific functionality to ease disk and memory bottlenecks. Applications and operating systems in turn must be able to take advantage of multiple CPUs. All three components are equally important.

schedule service—Supports and is required for use of the **at** command, which can schedule commands and programs to run on a computer at a specified date and time.

SCSI (small computer systems interface)—Computer interface developed to allow many different peripherals to attach to the computer externally or internally.

Security Accounts Manager (SAM)—A Windows NT protected subsystem that maintains the SAM database and provides an API for accessing the database.

security ID (SID)—A unique name that identifies a logged-on user to the security system of Windows NT. A security ID can identify either an individual user or a group of users.

segment—Network-level term used to describe a single subnet.

server—A LAN-based computer running administrative software that controls access to all or part of the network and its resources. A computer acting as a server makes resources available to computers acting as workstations on the network. For the X Window system of UNIX, the client/server relationship is reversed. Under the X Window system, this server definition becomes the client definition. See also *client*.

server service—A service in Windows NT that supplies an API for managing the Windows NT-based network software. Provides RPC support and file, print, and named pipe sharing.

service—A process that performs a specific system function and often provides an API for other processes to call. Services in Windows NT are RPC-enabled, meaning that their API routines can be called from remote computers.

session—A connection that two applications on different computers establish, use, and end. The Session layer performs name recognition and the functions needed to allow two applications to communicate over the network.

socket—Provides an end point to a connection; two sockets form a complete path. A socket works as a bidirectional pipe for incoming and outgoing data between networked computers. The Windows sockets API is a networking API tailored for use by Windows-based applications.

SPX (sequenced packet exchange)—Novell's protocol for guaranteed delivery or connection-based communications. Part of the IPX/SPX protocol suite that is the Novell default protocol.

stripe sets—The combination of 2 to 32 volumes that can allow for more speed due to the fact that they stripe the writing of data across numerous drives at one time.

striping—Software implementation of RAID that is natively supported by NT (see *RAID*).

subnet—Portion of an entire network that includes only devices sharing the same network address and/or collision domain.

synchronous I/O—The simplest way to perform I/O, by synchronizing the execution of applications with completion of the I/O operations that they request. When an application performs an I/O operation, the application's processing is blocked. When the I/O operation is complete, the application is allowed to continue processing. See also *asynchronous I/O*.

system default profile—For Windows NT Server, the user profile that's loaded when Windows NT is running and no user is logged on. When the Welcome dialog box is visible, the system default profile is loaded. See also *user default profile, user profile*.

T

TDI—See *transport driver interface*.

Telnet service—The service that provides basic terminal emulation to remote systems supporting the Telnet protocol over TCP/IP.

text file—A file containing only letters, numbers, and symbols. A text file contains no formatting information, except possibly linefeeds and carriage returns. Text files are also known as *flat files* and *ASCII files*.

text mode—See *character-based.*

thread—An executable entity that belongs to a single process, comprising a program counter, a user-mode stack, a kernel-mode stack, and a set of register values. All threads in a process have equal access to the processor's address space, object handles, and other resources. In Windows NT, threads are implemented as objects.

topology—The cabling and physical protocol scheme of a network.

transport driver interface (TDI)—In the networking model, a common interface for network components that communicate at the session layer.

transport protocol—Defines how data should be presented to the next receiving layer in the networking model and packages the data accordingly. It passes data to the network adapter card driver through the NDIS interface, and to the redirector through the transport driver interface.

trust relationship—Link between domains that enables pass-through authentication, in which a user has only one user account in one domain, yet can access the entire network. A trusting domain honors the logon authentications of a trusted domain.

U

unicode—A fixed-width, 16-bit character-encoding standard capable of representing all of the world's scripts.

uninterruptible power supply (UPS)—Device that provides continuous power to a server or other mission-critical device in the event of a power failure. Usually a battery contained in a metal case that the devices are plugged into (also called a *battery backup*).

UPS—See *uninterruptible power supply.*

user account—Consists of all the information that defines a user to Windows NT. This includes the username and password required for the user to log on, the groups in which the user account has membership, and the rights and permissions the user has for using the system and accessing its resources. See also *group.*

user default profile—For Windows NT Server, the user profile that's loaded by a server when a user's assigned profile can't be accessed for any reason, when a user without an assigned profile logs on to the computer for the first time, or when a user logs on as the Guest account. See also *system default profile, user profile.*

user mode—A nonprivileged processor mode in which application code runs.

user profile—Configuration information retained on a user-by-user basis. The information includes all the per-user settings of Windows NT, such as the desktop arrangement, personal program groups and the program items in those groups, screen colors, screen savers, network connections, printer connections, mouse settings, window size and position, and more. When a user logs on, the user's profile is loaded, and the user's environment in Windows NT is configured according to that profile.

user right—See *right*.

username—A unique name identifying a user account to Windows NT. An account's username can't be identical to any other group name or username of its own domain or workstation. See also *user account*.

V

validation—Authorization check of a user's logon information. When a user logs on to an account on a Windows NT Workstation computer, the authentication is performed by that workstation. When a user logs on to an account on a Windows NT Server domain, any server of that domain may perform that authentication. See also *trust relationship*.

virtual DOS machine (VDM)—A Windows NT protected subsystem that supplies a complete environment for MS-DOS and a console on which to run applications for MS-DOS or 16-bit Windows. A VDM is a Win32 application that establishes a complete virtual x86 (that is, 80386 or higher) computer running MS-DOS. Any number of VDMs can run simultaneously.

virtual memory—Space on a hard disk that Windows NT uses as if it were actually memory. Windows NT does this through the use of paging files. The benefit of using virtual memory is that you can run more applications at one time than your system's physical memory would otherwise allow. The drawbacks are the disk space required for the virtual-memory paging file and the decreased execution speed when swapping is required.

virtual memory manager—Responsible for mapping the virtual memory addresses needed by the applications into actual memory.

volume—A partition or collection of partitions that have been formatted for use by a file system.

W

WAN—See *wide area network*.

wide area network (WAN)—Network of computers and peripherals that covers a large area and requires long-distance equipment to maintain (leased phone lines, satellite uplink, frame relay, and so on).

Win32 API—A 32-bit application-programming interface for Windows NT. It updates earlier versions of the Windows API with sophisticated operating system capabilities, security, and API routines for displaying text-based applications in a window.

Windows on Win32 (WOW)—A Windows NT protected subsystem that runs within a VDM process. It provides an environment for 16-bit Windows capable of running any number of applications for 16-bit Windows under Windows NT.

Windows sockets—An IPC mechanism based on the WinSock specification and compatible with the Berkeley Sockets IPC under UNIX. The WinSock specification allows hardware and software vendors to design systems and applications that can access virtually any type of underlying network, including TCP/IP, IPX/SPX, OSI, ATM networks, wireless networks, and telephony networks.

wizard—Application that helps guide you through the process of creating a new service, object, or resource. These applications can also be found in applications and generally walk you through performing any new task step by step.

workgroup—Meant to allow small groups of users to create shared drives and peripherals on their own workstations and share those with others in their network.

workgroup post office—Rudimentary post office service, included with Windows NT, Windows 95, and Windows for Workgroups, which allows clients with the ability to access a Microsoft Mail post office to attach to the workgroup post office.

workstation—In general, a powerful computer having considerable calculating and graphics capability. For Windows NT, computers running the Windows NT Workstation operating system are called *workstations*, as distinguished from computers running Windows NT Server, which are called *servers*. See also *server, domain controller*.

workstation service—A service for Windows NT that supplies user-mode API routines to manage the Windows NT redirector. Provides network connections and communications.

WOW—The subsystem for running Windows for MS-DOS under Windows NT; sometimes also called *Win16 on Win32*.

X

x86-based computer—A computer using a microprocessor equivalent to an Intel 80386 or higher chip. Compare with *RISC-based computer*.

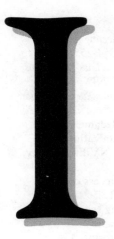

Index

H

hackers, 221
**HAL (hardware abstraction
layer), 8-9, 49, 746**
hard drives, 100, 700-702
  choosing, 109-110
  controllers, 101
    EIDE, 101-102
    IDE, 101-102
    intelligent, 104-105
    SCSI, 102-104
  Disk Administrator, 112,
    119
  duplexing, 124
  early warning features, 111
  fault tolerance, 105-109
  hot-pluggable, 111
  mapping, 343
  mirroring, 124
  NT installation, 76-78
    preparation, 62
    requirements, 59, 62
  partitions, 113, 750
    creating, 119-120
    DOS considerations,
     114-115
    extended, 114, 744
    primary, 113, 750
  RAID, 106, 124, 751
    level 0, 106, 648
    level 1, 106, 648-649
    level 4, 106-108
    level 5, 108-109,
     649-650
  self-maintenance, 111-112
  stripe sets, 105, 579-580
    creating, 123
    fault tolerance, 124
    parity, 125
  volumes, 115-116
    creating, 121
    sets, 121-123
hardware
  adapters
    installation, 63-64, 342
    Remoteboot support,
     548-549

    SNA Server support,
     416-417
    video adapters, 83
    WAN adapters,
     693-694
  buses, 104
  device drivers, 49
  Executive Services, 9,
    44-45
    I/O Manager, 46
    LPC facility, 47
    Object Manager, 46
    Process Manager, 47
    Security Reference
     Monitor, 47-48
    Virtual Memory
     Manager, 47
    Win32 subsystem,
     48-49
  failure recovery, 648-650
    disk striping, 648-650
    duplexing, 648-649
    online recovery servers,
     650-651
    RAID, 651
  fault tolerance, 105-109
  hard drives, 100
    choosing, 109-110
    controllers, 101-105
    Disk Administrator,
     112, 119
    early warning features,
     111
    hot-pluggable, 111
    partitions, 113-115,
     119-120, 750
    RAID, 124, 751
    self-maintenance,
     111-112
    stripe sets, 125
    volumes, 121-123
  hardware compatibility
  list, 684
    hard drives, 700-702
    LAN cards, 684-693
    SCSI controllers,
     694-700
    tape drives, 705-710

    UPSs, 702-705
    WAN adapters,
     693-694
    Web site, 684
  modems
    asynchronous, 295
    ISDN, 296-297
  monitors, 170
  NT requirements, 58-59
    disk space, 62
    hard drives, 59
    hardware settings
     checklist, 63-65
    Intel x86 systems, 60
    memory, 59-61
    processors, 59
    RISC systems, 60
  print devices, 156-157
  printer drivers, 158
  troubleshooting, 717-718
**hardware abstraction layer
(HAL), 8-9, 49, 746**
**Hardware Compatibility
List,** see HCL
**Hardware Compression field
(Backup Information
dialog box), 604**
**hardware-controlled RAID,
651**
**Hardware recognizer,
Registry settings, 562**
**/hc:off switch
(NTBACKUP command),
607**
**/hc:on switch
(NTBACKUP command),
607**
**HCL (Hardware Compat-
ibility List), 65**
  hard drives, 700-702
  LAN cards, 684-693
  SCSI controllers, 694-700
  tape drives, 705-710
  UPSs, 702-705
  WAN adapters, 693-694
  Web site, 65, 684
"heavy metal," 410

793

X-Y-Z

A V I A C O M   S E R V I C E

The Information SuperLibrary™

Bookstore

Search

What's New

Reference Desk

Software Library

Newsletter

Company Overviews

Yellow Pages

Internet Starter Kit

HTML Workshop

Win a Free T-Shirt!

Macmillan Computer Publishing

Site Map

Talk to Us

CHECK OUT THE BOOKS IN THIS LIBRARY.

You'll find thousands of shareware files and over 1600 computer books designed for both technowizards and technophobes. You can browse through 700 sample chapters, get the latest news on the Net, and find just about anything using our massive search directories.

All Macmillan Computer Publishing books are available at your local bookstore.

We're open 24-hours a day, 365 days a year.

You don't need a card.

We don't charge fines.

And you can be as LOUD as you want.

The Information SuperLibrary
http://www.mcp.com/mcp/   ftp.mcp.com

MACMILLAN COMPUTER PUBLISHING USA
A VIACOM COMPANY

Technical Support:

If you need assistance with the information in this book or with a CD/Disk accompanying the book, please access the Knowledge Base on our Web site at **http://www.superlibrary.com/general/support**. Our most Frequently Asked Questions are answered there. If you do not find the answer to your questions on our Web site, you may contact Macmillan Technical Support **(317) 581-3833** or e-mail us at **support@mcp.com**.

Windows NT 4 and Web Site Resource Library

— Sams Development Group

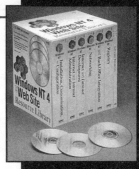

This comprehensive library is the most complete reference available for Windows NT and Web administration and development. Six volumes and more than 3,500 pages of key information about the Windows NT Registry, Web site administration and development, networking, BackOffice integration, and much more. Three bonus CD-ROMs include networking utilities, third-party tools, support utilities, Web site development tools, HTML templates, CGI scripts, and more!
Covers Windows NT Version 4, Internet/General/WWW Applications

Price: $149.99 USA/$209.95 CDN   *User Level: Accomplished—Expert*
ISBN: 0-672-30995-5   *3,200 pages*

Windows NT Server 4 Unleashed, Professional Reference Edition

— Jason Garms, et al.

Windows NT Server has been gaining tremendous market share over Novell, and the new upgrade—which includes a Windows 95 interface—is sure to add momentum to its market drive. *Windows NT Server 4 Unleashed, Professional Reference Edition* meets that growing market. It provides information on disk and file management, integrated networking, BackOffice integration, and TCP/IP protocols. CD-ROM includes source code from the book and valuable utilities.

Price: $69.99 USA/$98.95 CDN   *User Level: Accomplished—Expert*
ISBN: 0-672-31002-3   *1,776 pages*

Robert Cowart's Windows NT 4 Unleashed, Professional Reference Edition

— Robert Cowart

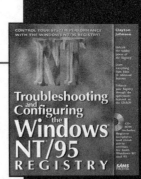

The only reference Windows NT administrators need to learn how to configure their NT systems for maximum performance, security, and reliability. This comprehensive reference explains how to install, maintain, and configure an individual workstation as well as connect computers with peer-to-peer networking. Includes advice on setting up and administering an NT server network, and focuses on the new and improved administration and connectivity features of version 4.0. CD-ROM includes source code, utilities, and sample applications from the book. Covers Windows NT 4 Server and Workstation.

Price: $59.99 USA/$84.95 CDN   *User Level: Intermediate—Expert*
ISBN: 0-672-31001-5   *1,400 pages*

Troubleshooting and Configuring the Windows NT/95 Registry

— Clayton Johnson

Written for system administrators who run networks with Windows NT Server, NT Workstation, and Windows 95, *Troubleshooting and Configuring the Windows NT/95 Registry* provides a complete reference for the Windows NT and 95 operating systems. Includes detailed coverage of Registry entries for both systems, noting instances when the entries differ. Offers complete troubleshooting sections outlining known problems and detailing their solutions. CD-ROM contains Registry entries and third-party utilities relating to the Registry for both Windows 95 and NT.

Price: $49.99 USA/$70.95 CDN   *User Level: Intermediate—Expert*
ISBN: 0-672-31066-x   *648 pages*

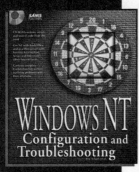

Windows NT 4 Administrator's Survival Guide

— *Rick Sant'Angelo*

This is the only survival guide an NT network administrator needs. Written by best-selling author Rick Sant'Angelo, this concise, easy-to-use guide provides all the information users need to successfully implement and maintain a Windows NT 4 server. Loaded with tips and notes on improving performance and saving money when implementing a Windows NT server. Guide to third-party products, logon scripts programming, technical terms, and commonly used NT utilities. CD-ROM includes demos of Windows NT applications, utilities, and source code from the book.

Price: $49.99 USA/ $70.95 CDN   *User Level: Accomplished—Expert*
ISBN: 0-672-31008-2   *900 pages*

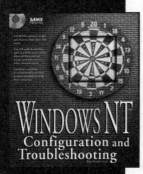

Windows NT Configuration and Troubleshooting

— *Robert Reinstein, et al.*

Written for system administrators, this book details how to use Windows NT with the other components of the BackOffice suite. It includes coverage of NT design, system management, Registry modification and management, troubleshooting, Internet support, and security issues. Teaches how to use NT with BackOffice and as a Web server with Internet Information Server and Microsoft's other Internet tools. Contains a complete troubleshooting section that outlines known problems with their solutions. CD-ROM contains scripts and source code from the book. Covers NT 4.0 and BackOffice.

Price: $59.99 USA/$84.95 CDN   *User Level: Accomplished—Expert*
ISBN: 0-672-30941-6   *1,200 pages*

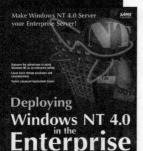

Deploying Windows NT 4 in the Enterprise

— *Jim Plas*

Windows NT is quickly becoming a recognized contender in the enterprise arena, and this must-have guide specifically addresses NT as an enterprise server—from LANs and WANs to multi-platform networks. Provides comprehensive coverage of server standardization, workstation standards, alternative clients, SNA connectivity, advanced trust relationships, and more. Discusses the challenges unique to large systems using the newest technologies, such as ATM and ISDN.

Price: $55.00 USA/$77.95 CDN   *User Level: Accomplished—Expert*
ISBN: 0-672-31038-4   *500 pages*

Teach Yourself Perl 5 for Windows NT in 21 Days

— *Tony Zhang & David Till*

Perl, a powerful programming language in the UNIX arena, can be used for manipulating text, generating reports, and performing system tasks. Assuming no prior programming knowledge, this easy-to-use guide shows readers how to use this language to quickly develop dynamic user interfaces into Windows NT databases. Extensive coverage of scripting model architecture, lists and array variables, subroutines, mathematical functions, scalar conversion functions, debugging, and more. CD-ROM is packed with author source code, sample scripts, and various third-party utilities.

Price: $39.99 USA/$56.95 CDN   *User Level: New—Casual*
ISBN: 0-672-31047-3   *912 pages*

Add to Your Sams Library Today with the Best Books for Programming, Operating Systems, and New Technologies

The easiest way to order is to pick up the phone and call

1-800-428-5331

between 9:00 a.m. and 5:00 p.m. EST.

For faster service please have your credit card available.

ISBN	Quantity	Description of Item	Unit Cost	Total Cost
0-672-30995-5		Windows NT 4 and Web Site Resource Library (6 Books/3 CD-ROMs) .	$149.99	
0-672-31002-3		Windows NT Server 4 Unleashed, Professional Reference Edition (Book/CD-ROM)	$69.99	
0-672-31001-5		Robert Cowart's Windows NT 4 Unleashed, Professional Reference Edition (Book/CD-ROM)	$59.99	
0-672-31066-X		Troubleshooting and Configuring the Windows NT/95 Registry (Book/CD-ROM)	$49.99	
0-672-31008-2		Windows NT 4 Administrator's Survival Guide (Book/CD-ROM)	$49.99	
0-672-30941-6		Windows NT Configuration and Troubleshooting (Book/CD-ROM)	$59.99	
0-672-31038-4		Deploying Windows NT 4 in the Enterprise	$55.00	
0-672-31047-3		Teach Yourself Perl 5 for Windows NT in 21 Days (Book/CD-ROM)	$39.99	
		Shipping and Handling: See information below.		
		TOTAL		

Shipping and Handling: $4.00 for the first book, and $1.75 for each additional book. If you need to have it NOW, we can ship product to you in 24 hours for an additional charge of approximately $18.00, and you will receive your item overnight or in two days. Overseas shipping and handling adds $2.00 per book. Prices subject to change. Call for availability and pricing information on latest editions.

201 W. 103rd Street, Indianapolis, Indiana 46290

1-800-428-5331 — Orders   1-800-835-3202 — FAX   1-800-858-7674 — Customer Service

Book ISBN 0-672-30987-4